Apple
PRESS

S0-DUS-059

Newton Programmer's Guide

For Newton 2.0

Addison-Wesley Publishing Company

Reading, Massachusetts   Menlo Park, California   New York
Don Mills, Ontario   Harlow, England   Amsterdam   Bonn
Sydney   Singapore   Tokyo   Madrid   San Juan
Paris   Seoul   Milan   Mexico City   Taipei

ISBN 0-201-47947-8
1 2 3 4 5 6 7 8 9-MA-0099989796
First Printing, September 1996

Library of Congress Cataloging-in-Publication Data

Newton programmer's guide : for Newton 2.0 / Apple Press.
     p. cm.
    Includes index.
    ISBN 0-201-47947-8
    1. Newton (Computer)—Programming.   I. Apple Press.
QA76.8.N48N48   1996
005.265—dc20

96-30960
CIP

Table of Contents

Chapter 2   Getting Started   2-1

Chapter 3   **Views**   3-1

Chapter 6	Pickers, Pop-up Views, and Overviews	6-1

Chapter 7   **Controls and Other Protos**   7-1

Chapter 8

Text and Ink Input and Display   8-1

Chapter 9	Recognition 9-1

Chapter 11   Data Storage and Retrieval   11-1

xvi

Chapter 16	Find 16-1

Chapter 17   **Additional System Services**   17-1

Chapter 19

Built-in Applications and System Data   19-1

Chapter 22   **Transport Interface**   22-1

Figures and Tables

Chapter 7   Controls and Other Protos   7-1

Chapter 8

Text and Ink Input and Display   8-1

About This Book

This book, *Newton Programmer's Guide*, is the definitive guide to Newton programming, providing conceptual information and instructions for using the Newton application programming interfaces.

This book is a companion to *Newton Programmer's Reference*, which provides comprehensive reference documentation for the routines, system prototypes, data structures, constants, and error codes defined by the Newton system. *Newton Programmer's Reference* is included on the CD-ROM that accompanies this book.

Who Should Read This Book

This guide is for anyone who wants to write NewtonScript programs for the Newton family of products.

Before using this guide, you should read *Newton Toolkit User's Guide* to learn how to install and use Newton Toolkit, which is the development environment for writing NewtonScript programs for Newton. You may also want to read *The NewtonScript Programming Language* either before or concurrently with this book. That book describes the NewtonScript language, which is used throughout the *Newton Programmer's Guide*.

To make best use of this guide, you should already have a good understanding of object-oriented programming concepts and have had experience using a high-level programming language such as C or Pascal. It is helpful, but not necessary, to have some experience programming for a graphic user interface (like the Macintosh desktop or Windows). At the very least, you should already have extensive experience using one or more applications with a graphic user interface.

Related Books

This book is one in a set of books available for Newton programmers. You'll also need to refer to these other books in the set:

■ *Newton Toolkit User's Guide*. This book comes with the Newton Toolkit development environment. It introduces the Newton development environment and shows how to develop applications using Newton Toolkit. You should read this book first if you are a new Newton application developer.

- *The NewtonScript Programming Language*. This book comes with the Newton Toolkit development environment. It describes the NewtonScript programming language.

- *Newton Book Maker User's Guide*. This book comes with the Newton Toolkit development environment. It describes how to use Newton Book Maker and Newton Toolkit to make Newton digital books and to add online help to Newton applications.

- *Newton 2.0 User Interface Guidelines*. This book contains guidelines to help you design Newton applications that optimize the interaction between people and Newton devices.

Newton Programmer's Reference CD-ROM

This book is accompanied by a CD-ROM disc that contains the complete text of *Newton Programmer's Reference*. *Newton Programmer's Reference* is the comprehensive reference to the Newton programming interface. It documents all routines, prototypes, data structures, constants, and error codes defined by the Newton system for use by NewtonScript developers.

The companion CD-ROM includes three electronic versions of *Newton Programmer's Reference*. The CD-ROM contains these items, among others:

- The complete *Newton Programmer's Reference* in QuickView format for the Mac OS — the same format used by the *Macintosh Programmer's Toolbox Assistant*. In this format, you can use the extremely fast full-text searching capabilities and ubiquitous hypertext jumps to find reference information quickly.

- The complete *Newton Programmer's Reference* in Windows Help format. This format provides quick and convenient access to the reference information for developers working on Windows platforms.

- The complete *Newton Programmer's Reference* in Adobe Acrobat format. This format provides a fully formatted book with page-numbered table of contents, index, and cross-references. You can print all or portions of the book, and you can also view it online. When viewing online, you can use the indexed search facilities of Adobe Acrobat Reader 2.1 for fast lookup of any information in the book.

The companion CD-ROM also includes an Adobe Acrobat version of this book, *Newton Programmer's Guide*, and a demo version of the Newton Toolkit development environment for the Mac OS.

Sample Code

The Newton Toolkit development environment, from Apple Computer, includes many sample code projects. You can examine these samples, learn from them, and experiment with them. These sample code projects illustrate most of the topics covered in this book. They are an invaluable resource for understanding the topics discussed in this book and for making your journey into the world of Newton programming an easier one.

The Newton Developer Technical Support team continually revises the existing samples and creates new sample code. The latest sample code is included each quarter on the Newton Developer CD, which is distributed to all Newton Developer Program members and to subscribers of the Newton monthly mailing. Sample code is updated on the Newton Development side on the World Wide Web (`http:/ /dev.info.apple.com/newton`) shortly after it is released on the Newton Developer CD. For information about how to contact Apple Computer regarding the Newton Developer Program, see the section "Developer Products and Support," on page xlvii.

The code samples in this book show methods of using various routines and illustrate techniques for accomplishing particular tasks. All code samples have been compiled and, in most cases, tested. However, Apple Computer does not intend that you use these code samples in your application.

To make the code samples in this book more readable, only limited error handling is shown. You need to develop your own techniques for detecting and handling errors.

Conventions Used in This Book

This book uses the following conventions to present various kinds of information.

Special Fonts

This book uses the following special fonts:

■ **Boldface**. Key terms and concepts appear in boldface on first use. These terms are also defined in the Glossary.

■ `Courier typeface`. Code listings, code snippets, and special identifiers in the text such as predefined system frame names, slot names, function names, method names, symbols, and constants are shown in the Courier typeface to distinguish them from regular body text. If you are programming, items that appear in Courier should be typed exactly as shown.

- *Italic typeface.* Italic typeface is used in code to indicate replaceable items, such as the names of function parameters, which you must replace with your own names. The names of other books are also shown in italic type, and *rarely*, this style is used for emphasis.

Tap Versus Click

Throughout the Newton software system and in this book, the word "click" sometimes appears as part of the name of a method or variable, as in `ViewClickScript` or `ButtonClickScript`. This may lead you to believe that the text refers to mouse clicks. It does not. Wherever you see the word "click" used this way, it refers to a tap of the pen on the Newton screen (which is somewhat similar to the click of a mouse on a desktop computer).

Frame Code

If you are using the Newton Toolkit (NTK) development environment in conjunction with this book, you may notice that this book displays the code for a frame (such as a view) differently than NTK does.

In NTK, you can see the code for only a single frame slot at a time. In this book, the code for a frame is presented all at once, so you can see all of the slots in the frame, like this:

```
{  viewClass: clView,
   viewBounds: RelBounds( 20, 50, 94, 142 ),
   viewFlags: vNoFlags,
   viewFormat: vfFillWhite+vfFrameBlack+vfPen(1),
   viewJustify: vjCenterH,

   ViewSetupDoneScript: func()
      :UpdateDisplay(),

   UpdateDisplay: func()
      SetValue(display, 'text, value);
};
```

If while working in NTK, you want to create a frame that you see in the book, follow these steps:

1. On the NTK template palette, find the view class or proto shown in the book. Draw out a view using that template. If the frame shown in the book contains a `_proto` slot, use the corresponding proto from the NTK template palette. If the frame shown in the book contains a `viewClass` slot instead of a `_proto` slot, use the corresponding view class from the NTK template palette.

2. Edit the `viewBounds` slot to match the values shown in the book.

3. Add each of the other slots you see listed in the frame, setting their values to the values shown in the book. Slots that have values are attribute slots, and those that contain functions are method slots.

Developer Products and Support

The *Apple Developer Catalog* (ADC) is Apple Computer's worldwide source for hundreds of development tools, technical resources, training products, and information for anyone interested in developing applications on Apple computer platforms. Customers receive the *Apple Developer Catalog* featuring all current versions of Apple development tools and the most popular third-party development tools. ADC offers convenient payment and shipping options, including site licensing.

To order products or to request a complimentary copy of the *Apple Developer Catalog*, contact

Apple Developer Catalog
Apple Computer, Inc.
P.O. Box 319
Buffalo, NY 14207-0319

Telephone	1-800-282-2732 (United States)
	1-800-637-0029 (Canada)
	716-871-6555 (International)
Fax	716-871-6511
AppleLink	ORDER.ADC
Internet	order.adc@applelink.apple.com
World Wide Web	http://www.devcatalog.apple.com

If you provide commercial products and services, call 408-974-4897 for information on the developer support programs available from Apple.

For Newton-specific information, see the Newton developer World Wide Web page at: `http://dev.info.apple.com/newton`

Undocumented System Software Objects

When browsing in the NTK Inspector window, you may see functions, methods, and data objects that are not documented in this book. Undocumented functions, methods, and data objects are not supported, nor are they guaranteed to work in future Newton devices. Using them may produce undesirable effects on current and future Newton devices.

Overview

This chapter describes the general architecture of the Newton system software, which is divided into three levels, as shown in Figure 1-1 (page 1-2).

The lowest level includes the operating system and the low-level communications system. These parts of the system interact directly with the hardware and perform basic operations such as memory management, input and output, and task switching. NewtonScript applications have no direct access to system services at this level.

The middle level consists of system services that NewtonScript applications can directly access and interact with to accomplish tasks. The system provides hundreds of routines that applications can use to take advantage of these services.

At the highest level are components that applications can use to construct their user interfaces. These reusable components neatly package commonly needed user interface objects such as buttons, lists, tables, input fields, and so on. These components incorporate NewtonScript code that makes use of the system services in the middle level, and that an application can override to customize an object.

Operating System

The Newton platform incorporates a sophisticated preemptive, multitasking operating system. The operating system is a modular set of tasks performing functions such as memory management, task management, scheduling, task to task communications, input and output, power management, and other low-level functions. The operating system manages and interacts directly with the hardware.

A significant part of the operating system is concerned with low-level communication functions. The communication subsystem runs as a separate task. It manages the hardware communication resources available in the system. These include serial, fax modem, AppleTalk networking, and infrared. The communication architecture is extensible, and new communication protocols can be installed and removed at run time, to support additional services and external devices that may be added.

Figure 1-1   System software overview

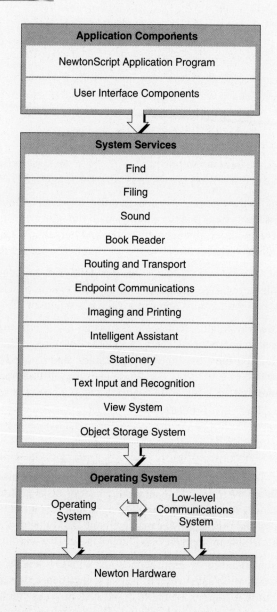

Another operating system task of interest is the Inker. The Inker task is responsible for gathering and displaying input from the electronic tablet overlaying the screen when the user writes on the Newton. The Inker exists as a separate task so that the Newton can gather input and display electronic ink at the same time as other operations are occurring.

All Newton applications, including the recognition system, built-in applications, and applications you develop, run in a single operating system task, called the Application task.

NewtonScript applications have no direct access to the operating system level of software. Access to certain low-level resources, such as communications, is provided by higher-level interfaces.

Memory

It is helpful to understand the use of random access memory (RAM) in the system, since this resource is shared by the operating system and all applications. Newton RAM is divided into separate domains, or sections, that have controlled access. Each domain has its own heap and stack. It is important to know about three of these domains:

- The operating system domain. This portion of memory is reserved for use by the operating system. Only operating system tasks have access to this domain.

- The storage domain. This portion of memory is reserved for permanent, protected storage of user data. All soups, which store the data, reside here, as well as any packages that have been downloaded into the Newton. To protect the data in the storage domain from inadvertent damage, it can only be accessed through the object storage system interface, described in Chapter 11, "Data Storage and Retrieval." If the user adds a PCMCIA card containing RAM, Flash RAM, or read-only memory (ROM) devices, the memory on the card is used to extend the size of the storage domain.

  The storage domain occupies special persistent memory; that is, this memory is maintained even during a system reset. This protects user data, system software updates, and downloaded packages from being lost during system resets. The used and free space in the storage domain is reported to the user in the Memory Info slip in the Extras Drawer.

- The application domain. This portion of memory is used for dynamic memory allocation by the handwriting recognizers and all Newton applications. A fixed part of this domain is allocated to the NewtonScript heap. The NewtonScript heap is important because most objects allocated as a result of your NewtonScript application code are allocated from the NewtonScript heap. These are the only memory objects to which you have direct access. The NewtonScript heap is shared by all applications.

CHAPTER 1

Overview

The system performs automatic memory management of the NewtonScript heap. You don't need to worry about memory allocation or disposal in an application. The system automatically allocates memory when you create a new object in NewtonScript. When references to an object no longer exist, it is freed during the next garbage collection cycle. The system performs garbage collection automatically when it needs additional memory.

The Newton operating system optimizes use of memory by using compression. Various parts of memory are compressed and decompressed dynamically and transparently, as needed. This occurs at a low level, and applications don't need to be concerned with these operations.

Packages

A **package** is the unit in which software is installed on and removed from the Newton. Packages can combine multiple pieces of software into a single unit. The operating system manages packages, which can be installed from PCMCIA cards, from a serial connection to a desktop computer, a network connection, or via modem. When a package comes into the Newton system, the system automatically opens it and dispatches its parts to appropriate handlers in the system.

A package consists of a header, which contains the package name and other information, and one or more **parts,** which contain the software. Parts can include applications, communication drivers, fonts, and system updates (system software code loaded into RAM that overrides or extends the built-in ROM code). A package can also export objects for use by other packages in the system, and can import (use) objects that are exported by other packages.

Packages are optionally stored compressed on the Newton. Compressed packages occupy much less space (roughly half of their uncompressed size), but applications in compressed packages may execute somewhat slower and use slightly more battery power, because of the extra work required to decompress them when they are executed.

For more information about packages, refer to Chapter 11, "Data Storage and Retrieval."

System Services

The Newton system software contains hundreds of routines organized into functional groups of services. Your application can use these routines to accomplish specific tasks such as opening and closing views, storing and retrieving data, playing sounds, drawing shapes, and so on. This section includes brief descriptions of the more important system services with which your application will need to interact. Note that communications services are described in a separate section following this one.

Object Storage System

This system is key to the Newton information architecture. The object storage system provides persistent storage for data.

Newton uses a unified data model. This means that all data stored by all applications uses a common format. Data can easily be shared among different applications, with no translation necessary. This allows seamless integration of applications with each other and with system services.

Data is stored using a database-like model. Objects are stored as **frames,** which are like database records. A frame contains named **slots,** which hold individual pieces of data, like database fields. For example, an address card in the Names application is stored as a frame that contains a slot for each item on the card: name, address, city, state, zip code, phone number, and so on.

Frames are flexible and can represent a wide variety of structures. Slots in a single frame can contain any kind of NewtonScript object, including other frames, and slots can be added or removed from frames dynamically. For a description of NewtonScript objects, refer to *The NewtonScript Programming Language.*

Groups of related frames are stored in **soups,** which are like databases. For example, all the address cards used by the Names application are stored in the Names soup, and all the notes on the Notepad are stored in the Notes soup. All the frames stored in a soup need not contain identical slots. For example, some frames representing address cards may contain a phone number slot and others may not.

Soups are automatically indexed, and applications can create additional indexes on slots that will be used as keys to find data items. You retrieve items from a soup by performing a query on the soup. Queries can be based on an index value or can search for a string, and can include additional constraints. A query results in a **cursor**—an object representing a position in the set of soup entries that satisfy the query. The cursor can be moved back and forth, and can return the current entry.

Soups are stored in physical repositories, called **stores.** Stores are akin to disk volumes on personal computers. The Newton always has at least one store—the internal store. Additional stores reside on PCMCIA cards.

The object storage system interface seamlessly merges soups that have the same name on internal and external stores in a **union** soup. This is a virtual soup that provides an interface similar to a real soup. For example, some of the address cards on a Newton may be stored in the internal Names soup and some may be stored in another Names soup on a PCMCIA card. When the card is installed, those names in the card soup are automatically merged with the existing internal names so the user, or an application, need not do any extra work to access those additional names. When the card is removed, the names simply disappear from the card file union soup.

The object storage system is optimized for small chunks of data and is designed to operate in tight memory constraints. Soups are compressed, and retrieved entries are not allocated on the NewtonScript heap until a slot in the entry is accessed.

You can find information about the object storage system interface in Chapter 11, "Data Storage and Retrieval."

View System

Views are the basic building blocks of most applications. A view is simply a rectangular area mapped onto the screen. Nearly every individual visual item you see on the screen is a view. Views display information to the user in the form of text and graphics, and the user interacts with views by tapping them, writing in them, dragging them, and so on. A view is defined by a frame that contains slots specifying view attributes such as its bounds, fill color, alignment relative to other views, and so on.

The view system is what you work with to manipulate views. There are routines to open, close, animate, scroll, highlight, and lay out views, to name just a few operations you can do. For basic information about views and descriptions of all the routines you can use to interact with the view system, refer to Chapter 3, "Views."

An application consists of a collection of views all working together. Each application has an **application base view** from which all other views in the application typically descend hierarchically. In turn, the base view of each application installed in the Newton descends from the system **root view.** (Think of the hierarchy as a tree structure turned upside down, with the root at the top.) Thus, each application base view is a **child** of the root view. We call a view in which child views exist the **parent** view of those child views. Note that occasionally, an application may also include views that don't descend from the base view but are themselves children of the root view.

The system includes several different primitive **view classes** from which all views are ultimately constructed. Each of these view classes has inherently different behavior and attributes. For example, there are view classes for views that contain text, shapes, pictures, keyboards, analog gauges, and so on.

As an application executes, its view frames receive messages from the system and exchange messages with each other. System messages provide an opportunity for a view to respond appropriately to particular events that are occurring. For example, the view system performs default initialization operations when a view is opened. It also sends the view a `ViewSetupFormScript` message. If the view includes a method to handle this message, it can perform its own initialization operations in that method. Handling system messages in your application is optional since the system performs default behaviors for most events.

Text Input and Recognition

The Newton recognition system uses a sophisticated multiple-recognizer architecture. There are recognizers for text, shapes, and gestures, which can be simultaneously active (this is application-dependent). An arbitrator examines the results from simultaneously active recognizers and returns the recognition match that has the highest confidence.

Recognition is modeless. That is, the user does not need to put the system in a special mode or use a special dialog box in order to write, but can write in any input field at any time.

The text recognizers can handle printed, cursive, or mixed handwriting. They can work together with built-in dictionaries to choose words that accurately match what the user has written. The user can also add new words to a personal dictionary.

Depending on whether or not a text handwriting recognizer is enabled, users can enter handwritten text that is recognized or not. Unrecognized text is known as ink text. Ink text can still be manipulated like recognized text—words can be inserted, deleted, moved around, and reformatted—and ink words can be intermixed with recognized words in a single paragraph. Ink words can be recognized later using the deferred recognition capability of the system.

The shape recognizer recognizes both simple and complex geometric objects, cleaning up rough drawings into shapes with straight lines and smooth curves. The shape recognizer also recognizes symmetry, using that property, if present, to help it recognize and display objects.

For each view in an application, you can specify which recognizers are enabled and how they are configured. For example, the text recognizer can be set to recognize only names, or names and phone numbers, or only words in a custom dictionary that you supply, among other choices.

Most recognition events are handled automatically by the system view classes, so you don't need to do anything in your application to handle recognition events, unless you want to do something special. For example, when a user writes a word in a text view, that view automatically passes the strokes to the recognizer, accepts the recognized word back, and displays the word. In addition, the view automatically handles corrections for you. The user can double-tap a word to pop up a list of other possible matches for it, or to use the keyboard to correct it.

For information on methods for accepting and working with text input, refer to Chapter 8, "Text and Ink Input and Display." For information on controlling recognition in views and working with dictionaries, refer to Chapter 9, "Recognition."

Stationery

Stationery is a capability of the system that allows applications to be extended by other developers. The word "stationery" refers to the capability of having different kinds of data within a single application (such as plain notes and outlines in the Notepad) and/or to the capability of having different ways of viewing the same data (such as the Card and All Info views in the Names file). An application that supports stationery can be extended either by adding a new type of data to it (for example, adding recipe cards to the Notepad), or by adding a new type of viewer for existing data (a new way of viewing Names file entries or a new print format, for example).

To support stationery, an application must register with the system a frame, called a data definition, that describes the data with which it works. The different data definitions available to an application are listed on the pop-up menu attached to the New button. In addition, an application must register one or more view definitions, which describe how the data is to be viewed or printed. View definitions can include simple read-only views, editor-type views, or print formats. The different view definitions available in an application (not including print formats) are listed on the pop-up menu attached to the Show button.

Stationery is well integrated into the NewtApp framework, so if you use that framework for your application, using stationery is easy. The printing architecture also uses stationery, so all application print formats are registered as a kind of stationery.

For more information about using stationery, see Chapter 5, "Stationery."

Intelligent Assistant

A key part of the Newton information architecture is the Intelligent Assistant. The Intelligent Assistant is a system service that attempts to complete actions for the user according to deductions it makes about the task that the user is currently performing. The Assistant is always instantly available to the user through the Assist button, yet remains nonintrusive.

The Assistant knows how to complete several built-in tasks; they are Scheduling (adding meetings), Finding, Reminding (adding To Do items), Mailing, Faxing, Printing, Calling, and getting time information from the Time Zones map. Each of these tasks has several synonyms; for example, the user can write "call," "phone," "ring," or "dial" to make a phone call.

Applications can add new tasks so that the Assistant supports their special capabilities and services. The Newton unified data model makes it possible for the Assistant to access data stored by any application, thus allowing the Assistant to be well integrated in the system.

For details on using the Intelligent Assistant and integrating support for it into your application, see Chapter 18, "Intelligent Assistant."

Imaging and Printing

At the operating system level, the Newton imaging and printing software is based on an object-oriented, device-independent imaging model. The imaging model is monochrome since the current Newton screen is a black-and-white screen.

NewtonScript application programs don't call low-level imaging routines directly to do drawing or image manipulation. In fact, most drawing is handled for applications by the user interface components they incorporate, or when they call other routines that display information. However, there is a versatile set of high-level drawing routines that you can call directly to create and draw shapes, pictures, bitmaps, and text. When drawing, you can vary the pen thickness, pen pattern, fill pattern, and other attributes. For details on drawing, refer to Chapter 13, "Drawing and Graphics."

The Newton text imaging facility supports Unicode directly, so the system can be easily localized to display languages using different script systems. The system is extensible, so it's possible to add additional fonts, font engines, and printer drivers.

The high-level interface to printing on the Newton uses a model identical to that used for views. Essentially, you design a special kind of view called a print format to specify how printed information is to be laid out on the page. Print formats use a unique view template that automatically adjusts its size to the page size of the printer chosen by the user. When the user prints, the system handles all the details of rendering the views on the printer according to the layout you specified.

The Newton offers the feature of deferred printing. The user can print even though he or she is not connected to a printer at the moment. An object describing the print job is stored in the Newton Out Box application, and when a printer is connected later, the user can then select that print job for printing. Again, this feature is handled automatically by the system and requires no additional application programming work.

For information on how to add printing capabilities to an application, refer to Chapter 21, "Routing Interface."

Sound

The Newton includes a monophonic speaker and can play sounds sampled at rates up to 22 kHz. You can attach sounds to particular events associated with a view, such as showing it, hiding it, and scrolling it. You can also use sound routines to play sounds synchronously or asynchronously at any other time.

Newton can serve as a phone dialer by dialing phone numbers through the speaker. The dialing tones are built into the system ROM, along with several other sounds that can be used in applications.

Besides the sounds that are built into the system ROM, you can import external sound resources into an application through the Newton Toolkit development environment.

For information about using sound in an application, see Chapter 14, "Sound."

Book Reader

Book Reader is a system service that displays interactive digital books on the Newton screen. Digital books can include multiple-font text, bitmap and vector graphics, and on-screen controls for content navigation. Newton digital books allow the user to scroll pages, mark pages with bookmarks, access data directly by page number or subject, mark up pages using digital ink, and perform text searches. Of course, the user can copy and paste text from digital books, as well as print text and graphics from them.

Newton Press and Newton Book Maker are two different development tools that you use to create digital books for the Newton. Nonprogrammers can easily create books using Newton Press. Newton Book Maker is a more sophisticated tool that uses a text-based command language allowing you to provide additional services to the user or exercise greater control over page layout. Also, using Book Maker, you can attach data, methods, and view templates to book content to provide customized behavior or work with the Intelligent Assistant.

The Book Maker application can also be used to create on-line help for an application. The installation of on-line help in an application package requires some rudimentary NewtonScript programming ability; however, nonprogrammers can create on-line help content, again using only a word processor and some basic Book Maker commands.

Refer to the book *Newton Book Maker User's Guide* for information on Book Reader, the Book Maker command language, and the use of Newton Toolkit to create digital book packages and on-line help. Refer to the *Newton Press User's Guide* for information on using Newton Press.

Find

Find is a system service that allows users to search one or all applications in the system for occurrences of a particular string. Alternatively, the user can search for data time-stamped before or after a specified date. When the search is completed, the Find service displays an overview list of items found that match the search criteria. The user can tap an item in the list and the system opens the corresponding application and displays the data containing the selected string. Users access the Find service by tapping the Find button.

If you want to allow the user to search for data stored by your application, you need to implement certain methods that respond to find messages sent by the system. You'll need to supply one method that searches your application's soup(s) for data and returns the results in a particular format, and another method that locates and displays the found data in your application if the user taps on it in the find overview. The system software includes routines and templates that help you support find in your application. For details on supporting the Find service, refer to Chapter 16, "Find."

Filing

The Filing service allows users to tag soup-based data in your application with labels used to store, retrieve, and display the data by category. The labels used to tag entries are represented as folders in the user interface; however, no true hierarchical filing exists—the tagged entries still reside in the soup. Users access the filing service through a standard user interface element called the file folder button, which looks like a small file folder.

When the user chooses a category for an item, the system notifies your application that filing has changed. Your application must perform the appropriate application-specific tasks and redraw the current view, providing to the user the illusion that the item has been placed in a folder. When the user chooses to display data from a category other than the currently displayed one, the system also notifies your application, which must retrieve and display data in the selected category.

The system software includes templates that help your application implement the filing button and the selector that allows the user to choose which category of data to display. Your application must provide methods that respond to filing messages sent by the system in response to user actions such as filing an item, changing the category of items to display, and changing the list of filing categories. For details on supporting the Filing service, refer to Chapter 15, "Filing."

Communications Services

This section provides an overview of the communications services in Newton system software 2.0.

The Newton communications architecture is application-oriented, rather than protocol-oriented. This means that you can focus your programming efforts on what your application needs to do, rather than on communication protocol details. A simple high-level NewtonScript interface encapsulates all protocol details, which are handled in the same way regardless of which communication transport tool you are using.

Overview

The communication architecture is flexible, supporting complex communication needs. The architecture is also extensible, allowing new communication transport tools to be added dynamically and accessed through the same interface as existing transports. In this way, new communication hardware devices can be supported.

The Newton communications architecture is illustrated in Figure 1-2.

Figure 1-2   Communications architecture

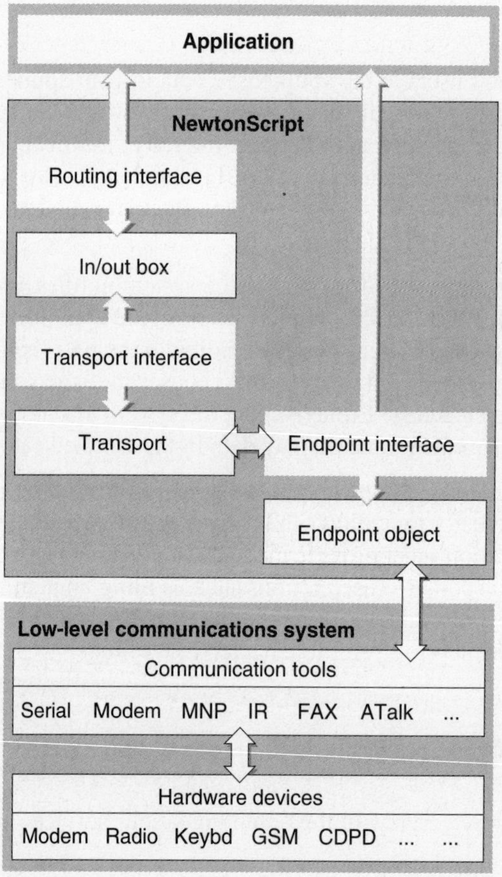

Figure 1-2 shows four unique communications interfaces available for you to use:

■ routing interface

■ endpoint interface

- transport interface

- communication tool interface

The first two, routing and endpoint interfaces, are available for NewtonScript applications to use directly.

The transport interface is a NewtonScript interface, but it isn't used directly by applications. A transport consists of a special kind of application of its own that is installed on a Newton device and that provides new communication services to the system.

The communication tool interface is a low-level C++ interface.

These interfaces are described in more detail in the following sections.

NewtonScript Application Communications

There are two basic types of NewtonScript communications an application can do. The most common type of communication that most applications do is routing through the In/Out Box. As an alternative, applications can use the endpoint interface to control endpoint objects.

Typically, an application uses only one of these types of communication, but sometimes both are needed. These two types of communication are described in the following sections.

Routing Through the In/Out Box

The routing interface is the highest-level NewtonScript communication interface. The routing interface allows an application to communicate with the In/Out Box and lets users send data and receive data from outside the system. In applications, users access routing services through a standard user interface element called the Action button, which looks like a small envelope. Users access the In/Out Box application through icons in the Newton Extras Drawer. The In/Out Box provides a common user interface for all incoming and outgoing data in the system.

The routing interface is best suited for user-controlled messaging and transaction-based communications. For example, the Newton built-in applications use this interface for e-mail, beaming, printing, and faxing. Outgoing items can be stored in the Out Box until a physical connection is available, when the user can choose to transmit the items, or they can be sent immediately. Incoming items are received in the In Box, where the user can get new mail and beamed items, for example.

For information on the routing interface, refer to Chapter 21, "Routing Interface."

The In/Out Box makes use of the transport and endpoint interfaces internally to perform its operations.

If you are writing an application that takes advantage of only the transports currently installed in the Newton system, you need to use only the routing

Communications Services   1-13 interface. You need to use the transport or endpoint interfaces only when writing custom communication tools.

Endpoint Interface

The endpoint interface is a somewhat lower-level NewtonScript interface; it has no visible representation to the Newton user. The endpoint interface is suited for real-time communication needs such as database access and terminal emulation. It uses an asynchronous, state-driven communications model.

The endpoint interface is based on a single proto—protoBasicEndpoint—that provides a standard interface to all communication tools (serial, fax modem, infrared, AppleTalk, and so on). The endpoint object created from this proto encapsulates and maintains the details of the specific connection. This proto provides methods for

- interacting with the underlying communication tool
- setting communication tool options
- opening and closing connections
- sending and receiving data

The basic endpoint interface is described in Chapter 23, "Endpoint Interface."

Low-Level Communications

There are two lower-level communication interfaces that are not used directly by applications. The transport and communication tool interfaces are typically used together (along with the endpoint interface) to provide a new communication service to the system.

These two interfaces are described in the following sections.

Transport Interface

If you are providing a new communication service through the use of endpoints and lower-level communication tools, you may need to use the transport interface. The transport interface allows your communication service to talk to the In/Out Box and to make itself available to users through the Action button (envelope icon) in most applications.

When the user taps the Action button in an application, the Action picker appears. Built-in transports available on the Action picker include printing, faxing, and beaming. Any new transports that you provide are added to this list.

For more information, refer to Chapter 22, "Transport Interface."

Communication Tool Interface

Underlying the NewtonScript interface is the low-level communications system. This system consists of a communications manager module and several code components known as communication tools. These communication tools interact directly with the communication hardware devices installed in the system. The communication tools are written in C++ and are not directly accessible from NewtonScript—they are accessed indirectly through an endpoint object.

The built-in communication tools include:

■ Synchronous and asynchronous serial

■ Fax/data modem (data is V.34 with MNP/V.42 and fax is V.17 with Class 1, 2, and 2.0 support)

■ Point-to-point infrared—called beaming (Sharp 9600 and Apple IR-enhanced protocols)

■ AppleTalk ADSP protocol

For information about configuring the built-in communication tools through the endpoint interface, refer to Chapter 24, "Built-in Communications Tools."

Note that the communications manager module, and each of the individual communication tools, runs as a separate operating system task. All NewtonScript code is in a different task, called the Application task.

The system is extensible—additional communication tools can be installed at run time. Installed tools are made available to NewtonScript client applications through the same endpoint interface as the built-in tools.

At some point, Apple Computer, Inc. may release the tools and interfaces that allow C++ communication tool development.

Application Components

At the highest level of system software are dozens of components that applications can use to construct their user interfaces and other nonvisible objects. These reusable components neatly package commonly needed user interface objects such as buttons, lists, tables, input fields, and so on. These components incorporate NewtonScript code that makes use of other system services, and which an application can override to customize an object.

These components are built into the Newton ROM. When you reference one of these components in your application, the code isn't copied into your application— your application simply makes a reference to the component in the ROM. This conserves memory at run time and still allows your application to easily override any attributes of the built-in component. Because you can build much of your application using these components, Newton applications tend to be much smaller in size than similar applications on desktop computers.

A simple example of how you can construct much of an application using components is illustrated in Figure 1-3. This simple application accepts names and phone numbers and saves them into a soup. It was constructed in just a few minutes using three different components.

The application base view is implemented by a single component that includes the title bar at the top, the status bar at the bottom, the clock and the close box, and the outer frame of the application. The Name and Phone input lines are each created from the same component that implements a simple text input line; the two buttons are created from the same button component. The only code you must write to make this application fully functional is to make the buttons perform their actions. That is, make the Clear button clear the input lines and make the Save button get the text from the input lines and save it to a soup.

Figure 1-3   Using components

The components available for use by applications are shown on the layout palette in Newton Toolkit. These components are known as **protos,** which is short for "prototypes." In addition to the built-in components, Newton Toolkit lets you create your own reusable components, called user protos. The various built-in components are documented throughout the book in the chapter containing information related to each proto. For example, text input protos are described in Chapter 8, "Text and Ink Input and Display;" protos that implement pickers and lists are described in Chapter 6, "Pickers, Pop-up Views, and Overviews;" and protos that implement controls and other miscellaneous protos are described in Chapter 7, "Controls and Other Protos."

The NewtApp framework consists of a special collection of protos that are designed to be used together in a layered hierarchy to build a complete application. For more information about the NewtApp protos, refer to Chapter 4, "NewtApp Applications."

Using System Software

Most of the routines and application components that comprise the Newton system software reside in ROM, provided in special chips contained in every Newton device. When your application calls a system routine, the operating system executes the appropriate code contained in ROM.

This is different from traditional programming environments where system software routines are accessed by linking a subroutine library with the application code. That approach results in much larger applications and makes it harder to provide new features and fix bugs in the system software.

The ROM-based model used in the Newton provides a simple way for the operating system to substitute the code that is executed in response to a particular system software routine, or to substitute an application component. Instead of executing the ROM-based code for some routine, the operating system might choose to load some substitute code into RAM; when your application calls the routine, the operating system intercepts the call and executes the RAM-based code.

RAM-based code that substitutes for ROM-based code is called a system update. Newton system updates are stored in the storage memory domain, which is persistent storage.

Besides application components, the Newton ROM contains many other objects such as fonts, sounds, pictures, and strings that might be useful to applications. Applications can access these objects by using special references called **magic pointers.** Magic pointers provide a mechanism for code written in a development system separate from the Newton to reference objects in the Newton ROM or in other packages. Magic pointer references are resolved at run time by the operating system, which substitutes the actual address of the ROM or package object for the magic pointer reference.

Magic pointers are constants defined in Newton Toolkit. For example, the names of all the application components, or protos, are actually magic pointer constants. You can find a list of all the ROM magic pointer constants in the Newton 2.0 Defs file, included with Newton Toolkit.

The NewtonScript Language

You write Newton applications in NewtonScript, a dynamic object-oriented language developed especially for the Newton platform, though the language is highly portable. NewtonScript is designed to operate within tight memory constraints, so is well suited to small hand-held devices like Newton.

NewtonScript is used to define, access, and manipulate objects in the Newton system. NewtonScript frame objects provide the basis for object-oriented features such as inheritance and message sending.

Newton Toolkit normally compiles NewtonScript into byte codes. The Newton system software contains a byte code interpreter that interprets the byte codes at run time. This has two advantages: byte codes are much smaller than native code, and Newton applications are easily portable to other processors, since the interpreter is portable. Newton Toolkit can also compile NewtonScript into native code. Native code occupies much more space than interpreted code, but in certain circumstances it can execute much faster.

For a complete reference to NewtonScript, refer to *The NewtonScript Programming Language*.

What's New in Newton 2.0

Version 2.0 of the Newton System Software brings many changes to all areas. Some programming interfaces have been extended; others have been completely replaced with new interfaces; and still other interfaces are brand new. For those readers familiar with previous versions of system software, this section gives a brief overview of what is new and what has changed in Newton 2.0, focusing on those programming interfaces that you will be most interested in as a developer.

NewtApp

NewtApp is a new application framework designed to help you build a complete, full-featured Newton application more quickly. The NewtApp framework consists of a collection of protos that are designed to be used together in a layered hierarchy. The NewtApp framework links together soup-based data with the display and editing of that data in an application. For many types of applications, using the NewtApp framework can significantly reduce development time because the protos automatically manage many routine programming tasks. For example, some of the tasks the protos support include filing, finding, routing, scrolling, displaying an overview, and soup management.

The NewtApp framework is not suited for all Newton applications. If your application stores data as individual entries in a soup, displays that data to the user in views, and allows the user to edit some or all of the data, then it is a potential candidate for using the NewtApp framework. NewtApp is well suited to "classic" form-based applications. Some of the built-in applications constructed using the NewtApp framework include the Notepad and the Names file.

Stationery

Stationery is a new capability of Newton 2.0 that allows applications to be extended by other developers. If your application supports stationery, then it can be extended by others. Similarly, you can extend another developer's application that supports stationery. You should also note that the printing architecture now uses stationery, so all application print formats are registered as a kind of stationery.

Stationery is a powerful capability that makes applications much more extensible than in the past. Stationery is also well integrated into the NewtApp framework, so if you use that framework for your application, using stationery is easy. For more information about stationery, see the section "Stationery" (page 1-8).

Views

New features for the view system include a drag-and-drop interface that allows you to provide users with a drag-and-drop capability between views. There are hooks to provide for custom feedback to the user during the drag process and to handle copying or moving the item.

The system now includes the capability for the user to view the display in portrait or landscape orientation, so the screen orientation can be changed (rotated) at any time. Applications can support this new capability by supporting the new ReorientToScreen message, which the system uses to alert all applications to re-layout their views.

Several new view methods provide features such as bringing a view to the front or sending it to the back, automatically sizing buttons, finding the view bounds including the view frame, and displaying modal dialogs to the user.

There is a new message, ViewPostQuitScript, that is sent to a view (only on request) when it is closing, after all of the view's child views have been destroyed. This allows you to do additional clean-up, if necessary. And, you'll be pleased to know that the order in which child views receive the ViewQuitScript message is now well defined: it is top-down.

Additionally, there are some new viewJustify constants that allow you to specify that a view is sized proportionally to its sibling or parent view, horizontally and/or vertically.

Protos

There are many new protos supplied in the new system ROM. There are new pop-up button pickers, map-type pickers, and several new time, date, and duration pickers. There are new protos that support the display of overviews and lists based on soup entries. There are new protos that support the input of rich strings (strings that contain either recognized characters or ink text). There are a variety of new scroller protos. There is an integrated set of protos designed to make it easy for you to display status messages to the user during lengthy or complex operations.

Generic list pickers, available in system 1.0, have been extended to support bitmap items that can be hit-tested as two-dimensional grids. For example, a phone keypad can be included as a single item in a picker. Additionally, list pickers can now scroll if all the items can't fit on the screen.

Data Storage

There are many enhancements to the data storage system for system software 2.0. General soup performance is significantly improved. A tagging mechanism for soup entries makes changing folders much faster for the user. You can use the tagging mechanism to greatly speed access to subsets of entries in a soup. Queries support more features, including the use of multiple slot indexes, and the query interface is cleaner. Entry aliases make it easy to save unique references to soup entries for fast access later without holding onto the actual entry.

A new construct, the virtual binary object, supports the creation and manipulation of very large objects that could not be accommodated in the NewtonScript heap. There is a new, improved soup change-notification mechanism that gives applications more control over notification and how they respond to soup changes. More precise information about exactly what changed is communicated to applications. Soup data can now be built directly into packages in the form of a store part. Additionally, packages can contain protos and other objects that can be exported through magic pointer references, and applications can import such objects from available packages.

Text Input

The main change to text input involves the use of ink text. The user can choose to leave written text unrecognized and still manipulate the text by inserting, deleting, reformatting, and moving the words around, just as with recognized text. Ink words and recognized words can be intermixed within a single paragraph. A new string format, called a rich string, handles both ink and recognized text in the same string.

There are new protos, `protoRichInputLine` and `protoRichLabelInputLine`, that you can use in your application to allow users to enter ink text in fields. In addition, the view classes `clEditView` and `clParagraphView` now support ink text. There are several new functions that allow you to manipulate and convert between regular strings and rich strings. Other functions provide access to ink and stroke data, allow conversion between strokes, points, and ink, and allow certain kinds of ink and stroke manipulations.

There are several new functions that allow you to access and manipulate the attributes of font specifications, making changing the font attributes of text much easier. A new font called the handwriting font is built in. This font looks similar to handwritten characters and is used throughout the system for all entered text. You should use it for displaying all text the user enters.

The use of on-screen keyboards for text input is also improved. There are new proto buttons that your application can use to give users access to the available keyboards. It's easier to include custom keyboards for your application. Several new methods allow you to track and manage the insertion caret, which the system displays when a keyboard is open. Note also that a real hardware keyboard is available for the Newton system, and users may use it anywhere to enter text. The system automatically supports its use in all text fields.

Graphics and Drawing

Style frames for drawing shapes can now include a custom clipping region other than the whole destination view, and can specify a scaling or offset transformation to apply to the shape being drawn.

Several new functions allow you to create, flip, rotate, and draw into bitmap shapes. Also, you can capture all or part of a view into a bitmap. There are new protos that support the display, manipulation, and annotation of large bitmaps such as received faxes. A new function, `InvertRect`, inverts a rectangle in a view.

Views of the class `clPictureView` can now contain graphic shapes in addition to bitmap or picture objects.

System Services

System-supplied Filing services have been extended; applications can now filter the display of items according to the store on which they reside, route items directly to a specified store from the filing slip, and provide their own unique folders. In addition, registration for notification of changes to folder names has been simplified.

Two new global functions can be used to register or unregister an application with the Find service. In addition, Find now maintains its state between uses, performs "date equal" finds, and returns to the user more quickly.

Applications can now register callback functions to be executed when the Newton powers on or off. Applications can register a view to be added to the user preferences roll. Similarly, applications can register a view to be added to the formulas roll.

The implementation of undo has changed to an undo/redo model instead of two levels of undo, so applications must support this new model.

Recognition

Recognition enhancements include the addition of an alternate high-quality recognizer for printed text and significant improvements in the cursive recognizer. While this doesn't directly affect applications, it does significantly improve recognition performance in the system, leading to a better user experience. Other enhancements that make the recognition system much easier to use include a new correction picker, a new punctuation picker, and the caret insertion writing mode (new writing anywhere is inserted at the caret position).

Specific enhancements of interest to developers include the addition of a recConfig frame, which allows more flexible and precise control over recognition in individual input views. A new proto, protoCharEdit, provides a comb-style entry view in which you can precisely control recognition and restrict entries to match a predefined character template.

Additionally, there are new functions that allow you to pass ink text, strokes, and shapes to the recognizer to implement your own deferred recognition. Detailed recognition corrector information (alternate words and scores) is now available to applications.

Sound

The interface for playing sounds is enhanced in Newton 2.0. In addition to the existing sound functions, there is a new function to play a sound at a particular volume and there is a new protoSoundChannel object. The protoSoundChannel object encapsulates sounds and methods that operate on them. Using a sound channel object, sound playback is much more flexible—the interface supports starting, stopping, pausing, and playing sounds simultaneously through multiple sound channels.

Built-in Applications

Unlike in previous versions, the built-in applications are all more extensible in version 2.0. The Notepad supports stationery, so you can easily extend it by adding new "paper" types to the New pop-up menu. The Names file also supports stationery, so it's easy to add new card types, new card layout styles, and new data items to existing cards by registering new data definitions and view definitions for the Names application. There's also a method that adds a new card to the Names soup.

The Dates application includes a comprehensive interface that gives you the ability to add, find, move, and delete meetings and events. You can get and set various kinds of information related to meetings, and you can create new meeting types for the Dates application. You can programmatically control what day is displayed as the first day of the week, and you can control the display of a week number in the Calendar view.

The To Do List application also includes a new interface that supports creating new to do items, retrieving items for a particular date or range, removing old items, and other operations.

Routing and Transports

The Routing interface is significantly changed in Newton 2.0. The system builds the list of routing actions dynamically, when the user taps the Action button. This allows all applications to take advantage of new transports that are added to the system at any time. Many hooks are provided for your application to perform custom operations at every point during the routing operation. You register routing formats with the system as view definitions. A new function allows you to send items programmatically.

Your application has much more flexibility with incoming items. You can choose to automatically put away items and to receive foreign data (items from different applications or from a non-Newton source).

The Transport interface is entirely new. This interface provides several new protos and functions that allow you to build a custom communication service and make it available to all applications through the Action button and the In/Out Box. Features include a logging capability, a system for displaying progress and status information to the user, support for custom routing slips, and support for transport preferences.

Endpoint Communication

The Endpoint communication interface is new but very similar to the 1.0 interface. There is a new proto, `protoBasicEndpoint`, that encapsulates the connection and provides methods to manage the connection and send and receive data. Additionally, a derivative endpoint, `protoStreamingEndpoint`, provides the capability to send and receive very large frame objects.

Specific enhancements introduced by the new endpoint protos include the ability to handle and identify many more types of data by tagging the data using data forms specified in the `form` slot of an endpoint option. Most endpoint methods can now be called asynchronously, and asynchronous operation is the recommended way to do endpoint-based communication. Support is also included for time-outs and multiple termination sequences. Error handling is improved.

Overview

There have been significant changes in the handling of binary (raw) data. For input, you can now target a direct data input object, resulting in significantly faster performance. For output, you can specify offsets and lengths, allowing you to send the data in chunks.

Additionally, there is now support for multiple simultaneous communication sessions.

Utilities

Many new utility functions are available in Newton 2.0. There are several new deferred, delayed, and conditional message-sending functions. New array functions provide ways to insert elements, search for elements, and sort arrays. Additionally, there's a new set of functions that operate on sorted arrays using binary search algorithms. New and enhanced string functions support rich strings, perform conditional substring substitution, tokenize strings, and perform case-sensitive string compares. A new group of functions gets, sets, and checks for the existence of global variables and functions.

Books

New Book Reader features include better browser behavior (configurable auto-closing), expanded off-line bookkeeping abilities, persistent bookmarks, the ability to remove bookmarks, and more efficient use of memory.

New interfaces provide additional ways to navigate in books, customize Find behavior, customize bookmarks, and add help books. Book Reader also supports interaction with new system messages related to scrolling, turning pages, installing books, and removing books. Additional interfaces are provided for adding items to the status bar and the Action menu.

Getting Started

This chapter describes where to begin when you're thinking about developing a Newton application. It describes the different kinds of software you can develop and install on the Newton and the advantages and disadvantages of using different application structures.

Additionally, this chapter describes how to create and register your developer signature.

Before you read this chapter, you should be familiar with the information described in Chapter 1, "Overview."

Choosing an Application Structure

When you create an application program for the Newton platform, you can use one of the following basic types of application structures:

- minimal predefined structure, by basing the application on a view class of `clView` or the `protoApp` proto
- highly structured, by basing the application on the NewtApp framework of protos
- highly structured and specialized for text, by building a digital book

Alternatively, you might want to develop software that is not accessed through an icon in the Extras Drawer. For example, you might want to install stationery, a transport, or some other kind of specialized software that does something like creating a soup and then removing itself.

These various approaches to software development are discussed in the following sections.

Minimal Structure

The minimalist approach for designing a Newton application starts with an empty or nearly empty container that provides little or no built-in functionality—thus the "minimalist" name. This approach is best suited for specialized applications that don't follow the "classic" form-based model. For example, some types of applications that might use this approach include games, utilities, calculators, and graphics applications.

The advantage of using the minimalist approach is that it's simple and small. Usually you'd choose this approach because you don't need or want a lot of built-in support from a comprehensive application framework, along with the extra size and overhead that such support brings.

The disadvantage of the minimalist approach is that it doesn't provide any support from built-in features, like the NewtApp framework does. You get just a simple container in which to construct your application.

To construct an application using the minimalist approach, you can use the view class `clView` or the proto `protoApp` as your application base view. The view class `clView` is the bare minimum you can start with. This is the most basic of the primitive view classes. It provides nothing except an empty container. The `protoApp` provides a little bit more, it includes a framed border, a title at the top, and a close box so the user can close it. For details on these objects, see `clView` (page 1-1) and `protoApp` (page 1-2) in *Newton Programmer's Reference*.

Neither of these basic containers provide much built-in functionality. You must add functionality yourself by adding other application components to your application. There are dozens of built-in protos that you can use, or you can create your own protos using NTK. Most of the built-in protos are documented in these two chapters: Chapter 6, "Pickers, Pop-up Views, and Overviews,"and Chapter 7, "Controls and Other Protos." Note also that certain protos in the NewtApp framework can be used outside of a NewtApp application. For information on NewtApp protos, see Chapter 4, "NewtApp Applications."

NewtApp Framework

NewtApp is an application framework that is well suited to "classic" form-based applications. Such applications typically gather and store data in soups, display individual soup entries to users in views, and allow the user to edit some or all of the data. For example, some types of applications that might use NewtApp include surveys and other data gathering applications, personal information managers, and record-keeping applications. Some of the built-in applications constructed using NewtApp include the Notepad, Names file, In/Out Box, Calls, and Time Zones.

The advantage of NewtApp is that it provides a framework of protos designed to help you build a complete, full-featured Newton application more quickly than if you started from scratch. The NewtApp protos are designed to be used together in a layered hierarchy that links together soup-based data with the display and editing of that data in an application. For many types of applications, using the NewtApp framework can significantly reduce development time because the protos automatically manage many routine programming tasks. For example, some of the tasks the protos support include filing, finding, routing, scrolling, displaying an overview, and soup management.

The disadvantage of NewtApp is that it is structured to support a particular kind of application—one that allows the creation, editing, and display of soup data. And particularly, it supports applications structured so that there is one data element (card, note, and so on) per soup entry. If your application doesn't lend itself to that structure or doesn't need much of the support that NewtApp provides, then it would be better to use a different approach to application design.

For details on using the NewtApp framework to construct an application, see Chapter 4, "NewtApp Applications."

Digital Books

If you want to develop an application that displays a large amount of text, handles multiple pages, or needs to precisely layout text, you may want to consider making a digital book instead of a traditional application. In fact, if you are dealing with a really large amount of text, like more than a few dozen screens full, then you could make your job much easier by using the digital book development tools.

Digital books are designed to display and manipulate large amounts of text and graphics. Digital books can include all the functionality of an application—they can include views, protos, and methods that are executed as a result of user actions. In fact, you can do almost everything in a digital book that you can do in a more traditional application, except a traditional application doesn't include the text layout abilities.

The advantage of using a digital book structure is that you gain the automatic text layout and display abilities of Book Reader, the built-in digital book reading application. Additionally, the book-making tools are easy to use and allow you to quickly turn large amounts of text and graphics into Newton books with minimal effort.

The disadvantage of using a digital book is that it is designed to support a particular kind of application—one that is like a book. If your application doesn't lend itself to that structure or doesn't need much of the text-handling support that Book Reader provides, then it would be better to use a different approach to application design.

For information on creating digital books using the Book Maker command language and/or incorporating NewtonScript code and objects into digital books, see *Newton Book Maker User's Guide*. For information on creating simpler digital books see *Newton Press User's Guide*.

Other Kinds of Software

There are other kinds of software you can develop for the Newton platform that are not accessed by the user through an icon in the Extras drawer. These might include new types of stationery that extend existing applications, new panels for the Preferences or Formulas applications, new routing or print formats, communication transports, and other kinds of invisible applications. Such software is installed in a kind of part called an auto part (because its part code is `auto`).

You can also install a special kind of auto part that is automatically removed after it is installed. The `InstallScript` function in the auto part is executed, and then it is removed. (For more information about the `InstallScript` function, see the section "Package Loading, Activation, and Deactivation" beginning on page 2-4.) This kind of auto part is useful to execute some code on the Newton, for example, to create a soup, and then to remove the code. This could be used to write an installer application that installs just a portion of the data supplied with an application. For example, you might have a game or some other application that uses various data sets, and the installer could let the user choose which data sets to install (as soups) to save storage space.

Any changes made by an automatically removed auto part are lost when the Newton is reset, except for changes made to soups, which are persistent.

For additional information about creating auto parts and other kinds of parts such as font, dictionary, and store parts, refer to *Newton Toolkit User's Guide*.

Package Loading, Activation, and Deactivation

When a package is first loaded onto the Newton store from some external source, the system executes the `DoNotInstallScript` function in each frame part in the package. This function gives the parts in the package a chance to prevent installation of the package. If the package is not prevented from being installed, next it is activated.

When a package containing an application or auto part is activated on the Newton, the system executes a special function in those parts: the `InstallScript` function. A package is normally activated as a result of installing it—by inserting a storage card containing it, by moving it from one store to another, by downloading it from a desktop computer, by downloading it via modem or some other communication device, or by soft resetting the Newton device. Packages can also exist in an inactive state on a Newton store, and such a package can be activated by the user at a later time.

When a package is deactivated, the system executes another special function in each of the application and auto parts in the package: the `RemoveScript` function. A package is normally deactivated when the card it resides on is removed, when it is moved to another store (it is deactivated then reactivated), or when the user deletes the application icon in the Extras Drawer. Packages can also be deactivated without removing them from the store.

When a package is removed as a result of the user deleting it from the Extras Drawer, the system also executes the DeletionScript function in each of the package frame parts. This occurs before the RemoveScript function is executed.

The following sections describe how to use these functions.

Loading

The DoNotInstallScript function in a package part is executed when a package is first loaded onto a Newton store from some external source (this does not include inserting a storage card containing the package or moving it between stores). This function applies to all types of frame parts (for example, not store parts).

This method gives the parts in the package a chance to prevent installation of the entire package. If any of the package parts returns a non-nil value from this function, the package is not installed and is discarded.

You should provide the user with some kind of feedback if package installation is prevented, rather than silently failing. For example, to ensure that a package is installed only on the internal store you could write a DoNotInstallScript function like the following:

```
func()
begin
    if GetStores()[0] <> GetVBOStore(ObjectPkgRef('foo)) then
    begin
    GetRoot():Notify(kNotifyAlert, kAppName,
            "This package was not installed.
            It can be installed only onto the internal store.");
    true;
    end;
end
```

Activation

The InstallScript function in a package part is executed when an application or auto part is activated on the Newton or whenever the Newton is reset.

This function lets you perform any special installation operations that you need to do, any initialization, and any registration for system services.

IMPORTANT

Any changes that you make to the system in the
InstallScript function must be reversed in the
RemoveScript function. For example, if you register your
application for certain system services or install print formats,
stationery, or other objects in the system, you must reverse
these changes and remove or unregister these objects in the
RemoveScript function. If you fail to do this, such changes
cannot be removed by the user, and if your application is on a
card, they won't be able to remove the card without getting a
warning message to put the card back. ▲

Only applications and auto parts use the InstallScript function. Note that the
InstallScript function takes one extra argument when used for an auto part.
Applications built using the NewtApp framework require special
InstallScript and RemoveScript functions. For details, see Chapter 4,
"NewtApp Applications."

Deactivation

The RemoveScript function in a package part is executed when an application or
auto part is deactivated.

This function lets you perform any special deinstallation operations that you need
to do, any clean-up, and any unregistration for system services that you registered
for in the InstallScript function.

Note that automatically removed auto parts do not use the RemoveScript
function since such auto parts are removed immediately after the
InstallScript is executed—the RemoveScript is not executed.

In addition to the RemoveScript function, another function, DeletionScript,
is executed when the user removes a package by deleting it from the Extras
Drawer. This function applies to all types of frame parts, and is actually executed
before the RemoveScript function.

The DeletionScript function is optional. It lets you do different clean-up
based on the assumption that the user is permanently deleting a package, rather
than simply ejecting the card on which it happens to reside. For example, in the
DeletionScript function, you might want to delete all the soups created by the
application—checking with the user, of course, before performing such an
irreversible operation.

Effects of System Resets on Application Data

Two kinds of reset operations—hard resets and soft resets—can occur on Newton devices. All data in working RAM (the NewtonScript heap and the operating system domain) is erased when a hard or soft reset occurs.

Unless a hard reset occurs, soups remain in RAM until they are removed explicitly, even if the Newton device is powered down. Soups are not affected by soft resets, as they are stored in the protected storage domain. The remainder of this section describes reset operations in more detail and suggests ways to ensure that your application can deal with resets appropriately.

A hard reset occurs at least once in the life of any Newton device—when it is initially powered on. The **hard reset** returns all internal RAM to a known state: all soups are erased, all caches are purged, all application packages are erased from the internal store, application RAM is reinitialized, the NewtonScript heap is reinitialized, and the operating system restarts itself. It's the end (or beginning) of the world as your application knows it.

Note
Data on external stores is not affected by a hard reset. ◆

A hard reset is initiated only in hardware by the user. Extreme precautions have been taken to ensure that this action is deliberate. On the MessagePad, the user must simultaneously manipulate the power and reset switches to initiate the hardware reset. After this is accomplished, the hardware reset displays two dialog boxes warning the user that all data is about to be erased; the user must confirm this action in both dialog boxes before the hard reset takes place.

It is extremely unlikely that misbehaving application software would cause a hard reset. However, a state similar to hardware reset may be achieved if the battery that backs up internal RAM is removed or fails completely.

It's advisable to test your application's ability to install itself and run on a system that has been initialized with a hard reset. The exact sequence of steps required to hard reset a Newton device is documented in its user guide.

Newton devices may also perform a soft reset operation. A **soft reset** erases all data stored by applications in the NewtonScript heap, for example all data stored in slots in views or other frames in memory. A soft reset also reinitializes the data storage system frames cache, while leaving soup data intact. Any frames in the cache are lost, such as new or modified entries that have not been written back to the soup. A soft reset can be initiated in software by the operating system or from hardware by the user.

When the operating system cannot obtain enough memory to complete a requested operation, it may display a dialog box advising the user to reset the Newton device. The user can tap the Reset button displayed in the dialog box to reset the system, or can tap the Cancel button and continue working.

The user may also initiate a soft reset by pressing a hardware button provided for this purpose. This button is designed to prevent its accidental use. On the MessagePad, for example, it is recessed inside the battery compartment and must be pressed with the Newton pen or similarly-shaped instrument.

A soft reset may also be caused by misbehaving application software. One way to minimize the occurrence of unexpected resets is to utilize exception-handling code where appropriate.

The only way applications can minimize the consequences of a soft reset is to be prepared for one to happen at any time. Applications need to store all permanent data in a soup and write changed entries back to the soup as soon as is feasible.

It's advisable to test your application's ability to recover from a soft reset. The exact sequence of steps required to soft-reset a particular Newton device is documented in its user guide.

Flow of Control

The Newton system is an event-driven, object-oriented system. Code is executed in response to messages sent to objects (for example, views). Messages are sent as a result of user events, such as a tap on the screen, or internal system events, such as an idle loop triggering. The flow of control in a typical application begins when the user taps on the application icon in the Extras Drawer. As a result of this event, the system performs several actions such as reading the values of certain slots in your application base view and sending a particular sequence of messages to it.

For a detailed discussion of the flow of control and the order of execution when an application "starts up," see the section "View Instantiation" beginning on page 3-26.

Using Memory

The tightly-constrained Newton environment requires that applications avoid wasting memory space on unused references. As soon as possible, applications should set to nil any object reference that is no longer needed, thereby allowing the system to reclaim the memory used by that object. For example, when an application closes, it needs to clean up after itself as much as possible, removing its references to soups, entries, cursors, and any other objects. This means you should set to nil any application base view slots that refer to objects in RAM.

IMPORTANT

If you don't remove references to unused soups, entries, cursors, and other objects, the objects will not be garbage collected, reducing the amount of RAM available to the system and other applications. ▲

Localization

If your application displays strings, and you want your application to run on localized Newton products, you should consider localizing your application. This involves translating strings to other languages and using other formats for dates, times, and monetary values.

There are some features of NTK that make string localization simple, allowing you to define the language at compile time to build versions in different languages without changing the source files. Refer to *Newton Toolkit User's Guide* for more information.

For details on localizing an application, see Chapter 20, "Localizing Newton Applications."

Developer Signature Guidelines

To avoid name conflicts with other Newton application, you need to register a single developer signature with Newton DTS. You can then use this signature as the basis for creating unique application symbols, soup names and other global symbols and strings according to the guidelines described in this section.

Signature

A **signature** is an arbitrary sequence of approximately 4 to 10 characters. Any characters except colons (:) and vertical bars(|) can be used in a signature. Case is not significant.

Like a handwritten signature, the developer signature uniquely identifies a Newton application developer. The most important characteristic of a signature is that it is unique to a single developer, which is why Newton DTS maintains a registry of developer signatures. Once you have registered a signature with Newton DTS it is yours, and will not be assigned to any other developer.

Getting Started

Examples of valid signatures include

```
NEWTONDTS
Joe's Cool Apps
1NEWTON2DTS
What the #$*? SW
```

How to Register

To register your signature, you need to provide the following information to the Newton Development Information Group at Apple.

```
Company Name:
Contact Person:
Mailing Address:
Phone:
Email Address:
Desired Signature 1st choice:
Desired Signature 2nd choice:
```

Send this information to the e-mail address

`NEWTONDEV@applelink.apple.com`

or send it via US Mail to:

NewtonSysOp
c/o: Apple Computer, Inc.
1 Infinite Loop, M/S: 305-2A
Cupertino, CA 95014
USA

Application Name

The **application name** is the string displayed under your application's icon in the Extras drawer. Because it is a string, any characters are allowed.

This name does not need to be unique, because the system does not use it to identify the application. For example, it is possible for there to be two applications named Chess on the market. The application name is used only to identify the application to the user. If there were in fact two applications named Chess installed on the same Newton device, hopefully the user could distinguish one from the other by some other means, perhaps by the display of different icons in the Extras drawer.

Examples of valid application names include

```
Llama
Good Form
2 Fun 4 U
Chess
```

Note
It's recommended that you keep your application
names short so that they don't crowd the names
of other applications in the Extras drawer. ◆

Application Symbol

The **application symbol** is created by concatenating the application name, a
colon (:), and your registered developer signature. This symbol is not normally
visible to the end user. It is used to uniquely identify an application in the system.
Because application symbols contain a colon (:), they must be enclosed by vertical
bars (|) where they appear explicitly in NewtonScript code.

Examples of valid application symbols include:

```
'|Llama:NEWTONDTS|
'|2 Fun 4 U:Joe's Cool Apps|
```

You specify the application symbol in the Output Settings dialog of NTK. At the
beginning of a project build, NTK 1.5 or newer defines a constant for your project
with the name kAppSymbol and sets it to the symbol you specify as the
application symbol. Use of this constant throughout your code makes it easier to
maintain your code.

At the end of the project build, if you've not created a slot with the name
appSymbol in the application base view of your project, NTK creates such a slot
and places in it the application symbol. If the slot exists already, NTK doesn't
overwrite it.

Package Name

The **package name** is usually a string version of the application symbol. The
package name may be visible to the user if no application name is provided.
Package names are limited to 26 characters, so this places a practical limit on the
combined length of application names and signatures.

Summary

View Classes and Protos

clView

```
aView := {
viewClass: clView, // base view class
viewBounds: boundsFrame, // location and size
viewJustify: integer, // viewJustify flags
viewFlags: integer, // viewFlags flags
viewFormat: integer, // viewFormat flags
...
}
```

protoApp

```
anApp := {
_proto: protoApp, // proto application
title: string, // application name
viewBounds: boundsFrame, // location and size
viewJustify: integer, // viewJustify flags
viewFlags: integer, // viewFlags flags
viewFormat: integer, // viewFormat flags
declareSelf: 'base, // do not change
...
}
```

Functions

Application-Defined Functions

```
InstallScript(partFrame) // for application parts
InstallScript(partFrame, removeFrame) // for auto parts
DeletionScript()
DoNotInstallScript()
RemoveScript(frame)
```

Views

This chapter provides the basic information you need to know about views and how to use them in your application.

You should start with this chapter if you are creating an application for Newton devices, as views are the basic building blocks for most applications. Before reading this chapter, you should be familiar with the information in *Newton Toolkit User's Guide* and *The NewtonScript Programming Language*.

This chapter introduces you to views and related items, describing

- views, templates, the view coordinate system, and the instantiation process for creating a view

- common tasks, such as creating a template, redrawing a view, creating special view effects, and optimizing a view's performance

- view constants, methods, and functions

About Views

Views are the basic building blocks of most applications. Nearly every individual visual item you see on the screen—for example, a radio button, or a checkbox—is a view, and there may even be views that are not visible. Views display information to the user in the form of text and graphics, and the user interacts with views by tapping them, writing in them, dragging them, and so on.

Different types of views have inherently different behavior, and you can include your own methods in views to further enhance their behavior. The primitive view classes provided in the Newton system are described in detail in Table 2-2 (page 2-4) in the *Newton Programmer's Reference*.

You create or lay out a view with the Newton Toolkit's graphic editor. The Newton Toolkit creates a template; that is, a data object that describes how the view will look and act on the Newton. Views are then created from templates when the application runs on the Newton.

This section provides detailed conceptual information on views and other items related to views. Specifically, it covers the following:

■ templates and views and how they relate to each other

■ the coordinate system used in placing views

■ components used to define views

■ application-defined methods that the system sends to views

■ the programmatic process used to create a view

■ new functions, methods, and messages added for 2.0 as well as modifications to existing view code

Templates

A **template** is a frame containing a description of an object. (In this chapter the objects referred to are views that can appear on the screen.) Templates contain data descriptions of such items as fields for the user to write into, graphic objects, buttons, and other interactive objects used to collect and display information. Additionally, templates can include **methods,** which are functions that give the view behavior.

Note
A template can also describe nongraphic objects like communication objects. Such objects have no visual representation and exist only as logical objects. ◆

An application exists as a collection of templates, not just a single template. There is a **parent** template that defines the application window and its most basic features. From this parent template springs a hierarchical collection of **child** templates, each defining a small piece of the larger whole. Each graphic object, button, text field, and so on is defined by a separate template. Each child template exists within the context of its parent template and inherits characteristics from its parent template, though it can override these inherited characteristics.

Within the Newton object system, a template for a view exists as a special kind of **frame;** that is, a frame containing or inheriting a particular group of **slots** (viewClass, viewBounds, viewFlags, and some other optional slots) that define the template's class, dimensions, appearance, and other characteristics. Templates are no different from any other frames, except that they contain or inherit these particular slots (in addition to others). For more information about frames, slots, and the NewtonScript language, see *The NewtonScript Programming Language.*

Views

Figure 3-1 shows a collection of template frames that might make up an application. The frame at the top represents the highest-level parent template. Each template that has children contains a `viewChildren` (or `stepChildren`) slot whose value is an array of references to its child templates.

Figure 3-1 Template hierarchy

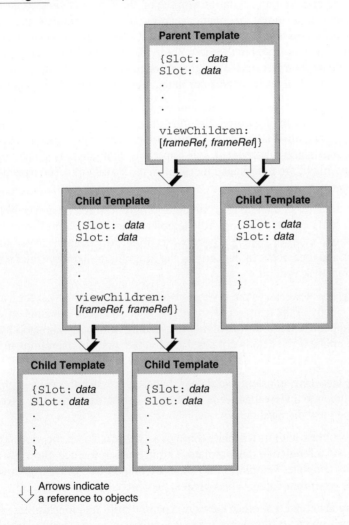

```
Parent Template

{Slot: data
Slot: data
  .
  .
  .

viewChildren:
[frameRef, frameRef]}
```

```
Child Template

{Slot: data
Slot: data
  .
  .
  .

viewChildren:
[frameRef, frameRef]}
```

```
Child Template

{Slot: data
Slot: data
  .
  .
  .
}
```

```
Child Template

{Slot: data
Slot: data
  .
  .
  .
}
```

```
Child Template

{Slot: data
Slot: data
  .
  .
  .
}
```

Arrows indicate
a reference to objects

Views

A template is a data description of an object. A **view** is the visual representation of the object that is created when the template is instantiated. The system reads the stored description in the template and creates a view on the screen—for example, a framed rectangle containing a title.

Besides the graphic representation you see on the screen, a view consists of a memory object (a frame) that contains a reference to its template and also contains transient data used to create the graphic object. Any changes to view data that occur during run time are stored in the view, not in its template. This is an important point— after an application has started up (that is, once the views are instantiated from their templates), all changes to slots occur in the view; the template is never changed.

This distinction between templates and views with respect to changing slot values occurs because of the NewtonScript inheritance mechanism. During run time, templates, containing static data, are prototypes for views, which contain dynamic data. To understand this concept, it is imperative that you have a thorough understanding of the inheritance mechanism as described in *The NewtonScript Programming Language.*

You can think of a template as a computer program stored on a disk. When the program starts up, the disk copy (the template) serves as a template; it is copied into dynamic memory, where it begins execution. Any changes to program variables and data occur in the copy of the program in memory (the view), not in the original disk version.

However, the Newton system diverges from this metaphor in that the view is not actually a copy of the template. To save RAM use, the view contains only a reference to the template. Operations involving the reading of data are directed by reference to the template if the data is not first found in the view. In operations in which data is written or changed, the data is written into the view.

Because views are transient and data is disposed of when the view is closed, any data written into a view that needs to be saved permanently must be saved elsewhere before the view disappears.

A view is linked with its template through a _proto slot in the view. The value of this slot is a reference to the template. Through this reference, the view can access slots in its template. Templates may themselves contain _proto slots which reference other templates, called **protos,** on which they are built.

Views are also linked to other views in a parent-child relationship. Each view contains a _parent slot whose value is a reference to its parent view; that is, the view that encloses it. The top-level parent view of your application is called the

application base view. (Think of the view hierarchy as a tree structure in which the tree is turned upside down with its root at the top. The top-level parent view is the root view.)

Figure 3-2 shows the set of views instantiated from the templates shown in Figure 3-1. Note that this example is simplified in that it shows a separate template for each view. In practice, multiple views often share a single template. Also, this example doesn't show templates that are built on other protos.

Figure 3-2 View hierarchy

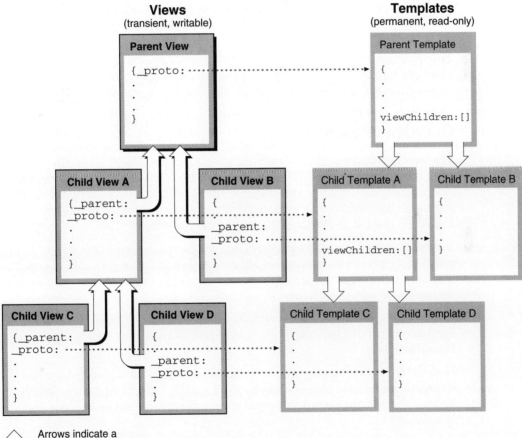

Arrows indicate a reference to parent/child

Arrows indicate a reference to protos

Figure 3-3 shows an example of what this view hierarchy might represent on the screen.

Figure 3-3   Screen representation of view hierarchy

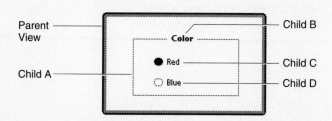

The application base view of each application exists as a child of the system **root view.** The root view is essentially the blank screen that exists before any other views are drawn. It is the ancestor of all other views that are instantiated.

Coordinate System

The view coordinate system is a two-dimensional plane. The (0, 0) **origin** point of the plane is assigned to the upper-left corner of the Newton screen, and coordinate values increase to the right and (unlike a Cartesian plane) down. Any pixel on the screen can be specified by a vertical coordinate and a horizontal coordinate. Figure 3-4 (page 3-7) illustrates the view system coordinate plane.

Views are defined by rectangular areas that are usually subsets of the screen. The origin of a view is usually its upper-left corner, though the origin can be changed. The coordinates of a view are relative to the origin of its parent view—they are not screen coordinates.

It is helpful to conceptualize the coordinate plane as a two-dimensional grid. The intersection of a horizontal and vertical grid line marks a point on the coordinate plane.

Note the distinction between points on the coordinate grid and pixels, the dots that make up a visible image on the screen. Figure 3-5 illustrates the relationship between the two: the pixel is down and to the right of the point by which it is addressed.

Figure 3-4   View system coordinate plane

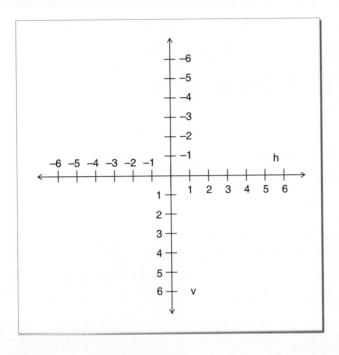

Figure 3-5   Points and pixels

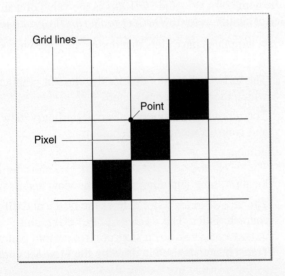

As the grid lines are infinitely thin, so a point is infinitely small. Pixels, by contrast, lie *between* the lines of the coordinate grid, not at their intersections.

This relationship gives them a definite physical extent, so that they can be seen on the screen.

Defining View Characteristics

A template that describes a view is stored as a frame that has slots for view characteristics. Here is a NewtonScript example of a template that describes a view:

```
{viewClass: clView,
viewBounds: RelBounds( 20, 50, 94, 142 ),
viewFlags: vNoFlags,
viewFormat:vfFillWhite+vfFrameBlack+vfPen(1),
viewJustify: vjCenterH,
viewFont: simpleFont10,
declareSelf: 'base,
debug: "dialer",
};
```

Briefly, the syntax for defining a frame is:

```
{slotName: slotValue,
  slotName: slotValue,
...};
```

where *slotName* is the name of a slot, and *slotValue* is the value of a slot. For more details on NewtonScript syntax, refer to *The NewtonScript Programming Language.*

Frames serving as view templates have slots that define the following kinds of view characteristics:

Class
: The viewClass slot defines the class of graphic object from which the view is constructed.

Behavior
: The viewFlags slot defines other primary view behaviors and controls recognition behavior.

Location, size, and alignment
: The viewBounds and viewJustify slots define the location, size, and alignment of the view and its contents.

Appearance
: The viewFormat slot defines the frame and fill characteristics. The viewFillPattern and viewFramePattern slots control custom patterns. Transfer modes used in drawing the view are controlled by the viewTransferMode slot.

Opening and closing animation effects

        The `viewEffect` slot defines an animation to be performed when the view is displayed or hidden.

Other attributes   Some other slots define view characteristics such as font, copy protection, and so on.

Inheritance links   The `_proto`, `_parent`, `viewChildren`, and `stepChildren` slots contain links to a view's template, parent view, and child views.

These different categories of view characteristics are described in the following sections.

Class

The `viewClass` slot defines the view class. This information is used by the system when creating a view from its template. The view class describes the type of graphic object to be used to display the data described in the template. The view classes built into the system serve as the primitive building blocks from which all visible objects are constructed. The view classes are listed and described in Table 2-2 (page 2-4) in the *Newton Programmer's Reference*.

Behavior

The `viewFlags` slot defines behavioral attributes of a view other than those that are derived from the view class. Each attribute is represented by a constant defined as a bit flag. Multiple attributes are specified by adding them together, like this:

```
vVisible+vFramed
```

Note that in the NTK viewFlags editor, multiple attributes are specified simply by checking the appropriate boxes.

Some of the `viewFlags` constants are listed and described in Table 2-4 (page 2-11) in the *Newton Programmer's Reference*. There are also several additional constants you can specify in the `viewFlags` slot that control what kinds of pen input (taps, strokes, words, letters, numbers, and so on) are recognized and handled by the view. These other constants are described in "Recognition" (page 9-1).

View behavior is also controlled through methods in the view that handle system messages. As an application executes, its views receive messages from the system, triggered by various events, usually the result of a user action. Views can handle system messages by having methods that are named after the messages. You control the behavior of views by providing such methods and including code that operates on the receiving view or other views.

For a detailed description of the messages that views can receive, and information on how to handle them, see "Application-Defined Methods" (page 3-26)."

Handling Pen Input

The use of the `vClickable` `viewFlags` constant to control pen input is important to understand, so it is worth covering here, even though it is discussed in more detail in "Recognition" (page 9-1). The `vClickable` flag must be set for a view to receive input. If this flag is not set for a view, that view cannot accept any pen input.

If you have a view whose `vClickable` flag is not set, pen events, such as a tap, will "fall through" that view and be registered in a background view that does accept pen input. This can cause unexpected results if you are not careful. You can prevent pen events from registering in the wrong view by setting the `vClickable` flag for a view and providing a `ViewClickScript` method in the view that returns non-`nil`. This causes the view to capture all pen input within itself, instead of letting it "fall through" to a different view. If you want to capture pen events in a view but still prevent input (and electronic ink), do not specify any other recognition flags besides `vClickable`.

If you want strokes or gestures but want to prevent clicks from falling through up the parent chain, return the symbol `'skip`. This symbol tells the view system not to allow the stroke to be processed by the parent chain, but instead allows the stroke to be processed by the view itself for recognition behavior.

Several other `viewFlags` constants are used to control and constrain the recognition of text, the recognition of shapes, the use of dictionaries, and other input-related features of views. For more information, refer to "Recognition" (page 9-1).

Location, Size, and Alignment

The location and size of a view are specified in the `viewBounds` slot of the view template. The `viewJustify` slot affects the location of a view relative to other views. The `viewJustify` slot also controls how text and pictures within the view are aligned and limits how much text can appear in the view (one line, one word, and so on).

The `viewOriginX` and `viewOriginY` slots control the offset of child views within a view.

View Bounds

The `viewBounds` slot defines the size and location of the view on the screen. The value of the `viewBounds` slot is a frame that contains four slots giving the view coordinates (all distances are in pixels). For example:

```
{left: leftValue,
 top: topValue,
 right: rightValue,
 bottom: bottomValue
}
```

leftValue   The distance from the left origin of the parent view to the left
                          edge of the view.

topValue   The distance from the top origin of the parent view to the top
                          edge of the view.

rightValue   The distance from the left origin of the parent view to the
                          right edge of the view.

bottomValue   The distance from the top origin of the parent view to the
                          bottom edge of the view.

Note

The values in the `viewBounds` frame are interpreted as
described here only if the view alignment is set to the default
values. Otherwise, the view alignment setting changes the way
`viewBounds` values are used. For more information, see "View
Alignment" (page 3-13). ◆

As shown in Figure 3-6, all coordinates are relative to a view's parent, they are not
actual screen coordinates.

Figure 3-6   Bounds parameters

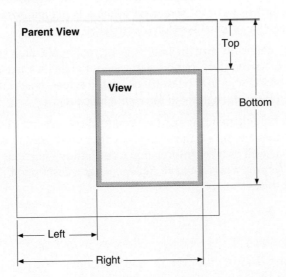

When you are using the Newton Toolkit (NTK) to lay out views for your application, the `viewBounds` slot is set automatically when you drag out a view in the layout window. If you are writing code in which you need to specify a `viewBounds` slot, you can use one of the global functions such as `SetBounds` or `RelBounds`, which are described in "Finding the Bounds of Views" (page 3-39).

View Size Relative to Parent Size

A view is normally entirely enclosed by its parent view. You shouldn't create a view whose bounds extend outside its parent's bounds. If you do create such a view, for example containing a picture that you want to show just part of, you need to set the vClipping flag in the viewFlags slot of the parent view.

If you do not set the vClipping flag for the parent view, the behavior is unpredictable. The portions of the view outside the parent's bounds may or may not draw properly. All pen input is clipped to the parent's bounds.

Note that the base views of all applications (all root view children, in fact) are automatically clipped, whether or not the vClipping flag is set.

If your application base view is very small and you need to create a larger floating child view, for example, a slip, you should use the BuildContext function. This function creates a special view that is a child of the root view. To open the view, you send the Open message to it.

Using Screen-Relative Bounds

Newton is a family of products with varying screen sizes. If you want your application to be compatible with a variety of individual Newton products, you should design your application so that it sizes itself dynamically (that is, at run time), accounting for the size of the screen on which it is running, which could be smaller or larger than the original Newton MessagePad screen.

You may want to dynamically size the base view of your application so that it changes for different screen sizes, or you may want it to remain a fixed size on all platforms. In the latter case, you should still check the actual screen size at run time to make sure there is enough room for your application.

You can use the global function GetAppParams to check the size of the screen at run time. This function returns a frame containing the coordinates of the drawable area of the screen, as well as other information (see "Utility Functions Reference" (page 23-1) in the *Newton Programmer's Reference* for a description). The frame returned looks like this:

```
{appAreaLeft: 0,
 appAreaTop: 0,
 appAreaWidth: 240,
 appAreaHeight: 320,
 ...}
```

The following example shows how to use the ViewSetupFormScript method in your application base view to make the application a fixed size, but no larger than the size of the screen:

```
viewSetupFormScript: func()
   begin
   local b := GetAppParams();
   self.viewbounds := RelBounds(
      b.appAreaLeft,
      b.appAreaTop,
      min(200, b.appAreaWidth),    // 200 pixels wide max
      min(300, b.appAreaHeight)); // 300 pixels high max
   end
```

Don't blindly size your application to the full extents of the screen. This might look odd if your application runs on a system with a much larger screen.

Do include a border around your application base view. That way, if the application runs on a screen that is larger than the size of your application, the user will be able to clearly see its boundaries.

The important point is to correctly size the application base view. Child views are positioned relative to the application base view. If you have a dynamically sizing application base view, make sure that the child views also are sized dynamically, so that they are laid out correctly no matter how the dimensions of the base view change. You can ensure correct layout by using parent-relative and sibling-relative view alignment, as explained in the next section, "View Alignment."

One additional consideration you should note is that on a larger screen, it may be possible for the user to move applications around. You should not rely on the top-left coordinate of your application base view being fixed. To prevent this from happening check your application's current location when you work with global coordinates. To do this, send the `GlobalBox` message to your application base view.

View Alignment

The `viewJustify` slot is used to set the view alignment and is closely linked in its usage and effects with the `viewBounds` slot.

The `viewJustify` slot specifies how text and graphics are aligned within the view and how the bounds of the view are aligned relative to its parent or sibling views. (**Sibling** views are child views that have a common parent view.)

In the `viewJustify` slot, you can specify one or more alignment attributes, which are represented by constants defined as bit flags. You can specify one alignment attribute from each of the following groups:

■ horizontal alignment of view contents (applies to views of class `clParagraphView` and `clPictureView` only)

■ vertical alignment of view contents (applies to views of class `clParagraphView` and `clPictureView` only)

- horizontal alignment of the view relative to its parent or sibling view
- vertical alignment of the view relative to its parent or sibling view
- text limits

For example, you could specify these alignment attributes for a button view that has its text centered within the view and is placed relative to its parent and sibling views:

```
vjCenterH+vjCenterV+vjSiblingRightH+vjParentBottomV+oneLineOnly
```

If you don't specify an attribute from a group, the default attribute for that group is used.

The view alignment attributes and the defaults are listed and described in Table 3-1. The effects of these attributes are illustrated in Figure 3-7, following the table.

Sibling setting are not used if the view has not previous setting, instead the parent settings are used.

Table 3-1   `viewJustify` constants

Constant	Value	Description
Horizontal alignment of view contents		
vjLeftH	0	Left alignment (default).
vjCenterH	2	Center alignment (default for `clPictureView` only).
vjRightH	1	Right alignment.
vjFullH	3	Stretches the view contents to fill the entire view width.
Vertical alignment of view contents[1]		
vjTopV	0	Top alignment (default).
vjCenterV	4	Center alignment (default for `clPictureView` only).
vjBottomV	8	Bottom alignment.
vjFullV	12	For views of the `clPictureView` class only; stretches the picture to fill the entire view height.
Horizontal alignment of the view relative to its parent or sibling view[2]		
vjParentLeftH	0	The left and right view bounds are relative to the parent's left side (default).

continued

Table 3-1 `viewJustify` constants (continued)

Constant	Value	Description
vjParentCenterH	16	The difference between the left and right view bounds is used as the width of the view. If you specify zero for left, the view is centered in the parent view. If you specify any other number for left, the view is offset by that much from a centered position (for example, specifying left = 10 and right = width+10 offsets the view 10 pixels to the right from a centered position).
vjParentRightH	32	The left and right view bounds are relative to the parent's right side, and will usually be negative.
vjParentFullH	48	The left bounds value is used as an offset from the left edge of the parent and the right bounds value as an offset from the right edge of the parent (for example, specifying left = 10 and right = –10 leaves a 10-pixel margin on each side).
vjSiblingNoH	0	(Default) Do not use sibling horizontal alignment.
vjSiblingLeftH	2048	The left and right view bounds are relative to the sibling's left side.
vjSiblingCenterH	512	The difference between the left and right view bounds is used as the width of the view. If you specify zero for left, the view is centered in relation to the sibling view. If you specify any other number for left, the view is offset by that much from a centered position (for example, specifying left = 10 and right = width+10 offsets the view 10 pixels to the right from a centered position).
vjSiblingRightH	1024	The left and right view bounds are relative to the sibling's right side.
vjSiblingFullH	1536	The left bounds value is used as an offset from the left edge of the sibling and the right bounds value as an offset from the right edge of the sibling (for example, specifying left = 10 and right = –10 indents the view 10 pixels on each side relative to its sibling).

Vertical alignment of the view relative to its parent or sibling view[3]

vjParentTopV	0	The top and bottom view bounds are relative to the parent's top side (default).

continued

Table 3-1 `viewJustify` constants (continued)

Constant	Value	Description
vjParentCenterV	64	The difference between the top and bottom view bounds is used as the height of the view. If you specify zero for top, the view is centered in the parent view. If you specify any other number for top, the view is offset by that much from a centered position (for example, specifying top = –10 and bottom = height–10 offsets the view 10 pixels above a centered position).
vjParentBottomV	128	The top and bottom view bounds are relative to the parent's bottom side.
vjParentFullV	192	The top bounds value is used as an offset from the top edge of the parent and the bottom bounds value as an offset from the bottom edge of the parent (for example, specifying top = 10 and bottom = –10 leaves a 10-pixel margin on both the top and the bottom).
vjSiblingNoV	0	(Default) Do not use sibling vertical alignment.
vjSiblingTopV	16384	The top and bottom view bounds are relative to the sibling's top side.
vjSiblingCenterV	4096	The difference between the top and bottom view bounds is used as the height of the view. If you specify zero for top, the view is centered in relation to the sibling view. If you specify any other number for top, the view is offset by that much from a centered position (for example, specifying top = –10 and bottom = height–10 offsets the view 10 pixels above a centered position).
vjSiblingBottomV	8192	The top and bottom view bounds are relative to the sibling's bottom side.
vjSiblingFullV	12288	The top bounds value is used as an offset from the top edge of the sibling and the bottom bounds value as an offset from the bottom edge of the sibling (for example, specifying top = 10 and bottom = –10 indents the view 10 pixels on both the top and the bottom sides relative to its sibling).

continued

Table 3-1   `viewJustify` constants (continued)

Constant	Value	Description
Text limits		
noLineLimits	0	(Default) No limits, text wraps to next line.
oneLineOnly	8388608	Allows only a single line of text, with no wrapping.
oneWordOnly	16777216	Allows only a single word. (If the user writes another word, it replaces the first.)
Indicate that a bounds value is a ratio		
vjNoRatio	0	(Default) Do not use proportional alignment.
vjLeftRatio	67108864	The value of the slot `viewBounds.left` is interpreted as a percentage of the width of the parent or sibling view to which this view is horizontally justified.
vjRightRatio	134217728	The value of the slot `viewBounds.right` is interpreted as a percentage of the width of the parent or sibling view to which this view is horizontally justified.
vjTopRatio	268435456	The value of the slot `viewBounds.top` is interpreted as a percentage of the height of the parent or sibling view to which this view is vertically justified.
vjBottomRatio	–536870912	The value of the slot `viewBounds.bottom` is interpreted as a percentage of the height of the parent or sibling view to which this view is vertically justified.
vjParentAnchored	256	The view is anchored at its location in its parent view, even if the origin of the parent view is changed. Other sibling views will be offset, but not child views with this flag set.

[1] For views of the `clParagraphView` class, the vertical alignment constants `vjTopV`, `vjCenterV`, and `vjBottomV` apply only to paragraphs that also have the `oneLineOnly` `viewJustify` flag set.

[2] If you are applying horizontal sibling-relative alignment and the view is the first child, it is positioned according to the horizontal parent-relative alignment setting.

[3] If you are applying vertical sibling-relative alignment and the view is the first child, it is positioned according to the vertical parent-relative alignment setting.

Figure 3-7   View alignment effects

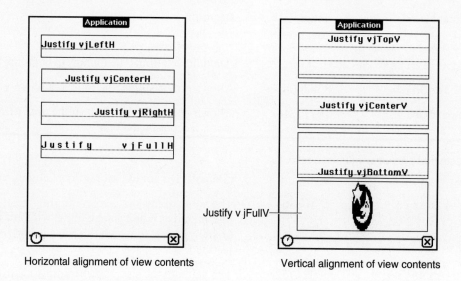

Horizontal alignment of view contents   Vertical alignment of view contents

Figure 3-7   View alignment effects (continued)

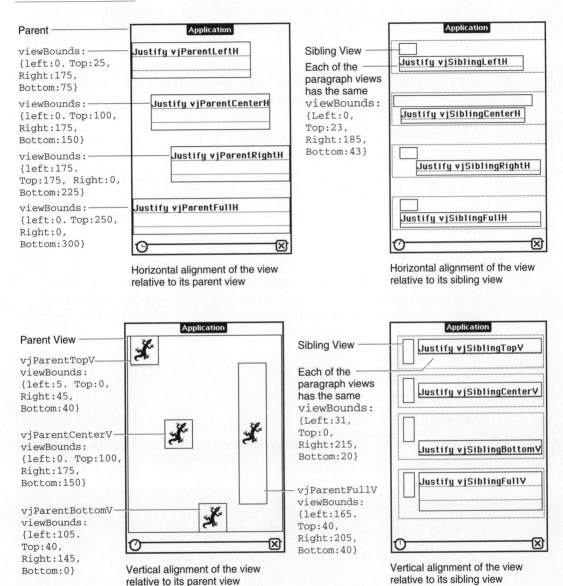

viewOriginX and viewOriginY Slots

These slots can be read but not written or set. Instead, use Setorigin to set the origin offset for a view. For more information, see "Scrolling View Contents" (page 3-41).

If you use these slots to specify an offset, the point you specify becomes the new origin. Child views are drawn offset by this amount. This is useful for displaying different portions of a view whose content area is larger than its visible area.

Appearance

The viewFormat slot defines view attributes such as its fill pattern, frame pattern, frame type, and so on. Custom fill and frame patterns are defined using the viewFillPattern and viewFramePattern slots.

The viewTransferMode slot controls the appearance of the view when it is drawn on the screen; that is, how the bits being drawn interact with bits on the screen.

View Format

The viewFormat slot defines visible attributes of a view such as its fill pattern, frame type, and so on. In the viewFormat slot, you can specify one or more format attributes, which are represented by constants defined as bit flags. You can specify one format attribute from each of the following groups:

- view fill pattern
- view frame pattern
- view frame thickness
- view frame roundness
- view frame inset (this is the white space between the view bounds and view frame)
- view shadow style
- view line style (these are solid or dotted lines drawn in the view to make it look like lined paper)

Multiple attributes are specified by adding them together like this:

```
vfFillWhite+vfFrameBlack+vfPen(2)+vfLinesGray
```

Note that the frame of a view is drawn just outside of the view bounding box, not within it.

The fill for a view is drawn before the view contents and the frame is drawn after the contents.

IMPORTANT

Many views need no fill pattern, so you may be inclined to set the
fill pattern to "none" when you create such a view. However, it's
best to fill the view with white, if the view may be explicitly
dirtied (in need of redrawing) and if you don't need a transparent
view. This increases the performance of your application because
when the system is redrawing the screen, it doesn't have to update
views behind those filled with a solid color such as white.
However, don't fill all views with white, since there is some small
overhead associated with fills; only use this technique if the view
is one that is usually dirtied.

Also, note that the application base view always appears opaque,
as do all child views of the root view. That is, if no fill is set for
the application base view, it automatically appears to be filled
with white. ▲

The view format attributes are listed and described in Table 2-5 (page 2-13) in the
Newton Programmer's Reference.

Custom Fill and Frame Patterns

Custom fill and custom view frame patterns are set for a view by using the
vfCustom flag, as shown in Table 2-5 (page 2-13) in the *Newton Programmer's
Reference*, and by using following two slots:

viewFillPattern

> Sets a custom fill pattern that is used to fill the view.

viewFramePattern

> Sets a custom pattern that is used to draw the frame lines
> around the view, if the view has a frame.

You can use custom fill and frame patterns by setting the value of the
viewFillPattern and viewFramePattern slots to a binary data structure
containing a custom pattern. A pattern is simply an eight-byte binary data structure
with the class 'pattern.

You can use this NewtonScript trick to create binary pattern data structures "on
the fly":

```
DefineGlobalConstant('myPat,SetLength(SetClass(Clone
   ("\uAAAAAAAAAAAAAAAA"),'pattern), 8));
```

This code clones a string, which is already a binary object, and changes its class to
'pattern. The string is specified with hexadecimal character codes whose binary
representation is used to create the pattern. Each two-digit hex code creates one
byte of the pattern.

Drawing Transfer Mode for Views

The viewTransferMode slot specifies the transfer mode to be used for drawing in the view. The transfer mode controls how bits being drawn are placed over existing bits on the screen. The constants that you can specify for the viewTransferMode slot are listed and described in Table 2-6 (page 2-14) in the *Newton Programmer's Reference*.

The transfer mode is used to specify how bits are copied onto the screen when something is drawn in a view. For each bit in the item to be drawn, the system finds the existing bit on the screen, performs a Boolean operation on the pair of bits, and displays the resulting bit.

The first eight transfer modes are illustrated in Figure 3-8. The last transfer mode, in addition to those shown, modeMask, is a special one, and its effects are dependent on the particular picture being drawn and its mask.

Figure 3-8   Transfer modes

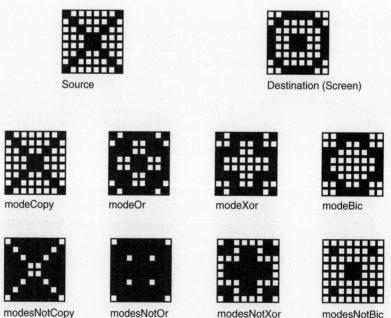

In Figure 3-8, the Source item represents something being drawn on the screen. The Destination item represents the existing bits on the screen. The eight patterns below these two represent the results for each of the standard transfer modes.

Opening and Closing Animation Effects

Another attribute of a view that you can specify is an animation that occurs when the view is opened or closed on the screen. If an effect is defined for a view, it occurs whenever the view is sent an `Open`, `Close`, `Show`, `Hide`, or `Toggle` message.

Use the `viewEffect` slot to give the view an opening or closing animation. Alternately, you can perform one-time effects on a view by sending it one of these view messages: `Effect`, `SlideEffect`, `RevealEffect`, or `Delete`. These methods are described in "Animating Views" (page 3-40).

The `viewEffect` slot specifies an animation that occurs when a view is shown or hidden. If this slot is not present, the view will not animate at these times. There are several predefined animation types. You can also create a custom effect using a combination of `viewEffect` flags from Table 2-7 (page 2-86) in *Newton Programmer's Reference*. To use one of the predefined animation types, specify the number of animation steps, the time per step, and the animation type, with the following values:

`fxSteps`(x)   In *x* specify the number of steps you want, from 1 to 15.

`fxStepTime`(x)   In *x* specify the number of ticks that you want each step to take, from zero to 15 (there are 60 ticks per second).

Specify one of the following values to select the type of animation effect desired:

- `fxCheckerboardEffect`—reveals a view using a checkerboard effect, where adjoining squares move in opposite (up and down) directions.

- `fxBarnDoorOpenEffect`—reveals a view from center towards left and right edges, like a barn door opening where the view is the inside of the barn.

- `fxBarnDoorCloseEffect`—reveals a view from left and right edges towards the center, like a barn door closing where the view is painted on the doors.

- `fxVenetianBlindsEffect`—reveals a view so that it appears behind venetian blinds that open.

- `fxIrisOpenEffect`—changes the size of an invisible "aperture" covering the view, revealing an ever-increasing portion of the full-size view as the aperture opens.

- `fxIrisCloseEffect`—like `fxIrisOpenEffect`, except that it decreases the size of an invisible "aperture" covering the view, as the aperture closes.

- `fxPopDownEffect`—reveals a view as it slides down from its top boundary.

- `fxDrawerEffect`—reveals a view as it slides up from its bottom boundary.

- `fxZoomOpenEffect`—expands the image of the view from a point in the center until it fills the screen; that is, the entire view appears to grow from a point in the center of the screen.

- fxZoomCloseEffect—opposite of fxZoomOpenEffect. This value shrinks the image of the view from a point in the center until it disappears or closes on the screen.

- fxZoomVerticalEffect—the view expands out from a horizontal line in the center of its bounds. The top half moves upward and lower half moves downward.

A complete viewEffect specification might look like this:

fxVenetianBlindsEffect+fxSteps(6)+fxStepTime(8)

You can omit the fxSteps and fxStepTime constants and appropriate defaults will be used, depending on the type of the effect.

Table 2-7 (page 2-86) in *Newton Programmer's Reference* lists the constants that you can use in the viewEffect slot to create custom animation effects. You combine these constants in different ways to create different effects. For example, the predefined animation type fxCheckerboardEffect is defined as:

fxColumns(8)+fxRows(8)+fxColAltPhase+fxRowAltPhase+fxDown

It is difficult to envision what the different effects will look like in combination, so it is best to experiment with various combinations until you achieve the effect you want.

Other Characteristics

Other view characteristics are controlled by the following slots:

viewFont	Specifies the font used in the view. This slot applies only to views that hold text, that is, views of the class clParagraphView. For more information about how to specify the font, see the section "Using Fonts for Text and Ink Display" (page 8-17) in "Text and Ink Input and Display"
declareSelf	When the template is instantiated, a slot named with the value of this slot is added to the view. Its value is a reference to itself. For example, if you specify declareSelf: 'base, a slot named base is added to the view and its value is set to a reference to itself. Note that this slot is not inherited by the children of a view; it applies only to the view within which it exists.

Inheritance Links

These slots describe the template's location in the inheritance chain, including references to its proto, parent, and children. The following slots are not inherited by children of the template.

_proto	Contains a reference to a proto template. This slot is created when the view opens.

_parent	Contains a reference to the parent template. This slot is created when the view opens. Note that it's best to use the `Parent` function to access the parent view at run time, rather than directly referencing the `_parent` slot.
stepChildren	Contains an array that holds references to each of the template's child templates. This slot is created and set automatically when you graphically create child views in NTK. This slot is for children that you add to a template.
viewChildren	Contains an array that holds references to each of a system proto's child templates. Because this slot is used by system protos, you should never modify it or create a new one with this name. If you do so, you may be inadvertently overriding the children of a system proto. An exception to this rule occurs for clEditView; you might want to edit the viewChildren slot of a clEditView. See Table 2-1, "View class constants," (page 2-2) in *Newton Programmer's Guide* for details.

The reason for the dual child view slots is that the `viewChildren` slot is used by the system protos to store their child templates. If you create a view derived from one of the system protos and change the `viewChildren` slot (for example, to add your own child templates programmatically), you would actually be creating a new `viewChildren` slot that would override the one in the proto, and the child templates of the proto would be ignored.

The `stepChildren` slot has been provided instead as a place for you to put your child templates, if you need to do so from within a method. By adding your templates to this slot, the `viewChildren` slot of the proto is not overridden. Both groups of child views are created when the parent view is instantiated.

If you are only creating views graphically using the Newton Toolkit palette, you don't need to worry about these internal details. The Newton Toolkit always uses the `stepChildren` slot for you.

You may see either `viewChildren`, `stepChildren`, or both slots when you examine a template at run time in the Newton Toolkit Inspector window. Child templates can be listed in either slot, or both. When a view is instantiated, all the child views from both of these two slots are also created. Note that the templates in the `viewChildren` slot are instantiated first, followed by the templates in the `stepChildren` slot.

If you are adding child views in a method that will not be executed until run time, you need to use the `stepChildren` slot to do this. If there isn't a `stepChildren` slot, create one and put your views there.

IMPORTANT

Remember that the `viewChildren` and `stepChildren` arrays contain templates, *not* views. If you try to send a message like `Hide` to one of the objects listed in this array, the system will probably throw an exception because it is not a view.

During run time, if you want to obtain references to the child views of a particular view, you must use the `ChildViewFrames` method. This method returns views from both the `viewChildren` and `stepChildren` slots. This method is described in "Getting References to Views" (page 3-32). ▲

Application-Defined Methods

As your application executes, it receives **messages** from the system that you can choose to handle by providing **methods** that are named after the messages. These messages give you a chance to perform your own processing as particular events are occurring.

For example, with views, the system performs default initialization operations when a view is instantiated. It also sends a view a `ViewSetupFormScript` message. If you provide a method to handle this message, you can perform your own initialization operations in the method. However, handling system messages in your application is optional.

The system usually performs its own actions to handle each event for which it sends your view messages. Your system message-handling methods do not override these system actions. You cannot change, delete, or substitute for the default system event-handling actions. Your system message-handling methods augment the system actions.

For example, when the view system receives a Show command for a view, it displays the view. It also sends the view the `ViewShowScript` message. If you have provided a `ViewShowScript` method, you can perform any special processing that you need to do when the view is displayed.

The system sends messages to your application at specific times during its handling of an event. Some messages are sent before the system does anything to respond to the event, and some are sent after the system has already performed its actions. The timing is explained in each of the message descriptions in "Application–Defined Methods" (page 2-65) in the *Newton Programmer's Reference*.

View Instantiation

View instantiation refers to the act of creating a view from its template. The process of view instantiation includes several steps and it is important to understand when and in what order the steps occur.

Declaring a View

Before diving into the discussion of view instantiation, it is important to understand the term **declaring.** Declaring a view is something you do during the application development process using the Newton Toolkit (NTK). Declaring a view allows it to be accessed symbolically from another view.

In NTK, you declare a view using the Template Info command. (Although the phrase "declaring a view" is being used here, at development time, you're really just dealing with the view template.) In the Template Info dialog, you declare a view by checking the box entitled "Declare To," and then choosing another view in which to declare the selected view. The name you give your view must be a valid symbol, and not a reserved word or the name of a system method.

You always declare a view in its parent or in some other view farther up the parent chain. It's best, for efficiency and speed, to declare a view in the lowest level possible in the view hierarchy; that is, in its parent view or as close to it as possible. If you declare a view in a view other than the parent view, it may get the wrong parent view. Because the view's parent is wrong, its coordinates will be wrong as well, so it will show up at the wrong position on screen.

Declaring a view simply puts the declared view in the named slot. See Appendix A, "The Inside Story on Declare," for a complete description. The slot name is the name of the view you are declaring. The slot value, at run time, will hold a reference to the declared view.

The base view of your application is always declared in the system root view. Note that the application base view is declared in a slot named with its application symbol, specified in the Application Symbol field of the Project Settings slip in NTK.

Why would you want to declare a view? When a view is declared in another view, it can be accessed symbolically from that other view. The NewtonScript inheritance rules already allow access from a view to its parent view, but there is no direct access from a parent view to its child views, or between child views of a common parent. Declaring a view provides this access.

For example, if you have two child views of a common parent, and they need to send messages to each other, you need to declare each of them in the common parent view. Or, if a parent view needs to send messages to one of its child views, the child view must be declared in the parent view.

One key situation requiring a declared view is when you want to send the Open message to show a nonvisible view. The Open message can only be sent to a declared view.

Declaring a view has a small amount of system overhead associated with it. This is why the system doesn't just automatically declare every view you create. You should only declare views that you need to access from other views.

For a more detailed technical description of the inner workings of declaring a view, see the Appendix, "The Inside Story on Declare."

Creating a View

A view is created in two stages. First, a view memory object (a frame) is created in RAM. This view memory object contains a reference to its template, along with other transient run-time information. In the following discussion, the phrase, "creating the view" is used to describe just this part of the process. Second, the graphic representation of the view is created and shown on the screen. In the following discussion, the phrase, "showing the view" is used to describe just this part of the process.

A view is created and shown at different times, depending on whether or not it is a declared view.

■ If the view is declared in another open (shown) view, it is created when the view in which it is declared is sent the Open message. For example, a child view declared in the parent of its parent view is created when that "grandparent" view is opened. Note, however, that the child view is not necessarily shown at the same time it is created.

■ If the view is not declared in any view, it is created and also shown when its immediate parent view is sent the Open message. (Note that if a nondeclared view's vVisible flag is not set, that view can never be created.)

Here is the view creation sequence for a typical application installed in the Newton Extras Drawer and declared in the system root view:

1. When your application is installed on the Newton device, its base view is automatically created, but not shown.

2. When the user taps on the icon representing your application in the Extras Drawer, the system sends the ButtonToggleScript message to the application's base view.

3. When the application is launched from the Extras Drawer, a view is created (but not shown yet) for each template declared in the base view. Slots with the names of these views are created in the base view. These slots contain references to their corresponding views.

4. The ViewSetupFormScript message is sent to the base view, viewFlags, viewFormat, viewBounds, viewJustify, and declareSelf slots, and so on, are read from the view template. The global bounds of the view are adjusted to reflect the effects of the viewJustifyflags, but the viewBounds values are not changed, and the ViewSetupChildrenScript message is sent to the base view.

5. The `viewChildren` and `stepChildren` slots are read and the child views are instantiated using this same process. As part of the process, the following messages are sent to each child view, in this order: `ViewSetupFormScript`, `ViewSetupChildrenScript`, and `ViewSetupDoneScript`.

6. The `ViewSetupDoneScript` message is sent to the view.

7. The view is displayed if its `vVisible viewFlags` bit is set.

8. The `ViewShowScript` message is sent to the view and then the `ViewDrawScript` message is sent to the view. (Note that the `ViewShowScript` message is not sent to any child views, however.)

9. Each of the child views is drawn, in hierarchical order, and the `ViewDrawScript` message is sent to each of these views, immediately after it is drawn.

As you can see from step 5, when a view is opened, all child views in the hierarchy under it are also shown (as long as they are flagged as visible). A nonvisible child view can be subsequently shown by sending it the `Open` message—as long as it has been declared.

Closing a View

When you send a view the `Close` message, the graphic representation of the view (and of all of its child views) is destroyed, but the view memory object is not necessarily destroyed. There are two possibilities:

■ If the view was declared, and the view in which it was declared is still open, the frame is preserved. You can send the view another `Open` or `Toggle` message to reopen it at a later time.

  A view memory object is finally destroyed when the view in which it was declared is closed. That is, when a view is closed, all views declared in it are made available for garbage collection.

■ If the view being closed was not declared, both its graphic representation and its view memory object are made available for garbage collection when it is closed.

When a view is closed, the following steps occur:

1. If the view is closing because it was directly sent the `Close` or `Toggle` message, the system sends it the `ViewHideScript` message. (If the view is closing because it is a child of a view being closed directly, the `ViewHideScript` message is not sent to it.)

2. The graphic representation of the view is removed from the screen.

3. The view is sent the `ViewQuitScript` message.

The view itself may or may not be marked for garbage collection, depending on whether or not it was declared.

View Compatibility

The following new functionality has been added for the 2.0 release of Newton System Software. See the *Newton Programmer's Reference* for complete descriptions on each new function and method.

New Drag and Drop API

A drag and drop API has been added. This API now lets users drag a view, or part of a view, and drop it into another view. See "Dragging and Dropping with Views" (page 3-40) for details.

New Functions and Methods

The following functions and methods have been added.

- AsyncConfirm creates and displays a slip that the user must dismiss before continuing.
- ButtonToggleScript lets the application perform special handling when its icon is tapped in the Extras Drawer.
- DirtyBox marks a portion of a view (or views) as needing redrawing.
- GetDrawBox returns the bounds of the area on the screen that needs redrawing.
- GlobalOuterBox returns the rectangle, in global coordinates, of the specified view, including any frame that is drawn around the view.
- ModalConfirm creates and displays a slip.
- MoveBehind moves a view behind another view, redrawing the screen as appropriate.
- StdButtonWidth returns the size that a button needs to be in order to fit some specified text.

New Messages

The following messages have been added.

- ReorientToScreen is sent to each child of the root view when the screen orientation is changed.
- ViewPostQuitScript is sent to a view following the ViewQuitScript message and after all of the view's child views have been destroyed.

New Alignment Flags

The viewJustify slot contains new constants that allow you to specify that a view is sized proportionally to its sibling or parent view, both horizontally and/or vertically.

A change to the way existing viewJustify constants work is that when you are using sibling-relative alignment, the first sibling uses the parent alignment settings (since it has no sibling to which to justify itself).

Changes to Existing Functions and Methods

The following changes have been made to existing functions and methods for 2.0.

- RemoveStepView. This function now removes the view template from the stepChildren array of the parent view. You do not need to remove the template yourself.

- SetValue. You can now use this global function to change the recognition behavior of a view at run time by setting new recognition flags in the viewFlags slot. The new recognition behavior takes effect immediately following the SetValue call.

- GlobalBox. This method now works properly when called from the ViewSetupFormScript method of a view. If called from the ViewSetupFormScript method, GlobalBox gets the viewBounds and ViewJustify slots from the view, calculates the effects of the sibling and parent alignment on the view bounds, and then returns the resulting bounds frame in global coordinates.

- LocalBox. This method now works properly when called from the ViewSetupFormScript method of a view. If called from the ViewSetupFormScript method, LocalBox gets the viewBounds and ViewJustify slots from the view, calculates the effects of the sibling and parent alignment on the view bounds, and then returns the resulting bounds frame in local coordinates.

- ViewQuitScript. When this message is sent to a view, it propagates down to child views of that view. In system software version 1.0, the order in which child views received this message and were closed was undefined.

  In system software version 2.0, the order in which this message is sent to child views is top-down. Also, each view has the option of having ViewPostQuitScript called in child-first order. The return value of the ViewQuitScript method determines whether or not the ViewPostQuitScript message is sent.

New Warning Messages

Warning messages are now printed to the inspector when a NewtonScript application calls a view method in situations where the requested operation is unwise, unnecessary, ambiguous, invalid, or just a bad idea.

Obsolete Functions and Methods

The following functions and methods are obsolete with version 2.0 of the Newton System Software:

- `Confirm`, which created and displayed an OK/Cancel slip. Use `AsyncConfirm` instead.

- `DeferredConfirmedCall` and `DeferredConfirmedSend` have both been replaced by `AsyncConfirm`.

Using Views

This section describes how to use the view functions and methods to perform specific tasks. See "Summary of Views" (page 3-47) for descriptions of the functions and methods discussed in this section.

Getting References to Views

Frequently, when performing view operations, you need access to the child or parent views of a view, or to the root view in the system. You need to use the `ChildViewFrames` and `Parent` methods as well as the `GetRoot` and `GetView` functions to return references to these "related" views.

To test whether an application is open or not, for example, you can use the `GetRoot` function and the application's signature, together with the global function `kViewIsOpenFunc`:

```
call kViewIsOpenFunc with (GetRoot().appsignature)
```

The `ChildViewFrames` method is an important method you must use if you need access to the child views of a view. It returns the views in the same order in which they appear in the view hierarchy, from back to front. The most recently opened views (which appear on top of the hierarchy) will appear later in the list. Views with the `vFloating` flag (which always appear above nonfloating views) will be at the end of the array.

Displaying, Hiding, and Redrawing Views

To display a view (and its visible child views), send it one of the following view messages:

- `Open`—to open the view
- `Toggle`—to open or close the view
- `Show`—to show the view if it had previously been opened, then hidden

To hide a view (and its child views), send it one of the following view messages:

- `Close`—to hide and possibly delete it from memory
- `Toggle`—to close or open the view
- `Hide`—to hide it temporarily

You can cause a view (and its child views) to be redrawn by using one of the following view messages or global functions:

- `Dirty`—flags the view as "dirty" so it is redrawn during the next system idle loop
- `RefreshViews`—redraws all dirty views immediately
- `SetValue`—sets the value of a slot and possibly dirties the view
- `SyncView`—redraws the view if its bounds have changed

Dynamically Adding Views

Creating a view dynamically (that is, at run time) is a complex issue that has multiple solutions. Depending on what you really need to do, you can use one of the following solutions:

- Don't create the view dynamically because it's easier to accomplish what you want by creating an invisible view and opening it later.
- Create the view by adding a new template to its parent view's `stepChildren` array in the `ViewSetupChildrenScript` method.
- Create the template and the view at run time by using the `AddStepView` function.
- Create the template and the view at run time by using the `BuildContext` function.
- If you want a pop-up list view, called a **picker,** use the `PopupMenu` function to create and manage the view.

These techniques are discussed in the following sections. The first four techniques are listed in order from easiest to most complex (and error prone). You should use the easiest solution that accomplishes what you want. The last technique, for creating a picker view, should be used if you want that kind of view.

Showing a Hidden View

In many cases, you might think that you need to create a view dynamically. However, if the template can be defined at compile time, it's easier to do that and flag the view as not visible. At the appropriate time, send it the Open message to show it.

The typical example of this is a slip, which you can usually define at compile time. Using the Newton Toolkit (NTK), simply do not check the vVisible flag in the viewFlags slot of the view template. This will keep the view hidden when the application is opened.

Also, it is important to declare this view in your application base view. For information on declaring a view, see the section "View Instantiation" (page 3-26).

When you need to display the view, send it the Open message using the name under which you have declared it (for example, myView:Open()).

This solution even works in cases where some template slots cannot be set until run time. You can dynamically set slot values during view instantiation in any of the following view methods: ViewSetupFormScript, ViewSetupChildrenScript, and ViewSetupDoneScript. You can also set values in a declared view before sending it the Open message.

Adding to the stepChildren Array

If it is not possible to define the template for a view at compile time, the next best solution is to create the template (either at compile time or run time) and add it to the stepChildren array of the parent view using the ViewSetupChildrenScript method. This way, the view system takes care of creating the view at the appropriate time (when the child views are shown).

For example, if you want to dynamically create a child view, you first define the view template as a frame. Then, in the ViewSetupChildrenScript method of its parent view, you add this frame to the stepChildren array of the parent view. To ensure that the stepChildren array is in RAM, use this code:

```
if not HasSlot(self, 'stepChildren) then
    self.stepChildren := Clone(self.stepChildren);
AddArraySlot(self.stepChildren, myDynamicTemplate);
```

The if statement checks whether the stepChildren slot already exists in the current view (in RAM). If it does not, it is copied out of the template (in ROM) into RAM. Then the new template is appended to the array.

All of this takes place in the ViewSetupChildrenScript method of the parent view, which is before the stepChildren array is read and the child views are created.

If at some point after the child views have been created you want to modify the contents of the `stepChildren` array and build new child views from it, you can use the `RedoChildren` view method. First, make any changes you desire to the `stepChildren` array, then send your view the `RedoChildren` message. All of the view's current children will be closed and removed. A new set of child views will then be recreated from the `stepChildren` array.

Also, note that reordering the `stepChildren` array and then calling `RedoChildren` or `MoveBehind` is the way to reorder the child views of a view dynamically.

For details on an easy way to create a template dynamically, see "Creating Templates" (page 3-36).

Using the AddStepView Function

If you need to create a template and add a view yourself at run time, use the function `AddStepView`. This function takes two parameters: the parent view to which you want to add a view, and the template for the view you want to create. The function returns a reference to the view it creates. Be sure to save this return value so you can access the view later.

The `AddStepView` function also adds the template to the parent's `stepChildren` array. This means that the `stepChildren` array needs to be modifiable, or `AddStepView` will fail. See the code in the previous section for an example of how to ensure that the `stepChildren` array is modifiable.

The `AddStepView` function doesn't force a redraw when the view is created, so you must take one of the following actions yourself:

- Send the new view a `Dirty` message.

- Send the new view's parent view a `Dirty` message. This is useful if you're using `AddStepView` to create several views and you want to show them all at the same time.

- If you created the view template with the `vVisible` bit cleared, the new view will remain hidden and you must send it the `Show` message to make it visible. This technique is useful if you want the view to appear with an animation effect (specified in the `viewEffect` slot in the template).

Do not use the `AddStepView` function in a `ViewSetupFormScript` method or a `ViewSetupChildrenScript` method—it won't work because that's too early in the view creation process of the parent for child views to be created. If you are tempted to do this, you should instead use the second method of dynamic view creation, in which you add your template to the `stepChildren` array and let the view system create the view for you.

To remove a view created by `AddStepView`, use the `RemoveStepView` function. This function takes two parameters: the parent view from which you want to remove the child view, and the view (not its template) that you want to remove.

For details on an easy way to create a template dynamically, see "Creating Templates" (page 3-36).

Using the BuildContext Function

Another function that is occasionally useful is `BuildContext`. It takes one parameter, a template. It makes a view from the template and returns it. The view's parent is the root view. The template is not added to any `viewChildren` or `stepChildren` array. Basically, you get a free-agent view.

Normally, you won't need to use `BuildContext`. It's useful when you need to create a view from code that isn't part of an application (that is, there's no base view to use as a parent). For instance, if your `InstallScript` or `RemoveScript` needs to prompt the user with a slip, you use `BuildContext` to create the slip.

`BuildContext` is also useful for creating a view, such as a slip, that is larger than your application base view.

For details on an easy way to create a template dynamically, see the next section, "Creating Templates"

Creating Templates

The three immediately preceding techniques require you to create templates. You can do this using NewtonScript to define a frame, but then you have to remember which slots to include and what kinds of values they can have. It's easy to make a mistake.

A simple way of creating a template is to make a user proto in NTK and then use it as a template. That allows you to take advantage of the slot editors in NTK.

If there are slots whose values you can't compute ahead of time, it doesn't matter. Leave them out of the user proto, and then at run time, create a frame with those slots set properly and include a `_proto` slot pointing to the user proto. A typical example might be needing to compute the bounds of a view at run time. If you defined all the static slots in a user proto in the file called `dynoTemplate`, you could create the template you need using code like this:

```
template := {viewBounds: RelBounds(x, y, width, height),
             _proto: GetLayout("DynoTemplate"),
             }
```

This really shows off the advantage of a prototype-based object system. You create a small object "on the fly" and the system uses inheritance to get the rest of the needed values. Your template is only a two-slot object in RAM. The user proto resides in the package with the rest of your application. The conventional, RAM-wasting alternative would have been:

```
template := Clone(PT_dynoTemplate);
template.viewBounds := RelBounds(x, y, width, height);
```

Note that for creating views arranged in a table, there is a function called `LayoutTable` that calculates all the bounds. It returns an array of templates.

Making a Picker View

To create a transient pop-up list view, or picker, you can use the function `PopupMenu`. This kind of view pops up on the screen and is a list from which the user can make a choice by tapping it. As soon as the user chooses an item, the picker view is closed.

You can also create a picker view by defining a template using the `protoPicker` view proto. See "Pickers, Pop-up Views, and Overviews" (page 6-1) for information on `protoPicker` and `PopupMenu`.

Changing the Values in viewFormat

You can change the values in the `viewFormat` slot of a view without closing and reopening a view. Use the `SetValue` function to update the view with new settings. For example:

```
SetValue(myView, 'viewFormat, 337)
// 337 = vfFillWhite + vfFrameBlack+vfPen(1)
```

`SetValue`, among other things, calls `Dirty` if necessary, so you don't need to call it to do a task that the view system already knows about, such as changing `viewBounds` or text slots in a view.

Determining Which View Item Is Selected

To determine which view item is selected in a view call `GetHiliteOffsets`. You must call this function in combination with the `HiliteOwner` function. When you call `GetHiliteOffsets`, it returns an array of arrays. Each item in the outer array represents selected subviews, as in the following example:

```
x:= gethiliteoffsets()
#440CA69                    [[{#4414991}, 0, 2],
                             [{#4417B01}, 0, 5],
                             [{#4418029}, 1, 3]]
```

Each of the three return values contains three elements:

■ Element 0: the subview that is highlighted. This subview is usually a clParagraphView, but you need to check to make sure. A clPolygonView is not returned here even if HiliteOwner returns a clEditView when a clPolygonView child is highlighted.

■ Element 1: the start position of the text found in the text slot of a clParagraphView.

■ Element 2: the end position of the text found in the text slot of a clParagraphView.

To verify that your view is a clParagraphView, check the viewClass slot of the view. The value returned (dynamically) sometimes has a high bit set so you need to take it into consideration using a mask constant, vcClassMask:

```
theviews.viewClass=clParagraphView OR
theView.viewClass - vcClassMask=clParagraphView
BAnd(thViews.viewClass, BNot(vcClassMask))=clParagraphView
```

If a graphic is highlighted and HiliteOwner returns a clEditView, check its view children for non-nil values of the 'hilites slot (the 'hilites slot is for use in any view but its contents are private).

Complex View Effects

If you have an application that uses ViewQuitScript in numerous places, your view may close immediately, but to the user the Newton may appear to be hung during the long calculations. A way to avoid this is to have the view appear open until the close completes.

You can accomplish this effect in one of two ways. First, put your code in ViewHideScript instead of ViewCloseScript. Second, remove the view's ViewEffect and manually force the effect at the end of ViewQuitScript using the Effect method.

Making Modal Views

A modal view is one that primarily restricts the user to interacting with that view. All taps outside the modal view are ignored while the modal view is open.

In the interest of good user interface design, you should avoid using modal views unless they are absolutely necessary. However, there are occasions when you may need one.

Typically, modal views are used for slips. For example, if the user was going to delete some data in your application, you might want to display a slip asking them to confirm or cancel the operation. The slip would prevent them from going to another operation until they provide an answer.

Use `AsyncConfirm` to create and display a slip that the user must dismiss before continuing. The slip is created at a deferred time, so the call to `AsyncConfirm` returns immediately, allowing the currently executing NewtonScript code to finish. You can also use `ModalConfirm` but this method causes a separate OS task to be created and doesn't return until after the slip is closed. It is less efficient and takes more system overhead.

Once you've created a modal view, you can use the `FilterDialog` or `ModalDialog` to open it. Using `FilterDialog` is the preferred method as it returns immediately. As with `ModalConfirm`, `ModalDialog` causes a separate OS task to be created.

Finding the Bounds of Views

The following functions and view methods calculate and return a `viewBounds` frame.

Run-time functions:

- `RelBounds`— calculates the right and bottom values of a view and returns a bounds frame.

- `SetBounds`—returns a frame when the left, top, right, and bottom coordinates are given.

- `GlobalBox`—returns the rectangle, in coordinates, of a specified view.

- `GlobalOuterBox`—returns the rectangle, in coordinates, of a specified view including any frame that is drawn around a view.

- `LocalBox`—returns a frame containing the view bounds relative to the view itself.

- `MoveBehind`— moves a view behind another view.

- `DirtyBox`— marks a portion of a view as needing redrawing.

- `GetDrawBox`— returns the bounds of an area on the screen that needs redrawing.

Compile-time functions:

- `ButtonBounds`—returns a frame when supplied with the width of a button to be placed in the status bar.

- `PictBounds`— finds the width and height of a picture and returns the proper bounds frame.

Animating Views

There are four view methods that perform special animation effects on views. They are summarized here:

- `Effect`—performs any animation that can be specified in the `viewEffect` slot.
- `SlideEffect`—slides a whole view or its contents up or down.
- `RevealEffect`—slides part of a view up or down.
- `Delete`—crumples a view and tosses it into a trash can.

Note that these animation methods only move bits around on the screen. They do not change the actual bounds of a view, or do anything to a view that would change its contents. When you use any of these methods, you are responsible for supplying another method that actually changes the view bounds or contents. Your method is called just before the animation occurs.

Dragging a View

Dragging a view means allowing the user to move the view by tapping on it, holding the pen down, and dragging it to a new location on the screen. To drag a view, send the view a `Drag` message.

Dragging and Dropping with Views

Dragging and dropping a view means allowing a user to drag an item and drop it into another view.

To enable dragging and dropping capability, you must first create a frame that contains slots that specify how the drop will behave. For example, you specify the types of objects that can be dropped into a view, if any. Examples include `'text` or `'picture`. See the *dragInfo* parameter to the `DragAndDrop` method (page 2-46) in the *Newton Programmer's Reference* for a complete description of the slots.

You must set up code to handle a drag and drop in one of two ways: either add code to create a frame and code to call `DragAndDrop`'s view method in each source and destination view that accepts a drag and drop message, or you can create a proto and use it as a template for each view.

Each view must also have the following methods. The system calls these methods in the order listed.

- `ViewGetDropTypesScript`— is sent to the destination view. It is called repeatedly while the pen is down. `ViewGetDropTypesScript` is passed the current location as the dragged item is moved from its source location to its destination location. An array of object types is also returned. In this method, you must return an array of object types that can be accepted by that location.

- `GetDropDataScript`— is sent to the source view when the destination view is found.

- `ViewDropScript`— is sent to the destination view. You must add the object to the destination view.

- `ViewDropMoveScript`— is sent to the source view. It is used when dragging an object within the same view. `ViewDropRemoveScript` and `ViewDropScript` are not called in this case.

- `ViewDropRemoveScript` — is sent to the source view. It is used when dragging an object from one view to another. You must delete the original from the source view when the drag completes.

Additional optional methods can also be added. If you do not include these, the default behavior occurs.

- `ViewDrawDragDataScript` — is sent to the source view. It draws the image that will be dragged. If you don't specify an image, the area inside the rectangle specified by the `DragAndDrop` bounds parameter is used.

- `ViewDrawDragBackgroundScript`— is sent to the source view. It draws the image that will appear behind the dragged image.

- `ViewFindTargetScript`— is sent to the destination view. It lets the destination view change the drop point to a different view.

- `ViewDragFeedbackScript`— is sent to the destination view. It provides visual feedback while items are dragged.

- `ViewDropDoneScript`— is sent to the destination view to tell it that the object has been dropped.

Scrolling View Contents

There are different methods of scrolling a view, supported by view methods you call to do the work. Both methods described here operate on the child views of the view to which you send a scroll message.

One method is used to scroll all the children of a view any incremental amount in any direction, within the parent view. Use the `SetOrigin` method to perform this kind of scrolling. This method changes the view origin by setting the values of the `viewOriginX` and `viewOriginY` slots in the view.

Another kind of scrolling is used for a situation in which there is a parent view containing a number of child views positioned vertically, one below the other. The `SyncScroll` method provides the ability to scroll the child views up or down the height of one of the views. This is the kind of scrolling you see on the built-in Notepad application.

In the latter kind of scrolling, the child views are moved within the parent view by changing their view bounds. Newly visible views will be opened for the first time, and views which have scrolled completely out-of-view will be closed. The viewOriginX and viewOriginY slots are not used.

For information about techniques you can use to optimize scrolling so that it happens as fast as possible, see "Scrolling" (page 3-46), and "Optimizing View Performance" (page 3-44).

Redirecting Scrolling Messages

You can redirect scrolling messages from the base view to another view. Scrolling and overview messages are sent to the frontmost view; this is the same view that is returned if you call GetView('viewFrontMost).

The viewFrontMost view is found by looking recursively at views that have both the vVisible and vApplication bits set in their viewFlags. This means that you can set the vApplication bit in a descendant of your base view, and as long as vApplication is set in all of the views in the parent chain for that view, the scrolling messages will go directly to that view. The vApplication bit is not just for base views, despite what the name might suggest.

If your situation is more complex, where the view that needs to be scrolled cannot have vApplication set or is not a descendant of your base view, you can have the base view's scrolling scripts call the appropriate scripts in the view you wish scrolled.

Working With View Highlighting

A highlighted view is identified visually by being inverted. That is, black and white are reversed.

To highlight or unhighlight a view, send the view the Hilite message.

To highlight or unhighlight a single view from a group, send the view the HiliteUnique message. (The group is defined as all of the child views of one parent view.)

To highlight a view when the current pen position is within it, send the view the TrackHilite message. The view is unhighlighted when the pen moves outside the view bounds. If the view is a button, you can send the view the TrackButton message to accomplish the same task.

To get the view containing highlighted data, you can call the global function HiliteOwner; to get the highlighted text use GetHiliteOffsets.

To highlight some or all of the text in a paragraph, you can use the SetHilite method.

To determine if a given view is highlighted, check the vSelected bit in the viewFlags. vSelected should not be set by your application, but you can test it to see if a view is currently selected (that is, highlighted.) If BAND(viewflags,vSelected) <> 0 is non-nil, the view is selected.

Creating View Dependencies

You can make one view dependent upon another by using the global function TieViews. The dependent view is notified whenever the view it is dependent on changes.

This dependency relationship is set up outside the normal inheritance hierarchy. That is, the views don't have to be related to each other in any particular way in the hierarchy. The views must be able to access each other, and so need references to each other. Declaring them to a common parent view is one way to accomplish this.

View Synchronization

View synchronization refers to the process of synchronizing the graphic representation of the view with its internal data description. You need to do this when you add, delete, or modify the children of a view, in order to update the screen.

Typically you would add or remove elements from the stepChildren array of a parent view, and then call one of the view synchronization functions to cause the child views to be redrawn, created, or closed, as appropriate. Remember that if you need to modify the stepChildren array of a view, the array must be copied into RAM; you can't modify the array in the view template, since that is usually stored in ROM or in a package. To ensure that the stepChildren array is in RAM, use this code:

```
if not HasSlot(self, 'stepChildren) then
    self.stepChildren := Clone(self.stepChildren);
```

To redraw all the child views of a view, you can send two different messages to a view: RedoChildren or SyncChildren. These work similarly, except that RedoChildren closes and reopens all child views, while SyncChildren only closes obsolete child views and opens new child views.

Laying Out Multiple Child Views

Two different methods are provided to help lay out a view that is a table or consists of some other group of child views.

To lay out a view containing a table in which each cell is a child view, send the view the message LayoutTable.

To lay out a view containing a vertical column of child views, send the view the message `LayoutColumn`.

Optimizing View Performance

Drawing, updating, scrolling, and performing other view operations can account for a significant amount of time used during the execution of your application. Here are some techniques that can help speed up the view performance of your application.

Using Drawing Functions

Use the drawing functions to draw lines, rectangles, polygons, and even text in a single view, rather than creating these objects as several separate specialized views. This technique increases drawing performance and reduces the system overhead used for each view you create. The drawing functions are described in "Drawing and Graphics" (page 13-1)

View Fill

Many views need no fill color, so you may be inclined to set the fill color to "none" when you create such a view. However, it's best to fill the view with white, if it may be individually dirtied and you don't need a transparent view. This increases the performance of your application because when the system is redrawing the screen, it doesn't have to update views behind those filled with a solid color such as white. However, don't fill all views with white, since there is some small overhead associated with fills; use this technique only if the view is one that is usually dirtied.

Redrawing Views

A view is flagged as dirty (needing redrawing) if you send it the `Dirty` message, or as a result of some other operation, such as calling the `SetValue` function for a view. All dirty views are redrawn the next time the system event loop executes. Often this redrawing speed is sufficient since the system event loop usually executes several times a second (unless a lengthy or slow method is executing).

However, sometimes you want to be able to redraw a view immediately. The fastest way to update a single view immediately is to send it the `Dirty` message and then call the global function `RefreshViews`. In most cases, only the view you dirtied will be redrawn.

If you call `RefreshViews` and there are multiple dirty views, performance can be significantly slower, depending on where the dirty views are on the screen and how many other views are between them. In this case, what is redrawn is the rectangle that is the union of all the dirty views (which might include many other nondirty views). Also, if there are multiple dirty views that are in different view hierarchies, their closest common ancestor view is redrawn, potentially causing many other views to be redrawn needlessly.

If you want to dirty and redraw more than one view at a time, it may be faster to send the `Dirty` message to the first view, then call `RefreshViews`, send the `Dirty` message to the second view, then call `RefreshViews`, and so on, rather than just calling `RefreshViews` once after all views are dirtied. The performance is highly dependent on the number of views visible on the screen, the location of the dirty views, and their positions in the view hierarchy, so it's best to experiment to find the solution that gives you the best performance.

Memory Usage

Each view that you create has a certain amount of system overhead associated with it. This overhead exists in the form of frame objects allocated in a reserved area of system memory called the NewtonScript heap. The amount of space that a frame occupies is entirely dependent on the complexity and content of the view to which it corresponds. As more and more views are created, more of the NewtonScript heap is used, and overall system performance may begin to suffer as a result.

This is not usually an issue with relatively simple applications. However, complex applications that have dozens of views open simultaneously may cause the system to slow down. If your application fits this description, try to combine and eliminate views wherever possible. Try to design your application so that it has as few views as possible open at once. This can increase system performance.

You should also be aware of some important information regarding hidden and closed views and the use of memory. This information applies to any view that is hidden, it has been sent the `Hide` message, or to any declared view that is closed but where the view it is declared in is still open. In these cases, the view memory object for the view still exists, even though the view is not visible on the screen. If the hidden or closed view contains large data objects, these objects continue to occupy space in the NewtonScript heap.

You can reduce memory usage in the NewtonScript heap by setting to `nil` those slots that contain large objects and that you don't need when the view is hidden or closed. You can do this in the `ViewHideScript` or `ViewQuitScript` methods, and then reload these slots with data when the view is shown or opened again, using the `ViewShowScript` or `ViewSetupFormScript` methods. Again, the performance impact of these techniques is highly application-dependent and you should experiment to see what works best.

Note that this information applies to the base view of your application, since it is automatically declared in the system root view. As long as it is installed in the Newton, slots that you set in the base view of your application will continue to exist, even after the application is closed. If you store large data objects in the base view of your application, you should set to nil those slots that aren't needed when the application is closed, since they are wasting space in the NewtonScript heap. It is especially important to set to nil slots that reference soups and cursors, if they are not needed, since they use relatively much space.

If your application is gathering data from the user that needs to be stored, store the data in a soup, rather than in slots in one of the application views. Data stored in soups is protected, while slots in views are transient and will be lost during a system restart.

For information on declaring views, see "View Instantiation" (page 3-26). For information on storing data in soups, see Chapter 11, "Data Storage and Retrieval."

Scrolling

Scrolling the contents of a view can sometimes seem slow. Here are some techniques you can use to improve the speed:

- Scroll multiple lines at a time, rather than just a single line at a time, when the user taps a scroll arrow.

- In general, reduce the number of child views that need to be redrawn, if possible. For example, make a list that is implemented as several paragraphs (separate views) into a single paragraph.

- Set the view fill to white. For more information, see "View Fill" (page 3-44).

Summary of Views

Constants

Class Constants

Constant	Value
clView	74
clPictureView	76
clEditView	77
clKeyboardView	79
clMonthView	80
clParagraphView	81
clPolygonView	82
clRemoteView	88
clPickView	91
clGaugeView	92
clOutline	105

viewFlags Constants

Constant	Value
vNoFlags	0
vVisible	1
vReadOnly	2
vApplication	4
vCalculateBounds	8
vClipping	32
vFloating	64
vWriteProtected	128
vClickable	512
vNoScripts	134217728

viewFormat Constants

Constant	Value
vfNone	0
vfFillWhite	1
vfFillLtGray	2
vfFillGray	3
vfFillDkGray	4
vfFillBlack	5
vfFillCustom	14
vfFrameWhite	16
vfFrameLtGray	32
vfFrameGray	48
vfFrameDkGray	64
vfFrameBlack	80
vfFrameDragger	208
vfFrameCustom	224
vfFrameMatte	240
vfPen (*pixels*)	*pixels* 256
vfLinesWhite	4096
vfLinesLtGray	8192
vfLinesGray	12288
vfLinesDkGray	16384
vfLinesBlack	20480
vfInset (*pixels*)	*pixels* 65536
vfLinesCustom	57344
vfShadow (*pixels*)	*pixels* 262144
vfRound (*pixels*)	*pixels* 16777216

CHAPTER 3

Views

viewTransferMode Constants

Constant	Value
modeCopy	0
modeOr	1
modeXor	2
modeBic	3
modeNotCopy	4
modeNotOr	5
modeNotXor	6
modeNotBic	7
modeMask	8

viewEffect Constants

Constant	Bit Flag	Integer Value
fxColumns(x)	$((x-1)$ << fxColumnsShift$)$	x-1
fxRows(x)	$((x-1)$ << fxRowsShift$)$	$(x-1)*32$
fxHStartPhase	$(1$ << fxHStartPhaseShift$)$	1024
fxVStartPhase	$(1$ << fxVStartPhaseShift$)$	2048
fxColAltHPhase	$(1$ << fxColAltHPhaseShift$)$	4096
fxColAltVPhase	$(1$ << fxColAltVPhaseShift$)$	8192
fxRowAltHPhase	$(1$ << fxRowAltHPhaseShift$)$	16384
fxRowAltVPhase	$(1$ << fxRowAltVPhaseShift$)$	32768
fxMoveH	$(1$ << fxMoveHShift$)$	65536
fxRight	fxMoveH	65536
fxLeft	fxHStartPhase+fxMoveH	66560
fxUp	fxVStartPhase+fxMoveV	133120
fxDown	fxMoveV	131072
fxMoveV	$(1$ << fxMoveVShift$)$	131072
fxVenetianBlindsEffect	fxRows(8)+fxDown	131296
fxDrawerEffect	fxUp	133120

continued

Constant	Bit Flag	Integer Value
fxCheckerboardEffect		
	fxColumns(8)+fxRows(8)+fxColAltVPhase+ fxRowAltHPhase+fxDown	155879
fxZoomVerticalEffect		
	fxColumns(1)+fxRows(2)+fxUp+ fxRowAltVPhase	165920
fxZoomCloseEffect		
	fxColumns(2)+fxRows(2)+fxUp+fxLeft	199713
fxZoomOpenEffect		
	fxColumns(2)+fxRows(2)+fxUp+fxLeft+ fxColAltHPhase+fxRowAltVPhase	236577
fxRevealLine	(1 << fxRevealLineShift)	262144
fxPopDownEffect		
	fxDown+fxRevealLine	393216
fxWipe	1 << fxWipeShift)	524288
fxBarnDoorCloseEffect		
	fxColumns(2)+fxColAltHPhase+ fxRowAltVPhase+fxRight+fxWipe	626689
fxBarnDoorOpenEffect		
	fxColumns(2)+fxColAltHPhase+ fxRowAltVPhase+fxLeft+fxWipe	627713
fxIrisCloseEffect		
	fxColumns(2)+fxRows(2)+fxUp+fxLeft+ fxRevealLine+fxWipe	986145
fxIrisOpenEffect		
	fxColumns(2)+fxRows(2)+fxUp+fxLeft+ fxColAltHPhase+fxRowAltVPhase+ fxRevealLine+fxWipe	1023009
fxFromEdge	(1 << fxFromEdgeShift)	1048576
fxSteps(x)	((num-1) << fxStepsShift)	$(x-1)*$ 2097152
fxStepTime(x)	((num) << fxStepTimeShift)	$x*33554432$

Functions and Methods

Getting References to Views

view:ChildViewFrames()
view:Parent()
GetRoot()
GetView(*symbol*)

Displaying, Hiding, and Redrawing Views

view:Open()
view:Close()
view:Toggle()
view:Show()
view:Hide()
view:Dirty()
RefreshViews()
SetValue(*view*, *slotSymbol*, *value*)
view:SyncView()
viewToMove:MoveBehind(*view*)

Dynamically Adding Views

AddStepView(*parentView*, *childTemplate*)
RemoveStepView(*parentView*, *childView*)
AddView(*parentView*, *childTemplate*)
BuildContext(*template*)

Making Modal Views

AsyncConfirm(*confirmMessage*, *buttonList*, *fn*)
ModalConfirm(*confirmMessage*, *buttonList*)
view:ModalDialog()
view:FilterDialog()

Setting the Bounds of Views

RelBounds(*left*, *top*, *width*, *height*)
SetBounds(*left*, *top*, *right*, *bottom*)
view:GlobalBox()
view:GlobalOuterBox()
view:LocalBox()
viewToMove:MoveBehind(*view*)
view:DirtyBox(*boundsFrame*)
view:GetDrawBox()
ButtonBounds(*width*)
PictBounds(*name*, *left*, *top*)

Animating Views

view:Effect(*effect*, *offScreen*, *sound*, *methodName*, *methodParameters*)
view:SlideEffect(*contentOffset*, *viewOffset*, *sound*, *methodName*,
                   methodParameters)

view:RevealEffect(*distance*, *bounds*, *sound*, *methodName*,
         methodParameters)
view:Delete(*methodName*, *methodParameters*)

Dragging a View
view:Drag(*unit*, *dragBounds*)

Dragging and Dropping an Item
view:DragAndDrop(*unit*, *bounds*, *limitBounds*, *copy*, *dragInfo*)

Scrolling View Contents
view:SetOrigin(*originX*, *originY*)
view:SyncScroll(*What*, *index*, *upDown*)

Working With View Highlighting
view:Hilite(*on*)
view:HiliteUnique(*on*)
view:TrackHilite(*unit*)
view:TrackButton(*unit*)
HiliteOwner()
GetHiliteOffsets()
view:SetHilite(*start, end, unique*)

Creating View Dependencies
TieViews(*mainView*, *dependentView*, *methodName*)

Synchronizing Views
view:RedoChildren()
view:SyncChildren()

Laying Out Multiple Child Views
view:LayoutTable(*tableDefinition*, *columnStart*, *rowStart*)
view:LayoutColumn(*childViews*, *index*)

Miscellaneous View Operations
view:SetPopup()
GetViewFlags(*template*)
Visible(*view*)
ViewIsOpen(*view*) //platform file function

Application-Defined Methods
ViewSetupFormScript()
ViewSetupChildrenScript()
ViewSetupDoneScript()
ViewQuitScript()
ViewPostQuitScript()
ViewShowScript()
ViewHideScript()
ViewDrawScript()
ViewHiliteScript(*on*)
ViewScrollDownScript()

```
ViewScrollUpScript()
ViewOverviewScript()
ViewAddChildScript(child)
ViewChangedScript(slot, view)
ViewDropChildScript(child)
ViewIdleScript()
```
sourceView:`ViewDrawDragDataScript`(*bounds*)
sourceView:`ViewDrawDragBackgroundScript`(*bounds, copy*)
destView:`ViewGetDropTypesScript`(*currentPoint*)
src: `ViewGetDropDataScript`(*dragType, dragRef*)
destView:`ViewDragFeedbackScript`(*dragInfo, currentPoint, show*)
sourceView:`ViewDropApproveScript`(*destView*)
sourceView:`ViewGetDropDataScript`(*dragType, dragRef*)
destView:`ViewDropScript`(*dropType, dropData, dropPt*)
sourceView:`ViewDropMoveScript`(*dragRef, offset, lastDragPt, copy*)
destView:`ViewFindTargetScript`(*dragInfo*)
sourceView:`ViewDropRemoveScript`(*dragRef*)
destView:`ViewDropDoneScript`()

NewtApp Applications

NewtApp is a collection of prototypes that work together in an application framework. Using these protos you can quickly construct a full-featured application that includes functionality like finding and filing.

Whether or not you have written an application for the Newton platform before, you should read this chapter. If you're new at writing Newton applications, you'll find that using NewtApp is the best way to start programming for the Newton platform. If you've created Newton applications before, the process of putting together a NewtApp application will be familiar, though you'll find the time required is significantly less.

Newton applications can be created with the NewtApp framework protos, which are described in this chapter, or by constructing them from protos described in almost every other chapter of this book. Chapter 2, "Getting Started," gives you an overview of the process.

Before reading this chapter you should be familiar with the concepts of views, templates, protos, soups, and stores. However, you don't need to know the details of the interfaces to these objects before proceeding with NewtApp. Simply read the first part of the appropriate chapters to get a good overview of the information. These subjects are covered in Chapter 3, "Views," Chapter 11, "Data Storage and Retrieval," Chapter 16, "Find," Chapter 15, "Filing," and Chapter 21, "Routing Interface."

To work with the examples in this chapter, you should also be familiar with Newton Toolkit (NTK) which is described in the *Newton Toolkit User's Guide*.

About the NewtApp Framework

You can construct an entire application by using the protos in the NewtApp framework, without recreating a lot of support code; that is, the code necessary for providing date and text searching, filing, setting up and registering soups, flushing entries, notifying the system of soup changes, formatting data for display, displaying views, and handling write-protected cards. You set the values of a prescribed set of slots, and the framework does the rest.

You can create most kinds of applications with the NewtApp framework. If your application is similar to a data browser or editor, or if it implements an automated form, you can save yourself a significant amount of time by using the NewtApp framework.

If you're creating a specialized application (for example, a calculator) or if you need to display more than one soup at a time, you shouldn't construct it with NewtApp, but should use the protos described in other chapters of this book. These chapters include Chapter 3, "Views," Chapter 6, "Pickers, Pop-up Views, and Overviews," Chapter 7, "Controls and Other Protos," Chapter 8, "Text and Ink Input and Display," Chapter 13, "Drawing and Graphics," Chapter 16, "Find," and Chapter 15, "Filing."

Some NewtApp protos work in nonframework applications. For example, you may want to update an existing application to take advantage of the functionality provided by the NewtApp slot view protos. Updating requires a bit of retrofitting, but it can be done. See "Using Slot Views in Non-NewtApp Applications" (page 4-22) for an example.

When you use the NewtApp framework protos, your user interface is updated as the protos change with new system software releases, thereby staying consistent with the latest system changes. In addition, the built-in code that manages system services for these protos is also automatically updated and maintained as the system software advances.

A NewtApp-based application can present many different views of your data. For example, the Show button displays different views of information; the New button creates new formats for data input.

NewtApp applications use a programming device known as **stationery**—a collective term for data definitions (known as dataDefs) and view definitions (known as viewDefs)—to enable this feature. You should use viewDefs to add different views of your data and dataDefs to create different data formats. Stationery is documented in Chapter 5; its use in a NewtApp application is demonstrated in this chapter.

The NewtApp Protos

When you put the application protos together in a programming environment like Newton Toolkit and set the values of slots, the framework takes care of the rest. Your applications automatically take advantage of extensive system management functionality with little additional work on your part. For example, to include your application in system-wide date searches, just set a slot in the base view of your application called dateFindSlot. (See "newtApplication" (page 3-8) in *Newton Programmer's Reference*.)

The parts of the NewtApp framework are designed to fit together using the two-part NewtonScript inheritance scheme. Generally speaking, the framework is constructed so the user interface components of your application (such as views and buttons) use proto inheritance to make methods and application-state variables, which are provided by NewtApp (and transparent to you), available to your application. Parent inheritance implements slots that keep track of system details.

Because the NewtApp framework structure is dependent on both the parent and proto structure of your application, it requires applications to be constructed in a fairly predictable way. Children of certain NewtApp framework protos are required to be particular protos; for example, the application base view must be a `newtApplication` proto.

▲ **WARNING**
When you override system service methods and functions be careful to use the conditional message send operator (`:?`) to avoid inadvertently overriding built-in functionality; otherwise, your code will break.

There may also be alternate ways to construct a NewtApp application, other than those recommended in this chapter and in Chapter 5, "Stationery." Be forewarned that applications using alternate construction methods are not guaranteed to work in the future. ▲

Figure 4-1 shows the four conceptual layers of NewtApp protos that you use to construct an application: the application base view, the layout view, the entry view, and the slot views.

Figure 4-1   The main protos in a NewtApp-based application

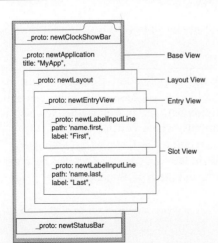

Note

This drawing does not depict the protos as they would appear in a
Newton Toolkit layout window. ◆

The basic NewtApp protos are defined here in very general terms. Note that unlike
Figure 4-1, this list includes the proto for storing data, which does not have a visual
representation in a layout file.

- The newtApplication proto is the application's base view. As in
  nonframework applications, the base view proto either contains or has
  references to all the other application parts.

- The newtSoup proto is used to create and manage the data storage soup for
  your application; it is not displayed.

- The newtLayout protos govern the overall look of your data.

- The newtEntryView protos is the view associated with current soup entry and
  is contained in the default layout view. A newtEntryView proto does not
  display on the screen, but instead manages operations on a soup.

- The slot views are a category of protos used to edit and/or display data from the
  slots in your application's soup entry frames.

About newtApplication

The newtApplication proto serves as the base view for your application; it
contains all other application protos. The allSoups slot of this proto is where you
set up the application soup (based on the newtSoup proto).

The functionality defined in this proto layer manages application-wide functions,
events, and globals. For example, the functionality for opening and registering
soups, dispatching events, and maintaining state information and application
globals is implemented in this proto layer.

Also managed by this proto layer are the application-wide user interface elements.

Application-wide Controls

Several control protos affect the entire application. Because of this, the protos are
generally placed in the newtApplication base view layer. The buttons include
the standard Information and Action buttons, as well as the New and Show
stationery buttons. Stationery buttons, which you can use to tie viewDefs and
dataDefs into your application, are defined in Chapter 5, "Stationery." The
NewtApp controls that should be in the newtApplication base view include the
standard status bar, the folder tab, and the A-Z alphabet tabs.

About newtSoup

Application data is stored in persistent structures known as soups in any Newton application. In a NewtApp application, soup definitions, written in the `newtApplication.allSoups` slot, must be based on the `newtSoup` proto.

Within a soup, data is stored in frames known as entries. In turn, entries contain the individual slots in which you store your application's data. The data in these slots is accessed by using a programming construct known as a cursor.

The `newtSoup` proto defines its own version of a set of the data storage objects and methods. If you are not already familiar with these concepts and objects, you should read the introductory parts of Chapter 11, "Data Storage and Retrieval," before trying to use the `newtSoup` proto.

The Layout Protos

Each NewtApp application must have two basic views of the application data, known as layouts, which are:

- an overview—seen when the Overview button is tapped
- a default view—seen when the application is first opened

Three kinds of layouts correspond to three basic application styles:

- the card (see `newtLayout`)
- the continuous roll (see `newtRollLayout`)
- the page (see `newtPageLayout`)

Card-based and roll-based applications differ in the number of entries each may have visible at one time. The built-in Names application is a card-based application. For this type of application, only one entry is displayed at a time. In contrast, the built-in Notes application, which is a roll-based application, can have multiple entries visible at once. They must be separated by a header, that incorporates Action and Filing buttons to make it obvious to which entry a button action should apply. Examples of card-based and a roll-based applications are shown in Figure 4-2.

Figure 4-2   A roll-based application (left) versus a card-based application

The page-based application is a hybrid of the card-based and roll-based applications. Like the card-based application, the page-based application shows only one entry at a time. However, unlike the card-based application but like the roll-based application, an entry may be longer than a screen's length. The built-in Calls application, shown in Figure 4-3, is an example of a page-based application.

Figure 4-3   Calls is an example of a page-based application

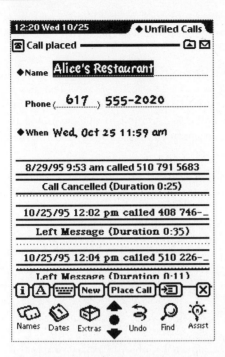

The overview protos are also layouts; they include the `newtOverLayout` and `newtRollOverLayout` protos.

The NewtApp framework code that governs soups, scrolling, and all the standard view functionality, is implemented in the layout protos. A main (default) view layout and an overview layout must be declared in the `allLayouts` slot of the `newtApplication` base view. See "newtApplication" (page 3-8) in *Newton Programmer's Reference* for details.

Your layout can also control which buttons show on the status bar; you can set the `menuLeftButtons` and `menuRightButtons` slots of the layout proto, along with the `statusBarSlot` of the base view (`newtApplication` proto). This control becomes important when more than one entry is shown on the screen, as in a roll-style application. For example, when multiple entries are showing on one screen, the Action and Filing buttons would not be on the status bar. Instead, they would be on the header of each entry, so the entry on which to perform an action is unambiguous.

The Entry View Protos

The entry view is the focal point for operations that happen on one soup entry frame at a time. These include functions such as displaying and updating data stored in the entry's slots.

The NewtApp framework has three entry view protos: newtEntryView, newtRollEntryView, and newtFalseEntryView. The newtEntryView and newtRollEntryView protos are used within a NewtApp application, while the newtFalseEntryView and newtRollEntryView protos allows you to use the framework's slot views in an application that is not based on the NewtApp framework.

The entry view also contains the user interface components that perform operations on one entry at a time. These components include the header bars, which are used as divider bars to separate multiple entries displayed simultaneously. This behavior happens in the Notes application. An example of the Notes application with multiple entries and header bars is shown in Figure 4-4.

Figure 4-4   Multiple entries visible simultaneously

Note that the header bar contains the Action and Filing buttons on its right side. These buttons appear on the header bar to prevent any ambiguity regarding the entry to be acted upon by those buttons.

In addition, the header bar contains a Title and icon on the left. When the icon is tapped, the Information slip appears, as shown in Figure 4-5. This slip is created from a `newtInfoBox` proto and displays an informational string, which it obtains from the `description` slot of the dataDef. See Chapter 5, "Stationery," for more information about dataDefs.

Figure 4-5   An Information slip

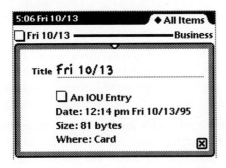

It is at the entry view level of your application that the specific slots for accessing and displaying data in your application soup are set up. The target entry, which is the entry to be acted on, is set in the entry view. The target view is then created by the entry view; the view in which the data in that entry appears. Finally, the data cursor is created by the entry view and is used to access the entries.

The entry view protos also contain important methods that act on individual entries. These methods include functionality for managing and changing existing data in the soup, such as the `FlushData` method.

About the Slot View Protos

The slot view protos retrieve, display, edit, and save changes to any type of data stored in the slots of your application soup's entry frame.

Unless they are contained by either a `newtEntryView` or a `newtFalseEntryView`, the slot views do not work. This is because the entry views are responsible for setting references to a specific entry. These references are used by the slot view to display data.

Slot views exist in two varieties: simple slot views and labelled input-line slot views. Both kinds of slot views are tailored to display and edit a particular kind of data which they format appropriately. For example, the number views (`newtNumberView` and `newtRONumberView`) format number data (according to the value of a `format` slot you set).

The labelled input-line slot view protos provide you with a label, which you may specify, for the input line. Additionally, the label may include a picker (pop-up menu).

These views also format a particular kind of data. To do this they use a special NewtApp object known as a filter to specify a value for the `flavor` slot of the labelled input-line slot views.

The filter object essentially acts as a translator between the target data frame (or more typically, a slot in that frame) and the text field visible to the user. For example, in the `newtDateInputLine` proto, a filter translates the time from a time-in-minutes value to a string, which is displayed. The filter then translates the string back to a time-in-minutes value, which is saved in the soup.

You can create custom filters by basing them on the proto `newtFilter` or on the other filters documented in Table 3-1 (page 3-60) in the *Newton Programmer's Reference*. You can also create custom labelled input-line slot views. See the example in "Creating a Custom Labelled Input-Line Slot View," beginning on page 4-24.

You can have your label input-line protos remember a list of recent items. To do so, all you need do is assign a symbol to the `'memory` slot of your template. This symbol must incorporate your developer signature. The system automatically maintains the list of recent items for your input line. To use the list, you need to use the same symbol with the `AddMemoryItem`, `AddMemoryItemUnique`, `GetMemoryItems`, and `GetMemorySlot` functions, which are described in Chapter 26, "Utility Functions."

In addition, one special slot view, called the `newtSmartNameView` proto, allows the user to choose a name from the soup belonging to the built-in Names application. It adds the pop-up menu item, Other, to the picker; when the user chooses Other from the `newtSmartNameView` proto, it displays the names in the Names application soup in a system-provided people picker.

After you choose a name and close the view displaying the Names soup, that name is displayed on the input line. The name is also put into the Picker menu. A `newtSmartNameView` proto is shown in Figure 4-6.

Figure 4-6   The smart name view and system-provided people picker

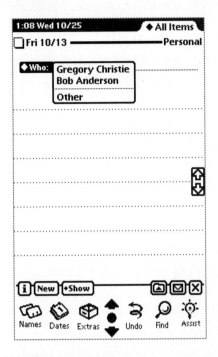

Stationery

Stationery, an extension you can add to any NewtApp application, is tightly integrated with the NewtApp framework.

Stationery consists of two components that work together: a data definition (dataDef) and a view definition (viewDef). The dataDef provides a definition of the data to be used in the stationery. It is registered in conjunction with its display component, which is a viewDef.

These extensions are available to the user through the New and Show stationery buttons in the NewtApp application. The names of the viewDefs are displayed in the Show menu. The New button is used either to propagate the new entry defined in the dataDef or to display the names of the dataDefs. For more detailed information, see Chapter 5, "Stationery."

NewtApp Compatibility

The NewtApp framework did not exist prior to version 2.0 of Newton system software. Applications created with NewtApp protos will not run on previous versions of the Newton system.

Some NewtApp protos are usable in your non-NewtApp applications. For example, there is a `newtStatusBarNoClose` proto, see page 3-29 in the *Newton Programmer's Reference*, that is unique to NewtApp, which may be used, without special provision, in a non-NewtApp application.

Other NewtApp protos—specifically the slot views—can function only within a simulated NewtApp environment. The mechanism for creating this setup is the `newtFalseEntryView` proto, described on page 3-44 in the *Newton Programmer's Reference*.

The slot views, documented in "Slot View Protos" (page 3-49) in *Newton Programmer's Reference*, provide convenient display and data manipulation functionality that you can use to your advantage in an existing application.

Using NewtApp

The protos in the NewtApp application framework can be used to

- create an application that has one data soup and can be built as a data viewer or editor
- add functionality to non-NewtApp applications
- create and incorporate stationery extensions

When you use the set of protos that make up the NewtApp application framework, you can quickly create an application that takes full advantage of the Newton system services.

In addition, many of the protos may be used in applications built without the framework. In particular, the slot views, used to display data, have built-in functionality you may wish to use.

The framework works best when used with stationery to present different views of and formats for the application's data. The sample application, described in the following sections uses a single piece of stationery, which consists of a dataDef with two viewDefs. Stationery is documented fully in Chapter 5, "Stationery."

The sample application is built using the Newton Toolkit (NTK) development environment. See *Newton Toolkit User's Guide* for more information about using NTK.

Constructing a NewtApp Application

The sample "starter" application presented here shows how to get a NewtApp application underway quickly. You may incorporate this sample code into your applications without restriction. Although every reasonable effort has been made to make sure the application is operable, the code is provided "as is." The responsibility for its operation is 100% yours. If you are going to redistribute it, you must make it clear in your source files that the code descended from Apple-provided sample code and you have made changes.

The sample is an application for gathering data that supports the system services routing, filing, and finding. It presents two views of the data to be collected: a required default view; "IOU Info" (and an alternate "IOU Notes" view); and a required overview. IOU Info and IOU Notes are stationery and appear as items in the Show button's picker. In addition, it shows how to implement the application in the three styles of NewtApp applications: card, page, and roll. See the DTS sample code for details.

The application starts with three basic NTK layout files:

- The application base view—a `newtApplication` proto.

- A default layout—one of the layout protos.

- An overview layout—either the `newtOverLayout` or `newtRollOverLayout` proto.

The application also contains the NTK layout files for the stationery, a dataDef, and its two corresponding viewDefs:

- `iouDataDef`

- `iouDefaultViewDef`

- `iouNotesViewDef`

The creation of these files is shown in Chapter 5, "Stationery."

A NewtApp application must include standard `InstallScript` and `RemoveScript` functions. Any icons must be included with a resource file; the example uses `CardStarter.rsrc`. In the example, there is also a text file, `Definitions.f`, in which application globals are defined. Neither the resource file nor the text file is required.

The basic view slots, `viewBounds`, `viewFlags`, and `viewJustify`, are discussed in Chapter 3, "Views," and are called out in the samples only when there is something unusual about them.

Using Application Globals

These samples use several application globals. When you use NTK as your development system, they are defined in a definitions file, which we named `Definitions.f`.

The values of the constants `kSuperSymbol` and `kDataSymbol` are set to the application symbol. They are used to set slots that must have unique identifying symbols. You are not required to use the application symbol for this purpose, but it is a good idea, because the application symbol is known to be unique.

One other global, unique to this application, is set. It is the constant kAppTitle, set to the string "Card Starter".

Using newtApplication

This proto serves as the template for the application base view. This section shows you how to use it to set up the

- application base view
- application soup
- status bar; for layout-level control of the appearance and disappearance of its buttons.
- layout slots
- stationery slots

Setting Up the Application Base View

The application base view template, newtApplication, should contain the basic application element protos. When you use NTK to create the layout for the newtApplication proto, you add to it a newtStatusBar proto (the status bar at the bottom of the application) and a newtClockShowBar (the folder tab across the top of the application).

Follow these steps to create the application base view:

1. Create a new layout and draw a newtApplication proto in it.

2. Place a newtStatusBar across the bottom of the layout.

3. Name the newtStatusBar proto status.

4. Place a newtClockShowBar proto across the top of the layout.

5. Save the layout file as baseView.t.

6. Name the layout frame baseView.

There are more than a dozen slots that need to be set in a newtApplication proto. Several of the newtApplication slots can be set quickly. Set these slots as follows:

- Set the title slot to kAppTitle. Note that you must define this constant.

- Set the appSymbol slot to kAppSymbol. This constant is automatically defined by NTK.

- Set the appObject slot to ["Item", "Items"].

- Set the appAll slot to "All Items". Note that you'll see this displayed on a folder tab.

■ Optional. Set the `statusBarSlot` to contain the declared name of the status bar so layouts can use it to control the buttons displayed on it. Use the symbol `'status` to set it.

If you wish to override a system message like `ViewSetupFormScript`, which is called before a view is displayed on the screen, make sure to call the inherited method at the end of your own `ViewSetupFormScript` method. Also, you may wish to add a `ReOrientToScreen` method to the `newtApplication` base view so your application can rotate to a landscape display. This message is sent to each child of the root view when the screen orientation is changed. See `ReOrientToScreen` (page 2-73) in *Newton Programmer's Reference* for details.

Finally, be sure to add the layout file `baseView.t` to your project and mark it as the application base view.

Tying Layouts Into the Main Application

The `allLayouts` slot in the `newtApplication` proto is a frame that contains symbols for the application's layout files. It must contain two slots, named `default` and `overview`, that refer to the two layout files used for those respective views.

The section "Using the Layout Protos," beginning on page 4-16, shows how to use the NewtApp layout protos to construct these files. Assume they are named Default Layout and Overview Layout for the purpose of setting the references to them in the `allLayouts` slot. The following code segment sets the `allLayouts` slot appropriately:

```
allLayouts:= {
            default: GetLayout("Default Layout"),
            overview: GetLayout("Overview Layout"),
            }
```

Setting Up the Application Soup

The `newtApplication` proto uses the values in its `allSoups` slot to set up and register your soup with the system.

The framework also looks in the `allSoups` slot to get the appropriate soup information for each layout. It does this by matching the value of the layout's `masterSoupSlot` to the name of a frame contained in the `newtApplication.allSoups` slot. See the section "Using the Layout Protos," following this one.

This application contains only one soup, though a NewtApp application can contain more than one. Each soup defined for a NewtApp application must be based on the `newtSoup` proto. The slots `soupName`, `soupIndices`, and `soupQuery` must be defined within the `allSoups` soup definition frame.

Use code similar to the following example to set the `allSoups` slot:

```
allSoups:=
{  IOUSoup: {_proto: newtSoup,
                soupName: "IOU:PIEDTS",
                soupIndices: [
                            {structure: 'slot,
                            path: 'title,
                            type: 'string},

                            {structure: 'slot,
                            path: 'timeStamp,
                            type: 'int},

                            { structure: 'slot,
                            path: 'labels,
                            type: 'tags }
                            ],

                soupQuery: {type: 'index, indexPath:
                            'timeStamp},
                soupDescr: "The IOU soup.",
                defaultDataType: '|BasicCard:sig|,}
}
```

Using the Layout Protos

Each NewtApp Application requires exactly two layouts: a default layout, displayed when the application is opened, and an overview layout, displayed when the Overview button is tapped.

The NewtApp framework layout proto you choose for your default view, sets up your application as either a card-, roll-, or page-style application.

Unique slots in the layout protos include:

■ `masterSoupSlot`

■ `forceNewEntry`

The `masterSoupSlot` is the most important. It contains a reference to the application soup in the `newtApplication.allSoups` slot, from which the layout gets its data.

■ The `forceNewEntry` slot allows your application to deal gracefully with the situation created when someone opens a folder that is empty. If the `forceNewEntry` slot is set to `true` in that situation, an entry is automatically created. Otherwise, an alert slip announces that there are no *items* in this list,

where *items* is replaced by the value of the `appObject` slot set in the
`newtApplication` base view. An example of this message from the Names
application is shown in Figure 4-7.

Figure 4-7   The message resulting from a `nil` value for `forceNewEntry`

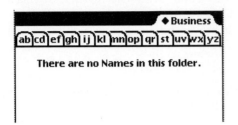

Using newtOverLayout

The slots you must set for an overview are shown in the Overview Layout browser
in Figure 4-8.

Figure 4-8   The overview slots

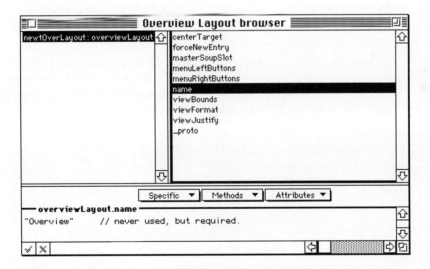

Follow these steps to create the required overview layout:

1. Open a new layout window and drag out a `newtOverLayout` proto.

2. Name it `Overview Layout`.

3. Set the `masterSoupSlot` to the symbol `'IOUSoup`. This correlates to the name of the soup as it is set up in the `newtApplication.allSoups` slot. See "Setting Up the Application Soup," beginning on page 4-15.

4. Add the `forceNewEntry` slot. Leave it with the default value `true`. This causes a new entry to be created if a user tries to open an empty folder.

5. Add a `viewFormat` slot and set the `Fill` value to `White`. This makes the data it displays look better and keeps anything from inadvertently showing through. In addition, the white fill improves the speed of the display and enhances view performance.

6. Set the name slot to a string like "Overview".

7. Add a `centerTarget` slot and set it to `true`. This assures that the entries are centered for display in the Overview.

Controlling Menu Buttons From Layouts

Once the name of the status bar is declared to the application base view (in the `newtApplication.statusBarSlot`), you may control the appearance and disappearance of buttons on the status bar, from the layout view, as needed.

To do this, you must specify which buttons should appear on the status bar by using the slots `menuLeftButtons` and `menuRightButtons`. Each of these is an array that must contain the name of the button proto(s) that you wish to appear on the menu bar's left and right sides. When you use these arrays, the button protos listed in them are automatically placed correctly on the status bar, according to the current human interface guidelines.

To appropriately set up the appearance of the status bar for display in the Overview, first add the optional slots `menuLeftButtons` and `menuRightButtons`. The buttons you name in these slots replace the menu bar buttons from the main layout, since the `statusBarSlot` is set there.

Set the `menuLeftButtons` slot to an array that includes the protos for the Information and New buttons. These buttons are automatically laid out on the status bar, going from left to right.

```
menuLeftButtons:=[
                newtInfoButton,
                newtNewStationeryButton,
                ]
```

Set the `menuRightButtons` slot to an array that includes the protos for the Action and Filing buttons. These buttons are automatically laid out on the status bar from right to left.

```
menuRightButtons:=[
                newtActionButton,
                newtFilingButton,
                ]
```

Be sure to add the Overview Layout template file to your NTK Project window.

Creating the Default Layout

This is the view you see upon opening the application. Since it will eventually contain views that display the data, it needs to know about the application soup.

The `masterSoupSlot` identifies the application soup to the layout proto. The symbol in this slot must match the name of a soup declared in the `allSoups` slot of the `newtApplication` base view, which was `IOUSoup`. In the layout it is used as a symbol to set the value of the `masterSoupSlot`.

Follow these steps to create the required default layout:

1. Open a new layout window in NTK and drag out a `newtLayout` proto.

2. Name it `default`.

3. Set the `masterSoupSlot` to the symbol `'IOUSoup`. This correlates to the name of the soup as it is set up in the `newtApplication.allSoups` slot. See "Setting Up the Application Soup," beginning on page 4-15.

4. Add a `forceNewEntry` slot. Leave the default value `true`. This causes a new entry to be created when a user tries to open an empty folder.

5. Set the `viewFormat` slot's Fill value to White. This makes the data it displays look better and keeps anything from inadvertently showing through. In addition, the white fill improves the speed of the display and enhances view performance.

Be sure to add the default template file to your NTK Project window.

Using Entry Views

Entry views are used as containers for the slot views that display data from the slots in the target entry of the application soup. They are also the containers for the different header bars. Note that entry views are not necessary in the overview layout, since the overview layout displays items as shapes.

The entry view sets values needed to locate the data to be displayed in the slot views it will contain. These values include references to the data cursor (the `dataCursor` slot), the soup entry that contains the stored data (the `target` slot), and the view to display data (the `targetView` slot).

Follow these steps to ready your application for the slot views:

1. Drag out a `newtEntryView` proto on top of the `newtLayout` proto.

2. Optional. Name it `theEntry`.

There are no unusual slots to set in an entry view. Therefore, you are ready to add the header and slot view protos.

3. Drag out a `newtEntryPageHeader` across the top of the `newtEntryView`.

4. Under the header, drag out a `newtStationeryView` proto that covers the rest of the entry view. This special view is not be visible; its function is to provide a bounding box for the viewDef that will eventually be displayed.

The layout should look like the screen shot shown in Figure 4-9.

Figure 4-9   The information button and picker.

Registering DataDefs and ViewDefs

Several slots in the `newtApplication` base view enable you to identify the stationery in your application. These slots include the `allViewDefs`, `allDataDefs`, and `superSymbol` slots.

Note
To see how to create the stationery used as part of this application, consult Chapter 5, "Stationery." The `allDataDefs` and `allViewDefs` slots, which are discussed here, contain references to those dataDefs and viewDefs. ◆

The `allDataDefs` and `allViewDefs` slots are assigned references to the NTK layout files containing your dataDefs and viewDefs. Once this is done, the NewtApp framework automatically registers your stationery with the Newton system registry when your application is installed on a Newton device.

Each `allDataDefs` and `allViewDefs` slot contains frames that are required to contain slots with identical names, to indicate the dataDefs and viewDefs that work together. (A dataDef must be registered with its set of viewDefs because dataDefs use viewDefs to display their data.)

In the `allDataDefs` slot is a frame containing a reference to the NTK layout template for a single dataDef. In the frame within the `allViewDefs` slot is the frame containing slots with references to all the viewDef layout templates that work with that dataDef.

The recommended way to name the corresponding `allDataDefs` and `allViewDefs` slots is to set the slot names to the data symbol constant, as shown in the following code examples.

Set the `allDataDefs` slot to return a frame with references to all the application's dataDefs, as follows:

```
result := {};

result.(kDataSymbol) := GetLayout("IOUDataDef");
// result.(kData2Symbol) := ... to add a 2nd DataDef
result;
```

Set the `allViewDefs` slot to return a frame with references to all the application's viewDefs, in a parallel manner, as shown in the following code:

```
result := {};

result.(kDataSymbol) := {
    default: GetLayout("IOUDefaultViewDef"),
    notes:   GetLayout("IOUNotesViewDef"),
    iouPrintFormat: GetLayout("IOUPrintFormat"),
    // Use for routing (beaming, mailing, transports):
    frameFormat: {_proto: protoFrameFormat},
};
// Use to add a 2nd DataDef:
// result.(kData2Symbol) := {...}

result;
```

A NewtApp application only accepts stationery when a dataDef has a `superSymbol` with a value matching the value of the `newtApplication` base view's `superSymbol` slot. For this reason you want the value of the `superSymbol` slot to be a unique symbol. This sample application uses the constant `kSuperSymbol`, which is set to the application symbol `'|IOU:PIEDTS|`, to set the `superSymbol` slot.

Using the Required NewtApp Install and Remove Scripts

An `InstallScript` function and `RemoveScript` function are required to register your NewtApp application with the system for the various system services. These scripts are boilerplate functions you should copy unaltered.

You should create a text file, which you save as `Install&Remove.f`, into which to copy the functions:

```
InstallScript := func(partFrame)
   begin
      partFrame.removeFrame :=
(partFrame.theForm):NewtInstallScript(partFrame.theForm);
   end;

RemoveScript := func(partFrame)
   begin
(partFrame.removeFrame):NewtRemoveScript(removeFrame);
   end;
```

This file should be the last one processed when your application is built. (In NTK this means that it should appear at the bottom of the Project file list.)

If you have included the stationery files built in Chapter 5, "Stationery," you may now build, download, and run your NewtApp application.

Using Slot Views in Non-NewtApp Applications

The NewtApp slot view protos have a lot of functionality built into them which you may want to use in a non-NewtApp application. You can do this by keeping your existing application base view, removing the existing entry view layer and its contents, replacing it with a `newtFalseEntryView` proto, and placing the slot views in the `newtFalseEntryView`.

The following requirements must be satisfied for slot views to work outside a NewtApp application:

- The parent of the `newtFalseEntryView` must have the following slots:
  - `target`
  - `targetView`
- The slot views must be contained in a `newtFalseEntryView` proto.
- The `newtFalseEntryView` must receive a `Retarget` message whenever entries are changed.

Modifying the Base View

This discussion assumes that you already have a base view set up as part of your NTK project and that a `newtFalseEntryView` will be added to it later. If that is the case, you already have slots set with specifications for a soup name, soup indices, a soup query, and a soup cursor (among numerous others.)

Certain slots must be added to these base view slots for your application to be able to utilize the false entry view and the slot views. First, you must be sure to add a `target` slot and `targetView` slot, so that the false entry view can set them when an entry is changed. Second, you should include a method that sends the `Retarget` message to the false entry view when an entry is changed. As an example, you may wish to implement the following method, or one like it:

```
baseView.DoReTargeting := func()
                    theFalseEntryView:Retarget()
```

There are several places in your code where this message could be sent. For instance, if your application scrolls through entries, you should send the `DoReTargeting` message, defined above, to `ViewScrollUpScript` and `ViewScrollDownScript`. Following is an example of a `ViewScrollUpScript` method that scrolls through soup entries:

```
func()
    begin
        EntryChange(target);
        cardSoupCursor:Prev();
        :ResetTarget();
        :DoRetargeting();
    end
```

Other places where you may want to send the `Retarget` message include a delete action method, a `ViewSetupDoneScript` method (which executes immediately before a view is displayed or redisplayed), or even the `ButtonClickScript` method of a button that generates new entries and thus changes the soup and its display.

Using a False Entry View

The example used here, in which the `newtFalseEntryView` is implemented, is a non-NewtApp application that supports the use of slot views. If you want to adopt slot views into an existing application, you must use `newtFalseEntryView`.

Once you have an application base view set up, you may add the following slots to your `newtFalseEntryView`:

- Add a `dataCursorSlot` and set it to the symbol `'cardSoupCursor`. This symbol should match a slot defined in your application base view. The slot may be omitted if your base application view's cursor slot is set to the default name `dataCursor`.

- Add a `dataSoupSlot` and set it to the symbol `'cardSoup`. This symbol should match a slot defined in your application base view. The slot may be omitted if your base application view's soup slot is set to the default name `dataSoup`.

■ Add a `soupQuerySlot` and set it to the symbol `'cardSoupQuerySpec`. This symbol should match a slot defined in your application base view. The slot may be omitted if your base application view's soup query slot is set to the default name `soupQuery`.

Finally, you should make sure to declare the `newtFalseEntryView` to the application base view so the base view can send `Retarget` messages to the false entry view when data is changed.

For more information about the `newtFalseEntryView` see the *Newton Programmer's Reference*.

Creating a Custom Labelled Input-Line Slot View

You may find situations in which you need to create a custom slot view to get one that does exactly what your application requires. For example, the NewtApp framework does not yet contain a slot view that can display a picture. This is possible after you know more about how the slot views work.

In general, a slot view performs the following functions:

■ Target data; that is, updates a soup entry from its contents and vice versa.

■ Format data by using a filter.

■ Allow you to place ("jam") the data from another soup entry in this slot view. Of the built-in slot views, the `newtSmartName` proto does this.

All slot views assume a soup entry has been set by the parent view as the value of the `target` slot. The `target` slot contains a reference to the soup entry. The soup entry contains the slot with the data to be displayed in a given slot view and stores the new data.

Slot views also require a `path` slot which refers to the specific slot within the `target` entry. The path expression must lead to a slot that holds the correct kind of data for a given slot view. For instance, the `path` slot of a `newtROTextDateView` proto must refer to a slot in an entry that contain a integer date.

In the label input-line slot view protos, formatting is accomplished by selecting the correct NewtApp data filter as the value of the slot view's `flavor` slot. Note that some of the NewtApp data filters also specify a particular system picker which will be available when you use the `popup` option for your slot view. See the DTS sample code to see how to create a new newt proto.

Summary of the NewtApp Framework

Required Code

Required InstallScript

```
InstallScript := func(partFrame)
begin
    partFrame.removeFrame := (partFrame.theForm):
                NewtInstallScript(partFrame.theForm);
end;
```

Required RemoveScript

```
RemoveScript := func(partFrame)
begin
    (partFrame.removeFrame):NewtRemoveScript(removeFrame);
end;
```

Protos

newtSoup

```
myNewtSoup := {
_proto: newtSoup, // NewtApp soup proto
soupName: "MyApp:SIG", // a string unique to your app.

soupIndices: [    //soup particulars, may vary
            {structure: 'slot, //describing a slot
            path: 'title, // named "title" which
            type: 'string}, //contains a string
        ...], // more descriptions may follow

soupQuery: {                        // a soup query
        type: 'index,
        indexPath:'timeStamp}, // slot to use as index

soupDescr:"The Widget soup."//string describing the soup
defaultDataType:'soupType ,   //type for your soup entry
```

```
AddEntry: //Adds the entry to the specified store
    func (entry, store) ...

AdoptEntry: // Adds entry to the application soup while
    func (entry, type) ... // preserving dataDef entry slots

CreateBlankEntry: // Returns a blank entry
    func () ...

DeleteEntry: // Removes an entry from its soup
    func (entry) ...

DuplicateEntry: // Clones and returns entry
    func (entry) ...

DoneWithSoup: // Unregisters soup changes and soup
    func (appSymbol) ...

FillNewSoup:    // Called by MakeSoup to add soup
    func ()    ...// values to a new soup

MakeSoup:       // Used by the newtApplication proto
    func (appSymbol) ... // to return and register a new soup

GetCursor: // Returns the cursor
    func ()    ...

SetupCursor:      // Sets the cursor to an entry in the
func (querySpec) ... // master soup

Query: // Performs a query on a newtSoup
    func (querySpec) ...

GetAlias: // Returns an entry alias.
    func (entry) ...

GetCursorPosition: // Returns an entry alias.
    func () ...

GoToAlias: // Returns entry referenced by the alias.
    func (alias) ...

}
```

newtApplication

```
myNewtAppBaseView := {
_proto: newtapplication, // Application base view proto
   appSymbol: '|IOU:DTS| //Unique application symbol
   title: "Roll Starter" // A string naming the app
   appObject: ["Ox", "Oxen"]// Array with singular and
        // plural strings describing application's data
   appAll: "All Notes" // Displayed in folder tab picker

   allSoups: { //Frame defining all known soups for app
            mySoup: {
            _proto: newtSoup,
            ...        }
        }

   allLayouts: {
            // Frame with references to layout files;
            // both default and overview required.
             default:GetLayout("DefaultLayoutFile"),
             overview:GetLayout("OverviewLayoutFile"),
        }

   scrollingEndBehavior:'beepAndWrap // How scrolling is
   // handled at end of view; can also be 'wrap, 'stop, or
   // 'beepAndStop.

   scrollingUpBehavior: 'bottom //Either 'top or 'bottom

   statusBarSlot: 'myStatusBar //Declare name to base so
                                //layouts may send messages

   allDataDefs: {'|appName:SIG|:GetLayout("yourDataDef")}
      //Frame with dataDef symbols as slot names. Slot
      // values are references to dataDef layout files.

   allViewDefs:
      {'|appName:SIG|: {default:GetLayout("yourViewDef")}}
   // Frame with dataDef symbols as slot names. Slot
   // values are references to frames of viewDef
   // layout files.

   superSymbol: '|appName:SIG| //Unique symbol identifying
                        //superSet of application's soups

   doCardRouting:true or 'onlyCardRouting //Enables
                                // filing and routing
```

```
        dateFindSlot: pathExpression // Enables dateFind for your
        // app. Path must lead to a slot containing a date.
        routeScripts:   //Contains default Delete and Duplicate
                        //route scripts.
        labelsFilter: //Set dynamically for filing settings
        layout:         // Set to the current layout
        newtAppBase: //Set dynamically to identify, for
            //instance, view to be closed when close box tapped
        retargetChain: // Dynamically set array of views
                        // to update.
        targetView: // Dynamically set to the view where
                    // target soup entry is displayed
        target: // Set to the soup entry to be displayed

AddEntryFromStationery: //Returns blank entry with class
    func (stationerySymbol)....// slot set to stationerySymbol

AdoptEntryFromStationery: // Returns entry with all slots
    func (adoptee, stationerySymbol, store)...// from adopted frame
                        //and class slot set to stationerySymbol

AdoptSoupEntryFromStationery: //Same as above plus
    func (adoptee, stationerySymbol, store, soup)... // you specify
                                        //soup & store

FolderChanged: //Changes folder tab to new value
    func (soupName, oldFolder, newFolder)....

FilterChanged: //Updates folder labels for each soup
    func ()         .... //in the allSoups frame.

ChainIn: //Adds views needing to be notified for
    func (chainSymbol) .... //retargeting to chainSymbol array.

ChainOut:                   //Removes views from
    func (chainSymbol) .... //chainSymbol array.

GetTarget:                  //Returns current soup entry.
    func ()         ....

GetTargetView:              //Returns view in which the
    func ()         .... // target entry is displayed.

DateFind: // Default DateFind method defined in framework.
        // Set dateFindSlot in base view to enable it.
    func (date, findType, results, scope, findContext)....
```

```
Find:      // Default Find method as defined in framework.
    func(text, results, scope, findContext)...

ShowLayout:// Switches display to specified layout.
    func(layout)...

NewtDeleteScript:// Deletes entry.
    func(entry, view)... // Referenced in routeScripts array

NewtDuplicateScript:// Duplicates entry.
    func(entry, view)... // Referenced in routeScripts array

GetAppState:// Gets app preferences, sets app, & returns
    func()... // prefs. Override to add own app prefs.

GetDefaultState:// Sets default app preferences.
    func()... // Override to add own app prefs.

SaveAppState:// Sets default app preferences.
    func()... // Override to add own app prefs.
```

newtInfoButton

```
infoButton := {          // The standard "i" info button
_proto: newtInfoButton,// Place proto in menuLeftButtons
DoInfoHelp:              //Opens online help book
    func()...,
DoInfoAbout:             //Either opens or closes an
    func()...,          // About view
DoInfoPrefs:            //Either opens or closes a
    func()...,}         // Preferences view
```

newtActionButton

```
actionButton := {        // the standard action button
_proto: newtActionButton } // place in menuRightButtons
```

newtFilingButton

```
filingButton := {        // the standard filing button
_proto: newtFilingButton } // place in menuRightButtons
```

newtAZTabs

```
myAZTab:= {              // the standard A-Z tabs
_proto: newtAZTabs,
PickActionScript:       //Default definition keys to
    func(letter)...}    // 'indexPath of allSoups soup query
```

newtFolderTab

```
myFolderTab:= {          // the plain folder tab
_proto: newtFolderTab }
```

newtClockFolderTab

```
myClockFolderTab:= {     // digital clock and folder tabs
_proto: newtClockFolderTab }
```

newtStatusBarNoClose

```
aStatusBarNoClose:= {      // status bar with no close box
_proto: newtStatusBarNoClose,
menuLeftButtons: [], //array of button protos
                    // laid out left to right
menuRightButtons: [], // array of button protos laid out
                    // right to left
```

newtStatusBar

```
aStatusBar:= {            // status bar with close box
_proto: newtStatusBar
menuLeftButtons: [], //array of button protos
                    // laid out left to right
menuRightButtons: [], // array of button protos laid out
                    // right to left }
```

newtFloatingBar

```
aFloatingBar:= {          // status bar with close box
_proto: newtFloatingBar,
menuButtons: [], // array of button protos }
```

newtAboutView

```
anAboutView:= {           // The about view
_proto: newtAboutView }
```

newtPrefsView

```
aPrefsView := {           // The preferences view
_proto: newtPrefsView  }
```

newtLayout

```
aBasicLayout := {           // The basic layout view
_proto: newtLayout,
    name: "",                    // Optional.
    masterSoupSlot: 'mainSoup, // Required.
        // Symbol referring to soup from allSoups slot
    forceNewEntry: true, //Forces new entry when empty
                        //folder opened.
    menuRightButtons:[], //Replaces slot in status bar
    menuLeftButtons:[], //Replaces slot in status bar
    dataSoup: 'soupSymbol,//Set to soup for this layout
    dataCursor: ,// Set to top visible entry; main cursor

FlushData:      //Flushes all children's entries
    func(),

NewTarget:      //Utility resets origin and
    func(),     // resets screen

ReTarget:       //Sets the dataCursor slot and resets
    func(setViews),// screen if setViews is true

ScrollCursor:   //Moves cursor delta entries and resets it.
    func(delta),

SetUpCursor:    //Sets cursor and returns entry.
    func(),

Scroller:       //Moves numAndDirection entries. Scrolls
    func(numAndDirection)...,//up if numAndDirection <0.

ViewScrollDownScript: // Calls scroller with the
    func()...,          //value of 1.

ViewScrollUpScript:  // Calls scroller with the
    func()...,          //value of -1.

DoRetarget():        // Calls the "right" retarget
    func()...,
            }
```

newtRollLayout

```
myRollLayout:= {  // Dynamically lays out child views
_proto: newtRollLayout, // using protoChild as default
   protoChild: GetLayout("DefaultEntryView"), // Default view
   name: "",                    // Optional.
   masterSoupSlot: 'mainSoup, // Required.
        // Symbol referring to soup from allSoups slot
   forceNewEntry: true, //Forces new entry when empty
                        //folder opened.
   menuRightButtons:[], //Replaces slot in status bar
   menuLeftButtons:[], //Replaces slot in status bar
   dataSoup: 'soupSymbol,//Set to soup for this layout
   dataCursor: ,// Set to top visible entry; main cursor


        // All newtLayout methods are inherited.
            }
```

newtPageLayout

```
myPageLayout:= { // Dynamically lays out child views
_proto: newtPageLayout, // using protoChild as default
   protoChild: GetLayout("DefaultEntryView"), // Default view
   name: "",                    // Optional.
   masterSoupSlot: 'mainSoup, // Required.
        // Symbol referring to soup from allSoups slot
   forceNewEntry: true, //Forces new entry when empty
                        //folder opened.
   menuRightButtons:[], //Replaces slot in status bar
   menuLeftButtons:[], //Replaces slot in status bar
   dataSoup: 'soupSymbol,//Set to soup for this layout
   dataCursor: ,// Set to top visible entry; main cursor


        // All newtLayout methods are inherited.
            }
```

newtOverLayout

```
myOverLayout:= { // Overview for page and card type layout
_proto: newtOverLayout
   centerTarget: nil, // True centers entry in overview
   masterSoupSlot: 'mainSoup, // Required.
        // Symbol referring to soup from allSoups slot
   name: "",                    // Required but not used.
```

```
    forceNewEntry: true, //Creates blank entry for layout
    menuRightButtons:[], //Replaces slot in status bar
    menuLeftButtons:[], //Replaces slot in status bar
    nothingCheckable: nil, //True suppresses checkboxes
Abstract: //Returns shapes for items in overviews
    func(targetEntry, bbox)..., //Override to extract text
GetTargetInfo: //Returns frame with target information
    func(targetType)...,
HitItem: //Called when overview item is tapped.
    func(index, x, y)...,

        // All newtLayout methods are inherited.
            }
```

newtRollOverLayout

```
myOverLayout := { // Overview for roll-type application
_proto: newtRollOverLayout //Same as newtOverLayout
    centerTarget: nil, // True centers entry in overview
    masterSoupSlot: 'mainSoup, // Required.
        // Symbol referring to soup from allSoups slot
    name: "",                   // Required but not used.
    menuRightButtons:[], //Replaces slot in status bar
    menuLeftButtons:[], //Replaces slot in status bar
    forceNewEntry: true, //Creates blank entry for layout
    nothingCheckable: nil, //True suppresses checkboxes
Abstract: //Returns shapes for items in overviews
    func(targetEntry, bbox)..., //Override to extract text
GetTargetInfo: //Returns frame with target information
    func(targetType)...,
HitItem: //Called when overview item is tapped.
    func(index, x, y)...,

            // All newtLayout methods are inherited.
            }
```

newtEntryView

```
anEntryView := {   // Invisible container for slot views
_proto: newtEntryView
    entryChanged: //Set to true for flushing
    entryDirtied: //Set to true if flush occurred
    target: //Set to entry for display
    currentDataDef: //Set to current dataDef
```

```
    currentViewDef: //Set to current viewDef
    currentStatView: //Set to current context of viewDef
StartFlush: // Starts timer that flushes entry
    func()...,
EndFlush: // Called when flush timer fires
    func()...,
EntryCool: // Is target read-only? True report
    func(report)..., //displays write-protected message
JamFromEntry: // Finds children's jamFromEntry and sends
    func(otherEntry)..., // message if found, then retargets
Retarget: // Changes stationery's display then sends
    func()...,//message on to child views
DoRetarget: // Calls the "right" retarget
    func()...,//
        }
```

newtFalseEntryView

```
aFalseEntryView:= {// Use as container for slot views in
_proto: newtFalseEntryView, // non-NewtApp applications.
    targetSlot: 'target, //Parent needs to have slots
    dataCursorSlot: 'dataCursor, //with names
    targetSlot: 'dataSoup, //that match each of
    dataSoup: 'soupQuery // these symbols.
// newtFalseEntryView inherits all newtEntryView methods.
        }
```

newtRollEntryView

```
aRollEntryView:= { // Entry view for paper roll-style apps
_proto: newtRollEntryView, //stationery required.
    bottomlessHeight: kEntryViewHeight, //Optional
// Inherits slots and methods from newtEntryView.
        }
```

newtEntryPageHeader

```
aPageHeader:= {  // Header bar for card or page-style apps
_proto: newtEntryPageHeader,
    // contains no additional slots or methods
        }
```

newtEntryRollHeader

```
aRollHeader:= {    // Header/divider bar for page or
                   // roll-style apps
_proto: newtEntryRollHeader,
   hasFiling: true // Nil is no filing or action buttons
   isResizable: true // Nil is no drag resizing
           }
```

newtEntryViewActionButton

```
anEntryActionButton:= {// Action button to use on headers
                     // and within entry views
_proto: newtEntryViewActionButton
           }
```

newtEntryViewFilingButton

```
anEntryFilingButton:= {// Filing button to use on headers
                     // and within entry views
_proto: newtEntryViewFilingButton
           }
```

newtInfoBox

```
anInfoBox:= {      // Floating view displayed when header
_proto: newtInfoBox, //icon tapped
   icon: ,// Optional, default provided.
   description: "",// Displayed in view next to icon.
           }
```

newtROTextView

```
readOnlyTextView:= {// All simple slot views based on this
_proto: newtROTextView,
   path: 'pathExpr,// Text stored and retrieved from here
   styles: nil,// Plain text.
   tabs: nil,// Tabs not enabled.
   jamSlot: 'jamPathExpr,// New path for JamFromEntry.
TextScript: // Returns a text representation of data
   func()..., //
JamFromEntry: // Retargets to jamPathExpr if not nil
   func(jamPathExpr)..., //
           }
```

newtTextView

```
editableTextView:= {// This is the editable text view
_proto: newtTextView,
    path: 'pathExpr,// Text stored/retrieved from here
    styles: nil,// Plain text.
    tabs: nil,// Tabs not enabled.
    jamSlot: 'jamPathExpr,// New path for JamFromEntry.
TextScript: // Returns a text representation of data
func()..., //
JamFromEntry: // Retargets to jamPathExpr if not nil
    func(jamPathExpr)..., //
                }
```

newtRONumView

```
readOnlyNumberView:= {// Read-only number view
_proto: newtRONumView,
    path: 'pathExpr,// Numbers stored/retrieved from here
    format: %.10g,// For 10-place decimal; you may change
    integerOnly: true,// Text to num conversion is int
TextScript: // Returns a text representation of data
func()..., //
JamFromEntry: // Retargets to jamPathExpr if not nil
    func(jamPathExpr)..., //
                }
```

newtNumView

```
editableNumberView:= {// Editable number view
_proto: newtNumView,
    path: 'pathExpr,// Numbers stored/retrieved from here
    format: %.10g,// For 10-place decimal; you may change
    integerOnly: true,// Text to num conversion is int
TextScript: // Returns a text representation of data
func()..., //
JamFromEntry: // Retargets to jamPathExpr if not nil
    func(jamPathExpr)..., //
                }
```

newtROTextDateView

```
readOnlyTextDateView:= {// Read-only text and date view. One
_proto: newtROTextDateView, //format slot must be non-nil
    path: 'pathExpr,// Data stored/retrieved from here
```

```
    longFormat: yearMonthDayStrSpec,// for LongDateStr
    shortFormat: nil,         // for ShortDateStr function
TextScript: // Returns a text representation of data
func()..., //
JamFromEntry: // Retargets to jamPathExpr if not nil
    func(jamPathExpr)..., //
            }
```

newtTextDateView

```
editableTextDateView:= {// Editable text and date view. One
_proto: newtTextDateView, //format slot must be non-nil
    path: 'pathExpr,// Data stored/retrieved from here
    longFormat: yearMonthDayStrSpec,// for LongDateStr
    shortFormat: nil,         // for ShortDateStr function
TextScript: // Returns a text representation of data
func()..., //
JamFromEntry: // Retargets to jamPathExpr if not nil
    func(jamPathExpr)..., //
            }
```

newtROTextTimeView

```
readOnlyTextTimeView:= {// Displays and formats time text
_proto: newtROTextTimeView,
    path: 'pathExpr,// Data stored/retrieved from here
    format: ShortTimeStrSpec,// for TimeStr function
TextScript: // Returns a text representation of data
func()..., //
JamFromEntry: // Retargets to jamPathExpr if not nil
    func(jamPathExpr)..., //
            }
```

newtTextTimeView

```
editableTextTimeView:= {// Editable time text
_proto: newtTextTimeView,
    path: 'pathExpr,// Data stored/retrieved from here
    format: ShortTimeStrSpec,// for TimeStr function
TextScript: // Returns a text representation of data
func()..., //
JamFromEntry: // Retargets to jamPathExpr if not nil
    func(jamPathExpr)..., //
            }
```

newtROTextPhoneView

```
readOnlyTextPhoneView:= {// Displays phone numbers
_proto: newtROTextPhoneView,
    path: 'pathExpr,// Data stored/retrieved from here
TextScript: // Returns a text representation of data
func()..., //
JamFromEntry: // Retargets to jamPathExpr if not nil
    func(jamPathExpr)..., //
            }
```

newtTextPhoneView

```
EditableTextPhoneView:= {// Displays editable phone numbers
_proto: newtTextPhoneView,
    path: 'pathExpr,// Data stored/retrieved from here
    TextScript: // Returns a text representation of data
    func()..., //
JamFromEntry: // Retargets to jamPathExpr if not nil
    func(jamPathExpr)..., //
            }
```

newtAreaCodeLine

```
protonewtAreaCodeLine : = {
_proto: protonewtAreaCodeLine,
flavor: newtPhoneFilter
access: 'query
label: string  //text to display in the highlight window
path: 'pathExpr,// Data stored/retrieved from here
}
```

newtAreaCodePhoneLine

```
protonewtAreaCodeLine : = {
_proto: protonewtAreaCodeLine,
flavor: newtPhoneFilter
access: 'query
label: string  //text to display in the highlight window
path: 'pathExpr,// Data stored/retrieved from here
}
```

newtROEditView

```
readOnlyEditView := {   // A text display view, which
                        // may have scrollers
_proto: newtROEditView,
   optionFlags: kNoOptions,          // disables scroller
                  //kHasScrollersOption enables scroller
   doCaret: true, //caret is autoset
   viewLineSpacing: 28,
   path: 'pathExpr,// Data stored/retrieved from here
ScrolltoWord: // Finds words, scrolls to it, and high-
   func(words, hilite)..., // lights it (if hilite is true)
            }
```

newteditView

```
editView := {            // A text edit view, which
                         // may have scrollers
_proto: newtEditView,
   optionFlags: kNoOptions,          // disables scroller
                  //kHasScrollersOption enables scroller
   doCaret: true, //caret is autoset
   viewLineSpacing: 28,
   path: 'pathExpr,// Data stored/retrieved from here
ScrolltoWord: // Finds words, scrolls to it, and high-
   func(words, hilite)..., // lights it (if hilite is true)
            }
```

newtCheckBox

```
checkBoxView := {      // A checkbox
_proto: newtCheckBox
   assert: true,// Data stored/retrieved from here
   negate: nil,// Data stored/retrieved from here
   path: 'pathExpr,// Data stored/retrieved from here
ViewSetupForm: // Is target.(path)= assert?
   func()..., //
ValueChanged: // Changes target.(path) value to its
   func()..., // opposite either true or false
            }
```

newtStationeryView

```
stationeryView := {        // Used as bounding box and container
                           // view for viewDef
_proto: newtStationeryView
        }
```

newtEntryLockedIcon

```
entryLockedIcon:= {  //Shows lock if slot is on locked media
_proto: newtEntryLockedIcon
    icon: nil,// Can also be: lockedIcon
Retarget : // displays either lock or unlocked icon
    func()...,
SetIcon: // Changes target.(path) value to its
    func()..., // opposite either true or false
        }
```

newtProtoLine

```
basicInputLine := {            // Base for input line protos
_proto: newtProtoLine,
    label: "",// Text for input line label
    labelCommands: ["", "",],// Picker options
    curLabelCommand: 1,// Integer for current command
    usePopup: true,// When true with labelCommands array
                   // picker is enabled
    path: 'pathExpr,// Data stored/retrieved from here
    access: 'readWrite,// Could be 'readOnly or 'pickOnly
    flavor: newtFilter,// Don't change
    memory: nil,             // most recent picker choices
ChangePopup: // change picker items before they display
    func(item, entry)..., //
UpdateText: // Used with Undo to update text to new text
    func(newText)..., //
        }
```

newtLabelInputLine

```
aLabelInputLine := {          // Labelled input line for text
_proto: newtLabelInputLine,
    label: "",// Text for input line label
    labelCommands: ["", "",],// Picker options
    curLabelCommand: integer,// Integer for current command
```

```
    usePopup: true,// When true with labelCommands array
                // picker is enabled
    access: 'readWrite,// Could be 'readOnly or 'pickOnly
    flavor: newtTextFilter,//
    memory: nil,            // most recent picker choices
    path: 'pathExpr,// Data stored/retrieved from here
ChangePopup: // change picker items before they display
    func(item, entry)..., //
UpdateText: // Used with Undo to update text to new text
    func(newText)..., //
            }
```

newtROLabelInputLine

```
aLabelInputLine:= {          // Labelled display line for text
_proto: newtROLabelInputLine,
    label: "",// Text for input line label
       flavor: newtTextFilter,//
    memory: nil,            // most recent picker choices
    path: 'pathExpr,// Data stored/retrieved from here
ChangePopup: // change picker items before they display
    func(item, entry)..., //
UpdateText: // Used with Undo to update text to new text
    func(newText)..., //
            }
```

newtLabelNumInputLine

```
aLabelNumberInputLine:= {     // Labelled number input line
_proto: newtLabelNumInputLine,
    label: "",// Text for input line label
    labelCommands: ["", "",],// Picker options
    curLabelCommand: integer,// Integer for current command
    usePopup: true,// When true with labelCommands array
                // picker is enabled
    access: 'readWrite,// Could be 'readOnly or 'pickOnly
    flavor: newtNumberFilter,//
    memory: nil,            // most recent picker choices
    path: 'pathExpr,// Data stored/retrieved from here
ChangePopup: // change picker items before they display
    func(item, entry)..., //
UpdateText: // Used with Undo to update text to new text
    func(newText)..., //
            }
```

newtROLabelNumInputLine

aDisplayLabelNumberInputLine:= {// Labelled number display line
_proto: newtROLabelNumInputLine,
    label: "",// Text for input line label
    flavor: newtNumberFilter,//
    path: 'pathExpr,// Data stored/retrieved from here
UpdateText: // Used with Undo to update text to new text
    func(*newText*)..., //
            }

newtLabelDateInputLine

editableLabelNumberInputLine:= {// Labelled date input line
_proto: newtLabelDateInputLine,
    label: "",// Text for input line label
    labelCommands: ["", "",],// Picker options
    curLabelCommand: *integer*,// Integer for current command
    memory: nil,   // most recent picker choices
    usePopup: true,// When true with labelCommands array
                // picker is enabled
    access: 'readWrite,// Could be 'readOnly or 'pickOnly
    flavor: newtDateFilter,//
    path: 'pathExpr,// Data stored/retrieved from here
ChangePopup: // change picker items before they display
    func(*item, entry*)..., //
UpdateText: // Used with Undo to update text to new text
    func(*newText*)..., //
            }

newtROLabelDateInputLine

displayLabelDateLine:= {   // Labelled number display line
_proto: newtROLabelDateInputLine,
    label: "",// Text for input line label
    flavor: newtDateFilter,// Don't change
    path: 'pathExpr,// Data stored/retrieved from here
UpdateText: // Used with Undo to update text to new text
    func(*newText*)..., //
            }

newtLabelSimpleDateInputLine

editableLabelSimpleDateLine:= {// Labelled date display line
                // accepts dates like 9/15 or 9/15/95

```
_proto: newtLabelSimpleDateInputLine,
    label: "",// Text for input line label
    access: 'readWrite,// Could be 'readOnly or 'pickOnly
    flavor: newtSimpleDateFilter,//
    path: 'pathExpr,// Data stored/retrieved from here
UpdateText: // Used with Undo to update text to new text
    func(newText)..., //
                }
```

newtNRLabelDateInputLine

```
pickerLabelDateInputLine:= {   // Input through DatePopup picker
_proto: newtNRLabelDateInputLine,
    label: "",// Text for input line label
    access: 'pickOnly,// Could be 'readOnly
    flavor: newtDateFilter,//
    path: 'pathExpr,// Data stored/retrieved from here
UpdateText: // Used with Undo to update text to new text
    func(newText)..., //
                }
```

newtROLabelTimeInputLine

```
displayLabelTimeLine:= {        // Labelled time display line
_proto: newtROLabelTimeInputLine,
    label: "",// Text for input line label
    flavor: newtTimeFilter,// Don't change
    path: 'pathExpr,// Data stored/retrieved from here
                }
```

newtLabelTimeInputLine

```
aLabelTimeInputLine:= {         // Labelled time input line
_proto: newtLabelTimeInputLine,
    label: "",// Text for input line label
    labelCommands: ["", "",],// Picker options
    curLabelCommand: integer,// Integer for current command
    usePopup: true,// When true with labelCommands array
                 // picker is enabled
    access: 'readWrite,// Could be 'readOnly or 'pickOnly
    flavor: newtTimeFilter,// Don't change
    memory: nil,              // most recent picker choices
    path: 'pathExpr,// Data stored/retrieved from here
ChangePopup: // change picker items before they display
    func(item, entry)..., //
```

```
UpdateText: // Used with Undo to update text to new text
    func(newText)..., //
              }
```

newtNRLabelTimeInputLine

```
pickerLabelTimeInputLine:= {   // Input through TimePopup picker
_proto: newtNRLabelTimeInputLine,
    label: "",// Text for input line label
    access: 'pickOnly,// Could be 'readOnly
    flavor: newtTimeFilter,// Don't change
    path: 'pathExpr,// Data stored/retrieved from here
UpdateText: // Used with Undo to update text to new text
    func(newText)..., //
              }
```

newtLabelPhoneInputLine

```
aLabelPhoneInputLine:= {       // Labelled phone input line
_proto: newtLabelPhoneInputLine,
    label: "",// Text for input line label
    usePopup: true,// When true with labelCommands array
                 // picker is enabled
    access: 'readWrite,// Could be 'readOnly or 'pickOnly
    flavor: newtPhoneFilter,// Don't change
    memory: nil,              // most recent picker choices
    path: 'pathExpr,// Data stored/retrieved from here
ChangePopup: // change picker items before they display
    func(item, entry)..., //
UpdateText: // Used with Undo to update text to new text
    func(newText)..., //
              }
```

newtSmartNameView

```
smartNameLine:= {             // protoPeoplePicker Input
_proto: newtSmartNameView, // from Names soup
    label: "",// Text for input line label
    access: 'readWrite,// Could be 'readOnly or 'pickOnly
    flavor: newtSmartNameFilter,// Don't change
    path: 'pathExpr,// Data stored/retrieved from here
UpdateText: // Used with Undo to update text to new text
    func(newText)...,
              }
```

CHAPTER 5

Stationery

Stationery, which consists of new data formats and different views of your data, may be built into an application or added as an extension. Once incorporated, these data formats and views are available through the pickers (pop-up menus) of the New and Show buttons.

Stationery works best when incorporated into a NewtApp application. It is part of the NewtApp framework and is tightly integrated into its structures. If you are building applications using the NewtApp framework, you'll probably want to read this chapter.

Before you begin you should already be familiar with the concepts documented in Chapter 4, "NewtApp Applications," as well as the concepts of views and templates, soups and stores, and system services like finding, filing, and routing. These subjects are covered in Chapter 3, "Views," Chapter 11, "Data Storage and Retrieval," Chapter 16, "Find," Chapter 15, "Filing," and Chapter 21, "Routing Interface."

The examples in this chapter use the Newton Toolkit (NTK) development environment. Therefore, you should also be familiar with NTK before you try the examples. Consult *Newton Toolkit User's Guide* for information about NTK.

This chapter describes:

- how to create stationery and tie it into an application
- how to create, register, and install an extension
- the stationery protos, methods, and global functions

About Stationery

Stationery application extensions provide different ways of structuring data and various ways to view that data. To add stationery to your application, you must create a **data definition**, also called a dataDef, and an adjunct **view definition**, also called a viewDef. Both of the stationery components are created as view templates, though only the viewDef displays as a view at run time. Stationery always consists of at least one dataDef which has one or more viewDefs associated with it.

A **dataDef** is based on the `newtStationery` proto and is used to create alternative data structures. The dataDef contains slots that define, describe, and identify its data structures. It also contains a slot, called `superSymbol`, that identifies the application into which its data entries are to be subsumed. It also contains a `name` slot where the string that names the dataDef is placed. This is the name that appears in the New picker. Note that each of the items shown in the New menu of the Notes application in Figure 5-1 is a dataDef name.

The **viewDef** is based on any general view proto, depending upon the characteristics you wish to impart, but must have a specified set of slots added to it. (For more information about the slots required in viewDefs and dataDefs, see the "Stationery Reference" chapter in *Newton Programmer's Reference*.) The viewDef is the view template you design as the input and display device for your data. It is the component of stationery that imparts the "look and feel" for that part of the application. Each dataDef must have at least one viewDef defined to display it, though it can have several.

You may include or add stationery to any NewtApp application or any application that already uses stationery. The stationery components you create appear as items in the pickers (pop-up menus) of the New and Show buttons.

The Stationery Buttons

The stationery buttons are necessary to integrate stationery definitions with an application. They must be in the application which is to display your stationery components. They are defined as part of the NewtApp framework and work only when included in a NewtApp application. (You can use the `newtStationeryPopupButton` proto to create your own non-NewtApp buttons.)

The New button offers new data formats generated from dataDefs. For example, the New button in the built-in Calls application creates one new data entry form by default; if it contained more dataDefs there would be a New picker available. The New button of the built-in Notes application offers a picker whose choices create a new Note, Checklist, or Outline format for entering notes. The example used in this chapter extends the built-in Notes application by adding the dataDef item IOU to the New menu, as shown in Figure 5-1.

Stationery

Figure 5-1   The IOU extension in the New picker

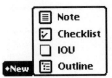

When you choose IOU from the New picker, an IOU entry is displayed, as shown in Figure 5-2.

Figure 5-2   The IOU extension to the Notes application

The Show button offers different views for the display of application data. These are generated by the viewDefs defined for an application. For example, the choices in the Show button of the built-in Names application include a Card and All Info view of the data. These views appear as shown in Figure 5-3.

Figure 5-3   The Show menu presents different views of application data

Stationery Registration

Your stationery, which may be built as part of an application or outside of an application (as an NTK auto part), must be registered with the system when an application is installed and unregistered when an application is uninstalled. DataDef and viewDef registry functions coordinate those stationery parts by registering the viewDef with its dataDef symbol, as well as its view template. The dataDef registry function adds its view templates to the system registry.

When it is part of a NewtApp application, stationery registration is done automatically–after you set slots with the necessary symbols. If you create your stationery outside of a NewtApp application, you must register (and unregister) your stationery manually by using the global functions provided for that purpose (`RegDataDef`, `UnRegDataDef`, `RegisterViewDef`, and `UnRegisterViewDef`) in the `InstallScript` and `RemoveScript` functions in your application part.

Once stationery is registered, applications can make use of those dataDefs whose `superSymbol` slot matches the application's `superSymbol` slot.

Getting Information about Stationery

By using the appropriate global function, you can get information about all the dataDefs and viewDefs that have been registered and thus are part of the system registry. These functions include `GetDefs`, `GetDataDefs`, `GetAppDataDefs`, `GetViewDefs`, and so on. For details on these functions, see *Newton Programmer's Reference*.

You can also obtain application-specific stationery information. This enables applications that are registered for stationery to be extended by other developers.

Compatibility Information

The stationery feature and programming interface is new in Newton OS version 2.0. It is not supported on earlier system versions.

Using Stationery

Stationery allows you to:

■ Create discrete data definitions and view definitions.

■ Extend your own and other applications.

■ Create print formats.

Designing Stationery

Whether you use stationery in an application or an auto part, it is important to keep the data and view definitions as discrete as possible. Encapsulating them, by keeping all references confined to the code in the data or view definition, will make them maximally reusable.

You should keep in mind that these extensions may be used in any number of future programming situations that you cannot foresee. If your stationery was created for an application (which you may have written at the same time), resist any and all urges to make references to structures contained in that application, thereby "hard-wiring" it to depend on that application. In addition, you should provide public interfaces to any values you want to share outside the dataDef.

If your stationery is designed for a NewtApp, the stationery soup entries, which are defined in the dataDef component of stationery, are adopted into the soup of a NewtApp application (via the `AdoptEntry` method) so that your stationery's slots are added to those already defined in the main application. This allows the stationery and the host application to have discrete soup structures. See the description of `AdoptEntry` (page 3-5) in *Newton Programmer's Reference*.

CHAPTER 5

The dataDef component of your stationery should use a `FillNewEntry` method to define its own discrete soup entry structure. Note that it is your responsibility to set a `class` slot within each entry. The value of the `class` slot must match the dataDef symbol and is used by the system when routing the entry (via faxing, mailing, beaming, printing, and so on). An example of how to use `FillNewEntry` follows.

Using FillNewEntry

You use the `FillNewEntry` method in your dataDef to create an entry structure that is tailored to your data. This approach is recommended when your stationery is implemented as part of a NewtApp application.

The `FillNewEntry` method works in conjunction with the NewtApp framework's `newtSoup.CreateBlankEntry` method. The `FillNewEntry` method takes a new entry, as returned by the `CreateBlankEntry` method, as a parameter. This is done with a `CreateBlankEntry` implementation put in the `newtApplication.allSoups` slot of your NewtApp application, as shown in the following example:

```
CreateBlankEntry: func()
   begin
   local newEntry := Clone({class:nil,
                            viewStationery: nil,
                            title: nil,
                            timeStamp: nil,
                            height: 176});
   newEntry.title := ShortDate(time());
   newEntry.timeStamp := time();
   newEntry;
   end;
```

This new entry contains an entry template. In the following code example, that new entry is passed as a parameter to the `FillNewEntry` method, which is implemented in the stationery's dataDef. `FillNewEntry` adds a slot named `kDataSymbol`, which contains an entry template for the stationery's data definition. It then adds a `class` slot to the new entry, which is set to the same constant (`kDataSymbol`). A `viewStationery` slot is then added and set to the same constant (only needed for vestigial compatibility with the Notes application). Finally, it adds a value to the `dueDate` slot of the `kDataSymbol` entry.

```
FillNewEntry: func(newEntry)
   begin
   newEntry.(kDataSymbol) :=
           Clone({who: "A Name",
                 howMuch: 42,
                 dueDate: nil});
```

```
newEntry.class := kDataSymbol;
newEntry.viewStationery := kDataSymbol;
newEntry.(kDataSymbol).dueDate:=time();
newEntry;
end;
```

Extending the Notes Application

You may extend an existing application, such as the built-in Notes application, by adding your own stationery. This is done by building and downloading an NTK auto part that defines your stationery extensions.

The sample project used to illustrate many of the following sections consists of these files, in the processing order shown:

- `ExtendNotes.rsrc`

- `ExtendNotes Definitions.f`

- `iouDataDef`

- `iouDefaultViewDef`

- `iouPrintFormat`

- `ExtendNotes Install & Remove.f`

Of these, the `iouDataDef`, `iouDefaultViewDef`, and `ExtendNotes Install & Remove.f` files are used in the examples in this chapter. The resource file (`ExtendNotes.rsrc`) contains the icon that is displayed next to the dataDef name in the New menu (as shown in Figure 5-1). The definitions file (`ExtendNotes Definitions.f`) is the file in which the constants, some of which are used in examples, are defined. Finally, the `iouPrintFormat` file defines a print format for the stationery.

Determining the SuperSymbol of the Host

Using stationery requires the presence of a matching `superSymbol` slot in both the host application and the dataDef component of your stationery. The value in the `superSymbol` slot is used to link a dataDef to an application.

If you do not know the value of the `superSymbol` slot for an application that is installed on your Newton device, you may use the global function `GetDefs` to see all the dataDefs that are registered by the system.

Stationery

A call to the global function GetDefs in the NTK Inspector window returns a series of frames describing dataDefs that have been registered with the system. An excerpt of the output from a call made in the Inspector window follows.

```
GetDefs('dataDef,nil,nil)

#44150A9  [{_proto: {@451},
            symbol: paperroll,
            name: "Note",
            superSymbol: notes,
            description: "Note",
            icon: {@717},
            version: 1,
            metadata: NIL,
            MakeNewEntry: <function, 0 arg(s) #46938D>,
            StringExtract: <function, 2 arg(s) #4693AD>,
            textScript: <function, 2 arg(s) #4693CD>},
          {_proto: {@451},
            symbol: calllog,
            name: "Calls",
            superSymbol: callapp,
            description: "Phone Message",
            icon: {@718},
            version: 1,
            metadata: NIL,
            taskSlip: |PhoneHome:Newton|,
            MakeNewEntry: <function, 0 arg(s) #47F9A9>,
            StringExtract: <function, 2 arg(s) #47F969>,
            textScript: <function, 2 arg(s) #47F989>},
          ...]
```

GetDefs and other stationery functions are documented in *Newton Programmer's Reference*.

Creating a DataDef

You create a dataDef by basing it on a newtStationery proto. In NTK it is created as a layout file, even though it is never displayed. The following steps lead you through the creation of the dataDef that is used to extend the built-in Notes application.

Note again that the data definition is adopted into an application's soup only when the application and dataDef have matching values in their superSymbol slots. For instance, when you are building a dataDef as an extension to the Notes application, as we are in this example, your dataDef must have 'notes as the value of its superSymbol slot.

The following example uses the constant kSuperSymbol as the value of the superSymbol slot. It is defined as follows in the Extend Notes Definition.f file:

```
constant kSuperSymbol := 'notes; // Note's SuperSymbol
```

Once you have created an NTK layout, named the template iouDataDef, and saved the file under the name iouDataDef, you may set the slots of the iouDataDef as follows:

- Set name to "IOU". This shows up in the New button's picker.

- Set superSymbol to the constant kSuperSymbol. This stationery can only be used by an application that has a matching value in the newtApplication base view's superSymbol slot.

- Set description to "An IOU entry". This string shows up in the information box that appears when the user taps the icon on the left side of the header, as shown in Figure 4-5 (page 4-9).

- Set symbol to kDataSymbol.

- Set version to 1. This is an arbitrary stationery version number set at your discretion.

- Remove the viewBounds slot; it's not needed since this object is not a view.

There are a number of methods defined within the newtStationery proto that you should override for your data type.

Defining DataDef Methods

The three methods MakeNewEntry, StringExtract, and TextScript are illustrated in this section. You use the method MakeNewEntry to define the soup entries for your dataDef; the method StringExtract is required by NewtApp overview scripts to return text for display in the overview; and TextScript is called by the routing interface to return a text description of your data.

The MakeNewEntry method returns a complete entry frame which will be added to some (possibly unknown) application soup. You should use MakeNewEntry, instead of the FillNewEntry method (which works in conjunction with the NewtApp framework's newtSoup.CreateBlankEntry), when your stationery is being defined as an auto part.

The example of MakeNewEntry used here defines the constant kEntryTemplate as a frame in which to define all the generic parts of the entry.

All the specific parts of the data definition are kept in a nested frame that has the name of the data class symbol, kDataSymbol. By keeping the specific definitions of your data grouped in a single nested frame and accessible by the class of the data, you are assuring that your code will be reusable in other applications.

Stationery

```
// Generic entry definition:
DefConst('kEntryTemplate, {
   class: kDataSymbol,
   viewStationery: kDataSymbol,// vestigial; for Notes
                              // compatibility
   title: nil,
   timeStamp: nil,
   height: 176,        // For page and paper roll-type apps
                       // this should be the same as height
                       // slot in dataDef and viewDefHeight
                       // slot in viewDef (if present)
});

// This facilitates writing viewDefs that can be reused
kEntryTemplate.(kDataSymbol) := {
   who: nil,
   howMuch: 0,
   dueDate: nil,
};

MakeNewEntry: func()
   begin
   local theNewEntry := DeepClone(kEntryTemplate);
   theNewEntry.title := ShortDate(time());
   theNewEntry.timeStamp := time();
   theNewEntry.(kDataSymbol).dueDate := time();
   theNewEntry;
   end;
```

The StringExtract method is called when an overview is generated and is expected to return a one or two-line description of the data. Here is an example of a StringExtract implementation:

```
StringExtract: func(item,numLines)
   begin
   if numLines = 1 then
      return item.title
   else
      return item.title&&item.(kDataSymbol).who;
   end;
```

The TextScript method is called by the routing interface to get a text version of an entire entry. It differs from StringExtract in that it returns the text of the item, rather than a description.

Here is an example:

```
TextScript: func(item,target)
   begin
   item.text := "IOU\n" & target.(kDataSymbol).who
              && "owes me" &&
              NumberStr(target.(kDataSymbol).howMuch);
   item.text;
   end;
```

Creating ViewDefs

ViewDefs may be based on any of the generic view protos. You could use, for instance, a `clView`, which has very little functionality. Or, if you wanted a picture to display behind your data, you could base your viewDef on a `clPictureView`.

Routing and printing formats are also implemented as viewDefs. You can learn more about using special protos to create routing and printing formats in Chapter 21, "Routing Interface."

Note that these are just a few examples of views you may use as a base view in your viewDef. Your viewDef will function as expected, so long as the required slots are set and the resulting view template is registered, either in the `allviewDefs` slot of the `newtApplication` base view or through the `InstallScript` function of an auto part.

You may create the viewDef for the auto part that extends the Notes application by using a `clView` as the base view. Create an NTK view template, named `iouDefaultViewDef`, in which a `clView` fills the entire drawing area. Then save the view template file (using the Save As menu item) as `iouDefaultViewDef`.

You can now set the slots as follows:

- Set the `name` slot to `"IOU Info"`. This string appears in the Show button, if there is one.

- Set the `symbol` slot to `'default`. At least one of the viewDefs associated with a dataDef must have `'default` as the value of its `symbol` slot.

- Set the `type` slot to `'viewer`. The three system-defined types for viewDefs are `'editor`, `'viewer`, and `'routeFormat`. You may define others as you wish.

- Set the `viewDefHeight` slot to 176 (of the four slot views that will be added to this viewDef, each is 34 pixels high plus an 8-pixel separation between them and an 8-pixel border at the bottom).

- Set the `viewBounds` slot to 0, 0, 0, 0.

- Set the `viewJustify` slot to horizontal parent full relative and vertical parent full relative.

Add the protos that will display the data and labels to the working application. The protos used here include:

- `newtSmartNameView`
- `newtLabelNumInputLine`
- `newtLabelDateInputLine`
- `newtLabelTimeInputLine`

You can read more about these protos in Chapter 4, "NewtApp Applications." They should be aligned as shown in Figure 5-4.

Figure 5-4   The default viewDef view template

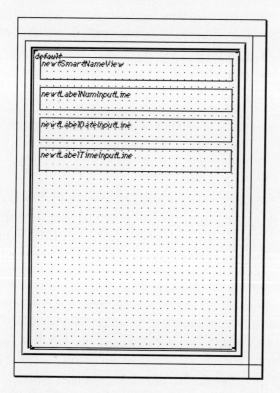

Set the slots of the `newtSmartNameView` as follows:

- Set the `label` slot to `"Who"`.
- Set the `path` slot to `[pathExpr: kDataSymbol, 'who]`. The path slot must evaluate to a slot in your data entry frame that contains a name (or a place to store one).
- Set the `usePopup` slot to `true`.

Set the slots of the newtLabelNumInputLine as follows:

- Set the label slot to "How Much".

- Set the path slot to [pathExpr: kDataSymbol, 'howMuch]. This path slot must evaluate to a slot in your data entry frame that contains a number (or a place to store one).

Add a newtLabelDateInputLine at the top of the default template so that it is aligned as shown. Then set the slots as follows:

- Set the label slot to "Date Due".

- Set the path slot to [pathExpr: kDataSymbol, 'dueDate]. This path slot must evaluate to a slot in your data entry frame that contains a date (or a place to store one).

Add a newtLabelTimeInputLine at the top of the default template so that it is aligned as shown. Then set the slots as follows:

- Set the label slot to "Due Time".

- Set the path slot to [pathExpr: kDataSymbol, 'dueDate]. This path must evaluate to a slot in your data entry frame that contains a time (or a place to store one).

Registering Stationery for an Auto Part

When your stationery is implemented in an auto part, you are responsible for registering and removing it. The following code samples show InstallScript and RemoveScript functions that use the appropriate global functions to register and unregister the viewDef and dataDef files in your auto part as it is installed and removed, respectively. Note that the print format file is also registered as a viewDef with the system.

```
InstallScript: func(partFrame,removeFrame)
   begin
   RegDataDef(kDataSymbol, GetLayout("iouDataDef"));
   RegisterViewDef(GetLayout("iouDefaultViewDef"),
                                     kDataSymbol);
   RegisterViewDef(GetLayout("iouPrintFormat"),
                                     kDataSymbol);
   end;

RemoveScript: func(removeFrame)
   begin
   UnRegisterViewDef('default, kDataSymbol);
   UnRegisterViewDef('iouPrintFormat, kDataSymbol);
   UnRegDataDef(kDataSymbol);
   end;
```

Using the MinimalBounds ViewDef Method

The MinimalBounds method must be used in a viewDef when the size of the entry is dynamic, as it is in a paper-roll-style or page-style application. It's not necessary for a card-style application, which has a fixed height; in that case you should set a static height for your viewDef in the viewDefHeight slot.

The MinimalBounds method is used to compute the minimal size for the enclosing bounding box for the viewDef at run time. The following is an example of a MinimalBounds implementation where the viewDef contains a newtEditView whose path slot is set to [pathExpr:kDataSymbol, 'notes]:

```
MinimalBounds: func(entry)
   begin
   local result := {left: 0, top: 0, right: 0,
                     bottom: viewDefHeight};

   // For an editView, make the bounds big enough to
   // contain all the child views.
   if entry.(kDataSymbol).notes then
      foreach item in entry.(kDataSymbol).notes do
         result := UnionRect( result, item.viewBounds );
   result;
   end;
```

Stationery Summary

Data Structures

ViewDef Frame

```
myViewDef := {
_proto: anyGenericView,
type: 'editor, // could also be 'viewer or a custom type
symbol: 'default, // required; identifies the view
name: string, // required; name of viewDef
version: integer, // required; should match dataDef
viewDefHeight: integer, // required, except in card-style
MinimalBounds:      // returns the minimal enclosing
    func(entry)..., // bounding box for data
SetupForm:          // called by ViewSetupFormScript;
    func(entry, entryView)..., //   use to massage data
}
```

Protos

newtStationery

```
myDataDef := { // use to build a dataDef
_proto: newtStationery,
description: string,   , // describes dataDef entries
height: integer, // required, except in card-style; should
                // match viewDefHeight
icon: resource,  // optional; used in header & New menu
name: string, // required; appears in New button picker
symbol: kAppSymbol, // required unique symbol
superSymbol: aSymbol, // identifies "owning" application
version: integer, // required; should match viewDef's version
FillNewEntry:      // returns a modified entry
    func(newEntry)...,
MakeNewEntry:      // used if FillNewEntry does not exist
    func()...,
StringExtract:     // creates string description
    func(entry, nLines)...,
TextScript:        // extracts data as text for routing
    func(fields, target)...,
}
```

newtStationeryPopupButton

```
aStatPopup := { // used to construct New and Show buttons
_proto: newtStationeryPopupButton,
form: symbol,      // 'viewDef or 'dataDef
symbols: nil,    // gathers all or specify:[uniqueSym,...]
text: string,       // text displayed in picker
types: [typeSym,...],// type slots of viewDefs
sorter: '|str<|,// sorted alphabetically by Sort function
shortCircuit: Boolean, // controls picker behavior
StatScript:       // called when picker item chosen
    func(stationeryItem)..., // define actions in this method
SetUpStatArray:// override to intercept picker items to
    func()...,   // be displayed
}
```

newtNewStationeryButton

```
aNewButton := { // the New button collects dataDefs
_proto: newtNewStationeryButton,
sorter: '|str<|,// sorted alphabetically by Sort function
shortCircuit: Boolean,// controls picker behavior
StatScript:        // called when picker item chosen
    func(stationeryItem)..., // define actions in this method
SetUpStatArray:// override to intercept picker items to
    func()...,   // be displayed
}
```

newtShowStationeryButton

```
aShowButton := { // the Show button collects viewDefs
_proto: newtShowStationeryButton,
types: [typeSym,...],// can specify type slots of viewDefs
sorter: '|str<|,// sorted alphabetically by Sort function
shortCircuit: Boolean,// controls picker behavior
StatScript:        // called when picker item chosen
    func(stationeryItem)..., // define actions in this method
SetUpStatArray:// override to intercept picker items to
    func()...,   // be displayed
}
```

Stationery

newtRollShowStationeryButton

```
aRollShowButton := { // the Show button in paper roll apps
_proto: newtRollShowStationeryButton,
types: [typeSym,...],// can specify type slots of viewDefs
sorter: '|str<|,// sorted alphabetically by Sort function
shortCircuit: Boolean,// controls picker behavior
StatScript:        // called when picker item chosen
    func(stationeryItem)..., // define actions in this method
SetUpStatArray:// override to intercept picker items to
    func()...,   // be displayed
}
```

newtRollShowStationeryButton

```
anEntryShowButton := { // Show button in paperroll apps
_proto: newtEntryShowStationeryButton,
types: [typeSym,...],// can specify type slots of viewDefs
sorter: '|str<|,// sorted alphabetically by Sort function
shortCircuit: Boolean,// controls picker behavior
StatScript:        // called when picker item chosen
    func(stationeryItem)..., // define actions in this method
SetUpStatArray:// override to change entry displayed
    func()..., // can display different view for each
}
```

Functions

```
RegDataDef(dataDefSym, newDefTemplate) // register dataDef
UnRegDataDef(dataDefSym) // unregister dataDef
RegisterViewDef(viewDef, dataDefSym)// register viewDef
UnRegisterViewDef(viewDefSym, dataDefSym) //unregister viewDef
GetDefs(form, symbols, types)// returns view or data defs array
GetDataDefs(dataDefSym)// returns dataDef
GetAppDataDefs(superSymbol)// returns an app's dataDefs
GetEntryDataDef(soupEntry) // returns the entry's dataDef
GetEntryDataView(soupEntry, viewDefSym)// returns the entry's
                              // viewDef
GetViewDefs (dataDefSym)  // returns viewDefs registered
                          // with the dataDef
GetDataView (dataDefSym, viewDefSym) // returns a specific
                  // viewDef of the dataDef
```

Pickers, Pop-up Views, and Overviews

This chapter describes how to use pickers and pop-up views to present information and choices to the user. You should read this chapter if you are

- creating your own pickers and pop-up views
- taking advantage of built-in picker and pop-up protos
- presenting outlines and overviews of data

Before reading this chapter, you should be familiar with the information in Chapter 3, "Views."

This chapter contains:

- an overview of pickers and pop-up views
- descriptions of the pickers and pop-up views used to perform specific tasks
- a summary of picker and pop-up view reference information

About Pickers and Pop-up Views

A **picker** or **pop-up view** is a view that pops up and presents a list of items from which the user can make selections. The view pops up in response to a user action such as a pen tap.

The distinction between a picker and a pop-up view is not important and has not been maintained in naming the protos, so the terms are used somewhat interchangeably. In the discussion that follows, picker is used for both terms.

The simplest picker protos handle the triggering and closing of the picker; for these protos, all you need to do is provide the items in the list. When the user taps a button, a label, or a hot spot in a picture, the picker view opens automatically. When the user makes a selection, the view closes automatically and sends a message with the index of the chosen item. If the user taps outside the picker, the view closes, with no selection having been made.

More sophisticated picker protos allow multiple selections and use a close box to dispatch the view.

With some picker protos, you must determine when and how the picker is displayed. You open a picker view by sending the Open message to the view, or by calling the PopupMenu function.

Your picker views can display

- simple text
- bitmaps
- icons with strings
- separator lines
- two-dimensional grids

The most sophisticated picker protos let you access built-in system soups as well as your own soups. Much of the behavior of these protos is provided by data definitions that iterate through soup entries, display a list, allow the user to see and modify the data, and add new entries to the soup.

Pickers and Pop-up View Compatibility

The 2.0 release of Newton system software contains a number of new picker protos and a replacement for the DoPopup global function.

New Pickers and Pop-up Views

Two new picker protos, protoPopupButton and protoPopInPlace, define text buttons that display pickers.

A new set of map pickers allows you to display various maps from which a user can select a location and receive information about it. The map pickers include the following:

- protoCountryPicker
- protoProvincePicker
- protoStatePicker
- protoWorldPicker

A set of new text pickers lets you display pop-up views that show text that the user can change by tapping the string and entering a new string. The protoDateTextPicker, for example, lets the user change a date. The text-picker protos include the following:

- protoTextPicker
- protoDateTextPicker

- `protoDateDurationTextPicker`

- `protoRepeatDateDurationTextPicker`

- `protoDateNTimeTextPicker`

- `protoTimeTextPicker`

- `protoDurationTextPicker`

- `protoTimeDeltaTimePicker`

- `protoMapTextPicker`

- `protoCountryTextPicker`

- `protoUSstatesTextPicker`

- `protoCitiesTextPicker`

- `protoLongLatTextPicker`

New date, time, and location pop-up views let the user specify new information in a graphical view—changing the date on a calendar, for example. These protos include the following:

- `protoDatePopup`

- `protoDatePicker`

- `protoDateNTimePopup`

- `protoDateIntervalPopup`

- `protoMultiDatePopup`

- `protoYearPopup`

- `protoTimePopup`

- `protoAnalogTimePopup`

- `protoTimeDeltaPopup`

- `protoTimeIntervalPopup`

A new number picker displays pickers from which a user can select a number. The new number picker is

- `protoNumberPicker`

A set of new overview protos allows you to create overviews of data; some of the protos are designed to display data from the Names soup. The data picker protos include the following:

- `protoOverview`

- `protoSoupOverview`

- `protoListPicker`

- `protoPeoplePicker`

- `protoPeoplePopup`

The following two protos are data types that support the `protoListPicker`:

- `protoNameRefDataDef`
- `protoPeopleDataDef`

Obsolete Function

The `DoPopup` global function used in system software version 1.x is obsolete; it is supported in version 2.0, but support is not guaranteed in future releases. Use the new `PopupMenu` function instead.

Picker Categories

The remainder of this chapter divides the pickers into a number of categories. The protos within each category operate in a related manner. General-purpose protos are used to create simple, general-purpose pickers and pop-up views. The remaining protos in the list are triggered by specific user actions or by events that you define:

- general-purpose pickers
- map pickers
- text pickers
- date, time, and location pickers
- number pickers
- picture picker
- overview protos
- roll protos

There is also a section discussing the view classes used with pickers.

General-Purpose Pickers

You use the protos described in this section to create simple, general-purpose pickers and pop-up views. Some of the following protos are triggered by specific user actions, while others are triggered by events that you define:

- The `protoPopupButton` picker is a text button that displays a picker when tapped. The button is highlighted while the picker is open. For information about the slots and methods for this picker, see "protoPopupButton" (page 5-4) in *Newton Programmer's Reference*. Figure 6-1 shows an example of a `protoPopupButton`.

Figure 6-1   A `protoPopupButton` example

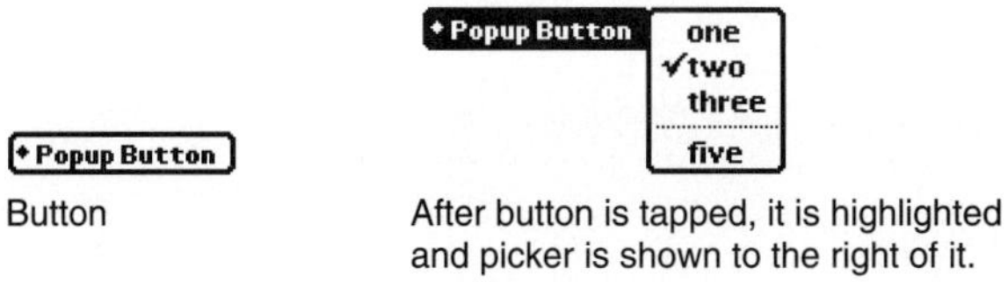

Button   After button is tapped, it is highlighted
                                and picker is shown to the right of it.

■ The `protoPopInPlace` picker is a text button that displays a picker when tapped. When the user chooses an item from the picker, the text of the chosen item appears in the button. For information about the slots and methods for this picker, see "protoPopInPlace" (page 5-6) in *Newton Programmer's Reference*. Figure 6-2 shows an example of a `protoPopInPlace`.

Figure 6-2   A `protoPopInPlace` example

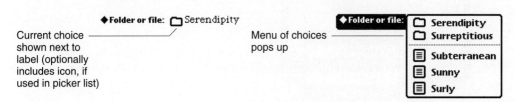

Button   After button is tapped,   After item is chosen from
                    picker is shown on top of it.   picker, it is shown in button

■ The `protoLabelPicker` is a label that displays a picker when tapped. The currently selected item in the list is displayed next to the label. For information about the slots and methods for this picker, see "protoLabelPicker" (page 5-8) in *Newton Programmer's Reference*. Figure 6-3 shows an example of a `protoLabelPicker`.

Figure 6-3   A `protoLabelPicker` example

Current choice
shown next to
label (optionally
includes icon, if
used in picker list)

Menu of choices
pops up

■ The `protoPicker` is a picker that displays anything from a simple text list to a two-dimensional grid containing shapes and text. For information about the slots and methods for this picker, see "protoPicker" (page 5-13) in *Newton*

Programmer's Reference. Figure 6-4 shows the types of objects you can display in a `protoPicker`.

Figure 6-4   A `protoPicker` example

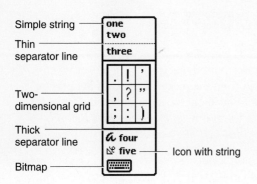

- The `protoGeneralPopup` is a pop-up view that has a close box. The view cancels if the user taps outside it. This can use this proto to construct more complex pickers. It is used, for example, as the basis for the duration pickers. For information about the slots and methods for this proto, see "protoGeneralPopup" (page 5-19) in *Newton Programmer's Reference*. Figure 6-5 shows an example of a `protoGeneralPopup`.

Figure 6-5   A `protoGeneralPopup` example

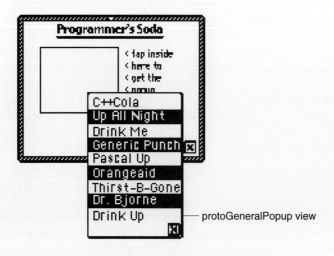

■ The `protoTextList` picker is a scrollable list of items. The user can scroll the list by dragging or scrolling with the optional scroll arrows and can choose one or more items in the list by tapping them. The scrollable list can include shapes or text. For information about the slots and methods for this picker, see "protoTextList" (page 5-20) in *Newton Programmer's Reference*. Figure 6-6 shows an example of a `protoTextList`.

Figure 6-6   A `protoTextList` example

■ The `protoTable` picker is a simple one-column table of text. The user can tap any item in the list to select it. For information about the slots and methods for this picker, see "protoTable" (page 5-24) in *Newton Programmer's Reference*. Figure 6-7 shows an example of a `protoTableList` picker.

Figure 6-7   A `protoTable` example

You define the format of the table using a `protoTableDef` object; see "protoTableDef" (page 5-27) in *Newton Programmer's Reference* for information. You define the format of each row using a `protoTableEntry` object; see "protoTableEntry" (page 5-29) in *Newton Programmer's Reference* for information.

Using protoGeneralPopup

As with most protos, you create a `protoGeneralPopup` object by using the NTK palette to draw one in your layout. After creating the object, you should remove the `context` and `cancelled` slots. The `viewBounds` should be (0, 0, width, height) for the box. The `New` method tries to set the bounds correctly, based on the recommended bounds passed to the call.

The protoGeneralPopup sends a pickCancelledScript to the callbackContext specified in the New method. However, it does not send a pickActionScript back; instead, it sends an Affirmative message to itself. You supply the method and decide what call to make to the context and what information to send back.

To put other objects in the protoGeneralPopup, just drag them out in NTK. For example, if you want a checkbox in your pop-up view, drag out a protoCheckbox. You can put anything in the pop-up view, including your own protos.

Since you have to assemble the information to send on an affirmative, you will likely end up declaring your content to the general pop-up.

The only slots you really need to set are Affirmative and viewBounds.

Affirmative is a function. Here's an example:

```
func()
begin
// Notify the context that the user has accepted the
// changes made in the popup
if context then
      context:?pickActionScript(changeData) ;
end
```

Map Pickers

You can use the pickers described in this section to display maps and allow the user to select countries, U.S. states, Canadian provinces, and cities. The Newton system software provides the following map picker protos:

- The protoCountryPicker displays a map of the world. When the user taps a country, the PickWorld message is sent to your view. For information about the slots and methods for this picker, see "protoCountryPicker" (page 5-30) in *Newton Programmer's Reference*. Figure 6-8 shows an example of a protoCountryPicker.

Figure 6-8   A `protoCountryPicker` example

■ The `protoProvincePicker` displays a map of North America. When the user taps a province, the `PickWorld` message is sent to your view. For information about the slots and methods for this picker, see "protoProvincePicker" (page 5-31) in *Newton Programmer's Reference*. Figure 6-9 shows an example of a `protoProvincePicker`.

Figure 6-9   A `protoProvincePicker` example

■ The `protoStatePicker` displays a map of North America. When the user taps a state, the `PickWorld` message is sent to your view. For information about the slots and methods for this picker, see "protoStatePicker" (page 5-32) in *Newton Programmer's Reference*. Figure 6-10 shows an example of a `protoStatePicker`.

Figure 6-10   A `protoStatePicker` example

■ The `protoWorldPicker` displays a map of the world. When the user taps a continent, the `PickWorld` message is sent to your view. For information about the slots and methods for this picker, see "protoWorldPicker" (page 5-34) in *Newton Programmer's Reference*. Figure 6-11 shows an example of a `protoWorldPicker`.

Figure 6-11   A `protoWorldPicker` example

Text Pickers

Text picker protos allow the user to specify various kinds of information by picking text representations. Each of these protos displays a label picker with a string that shows the currently selected data value. For example, `protoDurationTextPicker`, which lets the user set a duration, might have a label of "When" followed by a duration in the form "8:26 A.M. – 10:36 P.M."

When the user taps a text picker, the picker displays a pop-up view in which the user can enter new information. The Newton system software provides the following text picker protos:

- The `protoTextPicker` is a label picker with a text representation of an entry. When the user taps the picker, a customized picker is displayed. For information about the slots and methods for this picker, see "protoTextPicker" (page 5-35) in *Newton Programmer's Reference*. Figure 6-12 shows an example of a `protoTextPicker`.

Figure 6-12   A `protoTextPicker` example

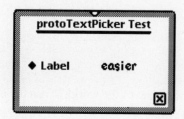

■ The `protoDateTextPicker` is a label picker with a text representation of a date. When the user taps the picker, a `protoDatePopup` is displayed, which allows the user to specify a different date. For information about the slots and methods for this picker, see "protoDateTextPicker" (page 5-37) in *Newton Programmer's Reference*. Figure 6-13 shows an example of a `protoDateTextPicker`.

Figure 6-13 A `protoDateTextPicker` example

■ The `protoDateDurationTextPicker` is a label picker with a text representation of a range of dates. When the user taps the picker, a `protoDateIntervalPopup` is displayed, which allows the user to specify a different range. For information about the slots and methods for this picker, see "protoDateDurationTextPicker" (page 5-40) in *Newton Programmer's Reference*. Figure 6-14 shows an example of a `protoDateDurationTextPicker`.

Figure 6-14   A `protoDateDurationTextPicker` example

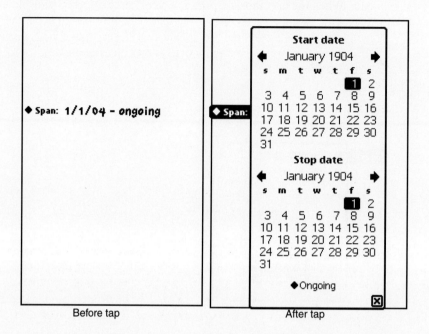

Before tap   After tap

- The `protoRepeatDateDurationTextPicker` is a label picker
  with a text representation of a range of dates. When the user taps the
  picker, a `protoDateIntervalPopup` is displayed, which allows the
  user to specify a different range. This proto differs from the
  `protoDateDurationTextPicker` in that the
  `protoRepeatDateDurationDatePicker` presents choices that are
  appropriate for the `repeatType` slot, and the duration displayed when the user
  taps a duration or stop date is given in units of the `repeatType`. Otherwise, it
  looks like the protoDateDurationTextPicker and popup shown in Appendix
  Figure 6-14. For information about the slots and methods for this picker,
  see "protoRepeatDateDurationTextPicker" (page 5-43) in *Newton Programmer's
  Reference*.

- The `protoDateNTimeTextPicker` is a label picker with a text
  representation of a date and time. When the user taps the picker, a
  `protoDateNTimePopup` is displayed, which allows the user to specify a
  different date and time. For information about the slots and methods for this
  picker, see "protoDateNTimeTextPicker" (page 5-46) in *Newton Programmer's
  Reference*. Figure 6-15 shows an example of a
  `protoDateNTimeTextPicker`.

Pickers, Pop-up Views, and Overviews

Figure 6-15   A `protoDateNTimeTextPicker` example

Before tap ——— **Label**   **9/27/95 2:15 pm**

After tap ———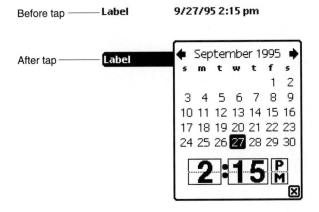

- The `protoTimeTextPicker` is a label picker with a text representation of a time. When the user taps the picker, a `protoTimePopup` is displayed, which allows the user to specify a different time. For information about the slots and methods for this picker, see "A `protoTimeTextPicker` example" (page 6-13) in *Newton Programmer's Reference*. Figure 6-16 shows an example of a `protoTimeTextPicker`.

Figure 6-16   A `protoTimeTextPicker` example

Before tap ——— **◆ Time   1:40 pm**

After tap ———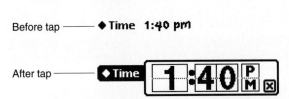

- The `protoDurationTextPicker` is a label picker with a text representation of a time range. When the user taps the picker, a `protoTimeIntervalPopup` is displayed, which allows the user to specify a different time range. For information about the slots and methods for this picker, see "protoDurationTextPicker" (page 5-51) in *Newton Programmer's Reference*. Figure 6-17 shows an example of a `protoDurationTextPicker`.

Figure 6-17   A `protoDurationTextPicker` example

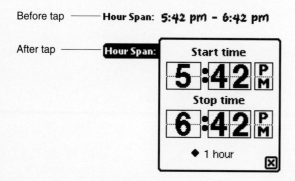

The `protoTimeDeltaTextPicker` is a label picker with a text representation of a time delta. When the user taps the picker, a `protoTimeDeltaPopup` is displayed, which allows the user to specify a different time delta. For information about the slots and methods for this picker, see "protoTimeDeltaTextPicker" (page 5-53) in *Newton Programmer's Reference*. Figure 6-18 shows an example of a `protoTimeDeltaTextPicker`.

Figure 6-18   A `protoTimeDeltaTextPicker` example

The `protoMapTextPicker` is a label picker with a text representation of a country. When the user taps the picker, a popup displays that allows the user to select a new country from an alphabetical list. For information about the slots and methods for this picker, see "protoMapTextPicker" (page 5-54) in *Newton Programmer's Reference*. Figure 6-19 shows an example of a `protoMapTextPicker`.

Figure 6-19   A `protoMapTextPicker` example

Before tap ——— Country: **Afghanistan**

After tap ———

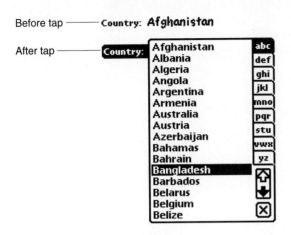

- The `protoCountryTextPicker` is the same as `protoMapTextPicker`.

- The `protoUSstatesTextPicker` is a label picker with a text representation of a U.S. state. When the user taps the picker, a popup displays that allows the user to select a new state from an alphabetical list. For information about the slots and methods for this picker, see "protoUSstatesTextPicker" (page 5-56) in *Newton Programmer's Reference*. Figure 6-20 shows an example of a `protoUSstatesTextPicker`.

Figure 6-20   A `protoUSstatesTextPicker` example

Before tap ——— ◆ **State:**   Arizona

After tap ———

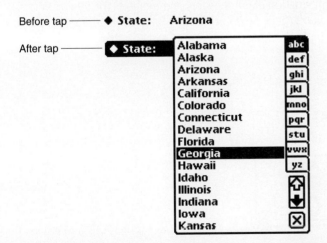

■ The `protoCitiesTextPicker` is a label picker with a text representation of a city. When the user taps the picker, a popup displays that allows the user to select a new city from an alphabetical list. For information about the slots and methods for this picker, see "protoCitiesTextPicker" (page 5-58) in *Newton Programmer's Reference*. Figure 6-21 shows an example of a `protoCitiesTextPicker`.

Figure 6-21   A `protoCitiesTextPicker` example

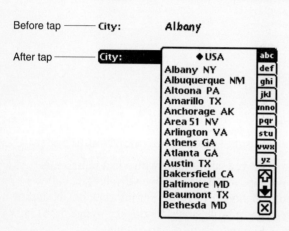

■ The `protoLongLatTextPicker` is a label picker with a text representation of longitude and latitude values. When the user taps the picker, a `longLatPicker` is displayed, which allows the user to select new longitude and latitude values. For information about the slots and methods for this picker, see "protoLongLatTextPicker" (page 5-61) in *Newton Programmer's Reference*. Figure 6-22 shows an example of a `protoLongLatTextPicker`.

Figure 6-22   A `protoLongLatTextPicker` example

Date, Time, and Location Pop-up Views

You can use the protos described in this section to present pop-up views to the user for setting or choosing specific types of values. The Newton System Software provides the following pop-up protos for date, time, and location values:

- The `protoDatePopup` allows the user to choose a single date. For information about the slots and methods for this proto, see "protoDatePopup" (page 5-63) in *Newton Programmer's Reference*. Figure 6-23 shows an example of a `protoDatePopup`.

Figure 6-23 A `protoDatePopup` example

June 1993
s m t w t f s
1 2 3 4 5
6 7 8 9 10 11 12
13 14 15 16 17 18 19
20 21 22 23 24 25 26
27 28 29 30
1993

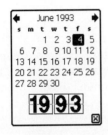

- The `protoDatePicker` allows the user to choose a single date when the date is likely to be relatively close to the current date. Changing the year is not easily done with this proto. For information about the slots and methods for this proto, see "protoDatePicker" (page 5-64) in *Newton Programmer's Reference*. Figure 6-24 shows an example of a `protoDatePicker`.

Figure 6-24 A `protoDatePicker` example

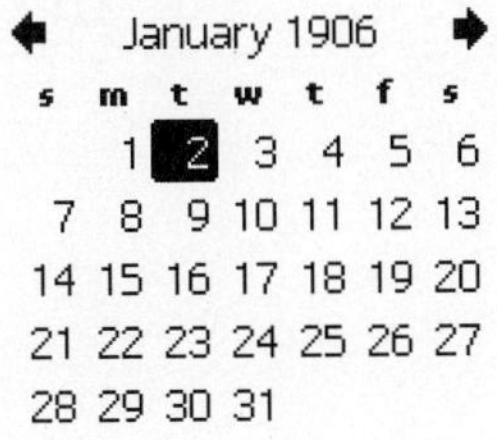

January 1906
s m t w t f s
1 2 3 4 5 6
7 8 9 10 11 12 13
14 15 16 17 18 19 20
21 22 23 24 25 26 27
28 29 30 31

■ The protoDateNTimePopup allows the user to choose a single date and time. For information about the slots and methods for this proto, see "protoDateNTimePopup" (page 5-67) in *Newton Programmer's Reference*. Figure 6-25 shows an example of a protoDateNTimePopup.

Figure 6-25 A protoDateNTimePopup example

■ The protoDateIntervalPopup allows the user to choose an interval of dates by specifying the start and stop dates. For information about the slots and methods for this proto, see "protoDateIntervalPopup" (page 5-69) in *Newton Programmer's Reference*. Figure 6-26 shows an example of a protoDateIntervalPopup.

Figure 6-26 A protoDateIntervalPopup example

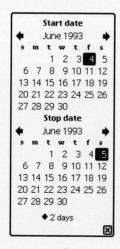

■ The `protoMultiDatePopup` allows the user to specify a range of dates. For information about the slots and methods for this proto, see "protoMultiDatePopup" (page 5-72) in *Newton Programmer's Reference*. Figure 6-27 shows an example of a `protoMultiDatePopup`.

Figure 6-27   A `protoMultiDatePopup` example

■ The `protoYearPopup` allows the user to choose a year. For information about the slots and methods for this proto, see "protoYearPopup" (page 5-73) in *Newton Programmer's Reference*. Figure 6-28 shows an example of a `protoYearPopup`.

Figure 6-28   A `protoYearPopup` example

■ The `protoTimePopup` allows the user to choose a time with a digital clock. For information about the slots and methods for this proto, see "protoTimePopup" (page 5-74) in *Newton Programmer's Reference*. Figure 6-29 shows an example of a `protoTimePopup`.

Figure 6-29   A `protoTimePopup` example

■ The `protoAnalogTimePopup` allows the user to choose a time with an analog clock. For information about the slots and methods for this proto, see "protoAnalogTimePopup" (page 5-76) in *Newton Programmer's Reference*. Figure 6-30 shows an example of a `protoAnalogTimePopup`.

Figure 6-30   A `protoAnalogTimePopup` **example**

■ The `protoTimeDeltaPopup` allows the user to choose a time period (a delta). For information about the slots and methods for this proto, see "protoTimeDeltaPopup" (page 5-78) in *Newton Programmer's Reference*. Figure 6-31 shows an example of a `protoTimeDeltaPopup`.

Figure 6-31   A `protoTimeDeltaPopup` **example**

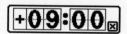

■ The `protoTimeIntervalPopup` allows the user to choose a time interval by specifying the start and stop times. For information about the slots and methods for this proto, see "protoTimeIntervalPopup" (page 5-79) in *Newton Programmer's Reference*. Figure 6-32 shows an example of a `protoTimeIntervalPopup`.

Figure 6-32   A `protoTimeIntervalPopup` **example**

Number Pickers

This section describes the protos available to allow users to pick numbers. The Newton system software provides the following protos for picking numbers:

■ The protoNumberPicker displays a picker from which the user can select a number. For information about the slots and methods for this picker, see "protoNumberPicker" (page 5-81) in *Newton Programmer's Reference*. Figure 6-33 shows an example of a protoNumberPicker.

Figure 6-33   A protoNumberPicker example

Picture Picker

This section describes the proto you can use to create a picture as a picker.

■ The protoPictIndexer picker displays a horizontal array of pictures, from which the user can choose. For information about the slots and methods for this picker, see "protoPictIndexer" (page 5-82) in *Newton Programmer's Reference*. Figure 6-34 shows an example of a protoPictIndexer.

Figure 6-34   A protoPictIndexer example

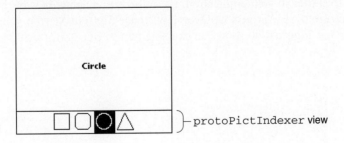

Overview Protos

You can use the protos described in this section to create overviews of data. An over-view allows the user to see all of data in a soup or an array scrolling list. The user can select individual items and open them to see the detail. Overview protos include:

- The `protoOverview` provides a framework for displaying an overview of the data in your application. Each overview item occupies one line, and the user can scroll the list and pick individual or multiple items. "Using protoOverview" (page 6-24) has information on using this proto. For further information about the slots and methods of `protoOverview`, see "protoOverview" (page 5-85) in *Newton Programmer's Reference*. Figure 6-35 shows an example of a `protoOverview`.

Figure 6-35   A `protoOverview` example

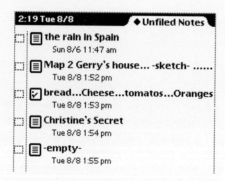

- The `protoSoupOverview` provides a framework for displaying an overview of soup entries in your application. For information about the slots and methods for this proto, see "protoSoupOverview" (page 5-90) in *Newton Programmer's Reference*. Figure 6-36 shows an example of a `protoSoupOverview`.

Figure 6-36   A `protoSoupOverview` example

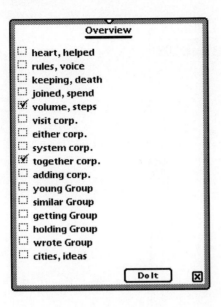

- The `protoListPicker` provides a scrollable list of items. Items can be from a soup, an array, or both. The user can select any number of items in the list. For information about the slots and methods for this proto, see "protoListPicker" (page 5-93) in *Newton Programmer's Reference*. "Using protoListPicker" (page 6-26) has a more extensive example and discusses how to use this proto. Figure 6-37 shows an example of a `protoListPicker`.

Figure 6-37   A `protoListPicker` example

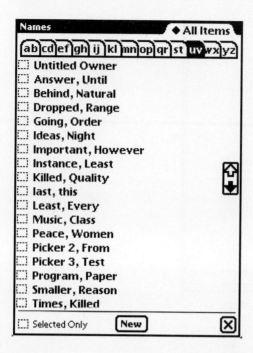

- The `protoPeoplePicker` displays a list of names and associated information from the Names application. For information about the slots and methods for this proto, see "protoPeoplePicker" (page 5-110) in *Newton Programmer's Reference*.

- The `protoPeoplePopup` is similar to the `protoPeoplePicker`, except that `protoPeoplePopup` displays the picker in a pop-up view. For information about the slots and methods for this proto, see "protoPeoplePopup" (page 5-111) in *Newton Programmer's Reference*.

Using protoOverview

The `protoOverview` was set up primarily to be the basis for `protoSoupOverview`. Because of that, you need to do some extra work to use just the `protoOverview`.

You need to define `Abstract`, `HitItem`, `IsSelected`, `SelectItem`, and `viewSetupChildrenScript` methods in your `protoOverview`. See "protoOverview" (page 5-85) in *Newton Programmer's Reference* for details.

You also need to define the following slot in your `protoOverview`:

cursor   This should be a cursor-like object.

You use the object stored in this slot to encapsulate your data. The cursor-like object must support the methods `Entry`, `Next`, `Move`, and `Clone`. An example is given below.

In addition, you must provide a mechanism to find an actual data item given an index of a displayed item. In general, you need some sort of saved index that corresponds to the first displayed item. See the example code in "HitItem" (page 5-88) in *Newton Programmer's Reference* for an example of how this is used.

You also should provide a mechanism to track the currently highlighted item, which is distinct from a selected item.

Since your data is probably in an array, you can use a "cursor" object like this:

```
{   items: nil,
    index: 0,

    Entry:func()
            begin
            if index < Length(items) then
                items[index];
            end,

    Next:  func()
            if index < Length(items)-1 then
            begin
                index := index + 1;
                items[index];
            end,

    Move:  func(delta)
            begin
                index := Min(Max(index + delta, 0),
                        kNumItems-1) ;
                items[index];
            end,

    Clone:func()
            Clone(self)}
```

The methods that you need to have in the cursor-like object are:

■ `Entry`, which returns the item pointed to by the "cursor."

■ `Next`, which moves the "cursor" to the next item and returns that item or, if there is no next item, `nil`.

- Move, which moves the "cursor" a given number of entries and returns that entry or, if there is no item in that place, nil.

- Clone, which returns a copy of the "cursor" that is modifiable independent of the original "cursor."

Using protoListPicker

The protoListPicker proto—documented in *Newton Programmer's Reference* (page 5-93)—provides a number of controls for finding specific entries, including folder tabs, alphabet tabs (azTabs), and scrolling arrows; any of these controls can be suppressed.

Like protoOverview, this proto manages an array of selected items. Any soup that can be queried by a cursor can be displayed, or elements from an array can be displayed.

Figure 6-38 shows a full-featured example of protoListPicker that displays a two-column list. The first column is used to select or deselect members, and the second column provides additional information that can be edited in place.

Figure 6-38   A ProtoListPicker example

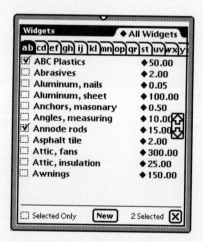

The checkbox at the bottom-left of the slip is used to either show every eligible item or to trim all unselected elements from the list. The New button at the bottom allows the immediate creation of another entry to be displayed. See Figure 6-39.

Figure 6-39 Creating a new name entry

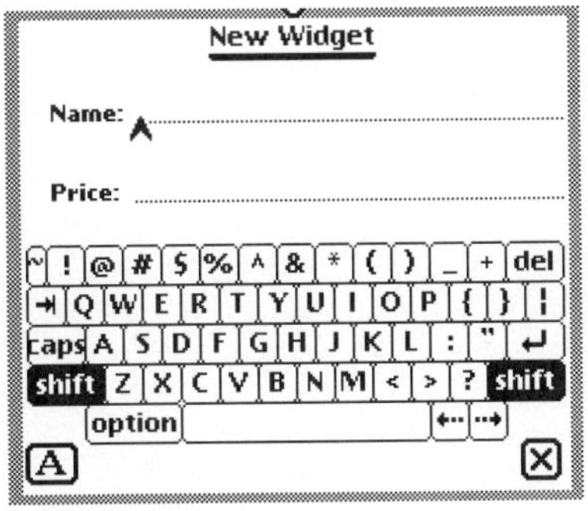

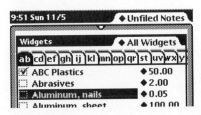

When the pen comes down in any column, the row/column cell inverts as shown in Figure 6-40.

Figure 6-40 Highlighted row

When the pen is released, if it is within the first column, the item is either checked to show that it is selected or unchecked to show that it is not. See Figure 6-41.

Figure 6-41 Selected row

When the pen tap is released within the second column, what happens next depends on the underlying data. If there are many options already available, a pop-up view is displayed to allow the user to select any option or enter a new one. See Figure 6-42.

Figure 6-42   Pop-up view displayed over list

If the user selects "Add new price" (or if there were one or no options already available to them), the user can enter a new price as shown in Figure 6-43.

Figure 6-43   Slip displayed for gathering input

The proto is driven by a frame contained in the `pickerDef` slot. This **picker definition** frame may or may not come from the data definition registry. The functionality it provides, however, is similar to that of any data definition: it offers all the hooks the proto needs to interpret and display the data without the proto itself knowing what the data is.

The chosen items are collected into an array, as described in "Name References" (page 5-1) in *Newton Programmer's Reference*, which can be stored separately from the original entries. Each selection is represented in the array by a name reference that contains all information needed to display or operate on the entries. The name reference is stored as part of the selection, along with an entry alias that refers to the original entry, if there is an original entry. (See "Entry Aliases" beginning on page 12-1 for basic information on these objects.)

The picker definition (described in the next section) is a data definition frame that is provides the routines to create a name reference from an entry, an entry alias, another name reference, a straight frame, or just to create a canonical empty name reference (if no data is provided). It also retrieves the data from a name reference. Finally, it provides some information about the name reference to support actions like tapping and highlighting.

You also need to define the soup to query. Both this and the query specification can be defined either in the data definition or in the list picker.

Using the Data Definitions Frame in a List Picker

The `pickerDef` slot of the list picker holds a data definition frame that determines the overall behavior of the list picker. This frame should be based on `protoNameRefDataDef` or `protoPeopleDataDef`, or at should least support the required slots.

Here is an example:

```
pickerDef:= {
    _proto:             protoNameRefDataDef,
    name:        "Widgets",
    class:       '|nameRef.widget|,
    entryType:        'widget,
    soupToQuery:"Widgets",
    querySpec:           {indexPath: 'name},
    columns:                kColumns,
};
```

Specifying Columns

The `columns` slot hold an array that determines how the columns in the list picker are displayed. Here's an example of column specification array:

```
columns:= [{
    fieldPath:'name,// path for field to display in column
    optional:true,// not required -- unnamed widget

    tapWidth:155},// width for checkbox & name combined

{
    fieldPath:'price,// path for field to display
                    in column
    optional:nil,// price is required

    tapWidth:0}];// width -- to right end of view
```

See "Column Specifications" (page 5-3) in *Newton Programmer's Reference* for details of the slots.

Having a Single Selection in a List Picker

The key to getting single selection is that single selection is part of the picker definition and not an option of protoListPicker. That means the particular class of nameRef you use must include single selection. In general, this requires creating your own subclass of the particular name reference class.

The basic solution is to create a data definition that is a subclass of the particular class your protoListPicker variant will view. That data definition will include the singleSelect slot. As an example, suppose you want to use a protoPeoplePopup that just picks individual people. You could use the following code to bring up a protoPeoplePopup that allows selecting only one individual at a time:

```
// register the modified data definition
RegDataDef('|nameref.people.single:SIG|,
  {_proto: GetDataDefs('|nameRef.people|), singleSelect:
true});

// then pop the thing
protoPeoplePopup:New('|nameref.people.single:SIG|,[],self,[
]);

// sometime later
UnRegDataDef('|nameref.people.single:SIG|);
```

For other types of protoListPickers and classes, create the appropriate subclass. For example, a transport that uses protoAddressPicker for e-mail messages might create a subclass of '|nameRef.email| and put that subclass symbol in the class slot of the protoAddressPicker.

Since many applications are likely to do this, you may cut down on code in your installScript and removeScript by registering your dataDef only for the duration of the picker. That would mean registering the class just before you pop the picker and unregistering after the picker has closed. You can use the pickActionScript and pickCanceledScript methods to be notified when to unregister the dataDef.

Having Preselected Items in a List Picker

If you want to have items that are initially selected in a list picker, use the viewSetupDoneScript to set up the selected array, rather than setting up the selected array in your viewSetupFormScript or viewSetupChildrenScript, then send the Update message to protoListPicker to tell it to update the display.

Validation and Editing in protoListPicker

The built-in validation mechanism is not designed to deal with nested soup information. In general, you gain more flexibility by not using a validationFrame in your pickerDef, even if you have no nested entries. Instead, you can provide your own validation mechanism and editors:

- define a Validate method in your picker definition
- define an OpenEditor method in your picker definition
- draw a layout for each editor you require

Here is how your Validate method should work. The following example assumes that *pickerDef.ValidateName* and *pickerDef.ValidatePager* have been implemented:

```
pickerDef.Validate := func(nameRef, pathArray)
begin
    // keep track of any paths that fail
    local failedPaths := [];

    for each index, path in pathArray do
    begin
        if path = 'name then
        begin
            // check if name validation fails
            if NOT :ValidateName(nameRef) then
                // if so, add it to array of failures
                AddArraySlot(failedPaths, path);
        end;
        else begin
            if NOT :ValidatePager(nameRef) then
                AddArraySlot(failedPaths, path);
        end;
    end;
    // return failed paths or empty array
    failedPaths;
end;
```

Here is how your OpenEditor method should work:

```
pickerDef.OpenEditor := func(tapInfo, context, why)
begin
    local valid = :Validate(tapInfo.nameRef,
tapInfo.editPaths) ;
    if (Length(valid) > 0) then
        // if not valid, open the editor
```

Pickers, Pop-up Views, and Overviews

```
                    // NOTE: returns the edit slip that is opened
                    GetLayout("editor.t"):new(tapInfo.nameRef,
                        tapInfo.editPaths, why, self, 'EditDone, context);
                else
                begin
                    // the item is valid, so just toggle the selection
                    context:Tapped('toggle);
                    nil;                              // Return <nil>.
                end; ..
            end;
```

The example above assumes that the base view of the layout editor.t has a New method that opens the editor and returns the associated view.

The editor can be designed to fit your data. However, we suggest that you use a protoFloatNGo that is attached to the root view using BuildContext. You are also likely to need a callback to the pickderDef so it can appropriately update the edited or new item. Finally, your editor needs to update your data soup using an Xmit soup method so that the list picker updates.

In the OpenEditor example above, the last three arguments are used by the editor to send a callback to the pickerDef from the viewQuitScript. The design of the callback function is up to you. Here is an example:

```
pickerDef.EditDone := func(nameRef, context)
begin
    local valid = :Validate(tapInfo.nameRef, tapInfo.editPaths) ;
    if (Length(valid) > 0) then
    begin
        // Something failed. Try and revert back to original
        if NOT :ValidatePager(nameRef) AND
            self.('[pathExpr: savedPagerValue, nameRef]) = nameRef then
                nameRef.pager := savedPagerValue.pager;

        context:Tapped(nil);// Remove the checkmark
    end;
    else
        // The nameRef is valid, so select it.
        context:Tapped('select);

    // Clear the saved value for next time.
    savedPagerValue := nil;
end;
```

Changing the Font of protoListPicker

The mechanism described here will probably change in the future. Eventually you may be able to set a `viewFont` slot in the list picker itself, just as you can set `viewLineSpacing` now. In the meantime, you need a piece of workaround code. You must set the `viewFont` of the list picker and also include this workaround code.

Give the list picker the following `viewSetupDoneScript`:

```
func()
begin
    if listBase then
       SetValue(listBase, 'viewFont, viewFont) ;

    inherited:?viewSetupDoneScript();
end;
```

This sets the `viewFont` of the `listbase` view to the view font of the list picker. You cannot rely on the `listbase` view always being there (hence the test).

Using protoSoupOverview

For the most part, you use this proto like `protoOverview`, except that it is set up to use a soup cursor, and, so, is easier to use. See "Using protoOverview" (page 6-24) for information.

Determining Which protoSoupOverview Item Is Hit

There is a method of `protoSoupOverview` called `HitItem` that is called whenever an item is tapped. The method is defined by the overview and you should call the inherited method. Also note that `HitItem` gets called regardless of where in the line a tap occurs. If the tap occurs in the checkbox (that is, if x is less than `selectIndent`), you should do nothing other than calling the inherited functions, because the inherited function will handle the tap, otherwise you should do something appropriate.

The method is passed the index of the item that is hit. The index is relative to the item displayed at the top of the displayed list. This item is always the current entry of the cursor used by `protoSoupOverview`, so you can find the actual soup entry by cloning the cursor and moving it.

```
func(itemIndex, x, y)
begin
    // MUST call the inherited method for bookkeeping
    inherited:HitItem(itemIndex, x, y);
```

```
   if x > selectIndent then
    begin
   // get a temporary cursor based on the cursor used
   // by soup overview
      local tCursor := cursor:Clone();

   // move it to the selected item
      tCursor:Move(itemIndex) ;

   // move the application's detail cursor to the
   // selected entry
      myBaseApp.detailCursor:Goto(tCursor:Entry());

   // usually you will close the overview and switch to
   // some other view
      self:Close();
    end;
   // otherwise, just let them check/uncheck
   // which is the default behavior
end
```

Displaying the protoSoupOverview Vertical Divider

The mechanism for bringing up the vertical divider line was not correctly implemented in protoSoupOverview. You can draw one in as follows:

```
// set up a cached shape for efficiency
mySoupOverview.cachedLine := nil;

mySoupOverview.viewSetupDoneScript := func()
begin
   inherited:?viewSetupDoneScript();

   local bounds := :LocalBox();
   cachedLine := MakeRect(selectIndent - 2, 0,
       selectIndent - 1, bounds.bottom);
end;

mySoupOverview.viewDrawScript := func()
begin
   // MUST call inherited script
   inherited:?viewDrawScript();

   :DrawShape(cachedLine,
      {penPattern: vfNone, fillPattern: vfGray});
end;
```

Roll Protos

You can use the protos described in this section to present roll views in your applications. A roll view is one that contains several discrete subviews that are arranged vertically. The roll can be viewed in overview mode, in which each subview is represented by a one-line description. Any or all of the subviews can be expanded to full size. The individual subviews are contained in objects based on protoRollItem.

The Newton system software provides the following roll protos:

■ The protoRoll provides a roll-like view that includes a series of individual items. The user can see the items either as a collapsed list of one-line overviews or as full-size views. When the user taps an overview line, all the full-size views are displayed, with the tapped view shown at the top of the roll. For information about the slots and methods for this proto, see "protoRoll" (page 5-112) in *Newton Programmer's Reference*. Figure 6-44 shows an example of a protoRoll.

Figure 6-44   A protoRoll example

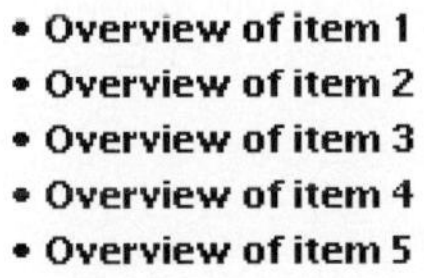

- Overview of item 1
- Overview of item 2
- Overview of item 3
- Overview of item 4
- Overview of item 5

■ The protoRollBrowser is similar to protoRoll, except that protoRollBrowser creates a self-contained application based on the protoApp, described in "protoApp" (page 1-2) in *Newton Programmer's Reference*. See "protoRollBrowser" (page 5-116) in *Newton Programmer's Reference* for information about the slots and methods for this proto. Figure 6-45 shows an example of a protoRollBrowser:

Figure 6-45   A `protoRollBrowser` example

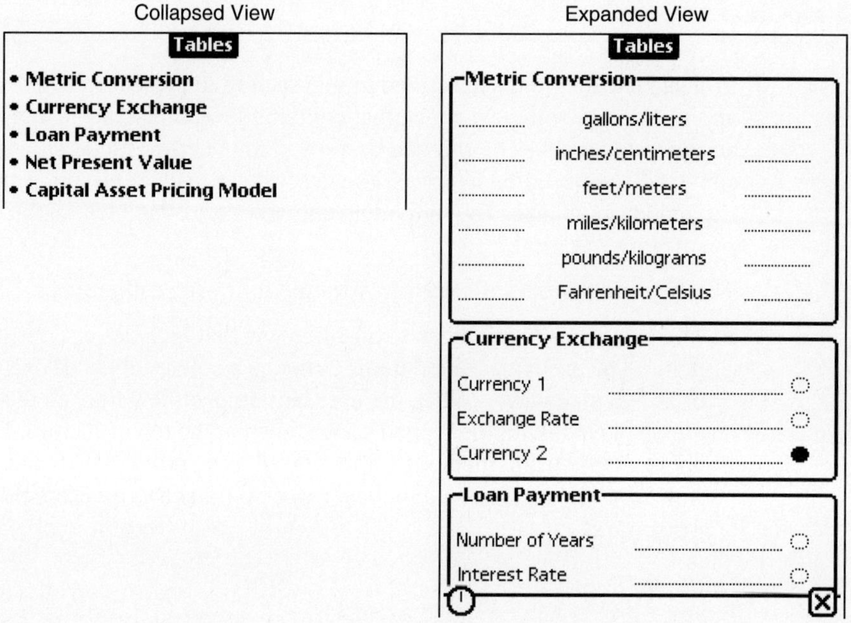

Collapsed View

Expanded View

View Classes

There are two view classes that you use for pickers:

- The `clOutline` view class displays an expandable text outline. Figure 6-46 shows an example.

Figure 6-46   Example of an expandable text outline

My First Heading
 First level 2 head
  Another level 2 head
   Wow—a third level!
Second main heading
Third main heading

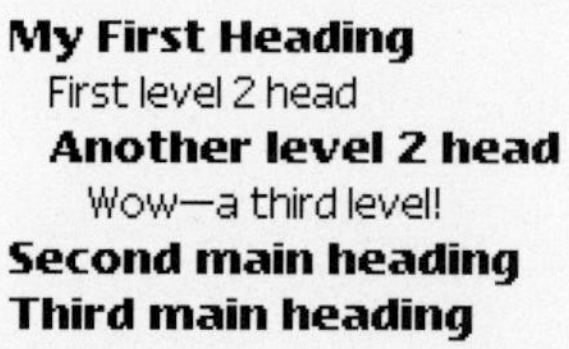

■ The `clMonthView` view class displays a monthly calendar. Figure 6-47 shows an example.

Figure 6-47   Example of a month view

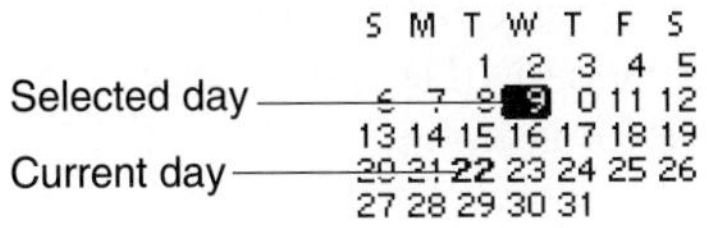

Specifying the List of Items for a Popup
==

You specify the item list for `protoPicker`, `protoTextList`, `protoPopUpButton`, `proptoPopupInPlace`, and `PopUpMenu` in an array. In the simplest case, this is an array of strings, but it can contain different kinds of items:

simple string   A string. You can control the pickability of a text item or add a mark to the display by specifying the text in a frame, as described in Table 6-1 (page 6-38).

bitmap   A bitmap frame or a NewtonScript frame, as returned from the `GetPictAsBits` compile-time function. You can control the pickability of the item or add a mark to the display by placing the bitmap in a frame, as described in Table 6-1 (page 6-38).

icon with string   A frame that specifies both a string and an icon, as described in Table 6-2 (page 6-38).

separator line   An instruction to display a line that runs the width of the picker. To display a dashed gray line, specify the symbol `'pickSeparator`. For a solid black line, specify the symbol `'pickSolidSeparator`.

two-dimensional grid
                    A frame describing the grid item, as described in Table 6-3 (page 6-39).

If all the items in the picker list cannot fit into the view, the user can scroll the list to see more items.

Table 6-1 describes the frame used to specify simple string and bitmap items in the picker list.

Pickers, Pop-up Views, and Overviews

Table 6-1   Item frame for strings and bitmaps

Slot name	Description
item	The item string or bitmap reference.
pickable	A flag that determines whether the item is pickable. Specify non-nil if you want the item to be pickable, or nil if you don't want the item pickable. Not-pickable items appear in the list but are not highlighted and can't be selected.
mark	A character displayed next to an item when it's chosen. Specify a dollar sign followed by the character you want to use to mark this item if it is chosen. For example, $\uFC0B specifies the check mark symbol. (You can use the constant kCheckMarkChar to specify the check mark character.)
fixedHeight	When you give a bitmap, you can give this slot for the first item in order to force all items to be the same size. If you use bitmaps in a list that can become large enough to scroll, you should specify the fixedHeight slot for every item. You can also use slot this for any item to specify a height different from other items.

Table 6-2 describes the frame used to specify a string with an icon in the picker list.

Table 6-2   Item frame for string with icon

Slot name	Description
item	The item string.
icon	A bitmap frame, as returned from the compile-time function GetPictAsBits. The bitmap is displayed to the left of the text, and the text is drawn flush against it, unless the indent slot is specified.

continued

Table 6-2 Item frame for string with icon (continued)

Slot name	Description
indent	An integer that defines a text indent to use for this item and subsequent icon/string items. This integer specifies the number of pixels to indent the text from the left side of the picker view. You can use it to line up a number of text items that may have icons of varying width. Specify –1 to cancel the indent effect for the current and subsequent text items. The icon is always centered within the indent width.
fixedHeight	You can give this slot for the first item in order to force all items to be the same size. If you use icons in a list that can become large enough to scroll, you should specify the fixedHeight slot for every item. You can also use this slot for any item to specify a height different from other items. (When you use PopupMenu, you must specify a fixedHeight slot for the first item, because PopupMenu ignores the height of the icon.)

Table 6-3 describes the frame required to specify a two-dimensional grid item in the picker list.

Table 6-3 Item frame for two-dimensional grid

Slot Name	Description
bits	A binary object representing the bitmap of the grid item. A bitmap is returned in the bits slot in the frame returned by the compile-time function GetPictAsBits. The bitmap is a complete picture of the grid item, including the lines between cells and the border around the outside of the cells. There must be no extra white space outside the border. Each cell must be the same size and must be symmetrical.
bounds	The bitmap bounds frame, from the bounds slot in the frame returned by GetPictAsBits.
width	The number of columns in the grid (must be non-zero).
height	The number of rows in the grid (must be non-zero).

continued

Table 6-3   Item frame for two-dimensional grid (continued)

Slot Name	Description
cellFrame	Optional. The width of the separator line between cells, used for highlighting purposes. If you don't specify this slot, the default is 1 pixel.
outerFrame	Optional. The width of the border line around the cells, used for highlighting purposes. If you don't specify this slot, the default is 2 pixels.
mask	Optional. A binary object representing the bits for a bitmap mask. This mask is used to restrict highlighting, or for special hit-testing. The mask must be exactly the same size as the bitmap. Cells in the grid are highlighted only if the position tapped is "black" in the mask.

Note

Picker items can include 1.x bitmaps but not 2.0 shapes. ◆

When a cell is highlighted in a two-dimensional picker item, only the part of the cell inside the cell frame lines is inverted. You can vary the highlighting effect by changing the values of the cellFrame and outerFrame slots, which control how much unhighlighted space to leave for the cell frame lines. An example of how these values affect cell highlighting is shown in Figure 6-48.

Figure 6-48   Cell highlighting example for protoPicker

cellFrame=1
outerFrame=2

cellFrame=3
outerFrame=3

cellFrame=0
outerFrame=0

Summary

The following sections summarize the reference information in this chapter.

General Picker Protos

protoPopupButton

```
aProtoPopupButton := {
_proto:                  protoPopupButton,
viewFlags:               flags,
viewBounds:              boundsFrame,
viewJustify:             justificationFlags,
text:                    string,      // text inside button
popup:                   array,       // items in list
ButtonClickScript:       function,    // called on button tap
PickActionScript:        function,    // returns item selected
PickCancelledScript:     function,    // user cancelled
...
}
```

protoPopInPlace

```
aProtoPopInPlace := {
_proto:                  protoPopInPlace,
viewBounds:              boundsFrame,
viewFlags:               constant,
viewJustify:             justificationFlags,
text:                    string,      // text inside button
popup:                   array,       // items in list
PickActionScript:        function,    // returns selected item
PickCancelledScript:     function,    // user cancelled
...
}
```

protoLabelPicker

```
aProtoLabelPicker := {
_proto:                  protoLabelPicker,
viewBounds:              boundsFrame,
viewFont:                fontSpec,
```

```
iconSetup:           icon frame,
labelCommands:       array,        // items in list
iconBounds:          boundsFrame,  // bounds of largest icon
iconIndent:          integer,      // indent of text from icon
checkCurrentItem:    Boolean,      // true to check selected item
indent:              integer,      // indent of picker from label
textIndent:          integer,      // indent of text
LabelActionScript:   function,     // returns selected item
TextSetup:           function,     // gets initial item
TextChanged:         function,     // called upon item value change
UpdateText:          function,     // call to change selected item
PickerSetup:         function,     // called when user taps label
Popit:               function,     // call to programmatically
                                   //  pop up picker
...
}
```

protoPicker

```
aProtoPicker := {
_proto:              protoPicker,
bounds:              boundsFrame,
viewBounds:          boundsFrame, // ignored
viewFlags:           constant,
viewFormat:          formatFlags,
viewJustify:         justificationFlags,
viewFont:            fontSpec,
viewEffect:          effectFlag,
pickItems:           array,    // items in list
pickTextItemHeight:  integer,  // height reserved for items
pickLeftMargin:      integer,  // margin from left of view
pickRightMargin:     integer,  // margin from right of view
pickTopMargin:       integer,  // margin above each item in
                               //   list
pickAutoClose:       Boolean,  // true to close list after pick
pickItemsMarkable:   Boolean,  // true to reserve space for
                               //   check mark before item
pickMarkWidth:       integer,  // space to reserve for marks
callbackContext:     view,     // view with pick scripts
PickActionScript:    function, // returns selected item
PickCancelledScript: function,    // user cancelled
SetItemMark:         function, // sets char for check marks
GetItemMark:         function, // gets char for check marks
...
}
```

Pickers, Pop-up Views, and Overviews

protoGeneralPopup

```
aProtoGeneralPopup := {
_proto:              protoGeneralPopup,
viewBounds:          boundsFrame,
viewFlags:           constant,
cancelled:           Boolean,     // true if user cancelled
                                  //  pop-up view
context:             view,        // view with pick scripts
New:                              // open pop-up view
Affirmative:         function,    // user taps pop-up view
PickCancelledScript: function,    // called in pop-up view
                                  //  cancelled
...
}
```

protoTextList

```
aProtoTextList := {
_proto:              protoTextList,
viewBounds:          boundsFrame,
viewFont:            fontSpec,
viewFormat:          formatFlags,
viewLines:           integer,     // number of lines to show
selection:           integer,     // index of selected item
selectedItems:       arrary,      // items in list
listItems:           array,       // strings or shapes in list
lineHeight:          array,       // height of lines in list
isShapeList:         Boolean,     // true if picts instead of text
useMultipleSelections:
                     Boolean,     // true for multiple select
useScroller:         Boolean,     // true to include scrollers
scrollAmounts:       array,       // units to scroll
DoScrollScript:      function,    // scrolls list by offset
ViewSetupFormScript: function,    // set up list
ButtonClickScript:   function,    // returns selected item
...
}
```

protoTable

```
aProtoTable := {
_proto:          protoTable,
viewBounds:      boundsFrame,
```

```
viewFormat:          formatFlags,
def:                 frame,       // protoTableDef table
                                  //  definition frame
scrollAmount:        integer,     // number of rows to scroll
currentSelection:    string,      // text of selected item
selectedCells:       array,       // selected cell indexes
declareSelf:         symbol,      // 'tabbase; do not change
ViewSetupFormScript: function,    // set up table
SelectThisCell:      function,    // called when cell is
selected
...
}
```

protoTableDef

```
aProtoTableDef := {
_proto: protoTableDef,
tabAcross:      integer,      // number of columns - must be 1
tabDown:        integer,      // number of rows in table
tabWidths:      integer,      // width of table
tabHeight:      integer,      // height of rows
tabProtos:      frame,        // references to row templates
tabValues:      integer/array, // value/array of values for
                               // rows
tabValueSlot:   symbol,       // slot to store tabValues in
tabUniqueSelection:Boolean,   // true for single selection
indentX:        integer,      // do not change: used internally
TabSetUp:       function,      // called before each row set up
...
}
```

protoTableEntry

```
aProtoTableEntry := {
_proto:             protoTableEntry,
viewClass:          clTextView,
viewFlags:          flags,
viewJustify:        justificationFlags,
viewTransferMode:   modeOr,
text:               string,      // text inside table
ViewClickScript:    function,    // sets current selection
ViewHiliteScript:   function,    // highlights selection
...

}
```

Map Pickers

protoCountryPicker

```
aProtoCountryPicker := {
_proto:       protoCountryPicker,
viewBounds:   boundsFrame,
autoClose:    Boolean,    // true to close picker on selection
listLimit:    integer,    // maximum items listed
PickWorld:    function,    // called when selection is made
...
}
```

protoProvincePicker

```
aProtoProvincePicker := {
_proto:       protoProvincePicker,
viewFlags:    constant,
autoClose:    Boolean,    // true to close picker on selection
listLimit:    integer,    // maximum items listed
PickWorld:    function,    // called when selection is made
...
}
```

protoStatePicker

```
aProtoStatePicker := {
_proto:       protoStatePicker,
viewFlags:    constant,
autoClose:    Boolean,    // true to close picker on selection
PickWorld:    function,    // called when selection is made
listLimit:    integer,    // maximum items listed
...
}
```

protoWorldPicker

```
aProtoWorldPicker := {
_proto:       protoWorldPicker,
viewBounds:   boundsFrame,
autoClose:    Boolean, // true to close picker on selection
listLimit:    integer,    // maximum items listed
PickWorld:    function, // called when selection is made
...
}
```

Text Picker Protos

protoTextPicker

```
aProtoTextPicker := {
_proto:                 protoTextPicker,
label:                  string,     // picker label
indent:                 integer,    // indent
labelFont:              fontSpec,   // font for label
entryFont:              fontSpec,   // font for picker line
Popit:                  function,   // user tapped picker
PickActionScript:       function,   // returns selected item
PickCancelledScript:    function,   // user cancelled picker
TextSetup:              function,   // returns text string
...
}
```

protoDateTextPicker

```
aProtoDateTextPicker := {
_proto:             protoDateTextPicker,
label:              string,     // picker label
date:               integer,    // initial and currently
                                // selected date
longFormat:         symbol,     // format to display date
shortFormat:        symbol,     // format to display date
PickActionScript:   function,   // returns selected item
PickCancelledScript:function,   // user cancelled picker
...
}
```

protoDateDurationTextPicker

```
aProtoDateDurationTextPicker := {
_proto:             protoDateDurationTextPicker,
label:              string,     // picker label
labelFont:          fontSpec,   // display font
entryFont:          fontSpec,   // picked entry font
startTime:          integer,    // initial start date
stopTime:           integer,    // initial end date
longFormat:         symbol,     // format to display date
shortFormat:        symbol,     // format to display date
```

```
PickActionScript:      function,   // returns selected item
PickCancelledScript: function,   // user cancelled picker
...
}
```

protoRepeatDateDurationTextPicker

```
aProtoRepeatDateDurationTextPicker := {
_proto:            protoRepeatDateDurationTextPicker,
label:             string,    // picker label
startTime:         integer,   // initial start date
stopTime:          integer,   // initial end date
longFormat:        symbol,    // format to display date
shortFormat:       symbol,    // format to display date
repeatType:        constant,  // how often meeting meets
mtgInfo:           constant,  // repeating meetings
PickActionScript: function,   // returns selected item
PickCancelledScript:function, // user cancelled picker
...
}
```

protoDateNTimeTextPicker

```
aProtoDateNTimeTextPicker := {
_proto:            protoDateNTimeTextPicker,
label:             string,    // picker label
date:              integer,   // initial date/time
format:            symbol,    // format to display time
longFormat:        symbol,    // format to display date
shortFormat:       symbol,    // format to display date
increment:         integer    // amount to change time
PickActionScript:  function,  // returns selected item
PickCancelledScript: function, // user cancelled picker
...
}
```

protoTimeTextPicker

```
aProtoTimeTextPicker := {
_proto:            protoTimeTextPicker,
label:             string,    // picker label
labelFont:         fontSpec,  // label display font
entryFont:         fontSpec,  // picked entry font
indent:            integer,   // amount to indent text
```

Summary

```
time:                   integer,    // initial start time
format:                 symbol,     // format to display time
increment:              integer,    // increment to change
                                    //  time for taps
PickActionScript:       function,   // returns selected item
PickCancelledScript:    function,   // user cancelled picker
...
}
```

protoDurationTextPicker

```
aProtoDurationTextPicker := {
_proto:                 protoDurationTextPicker,
label:                  string,     // picker label
startTime:              integer,    // initial start time
stopTime:               integer,    // initial end time
format:                 symbol,     // format to display time
increment:              integer,    // increment to change
                                    //  time for taps
PickActionScript:       function,   // returns selected item
PickCancelledScript:    function,   // user cancelled picker
...
}
```

protoTimeDeltaTextPicker

```
aProtoTimeDeltaTextPicker := {
_proto:                 protoTimeDeltaTextPicker,
label:                  string,     // picker label
time:                   integer,    // initial time
labelFont:              fontSpec,   // label display font
entryFont:              fontSpec,   // picked entry font
indent:                 integer,    //amount to indent text
increment:              integer,    // increment to change
                                    //  time for taps
minValue:               integer,    // minimum delta value
PickActionScript:       function,   // returns selected item
PickCancelledScript:    function,   // user cancelled picker
...
}
```

protoMapTextPicker

```
aProtoMapTextPicker := {
_proto:                 protoMapTextPicker,
label:                  string,     // picker label
labelFont:              fontSpec,   // label display font
entryFont:              fontSpec,   // picked entry font
indent:                 integer,    // amount to indent text
params:                 frame,
PickActionScript:       function,   // returns selected item
PickCancelledScript:    function,   // user cancelled picker
...
}
```

protoCountryTextPicker

```
aProtoCountryTextPicker := {
_proto:                 protoCountryTextPicker,
label:                  string,     // picker label
labelFont:              fontSpec,   // label display font
entryFont:              fontSpec,   // picked entry font
indent:                 integer,    // amount to indent text
params:                 frame,
PickActionScript:       function,   // returns selected item
PickCancelledScript:    function,   // user cancelled picker
...
}
```

protoUSstatesTextPicker

```
aProtoUSstatesTextPicker := {
_proto:                 protoUSstatesTextPicker,
label:                  string,     // picker label
labelFont:              fontSpec,   // label display font
entryFont:              fontSpec,   // picked entry font
indent:                 integer,    // amount to indent text
params:                 frame,
PickActionScript:       function,   // returns selected item
PickCancelledScript:    function,   // user cancelled picker
...
}
```

protoCitiesTextPicker

```
aProtoCitiesTextPicker := {
_proto:                 protoCitiesTextPicker,
label:                  string,      // picker label
labelFont:              fontSpec,    // label display font
entryFont:              fontSpec,    // picked entry font
indent:                 integer,     // amount to indent text
params:                 frame,
PickActionScript:       function,    // returns selected item
PickCancelledScript:    function,    // user cancelled picker
...
}
```

protoLongLatTextPicker

```
aProtoLongLatTextPicker := {
_proto:                 protoLongLatTextPicker,
label:                  string,      // picker label
latitude:               integer,     // initial latitude
longitude:              integer,     // initial longitude
labelFont:              fontSpec,    // label display font
entryFont:              fontSpec,    // picked entry font
indent:                 integer,     // amount to indent text
PickActionScript:       function,    // returns selected item
PickCancelledScript:    function,    // user cancelled picker
worldClock:             boolean      // do not change
...
}
```

Date, Time, and Location Pop-up Views

protoDatePopup

```
aProtoDatePopup := {
_proto:                 protoDatePopup,
New:                    function,    // creates pop-up view
PickActionScript:       function,    // returns selected item
PickCancelledScript:    function,    // user cancelled picker
...
}
```

protoDatePicker

```
aProtoDatePicker := {
_proto:         protoDatePicker,
selectedDates: array,      // selected date
DateChanged:   function,   // called when date is selected
Refresh:       function,   // update view with new dates
...
}
```

protoDateNTimePopup

```
protoDateNTimePopup := {
_proto:              protoDateNTimePopup,
New:                 function,   // creates pop-up view
NewTime:             function,   // called when time changes
PickActionScript:    function,   // returns selected item
PickCancelledScript: function,   // user cancelled picker
...
}
```

protoDateIntervalPopup

```
protoDateIntervalPopup := {
_proto:              protoDateIntervalPopup,
New:                 function,   // creates pop-up view
NewTime:             function,   // called when time changes
PickActionScript:    function,   // returns selected item
PickCancelledScript: function,   // user cancelled picker
...
}
```

protoMultiDatePopup

```
protoMultiDatePopup := {
_proto:              protoMultiDatePopup,
New:                 function,   // creates pop-up view
PickActionScript:    function,   // returns selected item
PickCancelledScript: function,   // user cancelled picker
...
}
```

protoYearPopup

```
protoYearPopup := {
_proto:             protoYearPopup,
New:                      function,    // creates pop-up view
NewYear:                  function,    // called when year changes
DoneYear:                 function,    // called on close box tap
PickCancelledScript: function,         // user cancelled picker
...
}
```

protoTimePopup

```
protoTimePopup := {
_proto:             protoTimePopup,
New:                      function,    // creates pop-up view
NewTime:                  function,    // called when time changes
PickActionScript:    function,         // returns selected item
PickCancelledScript: function,         // user cancelled picker
...
}
```

protoAnalogTimePopup

```
protoAnalogTimePopup := {
_proto:             protoAnalogTimePopup,
New:                      function,    // creates pop-up view
NewTime:                  function,    // called when time changes
PickActionScript:    function,         // returns selected item
PickCancelledScript: function,         // user cancelled picker
...
}
```

protoTimeDeltaPopup

```
protoTimeDeltaPopup := {
_proto:             protoTimeDeltaPopup,
New:                      function,    // creates pop-up view
PickActionScript:    function,         // returns selected item
PickCancelledScript: function,         // user cancelled picker
...
}
```

protoTimeIntervalPopup

```
protoTimeIntervalPopup := {
_proto:             protoTimeIntervalPopup,
New:                function,   // creates pop-up view
PickActionScript:   function,   // returns selected item
PickCancelledScript: function,  // user cancelled picker
...
}
```

Number Pickers

protoNumberPicker

```
aProtoNumberPicker := {
_proto:             protoNumberPicker,
minValue:           integer,   // minimum value in list
maxValue:           integer,   // maximum value in list
value:              integer,   // currently selected value
showLeadingZeros:   Boolean,   // true to show leading zeros
prepareForClick:    function,  // called after click is
                               //   processed

ClickDone:          function,  // called after click is
                               //   processed

...
}
```

Picture Picker

protoPictIndexer

```
aProtoPictIndexer := {
_proto:             protoPictIndexer,
viewBounds :        boundsFrame,
viewJustify:        justificationFlags,
viewFormat:         formatFlags,
icon:               bitmap,         // bitmap with objects
                                    //   arranged vertically
iconBBox:           boundsFrame,    // bitmap bounds within view
numIndices:         integer,        // # of objects in bitmap
curIndex:           integer,        // index of current item
IndexClickScript:   function,       // user taps bitmap

...
}
```

Summary

Overview Protos

protoOverview

```
aProtoOverview := {
_proto:              protoOverview,
viewBounds :         boundsFrame,
viewFlags :          constant,
viewFont :           fontSpec,
lineHeight:          integer,      // height of items in pixels
selectIndent:        integer,      // specifies left margin
nothingCheckable:    Boolean,      // true for no checkboxes
SelectItem:          function,     // to record selected items
SetupAbstracts:      function,     // set up entry
Abstract:            function,     // return shape given entry
HitItem:             function,     // called when item is tapped
IsSelected:          function      // Return true if the item is
                                   // selected
cursor:              cursor,       // cursor for the items
CheckState:          function,     // determines if selectable
Scroller:            function,     // implement scrolling here
SelectItem:          function,     // records selected items
viewSetupChildrenScript:
                     function,     // Calls SetupAbstracts
...
}
```

protoSoupOverview

```
aProtoSoupOverview := {
_proto:              protoSoupOverview,
autoDeselect:        Boolean,      // whether to deselect when
                                   // the pen leaves an item
cursor:              cursor,       // cursor for the entries
Scroller:            function,     // implement scrolling here
SelectItem:          function,     // records selected items
Abstract:            function,     // return shape given entry
IsSelected:          function,     // returns true if selected
ForEachSelected:     function,     // called for each selected
                                   //  item
...
}
```

protoListPicker

```
aProtoListPicker := {
_proto:          protoListPicker,
declareSelf :    symbol,        // Set to 'pickBase
defaultJustification :constant,
viewFlags :      constant,
viewBounds :     boundsFrame,
lineHeight:      integer,       // height of items in pixels
listFormat:      formatFlags,
pickerDef:       frame,         // defines list behavior
selected:        array,         // references to selected items
soupToQuery:     string,        // union soup to query
querySpec:       frame,         // query to use
selected:        array,         // modified as user selects
                                //   and deselects item
singleSelect:    Boolean,       // single selection if non-nil
suppressNew:     Boolean,       // suppress New button if non-nil
suppressScrollers:Boolean,      // suppress scroller if
                                //    non-nil
suppressAZTabs:    Boolean,     // suppress tabs if non-nil
suppressFolderTabs:Boolean,     // suppress if non-nil
suppressSelOnlyCheckbox:Boolean.// suppress if non-nil
suppressCloseBox:  Boolean,     // suppress if non-nil
suppressCounter:   Boolean,     // suppress if non-nil
reviewSelections:  Boolean,     // Selected Only if non-nil
readOnly:          Boolean,     // items are read-only if
                                //    non-nil
dontPurge:         Boolean,     // keep unselected refs if
                                //    non-nil
soupChangeSymbol:  symbol,      // for RegSoupChange method
SoupEnters:        function,    // syncs up changed soup
SoupLeaves:        function,    // syncs up changed soup
SetNowShowing:     function,    // set Selected Only
AddFakeItem:       function,    // add item to array; update
                                //   screen
GetSelected:       function,    // returns clone of selected
                                //    array

...
}
```

protoNameRefDataDef

```
aProtoNameRefDataDef := {
_proto:             protoNameRefDataDef,
name:               string,       // name to identify picker in
                                  // top left corner
class:              symbol,       // specify class for new name
                                  // references
entryType:          symbol,       // class for new soup entries
columns:            array,        // column specifications
singleSelect:       Boolean,      // single selection if non-nil
soupToQuery:        string,       // union soup to query
querySpec:          frame,        // query to use
validationFrame:    frame,        // checks validity of entry
MakeCanonicalNameRef:function, // make blank name ref
MakeNameRef:        function,     // make name reference
Get:                function,     // returns data from specified
                                  // object
GetPrimaryValue:function,         // retrieves data from object
HitItem:            function,     // called when item tapped
MakePopup:          function,     // called before making pop-up
                                  // view
Tapped:             function,     // called when tap has been
                                  // handled
New:                function,     // called when tap on New button
DefaultOpenEditor:function,    // open an edit view
OpenEditor:         function,     // open an custom edit view
NewEntry:           function,     // returns a new soup entry
ModifyEntry:        function,     // returns a modified soup entry
Validate:           function,     // validates paths
...
}
```

protoPeopleDataDef

```
aProtoPeopleDataDef := {
_proto:             protoPeopleDataDef,
entryType:          symbol,       // class for new soup entries
soupToQuery:        string,       // union soup to query
primaryPath:        symbol,       // the primary path column
primaryPathMapper:frame,          // maps entry class to data
Equivalent:         function,     // compares two name refs
```

```
Validate:          function,   // returns array of invalid
                               //   refs
ModifyEntryPath:   function,   // entry modification of Names
GetRoutingInfo:    function,   // retrieves routing info
GetItemRoutingFrame:function,  // converts routing info
GetRoutingTitle:   function,   // creates target string
PrepareForRouting:function,    // strips extra info
...
}
```

protoPeoplePicker

```
aProtoPeoplePicker := {
_proto:        protoPeoplePicker,
class:         symbol,    // type of data to display
selected:      array,     // references to selected items
...
}
```

protoPeoplePopup

```
aProtoPeoplePicker := {
_proto:        protoPeoplePicker,
class:         symbol,    // type of data to display
selected:      array,     // references to selected items
context:       symbol,    // view with PickActionScript
                          // method
options:       array,     // options for protoListPicker
PickActionScript: function,
                          // called when pop-up is closed
...
}
```

Roll Protos

protoRoll

```
aProtoRoll := {
_proto:        protoRoll,
viewFlags:     constant,
viewBounds:    boundsFrame,
items:         array,     // templates for roll items
```

```
allCollapsed:   Boolean,   // roll collapsed if non-nil
index:          integer,   // index of item to start
                           // display at
declareSelf:    symbol,    // 'roll — do not change
...
}
```

protoRollBrowser

```
aProtoRollBrowser := {
_proto:         protoRollBrowser,
viewBounds:     boundsFrame,
viewJustify:    justificationFlags,
viewFormat:     formatFlags,
title:          string,     // text for title at top of roll
rollItems:      array,      // templates for roll items
rollCollapsed:  Boolean,    // roll collapsed if non-nil
rollIndex:      integer,    // index of item to start
                            // display at
declareSelf:    symbol,     // 'base — do not change
...
}
```

protoRollItem

```
aProtoRollItem := {
_proto:         protoRollItem,
viewBounds:     boundsFrame,
viewJustify:    justificationFlags,
viewFormat:     formatFlags,
overview:       string,     // text for one-line overview
height:         integer,    // height of the view in pixels
stepChildren:   Boolean,    // child views for this roll item
...
}
```

View Classes

clOutlineView

```
myOutline:= {...
viewClass:      clOutline,
viewBounds:     boundsFrame,
```

```
browsers:        array,          // frame with array of outline
                                 //  items
viewFont:        fontSpec,
viewFlags :      constant,
viewFormat:      formatFlags,
clickSound:      frame,          // sound frame for taps
OutlineClickScript:function,     //called when user taps item
...
}
```

clMonthView

```
theMonth := {...
viewclass: clMonthView,
viewBounds:     boundsFrame,
viewflags:      constant,
labelFont:      fontSpec,
dateFont:       fontSpec,
selectedDates:  array,
viewSetupFormScript: function,
...
}
```

Functions

```
PopupMenu(list,  options)
IsNameRef(item)
AliasFromObj(item)
EntryFromObj(item)
ObjEntryClass(item)
```

Controls and Other Protos

Controls are software objects that provide various user interface capabilities, including scrolling, selection buttons, and sliders. You use the controls and other protos described in this chapter to add these features to your NewtonScript applications.

This chapter gives a general description of the controls and related protos provided in Newton System Software. For a detailed description of these protos, including the slots that you use to set to implement each, see "Controls Reference" (page 6-1) in *Newton Programmer's Reference*.

This chapter provides information about the following controls and protos:

- horizontal and vertical scrollers
- boxes and buttons
- alphabetical selection tabs
- gauges and sliders
- time-setting displays
- special views
- view appearance enhancements
- status bars

Controls Compatibility

The 2.0 release of Newton System Software includes a number of new protos, including:

- four new scroller protos: `protoHorizontal2DScroller`, `protoLeftRightScroller`, `protoUpDownScroller`, and `protoHorizontalUpDownScroller`
- two new buttons: `protoInfoButton` and `protoOrientation`
- two selection tab protos: `protoAZTabs` and `protoAZVertTabs`

- four new date and time protos: `protoDigitalClock`, `protoSetClock`, `protoNewSetClock`, and `protoAMPMCluster`

- two special view protos: `protoDragger` and `protoDragNGo`

Scroller Protos

Scrollers allow the user to move vertically or horizontally through a display that is bigger than the view. The Newton System Software provides a number of scrollers to allow users to scroll their views.

All scroller protos are implemented in the same way; that is, they use the same methods and slots. These scrollers are not linked or related to the scroll arrows on the built-in button bar. For individual descriptions of the scroller protos, see "Scroller Protos" (page 7-2) in *Newton Programmer's Reference*. This section describes how to implement scrollers in your applications.

The scroller protos do not perform the actual scrolling of data in a view; they simply display and maintain the arrows as the user taps them. To scroll data in a view, you can use the following protos in your applications:

- The `protoHorizontal2DScroller` is centered at the bottom of a view and provides both horizontal and vertical scroll arrows. For more information about the slots and methods for this scroller, see "protoHorizontal2DScroller" (page 6-2) in *Newton Programmer's Reference*. Figure 7-1 shows an example of a `protoHorizontal2DScroller` view.

Figure 7-1   A `protoHorizontal2DScroller` view

- The `protoLeftRightScroller` is centered at the bottom of a view and provides horizontal scroll arrows. For more information about the slots and methods for this scroller, see "protoLeftRightScroller" (page 6-5) in *Newton Programmer's Reference*. Figure 7-2 shows an example of a `protoLeftRightScroller` view.

Figure 7-2   A `protoLeftRightScroller` view

- The `protoUpDownScroller` is centered on the right side of a view and provides vertical scroll arrows. For more information about the slots and methods for this scroller, see "protoUpDownScroller" (page 6-5) in *Newton Programmer's Reference*. Figure 7-3 shows an example of a `protoHorizontal2DScroller` view.

Figure 7-3   A `protoUpDownScroller` view

- The `protoHorizontalUpDownScroller` is centered at the bottom of a view and provides vertical scroll arrows. For more information about the slots and methods for this scroller, see "protoHorizontalUpDownScroller" (page 6-6) in *Newton Programmer's Reference*. Figure 7-4 shows an example of a `protoHorizontalUpDownScroller` view.

Figure 7-4   A `protoHorizontalUpDownScroller` view

Implementing a Minimal Scroller

To implement a minimal scroller, all that you have to define is a `ViewScroll2DScript` method in your scroller template. This method is called whenever the user taps one of the scroll arrows in the scroller view. Your `ViewScroll2DScript` method must perform the actual scrolling of the contents of some other view, which you usually do by calling the `SetOrigin` method.

For more information on the `ViewScroll2DScript` method, see "ViewScroll2DScript" (page 6-3) in *Newton Programmer's Reference*. For more information on the `SetOrigin` method, see "SetOrigin" (page 2-48) in *Newton Programmer's Reference*.

Automatic Arrow Feedback

All of the scroller protos can provide visual feedback to the user indicating that there is more information to see. This feedback is handled automatically for your if you provide three additional slots in your scroller template: `scrollRect`, `viewRect`, and `dataRect`. Each of these slots is a bounds frame with the following form:

```
{left: 0, top: 0, right: 10, bottom: 10}
```

You usually create these bounds frame slots with the utility function `SetBounds`, which is described in "SetBounds" (page 2-34) in *Newton Programmer's Reference*.

When you use these slots, the scroller protos highlight the scrolling arrows automatically to indicate to the user that more data can be viewed by tapping on the highlighted arrows.

Each of the bounds frame slots serves a specific purpose in the scroller, as shown in Table 7-1. The next section provides several examples of setting the values of these slots for different scrolling effects.

Table 7-1   Scroller bounds frame slots

Slot name	Description
scrollRect	Specifies the scrollable area, which is the total area that the user can see, or scroll over, with the scroller.
viewRect	Specifies the part of the scrollable area that the user can see at any one time. This is usually smaller than the area specified by scrollRect.
dataRect	Specifies the portion of the scrollRect that contains data. In simple cases, this is the same as scrollRect.

Scrolling Examples

This section presents several simple examples of setting the bounds frame slots in your scroller to allow scrolling.

Scrolling Lines of Text

To scroll lines of text, you set the values of the three scroller bounds frames as required for your application. For example, if you have 20 text items in a vertical list and you want to show 6 of the items at a time, you need to set the slot values as follows:

```
scrollRect:  SetBounds(0, 0, 0, 20)    // 20 possible lines
viewRect:    SetBounds(0, 0, 0,  6)    // show 6 at a time
dataRect:    SetBounds(0, 0, 0, 20)
```

Scrolling in the Dates Application

Scrolling in the Dates application allows the user to see the 24 hours in a day, 7 hours at a time. When there is only interesting data in a certain range of the day, the application sets the `dataRect` for that time frame. This tells the scroller to blacken a scroll arrow when the data time frame is not displayed in the `viewRect`, providing additional visual feedback to the user.

```
scrollRect:  SetBounds(0, 0, 0, 24)    // 24 hours per day
viewRect:    SetBounds(0, 0, 0,  7)    // show 7 at a time
dataRect:    SetBounds(0, 0, 0, 10)    // meeting from 9-10
```

Scrolling In a Graphics Application

A final example shows scrolling in a graphics application. This example shows a total scrollable area of 200 pixels by 200 pixels, of which a 50 pixel by 50 pixel area is shown at any one time. In this example, an object of interest (data) is located at (100,100).

```
             // total area is 200 by 200
scrollRect:  SetBounds(  0,   0, 200, 200)
             // show a 50 by 50 area at a time
viewRect:    SetBounds(  0,   0,  50,  50)
             // there's something at location (100,100)
dataRect:    SetBounds(100, 100, 110, 110)
```

Scroll Amounts

Whenever the `ViewScroll2DScript` method is called, the scroller proto increments the `viewRect` by 1. For example, in the Dates application example, each time the user taps an arrow, the `viewRect` is moved up or down by 1 hour.

In the graphics application example, each time the user taps an arrow, the `viewRect` is moved up or down by 1 pixel. Since scrolling by 1 pixel at a time is too slow, you need to be able to adjust the scrolling amount for certain applications. To do so, you change the value of the `scrollAmounts` slot, which is an array of three values. The default value of this slot is:

```
[1, 1, 1]
```

The first value in the `scrollAmounts` array specifies the amount to scroll for a single tap. The second value specifies the amount to scroll when the user holds down on the arrow (accelerated scrolling), and the third value specifies the amount to scroll for a double tap. For a typical graphics application, you can use values like the following:

```
[10, 50, 50]
```

Keep in mind that if you set scrollAmounts to values other than the default, your method must check the value passed to it and scroll that amount.

Note

In general, you should discourage double-tapping, since inadvertently tapping twice can cause a double-tap action to occur. ◆

Advanced Usage

If you want more control over the arrow feedback, don't use the scrollRect, viewRect, or dataRect slots at all; instead, use the SetArrow and GetArrow methods.

For more information about the SetArrow method, see "SetArrow" (page 6-4) in *Newton Programmer's Reference*; for more on the GetArrow method, see "GetArrow" (page 6-4) in *Newton Programmer's Reference*.

Button and Box Protos

You use the protos described in this section to display text and picture buttons, checkboxes, and radio buttons. The Newton System Software provides a variety of button and box types for use in your applications.

Each of these protos uses specific methods to control its behavior. For many of the protos, the Newton System Software calls the ButtonClickScript when the button is tapped. You can define or redefine this method to generate the actions that you want associated with the button.

The Newton System Software calls certain methods for each of the protos described here. For information about which methods you need to define for each proto, see "Button and Box Protos" (page 6-6) in *Newton Programmer's Reference*.

For information about sizing and placement recommendations for your button and box protos, see *Newton 2.0 User Interface Guidelines*.

The following are the button and box protos that you can use in your applications:

■ The protoTextButton creates a rounded text button with text centered vertically and horizontally inside it. For more information about the slots and methods for this button, see "protoTextButton" (page 6-7) in *Newton Programmer's Reference*. Figure 7-5 shows an example of a protoTextButton view.

Figure 7-5   A protoTextButton view

My Button

■ The `protoPictureButton` creates a picture that is a button. For more information about the slots and methods for this button, see "protoPictureButton" (page 6-9) in *Newton Programmer's Reference*. Figure 7-6 shows an example of a `protoPictureButton` view.

Figure 7-6   A `protoPictureButton` view

Picture Buttons

■ The `protoInfoButton` includes an information button in a view. When the user taps this button, a picker containing information items appears. The picker includes the About, Help, and Prefs items. For more information about the slots and methods for this button, see "protoInfoButton" (page 6-10) in *Newton Programmer's Reference*. Figure 7-7 shows an example of a `protoInfoButton` view.

Figure 7-7   A `protoInfoButton` view

Information
Button

Picker displayed when
button is tapped

■ The `protoOrientation` is a text button that changes the screen orientation so that data on the screen can be displayed facing different directions. This proto is available only on Newton platforms that support changing the screen orientation. For more information about the slots and methods for this button, see "protoOrientation" (page 6-13) in *Newton Programmer's Reference*. Figure 7-8 shows an example of a protoOrientation view.

Figure 7-8   A `protoOrientation` view

[Rotate]

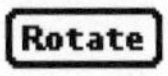

■ The `protoRadioCluster` groups a series of radio buttons into a cluster in which only one can be "on" at a time. For more information about the slots and methods for this proto, see "protoRadioCluster" (page 6-14) in *Newton Programmer's Reference*. This proto has no visual representation.

CHAPTER 7

Controls and Other Protos

- The `protoRadioButton` creates a radio button child view of a radio button cluster (based on `protoRadioCluster`). Each radio button is a small oval bitmap that is labeled with text. For more information about the slots and methods for this button, see "protoPictRadioButton" (page 6-18) in *Newton Programmer's Reference*. Figure 7-9 shows an example of several radio buttons in a cluster.

Figure 7-9   A cluster of `protoRadioButtons`

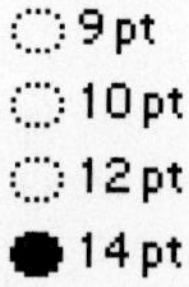

- The `protoPictRadioButton` creates a child view of a radio button cluster (based on `protoRadioCluster`). For more information about the slots and methods for this button, see "protoPictureButton" (page 6-9) in *Newton Programmer's Reference*. Figure 7-10 shows a cluster of `protoPictRadioButtons`.

Figure 7-10   A cluster of `protoPictRadioButtons`

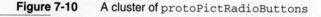

- The `protoCloseBox` allows the user to close the view. For more information about the slots and methods for this box, see "protoCloseBox" (page 6-20) in *Newton Programmer's Reference*. Figure 7-11 shows an example of a `protoCloseBox` view.

Figure 7-11   A `protoCloseBox` view

- The `protoLargeCloseBox` creates a picture button with an "X" icon that is used to close the view. For more information about the slots and methods for this box, see "protoLargeCloseBox" (page 6-22) in *Newton Programmer's Reference*. Figure 7-12 shows an example of a `protoLargeCloseBox` view.

Figure 7-12   A `protoLargeCloseBox` view

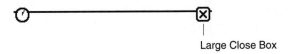

Large Close Box

Note
See *Newton 2.0 User Interface Guidelines* for information about when to use `protoCloseBox` and when to use `protoLargeCloseBox`. ◆

- The `protoCheckBox` creates a labeled checkbox with the label text to the right of the box. When the user taps the checkbox, a checkmark is drawn in it. For more information about the slots and methods for this box, see "protoCheckbox" (page 6-24) in *Newton Programmer's Reference*. Figure 7-13 shows an example of a `protoCheckBox` view.

Figure 7-13   A `protoCheckBox` view

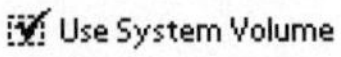

☑ Use System Volume

- The `protoRCheckBox` creates a labeled checkbox with the text to the left of the checkbox. When the user taps the checkbox, a checkmark is drawn in it. For more information about the slots and methods for this box, see "protoRCheckbox" (page 6-26) in *Newton Programmer's Reference*. Figure 7-14 shows an example of a `protoRCheckBox` view.

Figure 7-14   A `protoRCheckBox` view

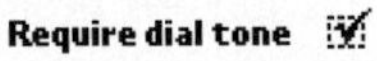

Require dial tone   ☑

Implementing a Simple Button

To provide a simple button in your application, pick a button proto to use, set the appropriate slots in the button object, and (in most cases) define one or more scripts for the button.

The following is an example of a template that includes `protoTextButton`:

```
aButton := {...
_proto: protoTextButton,
viewFont: ROM_fontSystem12Bold,
text: "My Button",

ButtonClickScript: func()
    Print("ouch!");

        // a handy way to fit a button around a string
ViewSetupFormScript: func()
    viewbounds := RelBounds(10, 60,
                    StdButtonWidth(self.text), 13);
...}
```

The above example creates the following button on the Newton screen:

My Button

When the user taps this button in the Inspector, "ouch" is printed to the Inspector.

You implement a picture button with a similar template, as shown in the following example:

```
pictButton := {...
_proto: protoPictureButton,
icon: namesBitmap,
viewBounds: SetBounds( 2, 8, 34, 40 ),

ButtonClickScript: func()
    cardfile:Toggle()
...}
```

For more information on implementing specific button and box protos, see "Button and Box Protos" (page 7-6) in *Newton Programmer's Reference*.

Selection Tab Protos

You can use the protos described in this section to display alphabetic selection tabs on the screen. There are two tab protos that you can use:

- The `protoAZTabs` displays alphabetical tabs arranged horizontally in a view. For more information about the slots and methods for this proto, see "protoAZTabs" (page 6-28) in *Newton Programmer's Reference*. Figure 7-15 shows an example of a `protoAZTabs` view.

Figure 7-15 A `protoAZTabs` view

ab cd ef gh ij kl mn op qr st uv wx yz

- The `protoAZVertTabs` displays alphabetical tabs arranged vertically in a view. For more information about the slots and methods for this proto, see "protoAZVertTabs" (page 6-29) in *Newton Programmer's Reference*. Figure 7-16 shows an example of a `protoAZVertTabs` view.

Figure 7-16 A `protoAZVertTabs` view

abc
def
ghi
jkl
mno
pqr
stu
vwx
yz

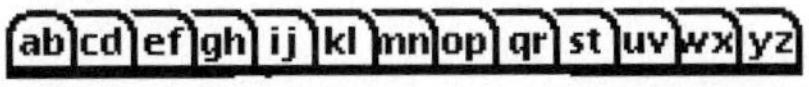

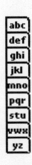

When the user taps in either of the tab protos, the proto calls the `PickLetterScript` method, passing in the letter that was tapped. The tabs protos and the `PickLetterScript` method are described in "Selection Tab Protos" (page 6-28) in *Newton Programmer's Reference*.

Gauge and Slider Protos

You can use the gauge and slider protos described in this section to display gauges. Each slider presents a gauge view that indicates the current progress in relation to the entire operation. There are three protos and one view class available for defining sliders:

- The `protoSlider` creates a user-settable gauge view, which looks like an analog bar gauge with a draggable diamond-shaped knob. For more information about the slots and methods for this proto, see "protoSlider" (page 6-33) in *Newton Programmer's Reference*. Figure 7-17 shows an example of a `protoSlider` view.

Figure 7-17   A `protoSlider` view

Large Close Box

- The `protoGauge` creates a read-only gauge view. For more information about the slots and methods for this proto, see "protoGauge" (page 6-35) in *Newton Programmer's Reference*. Figure 7-18 shows an example of a `protoGauge` view.

Figure 7-18   A `protoGauge` view

- The `protoLabeledBatteryGauge` creates a read-only gauge view that periodically samples the system battery and graphically shows the amount of power left. For more information about the slots and methods for this proto, see "protoLabeledBatteryGauge" (page 6-37) in *Newton Programmer's Reference*. Figure 7-19 shows an example of a `protoLabeledBatteryGauge` view.

Figure 7-19   A `protoLabeledBatteryGauge` view

Battery gauge

Battery

Battery charging

Charging

■ The clGaugeView class is used to display objects that look like analog bar gauges. Although the clGaugeView class is available, you should use the protoGauge to display bar gauges. purpose as is the protoGauge proto. For more information about the slots and methods for the protoGauge proto, see "protoGauge" (page 6-35) in *Newton Programmer's Reference*.

Figure 7-20   A clGaugeView view

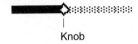

Knob

Implementing a Simple Slider

The clGaugeView class and the slider protos all have several slots to define the appearance and range of the slider:

■ The viewBounds slot specifies the size and location of the slider.

■ The viewValue slot specifies the current value of the slider.

■ The minValue slot specifies the minimum value of the slider, with a default value of 0.

■ The maxValue slot specifies the maximum value of the slider, with a default value of 100.

You can specify the initial value of a slider in the viewValue slot. However, you often need to look up the initial value; when this is the case, set the initial value of the slider in the ViewSetupFormScript method.

To implement a slider, define your template with the proto that you want to use, specify the appearance and range slots, and (optionally) assign an initial value in the ViewSetupFormScript method of the proto. For some protos, you need to define additional methods that respond to the user modifying the slider.

The following example is a template that uses protoSlider to allow adjustment of the current system volume:

```
SoundSetter := {...
_proto: protoSlider,
viewBounds: RelBounds( 12, -21, 65, 9),
viewJustify: vjParentBottomV,
maxValue: 4,

ViewSetupFormScript: func()
   self.viewValue := GetUserConfig('soundVolume);
```

```
ChangedSlider: func()
   begin
   SetVolume(viewValue);
   :SysBeep();
   end,
...}
```

The example above initializes the slider gauge to indicate the current system volume, which it retrieves from the user configuration that is maintained by the Newton System Software. The range of allowable volume values is from 0 (the default for minValue) to 4.

Whenever the user moves the slider and lifts the pen, the viewValue slot is updated and the ChangedSlider method is called. In the example, the ChangedSlider method resets the system volume to the new value chosen by the user and sounds a beep to provide the user with audible feedback.

For more information on the protoSlider and the ChangedSlider method, see "protoSlider" (page 6-33) in *Newton Programmer's Reference*.

Time Protos

You can use the time protos to allow the user to set time and date values. There are four time protos:

■ The protoDigitalClock time proto displays a digital clock with which the user can set a time value. For more information about the slots and methods for this proto, see "protoDigitalClock" (page 6-38) in *Newton Programmer's Reference*. Figure 7-21 shows an example of a protoDigitalClock view.

Figure 7-21   A protoDigitalClock view

■ The protoNewSetClock time proto displays an analog clock with which the user can set a time value. For more information about the slots and methods for this proto, see "protoNewSetClock" (page 6-40) in *Newton Programmer's Reference*. Figure 7-22 shows an example of a protoNewSetClock view.

Figure 7-22   A `protoNewSetClock` view

- The `protoSetClock` time proto also displays an analog clock with which the user can set a time value. Although this proto is still available for use, it has been updated to the `protoNewSetClock`, which you should use instead.

- The `protoAMPMCluster` time proto displays A.M. and P.M. radio buttons in a `protoNewSetClock` view. For more information about the slots and methods for this proto, see "protoAMPMCluster" (page 6-44) in *Newton Programmer's Reference*. Figure 7-23 shows an example of a `protoAMPMCluster` view.

Figure 7-23   A `protoAMPMCluster` view

○ am ● pm

Implementing a Simple Time Setter

To implement a time setter, define your template with the proto that you want to use, specify the initial time value to show in the clock, and define the `TimeChanged` method. You might also need to define additional slots or messages, as described in "Time Protos" (page 6-38) in *Newton Programmer's Reference*.

The following example is a template that uses `protoDigitalClock` to allow the user to specify a time:

```
clock := {...
 _proto: protoDigitalClock,
    time: 0,

TimeChanged: func()
    begin
            // add your code to respond to time change
    print(time);
    end,
```

```
                    // initialize with current time
ViewSetupFormScript: func()
   begin
   time := time();
   end,
...};
```

Special View Protos

You can use the protos described in this section to provide special-purpose views in your applications. There are seven special view protos:

- The protoDragger creates a view that can be dragged around the screen with the pen. For more information about the slots and methods for this proto, see "protoDragger" (page 6-45) in *Newton Programmer's Reference*. Figure 7-22 shows an example of a protoDragger view.

Figure 7-24   A protoDragger view

- The protoDragNGo creates a view that can be dragged around the screen with the pen. This is identical to protoDragger, except that protoDragNGo includes a close box in the lower-right corner of the view. For more information about the slots and methods for this proto, see "protoDragNGo" (page 6-47) in *Newton Programmer's Reference*. Figure 7-25 shows an example of a protoDragNGo view.

Figure 7-25   A protoDragNGo view

- The `protoDrawer` creates a view that looks and acts like the base view of the Extras Drawer. For more information about the slots and methods for this proto, see "protoDrawer" (page 6-49) in *Newton Programmer's Reference*.

- The `protoFloater` creates a draggable view that is horizontally centered within its parent view and floats above all other nonfloating sibling views within an application. For more information about the slots and methods for this proto, see "protoFloater" (page 6-49) in *Newton Programmer's Reference*.

- The `protoFloatNGo` creates a draggable view that is horizontally centered within its parent view and floats above all other nonfloating sibling views within an application. This is identical to `protoFloater`, except that `protoFloatNGo` includes a close box in the lower-right corner of the view. For more information about the slots and methods for this proto, see "protoFloatNGo" (page 6-51) in *Newton Programmer's Reference*.

- The `protoGlance` creates a text view that automatically closes itself after displaying for a brief period. For more information about the slots and methods for this proto, see "protoGlance" (page 6-52) in *Newton Programmer's Reference*. Figure 7-26 shows an example of a `protoGlance` view.

Figure 7-26   A `protoGlance` view

8/1/93 11:00 am 46 bytes

- The `protoStaticText` creates a one-line paragraph view that is read-only and left-justified. For more information about the slots and methods for this, see "protoStaticText" (page 6-54) in *Newton Programmer's Reference*. Figure 7-22 shows an example of a `protoStaticText` view.

Figure 7-27   A `protoStaticText` view

Static text

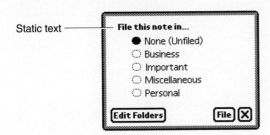

View Appearance Protos

You can use the protos described in this section to add to the appearance of your views in certain ways. There are three view appearance protos:

■ The `protoBorder` is a view filled with black. You can use this proto as a border, a line, or a black rectangle. For more information about the slots and methods for this proto, see "protoBorder" (page 6-56) in *Newton Programmer's Reference*. Figure 7-28 shows an example of a `protoBorder` view.

Figure 7-28   A `protoBorder` view

■ The `protoDivider` creates a divider bar that extends the whole width of its parent view. This proto also includes a text label. For more information about the slots and methods for this proto, see "protoDivider" (page 6-56) in *Newton Programmer's Reference*. Figure 7-29 shows an example of a `protoDivider` view.

Figure 7-29   A `protoDivider` view

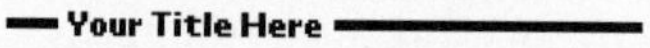

━ **Your Title Here** ━━━━━

■ The `protoTitle` creates a title centered above a heavy black line at the top of a view. You can optionally include an icon that appears to the left of the title text. For more information about the slots and methods for this proto, see "protoTitle" (page 6-58) in *Newton Programmer's Reference*. Figure 7-30 shows an example of a `protoTitle` view.

Figure 7-30   A `protoTitle` view

Icon ─────┼──── ◆ **My Application** ────┼─ Title

Status Bar Protos

You can use the protos described in this section to display a status bar at the bottom of a view. There are two status bar protos:

- The `protoStatus` creates a status bar, which includes a close button and an analog clock, at the bottom of a view. For more information about the slots and methods for this proto, see "protoStatus" (page 6-59) in *Newton Programmer's Reference*. Figure 7-31 shows an example of a `protoStatus` view.

Figure 7-31   A `protoStatus` view

- The `protoStatusBar` creates a status bar, which includes an analog clock, at the bottom of a view. This is identical to `protoStatus`, except that `protoStatusBar` does not include a close button. For more information about the slots and methods for this proto, see "protoStatusBar" (page 6-60) in *Newton Programmer's Reference*. Figure 7-32 shows an example of a `protoStatusBar` view.

Figure 7-32   A `protoStatusBar` view

Note

The new status bar protos `newtStatusBarNoClose` and `newtStatusBar`, are the preferred way to add a status bar to your applications. These protos, which are described in "NewtApp Applications" (page 4-1), simplify adding buttons and automate hiding the close box when your application is moved into the background. ◆

Summary

Scroller Protos

protoLeftRightScroller

```
aProtoLeftRightScroller := {
_proto: protoLeftRightScroller,
scrollView:     viewTemplate,
scrollRect:     boundsFrame,  // extent of scrollable area
dataRect:       boundsFrame,  // extent of data in the view
viewRect:       boundsFrame,  // extent of visible area
xPos:           integer,    // initial x-coord in scrollRect
yPos:           integer,    // initial y-coord in scrollRect
scrollAmounts:  array,      // line, page, dbl-click values
pageThreshhold: integer,      // lines before page scrolling
ViewScroll2DScript:  function, // called when arrows tapped
ViewScrollDoneScript: function, // called when scroll done
SetArrow:                function, // set scroll direction
GetArrow:                function, // returns scroll direction
...
}
```

protoUpDownScroller

```
aProtoUpDownScroller := {
_proto: protoUpDownScroller,
scrollView:     viewTemplate,
scrollRect:     boundsFrame, // extent of scrollable area
dataRect:       boundsFrame, // extent of data in the view
viewRect:       boundsFrame, // extent of visible area
xPos:           integer     // initial x-coord in scrollRect
yPos:           integer,    // initial y-coord in scrollRect
scrollAmounts:  array,      // line, page, dbl-click values
pageThreshhold: integer,      // lines before page scrolling
ViewScroll2DScript:  function, // called when arrows tapped
ViewScrollDoneScript: function, // called when scroll done
SetArrow:                function, // set scroll direction
GetArrow:                function, // returns scroll direction
...
}
```

protoHorizontal2DScroller

```
aProtoHorizontal2DScroller := {
_proto: protoHorizontal2DScroller,
scrollView:      viewTemplate,
scrollRect:      boundsFrame,// extent of scrollable area
dataRect:        boundsFrame,// extent of data in the view
viewRect:        boundsFrame,// extent of visible area
xPos:            integer,    // initial x-coord in scrollRect
yPos:            integer,    // initial y-coord in scrollRect
scrollAmounts: array,        // line, page, dbl-click values
pageThreshhold:integer,      // lines before page scrolling
ViewScroll2DScript: function, // called when arrows tapped
ViewScrollDoneScript:function, // called when scroll done
SetArrow:            function, // set scroll direction
GetArrow:            function, // returns scroll direction
...
}
```

protoHorizontalUpDownScroller

```
aProtoHorizontalUpDownScroller := {
_proto: protoHorizontalUpDownScroller,
scrollView:      viewTemplate,
scrollRect:      boundsFrame,// extent of scrollable area
dataRect:        boundsFrame,// extent of data in the view
viewRect:        boundsFrame,// extent of visible area
xPos:            integer,    // initial x-coord in scrollRect
yPos:            integer,    // initial y-coord in scrollRect
scrollAmounts: array,        // line, page, dbl-click values
pageThreshhold:integer,      // lines before page scrolling
ViewScroll2DScript: function, // called when arrows tapped
ViewScrollDoneScript:function, // called when scroll done
SetArrow:            function, // set scroll direction
GetArrow:            function, // returns scroll direction
...
}
```

Button and Box Protos

protoTextButton

```
aProtoTextButton := {
_proto: protoTextButton,
viewBounds:          boundsFrame,
viewFlags:           integer,    // viewFlags constants
text:                string,     // text inside the button
viewFont:            fontFlags,
viewFormat:          formatFlags,
viewJustify:         justificationFlags,
viewTransferMode:    integer,    // view transfer constants
ButtonClickScript:   function,   // when button is tapped
ButtonPressedScript: function,   // while button is pressed
...
}
```

protoPictureButton

```
aProtoTextButton := {
_proto: protoPictureButton,
viewBounds:          boundsFrame,
viewFlags:           integer,    // viewFlags constants
icon:                bitmap,     // bitmap to use for button
viewFormat:          formatFlags,
viewJustify:         justificationFlags,
ButtonClickScript:   function,   // when button is tapped
ButtonPressedScript: function,   // while button is pressed
...
}
```

protoInfoButton

```
aProtoInfoButton := {
_proto: protoInfoButton,
viewFlags:           integer,    // viewFlags constants
viewBounds:          boundsFrame,
viewJustify:         justificationFlags,
...
}
```

protoOrientation

```
aProtoOrientation := {
_proto: protoOrientation,
viewFlags:          integer,     // viewFlags constants
viewBounds:         boundsFrame,
viewJustify:        justificationFlags,
. . .
}
```

protoRadioCluster

```
aProtoRadioCluster := {
_proto: protoRadioCluster,
viewBounds:              boundsFrame,
clusterValue:            integer,     // value of selected button
InitClusterValue:        function,    // initialize cluster
ViewSetupFormScript:     function,    // set initial button
ClusterChanged:          function,    // called upon value change
SetClusterValue:         function,    // change selected button
. . .
}
```

protoRadioButton

```
aProtoRadioButton := {
_proto: protoRadioButton,
viewBounds:     boundsFrame,
viewFormat:     formatFlags,
text:           string,      // radio button text label
buttonValue:    integer,     // identifies button
viewValue:      integer,     // current value of radio button
. . .
}
```

protoPictRadioButton

```
aProtoPictRadioButton := {
_proto: protoPictRadioButton,
viewBounds:     boundsFrame,
viewFormat:     formatFlags,
viewJustify:    justificationFlags,
icon:           bitmap,      // bitmap for picture button
buttonValue:    integer,     // identifies button
```

```
viewValue:       integer,      // current value of radio button
ViewDrawScript:function,       // to highlight button
...
}
```

protoCloseBox

```
aProtoCloseBox := {
_proto: protoCloseBox,
viewFlags:        integer,     // viewFlags constants
viewBounds:       boundsFrame,
viewJustify:      justificationFlags,
viewFormat:       formatFlags,
ButtonClickScript:function,    // called before closing
...
}
```

protoLargeCloseBox

```
aProtoLargeCloseBox := {
_proto: protoLargeCloseBox,
viewFlags:        integer,     // viewFlags constants
viewBounds:       boundsFrame,
viewJustify:      justificationFlags,
viewFormat:       formatFlags,
ButtonClickScript:function,    // called before closing
...
}
```

protoCheckbox

```
aProtoCheckbox := {
_proto: protoCheckbox,
viewBounds:       boundsFrame,
viewFormat:       formatFlags,
viewFont:         fontFlags,   // font for text label
text:             string,      // the checkbox label
buttonValue:      value,       // value when box is checked
viewValue:        value,       // current value (nil=unchecked)
ValueChanged:     function,    // checkbox value changed
ToggleCheck:      function,    // toggles checkbox state
...
}
```

protoRCheckbox

```
aProtoRCheckbox := {
_proto: protoRCheckbox,
viewBounds:      boundsFrame,
viewFormat:      formatFlags,
viewFont:        fontFlags,   // font for text label
text:            string,      // the checkbox label
indent:          integer,     // pixels to indent box
buttonValue:     value,       // value when box is checked
viewValue:       value,       // current value (nil=unchecked)
ValueChanged:    function,    // checkbox value changed
ToggleCheck:     function,    // toggles checkbox state
...
}
```

Selection Tab Protos

protoAZTabs

```
aProtoAZTabs := {
_proto: protoAZTabs,
PickLetterScript: function,      // tab is tapped
SetLetter:        function,      // sets tab letter
...
}
```

protoAZVertTabs

```
aProtoAZVertTabs := {
_proto: protoAZVertTabs,
PickLetterScript: function,      // tab is tapped
SetLetter:        function,      // sets tab letter
...
}
```

Gauges and Slider Protos

protoSlider

```
aProtoSlider := {
_proto: protoSlider,
viewBounds:              boundsFrame,
```

```
viewValue:              integer,     // gauge value
minValue:               integer,     // minimum gauge value
maxValue:               integer,     // maximum gauge value
ViewSetupFormScript:    function,    // set initial gauge value
ChangedSlider:          function,    // slider moved
TrackSlider:            function,    // viewValue changed
...
}
```

protoGauge

```
aProtoGauge := {
_proto: protoGauge,
viewBounds:             boundsFrame,
viewValue:              integer,     // gauge value
minValue:               integer,     // minimum gauge value
maxValue:               integer,     // maximum gauge value
gaugeDrawLimits:        Boolean,     // non-nil for gray bg
ViewSetupFormScript:    function,    // set initial gauge value
...
}
```

protoLabeledBatteryGauge

```
aProtoLabeledBatteryGauge:= {
_proto: protoLabeledBatteryGauge,
viewBounds: boundsFrame,
...
}
```

clGaugeView

```
aClGaugeView:= {
viewBounds:             boundsFrame,
viewClass:              clGaugeView,
viewValue:              integer,     // value of gauge
viewFlags:              integer,     // viewFlags constants
viewFormat:             formatFlags,
minValue:               integer,     // min value of gauge
maxValue:               integer,     // max value of gauge
gaugeDrawLimits:        Boolean,     // non-nil for gray bg
ViewChangedScript:      function,    // gauge dragged
ViewFinalChangeScript:  function,    // gauge changed
...
}
```

Time Protos

protoDigitalClock

```
aProtoDigitalClock := {
_proto: protoDigitalClock,
viewFlags:      integer,        // viewFlags constants
viewBounds:     boundsFrame,
viewJustify:    justificationFlags,
increment:      integer,        // minutes to change on tap
time:           integer,        // initial or current time
wrapping:       Boolean,        // non-nil to wrap around day
                                //   boundaries
midnite:        Boolean,        // non-nil if 0 means midnight
                                //   tomorrow
Refresh:        function,       // update clock
TimeChanged:    function,       // called when time is changed
...
}
```

protoSetClock

```
aProtoSetClock := {
_proto: protoSetClock,
viewBounds:     boundsFrame,
viewFlags:      integer,        // viewFlags constants
viewFormat:     formatFlags,
hours:          integer,        // value set by hour hand
minutes:        integer,        // value set by minute hand
TimeChanged:    function,       // called when time is changed
...
}
```

protoNewSetClock

```
aProtoNewSetClock := {
_proto: protoNewSetClock,
viewBounds:     boundsFrame,
viewJustify:    justificationFlags,
time:           integer,        // initial or current time
annotations:    array,          // four strings to annotate
                                //   the clock face
supressAnnotations:Boolean,     // if slot exists, suppress
exactHour:      Boolean,        // adjust hour markers
```

```
Refresh:            function,    // update clock
TimeChanged:        function,    // called when time is changed
...
}
```

protoAMPMCluster

```
aProtoAMPMCluster := {
_proto: protoAMPMCluster,
viewBounds:     boundsFrame,
viewJustify:    justificationFlags,
time:           integer,    // specify time--required
...
}
```

Special View Protos

protoDragger

```
aProtoDragger := {
_proto: protoDragger,
viewBounds :    boundsFrame,
viewFlags:      integer,     // viewFlags constants
viewFormat:     formatFlags,
noScroll:       string,     // msg to display if no scrolling
noOverview:     string,     // msg to display if no overview
...
}
```

protoDragNGo

```
aProtoDragNGo := {
_proto: protoDragNGo,
viewBounds:     boundsFrame,
viewFlags:      integer,     // viewFlags constants
viewJustify:    justificationFlags,
viewFormat:     formatFlags,
noScroll:       string,     // msg to display if no scrolling
noOverview:     string,     // msg to display if no overview
...
}
```

protoDrawer

```
aProtoDrawer := {
_proto: protoDrawer,
viewFlags:     integer,      // viewFlags constants
viewBounds:    boundsFrame,
viewFormat:    formatFlags,
viewEffect:    effectFlags,
showSound:     soundFrame,// sound when drawer opens
hideSound:     soundFrame,// sound when drawer closes
...
}
```

protoFloater

```
aProtoFloater := {
_proto: protoFloater,
viewBounds:    boundsFrame,
viewFlags:     integer,      // viewFlags constants
viewJustify:justificationFlags,
viewFormat:    formatFlags,
viewEffect:    effectFlags,
noScroll:      string,       // msg to display if no scrolling
noOverview:    string,       // msg to display if no overview
...
}
```

protoFloatNGo

```
aProtoFloatNGo := {
_proto: protoFloatNGo,
viewFlags:      integer,       // viewFlags constants
viewBounds:     boundsFrame,
viewJustify:    justificationFlags,
viewFormat:     formatFlags,
viewEffect:     effectFlags,
noScroll:       string,       // msg to display if no scrolling
noOverview:     string,       // msg to display if no overview
...
}
```

protoGlance

```
aProtoGlance := {
_proto: protoGlance,
viewBounds:            boundsFrame,
viewJustify:           justificationFlags,
viewFormat:            formatFlags,
viewFont:              fontFlags,   // font for text
viewEffect:            effectFlags,
viewIdleFrequency:     integer,     // time view to remain open
text:                  string,      // text to appear in view
...
}
```

protoStaticText

```
aProtoStaticText:= {
_proto: protoStaticText,
viewBounds:            boundsFrame,
viewFlags:             integer,     // viewFlags constants
text:                  string,          // text to display
viewFont:              fontFlags,
viewJustify:           justificationFlags,
viewFormat:            formatFlags,
viewTransferMode:      integer,     // view transfer constants
tabs:                  array,   // up to eight tab-stop positions
styles:                array,   // font information
...
}
```

View Appearance Protos

protoBorder

```
aProtoBorder := {
_proto: protoBorder,
viewBounds:       boundsFrame,
viewFlags:        integer,     // viewFlags constants
viewFormat:       formatFlags,
...
}
```

protoDivider

```
aProtoDivider:= {
_proto: protoDivider,
viewBounds:      boundsFrame,
viewFlags:       integer,    // viewFlags constants
viewFont:        fontFlags,  // font for text
viewJustify:     justificationFlags,
viewFormat:      formatFlags,
title:           string,     // text on divider bar
titleHeight:     integer,    // height of divider
...
}
```

protoTitle

```
aProtoTitle := {
_proto: protoTitle,
viewJustify:        justificationFlags,
viewFormat:         formatFlags,
viewFont:           fontFlags,
title:              string,     // text of title
titleIcon:          bitMapFrame,
titleHeight:        integer,    // height of title
viewTransferMode:   integer,    // view transfer constants
...
}
```

Status Bar Protos

protoStatus

```
aProtoStatus := {
_proto: protoStatus,
...
}
```

protoStatusBar

```
aProtoStatusBar := {
_proto: protoStatusBar,
...
}
```

Text and Ink Input and Display

This chapter describes how the Newton system handles text and presents interfaces you can use to work with text in NewtonScript applications.

The material covers the following components of Newton text handling:

- handwritten text input
- keyboard text input
- views for text display
- fonts for text display

The first section of this chapter, "About Text," describes the basic terms and concepts needed to understand text processing on the Newton.

The second section, "Using Text," describes how to use the various input and display components to handle text in your applications.

For comprehensive reference information about the text-related constants, data structures, views, methods, and functions, see "Text and Ink Input and Display Reference" (page 7-1) in *Newton Programmer's Reference*.

About Text

This section describes the basic concepts, terms, and processes you need to understand to work with text in your applications.

About Text and Ink

The Newton allows you to process two forms of text input: **ink text** and **recognized text**. This section describes both forms of text input.

When the user writes a line of text on the Newton screen, the Newton system software performs a series of operations, as follows:

- The raw data for the input is captured as ink, which is also known as **sketch ink** or **raw ink.**

- Raw ink is stored as a sequence of **strokes** or stroke data.

- If the view in which the ink was drawn is configured for **ink text,** the recognition system groups the stroke data into a series of **ink words,** based on the timing and spacing of the user's handwriting. A user can insert, delete, and move ink words in the same way as recognized text. Ink words can be scaled to various sizes for display and printing. They can also be recognized at a later time, by a process known as **deferred recognition.**

- If the view in which the ink was drawn supports or is configured for text recognition, the ink words are processed by the recognition system into recognized text and displayed in a typeface.

The data describing the handwriting strokes of the ink word are stored as compressed data in a binary object. This **stroke data** can be accessed programmatically, using the stroke bundle methods described in "Recognition" (page 9-1) in *Newton Programmer's Guide*.

The recognition system and deferred recognition are described in "Recognition" (page 9-1).

Note
To provide maximum user flexibility for your applications, you are encouraged to allow ink text in all of your input views. ◆

Written Input Formats

Ink words can be intermixed with recognized text. This data, normally represented as **rich strings,** can be used anywhere that you might expect a standard string. Each ink word is encoded as a single character in a rich string, as described in "Rich Strings" (page 8-22).

You should use the **rich string format** to store data in a soup, because of its compact representation. You can safely use rich strings with all functions, including the string functions, which are documented in "Utility Functions" (page 26-1). Another data format, described in "Text and Styles" (page 8-25), pairs text strings with style data for viewing in text views.

Caret Insertion Writing Mode

Caret insertion writing mode is a text input mode that the user can enable or disable. When caret insertion mode is disabled, handwritten text is inserted into the view at the location where it is written. When caret insertion writing mode is enabled, handwritten text is inserted at the location indicated by the insertion caret, regardless of where on the screen it is drawn. Caret insertion writing mode is used automatically for keyboard text entry.

To enable or disable caret insertion writing mode, the user selects or deselects the "Insert new words at caret" option from the Text Editing Settings slip. You can display this slip by tapping the Options button in the Recognition Preferences slip.

Applications do not normally need to be aware of whether caret insertion writing mode is enabled or disabled. The one exception to this is at application startup time, when you might want to set the initial location of the insertion point. This is described in "Setting the Caret Insertion Point" (page 8-26).

There are a few caret insertion writing mode routines you can use to implement your own version of this mode. They are described in "Caret Insertion Writing Mode Functions and Methods" (page 7-47) in *Newton Programmer's Reference*.

Fonts for Text and Ink Display

The Newton system software allows you to specify the font characteristics for displaying text and ink in a paragraph view on the screen. The font information is stored in a font specification structure known as a **font spec.** The font specification for built-in ROM fonts can also be represented in a frame as a packed integer. Both of these representations are described in "Using Fonts for Text and Ink Display" (page 8-17).

The system provides a number of functions you can use to access and modify font attributes. These are described in "Text and Styles" (page 8-25).

About Text Views and Protos

There are a number of views and protos to use for displaying text and for receiving text input. For basic information about views, see "Views" (page 3-1).

The views and protos that you use for text are listed in Table 8-1.

Table 8-1   Views and protos for text input and display

View or Proto	Description
edit view	Use the `clEditView` class for basic text input and display. Objects of this class can display and/or accept text and graphic data. The `clEditView` automatically creates child `clParagraphView` views for text input and display and `clPolygonView` views for graphic input and display. You can also include `clPictureView` views in your `clEditViews`. For more information about this class, see "General Input Views" (page 8-6).
paragraph views	Use the `clParagraphView` class to display text or to accept text input. For more information about this class, see "Paragraph Views" (page 8-10).
lightweight paragraph views	If your paragraph view template meets certain criteria, the Newton system automatically creates a lightweight paragraph view for you. Lightweight paragraph views are read-only and use only one font, although they can contain ink. These views require significantly less memory than do standard paragraph views. For more information about lightweight paragraph views, see "Lightweight Paragraph Views" (page 8-11).
input line protos	You can use one of the input line protos to allow the user to enter a single line of text, as described in "Using Input Line Protos" (page 8-12).

About Keyboard Text Input

Your application can provide keyboards and keypads for user text input by creating an object from one of the keyboard view classes or protos:

■ The `clKeyboardView` class provides a keyboard-like array of buttons that the user can tap with the pen to perform an action. This class is described in "Keyboard Views" (page 8-26).

■ Use one of the keyboard protos to create keyboard views in your applications. These protos include the `protoKeyboard`, which creates a keyboard view that floats above all other views. The keyboard protos are also described in "Keyboard Views."

The Keyboard Registry

You need to register any custom keyboards or keypads that you create with the Newton system's keyboard registry. Caret insertion writing mode is used whenever the user enters text from a keyboard or keypad. When a registered keyboard or keypad is opened, the system knows to display the insertion caret at the proper location.

The Newton system also allows you to customize the behavior of the insertion caret and key presses by calling your application-defined methods whenever an action occurs in a registered keyboard or keypad.

For more information about the keyboard registry, see "Using the Keyboard Registry" (page 8-36).

The Punctuation Pop-up Menu

The user can tap the insertion caret to display a Punctuation pop-up menu. This menu, shown in Figure 8-1, provides an easy way to add punctuation when writing with the stylus.

Figure 8-1   The Punctuation pop-up menu

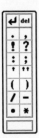

Choosing any item on the Punctuation pop-up menu inserts the appropriate character into the text, at the insertion caret. The bent arrow, at the top left, is a carriage return, and the blank box at the bottom indicates a space.

You can override this menu with your own caret pop-up menu, as described in "The Caret Pop-up Menu" (page 8-38).

Compatibility

One of the significant advances in software functionality in the Newton 2.0 system is the capacity to process ink in most views, which includes deferred recognition and the ability to mix text and ink together in rich string. This expands the behavior provided by Newton 1.x machines, which generally process written input immediately for recognition and display the resulting word in a typeface.

These additional capabilities made it necessary to extend the Recognition menu. The Newton 2.0 Recognition menu adds more input options and replaces the toggling Recognizer buttons of the Newton 1.x status bar.

The Newton 2.0 system also behaves slightly differently when merging text into paragraph views. When caret insertion writing mode is disabled, paragraphs no longer automatically insert carriage returns or tabs. This is true regardless of whether the user is entering text or ink words.

With Newton System 2.0, you can include images in your edit views. Edit views (clEditView) can now contain picture views (`clPictureView`) as child views

Any ink written on a 1.x machine can be dragged into a Newton System 2.0 paragraph and automatically converted into an ink word.

Notes, text, or ink moved from a Newton 1.x to a Newton with the 2.0 system works correctly without any intervention. However, the reverse is not true: you cannot insert a a card with 2.0 or later data into a 1.x machine.

The expando protos have become obsolete. These are `protoExpandoShell`, `protoDateExpando`, `protoPhoneExpando`, and `protoTextExpando`. These protos are still supported for 1.x application compatibility, but should not be used in new applications.

Using Text

This section describes how to use various features of text input and display on the Newton and provides examples of some of these features.

Using Views and Protos for Text Input and Display

This section describes the different views and protos to use in your applications for text input and display.

General Input Views

The `clEditView` view class is used for a view that can display and/or accept text and graphic data. Views of the `clEditView` class contain no data directly;

instead, they have child views that contain the individual data items. Text items are contained in child views of the class clParagraphView and graphics are contained in child views of the class clPolygonView.

A view of the clEditView class includes the following features:

- Automatic creation of clParagraphView or clPolygonView children as the user writes or draws in the view. These child views hold the data the user writes.

- Support for inclusion of clPictureView views, which are used for images.

- Text and shape recognition, selection, and gestures such as scrubbing, copying to clipboard, pasting from clipboard, duplicating, and others, as controlled by the setting of the viewFlags slot. The initial recognition is handled by the clEditView. A child clParagraphView or clPolygonView is created and that child view handles subsequent editing of the data.

- Drag and drop handling. A child view can be dragged (moved or copied) out of the clEditView and dropped into another clEditView, whose child it then becomes. Other views can be configured to handle data dragged from a clEditView, as described in "Views" (page 3-1).

- Clipboard support. A clParagraphView or clPolygonView child view can be dragged (moved or copied) to the clipboard, from which it can be pasted into another clEditView or clView, whose child it becomes.

- Automatic resizing of clParagraphView child views to accommodate added input. This feature is controlled by the vCalculateBounds flag in the viewFlags slot of those child views.

- Automatic addition of new words to existing paragraphs when caret insertion writing mode is disabled.

Views of the class clEditView are intended for user input of text, shape, image, and ink data. Consequently, views of this class expect that any child views have been defined and created at run time, not predefined by templates created in NTK.

If you need to include predefined child views in a clEditView, use the ViewSetupChildrenScript method of the clEditView to define the child views and set up the stepChildren array. You might need to do this, for example, if you store the data for child views in a soup, and you need to retrieve the data and rebuild the child views at run time. For more information, see "Including Editable Child Views in an Input View" (page 8-9).

The default font for a clParagraphView created by a clEditView is the font selected by the user on the Styles palette in the system.

The default pen width for a clPolygonView created by a clEditView is the width set by the user on the Styles palette.

The slots of clEditView are described in "General Input View (clEditView)" (page 7-12) in *Newton Programmer's Reference*.

Here is an example of a template defining a view of the clEditView class:

```
editor := {...
    viewClass: clEditView,
    viewBounds: {left:0, top:0, right:200, bottom:200},
    viewFlags: vVisible+vAnythingAllowed,
    viewFormat: vfFillWhite+vfFrameBlack+vfPen(1)+
                vfLinesLtGray,
    viewLineSpacing: 20,
    // methods and other view-specific slots
    viewSetupFormScript: func()...
...}
```

System Messages in Automatically Created Views

When a child view is automatically created by a clEditView, the vNoScripts flag is set in the viewFlags slot of the child view. This flag prevents system messages from being sent to a view.

This behavior is normally desirable for automatically created views, because they have no system message-handling methods and the system saves time by not sending the messages to them.

If you want to use one of these views in a manner that requires it to receive system messages, you need to remove the vNoScripts flag from the viewFlags slot of the view.

Creating the Lined Paper Effect in a Text View

A view of the clEditView class can appear simply as a blank area in which the user writes information. However, this type of view usually contains a series of horizontal dotted lines, like lined writing paper. The lines indicate to the user that the view accepts input. To create the lined paper effect, you must set the following slots appropriately:

viewFormat   Must include one of the vfLines... flags. This activates the line display.

viewLineSpacing
                 Sets the spacing between the lines, in pixels.

viewLinePattern
                 Optional. Sets a custom pattern that is used to draw the lines in the view. In the viewFormat slot editor in NTK, you must also set the Lines item to Custom to signal that you are using a custom pattern. (This sets the vfCustom<<vfLinesShift flag in the viewFormat slot.)

                 Patterns are binary data structures, which are described in the next section.

Defining a Line Pattern

You can define a custom line pattern for drawing the horizontal lines in a paragraph view. A line pattern is an eight-byte binary data structure with the class 'pattern.

To create a binary pattern data structure on the fly, use the following NewtonScript trick:

```
myPattern := SetClass( Clone("\uAAAAAAAAAAAAAAAA"),
                                        'pattern );
```

This code clones a string, which is already a binary object, and changes its class to 'pattern. The string is specified with hex character codes whose binary representation creates the pattern. Each two-digit hex code creates one byte of the pattern.

Including Editable Child Views in an Input View

For a child view of a clEditView to be editable, you need to follow certain rules:

■ The child view must reside in the viewChildren slot of the clEditView. You cannot store a child view's template in the stepChildren slot, as NTK normally does.

■ The child view must contain a viewStationery slot with an appropriate value, depending on the view class and data type. The acceptable values are shown in Table 8-2:

Table 8-2   viewStationery slot value for clEditView children

View class	View data type	Value of viewStationery slot
clParagraphView	text	'para
clPolygonView	recognized graphics	'poly
clPolygonView	ink	'ink
clPictureView	bitmap or picture object	'pict

■ Add the child view templates to the viewChildren array of the edit view and open the view or send it the RedoChildren message. Alternatively, you can add the child view with the AddView method and then send the Dirty message to the edit view.

IMPORTANT

You store view templates (not view objects) in the
`viewChildren` array of an edit view. ▲

Paragraph Views

The `clParagraphView` class displays text or accepts text input. It includes the following features:

- Text recognition
- Text correction
- Text editing, including scrubbing, selection, copying to the clipboard, pasting from the clipboard, and other gestures, including duplicating, as controlled by the setting of the `viewFlags` slot.
- Automatic word-wrapping.
- Support for the caret gesture, which adds a space or splits a word.
- Clipping of text that won't fit in the view. (An ellipsis is shown to indicate text beyond what is visible.)
- Use of ink and different text fonts (styles) within the same paragraph.
- Tab-stop alignment of text.
- Automatic resizing to accommodate added text (when this view is enclosed in a `clEditView`). This feature is controlled by the `vCalculateBounds` flag in the `viewFlags` slot.
- Automatic addition of new words written near the view when this view is enclosed in a `clEditView` and caret insertion writing mode is disabled.

The slots of `clParagraphView` are described in "Paragraph View (clParagraphView)" (page 7-15) in *Newton Programmer's Reference*.

Note that you don't need to create paragraph views yourself if you are accepting user input inside a `clEditView`. Just provide a `clEditView` and when the user writes in it, the view automatically creates paragraph views to hold text.

The following is an example of a template defining a view of the `clParagraphView` class:

```
dateSample := {...
   viewClass: clParagraphView,
   viewBounds: {left:50, top:50, right:200, bottom:70},
   viewFlags: vVisible+vReadOnly,
   viewFormat: vfFillWhite,
   viewJustify: oneLineOnly,
   text: "January 24, 1994",
```

```
// 8 chars of one font, 3 chars of another, 5 chars
// of another
styles: [8, 18434, 3, 12290, 5, 1060865],
...}
```

Paragraph views are normally lined to convey to the user that the view accepts text input. To add the lined paper effect to paragraph views, see "Creating the Lined Paper Effect in a Text View" (page 8-8).

Lightweight Paragraph Views

When you create a template using the `clParagraphView` class, and that template is instantiated into a view at run time, the system may create a specialized kind of paragraph view object, called a lightweight paragraph view. Lightweight paragraph views have the advantage of requiring much less memory than do standard paragraph views.

The system automatically creates a lightweight paragraph view instead of a standard paragraph view if your template meets the following conditions:

- The view must be read-only, which means that its `viewFlags` slot contains the `vReadOnly` flag.

- The view must not include any tabs, which means that the template does not contain the `tabs` slot.

- The view must not include multiple font styles, which means that the template does not contain the `styles` slot; however, the view can contain a rich string in its `text` slot. For information about rich strings, see "Rich Strings" (page 8-22).

- The `viewFlags` slot of the view must not contain the following flags: `vGesturesAllowed`, `vCalculateBounds`.

Note
Lightweight paragraph views can contain ink. ◆

Most paragraph views look the same after they are instantiated; that is, there is not normally a way to tell whether a particular paragraph view is a standard or a lightweight view. However, ink displayed in a lightweight paragraph view is displayed in a fixed font size.

Note
When laying out text in a lightweight paragraph view, the viewLineSpacing value is ignored. This is not generally a problem, since the line spacing dotted lines are normally used to indicate that the text can be edited, and text in a lightweight paragraph cannot be edited. ◆

Once a lightweight paragraph view has been instantiated, you cannot dynamically change the view flags to make it an editable view, or add multistyled text by providing a `styles` slot, since this type of view object doesn't support these features. If you need this functionality for an existing lightweight paragraph view, you'll have to copy the text out of it into an editable paragraph view.

Using Input Line Protos

Input line protos provide the user with single lines in which to enter data. There are four input line protos available:

- `protoInputLine` is a one-line input field that defines a simple paragraph view in which the text input is left-justified.

- `protoRichInputLine` is the text and ink equivalent of `protoInputLine`.

- `protoLabelInputLine` is a one-line input field that includes a text label and can optionally include a pop-up menu known as a **picker.**

- `protoRichLabelInputLine` is the text and ink equivalent of `protoLabelInputLine`.

protoInputLine

This proto defines a view that accepts any kind of text input and is left-justified. Below is an example of a what a `protoInputLine` looks like on the Newton screen:

The `protoInputLine` is based on a view of the `clParagraphView` class. It has no child views.

The following is an example of a template using `protoInputLine`:

```
myInput := {...
_proto: protoInputLine,
viewJustify: vjParentRightH+vjParentBottomV,
viewLineSpacing: 24,
viewBounds: SetBounds( -55, -33, -3, -3),
...}
```

The slots of the `protoInputLine` are described in "protoInputLine" (page 7-17) in *Newton Programmer's Reference.*

protoRichInputLine

This proto works exactly like `protoInputLine`. The only difference is that `protoRichInputLine` allows mixed ink and text input, as determined by the current user recognition preferences.

The slots of protoRichInputLine are described in "protoRichInputLine" (page 7-19) in *Newton Programmer's Reference*.

protoLabelInputLine

This proto defines a view that features a label, accepts any kind of input, and is left-justified. The protoLabelInputLine can optionally include a picker.

When the protoLabelInputLine does include a picker, the user selects a choice from the picker. That choice is entered as the text in the input line, and is marked with a check mark in the picker.

Figure 8-2 shows an example of a protoLabelInputLine with and without the picker option:

Figure 8-2   An example of a protoLabelInputLine

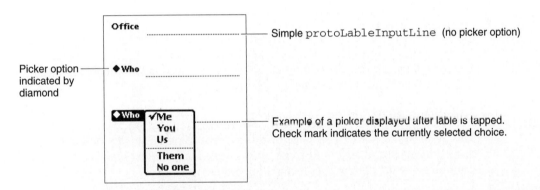

Picker option indicated by diamond

Simple protoLableInputLine (no picker option)

Example of a picker displayed after lable is tapped. Check mark indicates the currently selected choice.

The protoLabelInputLine is based on a view of the clParagraphView class. It has two child views:

■ The labelLine child view uses the protoStaticText proto to create the static text label and to activate the picker if the proto includes one.

■ The entryLine child view uses the protoInputLine proto to create the input field into which the user writes text. The text value entered into this field is stored in the text slot of this view.

You can have your label input line protos remember a list of recent items. To do this, assign a symbol that incorporates your developer signature to the 'memory slot of your prototype. The system automatically maintains the list of recent items for your input line. To access the list, use the same symbol with the AddMemoryItem, AddMemoryItemUnique, GetMemoryItems, and GetMemorySlot functions, which are described in "Utility Functions" (page 26-1).

IMPORTANT

You can programmatically access the value of the `text` slot for
the `protoLabelInputLine` with the expression
`entryLine.text`. If you update the text slot programmatically, you need to call the `SetValue` function to ensure that the
view is updated. Below is an example:

```
SetValue(entryLine, 'text, "new text")]
```

▲

The following is an example of a template using `protoLabelInputLine`:

```
labelLine := {...
_proto: protoLabelInputLine,
viewBounds: {top: 90, left: 42, right: 194, bottom: 114},
label: "Who",
labelCommands: ["Me", "You", "Us", 'pickseparator,
                "Them", "No one"],
curLabelCommand: 0,
...}
```

The slots of the `protoLabelInputLine` are described in "protoLabelInputLine"
(page 7-19) in *Newton Programmer's Reference*.

protoRichLabelInputLine

This proto works exactly like `protoLabelInputLine`. The only difference is
that `protoRichLabelInputLine` allows mixed ink and text input, as
determined by the current user recognition preferences.

The slots of the `protoRichLabelInputLine` are described in
"protoRichLabelInputLine" (page 7-22) in *Newton Programmer's Reference*.

Displaying Text and Ink

In addition to knowing about the views and protos that you can use for displaying
text and ink, you should understand how text and ink are displayed. This involves
the use of fonts, text styles, and rich strings. This section describes these objects
and how you can use them in your applications to control the display of text and ink.

Text and Ink in Views

When the user draws with the pen on the Newton screen, pen input data is captured
as ink, which is also known as sketch ink or raw ink.

What happens with the raw ink depends upon the configuration of the view in
which the input action was performed and the choices that the user made in the

Recognition menu. The view configuration is defined by the view flags and the (optional) recognition configuration (`recConfig`) frame of the view. The Recognition menu is shown in Figure 8-3.

Figure 8-3   The Recognition menu

When the `viewFlags` input flags and the `recConfig` frame of the view are set to accept both text and ink, the Recognition menu choices control what kind of data is inserted into the paragraph view.

Note that you can limit the choices that are available in the Recognition menu of your application, though this is rarely necessary or advisable.

The Recognition menu, recognition view flags, and the recognition configuration frame are described in "Recognition" (page 9-1).

Mixing Text and Ink in Views

Some views require textual input and cannot accept ink words. The recognition controls are not used by these text-only views, in which writing is always recognized and inserted as text. If the user drops an ink word into a text-only field, the ink word is automatically recognized before control returns to the user.

Edit views can handle both ink words and sketch ink. If an edit view receives an ink word, it either merges that word into an existing paragraph view or creates a new view for the ink word. If an edit view receives sketch ink, it creates a polygon view for the ink drawing.

You can also create fields that accepts only ink words. However, if the user types or drops recognized text into such a field, the recognized text remains recognized text.

You can set a paragraph view to accept either text or ink input with the following settings:

```
viewClass: clParagraphView,
   viewFlags:  vVisible + vClipping + vClickable +
               vGesturesAllowed + vCharsAllowed +
               vNumbersAllowed,
   recConfig: rcInkOrText
```

Note
The view flags are described in "Views" (page 3-1). The recognition view flags are described in "Recognition" (page 9-1). ◆

Although raw ink is intended mostly for drawing, the user can still write with raw ink by choosing "Sketches" from the Recognition menu. The recognizer automatically segments raw ink into ink words. The raw ink can subsequently be recognized, using deferred recognition. Unlike ink text, raw ink is not moved or resized after it is written.

When raw ink from a 1.x system is dragged into a paragraph view, each piece of ink is automatically converted into an ink word. This conversion is not reversible.

Note
You can use one of two representations for text and ink that are mixed together. The first and more common representation is as a rich string, as described in "Rich Strings" (page 8-22). The second representation, used in paragraph views, is as a text string with a corresponding series of matching style runs. This representation, which is used for editing operations in paragraph views, is described in "Text and Styles" (page 8-25). ◆

Ink Word Scaling and Styling

Ink words are drawn using the pen thickness that the user specifies in the Styles menu. After the ink words are drawn, they are scaled by the system software. The scaling value is specified in the Text Editing Settings menu, which the user can access by choosing Preferences from the Recognition menu.

The standard values for scaling ink words are 50 percent, 75 percent, and 100 percent. After the system performs scaling, it assigns a font style and size to the ink word. The initial style is plain. The initial size is proportional to the x-height of the ink word, as estimated by the recognizer. This size is defined so that an ink word of a certain size will be roughly the same size as a text word displayed in a font of that size. For example, an ink word of size 12 is drawn at roughly the same size as a text word in a typical 12-point font, as shown in Figure 8-4. The ink words in Figure 8-4 were first scaled to 50 percent of their written size.

Figure 8-4   Resized and recognized ink

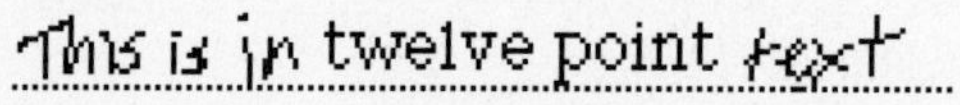

This is in twelve point text

You can modify the size at which ink words are displayed in two ways: by changing the scaling percentage or the font size. For example, suppose that you draw an ink word and the system calculates its font size, as written, at 36 point. If your ink text scaling is set to 50 percent, the ink word is displayed at half of the written size, which makes its font size 18 point. If you subsequently change the scaling of that ink word to 100 percent, its font size changes to 36 point.

If the user applies deferred recognition to the ink words, the recognized text is displayed in the current font family, size, and style, as specified in the Styles menu.

Note
There is a maximum ink word size. Ink words are scaled to the smaller of what would be produced by the selected scaling percentage or the maximum size. ◆

Constraining Font Style in Views

You can override the use of styles in a paragraph view so that all of the text in the paragraph is displayed with a certain font specification. To do this, use the `viewFont` slot of the paragraph view along with two of the text view flags.

If you include `vFixedTextStyle` in the text flags for a paragraph view, all recognized text in the view is displayed using the font family, point size, and character style specified for `viewFont`. This is the normal behavior for input fields.

If you include `vFixedInkTextStyle` in the text flags for a paragraph view, all ink words in the view are displayed using the point size and character style specified for `viewFont`. Note that the font family does not affect the display of ink words.

Note
Using the `vFixedTextStyle` or `vFixedInkTextStyle` flags does not modify the `'styles` slot of the view. However, if you use either of these flags, the system does not allow the user to change the text style for your paragraph view. ◆

The text view flags are described in "Text Flags" (page 7-2) in *Newton Programmer's Reference*.

Using Fonts for Text and Ink Display

Whenever recognized text is drawn on the Newton screen, the system software examines the font specification associated with the text to determine how to draw the text. The font specification includes the font family name, the font style, and the point size for the text. You can specify a font with a font frame or with a packed integer; both of these formats are described in this section.

The constants you can use in font specifications are shown in "Font Constants for Packed Font Integer Specifications" (page 7-4) in *Newton Programmer's Reference*.

The Font Frame

A font frame has the following format:

```
{family: familyName, face: faceNumber, size: pointSize}
```

For *familyName*, you can specify a symbol corresponding to one of the available built-in fonts, which are shown in Table 8-3.

Table 8-3   Font family symbols

Symbol	Font Family
'espy	Espy (system) font
'geneva	Geneva font
'newYork	New York font
'handwriting	Casual (handwriting) font

For *faceNumber*, you can specify a combination of the values shown in Table 8-4:

Table 8-4   Font style (face) values

Constant	Value	Font face
kFaceNormal	0x000	Normal font
kFaceBold	0x001	Bold font
kFaceItalic	0x002	Italic font
kFaceUnderline	0x004	Underline font
kFaceOutline	0x008	Outline font
kFaceSuperScript	0x080	Superscript font
kFaceSubscript	0x100	Subscript font

Note

Apple recommends using the normal, bold, and underline font styles. The other styles do not necessarily display well on Newton screens. ◆

For *pointSize*, use an integer that specifies the point size value.

The Packed Integer Font Specification

You can specify a font in one 30-bit integer. A packed integer font specification uses the lower 10 bits for the font family, the middle 10 bits for the font size, and the upper 10 bits for the font style. Since only the ROM fonts have predefined font family number constants, you can only specify ROM fonts in a packed value.

Using the Built-in Fonts

The system provides several constants you can use to specify one of the built-in fonts. These constants are listed in Table 8-5. The fonts shown in the table can be specified by the constant (usable at compile time only), by their font frame, or by an integer value that packs all of the font information into an integer (sometimes this is what you see at run time if you examine a `viewFont` slot in the NTK Inspector).

Table 8-5   Built-in font constants

Constant	Font frame	Integer value
ROM_fontsystem9	{family:'espy, face:0, size:9}	9216
ROM_fontsystem9bold	{family:'espy, face:1, size:9}	1057792
ROM_fontsystem9underline	{family:'espy, face:4, size:9}	4203520
ROM_fontsystem10	{family:'espy, face:0, size:10}	10240
ROM_fontsystem10bold	{family:'espy, face:1, size:10}	1058816
ROM_fontsystem10underline	{family:'espy, face:4, size:10}	4204544
ROM_fontsystem12	{family:'espy, face:0, size:12}	12288
ROM_fontsystem12bold	{family:'espy, face:1, size:12}	1060864

continued

Table 8-5   Built-in font constants (continued)

Constant	Font frame	Integer value
ROM_fontsystem12underline	{family:'espy, face:4, size:12}	4206592
ROM_fontsystem14	{family:'espy, face:0, size:14}	14336
ROM_fontsystem14bold	{family:'espy, face:1, size:14}	1062912
ROM_fontsystem14underline	{family:'espy, face:4, size:14}	4208640
ROM_fontsystem18	{family:'espy, face:0, size:18}	18432
ROM_fontsystem18bold	{family:'espy, face:1, size:18}	1067008
ROM_fontsystem18underline	{family:'espy, face:4, size:18}	4212736
simpleFont9	{family:'geneva, face:0, size:9}	9218
simpleFont10	{family:'geneva, face:0, size:10}	10242
simpleFont12	{family:'geneva, face:0, size:12}	12290
simpleFont18	{family:'geneva, face:0, size:18}	18434
fancyFont9 or userFont9	{family:'newYork, face:0, size:9}	9217
fancyFont10 or userFont10	{family:'newYork, face:0, size:10}	10241
fancyFont12 or userFont12	{family:'newYork, face:0, size:12}	12289
fancyFont18 or userFont18	{family:'newYork, face:0, size:18}	18433

continued

Table 8-5   Built-in font constants (continued)

Constant	Font frame	Integer value
editFont10	{family:'handwriting, face:0, size:10}	10243
editFont12	{family:'handwriting, face:0, size:12}	12291
editFont18	{family:'handwriting, face:0, size:18}	18435

The integers in Table 8-5 are derived by packing font family, face, and size information into a single integer value. Each NewtonScript integer is 30 bits in length. In packed font specifications, the lower 10 bits hold the font family, the middle 10 bits hold the font size, and the upper 10 bits hold the font style.

These three parts added together specify a single font in one integer value. You can use the constants listed in Table 8-6 at compile time to specify all of the needed information. To do this, add one constant from each category together to yield a complete font specification. At run time, of course, you'll need to use the integer values.

Table 8-6   Font packing constants

Constant	Value	Description
Font Family		
(none defined)	0	Identifies the System font (Espy)
tsFancy	1	Identifies the New York font
tsSimple	2	Identifies the Geneva font
tsHWFont	3	Identifies the Casual (Handwriting) font
Font Size		
tsSize (*pointSize*)	*pointSize* << 10	Specify the point size of the font in *pointSize*
Font Face		
tsPlain	0	Normal font
tsBold	1048576	Bold font

continued

Table 8-6   Font packing constants (continued)

Constant	Value	Description
tsItalic	2097152	Italic font
tsUnderline	4194304	Underlined normal font
tsOutline	8388608	Outline font
tsSuperScript	134217728	Superscript font
tsSubScript	268435456	Subscript font

Note that the "Casual" font uses the symbol `'handwriting` for its font family.

You can use the `MakeCompactFont` function at runtime to create a packed integer value from a specification of the font family, font size, and font face. You can only specify ROM fonts with the packed integer format. Here is an example:

```
fontValue := MakeCompactFont('tsSimple, 12, tsItalic)
```

If the font specified by the three parameters does not belong to a ROM font family, `MakeCompactFont` returns a font frame instead.

The `MakeCompactFont` function is described in "MakeCompactFont" (page 7-28) in *Newton Programmer's Reference*.

Rich Strings

Rich strings store text strings and ink in a single string. If you application supports user-input text or ink, you can use rich strings to represent all user data. You can convert between the text and styles pairs in paragraph views and rich strings. Text and styles pair are described in "Text and Styles" (page 8-25).

Rich strings are especially useful for storing text with embedded ink in a soup. You can use the rich string functions, described in "Rich String Functions" (page 8-24), to work with rich strings.

The system software automatically handles rich strings properly, including their use in performing the following operations:

- screen display

- sorting and indexing

- concatenation with standard functions such as `StrConcat` and `ParamStr`, described in "Utility Functions" (page 26-1)

- measuring

Important Rich String Considerations

Although the Newton system software allows you to use rich strings anywhere that plain strings are used, there are certain considerations to be aware of when using rich strings. These include:

■ Do not use functions that are not rich-string-aware. These include the `Length`, `SetLength`, `BinaryMunger`, and `StuffXXX` functions.

■ Use the `StrLen` function to find the length of a string.

■ Use the `StrMunger` function to perform operations that modify the length of a string, such as appending or deleting characters.

■ Do not assume that the rich string terminator character is the last character in a rich string object.

■ Do not truncate a rich string by inserting a string terminator character into the string.

■ Do not assign characters into a rich string, due to the presence of ink placeholder characters. Use the `SetChar` function instead of direct assignment.

■ Do not use undocumented string functions, which are not guaranteed to work with rich strings.

Using the Rich String Storage Format

Ink data is embedded in rich strings by inserting a placeholder character in the string for each ink word. Data for each ink word is stored following the string terminator character.

Each ink word is represented in the text portion of the rich string by the special character `kInkChar` (`0xF700`), which is a reserved Unicode character value.

The ink data for all ink words in the string follows the string terminator character. The final 32 bits in a rich string encode information about the rich string.

Note

The string in the `'text` slot of a paragraph view uses the `kParaInkChar` (`0xF701`) character as a placeholder character instead of the `kInkChar` code. The `'text` slot string is not a rich string but might contain ink word placeholders. See "Text and Styles" (page 8-25) for more information. ◆

Automatic Conversion of Rich Strings

Text is automatically converted from the rich string format to a text/styles pair whenever a paragraph is opened and the `SetValue` function is called with a rich string.

When a paragraph view is opened, the `'text` slot is first examined to determine whether or not the text contains any embedded ink. If so, new versions of the view's `'text` and `'styles` slots are generated and placed in the context frame of the view.

When `SetValue` is called with a string parameter that is a rich string, it is automatically decoded into a text and style pair. The result is stored in the view frame of the paragraph view.

Rich String Functions

You can use the rich string functions to convert and work with rich strings. Each of these functions, shown in Table 8-7, is described in "Rich String Functions and Methods" (page 7-31) in *Newton Programmer's Reference*.

Table 8-7   Rich string functions

Function or method name	Description
MakeRichString	Converts the data from two slots into a rich string. MakeRichString uses the text from the `'text` slot of the view and the `styles` array from the `'styles` slot of the view.
DecodeRichString	Converts a rich string into a frame containing a `'text` slot and a `'styles` slot. These slots can be placed in a paragraph view for editing or viewing.
ExtractRangeAsRichString	Returns a rich string for a range of text from a paragraph view.
IsRichString	Determines if a string is a rich string (i.e., contains ink).
view:GetRichString	Returns the text from a paragraph view as a rich string or plain string, depending on whether the paragraph view contains any ink.
StripInk	Strips any ink from a rich string. Either removes the ink words or replaces each with a specified replacement character or string.

Text and Styles

Within a paragraph view, text is represented in two slots: the 'text slot and the 'styles slot. The 'text slot contains the sequence of text characters in the paragraph, including an instance of the kParaInkChar placeholder character (0xF701) for each ink word.

The 'styles slot specifies how each **text run** is displayed in the paragraph. A text run is a sequence of characters that are all displayed with the same font specification. The 'styles slot consists of an array of alternating length and style information: one length value and one style specification for each text run. For ink words, the length value is always 1, and the style specification is a binary object that contains the ink data.

For example, consider the paragraph text shown in Figure 8-5.

Figure 8-5   A paragraph view containing an ink word and text

Try ~~this~~ one

In the paragraph view shown in Figure 8-5, the 'text slot contains the following sequence of Unicode characters:

```
'T' 'r' 'y' ' ' 0xF701 'o' 'n' 'e'
```

The 'styles slot for this paragraph consists of the following array:

```
styles: [4, 12289,   1, <inkData, length 42>, 4, 12289]
```

The first pair of values in the array, (4, 12289), covers the word "Try" and the space that follows it. The length value, 4, specifies that the text run consists of four characters. The packed integer font specification value 12289 specifies plain, 12-point, New York.

The second pair of values in the array, (1, inkData), covers the ink word. The length value is 1, which is always the case for ink words. The value inkData is a binary object that contains the compressed data for the handwritten "this" that is part of the text in the paragraph view. The data is automatically extracted from the tablet data as part of a preliminary recognition process that precedes word recognition.

The third and final pair of values in the 'styles slot array, (4, 12289), covers the word "one" and the space that precedes it. This text run is 4 characters long and is displayed 12 points high in the plain version of the New York font family.

Note
The packed integer font specification values
are shown in Table 8-6 (page 8-21). ◆

Setting the Caret Insertion Point

When you application starts up, you might want to establish the insertion point for keyboard entry in caret insertion writing mode. There are three functions that you can use for this purpose:

- to establish the insertion point in an input field, use the `SetKeyView` function, which is described in "SetKeyView" (page 7-43) in *Newton Programmer's Reference*.

- to establish the insertion point in an edit view, use the `PositionCaret` function, which is described in "PositionCaret" (page 7-49) in *Newton Programmer's Reference*.

- to establish the insertion point in an edit view or paragraph, you can use the `SetCaretInfo` function, which is described in "SetCaretInfo" (page 7-50) in *Newton Programmer's Reference*.

Using Keyboards

You can provide the user with on-screen keyboard input in your applications using the built-in keyboard views. You can also define new keyboard views and register them with the system, which will activate caret input when these views are opened.

Keyboard Views

There are four different floating keyboards built into the system root view. Each of the built-in keyboards can be accessed as a child of the root with a symbol.

To use the full alphanumeric keyboard, which is shown in Figure 8-6, use the symbol `'alphaKeyboard`.

Figure 8-6   The built-in alphanumeric keyboard

Text and Ink Input and Display

To use the numeric keyboard, which is shown in Figure 8-7, use the symbol
`'numericKeyboard`.

Figure 8-7 The built-in numeric keyboard

To use the phone keyboard, which is shown in Figure 8-8, use the symbol
`'phoneKeyboard`.

Figure 8-8 The built-in phone keyboard

To use the time and date keyboard, which is shown in Figure 8-9, use the symbol
`'dateKeyboard`.

Figure 8-9 The built-in time and date keyboard

An on-screen keyboard can be opened by the user with a double tap on an input
field. The kind of keyboard displayed is determined by what type of input field is
recognized. For example, a field in which only numbers are recognized would use
the numeric keyboard. The user can also open a keyboard from the corrector
pop-up list, which appears when you correct a recognized word.

If you want to open one of these keyboards programmatically, use code like the following to send it the Open message:

```
Getroot().alphaKeyboard:Open()
```

The keystrokes entered by the user are sent to the current key receiver view. There can be only one key receiver at a time, and only views of the classes clParagraphView and clEditView can be key receiver views. When a keyboard is open, a caret is shown in the key receiver view at the location where characters will be inserted.

The keyboard views are based on clKeyboardView, which is described in "Keyboard View (clKeyboardView)" (page 7-35) in *Newton Programmer's Reference*.

Using Keyboard Protos

The keyboard protos to provide users of your applications with on-screen keyboards with which to enter text. The following keyboard protos are available:

- protoKeyboard provides a standard keyboard view that floats above all other views.

- protoKeypad allows you to define a customized floating keyboard.

- protoKeyboardButton includes a keyboard button in a view.

- protoSmallKeyboardButton includes a small keyboard button in a view.

- protoAlphaKeyboard provides an alphanumeric keyboard that you can include in a view.

- protoNumericKeyboard provides a numeric keyboard that you can include in a view.

- protoPhoneKeyboard provides a phone keyboard that you can include in a view.

- protoDateKeyboardButton provides a time and date keyboard that you can include in a view.

protoKeyboard

This proto creates a keyboard view that floats above all other views. It is centered within its parent view and appears in a location that won't obscure the key-receiving view (normally, the view to which the keystrokes from the keyboard are to be sent). The user can drag the keyboard view by its drag-dot to a different location, if desired. Figure 8-10 shows an example of what a protoKeyboard looks like on the screen.

Figure 8-10   An example of a `protoKeyboard`

This proto enables the caret (if it is not already visible) in the key-receiving view while the keyboard is displayed. Characters corresponding to tapped keys are inserted in the key-receiving view at the insertion bar location. The caret is disabled when the keyboard view is closed.

This proto is used in conjunction with `protoKeypad` to implement a floating keyboard. The `protoKeyboard` proto defines the parent view, and `protoKeypad` is a child view that defines the key characteristics.

protoKeypad

This proto defines key characteristics for a keyboard view (`clKeyboardView` class). It also contains functionality that automatically registers an open keyboard view with the system. If you want to get this behavior in your custom keyboard, use `protoKeypad`.

You use this proto along with `protoKeyboard` to implement a floating keyboard. The view using the `protoKeypad` proto should be a child of the view using the `protoKeyboard` proto.

protoKeyboardButton

This proto is used to include the keyboard button in a view. This is the same keyboard button shown on the status bar in the notepad. Tapping the button causes the on-screen keyboard to appear. If the keyboard is already displayed, a picker listing available keyboard types is displayed. The user can tap one to open that keyboard.

Figure 8-11 shows an example of the keyboard button.

Figure 8-11   The keyboard button

protoSmallKeyboardButton

This proto is used to include a small keyboard button in a view. Tapping the button causes the on-screen keyboard to appear. If the keyboard is already displayed, a picker listing available keyboard types is displayed. The user can tap one to open that keyboard.

Figure 8-12 shows an example of the small keyboard button.

Figure 8-12   The small keyboard button

protoAlphaKeyboard

This proto is used to include an alphanumeric keyboard in a view. This is the same as the `'alphaKeyboard` keyboard view provided in the root view, as described in "Keyboard Views" (page 8-26). An example of `protoAlphaKeyboard` is shown in Figure 8-6 (page 8-26).

protoNumericKeyboard

This proto is used to include a numeric keyboard in a view. This is the same as the `'numericKeyboard` keyboard view provided in the root view, as described in "Keyboard Views" (page 8-26). An example of `protoNumericKeyboard` is shown in Figure 8-7 (page 8-27).

protoPhoneKeyboard

This proto is used to include a phone keyboard in a view. This is the same as the `'phoneKeyboard` keyboard view provided in the root view, as described in "Keyboard Views" (page 8-26). An example of `protoPhoneKeyboard` is shown in Figure 8-8 (page 8-27).

protoDateKeyboard

This proto is used to include a time and date keyboard in a view. This is the same as the `'dateKeyboard` keyboard view provided in the root view, as described in "Keyboard Views" (page 8-26). An example of `protoDateKeyboard` is shown in Figure 8-9 (page 8-27).

Defining Keys in a Keyboard View

When you define a keyboard view, you need to specify the appearance and behavior of each key in the keyboard. This section presents the definition of an example keyboard view, which is shown in Figure 8-13 (page 8-31).

The Key Definitions Array

Each keyboard view contains a key definitions array, which determines the layout of the individual keys in the keyboard. The key definitions array is an array of rows. Each row is an array of values that looks like this:

```
row0 := [ rowHeight, rowMaxKeyHeight,
    key0Legend, key0result, key0Descriptor,
    key1Legend, key1result, key1Descriptor,
    key2Legend, key2result, key2Descriptor,
    . . .
    ]
```

The first two elements describe the height to allot for the row (*rowHeight*) and the height of the tallest key in the row (*rowMaxKeyHeight*), in key units. These two measurements are often the same, but they may differ. Key units are described in "Key Dimensions" (page 8-35).

Next in the row array is a series of three elements for each key in the row:

■ *keyLegend*

■ *keyResult*

■ *keyDescriptor*

These values are described in the following sections.

Figure 8-13 shows the example keyboard view that is used to explain key definition in this section.

Figure 8-13   A generic keyboard view

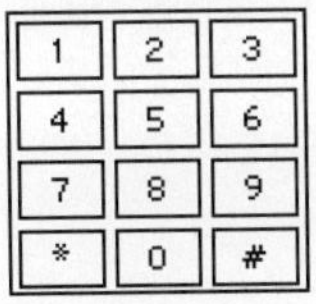

The following is the view definition of the keyboard shown in Figure 8-13. The values in the row arrays are explained in the remainder of this section.

```
row0 := [ keyVUnit, keyVUnit,
 "1",1, keyHUnit+keyVUnit+keyFramed+2*keyInsetUnit+keyAutoHilite,
 "2",2, keyHUnit+keyVUnit+keyFramed+2*keyInsetUnit+keyAutoHilite
 "3",3, keyHUnit+keyVUnit+keyFramed+2*keyInsetUnit+keyAutoHilite ];
```

```
row1 := [ keyVUnit, keyVUnit,
  "4",4,  keyHUnit+keyVUnit+keyFramed+2*keyInsetUnit+keyAutoHilite,
  "5",5,  keyHUnit+keyVUnit+keyFramed+2*keyInsetUnit+keyAutoHilite,
  "6",6,  keyHUnit+keyVUnit+keyFramed+2*keyInsetUnit+keyAutoHilite ];

row2 := [ keyVUnit, keyVUnit,
  "7",7,  keyHUnit+keyVUnit+keyFramed+2*keyInsetUnit+keyAutoHilite,
  "8",8,  keyHUnit+keyVUnit+keyFramed+2*keyInsetUnit+keyAutoHilite,
  "9",9,  keyHUnit+keyVUnit+keyFramed+2*keyInsetUnit+keyAutoHilite ];

row3 := [ keyVUnit, keyVUnit,
  "*",$*,  keyHUnit+keyVUnit+keyFramed+2*keyInsetUnit+keyAutoHilite,
  "0",0,  keyHUnit+keyVUnit+keyFramed+2*keyInsetUnit+keyAutoHilite,
  "#",$#,  keyHUnit+keyVUnit+keyFramed+2*keyInsetUnit+keyAutoHilite ];

keypad := {...
    viewClass: clKeyboardView,
    viewBounds: {left:65, top:65, right:153, bottom:145},
    viewFlags: vVisible+vClickable+vFloating,
    viewFormat: vfFrameBlack+vfFillWhite+vfPen(1),
    keyDefinitions: [ row0, row1, row2, row3 ],  // defined above
    keyPressScript: func (key)
        begin
        Print("You pressed " & key);
        end,
...}
```

The Key Legend

The key legend specifies what appears on the keycap. It can be one of the following types of data:

- ▪ nil, in which case the key result is used as the legend.

- ▪ A string, which is displayed centered in the keycap.

- ▪ A character constant, which is displayed centered in the keycap.

- ▪ A bitmap object, which is displayed centered in the keycap.

- ▪ An integer. The number is displayed centered in the keycap and is used directly as the key result, unless the keyResultsAreKeycodes slot is set to true, as described in the next section.

- ▪ A method. The method is evaluated and its result is treated as if it had been specified as the legend.

■ An array. An element of the array is selected and treated as one of the above data types. The index of the array element is determined by the value of the `keyArrayIndex` slot (which can be changed dynamically). Note that arrays of arrays are not allowed here, but an array can include any combination of other data types.

The Key Result

The key result is the value returned when the key is pressed. This value is passed as a parameter to the `keyPressScript` method. If this method doesn't exist, the result is converted (if possible) into a sequence of characters that are posted as key events to the key receiver view.

The key result element can be one of the following types of data:

■ A string, character constant, or bitmap object, which is simply returned.

■ An integer, which is returned. Alternately, if the `keyResultsAreKeycodes` slot is set to `true`, the integer is treated as a key code. In this case, the character corresponding to the specified key code is returned. If you are using keycodes, make sure to register your keyboard by including the `kKbdUsesKeycodes` view flag.

See Figure 8-14 (page 8-34) for the numeric key codes returned by each of the keys on a keyboard.

■ A method. The method is evaluated and its result is treated as if it had been specified as the result.

■ An array. An element of the array is selected and treated as one of the above data types. The index of the array element is determined by the value of the `keyArrayIndex` slot (which can be changed dynamically). Note that arrays of arrays are not allowed, but an array can include any combination of other data types.

Figure 8-14   Keyboard codes

The Key Descriptor

The appearance of each key in a keyboard is determined by its key descriptor. The key descriptor is a 30-bit value that determines the key size, framing, and other characteristics. The descriptor is specified by combining any of the constants shown in Table 8-8.

Table 8-8   Key descriptor constants

`keySpacer`	Nothing is drawn in this space; it is a spacer, not a key.
`keyAutoHilite`	Highlight this key when it is pressed.
`keyInsetUnit`	Inset this key's frame a certain number of pixels within its space. Multiply this constant by the number of pixels you want to inset, from 0–7 (for example, `keyInsetUnit*3`).

continued

Table 8-8   Key descriptor constants (continued)

`keyFramed`	Specify the thickness of the frame around the key. Multiply this constant by the number of pixels that you want to use for the frame thickness, from 0-3.
`keyRoundingUnit`	Specify the roundedness of the frame corners. Multiply this constant by the number of pixels that you want to use for the corner radius, from 0-15, zero being square.
`keyLeftOpen`	No frame line is drawn along the left side of this key.
`keyTopOpen`	No frame line is drawn along the top side of this key.
`keyRightOpen`	No frame line is drawn along the right side of this key.
`keyBottomOpen`	No frame line is drawn along the bottom side of this key.

`keyHUnit`
`keyHHalf`
`keyHQuarter`
`keyHEighth`
	A combination of these four constants specifies the horizontal dimension of the key in units. For details, see the next section.

`keyVUnit`
`keyVHalf`
`keyVQuarter`
`keyVEighth`
	A combination of these four constants specifies the vertical dimension of the key in units. For details, see the next section.

Key Dimensions

The width and height of keys are specified in units, not pixels. A key unit is not a fixed size, but is used to specify the size of a key relative to other keys. The width of a unit depends on the total width of all keys in the view and on the width of the view itself. Key widths and heights can be specified in whole units, half units, quarter units, and eighth units.

When it is displayed, the whole keyboard is scaled to fit entirely within whatever size view bounds you specify for it.

To fit the whole keyboard within the width of a view, the total unit widths are summed for each row, and the scaling is determined based on the widest row. This row is scaled to fit within the view width, giving an equal pixel width to each whole key unit. A similar process is used to scale keys vertically to fit within the height of a view.

Fractional key units (half, quarter, eighth), when scaled, must be rounded to an integer number of pixels, and thus may not be exactly the indicated fraction of a whole key unit. For example, if the keys are scaled to fit in the view bounds, a whole key unit ends up to be 13 pixels wide. This means that a key specified to have a width of 1 3/8 units (`keyHUnit+keyHEighth*3`) is rounded to 13 + 5, or 18 pixels, which is not exactly 1 3/8 *13.

Key dimensions are specified by summing a combination of horizontal and vertical key unit constants within the keyDescriptor. For example, to specify a key that is 2 3/4 units wide by 1 1/2 units high, specify these constants for keyDescriptor:

```
keyHUnit*2 + keyHQuarter*3 + keyVUnit + keyVHalf
```

Using the Keyboard Registry

If your application includes its own keyboard, you need to register it with the system keyboard registry. This makes it possible for the system to call any keyboard-related functions that you have defined and to handle the insertion caret properly.

The RegisterOpenKeyboard method of a view is for registering a keyboard for use with that view.

Use the UnregisterOpenKeyboard method of a view to remove the keyboard view from the registry. If the insertion caret is visible, calling this method hides it.

Note
The system automatically unregisters the keyboard when the registered view is hidden or closed. The protokeypad proto also automatically handles registration for you in its viewSetupDoneScript. You do not need to call the UnregisterOpenKeyboard method in these cases. ◆

You can use the OpenKeypadFor function to open a context-sensitive keyboard for a view. This function first attempts to open the keyboard defined in the view's _keyboard slot. If the view does not define a keyboard in that slot, OpenKeypadFor determines if the view allows only a single type of input, such as date, time, phone number, or numbers. If so, OpenKeypadFor opens the appropriate built-in keyboard for that input type. If none of these other conditions is met, OpenKeypadFor opens the alphaKeyboard keyboard for the view.

Note
The Newton System Software uses the OpenKeypadFor function to open a context-sensitive keyboard when the user double-taps on a view in which a _keyboard slot is defined. ◆

Theses methods and functions, as well as several others you can use with the keyboard registry in your applications, are described in "Keyboard Registry Functions and Methods" (page 7-44) in *Newton Programmer's Reference*.

Defining Tabbing Orders

You can define the tabbing order for an input view with the _tabChildren slot, which contains an array of view paths.

Each view path must specify the actual view that accepts the input. An example of a suitable path is shown here:

```
'myInputLine, 'myLabelInputLine.entryLine
```

When the user tabs through this list, it loops from end to beginning and, with reverse-tabbing, from beginning to end.

You can use the _tabParent slot to inform the system that you want tabbing in a view restricted to that view. Each view in which _tabParent is non-nil defines a tabbing context. This makes it possible to have several views on the screen at once with independent tabbing within each view. In this case, the user must tap in another view to access the tabbing order in that view.

For example, in Figure 8-15, there are two independent tabbing orders. The first consists of the input lines that contain the text "One," "Two," "Three," and "Four". The second tabbing order consists of the input lines that contain the text "Five" and "Six."

Figure 8-15   Independent tabbing orders within a parent view

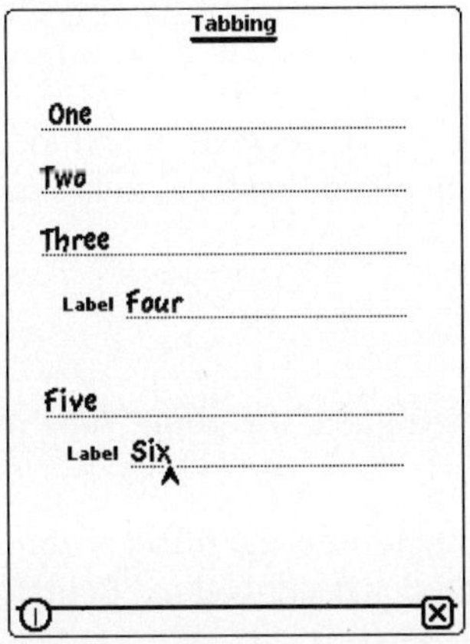

The user taps in any of the top four slots; thereafter, pressing the tab key on a keypad or external keyboard moves among the four slots in that tabbing order. If the user taps one of the bottom two slots, the tab key jumps between those two slots.

The slots _tabParent and _tabChildren can coexist in a view, but the _tabChildren slot takes precedence in specifying the next key view. If the current view does not define the _tabParent slot, the search moves upward from the current view until one of the following conditions is met:

■ a view descended from protoInputLine with a _tabParent slot is found.

■ a protofloater view is found

■ a view descended from `protoInputLine` with the `vApplication` flag set in the `viewFlags` slot

The Caret Pop-up Menu

Normally, when the user taps the insertion caret, the system-provided Punctuation pop-up Menu opens. However, you can override this with a pop-up menu of your own creation.

When the user taps the insertion caret, the system starts searching for a slot named `_caretPopup`. The search begins in the view owning the caret, and follows both the proto and parent inheritance paths. The default Punctuation pop-up is stored in the root view.

The `_caretPopup` slot must hold a frame containing two slots. The first slot, `pop`, defines a list of pop-up items suitable for passing to `DoPopup`. The second slot must contain a `pickActionScript`. If not, control passes to the punctuation pop-up, which has its own version of the `pickActionScript`. This routine then inserts a string, corresponding to the selected character at the caret, by using the function `PostKeyString`.

Handling Input Events

You sometimes need to respond to input events that occur in text views. This section describes how to test for a selection hit and respond to keystrokes and insertion events.

Testing for a Selection Hit

After the user taps the screen, you can determine if the point "hits" a specific character or word in a paragraph view.

The `view:PointToCharOffset` method returns the offset within the paragraph that is closest to the point (*x, y*). This method is described in "PointToCharOffset" (page 7-51) in *Newton Programmer's Reference*.

The `view:PointToWord` method returns a frame that indicates the position of the word within the paragraph that is closest to the point (*x, y*). This method is described in "PointToWord" (page 7-52) in *Newton Programmer's Reference*.

Note
Both of these functions return `nil` if the view is not a paragraph view. Also, the point you are testing must correspond to a visible position within the paragraph view; you cannot hit-test on off-screen portions of a view. ◆

Summary of Text

Text Constants and Data Structures

Text Flags

`vWidthIsParentWidth`	`(1 << 0)`
`vNoSpaces`	`(1 << 1)`
`vWidthGrowsWithText`	`(1 << 2)`
`vFixedTextStyle`	`(1 << 3)`
`vFixedInkTextSTyle`	`(1 << 4)`
`vExpectingNumbers`	`(1 << 9)`

Font Family Constants for Use in Frames

```
'espy
'geneva
'newYork
'handwriting
```

Font Face Constants for Use in Frames

`kFaceNormal`	`0x000`
`kFaceBold`	`0x001`
`kFaceItalic`	`0x002`
`kFaceUnderline`	`0x004`
`kFaceOutline`	`0x008`
`kFaceSuperScript`	`0x0080`
`kFaceSubScript`	`0x100`

Built-in Font Constants

`ROM_fontsystem9`	`9216`
`ROM_fontsystem9bold`	`1057792`
`ROM_fontsystem9underline`	`4203520`
`ROM_fontsystem10`	`10240`
`ROM_fontsystem10bold`	`1058816`

```
ROM_fontsystem10underline      4204544
ROM_fontsystem12              12288
ROM_fontsystem12bold          1060864
ROM_fontsystem12underline      4206592
ROM_fontsystem14              14336
ROM_fontsystem14bold          1062912
ROM_fontsystem14underline      4208640
ROM_fontsystem18              18432
ROM_fontsystem18bold          1067008
ROM_fontsystem18underline      4212736


simpleFont9                   9218
simpleFont10                  10242
simpleFont12                  12290
simpleFont18                  18434


fancyFont9 or
userFont9                     9217
fancyFont10 or
userFont10                    10241
fancyFont12 or
userFont12                    12289
fancyFont18 or
userFont18                    18433


editFont10                    10243
editFont12                    12291
editFont18                    18435
```

Font Family Constants for Packed Integer Font Specifications

```
tsFancy                       1
tsSimple                      2
tsHWFont                      3
```

Font Face Constants for Packed Integer Font Specifications

tsPlain	0
tsBold	1048576
tsItalic	2097152
tsUnderline	4194304
tsOutline	8388608
tsSuperScript	134217728
tsSubScript	268435456

Keyboard Registration Constants

kKbdUsesKeyCodes	1
kKbdTracksCaret	2
kKbdforInput	4

Key Descriptor Constants

keySpacer	(1 << 29)
keyAutoHilite	(1 << 28)
keyInsetUnit	(1 << 25)
keyFramed	(1 << 23)
keyRoundingUnit	(1 << 20)
keyLeftOpen	(1 << 19)
keyTopOpen	(1 << 18)
keyRightOpen	(1 << 17)
keyBottomOpen	(1 << 16)
keyHUnit	(1 << 11)
keyHHalf	(1 << 10)
keyHQuarter	(1 << 9)
keyHEighth	(1 << 8)
keyVUnit	(1 << 3)
keyVHalf	(1 << 2)
keyVQuarter	(1 << 1)
keyVEighth	(1 << 0)

Keyboard Modifier Keys

```
kIsSoftKeyboard          (1 << 24)
kCommandModifier         (1 << 25)
kShiftModifier           (1 << 26)
kCapsLockModifier        (1 << 27)
kOptionsModifier         (1 << 28)
kControlModifier         (1 << 29)
```

Views

clEditView

```
aClEditView:= {
viewBounds:              boundsFrame,
viewFlags:               constant,
viewFormat:              formatFlags,
viewLineSpacing:         integer,
viewLinePattern:         integer,

view:EditAddWordScript(form, bounds)
NotesText(childArray)
...
}
```

clParagraphView

```
aClEditView:= {
viewBounds:              boundsFrame,
viewFont:                fontFrame,
text:                    string,
viewFlags:               constant,
viewFormat:              formatFlags,
viewJustify:             constant,
tabs:                    array,        // tab stops
styles:                  array,        // style runs
textFlags:               constant,
copyProtection:          constant,
...
}
```

clKeyboardView

```
aClEditView:= {
_noRepeat:              constant,
viewBounds:             boundsFrame,
keyDefinitions:         array,      // defines key layout
viewFlags:              constant,
viewFormat:             constant,
keyArrayIndex:          array,      // key legends
keyHighlightKeys:       array,      // keys to highlight
keyResultsAreKeycodes:  Boolean,
keyReceiverView:        view,       // view for keystrokes
keySound:               soundFrame,
keyPressScript:         function
...
}
```

Protos

protoInputLine

```
aprotoInputLine:= {
_proto : protoInputLine,
viewBounds:             boundsFrame,
viewFlags:              constant,
text:                   string,
viewFont:               constant,
viewJustify:            constant,
viewFormat:             constant,
viewTransferMode:       constant,
viewLineSpacing:        integer,
viewLinePattern:        binary,     // 8-byte pattern
memory:                 symbol,

viewChangedScript:      function.
...
}
```

protoRichInputLine

```
aprotoRichInputLine:= {
_proto : protoRichInputLine,
viewBounds:             boundsFrame,
viewFlags:              constant,
```

```
text:                     string,
viewFont:                 constant,
viewJustify:              constant,
viewFormat:               constant,
viewTransferMode:         constant,
viewLineSpacing:          integer,
viewLinePattern:          binary,      // 8-byte pattern
memory:                   symbol,

viewChangedScript:        function,
...
}
```

protoLabelInputLine

```
aprotoLabelInputLine:= {
_proto : protoLabelInputLine,
viewBounds:               boundsFrame,
entryFlags:               constant,
label:                    string,
labelFont:                constant,
labelCommands:            array,       // strings for list
curLabelCommand:          integer,
indent:                   integer,
viewLineSpacing:          integer,
viewLinePattern:          binary,      // 8-byte pattern

textSetup:                function,
updateText:               function,
textChanged:              function,
setLabelText:             function,
setLabelCommands:         function,
labelClick:               function,
labelActionScript:        function,
...
}
```

protoRichLabelInputLine

```
aprotoRichLabelInputLine:= {
_proto : protoRichLabelInputLine,
viewBounds:               boundsFrame,
entryFlags:               constant,
label:                    string,
```

```
labelFont:              constant,
labelCommands:          array,      // strings for list
curLabelCommand:        integer,
indent:                 integer,
viewLineSpacing:        integer,
viewLinePattern:        binary,     // 8-byte pattern

textSetup:              function,
updateText:             function,
textChanged:            function,
setLabelText:           function,
setLabelCommands:       function,
labelClick:             function,
labelActionScript:      function,
...
}
```

protoKeyboard

```
aprotoKeyboard:= {
_proto : protoKeyboard,
saveBounds:             boundsFrame,
freeze:                 Boolean,
...
}
```

protoKeypad

```
aprotoKeypad:= {
_proto : protoKeypad,
keyDefinitions:         array,      // defines key layout
viewFont:               constant,
viewFormat:             constant,
keyArrayIndex:          integer,
keyHighlightKeys:       Boolean,
keyResultsAreKeycodes:  Boolean,
keyReceiverView:        constant,
keySound:               constant,
keyPressScript:         function,
...
}
```

protoKeyboardButton

```
aprotoKeyboardButton:= {
_proto : protoKeyboardButton,
viewFlags:              constant,
viewBounds:             boundsFrame,
viewJustify:            constant,
defaultKeyboard         symbol,
...
}
```

protoSmallKeyboardButton

```
aprotoSmallKeyboardButton:= {
_proto : protoSmallKeyboardButton,
viewFlags:              constant,
viewBounds:             boundsFrame,
viewJustify:            constant,
current:                symbol,
...
}
```

protoAlphaKeyboard

```
aprotoAlphaKeyboard:= {
_proto : protoAlphaKeyboard,
viewBounds:             boundsFrame,
viewJustify:            constant,
...
}
```

protoNumericKeyboard

```
aprotoNumericKeyboard:= {
_proto : protoNumericKeyboard,
viewBounds:             boundsFrame,
viewJustify:            constant,
...
}
```

protoPhoneKeyboard

```
aprotoPhoneKeyboard:= {
_proto : protoPhoneKeyboard,
viewBounds:              boundsFrame,
viewJustify:             constant,
...
}
```

protoDateKeyboard

```
aprotoDateKeyboard:= {
_proto : protoDateKeyboard,
viewBounds:              boundsFrame,
viewJustify:             constant,
...
}
```

Text and Ink Display Functions and Methods

This section summarizes the functions and methods you can use to work with text and ink in your applications.

Functions and Methods for Edit Views

*view:*EditAddWordScript (*form, bounds*)
NotesText (*childArray*)

Functions and Methods for Measuring Text Views

TextBounds (*rStr, fontSpec, viewBounds*)
TotalTextBounds (*paraSpec, editSpec*)

Functions and Methods for Determining View Ink Types

AddInk (*edit, poly*)
ViewAllowsInk (*view*)
ViewAllowsInkWords (*view*)

Font Attribute Functions and Methods

FontAscent (*fontSpec*)
FontDescent (*fontSpec*)
FontHeight (*fontSpec*)
FontLeading (*fontSpec*)
GetFontFace(*fontSpec*)
GetFontFamilyNum(*fontSpec*)
GetFontFamilySym(*fontSpec*)
GetFontSize(*fontSpec*)
MakeCompactFont(*family, size, face*)
SetFontFace(*fontSpec, newFace*)
SetFontFamily(*fontSpec, newFamily*)
SetFontParms (*fontSpec, whichParms*)
SetFontSize(*fontSpec, newSize*)

Rich String Functions and Methods

DecodeRichString(*richString, defaultFontSpec*)
*view:*ExtractRangeAsRichString(*offset, length*)
*view:*GetRichString()
IsRichString(*testString*)
MakeRichString(*text, styleArray*)
StripInk(*richString, replaceString*)

Functions and Methods for Accessing Ink in Views

GetInkAt(*para, index*)
NextInkIndex(*para, index*)
ParaContainsInk(*para*)
PolyContainsInk(*poly*)

Text and Ink Input and Display

Keyboard Functions and Methods

This section summarizes the functions and methods that you can use to work with keyboards in your applications.

General Keyboard Functions and Methods

GetCaretBox()
view:KeyboardInput()
KeyIn(*keyCode*, *down*)
PostKeyString(*view*, *keyString*)
SetKeyView(*view*, *offset*)

Keyboard Registry Functions and Methods

KeyboardConnected()
OpenKeyPadFor(*view*)
RegGlobalKeyboard(*kbdSymbol*, *kbdTemplate*)
view:RegisterOpenKeyboard(*flags*)
UnRegGlobalKeyboard(*kbdSymbol*)
view:UnregisterOpenKeyboard()

Caret Insertion Writing Mode Functions and Methods

GetRemoteWriting()
SetRemoteWriting(*newSetting*)

Insertion Caret Functions and Methods

GetCaretInfo()
GetKeyView()
view:PositionCaret(*x, y, playSound*)
SetCaretInfo(*view*, *info*)

Application-Defined Methods for Keyboards

ViewCaretChangedScript(*view, offset, length*)

Input Event Functions and Methods

This section summarizes the functions and methods that you can use to work with input events in your applications.

Functions and Methods for Hit-Testing

*view:*PointToCharOffset*(x,y)*
*view:*PointToWord*(x,y)*

Functions and Methods for Handling Insertions

*view:*HandleInsertItems*(insertSpec)*
InsertItemsAtCaret*(insertSpec)*

Functions and Methods for Handling Ink Words

GetInkWordInfo *(inkWord)*
*view:*HandleInkWord*(strokeBundle)*
*view:*HandleRawInk*(strokeBundle)*

Application-Defined Methods for Handling Ink in a View

*view:*ViewInkWordScript*(strokeBundle)*
*view:*ViewRawInkScript*(strokeBundle)*

Recognition

This chapter and Chapter 10, "Recognition: Advanced Topics," describe the use of the Newton recognition system. The recognition system accepts written input from views and returns text, ink text, graphical objects, or sketch ink to them.

This chapter describes how to use view flags to enable the recognition of text, shapes and gestures in views. If you are developing an application that must derive text or graphical data from pen input, you should become familiar with the contents of this chapter. Before reading this chapter, you should be familiar with NewtonScript message passing among views and the use of view flags to specify the characteristics of views, as described in Chapter 3, "Views."

You need not read Chapter 10, "Recognition: Advanced Topics," unless you need to provide unusual input views or specialized recognition behavior. (See that chapter's first page for a complete list of its topics.)

About the Recognition System

The Newton recognition system enables views to convert handwritten input into text or graphical shapes, and to take action in response to system-defined gestures such as taps and scrubs.

Any type of view can accept pen input, and different types of views provide different amounts of system-supplied behavior. Views based on the system-supplied `clEditView` and `clParagraphView` classes handle most forms of pen input automatically. Applications need not handle recognition events in these types of views explicitly unless they need to do something unusual. The `clView` class, on the other hand, provides no built-in recognition behavior. Views of this type must provide all recognition behavior themselves.

The system provides recognizer engines (also called **recognizers**) that classify pen input as clicks, strokes, gestures, shapes, or words. Each view can specify independently which recognizers it uses and how the recognition system is to process pen input that occurs within its boundaries. For example, you could configure a view to recognize text and shapes, or you might enable only text recognition in a view not intended to accept graphical input.

CHAPTER 9

Recognition

Although no recognizers are associated with clicks and strokes, they do pass through the recognition system, allowing your view to respond to them by means of optional `ViewClickScript` and `ViewStrokeScript` methods that you supply as necessary. The `ViewClickScript` method of a view that accepts pen input takes application-specific action when the pen contacts or leaves the surface of the screen within the view's boundaries. The `ViewStrokeScript` method performs application-specific processing of input strokes before they are passed on to the gesture, shape, or text recognizers.

The gesture recognizer identifies system-defined gestures such as scrubbing items on the screen, adding spaces to words, selecting items on the screen, and so on. Views based on the `clEditView` and `clParagraphView` classes (edit views and paragraph views, respectively) respond automatically to standard system-defined gestures; other kinds of views do not. Your view can provide an optional `ViewGestureScript` method to perform application-specific processing of system-defined gestures. You cannot define new gestures to the system.

Only views based on the `clEditView` class can recognize shapes. The shape recognizer uses symmetry found in input strokes to classify them as shapes. The shape recognizer may make the original shape more symmetrical, straighten its curves, or close the shape. There is no developer interface to shape recognition.

The system provides two text recognizers—one optimized for a printed handwriting style and another optimized for a cursive handwriting style. The printed text recognizer (also called the **printed recognizer**) requires that the user lift the pen from the screen between letters. The cursive text recognizer (also called the **cursive recognizer**) accepts cursive input (letters connected within a single word), printed input (disconnected letters within a single word), or any combination of these two kinds of input.

In views that recognize text, the system enables the printed recognizer by default unless the cursive recognizer is enabled explicitly. The user can specify the use of a particular text recognizer from within the Handwriting Recognition preferences slip. This user preference slip and others that affect recognition behavior are discussed in "User Preferences for Recognition" beginning on page 9-14.

Only one text recognizer can be active at a time—all views on the screen share the same text recognizer—but individual views can specify options that customize its behavior for a particular view. Individual views can also use any combination of other recognizers in addition to the specified text recognizer. Regardless of which text recognizer is in use, the recognition system limits the size of individual input strings to 32 characters—longer words may not be recognized correctly.

Although the Newton platform currently supports only its built-in recognizers, future versions of the system may permit the use of third-party recognizer engines.

The next section describes how the recognition system classifies input as text, shapes, or gestures.

Classifying Strokes

Recognition is an iterative process that compares raw input strokes with various system-defined models to identify the best matches for further processing. When the user writes or draws in an edit view or paragraph view that accepts user input, the system

- notifies the view that a pen event occurred within its boundaries.

- provides user feedback, in the form of electronic ink drawn on the screen as the pen moves across its surface.

- attempts to group strokes meaningfully according to temporal and spatial data.

A view that accepts pen input is notified of pen events within its boundaries by ViewClickScript messages that are sent when the pen contacts the screen and when it is lifted from the screen. Views based on the clEditView and clParagraphView classes handle these events automatically; other views may not, depending on the type of view in which the pen event occurred. Your view can supply an optional ViewClickScript method to take application-specific action in response to these events as necessary.

The electronic ink displayed as the pen moves across the screen is called **raw ink.** Raw ink is drawn in the same place on the screen as the original input strokes. Views based on the clParagraphView view class can be configured to replace the raw ink with another representation of the input strokes called ink text. **Ink text** is a version of the original strokes that has been scaled for display and formatted into paragraphs: spaces between groups of strokes are made uniform and groups of strokes are wrapped to the margins of the screen. The size to which ink text is scaled is specified by the user from the Text Editing Settings user preference slip. This user preference slip and others that affect recognition behavior are discussed in "User Preferences for Recognition" beginning on page 9-14.

The recognition system encapsulates raw input strokes in an object called a **stroke unit.** Stroke units cannot be examined directly from NewtonScript; however, you can pass them to functions that construct useful objects from them or perform recognition using the stroke data they contain.

Views configured to image input as ink text display a scaled representation of the original input strokes without performing any further processing; that is, they circumvent the remainder of the recognition process described here.

When stroke units are made available to a view that performs recognition, all of the recognizers enabled for the view compete equally to classify the input. Each recognizer compares the input to a system-defined model; if there is a match, the recognizer involved claims the stroke unit as its own.

Once a stroke unit is claimed by one of the recognizers, it is not returned to the other recognizers for additional classification; however, recognizers may combine multiple stroke units into meaningful groups. For example, certain letters (such as an uppercase *E*) might be composed of multiple strokes. The process of grouping input strokes is influenced by the user preference settings for handwriting style and letter styles.

The recognizer that claimed one or more stroke units returns to the view one or more interpretations of the strokes. The gesture and shape recognizers return only one interpretation to the view. The text recognizer usually returns multiple interpretations to the view.

Associated with each interpretation is a value, called the **score,** which indicates how well the input matched the system-defined model used by the recognizer that interpreted it. When multiple recognizers are enabled, the system selects the best interpretations based on their scores and the application of appropriate heuristics. For example, the text recognizer might choose between interpreting a stroke as a zero or as the letter *O* based on whether you have specified that the view accepts numeric or alphabetic input.

The recognizer that claimed the strokes places its best interpretations in another kind of unit that is returned to the view. The text recognizer returns *word units*, the shape recognizer returns *shape units*, and the gesture recognizer returns *gesture units*. Each of these units contains data representing one or more strokes. A **word unit** represents a single recognized word, a **shape unit** represents a single recognized shape, and a **gesture unit** represents a single recognized gesture, as shown in Figure 9-1. The next several sections describe how the system handles each of these units.

Gestures

When the recognition system returns a gesture unit to the view, the view performs the action associated with that gesture automatically. The action taken is dependent on the kind of view that received the gesture unit.

Edit views and paragraph views respond automatically to system-defined gestures such as scrubbing items on the screen, adding spaces to words, selecting items on the screen, and so on. Other kinds of views may do nothing in response to a particular gesture.

You can provide an optional `ViewGestureScript` method to take action in response to any standard gesture. For example, you can use this method to respond to gestures in views that are not paragraph views or edit views. You can also use this method to override or augment the standard behavior of a particular view in response to system-defined gestures. At present, you cannot define custom gestures to the system.

Figure 9-1   Recognizers create units from input strokes

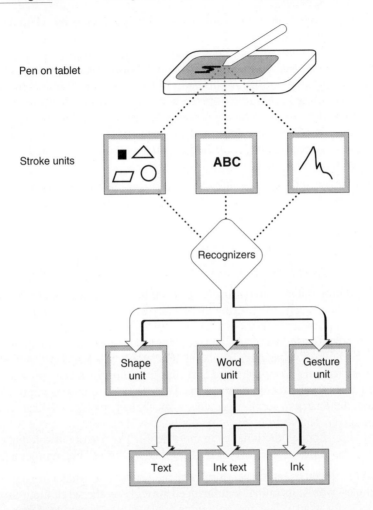

Pen on tablet

Stroke units

ABC

Recognizers

Shape unit

Word unit

Gesture unit

Text

Ink text

Ink

Shapes

When the recognition system returns a shape unit to the view, the shape is displayed as the `clPolygonView` child view of a `clEditView` view. The shape unit contains a single, cleaned-up version of the original strokes. The shape recognizer may make the original shape more symmetrical, straighten its curves, or close the shape.

There is no developer interface to shape recognition. To manipulate shapes returned by the recognition system, you must extract polygon view children from edit views yourself. You can do so from within an optional `ViewAddChildScript` method that you supply. The system invokes this method for each `clPolygonView` or `clParagraphView` child added to an edit view.

Text

When the recognition system returns a word unit to a view based on the `clParagraphView` or `clEditView` classes, the view displays or uses the best interpretation of the original input strokes. Paragraph views display words directly; edit views create a `clParagraphView` child automatically to display text that the recognition system returns. Additionally, the recognition system constructs a correction information frame from the word unit and saves learning data as appropriate. For more information, see "Correction and Learning" (page 9-13) and "Accessing Correction Information"(page 10-23). Your view can provide an optional `ViewWordScript` method to perform application-specific processing of the word unit.

The set of possible interpretations that the text recognizer returns to a view is affected by

■ the text recognizer that the view uses to interpret the input strokes

■ options you have specified for the text recognizer in use

■ the dictionaries that are available to the view for recognition use

A **dictionary** is a system construct against which the user's input strings are matched, as a means of ensuring the validity of the text recognizer's output. The system supplies dictionaries that define names, places, dates, times, phone numbers, and commonly used words to the text recognizers. The user can expand the system's built-in vocabulary by adding new words to a RAM-based user dictionary accessed from the Personal Word List slip. In addition, you can provide custom dictionaries for the recognition system's use. For example, you might create a custom dictionary to supply specialized vocabulary, such as medical or legal terminology. The section "System Dictionaries" beginning on page 9-11 describes the system-supplied dictionaries in more detail. The use of custom dictionaries for recognition is described in "Using Custom Dictionaries" beginning on page 10-24.

Although the interpretations returned by the printed recognizer are never limited to dictionary words, its output is influenced strongly by the set of dictionaries available for its use. The interpretations returned by the cursive recognizer can be restricted to those words appearing in the set of dictionaries available for its use; however its default behavior is to return non-dictionary words in addition to words appearing in available dictionaries.

Options specified for the currently enabled recognizer may also influence the interpretations it returns to the view. For example, the cursive recognizer's default settings enable its letter-by-letter recognition option, to increase the likelihood of its returning strings not in the currently available set of dictionaries. The user can control this option and others from within the Handwriting Settings preferences slip.

Note that even when the cursive and printed recognizers are configured similarly, the results they return for the same input may differ. For example, using the cursive recognizer's letter-by-letter option may produce different results than using the printed recognizer (which always provides letter-by-letter recognition.) Options for both recognizers are described throughout this chapter and in Chapter 10, "Recognition: Advanced Topics."

Unrecognized Strokes

If the input strokes are not recognized, the system encapsulates them in an object known as a stroke bundle. A **stroke bundle** is a NewtonScript object that encapsulates stroke data for multiple strokes. The strokes in the bundle have been grouped by the system according to temporal and spatial data gathered when the user first entered them on the screen. You can access the information in stroke bundles to provide your own form of deferred recognition, or to examine or modify stroke data before it is recognized. For information on using stroke bundles, see Chapter 10, "Recognition: Advanced Topics."

Stroke bundles may be returned to the view under any of the following circumstances:

- No recognizers are enabled for the view.

- Recognizers are enabled for the view but recognition fails.

- The view is configured to image input as ink text.

- The view's vStrokesAllowed flag is set and a ViewStrokeScript method is provided.

When the system passes a stroke bundle to a clEditView view, the view images the strokes in the bundle as ink text or sketch ink. Other kinds of views may require you to provide code that displays the strokes.

When no recognizers are enabled for a clEditView view, it displays input as sketch ink. Input views for which no recognizers are enabled are not as unusual as they might seem at first; for example, you might provide a view that accepts stroke input without performing recognition as a means of capturing the user's handwritten signature. And some views, such as those used in the built-in Notepad application, allow the user to enable and disable recognizers at will.

When recognizers are enabled for the view but recognition fails, the view may return ink text or sketch ink. Recognition may fail if input strokes are too sloppy to classify or if the view is not configured correctly for the intended input. For more information, see "Recognition Failure" beginning on page 9-11.

When the view is configured to display input as ink text, the system skips the remainder of the recognition process—it does not attempt to further classify the input strokes as letters or words. Instead, the view simply images the strokes as ink text.

The most important difference between ink text and sketch ink has to do with how these two forms of ink are represented. Ink text is inserted into existing text in paragraph views in the same way as recognized words are: as the contents of a clParagraphView view child. Ink text automatically wraps to the paragraph boundaries, just as recognized text does. Ink text is also usually reduced in size when it is drawn, according to the user preference specified by the Ink Text Scaling item in the Text Editing preferences slip. Sketch ink, on the other hand, is treated as a graphic: it is inserted into the view as a clPolygonView view child. Sketch ink is always drawn at full size, and in the position at which it was written on the screen.

Thus, stroke bundles are normally returned only to views that do not perform recognition. To cause the system to always return stroke bundles to the view (in addition to any word units, gesture units or shape units that may be passed to the view), set the view's vStrokesAllowed flag and provide a ViewStrokeScript method, as described in "Customized Processing of Input Strokes" beginning on page 10-40.

The recognition system's classification of user input is essentially a process of elimination. Enabling and configuring only the recognizers and dictionaries appropriate to a particular context is the primary means by which you optimize the recognition system's performance within your application.

Enabling Recognizers

Each view has a viewFlags slot that contains a bit field. The bits in this field specify characteristics that the view does not inherit from its view class, such as its recognition behavior. When you set a view flag, it sets bits in this field to enable combinations of recognizers and dictionaries suited to the input you anticipate the view to receive.

Not all of the bits in this field affect recognition; some are used to set other characteristics, such as the view's placement on the screen. The bits in this field that affect the recognition system are referred to as the view's **input mask.** When the view is constructed at run time, the system copies the input mask bits and other view flags' bits into the view's viewFlags slot. shows the relationship of recognition-related view flags to bits in the viewFlags slot.

You can set bits in the viewFlags slot from within the graphical view editor in Newton Toolkit or you can set them programmatically from within your own NewtonScript code. Either approach allows you to set combinations of bits to produce a variety of behaviors.

This book uses the NewtonScript approach for all examples. For information on using the graphical view editor in Newton Toolkit, see *Newton Toolkit User's Guide*.

Figure 9-2   Recognition-related view flags

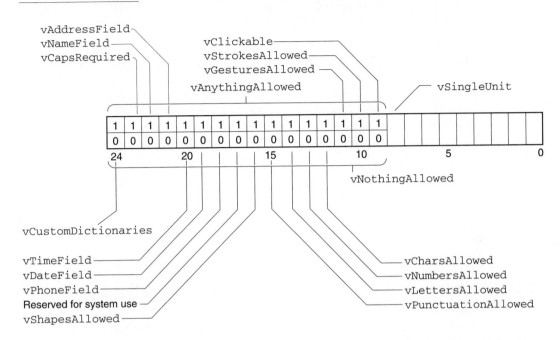

View Flags

The system supplies a number of constants, called **view flags**, which are used to set bits in a view's `viewFlags` slot programmatically. In general, each of these flags activates a combination of recognizers and dictionaries suited to recognizing a particular kind of input. Thus, a view's view flags specify the kinds of data it is likely to recognize successfully. For a summary of the view flags that affect recognition, see "Constants" (page 9-31).

There are two ways to set view flags from NewtonScript: you can place view flag constants in your view template's `viewFlags` slot or you can supply a recognition configuration (`recConfig`) frame for the view. Occasionally, the use of both techniques is appropriate, but in most cases you'll use only one or the other.

Recognition Configuration Frames

Recognition configuration frames (`recConfig` frames) provide an alternate programmatic interface to the recognition system. They can be used to provide any behavior that view flags provide, and can also be used to provide specialized recognition behaviors that view flags cannot. For example, view flags generally set multiple bits in the input mask to produce a particular behavior. You can use a recConfig frame to set individual bits in the input mask, allowing you to control aspects of recognition behavior that view flags do not.

Some features of the recognition system require the use of a recConfig frame. For example, to create a view that provides single-letter input areas suitable for accepting pen input in a crossword puzzle application, you must supply a recConfig frame that provides an rcGridInfo frame. The system-supplied rcGridInfo frame is used to specify the location of one or more single-letter input views.

This chapter focuses on the use of view flags to configure recognition. The use of recConfig frames is described in Chapter 10, "Recognition: Advanced Topics." System-supplied recConfig frames are described in "System-Supplied recConfig Frames" (page 8-18) in *Newton Programmer's Reference*.

View Flags vs. RecConfig Frames

In most cases, view flags provide the easiest and most efficient way to configure the recognition system. Although recConfig frames provide more flexible and precise control over the configuration of recognition behavior, they require more effort to use correctly.

It is recommended that you use view flags to configure recognition unless you need some special recognition behavior that they cannot provide. Examples of such behavior include constraining recognition on a character-by-character basis, implementing customized forms of deferred recognition, and defining baseline or grid information.

The rest of this chapter discusses configuration of the recognition system only in terms of the view flag model. You need to read this material even if you plan to use recConfig frames in your application, because the description of recConfig frames in Chapter 10, "Recognition: Advanced Topics," assumes an understanding of the view flag model upon which these frames are based.

Where to Go From Here

If you're anxious to begin experimenting with view flags, you can skip ahead to "Using the Recognition System" beginning on page 9-21 and test the effects of various flags using the viewFlags sample application provided with Newton Toolkit. However, it is recommended that you read the rest of this section before attempting to work with the recognition system.

Recognition Failure

Recognition may fail when the handwritten input is too sloppy for the system to make a good match against its internal handwriting model, when the view is not configured correctly for the intended input, or (in the case of dictionary-based recognition only) when none of the interpretations of the input strokes match a dictionary entry. In such cases, the recognition system may return sketch ink or ink text.

Ink text looks similar to sketch ink; however, ink text is scaled and placed in a `clParagraphView` view as text. Sketch ink is not placed in a paragraph but drawn in a `clPolygonView` view on top of anything else that appears in the polygon view's `clEditView` parent. Both ink text and sketch ink hold stroke data that can be used to recognize the strokes at another time. Deferred recognition—the process of recognizing saved ink at a later time—is described in more detail in "Deferred Recognition" (page 10-5), in Chapter 10, "Recognition: Advanced Topics."

System Dictionaries

The system supplies a variety of dictionaries against which names, places, dates, times, phone numbers, and commonly used words are matched. There are two kinds of dictionaries used for text recognition: enumerated and lexical. An **enumerated dictionary** is simply a list of strings that can be matched. A **lexical dictionary** specifies a grammar or syntax that is used to classify user input. The kind of dictionary used for a particular task is dependent upon task-specific requirements. For example, it would be impractical to create an enumerated dictionary of phone numbers; however, the clearly defined format imposed on these numbers makes them ideal candidates for definition in a lexical dictionary.

The specific set of dictionaries that the system provides for a particular purpose generally varies according to the user's locale. For example, because currency formats vary from country to country, the particular lexical dictionary that the system uses for matching monetary values may change according to the current locale. However, you usually need not be concerned with the specific set of dictionaries used by a particular locale. For more information, see Chapter 20, "Localizing Newton Applications."

Dictionaries can be in ROM or in RAM (internal or card-based). Most of the system-supplied dictionaries are in ROM; however, the user dictionary resides in RAM.

Applications must never add items to the user dictionary without the user's consent. The user dictionary is intended to be solely in the user's control—adding items to it is akin to changing the user's handwriting preferences or Names entries. It's also important to leave room for users to store their own items.

IMPORTANT

An excessively large user dictionary can slow the system when performing searches that are not related to your application. It is therefore recommended that applications do not add items to the user dictionary at all. ▲

The system supports a total of about 1,000 items in the RAM-based user dictionary (also known as the review dictionary). Note that this number may change in future Newton devices. A persistent copy of the user word list is kept on the internal store in the system soup. The user dictionary is loaded into system memory (not the NewtonScript heap or store memory) when the system restarts and saved when the user closes the Personal Word List slip. For more information, see "Working With the Review Dictionary" (page 10-30).

A separate dictionary called the **expand dictionary** allows you or the user to define word expansions that are substituted for abbreviations automatically. The substitution takes place after the abbreviation has been recognized, but before it has been displayed. For example, you could specify that the string *w/* be expanded to the string *with,* or the string *appt* expand to *appointment.* In addition to permitting the substitution of an entirely different string for the one recognized, the expand dictionary can be used to correct recurring recognition mistakes or misspellings automatically.

The expand dictionary is not used directly by the recognition system. Instead, each word to be expanded is added to both the user dictionary and the expand dictionary. Then the user dictionary and any appropriate additional dictionaries are used to perform stroke recognition. Before the recognizer returns the list of recognized words to the view, it determines whether any of the items in the list are present in the expand dictionary. If so, the expanded version of the word is inserted into the list of recognized words before the original version of the word. The original version is also included in the list, just in case the user doesn't want to expand the word.

As words not present in any of the currently enabled dictionaries are recognized, the auto-add mechanism may add them to the user dictionary automatically. This feature is enabled when the cursive recognizer is active, but not when the printed recognizer is active. (Although both recognizers use dictionaries to improve accuracy, the use of dictionaries does not benefit the printed recognizer enough to justify default use of the auto-add mechanism.) You can improve the printed recognizer's treatment of problematic words by making them available from a dictionary, but it is recommended that you create a custom dictionary that provides those words; the user dictionary is intended to be under the user's control.

The **auto-add dictionary** is a list of words that have been added to the user dictionary automatically. If the auto-add dictionary is not empty, the Recently Written Words slip displays its contents when the user opens the Personal Word List slip. The Recently Written Words slip prompts the user to indicate whether each of the words it displays should remain in the user dictionary. To encourage the user to make individual decisions about each word in the list, this slip does not permit selection.

Although the Recently Written Words slip asks the user whether to add words to the Personal Word List, the words have already been added to both the user dictionary and the auto-add dictionary by the time they are displayed in this slip if the cursive recognizer is in use. Rather than actually adding words to any dictionaries, this slip actually removes those words that the user does not confirm as candidates for addition to the user and auto-add dictionaries.

Note
When the printed text recognizer is in use, the automatic addition of words to the user dictionary and the auto-add dictionary is disabled. ◆

The size of the auto-add dictionary is limited to 100 words. A persistent copy of the auto-add dictionary is kept on the internal store in the system soup. The auto-add dictionary is loaded in system memory (not the NewtonScript heap or store memory) when the system restarts and saved when the user opens or edits the Recently Written Words slip. For more information, see "Working With the Review Dictionary" beginning on page 10-30.

Another dictionary, the symbols dictionary, is always enabled for any view that performs text recognition. This dictionary includes alphabetic characters, numerals, and some punctuation marks. Use of this dictionary permits the user to correct single characters by writing over them on the screen.

Correction and Learning

When the recognition system returns a word unit to the view, it constructs a correction information frame from the word unit and may save learning data as well. The correction information frame holds information used to correct misrecognized words. Learning data is used by the system to improve the cursive recognizer's accuracy.

The system provides a developer interface to the information in the correction information frame, as well as a user interface to a subset of this data. For complete descriptions of the protoCorrectInfo, protoWordInfo and protoWordInterp system prototypes that provide access to correction information, see "Recognition System Prototypes" (page 8-31) in *Newton Programmer's Reference*

The picker (popup menu) shown in Figure 9-3 provides the user interface to correction information. This picker is displayed automatically when the user double-taps a previously recognized word. This picker's items include

■ the five best interpretations returned by the recognizer.

■ the alternative capitalization of the most highly scored interpretation.

- the expansions of words that match entries in the expansion dictionary.
- a graphical representation of the original input strokes as ink.
- buttons for the soft keyboard and text-corrector views.
- a Try Letters button when the cursive recognizer is active.

Figure 9-3   Text-corrector picker

The words in this list are one example of correction information stored by the system as it recognizes words. In addition to word lists, correction information includes the original stroke data and information known as *learning data.*

Learning data is information gathered as the user corrects misrecognized words. It is used to modify the system's internal handwriting model to more closely match the way the user actually writes. This information is called *learning data* because the system can be said to learn various characteristics of the user's handwriting style, with a resulting increase in recognition accuracy. Not all recognizers return learning data.

User Preferences for Recognition

The user can specify several preferences that affect the overall configuration of the recognition system. This information is provided for reference purposes only; generally, you should not change the user's recognition preferences settings.

This section describes only those user preferences for which the system provides a NewtonScript interface. It does not provide a comprehensive summary of the user interface to recognition, which may vary on different Newton devices. For a description of the user interface to a particular Newton device, see the user manual for that device.

The user preference settings for recognition that this section describes are stored as the values of slots in a system-maintained frame that holds user configuration data. These slots are described in "System-Wide Settings" (page 8-2) in *Newton Programmer's Reference*.

The user preference settings described here may be affected by the setting of a `protoRecToggle` view associated with the view performing recognition. For a description of this view, see "RecToggle Views" beginning on page 9-18.

Recognition-oriented user preference settings may also be overridden by a `recConfig` frame associated with the view performing recognition. For complete information on `recConfig` frames, see Chapter 10, "Recognition: Advanced Topics."

Handwriting Recognition Preferences

The Handwriting Recognition preferences slip shown in Figure 9-4 specifies the overall characteristics of the user's handwriting. In general, you should not override the user settings specified in this slip.

The Printing and Cursive radio buttons specify whether a printed or cursive style of lettering is used. This system-wide setting enables either the printed or cursive recognizer by setting the value of the `letterSetSelection` slot in the system's user configuration data. It is strongly recommended that you do not change this setting.

The user can also specify the amount of blank space the recognizer may find between words; this setting influences the recognition system's initial grouping of stroke data. The value returned by the slider control in this slip is kept in the `letterSpaceCursiveOption` slot in the system's user configuration data. This value may be overridden by views that perform recognition.

Figure 9-4   Handwriting Recognition preferences

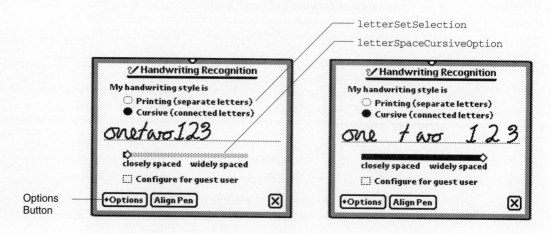

Checking the "Configure for guest user" checkbox causes the system to

■ save all current recognition system settings.

■ save the owner's learning data.

■ temporarily reset all recognition system preferences to their default values.

■ learn the guest user's writing style as misrecognized words are corrected if the cursive recognizer is in use. (The printed recognizer does not use learning data.)

When the user deselects the "Configure for guest user" checkbox, the guest user's learning data is discarded and the original user's learning data, preferences, and other settings are restored. Note that the system's use of the auto-add mechanism is not affected by the setting of this checkbox—when the cursive recognizer is enabled, the system always adds new words to the auto-add dictionary.

The Options button displays a picker from which the user can access options for various preferences. The items included in this picker vary according to whether the printed or cursive recognizer is enabled. When the cursive recognizer is enabled, this picker provides the Text Editing Settings, Handwriting Settings, Letter Shapes, and Fine Tuning items. When the printed recognizer is enabled, this picker provides only the Text Editing Settings and Fine Tuning items. Because the system provides no developer interface to the Letter Shapes slip, it is not discussed here.

Figure 9-5 shows the Text Editing Settings slip that is displayed for both the printed and cursive recognizers. Of the adjustments available from the Text Editing Settings slip, the "Add new words to Personal Word List" checkbox is of interest to developers. The cursive recognizer adds new words to the RAM-based user dictionary automatically when this checkbox is selected. The printed recognizer never adds new words automatically, regardless of the setting of this checkbox. You can always add new words to the user dictionary programmatically, regardless of which recognizer is enabled. To display or edit the personal word list, the user taps the book icon on the soft keyboard.

Figure 9-5   Text Editing Settings slip

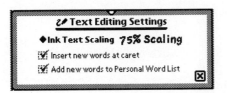

The system provides two versions of the Fine Tuning slip, one for each of the cursive and printed text recognizers, as shown in Figure 9-6. Both slips provide a "Transform my handwriting" slider control that allows the user to fine-tune the system's use of temporal cues to determine when a group of strokes is complete. This slider sets the value of the `timeoutCursiveOption` slot in the system's user configuration data.

Figure 9-6   Fine Tuning handwriting preferences slips

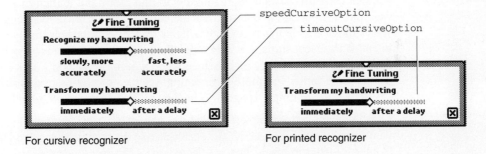

The Fine Tuning slip used by the cursive recognizer includes an additional slider that allows the user to trade some measure of accuracy for a faster response from the recognizer. The "Recognize my handwriting" slider sets the value of the `speedCursiveOption` slot in the system's user configuration data.

When the cursive recognizer is enabled, the Options button in the Handwriting Recognition preferences slip provides access to the Handwriting Settings slip shown in Figure 9-7.

Figure 9-7   Handwriting Settings slip

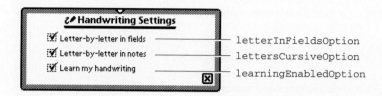

When the "Learn my handwriting" checkbox is selected, the system sets the value of the `learningEnabledOption` slot in its user configuration data to `true`. When this slot holds the value `true`, the system modifies its internal handwriting model as the user corrects misrecognized words when the cursive recognizer is enabled. The printed recognizer does not provide or use learning data.

The user can cause the cursive recognizer to perform character-based recognition (rather than dictionary-based recognition) in certain kinds of views by selecting the "Letter-by-letter in fields" or "Letter-by-letter in notes" checkboxes in the Handwriting Settings slip. (The printed recognizer can always return character combinations that do not appear in dictionaries.)

The "Letter-by-letter in fields" checkbox enables the cursive recognizer's letter-by-letter option in `protoLabelInputLine` views that use this recognizer. The intended use of this flag is to permit the user to enable letter-by-letter recognition automatically for views that are unlikely to find user input in dictionaries. For example, an application that restricts the cursive recognizer to returning dictionary words might enable this recognizer's letter-by-letter option selectively for views intended to accept surnames. When the "Letter-by-letter in fields" box is selected, the value of the `letterInFieldsOption` slot in the system's user configuration data is set to `true`. For more information, see the description of this slot in "System-Wide Settings" (page 8-2) in *Newton Programmer's Reference*.

The "Letter-by-letter in notes" checkbox enables letter-by-letter recognition for views based on the `clEditView` class that use the cursive recognizer. When the "Letter-by-letter in notes" box is selected, the `lettersCursiveOption` slot in the system's user configuration data is set to `true`. The built-in Notes application and notes associated with items in the Names and Dates applications demonstrate this behavior. For more information, see the `lettersCursiveOption` description in "System-Wide Settings" (page 8-2) in *Newton Programmer's Reference*.

RecToggle Views

The `protoRecToggle` view is a button that allows the user to control the recognition behavior of one or more views easily. This button is usually provided as a child of your application's status bar. When the user taps this button, it displays a picker from which the user can choose recognition behaviors that you specify. When this picker is collapsed, the appearance of the button indicates the current recognition settings for the view or views that it controls. Figure 9-8 shows the appearance of typical `protoRecToggle` view when it is collapsed and when it is expanded to display the pick list of recognizers it can enable.

Figure 9-8   Use of `protoRecToggle` view in the Notes application

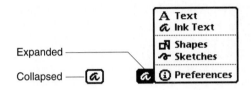

The default picker provides all of the items shown in Figure 9-8 in the order illustrated. You can specify that this picker display a subset of these items in the order you specify.

The topmost item in the picker indicates the recognizer that the `recToggle` view enables by default; unless you specify otherwise, the `recToggle` view enables the text recognizer by default, as shown in the figure.

You can also provide code that restores the user's most recent `recToggle` setting or initializes the `recToggle` to a predetermined setting each time your application opens.

The picker's Preferences item opens the Handwriting Recognition user preferences slip by default.

For more information on `protoRecToggle` views, see Chapter 10, "Recognition: Advanced Topics," as well as the description of this prototype in *Newton Programmer's Reference*.

Flag-Naming Conventions

This section describes conventions used to name recognition-related view flags, as well as the significance of the use of the words `Field` and `Allowed` in flag names.

The Entry Flags area of the Newton Toolkit (NTK) view editor actually sets view flags. The distinction that Newton Toolkit makes between "view flags" and "entry flags" is an artifact of the way certain views create child views dynamically at run time.

For example, when the user taps a `protoLabelInputLine` view, it creates and opens a `clParagraphView` child that is the input line view in which text recognition takes place. The Entry Flags area of the NTK screen specifies the view flags for this dynamically created child view separately from the view flags for the container view in which it appears. When the system creates the child view, it copies the Entry Flags bits into the child view's `viewFlags` slot.

For simplicity's sake, this chapter refers to all recognition-oriented flags as "view flags." This chapter and its corresponding section of the *Newton Programmer's Reference* document all such flags as view flags.

Although the NTK view editor describes `vAnythingAllowed` as a "flag" it is actually a mask that sets all bits in a `clEditView` view's input mask. This chapter refers to this construct as the "`vAnythingAllowed` mask." See (page 9-8) for a graphical depiction of the relationships between bits in the input mask and recognition-related view flags.

The use of `Field` in the names of some flags and `Allowed` in others is meant to reflect these flags' intended use, rather than a functional difference.

The "field" flags are intended for setting up input views that accept a single kind of input, such as dates. For example, setting the `vDateField` flag specifies that the view accepts numeric input in a format commonly used for dates in the current locale. Setting this flag enables the set of dictionaries appropriate for recognizing such input.

On the other hand, the more inclusive "allowed" flags are intended for use with views that must recognize several kinds of input; for example, setting the `vNumbersAllowed` flag specifies that the view accepts a wide range of numeric input, such as currency values, times, and dates. Setting the `vNumbersAllowed` flag alone, then, enables a more inclusive set of dictionaries than obtained by setting the `vDateField` flag alone.

Despite differences in naming conventions (and despite the fact that the Field Type popup menu in the NTK view editor considers these flags mutually exclusive), the "field" and "allowed" flags can be mixed in any combination. Keep in mind, though, that the more choices the recognizer has, the more opportunity it has to make the wrong choice.

Recognition Compatibility

In addition to the cursive recognizer available in previous systems, version 2.0 of system software adds a recognizer optimized for printed characters. This recognizer, represented by the Printed radio button in the Handwriting Recognition preferences slip, is the default text recognizer used when you or the user do not specify otherwise.

Selecting the Cursive radio button in the Handwriting Recognition preferences slip equates to selecting the Mixed Cursive and Printed radio button available in previous versions of this slip: the cursive recognizer is enabled, all printed and cursive letter styles in the system's handwriting model are enabled, and the system disables unused letter styles over time as the user corrects misrecognized words.

The default settings of the cursive recognizer in version 2.0 enable this recognizer's letter-by-letter recognition option. Previous versions of the system disabled this option by default, causing the cursive recognizer to return only words appearing in the set of dictionaries available to the view performing recognition.

The `protoLetterByLetter` prototype, which appears at the lower-left corner of the screen in the Notepad application on the MessagePad 100 and MessagePad 110, is obsolete. It has been replaced by the `protoRecToggle` prototype. For more information, see "RecToggle Views" (page 9-18).

Prior to version 2.0 of Newton system software, correction information was not accessible from NewtonScript. Version 2.0 of Newton system software makes this information available as frame data. For more information, see "Correction and Learning" (page 9-13).

Combining the `vLettersAllowed` flag with flags used to specify recognition of numeric values (such as `vPhoneField`, `vNumbersAllowed`, `vDateField`, `vTimeField`, and `vAddressField`) produced undesirable results in system software prior to version 2.0. System software version 2.0 supports these kinds of view flag combinations.

Deferred recognition—the ability to convert strokes to text at some time other than when the strokes are first entered on the screen—was introduced in Newton system software version 1.3 with no application programming interface. Version 2.0 of Newton system software provides a NewtonScript interface to this feature.

Using the Recognition System

This section describes how to use view flags to enable recognition in views. This chapter discusses only those view flags that interact with the recognition system. For a summary of these view flags, see "Constants" (page 9-31). For information on other kinds of view flags, see Chapter 3, "Views." For complete descriptions of all view flags, see *Newton Programmer's Reference*.

For information on the use of `recToggle` views, `recConfig` frames and advanced features of the recognition system, see Chapter 10, "Recognition: Advanced Topics."

Types of Views

The kind of view that you use to recognize input affects the amount of work you'll have to do to support recognition. Views based on the `clEditView` class handle most recognition events automatically once you've specified their intended recognition behavior by setting view flags or providing a `recConfig` frame. Specifically, `clEditView` views create `clParagraphView` or `clPolygonView` child views automatically as required to display output from the recognition system. To use other kinds of views for recognition, you may need to provide `viewXxxScript` methods that create these child views and respond in other ways to recognition system events.

Configuring the Recognition System

You can take the following approaches to configuring the recognition system:

- Set view flags only. This approach works well for most applications and is described in this chapter.

- Set view flags and allow the user to configure recognition from a `protoRecToggle` view that you provide. The easiest way to do this is by setting the `vAnythingAllowed` mask, which is described in this chapter. This approach supports the use of ink text in `clEditView` views. Use of the `protoRecToggle` view is described in Chapter 10, "Recognition: Advanced Topics."

- Set view flags and supply a recognition configuration frame based on `ROM_rcInkOrText`. This approach supports ink text in `clEditView` views. You should provide a `protoRecToggle` view as well, to allow the user to switch easily between text and ink text.

- Supply a recognition configuration frame of some other kind. This approach offers you the most control and flexibility, but also requires the most work to implement. The difficulty of enabling ink text according to the value of a `protoRecToggle` view depends on the particular implementation of your `recConfig` frame. Recognition configuration frames are described in Chapter 10, "Recognition: Advanced Topics."

- Use the `RecogSettingsChanged` message sent by the `protoRecToggle` view to enable recognition behaviors dynamically. This technique is described in Chapter 10, "Recognition: Advanced Topics."

Except where noted otherwise, all of the flags described in this chapter are set in the view's `viewFlags` slot. When setting the values of `viewFlags` slots, remember that in order to produce useful behavior you may need to set other bits in addition to the recognition-oriented ones that this chapter describes. To preserve settings that your view's `viewFlags` slot inherits from its view class, you should logically OR changes to bits in this slot.

For information on non-recognition view flags provided by the system, see Chapter 3, "Views."

Obtaining Optimum Recognition Performance

To obtain the most accurate results from the recognition system, you must define as precisely as possible the type of input that the view is to recognize. Aside from potentially introducing errors, enabling superfluous recognizers may slow the recognition system's performance.

The view flags that enable text recognition also enable dictionaries suited to recognizing particular kinds of input, such as dates, phone numbers, and so on. Some view flags activate multiple dictionaries, and the sets of dictionaries activated by various flags may overlap. The system shows no preference towards any single dictionary in a set except for a slight weighting of results in favor of words found in the user dictionary, which most view flags enable.

The specific dictionaries that a particular flag enables varies according to the user's locale and the ROM version of the Newton device. You usually need not be concerned with this implementation detail, nor should you rely on the presence of a particular dictionary when setting view flags.

When you need to control precisely which dictionaries a view uses for recognition, you can set its `vCustomDictionaries` flag and use a `dictionaries` slot to specify explicitly which dictionaries are to be used. For information about custom dictionaries, see "Using Your RAM-Based Custom Dictionary" (page 10-28), in Chapter 10, "Recognition: Advanced Topics." For information about locale and the recognition system, see "How Locale Affects Recognition" (page 20-2), in Chapter 20, "Localizing Newton Applications."

For best performance, you need to specify the minimum combination of recognizers and dictionaries required to process the kind of input you expect the view to receive. This equates to enabling the minimum set of view flags that allow the view to recognize appropriate input correctly. By restricting the possible interpretations returned by the recognition system to only those that are appropriate for a particular view, you increase the system's chances of interpreting the input correctly. For example, when configuring a view for the entry of numeric data, you would not specify that the recognition system return alphabetic characters to that view.

The printed and cursive text recognizers appear nearly identical to NewtonScript applications. The main difference between them is that while the cursive recognizer can be made to use the value of the `viewFlags` slot as a strict definition of what it can recognize, the printed recognizer uses this value as only a hint—that is, it can always return values not specified by the input view's view flags. When configuring views for text recognition, you should set view flags that describe the input you anticipate the view to receive and then verify that you obtain acceptable results from both text recognizers.

Because the printed recognizer lets you write anything in the input view, it may be difficult to determine whether your `viewFlags` settings are appropriate when this recognizer is enabled; the cursive recognizer usually provides better feedback in this regard. If necessary, you can provide a `ViewWordScript` or `ViewChangedScript` method that validates the recognizer's output; this method can be especially useful when working with the printed recognizer.

Accepting Pen Input

When setting up any view, you must specify whether it accepts pen input at all. If you set the `vNothingAllowed` flag (or turn off all recognition-oriented flags), the view does not accept pen input. If you want the view to accept pen input, you must set the `vClickable` flag in its `viewFlags` slot. Setting this flag only causes the view to accept pen taps and send `ViewClickScript` messages; it does not enable ink handling or send messages to any of the unit-handling methods that provide recognition behavior.

Setting the `vClickable` flag specifies that the view system is to send the `ViewClickScript` message to the view once for each pen tap that occurs within the view. Note that this is the case only when `vClickable` is the only flag set for the view—other flags, such as the `vCustomDictionaries` flag, set the `vClickable` bit in the view's input mask also.

When this flag is set, the system sends additional messages to the view to signal taps, strokes, gestures, and words. All pen input is signaled by the `ViewClickScript` message, which indicates that the pen contacted the screen or was lifted from it within the boundaries of the view. If you supply a `ViewClickScript` method, it should return `true` to indicate that the message was handled, or `nil` to pass the message on to another view. If this message is not handled by the view and additional recognition flags are set, other messages may be sent to the view, depending on what was written. These other messages include `ViewStrokeScript`, `ViewGestureScript`, and `ViewWordScript`—in that order, if all are sent.

Each of the corresponding input-related view methods accept as an argument a unit object passed to it by the system. The unit contains information about the pen input. You cannot examine the unit directly from NewtonScript, but you can pass it to other system-supplied functions that extract information from it such as the beginning and ending points of the stroke, an array of stroke points, the stroke bounds, and so on.

Taps and Overlapping Views

When views overlap, taps can "fall through" from the top view to the one beneath, causing unexpected results. For example, when the user taps in an area of the top view that doesn't handle taps, and the view beneath provides a button in the vicinity of the tap, the button may be activated unintentionally.

You can solve this problem by setting the top view's vClickable flag without providing a ViewClickScript method. (The top view need not handle the taps, only prevent them from being passed on to the other view.)

Recognizing Shapes

The vShapesAllowed flag enables the recognition of geometric shapes such as circles, straight lines, polygons, and so on. Do not set this flag for views that handle text input only. This flag is intended for use only in views based on the clEditView class. The clEditView class provides the built-in Notepad application's note stationery with much of its recognition behavior.

The shapes displayed on the screen are clPolygon views returned as the children of the clEditView that accepted the input strokes. There is no developer interface to shape recognition; to manipulate shapes returned by the recognition system, you must extract the polygon views from the edit view yourself. In some cases, you may find the ViewAddChildScript method useful for this purpose. The ViewAddChildScript message is sent when a child view is added to a view.

When multiple shapes are returned to an edit view, its ViewAddChildScript method is called once for each shape.

When multiple ink text words are returned to an edit view, the ViewAddChildScript method is invoked when the clParagraphView that holds the ink text is added as the child of the edit view, but this method is not invoked as ink text words are added to the paragraph view.

In views not based on the clEditView class, the arrival of each ink word is signalled by a ViewInkWordScript message.

Recognizing Standard Gestures

Setting the vGesturesAllowed flag supplies system-defined behavior for the gestures tap, double tap, highlight, scrub, line, caret, and caret-drag. Most input views set the vGesturesAllowed flag, as they need to respond to standard gestures such as scrubbing to delete text or ink. At present, you cannot define new gestures to the system.

When the vGesturesAllowed flag is set, the gesture recognizer invokes the view's ViewGestureScript method before handling the gesture. Normally, you don't need to supply a ViewGestureScript method for clEditView or clParagraphView views. These views handle all system-defined gestures automatically.

Your ViewGestureScript method is invoked only for gestures that the view system does not handle automatically. For information on intercepting standard gestures before the view system handles them, see "Customized Processing of

Double Taps" beginning on page 10-41. See also "ViewGestureScript" (page 8-71) in *Newton Programmer's Reference*.

Combining View Flags

Generally, you must combine multiple view flags to produce useful recognition behavior. For example, most views that accept user input set the vClickable flag to enable pen input and the vGesturesAllowed flag to enable recognition of standard gestures such scrubbing and inserting spaces.

Except where noted otherwise, the NewtonScript "plus" operator (+) is used to combine view flags, as in the following code fragment.

```
myViewTemplate :=
    {
    // recognize taps, gestures, and shapes
    viewFlags: vClickable+vGesturesAllowed+vShapesAllowed,
    …}
```

Note
Most combinations of view flags include the vClickable flag.
If you do not set the vClickable flag, the view does not accept
pen input at all. ◆

Sometimes a particular combination of view flags produces results that seem incorrect. For example, you might be surprised to discover that a view setting only the flags vClickable+vLettersAllowed can occasionally recognize numeric values. (The vLettersAllowed flag enables the recognition of single text characters by the cursive recognizer.) This behavior is caused by the presence of the symbols dictionary in the set of dictionaries available to the view. The symbols dictionary includes alphabetic characters, numerals and some punctuation marks. Most view flags enable this dictionary to support the correction of single letters or numerals by overwriting. As a side effect, it becomes possible to recognize extraneous characters or numerals in fields that ostensibly should not support such input. This behavior is rarely a problem, however, because the recognition system is designed to show a strong preference for "appropriate" interpretations of input as defined by the view flags set for the view.

Although you might expect that the presence of the symbols dictionary would allow a view setting only the flags vClickable+vNumbersAllowed to return alphabetic characters, this behavior is quite difficult to produce. Views that set the vNumbersAllowed flag show a much stronger preference for single-digit numbers than single alphabetic characters. However, letters that do not look similar to numeric values—for example, the letter *W*—may produce this particular form of misrecognition.

When troubleshooting recognition errors, remember that view flags may enable multiple dictionaries and that the sets of dictionaries enabled by various flags may overlap.

As a general rule, the fastest and most accurate recognition occurs when the fewest recognizers and dictionaries necessary to successfully analyze the input are enabled. Enabling unnecessary recognizers and dictionaries may decrease the speed and accuracy with which recognition is performed.

Recognizing Text

The vCharsAllowed and vLettersAllowed flags enable text recognition in views that accept pen input. Either flag enables the text recognizer specified by the Handwriting Recognition preferences slip.

Each of these flags specifies different recognition options and dictionary sets. The unique behaviors associated with each flag are demonstrated most clearly by the cursive recognizer. The cursive recognizer can be made to return only words present in the set of dictionaries available to the view performing recognition. In contrast, the printed recognizer can always return words or letter combinations that are not present in dictionaries.

The vCharsAllowed flag enables a default set of dictionaries that provide vocabulary used in common speech, names of days, names of months, proper names, and words in the user dictionary. When the vCharsAllowed flag is set and the vLettersAllowed flag is not, the cursive recognizer returns only words that appear in the set of dictionaries available to the view performing recognition.

Note that the complete set of dictionaries available to the view may include those enabled by other flags. For example, the NTK view editor provides a Field Type popup menu that allows you to specify whether the view is to accept phone, date, time, address or name data. The choices in this menu set the vPhoneField, vDateField, vTimeField, vAddressField and vNameField flags, respectively. Each of these flags enables one or more dictionaries suited to recognizing the specified input data. Custom dictionaries may also be made available to the view performing recognition by setting the vCustomDictionaries flag and providing a valid dictionaries slot in the view that performs recognition.

The vLettersAllowed flag enables the cursive recognizer's letter-by-letter recognition option. When the vLettersAllowed flag is set, the cursive recognizer may return words not appearing in dictionaries as well as nonword letter combinations. Note that this configuration increases the cursive recognizer's chances of misrecognizing words that appear in the set of dictionaries available to it.

Although both text recognizers provide a letter-based recognition feature, the two recognition engines are completely distinct. Consequently, the results produced by the cursive recognizer's letter-by-letter option may be different from those returned by the printed recognizer for the same input data.

Although the printed recognizer can always return non-dictionary words, it does make extensive use of the dictionaries available to the view for recognition. Users may improve the printed recognizer's accuracy for problematic non-dictionary words by adding them to the user dictionary. You can supply custom dictionaries to improve the recognition of specialized vocabulary. It is recommended that applications do not add words to the user dictionary.

Recognizing Punctuation

The vPunctuationAllowed flag permits the cursive recognizer to return common punctuation marks such as the period (.); comma (,); question mark (?); single quotation marks (' and '); double quotation marks (" and "); and so on. The printed recognizer can always return these characters, regardless of whether this flag is set.

Views restricted to the entry of phone numbers, dates, or times need not set the vPunctuationAllowed flag because the vPhoneField, vDateField, and vTimeField flags already allow the entry of appropriate punctuation.

The cursive recognizer can also apply some simple rules when deciphering ambiguous input; for example, it can make use of the fact that most punctuation marks follow rather than precede words.

Suppressing Spaces Between Words

Setting the vSingleUnit flag causes the recognition system to ignore spatial information when grouping input strokes as words; instead, the system relies on temporal cues to determine when the user has finished writing a word. When this flag is set, the recognizer ignores short delays, such as those that occur between writing the individual characters in a word. Longer delays cue the recognizer to group the most recently completed set of strokes as a word. The amount of time considered to be a longer delay is a function of the speed of the processor and the recognition system, as well as the value of the timeoutCursiveOption user preference.

The vSingleUnit flag is useful for views in which the presence of gratuitous spaces may confuse the recognizer; for example, phone number entry fields usually suppress the recognition of spaces. If you want to suppress all spaces in the displayed text, you can use the vNoSpaces flag in conjunction with the vSingleUnit flag.

Rather than suppressing the input of spatial cues, the vNoSpaces flag suppresses the insertion of spaces between groups of strokes or recognized text in views based on the clParagraphView class. This post-processing flag does not restrict the interpretation of the input strokes or affect word segmentation, as the vSingleUnit flag does.

The vNoSpaces flag must appear in an evaluate slot named textFlags that you create in the view. The vSingleUnit flag appears in the view's viewFlags slot, as usual.

Forcing Capitalization

The vCapsRequired flag directs the system to capitalize the first letter of each word returned by the recognizer before displaying the text in the view.

Setting the vCapsRequired flag does not affect the recognizer's behavior—it affects post-processing performed on the recognizer's output before it is returned to the view.

Justifying to Width of Parent View

Setting the vWidthIsParentWidth flag for a view based on the clParagraphView class causes the view to extend its right boundary to match that of its parent automatically.

The vWidthIsParentWidth flag must appear in an evaluate slot named textFlags that you create in the view.

Like other flags set in the textFlags slot, the vWidthIsParentWidth flag does not affect the recognizer's behavior—it affects post-processing performed on the recognizer's output before it is returned to the view.

Restricting Input to Single Lines or Single Words

Including the oneLineOnly flag in your view's viewJustify slot causes the view to accept only a single line of text input, with no word wrapping provided.

You can restrict input to a single word by including the oneWordOnly flag in the view's viewJustify slot. If this flag is set, the view replaces the currently displayed word with the new one when the user writes in the view. You can also restrict input to single characters by using this flag in conjunction with a custom dictionary of single letters.

For more information on these flags, see their descriptions in Chapter 3, "Views." For information on the use of custom dictionaries, see "Using Custom Dictionaries" beginning on page 10-24.

Validating Clipboard and Keyboard Input

It is possible for the user to enter invalid values in fields by dragging text from the Clipboard or by using a keyboard to type in the field. For example, setting the vPhoneField flag normally restricts input to numeric values in phone number formats; however, the user can still enter invalid values in such a field by dragging or typing them. To prevent invalid input by these means, you can implement a `ViewChangedScript` method that validates its view's input.

Using the vAnythingAllowed Mask

The `vAnythingAllowed` mask can be used only with views based on the `clEditView` class. When used by itself, this mask sets all of the bits in the view's input mask, potentially enabling all of the system-supplied recognizers and dictionaries. However, the actual recognition behavior of views that use this mask varies according to current user preference settings.

For a view that sets the `vAnythingAllowed` mask, the recognition system replaces the set of view flags you've specified with a set of flags derived from the current settings of user preferences that affect recognition.The actual set of recognizers enabled for the view is controlled by

- user preferences specified in the system's user configuration data.
- the application's `protoRecToggle` view, if it has one.
- the view's `recConfig` frame, if it has one.

Slots in the system's user configuration data specify recognition behaviors that all views inherit. However, an optional `protoRecToggle` view can specify different behaviors for individual views by overriding values inherited from user configuration data. Similarly, each view can provide a `recConfig` frame that overrides settings specified by the `protoRecToggle` view or the system's user configuration data.

Thus, in practice, the `vAnythingAllowed` mask usually is not what its name implies: if any bit in this mask is turned off (by another flag, or by a `recToggle` view, for example), the input mask is no longer `vAnythingAllowed`.

The built-in Notepad application provides a good example of the behavior of views that use the `vAnythingAllowed` mask, including the use of a `protoRecToggle` view to change recognition settings.

Summary

Constants

Text Recognition View Flags

Constant	Value	Description
vCharsAllowed	1 << 12 or 0x01000	Enables default text recognizer and default dictionary set.
vLettersAllowed	1 << 14 or 0x04000	Enables letter-by-letter text recognition.
vAddressField	1 << 21 or 0x0200000	Enables recognizers and dictionaries suitable for the input of address data in the current locale.
vNumbersAllowed	1 << 13 or 0x02000	Enables the recognition of numeric characters, monetary values (for example, $12.25), decimal points, and signs (+ or −).
vNameField	1 << 22 or 0x0400000	Enables text recognition optimized for name data; usually combined w/ vCapsRequired.
vCustomDictionaries	1 << 24 or 0x01000000	Enables text recognition using dictionaries specified by the view's dictionaries slot.
vPunctuationAllowed	1 << 15 or 0x08000	Enables recognition of punctuation marks by the cursive recognizer. (Printed recognizer always recognizes punctuation marks.)
vCapsRequired	1 << 23 or 0x0800000	Forces capitalization of the first character of each recognized word.

Non-Text Recognition View Flags

Constant	Value	Description
vNothingAllowed	0x00000000 or 0x0000	The view accepts no handwritten or keyboard input.
vAnythingAllowed	65535 << 9 or 0x01FFFE00	Recognize any input. Use only for views based on the clEditView class.
vClickable	1 << 9 or 0x0200	Accept taps and send ViewClickScript message to the view once for each tap that occurs within the view.
vStrokesAllowed	1 << 10 or 0x0400	Accept stroke input and send the ViewStrokeScript message at the end of each stroke.
vGesturesAllowed	1 << 11 or 0x0800	Recognize gesture strokes such as scrub, highlight, tap, double tap, caret, caret-drag, and line. Send the ViewGestureScript message when the view recognizes a gesture that it does not handle automatically.
vShapesAllowed	1 << 16 or 0x010000	Enables shape recognition. Use only for views based on the clEditView class.
vSingleUnit	1 << 8 or 0x0100	Disable the use of spatial cues (distance between strokes). Meaningful for text recognizers only.
vNoSpaces	1 << 1 or 0x0002	Directs a view based on the clParagraphView class to not insert spaces between existing text and new text.
vWidthIsParentWidth	1 << 0 or 0x0001	Extend right boundary of clParagraphView view to match that of its parent.

View Flags Enabling Lexical Dictionaries

Constant	Value	Description
vNumbersAllowed	1 << 13 or 0x02000	Enables recognition of numbers, monetary values (for example, $12.25), decimal points, and mathematical signs (+ and –).
vPhoneField	1 << 18 or 0x040000	Enables recognition of phone numbers. Note that the set of lexical dictionaries enabled by this flag varies with the text recognizer currently in use.
vDateField	1 << 19 or 0x080000	Enables recognition of date formats (such as March 3-95), names of months, and names of days.
vTimeField	1 << 20 or 0x0100000	Enables recognition of times.

Data Structures

Recognition-Related User Configuration Slots

Use the GetUserConfig and SetUserConfig global functions to access these slots.

Slot name	Notes
letterSetSelection	Text recognizer in use.
learningEnabledOption	true enables cursive learning.
letterSpaceCursiveOption	Space between stroke groups.
timeoutCursiveOption	Time between individual strokes.
speedCursiveOption	Time spent analyzing input.
letterInFieldsOption	true enables cursive recognizer's letter-by-letter option in protoLabelInputLine views.
lettersCursiveOption	true enables cursive recognizer's letter-by-letter option in built-in Names and Dates applications' protoLabelInputLine views.
doAutoAdd	true adds new words to user dictionary and auto-add dictionary automatically.

continued

Slot name	Notes
doTextRecognition	true enables text recognition unconditionally.
doShapeRecognition	true enables shape recognition unconditionally.
doInkWordRecognition	true causes text recognizer to return ink text rather than sketch ink.

CHAPTER 10

Recognition:
Advanced Topics

This chapter describes advanced uses of the Newton recognition system. If you are developing an application that supports ink text, implements specialized recognition system behavior, or provides unusual input views, you'll need to understand one or more topics presented here. This chapter describes

- the use of recConfig frames. An individual view can use a recConfig frame to specify its own recognition behavior, support ink text, specify baseline information, support deferred recognition, and define input areas for single letters.

- the use of text-corrector views and text-correction information.

- the programmatic manipulation of system dictionaries and custom dictionaries.

Before reading this chapter, you should understand the contents of Chapter 9, "Recognition," which provides an overview of the recognition system and describes how to implement its most common behaviors. Depending on your application development goals, you may also find it helpful to be familiar with soups, as described in Chapter 11, "Data Storage and Retrieval."

About Advanced Topics in Recognition

This section provides conceptual information regarding

- how views configure recognizers and dictionaries based on the interaction of view flags, recConfig frames, recToggle views, and recognition-related user preferences.

- the use of protoCharEdit views.

- deferred recognition.

How the System Uses Recognition Settings

A number of settings that control the behavior of the various recognizers are specified by the system's user configuration data. All views that perform recognition inherit behavior from these values, which is why it's rarely appropriate for individual applications to change these system-wide settings. Instead, individual views can customize their own recognition behavior by using a recConfig frame or recToggle view to override these inherited values locally.

In practice, most views' recognition behavior is defined by a combination of inherited and overridden values. For example, because most users tend not to change the speed at which they write, it's common for views to use inherited values for the timeoutCursiveOption slot, which specifies the relative delay required to consider a group of input strokes complete. At the same time, individual views may customize certain recognition settings by overriding values that would otherwise be inherited from the system's user configuration data. For example, a view can use a recConfig frame to disable the automatic addition of new words to the user dictionary.

A view based on the protoRecToggle system prototype provides another way to override inherited recognition settings. This view provides a picker that allows the user to change recognition settings easily. Each view controlled by this picker must provide a _recogSettings slot that the picker sets according to the user's current choice of recognition settings. The value in the _recogSettings slot overrides values inherited from the system's user configuration data.

Your application supplies only one _recogSettings slot for each recToggle view it provides. Because views use parent inheritance to find a _recogSettings slot, a single recToggle view and a single _recogSettings slot can control the recognition behavior of one view or multiple views, depending on the _recogSettings slot's position in the view hierarchy. For more information, see "Creating the _recogSettings Slot" beginning on page 10-20.

You can also provide an optional RecogSettingsChanged method in the _parent chain of any view controlled by the recToggle view. If a RecogSettingsChanged method is provided, the recToggle view sends this message to self when the user chooses an item in the recToggle picker. Your RecogSettingsChanged method can perform any application-specific task that is appropriate; typically, this method reconfigures recognition settings in response to the change in the recToggle view's state.

Finally, any view can provide an optional recConfig frame that specifies the view's recognition behavior at the local level.

Although recConfig frames have thus far been presented as simply an alternate interface to the recognition system, they are actually used internally by the system to represent the recognition behavior of each view. When the user writes, draws, or gestures in a view, the system builds a recConfig frame that specifies the precise settings of all the recognizers needed for the view. If you supply a recConfig frame for the view, the recConfig frame that the system builds is based on the recConfig frame you have supplied and any recognition-related user preferences that may apply.

On the other hand, if the view does not supply a recConfig frame, the recognition system builds one based on the set of view flags enabled for that view, the contents of its dictionaries slot (if present) and any recognition-related user preferences that may apply. Thus, every view that performs recognition is eventually associated with a recConfig frame that the system uses to perform setup tasks when the view is opened.

Note that the recConfig frame actually used to configure recognition is the one that the system builds, not the one that you supply. The recConfig frame that you supply is referenced by the _proto slot of the recConfig frame that the system builds.

The recConfig frame built by the system is passed to a *recognition area*, which is an object used internally by the system to describe the recognition characteristics of one or more views. Because similar views can share an area, the use of recognition areas minimizes the reconfiguration of the recognition system required to respond to changes in views on the screen.

A small number of recognition areas are kept in a cache. You can change the recognition behavior of a view dynamically by specifying new recognition settings and invalidating the area cache. The next time the view accepts input, the system builds a new recognition area reflecting its currently-specified recognition behavior and the dictionaries it is to use for recognition.

In addition to providing an efficient and flexible means of configuring the recognition system programmatically, recConfig frames provide support for future expansion of the recognition system. The recConfig frame allows applications to specify recognition configurations in a uniform way that is not dependent on the use of any particular recognizer engine. Although the Newton platform currently supports only its built-in recognizers, future versions of the system may permit the use of third-party recognizer engines.

The system provides several standard recConfig frames that can be placed in your view's recConfig slot or used as a starting point for building your own recConfig frames. For descriptions of system-supplied recConfig frames, see "System-Supplied recConfig Frames" (page 8-18) in *Newton Programmer's Reference*.

In summary, the recognition behavior that a view exhibits is ultimately determined by a combination of the following values:

■ values inherited from the system's user configuration data.

■ values in the view's viewFlags and entryFlags slots.

■ values in the view's dictionaries slot when the vCustomDictionaries flag is set.

■ values specified by an optional recToggle view, which may override values inherited from user configuration data or supply additional values.

■ values specified by an optional `recConfig` frame, which may override values inherited from user configuration data, override values specified by a `recToggle` view, or supply additional values.

ProtoCharEdit Views

The `protoCharEdit` system prototype provides a comb-style entry view (or *comb view*) that allows the user to edit individual characters in words easily.

Figure 10-1   Example of `protoCharEdit` view

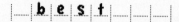

Individual character positions (or *cells*) in the comb view are delimited by vertical dotted lines. Each cell that can be edited has a dotted line beneath it to indicate that it can be changed. The user can edit a character by writing a new character over one currently occupying a cell; the recognized value of the character is displayed in the cell. When the user taps a cell, it displays a picker containing the best interpretations of the input strokes. The user can correct the character in that position by choosing an item from the picker.

The user can delete an individual character by tapping it and then selecting "Delete" from the picker that is displayed. Alternatively, the user can delete one or more characters by writing the scrub gesture over one or more cells.

The user can insert a space by tapping on the cell at the position that the new space is to occupy and choosing Insert from the picker that is displayed.

Alternatively, the user can enter the caret gesture in a cell to perform the same operation. When an insertion takes place in a cell already occupied by a character, the comb view shifts that character and those comprising the rest of the word to the right.

Tapping a blank cell before or after a word in the comb view displays a list of punctuation characters that may be appropriate for that position.

The recognition behavior of a `protoCharEdit` view is controlled by values you supply in an optional `template` slot. If this slot's value is `nil`, the comb view is said to be **unformatted** because input is not restricted in any way. The recognition behavior of an unformatted comb view is similar to that of the text-corrector view provided by the built-in Notepad application: all characters are allowed, insertion and deletion are supported fully, and spaces are added at the ends of words to allow them to be extended.

A **formatted comb view** utilizes a template you define which specifies characteristics of the view's behavior or appearance. A comb view's template may specify an initial value for the string that the view displays, the editing characteristics for each position in the comb view, and filters that restrict the values recognized in each of these positions. The template may also define methods for initializing and post-processing the string displayed by the comb view. These methods may be useful when the string displayed in the comb needs to be different from the input string or when an externally-displayed string must differ from its internal representation.

When the user taps a character in a formatted comb view, it displays the list of characters specified by its template, if that list contains ten or fewer items. (Note that this value may change in future platforms.) Otherwise, it displays the list of top-ranking alternate interpretations returned by the text recognizer.

Ambiguous Characters in protoCharEdit Views

Because there are several characters that are ambiguous in appearance—for example, the value zero (0) and the letter *O*, or the value one (1) and the letter *L*—the built-in system fonts provide enhanced versions of these characters that improve their readability. However, continuous use of these characters can be distracting to the user. Thus, these fonts contain character codes that map to alternate versions of the ambiguous characters, and the system provides functions for mapping between the codes for the normal and enhanced characters. For more information, see the descriptions of the `MapAmbiguousCharacters` and `UnMapAmbiguousCharacters` functions under "protoCharEdit Functions and Methods" (page 8-47) in *Newton Programmer's Reference*.

Deferred Recognition

Deferred recognition is the ability to convert strokes to text at some time other than when the strokes are first entered on the screen. Views that are to perform deferred recognition must be capable of capturing ink text or ink. For example, a view that bases its `recConfig` frame on the system-supplied `ROM_InkOrText` frame and uses a `protoRecToggle` view to configure the recognition system need not do anything more to provide the deferred recognition feature.

This section describes the user interface to deferred recognition and then provides a programmer's overview of this feature.

User Interface to Deferred Recognition

A view that performs deferred recognition uses the same settings as it would for real-time text recognition: a combination of settings specified by user preferences and settings specified by the view flags or `rccConfig` frame associated with the view in which recognition takes place.

The user can enter unrecognized ink by enabling ink text or sketch ink. In this mode, strokes appear as ink. To convert the ink to text, the user double-taps the ink word; the user can cause multiple words to be recognized by selecting them beforehand and then double-tapping the selection. The recognition system responds by inverting the ink word or selection, as shown in Figure 10-2, and returning the recognized text, which replaces the selection.

Figure 10-2   User interface to deferred recognition, with inverted ink

Programmer's Overview of Deferred Recognition

Deferred recognition is available in views based on the clEditView class or clParagraphView views that support ink text. This feature works with any amount of input, from a single letter to a full page of text.

To initiate deferred recognition, the user double-taps the child views that display the ink to be recognized. The recognized text is added to an edit view as if the user had just written it. That is, a new clParagraphView child is added, or the recognized text is appended to a nearby clParagraphView. After the recognized text has been added, the original view containing the sketch ink or the ink text is removed from its edit view parent.

Deferred recognition also invokes the ViewAddChildScript and ViewDropChildScript methods of the recognized text and unrecognized ink views. Words added to nearby paragraphs invoke ViewChangedScript methods for those paragraphs, updating the text slot in those views; for some paragraph views, the viewBounds slot is updated as well.

You can pass recConfig frames to the global functions Recognize, RecognizePara, and RecognizePoly to implement your own form of deferred recognition. For more information, see "Deferred Recognition Functions" (page 8-89) in *Newton Programmer's Reference*.

Compatibility Information

The `ReadDomainOptions` function is obsolete. It has been replaced by the `ReadCursiveOptions` function.

The `AddToUserDictionary` function is obsolete. It has been replaced by the `AddWord` method of the review dictionary.

Two new dictionary constants, `kMoneyOnlyDictionary` and `kNumbersOnlyDictionary`, provide access to new lexical dictionaries used for recognizing monetary and numeric values, respectively.

Most lexical dictionaries are no longer locale-specific—aside from a few exceptions, each lexical dictionary is used for all locales. For detailed information, see "System-Supplied Dictionaries" (page 8-16) in *Newton Programmer's Reference*.

All of the dictionary information provided by previous versions of system software is still present in version 2.0; however, certain dictionary constants now provide a superset of the information they previously referenced, as follows:

- The `kLastNamesDictionary` is obsolete. This information is now included in the `kSharedPropersDictionary` dictionary.

- The `kLocalCompaniesDictionary` constant is obsolete.This information is now included in the `kSharedPropersDictionary` dictionary.

- The `kLocalStatesAbbrevsDictionary` constant is obsolete.This information is now included in the `kSharedPropersDictionary` dictionary.

- The `kDateLexDictionary` constant is obsolete. It has been replaced by the `kLocalDateDictionary` constant.

- The `kTimeLexDictionary` constant is obsolete. It has been replaced by the `kLocalTimeDictionary` constant.

- The `kMoneyLexDictionary` constant is obsolete. This information is now included in the `kLocalNumberDictionary` dictionary.

- The `kNumberLexDictionary` constant is obsolete. This information is now included in the `kLocalNumberDictionary` dictionary.

Using Advanced Topics in Recognition

This section describes how to provide advanced recognition behaviors. It presumes understanding of conceptual material provided in this and other chapters. Topics discussed here include

- using `recConfig` frames to specify recognition behavior

- changing the recognition behavior of views dynamically

- using `protoRecToggle` views to specify recognition behavior
- defining single-letter input areas within a view
- accessing text correction information
- using custom dictionaries for recognition
- manipulating the review dictionary (includes the user dictionary, expand dictionary, and auto-add dictionary)
- using `protoCharEdit` views for correcting text
- using stroke bundles

Using recConfig Frames

This section describes how to use a `recConfig` frame to specify a view's recognition behavior. Note that the use of view flags is generally the best (and simplest) way to configure views to recognize common input such as words and shapes. You need not use a `recConfig` frame unless you require some recognition behavior that cannot be provided using the view's `viewFlags` and `dictionaries` slots. For example, the use of a `recConfig` frame is required for views that restrict recognition of individual characters to a specified set, or implement customized forms of deferred recognition.

This section describes the use of `recConfig` frames for

- enabling recognizers
- supporting ink text
- fine-tuning recognition options
- specifying the dictionaries used for recognition

A `recConfig` frame can be used to specify any set of recognizers and dictionaries, including combinations not supported by the view flag model; however, views controlled by `recConfig` frames are subject to the same limitations as all views that perform recognition:

- The text recognizer (printed or cursive) made available to all views is determined by the value of the `letterSetSelection` slot in the system's user configuration data. Individual views cannot override this system-wide setting.

- The system's ability to save learning data is enabled by the value of the `learningEnabledOption` slot in the system's user configuration data. Individual views cannot override this system-wide setting.

Do not include `letterSetSelection` or `learningEnabledOption` slots in your `recConfig` frame.

Creating a recConfig Frame

For any view that is to use a `recConfig` frame, you must supply a `recConfig` slot, usually by defining it in your view's template. The frame in your view's `recConfig` slot must be modifiable; that is, it must be RAM-based. When your view template supplies a `recConfig` frame, the view system builds a RAM-based `recConfig` frame along with the view—you need not do anything more to cause the view to use the `recConfig` frame.

To create your own `recConfig` frame at run time, you need to call the `PrepRecConfig` function to create a RAM-based `recConfig` frame that the system can use. Although you could obtain similar results by cloning a `recConfig` frame that your view template defines, using the `PrepRecConfig` function is more efficient:

■ The `PrepRecConfig` function creates a smaller frame than that obtained by cloning your view template's `recConfig` frame.

■ The frame that the `PrepRecConfig` function returns can be used as it is by the recognition system. Any other frame that you place in the view's `recConfig` slot is used by the system to create the `recConfig` frame actually used by the view, with the result being the creation of two frames in RAM rather than just one.

■ Consistent use of this function to create `recConfig` frames saves RAM by permitting similar `recConfig` frames to share the same frame map.

A function similar to the `PrepRecConfig` function, the `BuildRecConfig` function, is provided for debugging use. Do not use the `BuildRecConfig` function to create your RAM-based `recConfig` frame. The argument to the `BuildRecConfig` function is the view itself, rather than its `recConfig` frame. This function builds an appropriate `recConfig` frame for the specified view, regardless of whether the view defines one. The system does not use the `recConfig` frame that this function returns, however—as stated previously, this frame is for debugging use only.

IMPORTANT

The contents of the `inputMask` slot in the view's `recConfig` frame must match the input mask (the recognition-related bits) provided by the view's `viewFlags` slot. For more information on this slot and others that the `recConfig` frame may contain, see "protoRecConfig" (page 8-36) in *Newton Programmer's Reference*. ▲

You can base your `recConfig` frame on one of the system-supplied `recConfig` frames by simply placing the appropriate constant in your view template's `recConfig` slot. Alternatively, you can place in this slot a frame that uses its `_proto` slot to reference one of the system-supplied `recConfig` frames. A third way to define a `recConfig` frame is to supply all necessary values yourself. The exact complement of slots and values required is determined by the recognition features your `recConfig` frame is intended to supply; for more information, including complete descriptions of the system-supplied `recConfig` frames, see "System-Supplied recConfig Frames" (page 8-18) in *Newton Programmer's Reference*.

Once you've created a RAM-based `recConfig` frame, you must cause the recognition system to use it. This process is described in "Changing Recognition Behavior Dynamically" beginning on page 10-17. For a code example showing how to create a `recConfig` frame based on one of the system-supplied prototypes, see "Creating Single-Letter Input Views" beginning on page 10-15.

Using RecConfig Frames to Enable Recognizers

To enable or disable recognizers unconditionally, supply appropriate values for the `doTextRecognition`, `doShapeRecognition`, or `doInkWordRecognition` slots your view's `recConfig` frame provides. For descriptions of these slots, see "protoRecConfig" (page 8-36) in *Newton Programmer's Reference*.

For some operations, you may wish to restrict the recognizers that the user can enable in a view while still respecting the rest of the preferences indicated in the system's user configuration data. The optional slots `allowTextRecognition` and `allowShapeRecognition` in the view's `recConfig` frame are intended for use with views having an input mask that is `vAnythingAllowed`. For complete descriptions of these slots, see "protoRecConfig" (page 8-36) in *Newton Programmer's Reference*. Note that you can also allow the user to set the values of these slots from a `protoRecToggle` view instead of setting them yourself in the `recConfig` frame.

Views that use the `allow`*Something*`Recognition` slots allow the user to turn on only the recognizers that you specify while respecting all other user preferences. Any subset of `allow`*Something*`Recognition` slots can be specified to allow the user to enable any appropriate combination of recognizers from the `protoRecToggle` view or user preferences.

For example, setting the value of the `allowTextRecognition` slot to `true` allows the user to enable the text recognizer in the view controlled by the `recConfig` frame while the `doTextRecognition` slot in the system's user configuration data holds a non-`nil` value.

Returning Text, Ink Text or Sketch Ink

This section discusses the use of `recToggle` views with system-supplied view classes and `recConfig` frames to provide views that can display text, ink text, or sketch ink.

Sketch ink, like shapes, is displayed only in views based on the `clEditView` class. As a rule of thumb, consider sketch ink and ink text to be mutually exclusive when configuring recognition in views; for best results, configure your input view to recognize only one of these two data types.

Views based on the `clEditView` class handle sketch ink and ink text automatically. For other views, the system invokes the view's `ViewInkWordScript` or `ViewRawInkScript` method when ink arrives. For more details, see the descriptions of these methods in *Newton Programmer's Reference*.

The system-supplied `ROM_rcInkOrText` constant provides a ready-to-use `recConfig` frame that allows views based on the `clParagraphView` class to contain ink text in addition to normal text. To use this `recConfig` frame to create a view that supports ink text, you'll need to take the following steps:

■ Create a view template that protos from the `clParagraphView` class.

■ In your view template, create a `recConfig` slot that holds the `ROM_rcInkOrText` constant. For more information, see "Creating a recConfig Frame" beginning on page 10-9.

■ Provide a `protoRecToggle` view that allows the user to choose text or ink text settings; if your application provides a status bar, you need to provide the `recToggle` view as one of its children. For more information, see "Creating the recToggle View" beginning on page 10-19.

■ Provide a `_recogSettings` slot at an appropriate position in the `recToggle` view's `_parent` chain. For more information see "Creating the _recogSettings Slot" beginning on page 10-20.

Normally, the input view tries to recognize input using all currently enabled recognizers. If no recognizers are enabled or if recognition fails for some reason—for example, due to messy input or some sort of error—then the view system converts the input strokes into ink. The `doInkWordRecognition` slot in the input view's `recConfig` frame specifies the kind of ink that the system creates from the input strokes.

When the `doInkWordRecognition` slot holds a non-`nil` value, the system returns ink text; when this slot holds the `nil` value, the system returns sketch ink. This slot is described fully in "protoRecConfig" (page 8-36) in *Newton Programmer's Reference*. Table 10-1 on page 10-12 summarizes the kinds of data returned by the recognition system when recognition fails in an edit view or paragraph view that is controlled by a `recToggle` view.

Note that when the input view is set to recognize shapes, the smoothed and cleaned up ink that is returned may be ink text but is more likely to be a curve shape. Aside from the failure of shape recognition, the only time raw ink is returned to the view is when its associated `recToggle` is set to "Sketches".

Table 10-1 Recognition failure in paragraph or edit view controlled by `recToggle`

Recognizer enabled by `recToggle` view	Returns on failure
Text	Ink text
Ink text	Ink text (does not fail)
Shapes	Sketch ink, smoothed
Sketch ink	Nothing (occurs rarely)

As an alternative to using a `recConfig` frame to provide support for ink text, you can set your `clParagraphView` view's `vAnythingAllowed` mask. Although this is truly the easiest way to support ink text, it is less-preferred because it provides you the least control over the view's recognition behavior. A variation on this approach that may provide better performance is to enable an appropriate set of view flags rather than setting the `vAnythingAllowed` mask. The best way to support ink text, however, is through the use of a `recConfig` frame that provides appropriate values.

Regardless of the approach you take to provide ink text support, you should test your view's recognition behavior under both text recognizers, and under any other configurations your `recToggle` view provides.

To support both ink text and sketch ink in a single view, or to take other application-specific action in response to changes in the state of a `recToggle` view, your view can provide a `RecogSettingsChanged` method that reconfigures the its recognition behavior dynamically. For more information, see "Changing Recognition Behavior Dynamically" beginning on page 10-17.

For more information on `protoRecToggle` views, see "Using protoRecToggle Views" beginning on page 10-19. For detailed descriptions of `recConfig` frames, see "protoRecConfig" (page 8-36) and "System-Supplied recConfig Frames" (page 8-18) in *Newton Programmer's Reference*.

Fine-Tuning Text Recognition

To fine-tune either text recognizer's interpretation of input strokes, you can add the optional `speedCursiveOption`, `timeoutCursiveOption`, and `letterSpaceCursiveOption` slots to the `recConfig` frame. These mechanisms for controlling recognizer behavior may affect various recognizers differently. For more information, see "protoRecConfig" (page 8-36) in *Newton Programmer's Reference*. For a discussion of the `dictionaries` slot, see "Using Your RAM-Based Custom Dictionary" beginning on page 10-28.

Manipulating Dictionaries

You can control the view's use of dictionaries by including in your `recConfig` frame the `dictionaries`, `rcSingleLetters`, or `inhibitSymbolsDictionary` slots as appropriate. These slots are described in "protoRecConfig" (page 8-36) in *Newton Programmer's Reference*.

Single-Character Input Views

When recognizing single characters, the recognizer sometimes has difficulty determining individual characters' baseline or size; for example, it can be difficult to distinguish between an upper case *P* and a lower case *p* when relying strictly on user input. If you know where the user will be writing with respect to a well-defined baseline, you can provide an `rcBaseInfo` or `rcGridInfo` frame to specify to the recognition system precisely where characters are written.

The rcBaseInfo Frame

The `rcBaseInfo` frame is especially valuable in improving the recognition of single characters, for which it is sometimes difficult to derive baseline or letter-size values from user input.

Figure 10-3 depicts the editing box that an `rcBaseInfo` frame defines.

Figure 10-3   Single-character editing box specified by `rcBaseInfo` frame

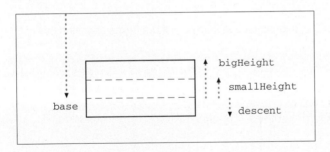

The NewtonScript code used to create the baseline information for the editing box shown in Figure 10-3 looks like the following example.

```
rcBaseInfo := {
   base:     140, // global y-coordinate of baseline
   smallHeight:15, // height of a lower case x
   bigHeight:30, // height of an upper case X
   descent:15, // size of descender below baseline
   };
```

To obtain the best performance and to conserve available memory, create your `rcBaseInfo` frame by cloning the frame provided by the `ROM_canonicalBaseInfo` constant. Store your frame in a slot named `rcBaseInfo` in your input view's `recConfig` frame.

For a detailed description of the `rcBaseInfo` frame, see "Data Structures Used in recConfig Frames" (page 8-24) in *Newton Programmer's Reference*.

The rcGridInfo Frame

The `rcGridInfo` frame allows you to define the position of one or more single-letter input areas within a single input view. Its purpose is to facilitate the creation of views having multiple single-letter input areas, such as might be used by a crossword puzzle application. Providing a separate view for each single letter input area would be extremely inefficient; the use of an `rcGridInfo` frame allows you to draw one view that provides the illusion of many input views, by defining to the recognizer the size of an individual input area and the spacing between input areas.

Figure 10-4 depicts an example of the grid that an `rcGridInfo` frame defines. The boxes shown in this figure are not views themselves, just lines on the screen that indicate the location of the input areas to the user. The recognition behavior is provided by the view that draws these boxes; the `rcGridInfo` frame helps the recognizer determine the precise location of user input, and, consequently, where to display its output. By providing the proper slots, you can use an `rcGridInfo` frame to define a row, column, or matrix (as shown in the figure) of single-letter input areas within a view.

Figure 10-4   Two-dimensional array of input boxes specified by `rcGridInfo` frame

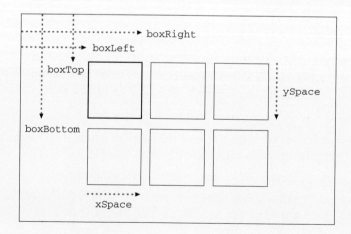

If you provide a grid in which the user is to write characters or words, you need to use an `rcGridInfo` frame to define the grid to the text recognizer. For example, the `protoCharEdit` system prototype uses an `rcGridInfo` frame internally to define the input areas (cells) in the comb view it provides.

The recognizer uses the information in an `rcGridInfo` frame to make character-segmentation decisions. You can use the `rcGridInfo` frame in conjunction with an `rcBaseInfo` frame to provide more accurate recognition within boxes in a single view. Recognition in the most recently used grid box begins as soon as the user writes in a new box in the grid.

The NewtonScript code used to create the grid shown in Figure 10-4 looks like the following example.

```
rcGridInfo := {
    boxLeft: 100,// x coordinate of left of top-left box
    boxRight:145,// x coordinate of right of top-left box
    xSpace:55,// x distance from boxLeft to boxLeft
    boxTop: 50,// y coordinate of top of top-left box
    boxBottom:95,// y coordinate of bottom of top-left box
    ySpace:55// y distance from boxTop to boxTop
    };
```

To obtain the best performance and to conserve available memory, create your `rcGridInfo` frame by cloning the frame provided by the `ROM_canonicalCharGrid` constant. Store your frame in a slot named `rcGridInfo` in your view's `recConfig` frame.

For a detailed description of the `rcGridInfo` frame, see "Data Structures Used in recConfig Frames" (page 8-24) in *Newton Programmer's Reference*

Creating Single-Letter Input Views

The following code fragment creates a single-letter input view's `recConfig` frame. This frame, which includes `rcBaseInfo` and `rcGridInfo` frames, is based on the `ROM_rcSingleCharacterConfig` frame supplied by the system.

```
// specify box (or horizontal array of boxes)
// into which character(s) are written.

myView := {
      recConfig: ROM_rcsinglecharacterconfig,
   ...}

// height of a lowercase letter
constant kSmallHeight := 11;
```

Recognition: Advanced Topics

```
// indent from left of view to first letter
constant kBoxIndent := 4;
// width of a single box in the grid
constant kCellWidth := 24;

// create editable recConfig frame and set initial values
myView.ViewSetupDoneScript := func()
   begin
      // prebuild RAM copy that we can change
      recConfig := PrepRecConfig(recConfig);

      // set these same flags in myView.viewFlags
      recConfig.inputMask :=
         vClickable+vGesturesAllowed+vCustomDictionaries;

      // get global bounds of enclosing view
      local box := :GlobalBox();
      // calc left edge of boxes in grid
      local leftX := box.left + kBoxIndent;

      // specify baseline and expected letter height
      recConfig.rcBaseInfo :=
         {
         // baseline for writing
         base: box.top + viewLineSpacing,
         // height of a small letter
         smallHeight: kSmallHeight,
         };

      // specify horizontal info for an array of boxes
      recConfig.rcGridInfo :=
         {
         // left edge of first box
         boxLeft: leftX,
         // right edge of first box
         boxRight: leftX + kCellWidth,
         // width to left edge of next box
         xSpace: kCellWidth,
         };

      // use new settings
      PurgeAreaCache();
   end;
```

The `PurgeAreaCache` function causes the recognition system to adopt the settings that the `recConfig` frame specifies. This function is explained in more detail in the next section, "Changing Recognition Behavior Dynamically."

Normally, you need not call the `PurgeAreaCache` function when specifying a `recConfig` frame as part of a view's template. However, you must call this function to change a `recConfig` frame at run time. For example, the previous code fragment calculates values determining the size and location of the grid view according to the size of the enclosing parent view; thus, the parent view must already exist before the grid view's `recConfig` frame can be constructed. Therefore, the grid view's `recConfig` frame is constructed from within the `ViewSetupDoneScript` method of the parent view that encloses the grid view. At the time the `viewSetupDoneScript` method is executed, the system has already used the `recConfig` frame supplied by the enclosing view's template. In order to cause the system to use the new `recConfig` frame—the one that defines the grid view—the `ViewSetupDoneScript` method must call the `PurgeAreaCache` function.

Changing Recognition Behavior Dynamically

To change a view's recognition behavior dynamically, you must indicate the view's new configuration (by setting view flags, changing the view's `dictionaries` slot, or defining a `recConfig` frame) and make the recognition system use the new settings. The system supplies three functions that you can use to make the system adopt new recognition settings; each is appropriate for a particular situation.

The function you use to adopt new settings depends on whether you are changing the recognition behavior of all views or just changing the behavior of individual views. Changes to user preferences for recognition affect the recognition behavior of all views. On the other hand, changing the value of a single view's `viewFlags` or `recConfig` slot affects that view only.

Note
It is recommended that you do not change any user settings without confirmation from the user. ◆

To change the recognition behavior of a single view dynamically, use the global function `SetValue` to change the value of the view's `viewFlags` slot or `recConfig` slot. In addition to setting the new value, the `SetValue` function invalidates the area cache, which is a buffer that stores a small number of recognition areas. Your changes to recognition behavior are incorporated when the recognition area for your view is rebuilt.

▲ **WARNING**

The SetValue function may not be appropriate for
setting the entryFlags slot in views that do not
have a viewFlags slot. In these kinds of views, set the
value of the entryFlags slot directly and then call the
PurgeAreaCache function to invalidate the area cache. If you
have changed values in the system's user configuration data, call
the ReadCursiveOptions function instead of the
PurgeAreaCache function. ▲

You can also use the PurgeAreaCache function to invalidate the area cache. This
function provides an efficient way to force the reconstruction of recognition areas
after you've changed the values of slots in multiple views. Note, however, that this
function does not resynchronize the recognition system with changes in the
system's user configuration data. Do not call PurgeAreaCache to effect changes
in user preferences for recognition.

User preferences that affect recognition behavior are saved as slot values in the
system's user configuration data. Some of these values, such as that of the
timeoutCursiveOption slot, affect all views; others affect only views that set
the vAnythingAllowed mask. For detailed information about the slot you need
to set, see its description in "System-Wide Settings" (page 8-2) in *Newton
Programmer's Reference*.

When setting user preferences for recognition, do not modify the system's user
configuration data directly. Instead, use the GetUserConfig and
SetUserConfig global functions to manipulate user configuration values.

After calling the SetUserConfig function to set one or more new values, you
must call the ReadCursiveOptions function to cause the recognition system to
use the new values. Do not call the PurgeAreaCache function after changing
values in the system's user configuration data—this function does not even test for
changes to user preferences. Because the ReadCursiveOptions function
invalidates the area cache, you need not call the PurgeAreaCache function after
calling the ReadCursiveOptions function.

IMPORTANT

The view's viewFlags slot must contain the same recognition
flags as the inputMask slot in its recConfig frame. Certain
view system operations depend on the viewFlags slot being set
up properly. ▲

Using protoRecToggle Views

A `protoRecToggle` view changes the recognition behavior of views by overriding values inherited from the system's user configuration data. Note that values in the view's `recConfig` frame override settings specified by the `protoRecToggle` view.

The `protoRecToggle` view is usually used with `clEditView` views that set the `vAnythingAllowed` mask or `clParagraphView` views that support ink text.

Take the following steps to use a `protoRecToggle` view.

- Create the `recToggle` view in NTK. If your application has a status bar, you need to provide the `recToggle` view as a child of the status bar.

- Configure input views appropriately to support the choices your `recToggle` view provides. To do so, you need to provide an appropriate `recConfig` frame or set the `vAnythingAllowed` mask for each view that is to be controlled by the `recToggle` view.

- Provide a `_recogSettings` slot at a place in the `_parent` chain that allows each view controlled by the `recToggle` view to inherit this slot.

You can take the following optional steps to customize your `recToggle` view's appearance or behavior:

- Provide a `_recogPopup` slot specifying the items to be included in the `protoRecToggle` picker.

- Implement a `RecogSettingsChanged` method in the `_parent` chain of any view controlled by the `recToggle` view.

The next several sections describes these steps in detail.

Creating the recToggle View

To create a `recToggle` view, you'll first need to sketch it out in the NTK layout editor. When you do so, you'll notice that regardless of where you draw it, the view will appear in the upper-left corner of the layout. This is because the `recToggle` view is intended to be displayed as a child of the status bar in applications that have one.

When a recToggle view is a child of your application's status bar, the view system positions the `recToggle` view on the status bar automatically, ignoring the value of the `recToggle` view template's `viewBounds` slot in the process. When the `recToggle` view is not a child of the status bar, you must create a `viewBounds` slot for it and set appropriate values for this slot.

Configuring Recognizers and Dictionaries for recToggle Views

Regardless of whether you use a recConfig frame or view flags to specify your view's recognition behavior, the view must be capable of enabling recognizers and dictionaries appropriate for each choice in the recToggle picker. If your view does not support all of the recognition settings provided by the default recToggle view, you need to provide a _recogPopup slot that restricts the choices appearing in the picker that the recToggle view displays. For more information, see "Providing the _recogPopup Slot" beginning on page 10-22.

If you are using a recConfig frame to specify your view's recognition behavior, you can place the ROM_rcPrefsConfig constant in your recConfig frame's _proto slot to provide a general-purpose recConfig frame that allows recognition of all forms of pen input. Note that you must also enable recognition behavior and dictionaries as appropriate in order to produce useful behavior.

Creating the _recogSettings Slot

Applications that use a recToggle view must provide a _recogSettings slot in a view that is a parent to both the recToggle view and the input view it controls. Your view template should specify an initial value of nil for this slot. Each time the user chooses an item from the recToggle picker, it saves a value representing its current setting in this slot. You can preserve the user's recognition settings by saving the contents of this slot when your application closes and restoring this slot's value when your application reopens.

When a single recToggle view controls recognition for all of your application's views, the _recogSettings slot can reside in the application's base view, as shown in Figure 10-5.

This approach can be used to synchronize the recognition behavior of multiple views; for example, the built-in Notes application uses a single recToggle view to control the recognition behavior of all currently visible notes. All of the views controlled by a single recToggle view must provide the same set of recognizers and dictionaries.

When each of several recToggle views must control individual input views, you must provide a _recogSettings slot for each recToggle view at an appropriate place in the _parent chain of each view that performs recognition, as shown in Figure 10-6.

Figure 10-5   One `recToggle` controls all views

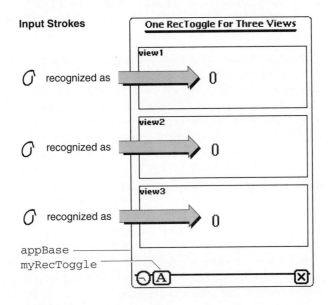

Figure 10-6   Each `recToggle` view controls a single input view

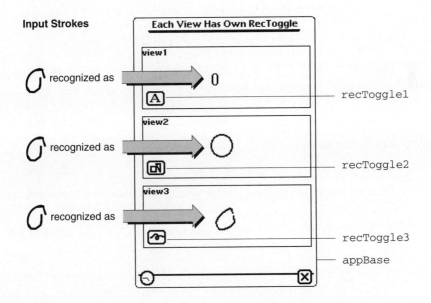

When the view receives input, it uses parent inheritance to find configuration information. If a _recogSettings slot exists in the view's _parent chain, the view uses the value of this slot, along with values supplied by an optional recConfig frame and values inherited from the system's user configuration data.

The recToggle view's ViewSetupFormScript method uses the value of the _recogSettings slot to set the state of the recToggle view. To restore the recognition settings that were in effect the last time your application was used, you can save the value of the _recogSettings slot when the application closes and restore the value of this slot when the application reopens. If you prefer that the recToggle view always open to a default setting, rather than a saved one, you can place the value nil in the _recogSettings slot when your application opens.

Providing the _recogPopup Slot

You can customize the appearance and behavior of your recToggle view by providing a _recogPopup slot in its view template. This slot contains an array of symbols corresponding to items included in the picker that the recToggle view displays. The first item in the array appears at the top of the picker and specifies the default recognizer enabled by the recToggle view. The picker includes subsequent items in the order in which they appear in the array.

Table 10-2 summarizes the symbols that may appear in the _recogPopup slot, along with the corresponding item each produces in the recToggle picker.

Table 10-2   Symbols appearing in the _recogPopup slot

Symbol	Represents	Picker item
'recogText	Text recognizer	Text
'recogInkText	Ink text	Ink Text
'recogShapes	Shape recognizer	Shapes
'recogSketches	Raw ink	Sketches
'recToggleSettings	Handwriting Recognition preferences slip	Preferences
'pickSeparator	No selection	Dashed line

To specify that the recToggle view enable a default recognizer other than the one specified by the first symbol in the _recogPopup array, your recToggle view's template can provide a defaultItem slot. This slot holds an integer value specifying the array element to be used as the default.

Avoid including inappropriate items in the `recToggle` popup, such as an ink text item for a view that does not support ink text. It is your responsibility to ensure that the `_recogPopup` array includes only symbols representing valid choices for the view that the `recToggle` configures.

Accessing Correction Information

As words are recognized, the system saves correction information that includes

- the stroke bundle. (See "Unrecognized Strokes" on page 9-7.)

- alternate interpretations returned by the recognizer. (See "Classifying Strokes" on page 9-3.)

- learning data. (See "Correction and Learning" on page 9-13.)

You can call the `GetCorrectInfo` global function at any time to obtain correction information for recently-recognized words. This function returns a `correctInfo` frame based on the `protoCorrectInfo` system prototype.

The `info` slot in the `correctInfo` frame holds an array of `wordInfo` frames based on the `protoWordInfo` system prototype. Each `wordInfo` frame represents a single written word.

The `max` slot in the `correctInfo` frame specifies the maximum number of words for which it holds correction information. When adding a new element to the `info` array will cause this array to exceed the size specified by the `max` slot, the system removes the first element of the `info` array, uses its learning data if necessary, and adds the new `wordInfo` frame to the `info` array.

The `correctInfo` frame provides a number of methods that you can use to manipulate its contents; for more information, see "CorrectInfo Functions and Methods" (page 8-54) in *Newton Programmer's Reference*.

Each `wordInfo` frame specifies the following information:

- the view that contains the word.

- the position of the word within the `clParagraphView` view that displays it.

- the list of alternate interpretations of the input strokes.

- an identifier specifying the recognizer that interpreted the input.

- a stroke bundle (optional).

- learning data (optional).

As an alternative to obtaining `wordInfo` frames from the `correctInfo` frame, you can extract these frames from the word unit passed to an optional `ViewWordScript` method that your view provides. For a description of this method, see "Application-Defined Recognition Methods" (page 8-66) in *Newton Programmer's Reference*.

The `wordInfo` frame provides methods that you can use to manipulate its contents; for more information, see "WordInfo Methods" (page 8-62) in *Newton Programmer's Reference*.

The alternate interpretations of a recognized word are provided as `wordInterp` frames based on the `protoWordInterp` system prototype. An array of `wordInterp` frames resides in the `wordInfo` frame's `words` slot.

Each `wordInterp` frame contains the following information:

- a string that is one interpretation of the original input strokes.

- a score indicating the recognizer's confidence in the accuracy of the interpretation.

- the dictionary identifier of the recognized word (for internal use only).

- the position occupied by this word in the original list of interpretations returned by the recognizer.

For more information, see the descriptions of the `protoCorrectInfo`, `protoWordInterp`, and `protoWordInfo` prototypes in *Newton Programmer's Reference*.

You can provide an optional `ViewCorrectionPopupScript` method that modifies or replaces the picker that displays correction information when a word is double-tapped. For a description of this method, see "Application-Defined Recognition Methods" (page 8-66) in *Newton Programmer's Reference*.

Using Custom Dictionaries

In addition to the system-supplied dictionaries, your application can use custom dictionaries to facilitate the recognition of specialized vocabulary such as medical or legal terms. It's relatively easy to create a RAM-based enumerated dictionary at run time; however, this approach is not recommended for dictionaries containing more than a few words.

Note that you cannot cause the built-in applications (Names, Dates and so on) to use custom dictionaries. The only way to enable these applications to recognize specialized terminology is to add words to the user dictionary. However, you are strongly discouraged from doing so, because each entry added to the user dictionary reduces the amount of system RAM available to the user. For more information, see "System Dictionaries" beginning on page 9-11.

Creating a Custom Enumerated Dictionary

To create a custom enumerated dictionary, you must populate a blank RAM-based dictionary with your dictionary items. Dictionary items can come from a number of places: they might be elements of your own array of strings stored in the application's NTK project data; they might be represented as binary resource data in your application's NTK project; they might be supplied by the user in an input line view; they might even arrive as serial data. Because dictionary items can originate from a number of sources, the example here presumes that you know how to store your word strings and pass them, one at a time, to the `AddWordToDictionary` function. This function adds its argument to the specified custom dictionary.

The `AddWordToDictionary` function does not place any restrictions on the strings to be entered in the dictionary; however, your intended use of the dictionary entry may influence its content. For nonrecognition purposes, such as validating input to a field, any string is a valid dictionary entry. For use in stroke recognition, strings in enumerated dictionaries must not include spaces. The printed recognizer accepts the full set of ASCII characters; the cursive recognizer does not. Digits or non-alphabetic characters in dictionary entries used by the cursive recognizer must appear in the input string in order to be recognized. Do not use the `AddWordToDictionary` function to add items to the review dictionary; use the appropriate `reviewDict` methods instead.

You can take the following steps to create a RAM-based enumerated dictionary at run time:

1. Use the global function `NewDictionary` to create a new empty dictionary.

2. Use the global function `AddWordToDictionary` to add dictionary items to the new dictionary.

3. Use the global function `GetDictionaryData` to create a binary representation of the completed dictionary, which can then be stored in a soup.

Another way to do this is to create a new dictionary and restore its data from a soup.

The next several sections describe the numbered steps in greater detail. Following this discussion, the section "Restoring Dictionary Data From a Soup" (page 10-28), describes how to restore an existing dictionary from soup data.

Creating the Blank Dictionary

You can create a blank RAM-based dictionary anywhere in your application that makes sense; a common approach is to take care of this in the `ViewSetupFormScript` method of the application's base view. You must also create a slot in which to store the RAM-based dictionary. The following code fragment creates a dictionary in the `mySpecialDictionary` slot.

```
ViewSetupFormScript := func()
begin
    mySpecialDictionary := NewDictionary('custom);
end
```

This code example uses the `NewDictionary` function to create a blank dictionary in the `mySpecialDictionary` slot. The `NewDictionary` function accepts the symbol `'custom` as its argument, which specifies that the new dictionary is for this application's use only.

Note
Although the token returned by the `NewDictionary` function currently evaluates to an integer in the NTK Inspector, the type of value returned by this function may change on future Newton devices. Do not rely on the `NewDictionary` function returning an integer. ◆

Adding Words to RAM-Based Dictionaries

Once you have created a blank dictionary, you need to populate it with your dictionary items. You can use the `AddWordToDictionary` function to add a specified string to a specified RAM-based dictionary.

The first argument to this function is the identifier of the dictionary to which the string is to be added; this identifier is returned by the `NewDictionary` function. The previous code example stored this identifier in the `mySpecialDictionary` slot.

The second argument to this function is the string to be added to the dictionary. If this argument is not a string, the `AddWordToDictionary` function throws an exception. If the word is added successfully, this function returns `true`. If the specified word cannot be added, this function returns `nil`.

The `AddWordToDictionary` function may return `nil` when the word to be added is already present in the specified dictionary, or it may return `nil` because of resource limitations. It is possible to run out of system memory for dictionaries, with potentially serious consequences. Do not rely on a specific number of dictionary entries as the maximum amount that may be added safely. It is strongly recommended that you use custom dictionaries sparingly and keep them as small as possible, taking into account the possibility that other applications may require system memory for their own dictionaries or for other uses.

To populate the dictionary, you need to call the `AddWordToDictionary` function once for each item to be added. There are many ways to call a function iteratively; the best approach for your needs is an application-specific detail that cannot be anticipated here. The following code example shows one way to populate a blank dictionary.

```
myAdder:= func()
begin
    local element;
    // items slot contains an array of dictionary strings
    foreach element in items do
        AddWordToDictionary(mySpecialDictionary, element);
end
```

This approach works well for small dictionaries; for most large dictionaries, however, it is far more efficient to populate the dictionary from saved soup data. You should store custom dictionary data in a soup so that it is safely stored and persistent across soft resets.

IMPORTANT

Do not use the `AddWordToDictionary` global function to add words to the review dictionary; instead, use the appropriate review dictionary methods. ▲

Removing Words From RAM-Based Dictionaries

You can use the `DeleteWordFromDictionary` function to remove a specified word from a specified RAM-based dictionary. Note that this function does not make permanent changes to soups. After calling this function you must write your changes to the appropriate soup.

IMPORTANT

Do not use the `DeleteWordFromDictionary` function to remove words from the review dictionary; instead, use the appropriate review dictionary methods. ▲

Saving Dictionary Data to a Soup

Once you have added all of your dictionary entries, your RAM-based custom dictionary is ready for use. However, it would be inefficient to build it from scratch each time you need it, especially if it is large. Instead, you can store a binary representation of the dictionary data in a soup and use this soup data to restore the custom dictionary.

The `NewDictionary` function returns an identifier used to reference the dictionary; in the previous example, this identifier was stored in the `mySpecialDictionary` slot defined in the base view of the application. You can pass this identifier as the `GetDictionaryData` function's argument. This function returns a binary representation of the dictionary data (the words or items). You can then place this binary object in a slot in a frame and add the frame to a soup. The following code fragment assumes that the soup `kSoupName` is a valid soup created according to the Newton DTS soup-creation guidelines.

```
// get a soup in which to save the data
mySoup := GetUnionSoupAlways (kSoupName);
// create binary representation of dictionary data
local dict := GetRoot().appSym.mySpecialDictionary;
local theObj:= GetDictionaryData(dict);
```

```
// store the dictionary data
dictData := {data:theObj};
mySoup:AddXmit(dictData, nil);
```

Restoring Dictionary Data From a Soup

To use the dictionary, your application needs to retrieve the dictionary data object from the soup and use the global function `SetDictionaryData` to install the data in an empty dictionary. This is typically done in the application part's `InstallScript` function or in the `ViewSetupFormScript` method of the view that uses the custom dictionary, as shown in the following code example:

```
// make new blank dictionary
mySpecialDictionary := NewDictionary('custom);
// get the dictionary data from the soup
// structure of query depends on how you store data
dataCursor:= dictDataSoup:Query(querySpec);
// how you get entry depends on how you store data
myBinaryData := dataCursor:entry();
// put data in dictionary
SetDictionaryData(mySpecialDictionary, myBinaryData);
```

Note that RAM-based dictionaries are lost when the system resets. However, the system calls your application part's `InstallScript` function after a reset. This function can determine whether the dictionary exists and recreate it if necessary. Because this function is also called when a card with your application on it is inserted, as well as when the application is installed initially, it provides an ideal place from which to install your custom dictionary.

Using Your RAM-Based Custom Dictionary

Take the following steps to make your RAM-based dictionary available to each view that is to use it for recognition:

1. Set the view's `vCustomDictionaries` flag.

2. Create a `dictionaries` slot. You can create this slot in the view itself or in its `recConfig` frame.

3. Place your dictionary's identifier in the `dictionaries` slot.

To enable the use of custom dictionaries, you must set the `vCustomDictionaries` flag for the view that is to use the custom dictionary. This flag indicates that the view has access to a slot named `dictionaries` that specifies dictionaries to be used for recognition. The dictionaries specified in this slot are used in conjunction with any other dictionaries that may be specified for this view's use.

In addition to setting the view's vCustomDictionaries flag, you need to create a dictionaries slot in either the view or its recConfig frame. The dictionaries slot stores a single dictionary identifier or an array of dictionary identifiers. You need to install the custom dictionary in this slot using code similar to the following example.

```
// vCustomDictionaries flag already set
dictionaries := mySpecialDictionary;
```

To use system-supplied dictionaries in addition to your custom dictionary, you can enable additional view flags in the Entry Flags editor in NTK or set these additional flags procedurally. If you prefer to set view flags procedurally, you must use the Bor function to bitwise OR the vCustomDictionaries flag with any bits already set in the viewFlags slot. In either case, your custom dictionary must still be specified in the dictionaries slot.

Note that some view flags enable combinations of system dictionaries. If you want to specify explicitly which system dictionaries the view can use, set no dictionary-enabling flags other than the vCustomDictionaries flag and use system-supplied dictionary ID constants to add specific dictionaries to the dictionaries slot. For descriptions of the system-supplied dictionary ID constants, see "System-Supplied Dictionaries" (page 8-16) in *Newton Programmer's Reference*.

The following code fragment shows how you can specify dictionaries explicitly by including the appropriate constants as elements of the array in the dictionaries slot.

```
dictionaries :=[mySpecialDictionary, kUserDictionary,
                kCommonDictionary]
```

Regardless of the order of elements in the dictionaries array, the system always searches the user dictionary first. The system then searches all of the specified dictionaries in the order that they appear in the dictionaries array. In general, the order in which this array's items appear is not critical, except in the case of conflicting capitalization information for representations of the same word in multiple dictionaries. When multiple dictionary entries match the input, the system uses the first dictionary entry that was matched.

Note that the printed recognizer can always return words not present in dictionaries. Only the cursive recognizer may be restricted to returning only words present in dictionaries (and then only when letter-by-letter recognition is not enabled). To test your dictionary settings, use the cursive recognizer while its letter-by-letter option is disabled.

Removing Your RAM-Based Custom Dictionary

It is recommended that you remove your custom dictionary when it is no longer needed, such as when your application is removed. The `DisposeDictionary` function removes a specified RAM-based dictionary.

The `DisposeDictionary` function accepts one argument, the dictionary identifier returned by `NewDictionary`. If this identifier was stored in a slot named `mySpecialDictionary`, a line of code similar to the following example would be used to remove the custom dictionary.

```
DisposeDictionary(mySpecialDictionary);
```

Using System Dictionaries Individually

The system provides several constants that you can use to refer to system dictionaries conveniently; see "System-Supplied Dictionaries" (page 8-16) in *Newton Programmer's Reference*. You can set the `vCustomDictionaries` flag and place one or more of these constants in your view's `dictionaries` slot to specify explicitly the vocabulary it can recognize, such as first names only or names of days and months only. Note that a single constant may represent multiple dictionaries; for example, when the `kCommonDictionary` constant is specified, the system may actually add several dictionaries to the set that the view uses for recognition. The rest of this section describes the use of individual system dictionaries.

The `vNumbersAllowed` flag enables both the numeric lexical dictionary and the monetary lexical dictionary. To create a view that recognizes numeric values but not monetary values, set the `vCustomDictionaries` flag and place the `kNumbersOnlyDictionary` constant in the view's `dictionaries` slot.

Note that both the `vCustomDictionaries` and `vCharsAllowed` flags enable text recognition. The difference between these flags is in the set of dictionaries they enable. The `vCustomDictionaries` flag enables only those dictionaries specified by the `dictionaries` slot of the view performing recognition. The `vCharsAllowed` flag, on the other hand, enables several system-supplied dictionaries. To avoid unexpected results when working with custom dictionaries, be aware that setting other flags may enable additional dictionaries. Remember, also, that the printed recognizer can always return words not appearing in dictionaries.

Working With the Review Dictionary

The review dictionary object provides methods for manipulating the contents of the user dictionary (personal word list), and the expand dictionary. Although the auto-add dictionary is also part of the review dictionary, the auto-add dictionary has its own interface.

Do not use the global functions `AddWordToDictionary` and `RemoveWordFromDictionary` to make changes to the review dictionary; instead, use the appropriate review dictionary methods.

The dictionaries themselves are stored as entries in the system soup. This section describes how to manipulate these dictionaries programmatically. All of the functions and methods named in this section are described completely in "User Dictionary Functions and Methods" beginning on page 10-54.

Retrieving the Review Dictionary

To manipulate the contents of the user dictionary or expand dictionary, you send messages to the `reviewDict` object, which resides in the root view.

To obtain a reference to the `reviewDict` object, you can use code similar to the following example.

```
local reviewDict := GetRoot().reviewDict;
```

Note
Future versions of the system are not guaranteed to have the `ReviewDict` slot. You must verify that the returned value is non-nil before using it. ◆

You usually do not need to load the review dictionary into RAM yourself—the system does so automatically when it is reset and most flags that enable text recognition include the user dictionary automatically in the set of dictionaries they enable. You usually do not need to load the auto-add or expand dictionaries explicitly, either—the user dictionary consults these additional dictionaries automatically. However, the `LoadUserDictionary`, `LoadExpandDictionary`, and `LoadAutoAddDictionary` functions are provided for your convenience.

For general information about the user dictionary, expand dictionary and auto-add dictionary, see "System Dictionaries" beginning on page 9-11.

Displaying Review Dictionary Browsers

You can send the `Open` message to the `reviewDict` object to display the Personal Word List slip. If words have been added to the auto-add dictionary, this function displays the Recently Written Words slip automatically as well.

To display the Recently Written Words slip alone, send the `Open` message to the `autoAdd` object residing in the system's root view, as shown in the following example.

```
local auto := GetRoot().autoAdd:Open();
if auto then auto:Open();
```

Note

Future versions of the system are not guaranteed to have the
`autoAdd` slot. You must verify that the returned value is non-`nil`
before using it. ◆

Adding Words to the User Dictionary

The following code fragment uses the `AddWord` method of the `reviewDict`
object to add words to the user dictionary. After adding one or more words, you
must call the `SaveUserDictionary` function to make your changes to the user
dictionary's system soup entry persistent.

```
local reviewDict := GetRoot().reviewDict;
if reviewDict then
    begin
        reviewDict:AddWord("myWord");
        reviewDict:AddWord("myOtherWord");
        SaveUserDictionary();
    end;
```

The `AddWord` method returns `true` if the word was added successfully and
returns `nil` if the word was not added; however, this function may also return `nil`
due to resource limitations.

It is possible to run out of system memory for dictionaries, with potentially serious
consequences. Do not rely on a specific number as the maximum amount of
dictionary entries that may be added safely.

If the Personal Word List slip is open when you add words to the user dictionary,
its display is updated automatically. An undo action is posted for this update.

IMPORTANT

Do not use the `AddWordToDictionary` global function to add
words to the review dictionary. ▲

Removing Words From the User Dictionary

The following code fragment uses the `RemoveWord` method of the `reviewDict`
object to remove a word from the user dictionary. After deleting the word, you
must call the `SaveUserDictionary` function to write the changes to the user
dictionary's system soup entry.

```
local reviewDict := GetRoot().ReviewDict;
if reviewDict then
    begin
        reviewDict:RemoveWord("myWord");
        reviewDict:RemoveWord("myOtherWord");
        SaveUserDictionary();
    end;
```

The `RemoveWord` method returns `true` if the word was removed successfully and returns `nil` if the word was not removed. This method returns `nil` and does not remove the specified word if there are differences in case between the word in the dictionary and the word passed as the argument to the `RemoveWord` method. This method also returns `nil` when the word to be removed is not present in the review dictionary.

IMPORTANT

Do not use the `RemoveWordFromDictionary` global function to make changes to the review dictionary; instead, use the appropriate review dictionary methods. ▲

Adding Words to the Expand Dictionary

The expand dictionary (the dictionary that defines word expansions) is kept in RAM, and its size is limited to 256 words. To manipulate the expand dictionary, you send messages to the `reviewDict` object residing in the root view. The system provides methods for adding words and their associated expansions to this dictionary; retrieving the expansions associated with words; removing words and expansions from this dictionary; and saving expansion dictionary changes to the system soup.

To add a word and its expansion to the expand dictionary, you must send the `AddExpandWord` message to the `reviewDict` object. Words added to the expand dictionary must first be recognized and present in the user dictionary. If necessary, you can use the `AddWord` method of the `reviewDict` object to add the word to the user dictionary before adding it to the expand dictionary. After adding one or more words to the expand dictionary, you must call the `SaveExpandDictionary` function to write your changes to the system soup, as the following code fragment illustrates.

```
local reviewDict := GetRoot().ReviewDict;
// word must be present in user dict before adding to expand dict
if reviewDict then
    begin
        if not LookupWordInDictionary(reviewDict, "BTW") then
            begin
                reviewDict:AddWord("BTW");
                SaveUserDictionary();
            end;
        reviewDict:AddExpandWord("BTW", "by the way");
        // write changes to system soup
        SaveExpandDictionary();
    end;
```

Removing Words From the Expand Dictionary

Normally, words are added to both the expand dictionary and the user dictionary simultaneously. As a result, words removed from the expand dictionary generally must also be removed from the user dictionary. The following code fragment uses the RemoveWord method to remove a word from both the expand and the user dictionaries. After deleting the word, you must call the SaveUserDictionary function to write the changes to the system soup.

```
local reviewDict := GetRoot().ReviewDict;
if reviewDict then
   begin
      // remove word & expansion from dictionaries
      reviewDict:RemoveWord("BTW");
      SaveUserDictionary();
   end;
```

Retrieving Word Expansions

The following code fragment uses the GetExpandedWord method of the reviewDict object to retrieve the expansion associated with a specified word. This method returns nil if the specified word is not found in the expand dictionary.

```
local reviewDict := GetRoot().ReviewDict;
if reviewDict then
   local theExpansion := reviewDict:GetExpandedWord("BTW");
```

Retrieving the Auto-Add Dictionary

The auto-add dictionary (the list of new words to add to the user dictionary automatically) resides in RAM and its size is limited to 100 words. The system adds new words to this dictionary automatically when the cursive recognizer is enabled and the Add New Words to Personal Word List checkbox in the Text Editing Settings preferences slip is selected.

The Recently Added Words slip provides the NewtonScript interface to the auto-add dictionary. You can use code similar to the following example to obtain a reference to the RecentlyAdded Words slip.

```
local autoAddDict := GetRoot().AutoAdd;
```

Note
Future versions of the system are not guaranteed to have this slot. You must verify that the returned value is non-nil before using it. ◆

Usually, you do not need to load the auto-add dictionary into RAM yourself—the system does so automatically whenever the Personal Word List slip is opened or the system is reset. However, the system provides the `LoadAutoAddDictionary` function for your convenience.

Disabling the Auto-Add Mechanism

When the cursive recognizer is enabled, words not appearing in any of the currently enabled dictionaries are added to the auto-add and user dictionaries automatically as they are recognized or corrected. The value of the `doAutoAdd` slot in the system's user configuration data controls this default behavior.

However, not all input to a view is appropriate to add to dictionaries; for example, consider a spreadsheet that allows the user to select cells by entering row and column numbers—you wouldn't want to add these strings to the dictionaries as they are recognized. To disable the automatic addition of new words to the user and auto-add dictionaries, you can use either of the following techniques:

- Set the `_noautoadd` slot in the view or its `recConfig` frame to a non-`nil` value.

- Set the `_noautoadd` slot in the word's `wordInfo` frame to a non-`nil` value. You can get a word's `wordInfo` frame by calling the `GetCorrectionWordInfo` function from within the view's `ViewWordScript` method.

Alternatively, you can set the value of the `doAutoAdd` slot in the system's user configuration data to `nil` and call the `ReadCursiveOptions` function; however, it is not recommended that you change user configuration settings without first obtaining confirmation from the user.

Adding Words to the Auto-Add Dictionary

The `AddAutoAdd` function adds a specified word to both the user and auto-add dictionaries. This function returns the value `true` after adding the word successfully. The word is not added if its unpunctuated form is present in the standard set of dictionaries enabled by the `vCharsAllowed` flag.

If the auto-add dictionary already contains its maximum of 100 words, this function does not add the new word but displays the notify icon instead. When the user taps the notify icon, it posts a notify action that displays the Recently Written Words slip. The user can then edit the Recently Written Words slip before attempting to add more words; if the user responds immediately, no new words are lost. For more information on the notify icon and notify actions, see Chapter 17, "Additional System Services."

Removing Words From the Auto-Add Dictionary

The RemoveAutoAdd function deletes a specified word from both the user and auto-add dictionaries. This function returns true if the word was removed and returns nil if the word was not removed. This method does not remove the word if it is not present in the auto-add dictionary or if there are case inconsistencies between the argument to this function and the word actually found in the dictionary.

Using protoCharEdit Views

The protoCharEdit proto provides a comb-style view that facilitates the correction of individual characters in misrecognized words. The view provided by this proto uses an rcGridInfo frame internally to provide a horizontal row of single-character input areas. The system-supplied corrector available from the picker displayed when the user taps a recognized word makes use of this view. Figure 10-7 illustrates a typical protoCharEdit view.

Figure 10-7   Example of a protoCharEdit view

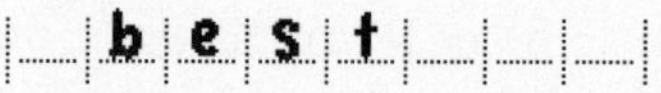

This section describes how to position a protoCharEdit view, how to manipulate the text string it displays, and how to restrict its input to a specified set of characters.

Positioning protoCharEdit Views

There are two ways to position a protoCharEdit view within its parent view. You can set the values of its top and left slots to values that position it at the top left corner of the view, or you can provide a similar value for its viewBounds slot.

If you specify the values of the top and left slots, then the ViewSetupFormScript method of the protoCharEdit view supplies an appropriate value for the viewBounds slot based on the values of the cellHeight, cellWidth, and maxChars slots. On the other hand, if you provide the values of the viewBounds and cellWidth slots, then this view supplies appropriate values for the maxChars and cellHeight slots for you. This proto provides useful default values for the cellWidth and cellHeight slots; it is recommended that you do not change these values.

The technique you use depends on how you want to set the slots that this proto provides. For detailed information, see "protoCharEdit" (page 8-41) in *Newton Programmer's Reference*.

Manipulating Text in protoCharEdit Views

The default view provided by the `protoCharEdit` proto is an unformatted comb view (see page 10-4). You can provide an optional template that customizes this view's appearance and behavior. The template itself is a frame residing in the view's `template` slot. This frame may provide the following slots and methods:

- The template's `filter` slot defines a set of permissible input values. For example, a view for correcting phone numbers might restrict the set of permissible characters to numerals.

- The template's `format` slot can specify the length of the comb view and the editing characteristics of its entry fields. For example, the phone number correction view might use a format template to restrict input to a fixed number of characters and make certain entry fields non-editable. When the comb view erases invalid characters it displays the animated cloud and plays the `ROM_poof` sound that normally accompanies the scrub gesture.

- The template's `text` slot supplies a string to be displayed initially when the comb view opens. The comb view retrieves this value when its `ViewSetupFormScript` is executed.

- You can also supply optional `SetupString` and `CleanupString` functions that manipulate the string in the `text` slot.

For complete descriptions of these slots, see "Template Used by ProtoCharEdit Views" (page 8-45) and "Application-Defined protoCharEdit Template Methods" (page 8-52) in *Newton Programmer's Reference*.

The system also provides several global functions that are useful for manipulating `protoCharEdit` views and the strings they display.

To change the comb view's text string or template dynamically, call the `UseTextAndTemplate` function after setting appropriate values for the `text` or `template` slots. Alternatively, you can use the `SetNewWord` or `SetNewTemplate` and `UseNewWord` or `UseNewTemplate` functions to perform the same operations; in fact, calling these functions yourself is faster than calling the `UseTextAndTemplate` function.

To get the current value of the text in the comb view, you can send the `CurrentWord` message to the view. You must not use the value of the `text` slot directly, because unformatted comb views may add extra spaces to the string in this slot. To get a special version of the text that is formatted for display in a view other than the comb view, use the `GetWordForDisplay` function. If you are using a template, this function may return the string in a more standardized format, because it calls the template's optional `CleanupString` function before returning the string.

You may also need to know the boundaries of the word in the text slot when working with certain protoCharEdit methods and functions. The protoCharEdit view's wordLeft and wordRight slots provide indexes into the text string that you can use to determine the boundaries of a substring suitable for external display or for use as an argument to these routines. The wordLeft slot contains the index of the first externally-displayed character in the text slot. The wordRight slot contains the index of the position immediately following the last externally-displayed character in the text slot. For example, when the text slot holds the "one " string, 1 is the value of the wordLeft slot and 4 is the value of the wordRight slot. The dispLeft slot contains the index of the first character in the text slot that is displayed—this character occupies the leftmost position in the comb view. The dispLeft slot normally has the value 0, but after scrolling it may have values greater than 0. The dispIndent slot is the offset from the leftmost edge of the view to the leftmost edge of the first character displayed.

For more information, see "protoCharEdit Functions and Methods" (page 8-47) in *Newton Programmer's Reference*.

Restricting Characters Returned by protoCharEdit Views

This section provides code examples illustrating the use of templates to restrict the set of characters that may appear in a comb view. Note that templates post-process the characters returned by the recognition system before the view displays them, rather than limiting the set of characters that the view can recognize.

The templates defined by the following code fragments are intended to serve as examples only. The system provides templates that handle formatting conventions for dates, times, phone numbers, and numeric values properly according to the user's locale. For complete descriptions of these templates, see "System-Supplied protoCharEdit Templates" (page 8-46) in *Newton Programmer's Reference*.

The following code example defines a template for a date field:

```
digits  :=   "0123456789";// filters[0]
digits1 :=   "01";        // filters[1]
digits3 :=   "0123";      // filters[2]

dateTemplate := {
   string:"  /  /  ",// slashes locked by "_" in format
   format:"10_20_00",// indexes into filters array
   filters:[digits, digits1, digits3],
   };
```

This example template is used in a protoCharEdit view that specifies a value of 8 or more for its maxChars slot; hence, the eight-character strings in the format and string slots.

The cells in this example template use filters defined by the `format` and `filters` slots to restrict input to valid values.

The `format` slot specifies the valid input for each position in the comb view. Each character in the `format` string is an index into the `filters` array. In this example, the first position in the comb view is filtered by the element 1 of the `filters` array, which is the `digits1` template; the second position is filtered by element 0 of the `filters` array, which is the `digits` template.

You can write-protect any position in the comb view by placing an underscore (_) in the appropriate position in the `format` string. In this example, the string positions that display slashes between the digits of the date field do not allow input. These are indicated by the underscores at corresponding positions in the `format` string.

The `text` slot is not used by `protoCharEdit` views, but may be used as a default value by optional `SetupString` and `CleanupString` methods that your template supplies.

Note that the template itself does not restrict any values unnecessarily. For example, it is not wise to restrict date values according to the value of the month, because the user might enter the date before the month or the month value might not be recognized correctly. Instead, you can define a `CleanupString` function that examines the input string and indicates an error condition or modifies the string.

The following code fragment provides examples of typical `SetupString` and `CleanupString` functions.

```
myTemplate := {
    format:"0000001",
    string:"      0",
    filters: [kMyDigitsOrSpace, kMyDigits],

    SetupString: func(str) begin
        // pad string to 5 digits
        if StrLen(str) < 7 then
            StrMunger(str,0,0,string,0,7-StrLen(str));
        str;
    end,

    CleanupString: func(str) begin
        // replace spaces with zeros
        StrReplace(str, " ", "0", nil);
        // trim leading zeros
        str := NumberStr(StringToNumber(str));
        str;
    end,
};
```

Customized Processing of Input Strokes

Setting the vStrokesAllowed flag provides the view with a means of intercepting raw input data for application-specific processing. If this flag is set, strokes are passed one at a time as the argument to the view's ViewStrokeScript method. Your ViewStrokeScript method can then process the strokes in any manner that is appropriate. The view's ViewStrokeScript method is invoked when the user lifts the pen from the screen at the end of each input stroke.

Both the vGesturesAllowed and vStrokesAllowed flags invoke methods that can be used to provide application-specific handling of gestures. However, the vGesturesAllowed flag supplies system-defined behavior for the gestures tap, double-tap, highlight, and scrub in clEditView and clParagraphView views, while the vStrokesAllowed flag does not provide any behavior that you don't implement yourself, regardless of the kind of view performing recognition.

For example, clEditView and clParagraphView views handle system-defined gestures automatically. Thus, scrubbing in a clParagraphView view that sets the vGesturesAllowed flag does not invoke the ViewGestureScript method because the view handles this gesture automatically. On the other hand, a clView view would need to supply a ViewGestureScript method to process the scrub gesture because this kind of view does not provide any gesture-handling behavior of its own. Finally, remember that any view setting the vStrokesAllowed flag must also supply a ViewStrokeScript method.

Setting these flags causes the recognition system to send messages such as ViewClickScript or ViewStrokeScript, passing a unit (an object that describes the interaction of the pen with the tablet) as the argument to the corresponding methods. Units are only valid when accessed from within the methods invoked during the recognition process—you cannot save them for later use. However, you can distribute the processing of unit data as appropriate; for example, you might call the GetPointsArray function from within your ViewClickScript method and use the result later in your ViewIdleScript method.

IMPORTANT

Do not save units for later use—they are valid only during the recognition process. After the user interaction is complete and the various scripts utilizing a particular unit have returned, the memory allocated for that unit is freed explicitly. Subsequent use of the unit may produce bus errors or loss of significant data. ▲

Customized Processing of Double Taps

To process double taps reliably, your view's `ViewGestureScript` method can test for the presence of the `aeDoubleTap` gesture. The gesture recognizer measures time between pen events reliably even when the main NewtonScript thread is busy.

The recognition system considers a second tap to be part of a double tap when it occurs within a specified amount of time and distance relative to the first tap.

The second tap must be within 6 pixels of the first to be considered part of a double tap. Any stroke longer than 6 pixels is not recognized as a tap (or as the second tap). Measurement of the distance between taps is based on the midpoint of the start and end points of the stroke.

The amount of time that determines whether a second tap is considered part of a double tap is specified by the value of the `timeoutCursiveOption` slot in the system's user configuration data. This value ranges between 15 and 60 ticks, with a default value of 45 ticks. The user sets the value of this slot by moving the "Transform my handwriting" slider in the Fine Tuning slip. The Fine Tuning slip is available from the picker displayed by the Options button in the Handwriting Recognition preferences slip.

Your `ViewGestureScript` method is called only if the view does not handle the gesture automatically. Your `ViewGestureScript` method should return the value `true` to avoid passing the gesture unit to other `ViewGestureScript` methods, such as those supplied by views in the `_parent` chain. If you do want to pass the gesture unit to other views, your method should return the value `nil`.

Changing User Preferences for Recognition

When you must make system-wide changes in recognition behavior, you can set the values of slots in the system's user configuration data to do so. However, in most cases it is more appropriate to change the behavior of individual views, rather than system-wide settings. For information on using `recConfig` frames to specify the recognition behavior of individual views, see "Using recConfig Frames" beginning on page 10-8.

Take the following steps to change recognition settings used by all views:

1. Call the `SetUserConfig` function to set the values of one or more slots in the system's user configuration data. For a complete listing of the recognition-related slots, see "System-Wide Settings" (page 8-2) in *Newton Programmer's Reference*.

2. Call the `ReadCursiveOptions` function to cause the system to use the new settings.

Note

Normally, slot values in the system's user configuration
data are set by the user from various preference slips.
It is strongly recommended that you do not change any
user preferences without first obtaining confirmation from
the user. ◆

Modifying or Replacing the Correction Picker

Views that recognize text can provide an optional `ViewCorrectionPopupScript`
method that modifies or replaces the picker displayed when a recognized word is
double-tapped. For more information, see "ViewCorrectionPopupScript" (page 8-75)
in *Newton Programmer's Reference*.

Using Stroke Bundles

The system provides functions that allow you to retrieve or manipulate stroke data,
such as the tablet points from each stroke. You can access these points in one of
two resolutions: **screen resolution** or **tablet resolution.** In screen resolution, each
coordinate value is rounded to the nearest screen pixel. In tablet resolution, each
coordinate has an additional three bits of data.

To access the ink in a view, use one of the functions documented in "Text and Ink
Input and Display Reference" (page 7-1) in *Newton Programmer's Reference*.
Functions that allow you to manipulate ink include the `ParaContainsInk`,
`PolyContainsInk`, and `GetInkAt` functions.

To perform deferred recognition on the strokes in a stroke bundle, pass the stroke
bundle to one of the `Recognize`, `RecognizePara` or `RecognizePoly`
functions. For more information, see "Deferred Recognition" on page 10-5.

The system software provides a number of functions for working with stroke
bundles. These functions allow you to extract information from a stroke bundle and
convert the information in stroke bundles into other forms. The stroke bundle
functions are documented in "Stroke Bundle Functions and Methods" (page 8-83)
in *Newton Programmer's Reference*.

Stroke Bundles Example

This section shows an example of working with stroke bundles before they are
passed to the view performing recognition. One way to do this, as shown in the
following code fragment, is to implement the `ViewInkWordScript` method
of an input view. The `ViewInkWordScript` method is described in
"ViewInkWordScript" (page 7-56) in *Newton Programmer's Reference*.

Recognition: Advanced Topics

```
GetKeyView().viewInkWordScript := func(strokeBundle) begin
   // convert the stroke bundle into an ink word
local inkPoly := CompressStrokes(strokeBundle);
local inkWord := inkPoly.ink;
local textSlot := "\uF701";
local stylesSlot := [1, inkWord];
local root := GetRoot();
   // create a rich string with the ink word in it
local appendString := MakeRichString(textSlot,
                                     stylesSlot);
   // append the rich string to myRichString
if root.myRichString then
root.myRichString := root.myRichString && appendString;
else
root.myRichString := appendString;
   // return nil so default handling still happens
nil;
end;
```

This implementation converts the stroke bundle into an ink word, creates a rich string that includes the ink word, and appends that rich string to a rich string that is stored in the root (`myRichString`). The method then returns `nil`, which allows the built-in handling of the stroke bundle to occur.

Summary of Advanced Topics in Recognition

See also "Summary" beginning on page 9-31 in Chapter 9, "Recognition."

Constants

See also Chapter 9, "Recognition," which includes the following summaries: "Text Recognition View Flags" on page 9-31; "Non-Text Recognition View Flags" on page 9-32; and "View Flags Enabling Lexical Dictionaries" on page 9-33.

```
kStandardCharSetInfo // cursive recognizer
kUCBlockCharSetInfo   // printed recognizer
ROM_canonicalBaseInfo // System-supplied rcBaseInfo frame
ROM_canonicalCharGrid // System-supplied rcGridInfo frame
```

Enumerated Dictionaries

Dictionary ID Constant	Value	Contents
kUserDictionary	31	Words added by the user.
kCommonDictionary	0	Commonly-used words.
kCountriesDictionary	8	Names of countries.
kDaysMonthsDictionary	34	Names of days and months.
kFirstNamesDictionary	48	First names.
kLocalCitiesDictionary	41	Names of cities.
kLocalPropersDictionary[1]	2	Proper names.
kLocalStatesDictionary	43	Names of states, provinces, etc.
kSharedPropersDictionary	1	Proper names, company names, state or province names and abbreviations.

[1] Locale-specific dictionary

Lexical Dictionaries

Dictionary ID Constant	Value	Contents
kLocalDateDictionary	110	Date formats.
kLocalNumberDictionary[1]	113	Currency and numeric formats.
kLocalPhoneDictionary	112	Phone number formats.
kLocalTimeDictionary	111	Time formats.
kMoneyOnlyDictionary[1]	118	Currency values and formats.
kNumbersOnlyDictionary[1]	117	Numeric values and formats.
kPostalCodeDictionary	116	Postal code formats.

[1] Locale-specific dictionary

System-Supplied RecConfig Frames

RecConfig Constant	Behavior of recConfig frame
ROM_rcInkOrText	Recognize ink text or text.
ROM_rcPrefsConfig	Recognize according to user settings.
ROM_rcDefaultConfig	None; you supply slot values.
ROM_rcSingleCharacterConfig	Recognize single characters.
ROM_rcTryLettersConfig	Recognize letter-by-letter.
ROM_rcRerecognizeConfig	Deferred recognition.
rcBaseInfo	Defines baseline.
rcGridInfo	Defines single-letter input view.

Data Structures

See also Chapter 9, "Recognition," which includes the following summaries:
"Recognition-Related User Configuration Slots" on page 9-33;

RecConfig Frame

See protoRecConfig in "Recognition System Prototypes" beginning on
page 10-49.

System-Supplied RecConfig Frames

```
// recognize ink or text
ROM_rcInkOrText :=
    {
    // allow user to enable text recog from recToggle
    allowTextRecognition: true, // default
    // return ink text when text recognizer disabled
    doInkWordRecognition: true, // default
    …}

// recognize according to user prefs
ROM_rcPrefsConfig :=
    {
    // allow user to enable text recog from recToggle
    allowTextRecognition: true, // default
    // allow user to enable shape recog from recToggle
    allowShapeRecognition: true, // default
    …}

// generic recConfig frame - you supply useful values
ROM_rcDefaultConfig :=
    {
    // true enables recognition of punctuation marks
    punctuationCursiveOption: nil, // default
    // list of dictionaries used for recognition
    dictionaries: nil, // default
    // true enables letter-by-letter option
    rcSingleLetters: nil, // default
    // Holds an rcBaseInfo frame
    rcBaseInfo: nil, // default
    // bitfield specifying recognition configuration
    inputMask: 0x0000, // default
    …}

// use as-is to configure single-character input views
ROM_rcSingleCharacterConfig :=
    {
    // do not change value of this slot
    _proto: ROM_rcDefaultConfig, // default
    //interpret all input strokes as a single word
    letterSpaceCursiveOption: nil, // default
    // enable letter-by-letter option
    rcSingleLetters: true, // default
```

```
// use custom dictionaries only
inputMask: vCustomDictionaries, // default
// dictionaries to use for recognition
dictionaries: kSymbolsDictionary, // default
// don't enable symbols dictionary twice
inhibitSymbolsDictionary: true // default
…}
```

```
// recognize letter-by-letter instead of w/ dictionaries
ROM_rcTryLettersConfig :=
    {
    // do not change value of this slot
    _proto: ROM_rcDefaultConfig, // default
    //interpret all input strokes as a single word
    letterSpaceCursiveOption: nil, // default
    // recognize non-dictionary words and numbers
    inputMask: vLettersAllowed+vNumbersAllowed, // default
    …}
// use as-is to implement your own form of deferred recog
ROM_rcRerecognizeConfig :=
    {
    // use value of doTextRecognition slot
    allowTextRecognition: true, // default
    // text recognition enabled
    doTextRecognition: true, // default
    // amount of time to spend analyzing input
    speedCursiveOption: 2, // default
    // do not segment strokes
    letterSpaceCursiveOption: nil, // default
    …}
```

Supporting Frames Used In RecConfig Frames

```
// specifies baseline info to recognizer
rcBaseInfo :=
    {
    // y-coordinate of the view's baseline
    // in screen coords (global coords).
    base: int,
    // Positive offset (in pixels) from base
    // to the top of a lowercase "x"
    smallHeight: int,
```

```
    // Positive offset (in pixels) from base
    // to the top of an uppercase "X"
    bigHeight: int,
    // Positive offset (in pixels) from base
    // to the bottom of a lowercase "g"
    descent: int,
    …}

// use w/ rcBaseInfo to define grids of input cells
rcGridInfo :=
    {// all coordinates are global (screen) coordinates
    // coord of left edge of upper-left box in grid
    boxLeft: int,
    // coord of right edge of upper-left box in grid
    boxRight: int,
    // distance in pixels from one boxLeft to next boxLeft
    xSpace: int,
    // coord of topmost edge of upper-left box in grid
    boxTop: int,
    // coord of bottom edge of upper-left box in grid
    boxBottom: int,
    // distance in pixels from one boxTop to next boxTop
    ySpace: int
    }
```

ProtoCharEdit Template

```
aCharEditTemplate :=
    {
    format: string, // string array indexes or underscores
    filters: [str1, str2, … strN], // valid input values
    string: string // initial string to display
    // optional method you supply
    // sets value of charEditView.text slot
    SetupString: func (str) begin … end,
    // optional method you supply
    // formats charEditView.text string for ext display
    CleanupString: func (str)begin … end
    }
```

System-Supplied ProtoCharEdit Templates

```
GetLocale().phoneFilter // phone number template
GetLocale().dateFilter // date template
GetLocale().timeFilter // time template
ROM_numberFilter // general-purpose integer template
```

Stroke Bundle Frame

```
aStrokeBundle :=
    {
    //bounding rectangle of ink strokes
    bounds: {top, left, right, bottom},
    // strokes in the bundle
    strokes: [ binaryObj1, binaryObj2, ... binaryObjN]
    }
```

Recognition System Prototypes

protoRecConfig

```
aRecConfigFrame := {
    // enabled recognizers and dicts
    inputMask: bitField,
    // true enables text recog if doTextRecognition
    // is also true
    allowTextRecognition: Boolean,
    // true enables shape recog if doShapeRecognition
    // is also true
    allowShapeRecognition: Boolean,
    // true enables text recognition unconditionally
    doTextRecognition: Boolean,
    // true enables shape recognition unconditionally
    doShapeRecognition: Boolean,
    // true enables ink text unconditionally
    doInkWordRecognition: Boolean,
    // amount of time to spend recognizing input
    speedCursiveOption: int,
    // relative amount of time between distinct strokes
    timeoutCursiveOption: int,
    // true enables letter-by-letter option
    letterSpaceCursiveOption: Boolean,
```

```
// dictionaries to use when vCustomDictionaries is set
// single values need not reside in an array
dictionaries: [dictId1, dictID2, … dictIdN],
// optional baseline info
rcGridInfo: frame,
// optional single-letter input view info
rcSingleLetters: frame,
// true disables symbols dictionary
inhibitSymbolsDictionary: Boolean,
…}
```

protoRecToggle

```
aRecToggleView :=
    {
    // current setting of recToggle view
    // this slot may be provided by _parent chain
    _recogSettings: systemSuppliedValue,
    // order of items in recToggle picker
    _recogPopup: [sym1, sym2 … symN],
    // optional index into _recogPopup array
    defaultItem: int,
    …}
```

protoCharEdit

```
aCharEditView :=
    {
    // screen coordinates of top edge of comb view
    top:int, // Required when viewBounds not provided
    // screen coordinates of left edge of comb view
    left: int, // Required when viewBounds not provided
    // dimensions & placement of comb view
    viewBounds: frame, // Required when top & left not provided
    // maximum number of cells in comb view; default value is 8
    maxChars: int, // Required; sys provides if you provide viewBounds
    // true causes comb view to display divider lines between cells
    frameCells: Boolean,// Optional; default value is nil
    // width of a cell in pixels; must be even number; default is 12
    cellWidth: int, // system calculates from your top & left values
    // pixels of blank space between cells in comb view
    cellGap: int, // system-provided default value is 6
    // pixels from top of viewBounds to dotted line at bottom of comb
    viewLineSpacing: int, // system-provided default is 30
```

```
// height of cells in pixels
cellHeight: int, // system-provided default is 50
// recConfig frame specifying this view's recog behavior
recConfig: frame, // system provides default
// specifies appearance & behavior of formatted comb view
template: frame, // optional protoCharEdit template
// string displayed when view opens; arg to SetupString method
text: string, // optional
// index of leftmost non-space character in comb view
wordLeft: int, // system-provided value
// index of cell to the right of rightmost non-space character
wordRight: int, // system-provided value
// index into text slot of character occupying leftmost cell
dispLeft: int, // system-provided value; changes after scrolling
// offset in pixels from leftmost edge of comb view
// to leftmost edge of first cell displayed
dispIndent: int,
// return word from comb view w/out leading/trailing spaces
CurrentWord: function,
// return cleaned-up version of word suitable for ext display
GetWordForDisplay: function, // calls CleanupString if provided
// deletes specified text from comb view
DeleteText: function,
// scrolls contents of comb view left or right as specified
Scroll: function,
// makes comb view use current values of text & template slots
UseTextAndTemplate: function,
// Sets the string displayed by the comb view
SetNewWord: function,
// performs internal initialization using current values of
// text and template slot; call after calling SetNewWord
UseNewWord: function,
// Returns true when template's format slot is non-nil
FixedWord: function,
// Returns number of chars residing in templates format slot
FixedWordLength: function,
// optional app-defined methods
// you supply optional fn to update external display
DisplayExternal: function, // message sent when comb view changes
// you supply optional fn to save your undo info
SaveUndoState: function, // message sent when comb view changes
// you supply optional fn to do app-specific tasks for undo
RestoreUndoState: function, // msg sent to undo comb view changes
...}
```

protoCharEdit Templates

```
ROM_numberFilter // general-purpose numeric template
GetLocale().timeFilter // time template
GetLocale().dateFilter// date template
GetLocale().phoneFilter // phone numnber template
```

ProtoCharEdit Functions

```
MapAmbiguousCharacters(str)
UnmapAmbiguousCharacters(str)
```

ProtoCorrectInfo

```
aCorrectInfoFrame :=
    {
    info: [frame1, frame2 … frameMax] // wordInfo frames
    // maximum number of frames in info array
    max: 10, // default value
    // system-supplied methods
    Offset: function, // move, merge or delete wordInfo
    // remove view's wordInfo from correctInfo
    RemoveView: function,
    // return wordInfo frame at specified offset
    Find: function,
    // return wordInfo frame at specified offset,
    // creating one if none found
    FindNew: function,
    // extract wordInfo from unit & add to correctInfo
    AddUnit: function,
    // add specified wordInfo to correctInfo
    AddWord: function,
    // delete range of wordInfo frames from correctInfo
    Clear: function,
    // copy range of wordInfo frames from view
    // into a new correctInfo frame
    Extract: function,
    // copy range of wordInfo frames from source
    // correctInfo frame into dest correctInfo frame
    Insert: function,
    …}
```

ProtoWordInfo

```
aWordInfoFrame :=
    {
    // ID of view that owns this data; returned by GetViewID
    id: int,
    // first char's offset into clParagraphView view
    Start: int,
    // last char's offset into clParagraphView view
    Stop: int,
    flags: forSystemUseOnly, // do not use this slot
    unitID: forSystemUseOnly, // do not use this slot
    // array of wordInterp frames; see page 10-53
    words: [wordInterp1, wordInterp2, … wordInterpN]
    // stroke data from original input
    strokes: strokeBundleFrame, // see page 10-49
    unitData: forSystemUseOnly, // do not use this slot
    // sets list of words held by this wordInfo frame
    SetWords: function,
    // returns array of strings held by wordInterp frames
    GetWords: function,
    // Adds first word in this word list to auto-add and user dicts
    AutoAdd: function,
    // Removes first word in this list from auto-add and user dicts
    AutoRemove: function,
    }
```

protoWordInterp

```
aWordInterpFrame :=
    {
    // one interpretation of input strokes
    word: string,
    // recognizer's confidence in this interpretation
    score: int, // 0 is good score, 1000 is bad score
    // dictionary id of recognized word
    label: int, // internal use only
    // this word's rank in orig list of interpretations
    index:int, // internal use only
    }
```

Additional Recognition Functions and Methods

Dictionary Functions

AddWordToDictionary(*dictionary, wordString*)
DeleteWordFromDictionary(*dictID,word*)
DisposeDictionary(*dictionary*)
GetDictionaryData(*dictionary*)
GetRandomWord(*minLength, maxLength*)
LookupWordInDictionary(*dictID,word*)
NewDictionary(*dictionaryKind*)
SaveUserDictionary()
SetDictionaryData(*dictionary, binaryObject*)

User Dictionary Functions and Methods

AddAutoAdd(*word*)
RemoveAutoAdd(*word*)
reviewDict:AddWord(*word*)
reviewDict:RemoveWord(*word*)
LoadUserDictionary()
SaveUserDictionary()
reviewDict:AddExpandWord(*word, expandedWord*)
reviewDict:GetExpandedWord(*word*)
reviewDict:RemoveExpandedWord(*word*)
LoadExpandDictionary()
SaveExpandDictionary()

Recognition Functions

BuildRecConfig(*viewRef*)
GetPoint(*selector, unit*)
GetPointsArray(*unit*)
GetScoreArray(*unit*)
GetViewID(*viewRef*)
GetWordArray(*unit*)
StrokeBounds(*unit*)
StrokeDone(*unit*)
PurgeAreaCache()

Deferred Recognition Functions

Recognize(*strokes*, *config*, *doGroup*)
RecognizePara(*para*, *start*, *end*, *hilite*, *config*)
RecognizePoly(*poly*, *hilite*, *config*)

Application-Defined Methods

view:ViewClickScript(*stroke*)
view:ViewStrokeScript(*stroke*)
view:ViewGestureScript(*stroke*, *gesture*)
view:ViewWordScript(*stroke*)

CorrectInfo Functions

GetCorrectInfo() // return correctInfo frame
// return view identifier for use w/ correctInfo methods
GetViewID(*view*)
// extract wordInfo from word unit
GetCorrectionWordInfo(*wordUnit*) // call in ViewWordScript

Inker Functions

InkOff(*unit*)
InkOffUnHobbled(*unit*)
SetInkerPenSize(*size*)

Stroke Bundle Functions and Methods

CompressStrokes(*strokeBundle*)
CountPoints(*stroke*)
CountStrokes(*strokeBundle*)
ExpandInk(*poly, format*)
ExpandUnit(*unit*)
GetStroke(*strokeBundle, index*)
GetStrokeBounds(*stroke*)
GetStrokePoint(*stroke, index, point, format*)
GetStrokePointsArray(*stroke, format*)
InkConvert(*ink, outputFormat*)
MakeStrokeBundle(*strokes, format*)
MergeInk(*poly1, poly2*)
PointsArrayToStroke(*pointsArray, format*)
SplitInkAt(*poly, x, slop*)
StrokeBundleToInkWord(*strokeBundle*)

Data Storage and Retrieval

The Newton operating system supplies a suite of objects that interact with each other to provide data storage and retrieval services. This chapter describes the use of these objects—stores, soups, cursors, and entries—to save and retrieve data. If you are developing an application that saves data, retrieves data, or provides preexisting data, you should familiarize yourself with the contents of this chapter.

Before reading this chapter, you should understand the following sections in Chapter 1, "Overview."

- "Memory" on page 1-3 describes the use of random access memory (RAM) by the operating system and applications.

- "Packages" on page 1-4 describes the object that encapsulates code, scripts, and resources as a Newton application.

- "Object Storage System" on page 1-5 provides a brief introduction to the most important data storage objects provided by the Newton operating system.

About Data Storage on Newton Devices

This section introduces Newton data storage objects and describes their interaction and use. Additional special-purpose data storage objects are described in Chapter 12, "Special-Purpose Objects for Data Storage and Retrieval."

Introduction to Data Storage Objects

Newton devices represent data as objects. The NewtonScript programming language provides four basic object types that applications can use to represent data:

Immediate   A small, immutable object such as a character, integer or Boolean value.

Binary   Raw binary data.

Array   A collection of object references accessed from a numerical index.

Frame   A collection of object references accessed by name.

Because immediates, binaries, and arrays are object representations of data types common to many programming languages, they are not discussed further here. For complete descriptions of these objects, see *The NewtonScript Programming Language*.

The frame is of particular interest, however, as it can contain any of the other objects and is the only NewtonScript object to which you can send messages. In addition, the following characteristics of frames make them a particularly flexible and efficient way to store data:

- Frames are sized dynamically—they grow and shrink as necessary.

- All frames support a common set of predefined NewtonScript data types that allows them to share most data virtually transparently.

- Dissimilar data types can be stored in a single frame.

Like a database record, a frame stores data items. An individual data item in the frame is held in a **slot,** which may be thought of as a field in the database record. Unlike database records, however, frames need not contain the same complement of slots.

Any slot can hold any NewtonScript data type, including strings, numeric formats, arrays, and binary objects. Note that NewtonScript does not require that slots declare a datatype. Slots are untyped because every NewtonScript object stores datatype information as part of the object itself. (NewtonScript variables need not declare a type, either, for the same reason.)

Slots can also hold other frames, as well as references to frames, slots, and NewtonScript objects. A frame's ability to reference other frames from its slots allows it to inherit attributes and behaviors from ROM-based objects known as system prototypes or "protos." This feature of the object system also provides dynamic slot lookup and message-passing between frames. For detailed descriptions of NewtonScript syntax, system-supplied data types, dynamic slot lookup, message-passing, and inheritance in NewtonScript, see *The NewtonScript Programming Language*.

Other than the requirement that data must reside in a slot, frames don't impose any structure on their data. In practical use, though, the slots in a frame tend to be related in some way, usually holding related data and methods which operate on that data. In this way, the frame exemplifies the classic object-oriented programming definition of an "object." Frames do not implement data-hiding, however, nor do they necessarily encapsulate their data.

RAM-based frames are not persistent until they are saved in a data structure called a **soup,** which is an opaque object that provides a persistent, dynamic repository for data. Unless removed intentionally, soups remain resident on the Newton device even when the application that owns them is removed.

The only NewtonScript object you can save in a soup is a frame; recall, however, that any slot in the frame can hold any NewtonScript data type and multiple data types can reside in a single frame. The object system does not impose any limitations on the number of frames or the kinds of data that may reside in a soup. In practical use, though, the items in a soup generally have some relationship to one another.

Soups are made available to the system in a variety of ways. Applications may create them on demand, they may be installed along with an application, or the user may introduce them by inserting a storage card in the Newton device.

The soup resides on a **store,** which is a logical data repository on a physical storage device. A store may be likened to a disk partition or volume on a conventional computer system; just as a disk can be divided logically into multiple partitions, a physical storage device can house multiple stores. The Newton platform supports a single internal store and one or more external stores on PCMCIA devices. Applications can use as many soups as they need, subject to the availability of memory space on stores and in the NewtonScript heap.

Each store is identified by a name, which is not necessarily unique, though each store has a nearly unique random number identifier called a **signature.** The store's signature is assigned by the system when the store is created.

Soups can reside on internal or external stores; a special kind of object, the **union soup,** represents multiple soups as a single entity, regardless of their locations on various physical stores. For example, when a PCMCIA card is installed, application data may be distributed between the internal and card-based soups. The union soup object provides a way to address multiple soups having the same name as a single "virtual" soup. Figure 11-1 illustrates the concept of a union soup graphically.

It's important to understand that there is only one kind of soup object in the system; a union soup object simply represents the logical association of multiple soup objects. In other words, aside from their logical association with other soups in the union, a union soup's constituent soups (also called *member soups*) are no different from soups that are not part of a union. Unless specifically noted otherwise, anything said about soups in this text applies equally to union soups.

Figure 11-1   Stores, soups and union soups

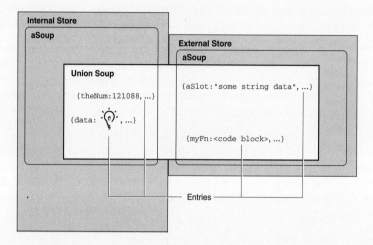

In general, you'll want to use union soups for most purposes, especially for saving most data the user creates with your application. Applications must allow the user to choose whether to save new data on the internal or external store; using union soups makes this easy to do.

An application creates a union soup by registering a **soup definition** frame with the system; registering the soup definition causes the system to return a union soup object to which the application can send messages that save and retrieve data. This object may represent a new soup, one created previously, or no soups (if, for some reason, all of the union's member soups are unavailable). For a detailed discussion of soup creation, see "Soups" beginning on page 11-7.

All soups save frame data as objects called entries. An **entry** is a frame that has been added to a soup by means of any of several system-supplied methods provided for this purpose. Note that you cannot create a valid entry by simply adding certain slots and values to a frame—the system must create the entry for you from a frame presented as an argument to one of the entry-creation methods.

Returning to the database analogy, you can think of entries as individual records in the database, and you can think of the soup as the database itself. Like a database, a soup is opaque—you retrieve data by requesting it, rather than by examining its records directly.

Your request for soup data takes the form of a `Query` message sent to the soup or union soup object. The `Query` method accepts as its argument a frame known as the **query specification** or **query spec.** The query spec describes the kind of information the query returns. The order in which soups return data items is imposed by an **index** you define for a specified soup.

If you've ever used an array, you are already familiar with the concept of an index. Each element of the array is associated with a unique numeric value called a **key**. These key values can be sorted, thus imposing order on their associated data items (the elements of the array). In the case of a common array, a single numeric index sorts the array elements in ascending key order.

Key values can also be used to reference or retrieve an indexed item. For example, arrays allow you to reference or retrieve the data at a particular position in the array without regard to the actual content stored at that position. Soup indexes provide similar capabilities for soup data: they allow you to find and sort soup entries associated with specified key values without specific knowledge of the data associated with a particular key value.

You can index soup entries on any slot value you need to use as a key for extracting them from the soup. For example, you could retrieve entries having a certain creation date, or entries in which a particular string is present, and so on. Soups can be created with a set of default indexes you specify and you can also add new indexes to existing soups. Indexes are discussed in more detail in "Indexes" beginning on page 11-8.

A soup responds to a query by returning a **cursor** object that iterates over the set of entries meeting the criteria defined by the query spec. Cursors are updated dynamically: if soup entries meeting the search criteria are added or deleted after the original query is made, these changes are reflected automatically in the set of entries that the cursor returns.

The cursor responds to messages that position it within the set of entries it references and extract individual entries from this set. Until an entry is extracted from the cursor, its data resides in the soup that was queried to generate the cursor.

The first time a slot in the entry is referenced—whether to read its value, set its value, or to print its value in the Inspector—the system creates a normal frame from it that is referenced by a special area of the NewtonScript heap known as the **entry cache.** Changes to the entry's soup data are actually made in the cached frame, not the permanent store; hence, changes to a soup entry are not persistent until the cached frame is written back to a soup. This scheme makes it simple to undo the changes to a soup entry—the system simply throws away the cached frame and restores references to the original, unmodified soup entry.

Because the frame-based storage model facilitates the sharing of data, the system provides a soup change notification mechanism that you can use to advise other objects of changes to soups or soup data. All the methods that add, modify, or delete soups or soup entries provide the option to execute registered callback functions in response to changes in specified soups. Soup changes for which applications might require notification include creating soups; deleting soups; and adding, removing, or changing individual soup entries. The soup change notification mechanism is discussed in more detail in "Using Soup Change Notification" beginning on page 11-63.

In summary, most applications that work with dynamic data perform the following operations, which are described in this chapter:

- creating and using frames
- storing frames as soup entries
- querying soups to retrieve sets of entries
- using cursor objects to work with sets of soup entries
- extracting individual entries from cursor objects
- manipulating individual soup entries as frame objects
- returning modified entries to the soup from which they came
- notifying other applications of changes to soups

Where to Go From Here

You should now have a general understanding of how stores, soups, queries, cursors, and entries interact. It is strongly recommended that you read the remainder of this section now—it provides important details you'll need to know in order to work with the Newton data storage system. However, if you are anxious to begin experimenting with Newton data storage objects, you can skip ahead to "Programmer's Overview" on page 11-25 and read the remainder of this section at another time.

Stores

Although soups and packages reside on stores, the occasions on which you'll need to interact with stores directly are rare—the system manages hardware interaction for you, creates union soups automatically as needed, and provides a programming interface that allows you to perform most union soup operations without manipulating the stores on which individual member soups reside. Occasionally, you may need to message a store directly in order to create or retrieve a soup that is not part of a union, or you may need to pass a store object as an argument to certain methods; otherwise, most applications' direct interaction with stores is limited.

In general, only specialized applications that back up and restore soup data need to manipulate stores directly. However, the system provides a complete developer interface to stores, as documented in "Data Storage and Retrieval Reference" (page 9-1) in *Newton Programmer's Reference*.

For information on using store objects, see "Using Stores" beginning on page 11-29.

Packages

A **package** is the basic unit of downloadable Newton software: it provides a means of loading code, resources, objects, and scripts into a Newton device. Most Newton applications are shipped as packages that can be installed on a Newton device by applications such as Newton Package Installer or Newton Backup Utility.

Packages can be read from a data stream or directly from memory. For example, Newton Connection Utility uses a data stream protocol to load a package into the Newton system from a MacOS or Windows computer. However, it is much more common to use packages directly from memory, as the user does after the package has been installed on the Newton device.

For a more detailed discussion of packages, see "Parts" on page 12-3 in Chapter 12, "Special-Purpose Objects for Data Storage and Retrieval."

Soups

This section provides important background information about soup objects. Topics discussed here include

- soups vs. union soups
- related data structures such as soup definitions, indexes, index specification frames, and tags
- automatic creation of soups
- saving user preferences in the system soup

Applications using soup-based data storage must respect the user's default store preferences for writing soup entries and create soups only as necessary. The use of union soups makes it easy to observe these requirements. Union soups provide methods that respect the user's default store preferences automatically when adding new entries. These ROM-based methods are also much faster than equivalent NewtonScript code. Union soups also provide methods you can use on those occasions when you must specify the store on which to save soup entries.

Another good reason to use union soups is that applications almost never need to create them explicitly. Once a soup definition is registered with the system, individual members of the union soup it defines are created automatically as needed.

A **soup definition** is a frame that provides information about a particular union soup. The soup definition supplies descriptive information about the union soup and information required to create its member soups.

The soup definition frame specifies a name that identifies the soup to the system, a user-visible name for the soup, a symbol identifying the application that "owns" the soup, a user-visible string that describes the soup, and an array of index specification frames defining the default set of indexes with which the soup is created. For a complete description of the slots in the soup definition frame, see the section "Soup Definition Frame" (page 9-2) in *Newton Programmer's Reference.*

Methods that add an entry to a union soup use the information in its soup definition to create a member soup to hold the new entry if the member soup is not present on the appropriate store at the time the entry is added. If a member of the union is present on the specified store, the new entry is added to the existing member soup and a new soup is not created. In most cases, the store in question is specified by the user's preferences for the default storage of new data items; if necessary, however, you can specify by store the member soup in which the new entry is to reside. Note also that you can create union soup members explicitly, if necessary.

If no frames have ever been added to a particular union soup, the union's member soups may not exist at all. You can add entries to a union soup in this state (member soups are created automatically), but you cannot query a union soup that has no members.

Member soups may be unavailable for other reasons, as well. For example, the user might have removed a member soup temporarily by ejecting the card on which it resides or might have removed the soup permanently by scrubbing it in the Extras Drawer.

The descriptive information in a soup definition frame can be used to supply information about a soup for use by the system, applications, or the user. For example, this information can be used to make the user aware of a particular soup's owner and function before allowing the user to delete the soup.

To make a soup definition available for use, you must first register it with the system. For information on registering and unregistering soup definitions, see the section "Registering and Unregistering Soup Definitions" beginning on page 11-33.

NewtApp applications also make use of soup definitions; for more information, see Chapter 4, "NewtApp Applications."

Indexes

An **index** is a data structure that provides random access to the entries in a soup as well as a means of ordering those entries. A designated value extracted from each soup entry is stored separately in the soup's index as the **index key** for that entry. Because the system can retrieve and sort index key values without reading their associated soup entries into memory, indexes provide a fast and efficient means of finding soup entries.

The system maintains all indexes automatically as soup entries are added, deleted, or changed. Thus, index data is always up-to-date and readily available.

You can create your own specialized indexes for any soup. You need to create an index for each slot or set of slots on which the soup will be searched frequently. It is preferable to define your indexes in the appropriate soup definition, but you can add indexes to an existing soup if necessary.

An index generated against a single key value is called a **single-slot index.** A single-slot index selects and sorts soup entries according to the value of a single slot specified when the index is created. An index generated against multiple key values is called a **multiple-slot index.** A multiple-slot index can select and sort soup entries according to the values of multiple slots. A multiple-slot index can associate up to a total of six key values with each entry it indexes. You can create multiple indexes for any soup.

The characteristics of an index are specified by an **index specification frame** or **index spec.** The values in the index spec frame indicate the kind of index to build, which slot values to use as index data, and the kind of data stored in the indexed slots. The precise format of the index spec frame varies according to whether it defines a single-slot index or a multiple-slot index. For complete descriptions of index specs, see "Single-Slot Index Specification Frame" on page 9-5 and "Multiple-Slot Index Specification Frame" (page 9-6) in *Newton Programmer's Reference*.

A **tag** is an optional developer-defined symbol used to mark one or more soup entries. Tags reside in a developer-specified slot that can be indexed, with the results stored in a special index called the **tags index.**

The tags index is used to select soup entries according to their associated symbolic values without reading the entries into memory; for example, one could select the subset of entries tagged `'business` from the `ROM_CardFileSoupName` soup used by the built-in Names application. In fact, "filing" Newton data items in "folders" is a user-interface illusion—the data really resides in soup entries and its display is filtered for the user according to the tags associated with each soup entry.

Note that the system allows only one tags index per soup. Each soup can contain a maximum of 624 tags. The system treats missing tags as `nil` values. For more information, see "Tag-based Queries" on page 11-14.

A **tags index specification frame,** or **tags index spec,** defines the characteristics of a soup's tags index. Like an index spec, a tags index spec can be used to create a default tags index on a new soup or add a tags index to an existing soup. For a complete description of the slots in a tags index spec frame, see the section "Tags Index Specification Frame" (page 9-8) in *Newton Programmer's Reference*.

To better support the use of languages other than English, soup indexes and queries can be made sensitive to case and diacritical marks in string values. (Normally, string comparison in NewtonScript is insensitive to case and diacritics.) This behavior is intended to allow applications to support the introduction of non-English data easily; for example, the user might insert a PCMCIA card containing data from a different locale. To take advantage of this behavior, the application must create an internationalized index for the soup and the query must request the alternate sorting behavior explicitly in its query spec. For more information, see "Internationalized Sorting Order for Text Queries" on page 11-45.

Saving User Preference Data in the System Soup

Most of the time you'll want to store data in union soups, but one task for which union soups are not suitable is the storage of your application's user preferences data. There are several good reasons for always saving user preferences data on the internal store:

- If your application is on a card that is moved from one Newton device to another, it acts the way the users of the respective Newton devices think it should.

- It rarely makes sense to distribute preferences data among several storage cards.

- It's difficult to guarantee that your application will always have access to any particular card.

- If your application is on the internal store and it simply adds preference data to the default store, the preference data could be saved on an external store that becomes unavailable to the application when a card is ejected.

Hence, the built-in ROM_SystemSoupName soup on the internal store is usually the ideal place to keep your application's preference data. The GetAppPrefs function allows you to get and set your application's preferences frame in this soup. For more information, see the description of this function in Chapter 26, "Utility Functions." For more information about the ROM_SystemSoupName soup itself, see Chapter 19, "Built-in Applications and System Data."

Queries

To retrieve entries from a soup or union soup, you perform a **query** by sending the Query message to the soup or union soup. The Query method accepts as its argument a frame known as a **query specification** or **query spec.** The query spec defines criteria for the inclusion of entries in the query result. You can think of the query spec as a filter that the Query method uses to select a subset of the soup's data. Queries can test index key values or string values and perform customized tests that you define.

A single query spec can specify multiple criteria that entries must meet in order to be included in the result of the query. For example, you can specify that your query return all entries created after a certain date that are tagged 'business but do not contain the "paid" string. For instructional purposes, this chapter discusses separately each test that a query spec may include.

Querying for Indexed Values

Queries can retrieve items according to the presence of one or more index keys and can test key values as well. A query that tests for the presence or value of an index key is called an **index query.**

Soups that have single-slot indexes allow queries to use a single index key to select soup entries. Detailed information is provided in "Querying on Single-Slot Indexes" beginning on page 11-39.

Soups that have multiple-slot indexes allow queries to use multiple index keys to select soup entries. Detailed information is provided in "Querying on Multiple-Slot Indexes" beginning on page 11-47.

Index queries can be based only on slot names for which an index has been generated. For example, to select entries according to the presence of the `foo` slot, the soup that receives the `Query` message must be indexed on the `foo` slot. Entries not having a `foo` slot are not included in the set of entries referenced by the `foo` index.

Although the entries in the soup are not actually in any particular order themselves, the index keys associated with them can be sorted in a specific order that is defined for each NewtonScript data type. Thus, you can envision the contents of an index as a sequence of entries arranged in key order, as shown in Figure 11-2.

Figure 11-2   An index provides random access and imposes order

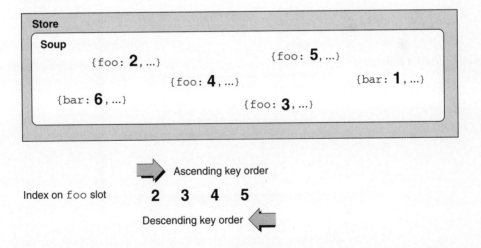

The `aSoup` soup shown in Figure 11-2 is indexed on the `foo` slot, which means that the value of each entry's `foo` slot is used as its index key. Only those entries containing a `foo` slot are included in this index. By sorting key values, the index imposes order on their corresponding soup entries, which are otherwise unordered.

Indexes sort key values in ascending order unless the index spec frame used to create a particular index specifies descending order.

Begin Keys and End Keys

Because index keys are sorted by value, you can improve the speed of an index query significantly by limiting the range of index key values it tests. One way to do this is to eliminate from the search any index key values that fall outside specified minimum or maximum values. For example, you can specify a minimum index key value used to select the first entry to be tested, causing the query to "skip over" all lesser-valued index keys. A minimum value used in this way is defined in the query spec as a beginKey value.

Similarly, you can specify a maximum index key value to be used in selecting the last entry to be tested, causing the query to ignore entries having index keys of greater value. A maximum value used in this way is defined in the query spec as an endKey value.

You can use these optional beginKey and endKey values together to specify a subrange of index key values, as shown in Figure 11-3. Note that if an endrange value is not specified, it is unbounded; for example, if you don't specify an endKey value the query result potentially includes all entries through the end of the index.

Figure 11-3   Using beginKey and endKey values to specify an index subrange

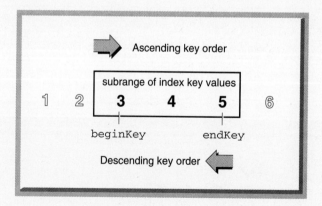

You can also define a special kind of key that is itself excluded from the valid subrange of index values. These keys are defined as beginExclKey and endExclKey values in the query spec. Figure 11-4 depicts the use of beginExclKey and endExclKey values to define the same index subrange shown in Figure 11-3. Note that you cannot specify both the inclusive and exclusive forms of the same endrange selector; for example, a single query spec cannot specify both a `beginKey` value and a `beginExclKey` value.

Another important point to understand is that there is only one `beginKey` or `beginExclKey` value, and only one `endKey` or `endExclKey` value associated with any query and the cursor it returns.

Figure 11-4 Using `beginExclKey` and `endExclKey` values to specify a subrange

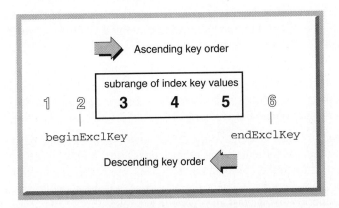

Each `beginKey`, `beginExclKey`, `endKey`, or `endExclKey` specification evaluates to a single value that has a unique position in the sorted index key data. This position marks one end of the range over which the cursor iterates. The cursor never moves to a position outside the range specified by these keys.

If any endrange selectors are defined for a query, the relationship of the cursor's entries to the endrange selectors may be summarized as follows:

entry > `beginExclKey`
entry ≥ `beginKey`
entry ≤ `endKey`
entry < `endExclKey`

You can think of these values as being used by the system in an inequality expression to specify the range of the cursor; for example,

`beginKey` ≥ *entry* < `endExclKey`

Note that if a valid entry is not found at the key value specified for an endrange selector, the cursor is positioned on the nearest entry in index key order that falls within the range specified by the endrange selectors. For example, if a valid entry is not found at the key value specified for a `beginKey` or `beginExclKey` value, the cursor is positioned on the next valid entry in index key order. Similarly, if a valid entry is not found at the key value specified for an endKey or endExclKey value, the cursor is positioned on the previous valid entry in index key order. (The cursor is never positioned beyond the endKey value or before the beginKey value.)

For information on using index queries, see "Querying on Single-Slot Indexes" beginning on page 11-39 and "Querying on Multiple-Slot Indexes" beginning on page 11-47.

Tag-based Queries

Index queries can also include or exclude entries according to the presence of one or more tags. A **tag** is an optional developer-defined symbol that resides in a specified slot in the soup entry.

The symbols used as tags are stored as the key values in the soup's **tags index.** As with any other index, the system maintains the tags index automatically and queries can test values in this index without reading soup entries into memory. Thus, tag-based queries are quick and efficient.

Unlike other indexes, the tags index alone cannot be used as the basis of an index query—it does not sort entries (as other indexes do), it only selects or eliminates entries according to their associated tag values. However, you need not specify an additional index in order to query on tag values; when a separate index is not specified, queries on tags test all entries in the soup.

The tags for which the query tests are specified by a **tags query specification frame** or **tags query spec** supplied as part of the query spec. The tags query spec can specify set operators such as not, any, equal, and all to create complex filters based on tag values. For example, you could use these operators to query for entries having the 'USA or 'west tags that do not have the 'California tag.

The set operators used by tags query specs are described in greater detail in "Tag-based Queries" beginning on page 11-14 of this book and "Tags Query Specification Frame" (page 9-13) in *Newton Programmer's Reference*.

Customized Tests

The use of indexes, begin keys, end keys, and tags provides sufficient control over query results for most uses; however, you can specify additional customized tests when necessary. These tests take the form of an indexValidTest or validTest function that you define in the query spec.

The indexValidTest function tests the index key values associated with each entry in the range of values over which the cursor iterates. This function returns nil for an entry that is to be rejected, and returns any non-nil value for an entry that is to be included in the results of the query. Like all tests that manipulate index key values, `indexValidTest` functions are fast and efficient because index key values are always kept in memory.

Another kind of customized test, the `validTest` function, works like the `indexValidTest` function but tests the soup entry itself rather than its associated index key value. To perform this test, the query must actually read the soup entry into the NewtonScript heap, which takes more time and uses more memory than tests which operate on index key values only. Thus, for performance reasons, `validTest` functions should be used only when absolutely necessary. It is strongly suggested that you use index-based approaches to limit the range of entries passed to the `validTest` function.

For information on using `indexValidTest` and `validTest` functions, see "Querying on Single-Slot Indexes" beginning on page 11-39.

Text Queries

Queries can also select entries according to the presence of one or more specified strings. For instructional purposes, this section describes separately each of the text searches that queries can perform—remember, though, that a single query spec can specify multiple tests for the query to perform on each soup entry it examines.

A **words query** tests all strings in each soup entry for a word beginning or for an entire word. A **text query** is similar to a words query but its test is not limited to word boundaries.

The default behavior for a words query is to test for word beginnings. For example, a words query on the string `"smith"` would find the words `"smithe"` and `"smithereens"`. The word `"blacksmith"` would not be included in the results of the search because the string `"smith"` is not at a word beginning. Because words queries are not case sensitive, the word `"Smithsonian"` would also be found by this query.

If you specify that the words query match only entire words, it returns only entries containing the entire word `"smith"` or `"Smith"` and does not return any other variations. You can also specify explicitly that the query be sensitive to case and diacritics, causing it to return only the `"smith"` entry.

A words query is slower than a similar index query because it takes some time to test all the string values in a soup entry. For information about performing words queries, see "Querying for Text" beginning on page 11-43.

A **text query** is similar to a words query but its test is not limited to word boundaries; that is, it tests all strings in each soup entry for one or more specified strings, regardless of where they appear in the word. For example, a words query on the string `"smith"` would find the words `"smithe"` and `"smithereens"` as well as the word `"blacksmith"`. Because text queries are not case sensitive unless this behavior is requested explicitly, the words "blackSmith" and "Smithsonian" would also be found by this query.

A text query is slower than its words query counterpart. Text queries do not require significantly more heap space than other kinds of queries.

For more information about performing text queries, see "Querying for Text" beginning on page 11-43.

Cursors

The Query method returns a **cursor,** which is an object that iterates over the set of entries satisfying the query spec and returns entries in response to the messages it receives. Cursors return entries in index key order. As entries in the soup are added, deleted, and changed, the set of entries the cursor references is updated dynamically, even after the original query has been performed.

Recall that after selecting a subrange of all entries in the soup, a query can use various tests to eliminate certain entries within that range. If viewed within the context of the entire soup index, the final set of valid entries is discontiguous—that is, it includes gaps occupied by entries that did not meet the criteria established by the query spec. However, the cursor presents this subset as a continuous range of entries, as depicted in Figure 11-5.

Initially, the cursor points to the first entry in index order that satisfies the query. The cursor supplies methods that allow you to determine its current position, retrieve the entry referenced by its current position, or specify a new position. The cursor may be moved incrementally, moved to the position occupied by a specified entry or key, or reset to an initial position that is not necessarily the first entry in the valid set. Note that it is possible to move the cursor incrementally to a position outside the valid range of entries, in which case the cursor returns nil instead of an entry.

For information about using cursors, see "Using Cursors" beginning on page 11-53.

Figure 11-5 Cursor presents discontiguous index key values contiguously

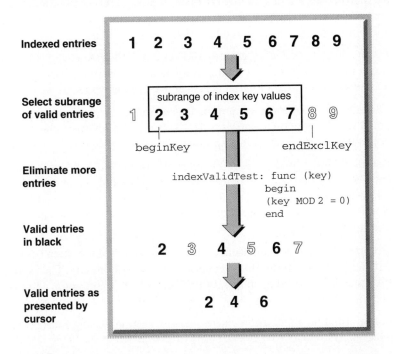

Entries

An **entry** is a special kind of frame that resides in a soup. Valid entries can be created only by system-supplied methods provided for this purpose—you cannot create an entry by creating a frame having certain slots and values. The entry that these methods create consists of the frame presented to the entry-creation method, along with copies of any data structures the frame references, as well as copies of any data structures those structures reference, and so on. An exception to this rule is that _proto slots are not saved in soup entries. Circular references within an entry are allowed.

Data Storage and Retrieval

All frames are compressed automatically when they are stored as soup entries and all soup entries are decompressed when they are referenced. The automatic compression and decompression of soup data reduces the amount of storage space and run-time memory required by Newton applications.

If you add a frame that references another entry, the referenced entry is copied as a frame into the new soup entry that is created. Similarly, if you move that entry to another store, any data it references is moved to the new store as well.

The only way to retrieve an entry is to send the `Query` message to the soup or union soup in which the entry resides. This method returns a cursor, which is an object that returns entries in response to messages it receives.

As first returned by the cursor, the entry is a frame that holds references to the entry's data. Soup data referenced by this frame is not decompressed until it is referenced—for example, to get or set the value of one of the entry's slots. When a slot in the entry is referenced, the system constructs the entire entry frame in the NewtonScript heap.

Decompressed entries are cached in RAM until they are written back to the soup. Applications can modify these cached entry frames directly. The system supplies functions for modifying entries, writing them back to the soup, and manipulating them in other ways.

For information about using entries, see the section "Using Entries" beginning on page 11-57.

Alternatives to Soup-Based Storage

Although soup-based data storage offers many advantages, you may improve your application's performance or reduce its RAM requirements by storing data in other formats.

There are a wide variety of trade-offs to consider when choosing a structure to represent your application data. You are strongly advised to conduct realistic tests with the actual data set your application uses before committing to the use of a particular data structure. It's also recommended that you design your application in a way that allows you to experiment with the use of various data structures at any point in its development.

When choosing schemes for storing your application's data, you need to consider factors such as:

- the kind of data to be saved
- the quantity of data to be saved
- how the application accesses the data

The most important factor to consider with respect to the kind of data is whether the data is static or dynamic. You must use soups to store dynamic data, but a number of options are available for storing static data. You will probably find that certain structures lend themselves more naturally than others to working with your particular data set.

Especially for large data sets, space-efficiency may influence your choice of one data structure over another. In some cases, you may need to consider trade-offs between space requirements and speed or ease of access.

Data access issues include questions such as whether the data structure under consideration facilitates searching or sorting the data. For example, soups provide powerful and flexible mechanisms for searching and sorting soup entry data.

Dynamic Data

Data your application gathers from the user must be stored in soups. Within individual soup entries, you are free to store data in whatever manner best suits your application's needs.

Because each entry in a soup is a frame, the price you pay for using soup-based storage can be measured in terms of

■ the time required to find slots at run time

■ the memory space required to expand soup entries

■ the memory space required to store the expanded entry frames on the NewtonScript heap

For many uses, the benefits offered by soups outweigh these costs; however, other approaches may be more suitable for certain data sets, especially large sets of read-only data.

For example, a large, read-only list of provinces and postal codes is saved most compactly as a single array, frame, or binary object residing in a slot in the application base view's template or in the application package itself. Information stored in this way is compressed along with your application package and is not brought into the NewtonScript heap when it is accessed. The primary disadvantages of this scheme are that the data set is read-only and the conveniences provided by soup queries are not available.

Static Data

Read-only or static data can be stored in packages held in protected memory on the Newton. There are a variety of reasons you might store data in a package rather than in a soup:

■ Storing static data in a compressed package rather than in a soup helps to conserve store space and NewtonScript heap space.

■ Although the user might enter data dynamically, there might be a large initial set of data your application needs to provide. Again, it's more efficient to supply this as package data rather than as soup data.

■ You can supply multiple static data sets as separate packages to allow the user to load some subset of that data. For example, a travel guide application might keep data for individual countries in separate packages.

If your application makes use of a large initial data set to which the user can make additions, you might consider a hybrid approach: keep the initial data set in your base view's template and use a soup only for the user's additions.

A special-purpose object called a store part allows you to provide read-only soups as package data; however, a soup residing on a store part cannot participate in a union. For information about store parts, see Chapter 12, "Special-Purpose Objects for Data Storage and Retrieval."

If you decide not to store your data in a soup, consider the following points:

■ Don't be too quick to discount frames as your data structure of choice—slot lookup is very fast.

■ Storing data as a binary object can help you avoid some of the overhead associated with array and frame data structures. In general, binary objects may let you store your data more compactly, but make it more difficult to access: you'll need to use the various Extract*DataType* functions to retrieve items. Note that the ExtractCString and ExtractPString functions create a string object in the NewtonScript heap for each string extracted from a binary object.

■ Consider storing symbols for repeated strings rather than storing the strings themselves. When you define a symbol for an object (such as a string or frame), only one instance of the object is stored in the application package, and all the symbols reference that instance. Remember that symbols are limited to 7-bit ASCII values. Symbols (slot names) can include nonalphanumeric ASCII characters if the name is enclosed by vertical bars; for example, the space in the symbol '|Chicken Little| would normally be illegal syntax, but the vertical bars suppress the usual evaluation of all characters they enclose.

Compatibility Information

This section provides version 2.0 compatibility information for applications that use earlier versions of the data storage and retrieval interface.

Obsolete Store Functions and Methods

The following store methods and functions are obsolete:

```
store:CreateSoup (soupName, indexArray) // use CreateSoupFromSoupDef
RemovePackage(pkgFrmOrID) // use SafeRemovePackage instead
store:RestorePackage(packageObject) // use SuckPackageFromBinary instead
```

Soup Compatibility Information

This section contains compatibility information regarding

- the new soup format introduced with version 2.0 of the Newton operating system
- obsolete soup functions and methods
- the new soup change notification mechanism introduced in version 2.0 of the Newton operating system
- soup information frame changes
- null union soups on Newton 1.x devices

New Soup Format

Because 2.0 soup formats are incompatible with earlier versions of the Newton data storage model, the system implements the following soup-conversion strategy:

- When a 1.x data set is introduced to a Newton 2.0 system, the system allows the user to choose read-only access or permanent conversion of the 1.x soup data to the Newton 2.0 format.
- Older systems display a slip that says "This card is too new. Do you want to erase it?" when a Newton 2.0 soup is introduced to the system.

Obsolete Soup Methods and Functions

The system's approach to creating soups automatically has changed with version 2.0 of Newton system software. In previous versions of the system, any soup registered by the `RegCardSoups` method was created automatically on any PCMCIA card lacking that soup, even when the user specified that new items be written by default to the internal store. The result was a proliferation of unused, "empty" soups on any PCMCIA card introduced to the system.

Version 2.0 of Newton system software creates the members of union soups automatically only when they are actually needed to store data. Thus, the `RegCardSoups`, `SetupCardSoups`, `RegisterCardSoup`, and `UnRegisterCardSoup` functions have been made obsolete by the `RegUnionSoup` and `UnRegUnionSoup` functions. Similarly, the `CreateSoup` store method has been made obsolete by the `RegUnionSoup` function. For more information, see "Soups" beginning on page 11-7.

The following soup methods and functions are obsolete:

```
SetupCardSoups() // use RegUnionSoup instead
RegisterCardSoup(soupName, indexArray,
                    appSymbol, appObject) // useRegUnionSoup instead
UnRegisterCardSoup(soupName)// use UnRegUnionSoup instead
BroadcastSoupChange(soupNameString) // use -xmit methods or
                                    // XmitSoupChange fn instead
UnionSoupIsNull(unionSoup)// no null uSoups from GetUnionSoupAlways
GetUnionSoup(soupNameString)// use GetUnionSoupAlways instead
soup:Add(frame) // use -xmit version instead
soup:AddIndex(indexSpec) // use -xmit version instead
soupOrUSoup:AddTags(tagsToAdd)// use -xmit version instead
unionSoup:AddToDefaultStore(frame)// use -xmit version instead
soup:AddWithUniqueId(frame)// use -xmit version instead
sourceSoup:CopyEntries(destSoup)// use -xmit version instead
soup:RemoveAllEntries() // use -xmit version instead
soup:RemoveFromStore() // use -xmit version instead
soup:RemoveIndex(indexPath) // use -xmit version instead
soupOrUSoup:RemoveTags(tagsToRemove)// use -xmit version instead
soup:SetInfo(slotSymbol) // use -xmit version instead
```

New Soup Change Notification Mechanism

Applications no longer modify system data structures directly to register and unregister with the soup change notification mechanism. Instead, they use the RegSoupChange and UnRegSoupChange global functions provided for this purpose.

In addition to the new registration and unregistration functions, the soup change mechanism provides additional information about the nature of the change and allows applications to register callback functions to be executed whenever a particular soup changes. Consequently, the global function BroadcastSoupChange is obsolete.

For more details, see the section "Using Soup Change Notification" beginning on page 11-63.

Soup Information Frame

Soups created from a soup definition frame carry a default soup information frame that holds a copy of the soup definition frame. Soups created by the obsolete global function RegisterCardSoup have a default soup information frame that contains only the slots applications and itemNames.

Soups created by the obsolete store method CreateSoup do not contain a default soup information frame.

Null Union Soups

Under unusual circumstances a 1.x application may encounter a union soup that doesn't contain any member soups. A soup in this state is referred to as a **null union soup.** Queries on a null union soup fail. Attempts to add entries to a missing member soup also fail if a soup definition for that soup has not been registered. Null union soups should not normally occur with 1.x applications and cannot occur with applications that use the 2.0 union soup interface correctly.

Null union soups are most often found in the aftermath of a debugging session— for example, if in the NTK Inspector you have deleted various soups (to test the cases in which your application needs to create its own soups) and neglected to restore things to their normal state.

Null union soups can also occur as a result of the application soup not being created properly. Normally, when a card is ejected, the internal store member of a union soup is left behind or a soup definition for creating that soup is available. When this is not the case, the union soup reference to the internal store member is null when the card is ejected. If you follow the guidelines outlined in "Registering and Unregistering Soup Definitions" on page 11-33 this problem does not occur.

Null union soups can also occur when another application deletes one or more soups that your application uses. Any application that deletes soups should at least transmit a soup change notification, thereby allowing your application to deal with the change appropriately.

When your application is running on a 1.x unit or when no soup definition exists for a union soup, it is appropriate to test for a constituent soup's validity before trying to add an entry to it. Simply loop through the array of stores returned by the GetStores function, sending the IsValid message to each of the constituent soups in the union.

Query Compatibility Information

Version 2.0 of Newton system software provides a more powerful query mechanism while at the same time simplifying the syntax of queries. Although old-style query syntax is still supported, you'll probably want to revise your application code to take advantage of the features new-style queries provide. The following list summarizes changes to queries. The remainder of this section explores query compatibility issues in more detail.

```
Query (soupOrUSoup, querySpec) // use soupOrUSoup:Query(querySpec) instead

querySpec := {type : symbol, // obsolete, do not use
              startKey: keyValue, // use beginKey or beginExclKey
              endTest: keyValue, // endKey or endExclKey instead
              ... }
```

Query Global Function Is Obsolete

Queries are now performed by the Query method of soups or union soups; however, the Query global function still exists for compatibility with applications using version 1.x of the Newton application programming interface. The Query method accepts the same query specification frame argument that the Query global function did; however, version 2.0 query specs provide additional features that 1.x queries do not. For examples of the use of the Query method, see "Using Queries" beginning on page 11-38. For a complete description of the query spec frame and its slots, see "Query Specification Frame" (page 9-9) in *Newton Programmer's Reference*.

Query Types Obsolete

Query specs no longer require a type slot; if this slot is present, it is ignored.

StartKey and EndTest Obsolete

Because the order in which the cursor returns entries is determined entirely by index values, specifying key values is sufficient to determine a range. Hence, the use of an endTest function in a query spec is always unnecessary. Instead, your query spec should specify an endKey or endExclKey value.

The endTest function was sometimes used for other purposes, such as stopping the cursor after the visible portion of a list had been filled; however, this sort of test is best performed outside the cursor to optimize performance. The caller of the cursor's Next method should be able to determine when to stop retrieving soup entries without resorting to the use of an endTest function.

When a cursor is generated initially and when it is reset, it references the entry having the lowest index value in the set of entries in the selected subset. Thus, it is usually unnecessary to use a start key, although this operation still works as in earlier versions of system software. For those occasions when it is necessary to start the cursor somewhere in the middle of the range, the use of a start key can be simulated easily by invoking the cursor's GotoKey method immediately after generating or resetting the cursor.

Queries on Nil-Value Slots Unsupported

In Newton system software prior to version 1.05, storing a value of nil in the indexed slot of an entry returns nil to the query for that entry; that is, the query fails to find the entry. To work around this problem in older Newton systems, make sure your indexed slots store appropriate values.

In Newton system software version 2.0, the behavior of queries on nil-value slots is unspecified. For best performance, make sure your indexed slots store appropriate values.

Heap Space Requirements of Words and Text Queries

On systems prior to version 2.0, words and text queries generally require more memory than index queries, because each entry to be tested must first be read into the NewtonScript heap. System software version 2.0 uses virtual binary objects to reduce the memory requirements of words and text queries significantly; however, you need not be familiar with these objects yourself in order to query on string values. Virtual binary objects are described in Chapter 12, "Special-Purpose Objects for Data Storage and Retrieval."

Obsolete Entry Functions

The following entry functions are obsolete:

```
EntryChange(entry) // use -xmit version instead
EntryCopy(entry, newSoup) // use -xmit version instead
EntryMove(entry, newSoup)// use -xmit version instead
EntryRemoveFromSoup(entry)// use -xmit version instead
EntryReplace(oldEntry, newEntry)// use -xmit version instead
EntryUndoChanges(entry)// use -xmit version instead
```

Obsolete Data Backup and Restore Functions

The utility functions and methods in the following list are obsolete. Note that these functions and methods are intended for use only by utility programs that back up and restore Newton data.

```
soup:AddWithUniqueId (entry)// use -xmit version instead
soup:SetAllInfo (frame)// use -xmit version instead
EntryChangeWithModTime(entry)// use -xmit version instead
EntryReplaceWithModTime(original, replacement)// use -xmit version
```

Using Newton Data Storage Objects

This section describes how to use the most common Newton data storage objects and methods. It presumes knowledge of the material in preceding sections. This section begins with a programmer's overview, which is followed by sections providing detailed explanations of the use of stores, soups, queries, cursors, and entries.

Programmer's Overview

This section provides a code-level overview of common objects, methods, and functions that provide data storage and retrieval services to Newton applications.

Data Storage and Retrieval

This section presumes understanding of the material in "About Data Storage on Newton Devices" beginning on page 11-1.

Most applications store data as frames that reside in soup entries. You can create a frame by simply defining it and saving it in a variable, a constant, or a slot in another frame. For example, the following code fragment defines a frame containing the aSlot and otherSlot slots. The frame itself is stored in the myFrame variable. For all practical purposes you can treat variables that hold NewtonScript objects as the objects themselves; hence, the following discussion refers to the frame saved in the myFrame variable as the myFrame frame.

```
myFrame := {aSlot: "some string data", otherSlot: 9258};
```

The myFrame frame contains two slots: the aSlot slot stores the "some string data" string and the otherSlot slot stores the 9258 integer value. Because every NewtonScript object encapsulates its own class data, you need not declare types for NewtonScript data structures, including slots.

Frames are not persistent unless stored as soup entries. To add the myFrame frame to a soup, you must send a message to the appropriate soup object. You can obtain a soup or union soup object by creating a new one or by retrieving a reference to one that is already present.

To create a new union soup, use the RegUnionSoup function to register its soup definition with the system. The system uses this definition to create the union's member soups as needed to store soup entries.

The following code fragment saves the union soup object RegUnionSoup returns in the myUSoup local variable. You might place code like this example in your application (form) part's InstallScript function or your application base view's ViewSetupFormScript method:

```
local aSlotIndexSpec := {structure: 'slot, path: 'aSlot,
                    type: 'string};
local otherSlotIndexSpec := {structure: 'slot, path: 'otherSlot,
                    type: 'int};
local mySoupDef := {name: "mySoup:mySig",
                 userName: "My Soup",
                 ownerApp: '|MyApp:MySig|,
                 ownerAppName : "My Application",
                 userDescr: "This is the My Application soup.",
                 indexes: [aSlotIndexSpec,otherSlotIndexSpec]
                 };
local myUsoup := RegUnionSoup('|MyApp:MySig|,mySoupDef);
```

Note the use of the mySig developer signature as a suffix to ensure the uniqueness of the values of the name and ownerApp slots. For more information regarding developer signatures, see Chapter 2, "Getting Started."

When creating soups from within your application (form) part's InstallScript function, remember that this function calls the EnsureInternal function on all values it uses. Thus, instead of passing references such as partFrame.theForm.myMainSoupDef to the RegUnionSoup function, paste a local copy of your soup definition into your application part's InstallScript function for its use.

The RegUnionSoup function uses the value of your soup definition's name slot to determine whether a particular soup definition has already been registered. You need not be concerned with registering a soup definition twice as long as you don't register different soup definitions that have the same name. An application that registers a soup definition when it opens can always use the union soup object returned by the RegUnionSoup function—if the union soup named by the soup definition exists, this function returns it; otherwise, this function uses the specified soup definition to create and return a new union soup.

The next code fragment uses the AddToDefaultStoreXmit function to add the myFrame frame to the myUSoup union soup. This function creates a new member soup to hold the entry if necessary. The soup is created on the store indicated by the user preference specifying where new items are kept.

```
myUSoup:AddToDefaultStoreXmit(myFrame, '|MyApp:MySig|);
```

At this point, we have created a soup on the store specified by the user and added an entry to that soup without ever manipulating the store directly.

Because you'll often need to notify other applications—or even your own application—when you make changes to soups, all the methods that modify soups or soup entries are capable of broadcasting an appropriate soup change notification message automatically. In the preceding example, the AddToDefaultStoreXmit method notifies applications registered for changes to the myUSoup union soup that the '|MyApp:MySig| application added an entry to this union soup. For more information, see "Callback Functions for Soup Change Notification" (page 9-14) in *Newton Programmer's Reference*.

Most of the time, your application needs to work with existing soups rather than create new ones. You can use the GetUnionSoupAlways function to retrieve an existing soup by name.

Once you have a valid soup object, you can send the Query message to it to retrieve soup entries. The Query method accepts a query specification frame as its argument. This frame defines the criteria soup entries must meet in order to be retrieved by this query. Although you can pass nil as the query spec in order to retrieve all the entries in a soup, usually you'll want to retrieve some useful subset of all entries. For example, the following code fragment retrieves from myUsoup all entries having an aSlot slot. For an overview of the use of query specifications, see "Using Queries" beginning on page 11-38.

```
// get from myUSoup all entries having an aSlot slot
local myCursor := myUSoup:Query({indexPath: 'aSlot});
```

The Query method returns a cursor object that iterates over the set of soup entries satisfying the query specification passed as its argument. You can send messages to the cursor to change its position and to retrieve specified entries, as shown in the following example. For an overview of cursor-manipulation functions, see "Moving the Cursor" beginning on page 11-55.

```
// move the cursor two positions ahead in index order
myCursor:Move(2);
// retrieve the entry at the cursor's current position
local myEntry := myCursor:Entry();
```

For the purposes of discussion, assume that the cursor returned the entry holding the myFrame frame. When accessing this frame, use the NewtonScript dot operator (.) to dereference any of its slots. In the current example, the expression myEntry.aSlot evaluates to the "some string data" value and the expression myEntry.otherSlot evaluates to the 9258 value.

As soon as any slot in the entry is referenced, the system reads entry data into a cache in memory and sets the myEntry variable to reference the cache, rather than the soup entry. This is important to understand for the following reasons:

■ Referencing a single slot in an entry costs you time and memory space, even if you only examine or print the slot's value without modifying it.

■ Changing the value of a slot in the entry really changes the cached entry frame, not the original soup entry; changes to the soup entry are not persistent until the cached entry frame is written back to the soup, where it takes the place of the original entry.

You can treat the cached entry frame as the myFrame frame and assign a new value to the aSlot slot directly, as shown in the following code fragment:

```
myEntry.aSlot := "new and improved string data";
```

To make the changes permanent, you must use EntryChangeXmit or a similar function to write the cached entry frame back to the soup, as in the following example:

```
EntryChangeXmit(myEntry, '|MyApp:MySig| );
```

Like the other functions and methods that make changes to soups, the EntryChangeXmit function transmits an appropriate soup change notification message after writing the entry back to its soup; in this case, the notification specifies that the '|MyApp:MySig| application made an 'entryChanged change to the soup. (All entries store a reference to the soup in which they reside, which is how the EntryChangeXmit method determines which soup changed.)

You can use the `EntryUndoChangesXmit` function to undo the changes to the soup entry if you have not yet written the cached entry back to the soup. Because this function throws away the contents of the entry cache, referencing a slot in the entry after calling the `EntryUndoChangesXmit` function causes entry data to be read into the cache again.

Most applications unregister their soup definitions when they are closed or removed. To facilitate the automatic creation of soups when the user files or moves soup entries in the Extras drawer, you may want your soup definition to remain registered while your application is closed—to unregister only when your application is removed, call the `UnRegUnionSoup` function from your application (`form`) part's `DeletionScript` function.

The following code example uses the `UnRegUnionSoup` function to unregister a soup definition. Because a single application can create multiple soups and soup definitions, soup definitions are unregistered by name and application symbol:

```
// usually in your app part's DeletionScript fn
UnRegUnionSoup("mySoup:mySig",'|MyApp:MySig|);
```

Using Stores

Because the system manages stores automatically, most NewtonScript applications' direct interaction with store objects is limited. This section describes the use of system-supplied functions and methods for

- getting store objects
- retrieving packages from stores
- testing stores for write protection
- getting and setting store information

Procedures for manipulating other objects that reside on stores (such as soups, store parts and virtual binary objects) are described in "Using" sections for each of these objects; for detailed information, see "Using Soups" on page 11-32; "Using Virtual Binary Objects" on page 12-8; and "Using Store Parts" on page 12-12.

Store Object Size Limits

The system imposes a hard upper limit of 64 KB on store object sizes for any kind of store. SRAM-based stores impose a further limitation of 32 KB on block size. Trying to create an entry larger than 32 KB causes the system to throw `|evt.ex.fr.store|` exceptions. These limits apply to the encoded form the data takes when written to a soup, which varies from the object's size in the NewtonScript heap.

Referencing Stores

The GetStores global function returns an array of references to all currently available stores. You can send the messages described in this section to any of the store objects in this array.

```
local allStores := GetStores();
```

▲ **WARNING**
Do not modify the array that the GetStores function returns. ▲

You can reference individual stores in the array by appending an array index value to the GetStores call, as in the following code example:

```
local internalStore := GetStores()[0];
```

The first element of the array returned by the GetStores function is always the internal store; however, the ordering of subsequent elements in this array cannot be relied upon, as it may vary on different Newton devices.

IMPORTANT
Don't call the GetStores function from your application's RemoveScript method, or you may find yourself looking at the "Newton needs the card…" slip. You can avoid this situation by using the IsValid store method to test the validity of a store object before sending messages to it. ▲

Retrieving Packages From Stores

The GetPackages global function returns an array of packages currently available to the system; this array contains packages that reside on any currently available store.

To determine the store on which a specified package resides, test the value of the store slot in the package reference information frame associated with the package. This frame is returned by the GetPkgRefInfo function.

To load a package procedurally, use either of the store methods SuckPackageFromBinary or SuckPackageFromEndpoint. For more information, see the descriptions of these methods in "Data Storage and Retrieval Reference" (page 9-1) in *Newton Programmer's Reference*.

Testing Stores for Write-Protection

The store methods CheckWriteProtect and IsReadOnly determine whether a store is write-protected. The former throws an exception when it is passed a reference to a write-protected store, while the latter simply returns the value nil for such stores. Do not use the global function `IsReadOnly` to test store objects; use only the `IsReadOnly` store method for this purpose.

Getting or Setting the Default Store

The default store is that store designated by the user as the one on which new data items are created. Normally, applications using union soups do not need to get or set the default store. The system-supplied functions that accept union-soup arguments handle the details of saving and retrieving soup data according to preferences specified by the user.

If for some reason you need to get or set the default store yourself, you can utilize the `GetDefaultStore` and `SetDefaultStore` global functions.

Note
Do not change the default store without first notifying the user. ◆

Getting and Setting the Store Name

Normal NewtonScript applications rarely need to get or set store names. A store's name is the string that identifies the store in slips displayed to the user. The default name for the internal store is "Internal" and a PCMCIA store is named "Card" by default. The store methods `GetName` and `SetName` are used to get and set the names of stores.

The following example uses the `GetName` method to obtain a string that is the name of the internal store:

```
//returns the string "Internal"
GetStores()[0]:GetName();
```

Before attempting to set the store's name or write any other data to it, you can use the store methods `IsReadOnly` or `CheckWriteProtect` to determine whether the store can be written.

▲ WARNING
Renaming a store renders invalid all aliases to entries residing on that store. See "Using Entry Aliases" on page 12-7. ▲

Accessing the Store Information Frame

Each store may hold an optional information frame that applications can use to save information associated with the store itself. Note that unless an application stores data in this frame, it may not exist on every store.

The `GetInfo` and `SetInfo` store methods are intended for use by backup/restore applications only; most applications need not use them at all. The `GetInfo` store method retrieves the value of a specified slot in the store information frame. Its corollary, the SetInfo store method, writes the value of a specified slot in this frame.

Using Soups

This section discusses the functions and methods used to work with soup objects. Individual entries in soups and union soups are manipulated by means of queries, cursors, and entry functions, as described in subsequent sections of this chapter. This section describes procedures for

- creating soups and indexes

- retrieving existing soups

- indexing existing soups

- reading and writing soup data

- accessing information about the soup itself and the store on which it resides

- removing soups

Naming Soups

When creating soups, you need to follow certain naming conventions in order to avoid name collisions with other applications' soups. Following these conventions also makes your own soups more easily identifiable.

If your application creates only one soup, you can use your package name as the name of its soup. Your package name is created by using a colon (:) to append your package's Extras Drawer name to your unique developer signature. For example, if your developer signature is "myCompany" and you are creating a package that appears in the Extras Drawer with the name "foo", concatenating these two values produces the "foo:myCompany" package name.

If your application creates multiple soups, use another colon, followed by your package name, as a suffix to a descriptive soup name. For example, "soup1:foo:myCompany" and "soup2:foo:myCompany" would be acceptable soup names unlikely to duplicate those used by other applications.

Normally, each soup appears under its own icon in the Extras Drawer. If your application creates multiple soups, it is recommended that you group them under a single Extras Drawer icon. For more information, see "About Icons and the Extras Drawer" on page 19-38 in Chapter 19, "Built-in Applications and System Data."

For additional information regarding naming conventions for your developer signature and other items, see "Developer Signature Guidelines" on page 2-9 in Chapter 2, "Getting Started."

Registering and Unregistering Soup Definitions

The `RegUnionSoup` global function registers a soup definition with the system and returns a union soup object to which you can send messages. Once the soup definition is registered, various union soup methods create the union's member soups as needed to save entries. A corollary function, `UnRegUnionSoup`, unregisters a specified soup definition.

You can register a soup definition with the system any time before your application needs to access the soup it defines. If your application is the only one using your soup, you need only ensure that its definition is registered while the application is actually open. Normally, code that registers soup definitions is provided by your application part's `InstallScript` function or your application base view's `ViewSetupFormScript` method. You need not be concerned with registering a soup definition twice as long as you don't register different soup definitions that have the same name.

Code to unregister soup definitions is usually provided either by your application base view's `ViewQuitScript` method (to unregister when the application closes) or your application part's `DeletionScript` function (to unregister only when the application is removed.) An application that allows the user to file or move data items from the Extras Drawer should allow its soup definitions to remain registered while the application is closed, unregistering them only when the application is removed. For more information on manipulating soup entries from the Extras Drawer, see "About Icons and the Extras Drawer" on page 19-38 in Chapter 19, "Built-in Applications and System Data."

Your application can also call the `RegUnionSoup` function to retrieve its own union soups that already exist. If you call `RegUnionSoup` on a soup definition that is already registered, this function replaces the currently registered soup definition with the new one and returns the union soup named by the soup definition passed as its argument; if that union soup does not exist, this method uses the soup definition passed as its argument to create a new union soup that it returns. Alternatively, you can call the `GetUnionSoupAlways` global function to retrieve any extant union soup, not just those your application registers. For more information, see "Retrieving Existing Soups" beginning on page 11-34.

To use the `RegUnionSoup` function, you might put code like the following example in the `ViewSetupFormScript` method of your application's base view:

```
local mySoupDef := {name: "mySoup:mySig",
                userName: "My Soup",
                ownerApp: '|MyApp:MySig|,
                ownerAppName : "My Application",
                userDescr: "This is the My Application soup.",
```

```
              indexes: [{structure: 'slot, path: 'aSlot,
                         type: 'string}]
              };
```

```
// register soup or retrieve already-registered soup
   local myUsoup := RegUnionSoup('|myApp:mySig|, mySoupDef);
```

You can unregister a soup definition whenever you no longer need to create the soup it defines. If your application is the only one that uses your soup, you need only ensure that its definition is registered while the application is actually open. If other applications use your soup, you may wish to leave its definition registered even after your application is closed or removed; however, most applications unregister their soup definitions at one of these times, if only to make that much more memory available to other applications.

The following code fragment illustrates the use of the UnRegUnionSoup function:

```
// unregister my soup def
   UnRegUnionSoup (mySoupDef.Name, '|myApp:mySig|);
// don't forget to set all unused references to nil
   myUsoup := nil;
```

Retrieving Existing Soups

To retrieve your own union soups, you can use the RegUnionSoup function as described in "Registering and Unregistering Soup Definitions" beginning on page 11-33. Alternatively, you can call the GetUnionSoupAlways global function to retrieve any union soup by name.

Use of the GetUnionSoupAlways global function is straightforward, as the following example shows. Note that you can pass system-supplied constants to this function to retrieve soups used by the system and the built-in applications. For more information, see Chapter 19, "Built-in Applications and System Data."

```
// retrieve "mySoup:mySig" union soup by name
local myUSoup := GetUnionSoupAlways("mySoup:mySig");
// retrieve soup used by built-in Names application
local names := GetUnionSoupAlways(ROM_CardFileSoupName);
```

Note that you can use the IsInstance utility function to determine whether a specified soup is a union soup. Pass either of the symbols 'PlainSoup or 'UnionSoup as the value of the *class* parameter to this function, as shown in the following code fragment.

```
IsInstance(mySoup, 'UnionSoup);
```

Adding Entries to Soups

This section describes how to add a frame to a union soup or a specified member soup in a union. For information on creating union soups, see "Registering and Unregistering Soup Definitions" on page 11-33. For information on retrieving union soups, see "Retrieving Existing Soups" on page 11-34.

You can use either of the `AddToDefaultStoreXmit` or `AddToStoreXmit` methods to save frames as soup entries. Both of these methods create a single soup in which to save the new entry when the appropriate member of the union is not already present on the store. The `AddToDefaultStoreXmit` method adds its entry to the member soup on the store specified by the user as the destination for new entries. The `AddToStoreXmit` method allows you to specify according to store the member soup to which it adds the new entry.

Methods that create soup entries—such as the `AddToDefaultStoreXmit`, `AddToStoreXmit`, and `AddXmit` methods—destructively modify the frame presented as their argument to transform it into a soup entry. Thus, any frame passed to these methods must allow write access. If the original frame must remain unmodified, pass a copy of it to these methods.

The following code fragment saves a frame in the default store member of the `myUsoup` union by sending the `AddToDefaultStoreXmit` message to the union soup object that the `RegUnionSoup` function returns:

```
// register soup def'n or get reference to already registered soup
   local myUsoup := RegUnionSoup('|myApp:mySig|, mySoupDef);
// add the entry and transmit notification
   local myEntry := myUSoup:AddToDefaultStoreXmit(
               {aSlot:"my data"}, // frame to add to soup
               '|myApp:mySig|); // app that changed soup
```

The following code fragment saves a frame in the internal store member of the `myUsoup` union by sending the `AddToStoreXmit` message to the union soup object that the `GetUnionSoupAlways` function returns:

```
// get pre-existing uSoup by name
   local myUSoup := GetUnionSoupAlways("mySoup:mySig");
// add entry to member on internal store and transmit notification
   local myEntry := myUSoup:AddToStoreXmit(
               {aSlot:"my data"}, // frame to add to soup
               (GetStores()[0]), // add to member on internal store
               '|myApp:mySig|); // app that changed soup
```

After creating the new soup entry, these methods transmit a soup change notification message. To suppress the soup change notification message that -Xmit functions and methods transmit, pass nil as the value of their *changeSym* argument. For more information, see "Using Soup Change Notification" beginning on page 11-63; also see the descriptions of the AddToDefaultStoreXmit and AddToStoreXmit methods in "Soup Functions and Methods" (page 9-35) in *Newton Programmer's Reference*.

Normally the member soups in a union are created automatically by the system as needed to save frames as soup entries. If you need to force the creation of a union soup member on a specified store without adding an entry to the new member soup, use the GetMember union soup method to do so. For more information, see the description of this method in "Soup Functions and Methods" (page 9-35) in *Newton Programmer's Reference*.

Adding an Index to an Existing Soup

Normally, applications create an index for each slot or set of slots on which a soup may be searched frequently. Although the soup's indexes are usually created along with the soup itself, you may occasionally need to use the AddIndexXmit method to add an index to an already existing soup and transmit a soup change notification message. Indexes must be added individually—you can't pass arrays of index specs to the AddIndexXmit method.

▲ **WARNING**

You cannot query a union soup on an index that is not present in all its member soups. Sending the AddIndexXmit message to a union soup adds the specified index to all soups currently available to the union; however, any soup introduced to the union subsequently has only its original complement of indexes, which may not include the index this method added. Similarly, any member soup created by the system has only the indexes specified by its soup definition, which may not include the index this method added. ▲

The following code fragment adds an index to the "mySoup:myApp" union soup, enabling queries to search for integer data in that soup's mySlot slot:

```
// get my union soup
   local myUSoup := GetUnionSoupAlways("mySoup:mySig");
// add a new single-slot index on the'mySlot slot
   local myISpec := {structure:'slot, path:'mySlot, type:'int};
   local myUSoup:AddIndexXmit(myISpec,'|myApp:mySig|);
```

▲ **WARNING**

Each soup has only one tags index; if you add a tags index to a
soup that already has one, it replaces the original tags index. For
more information, see the description of the AddIndexXmit
method (page 9-42) in *Newton Programmer's Reference.* ▲

Removing Soups

When the user scrubs your application's icon in the Extras Drawer, the system
sends a DeletionScript message to your application. The DeletionScript
function is an optional function that you supply in your application's form part.
This function accepts no arguments. You can remove your application's soups from
within this function by invoking the RemoveFromStoreXmit soup method. The
RemoveFromStoreXmit method is defined only for single soups; in other words,
you must remove each member of a union soup separately.

For more information on the DeletionScript method, see the *Newton Toolkit
User's Guide.* See also "RemoveFromStoreXmit" (page 9-47) in *Newton
Programmer's Reference.*

Do not delete soups from within your application's viewQuitScript method—
user data needs to be preserved until the next time the application is run. For
similar reasons, do not remove soups from within your application's
RemoveScript method. This method does not distinguish between removing
software permanently (scrubbing its icon in the Extras Drawer) and removing
software temporarily (ejecting the PCMCIA card.)

Using Built-in Soups

The soup-based data storage model makes it easy for applications to reuse existing
system-supplied soups for their own needs and to share their own soups with other
applications. Refer to Chapter 19, "Built-in Applications and System Data," to see
descriptions of the soups used by the applications built into the Newton ROM. You
can also use these descriptions as a model for documenting the structure of your
application's shared soups.

Making Changes to Other Applications' Soups

You should avoid changing other applications' soups if at all possible. If you must
make changes to another application's soup, be sure to respect the format of that
soup as documented by its creator. When possible, confine your changes to a single
slot that you create in any soup entry you modify.

When naming slots you add to other applications' soups, exercise the same caution
you would in naming soups themselves—use your application name and developer
signature in the slot name to avoid name-space conflicts.

This approach provides the following benefits:

■ It prevents your application from inadvertently damaging another application's data.

■ It helps your application avoid name conflicts with other applications' slots.

■ It prevents soups from becoming cluttered with excessive numbers of entries.

■ It facilitates removal of your application's data.

Note that when you makes changes to other applications' soups you should transmit notification of the changes by means of the mechanism described in "Using Soup Change Notification" beginning on page 11-63.

Adding Tags to an Existing Soup

You can add tags only to a soup that has a tags index. To add new tags to a soup that already has a tags index, simply add to the soup an entry that uses the new tags—the tags index is updated automatically to include the new tags.

Adding a tags index to an existing soup is like adding any other kind of index: simply pass the appropriate index spec to the soup's AddIndexXmit method. Remember, however, that the system allows only one tags index per soup. If you try to add another tags index to that soup, you'll replace the original tags index. It's quite easy to add new tags to a soup that already has a tags index, so you'll rarely need to replace a soup's tags index.

Using Queries

To retrieve soup entries, you need to query a soup or union soup object by sending the Query message to it. The Query method accepts a query specification frame, or query spec, as its argument. The query spec specifies the characteristics that soup entries must have in order to be included in the query result.

Note

For instructional purposes, this section describes each item that may appear in a query specification separately. Normally, a single query spec defines multiple criteria that soup entries must meet to be included in the results of the query; for example, you can create a single query spec that specifies tests of index key values, string values, and tags. ◆

This section describes how to perform various queries to retrieve soup data. It includes examples of

■ simple queries on index values, tags, or text

■ the use of ascending and descending indexes

- the use of internationalized sorting order
- queries on multiple-slot indexes

Querying Multiple Soups

Soups having the same name can be associated logically by a union soup object. To retrieve entries from all the available soups in a union, just send the Query message to the union soup object.

You must query differently named soups separately, however. For example, before scheduling a meeting, you might send the Query message to the ROM_CardfileSoup soup for information regarding its participants, and send another Query message to the ROM_CalendarSoupName soup to determine whether you have conflicting appointments at the proposed meeting time.

Entry aliases provide a handy way to save references to soup entries. You can use entry aliases to reference entries from different soups more easily. For more information, see "Using Entry Aliases" on page 12-7.

Querying on Single-Slot Indexes

This section provides code examples illustrating a variety of queries on single-slot indexes. For more information on indexes, see "Introduction to Data Storage Objects" on page 11-2 and "Indexes" on page 11-8.

The following code fragment presents an example of the simplest kind of index query—it returns all entries in the soup:

```
local myUSoup := GetUnionSoupAlways("mySoup:mySig");
local allEntriesCursor := myUSoup:Query(nil);
```

When nil is passed as the query spec, as in the example above, the query result potentially includes all entries in the soup. The cursor generated by such a query returns entries in roughly the same order that they were added to the soup; however, this sorting order is not guaranteed because the system recycles the values it uses to identify entries internally. The only way to guarantee that entries are sorted in the order they were added to a soup is to index them on your own time stamp slot.

Most situations will require that you query for a subset of a soup's entries, rather than for all of its entries. That is, you'll want to include or exclude entries according to criteria you define. For example, you might want to find only entries that have a certain slot, or entries in which the value of a specified slot falls within a certain range. The next several examples illustrate the use of single-slot index queries for these kinds of operations.

To find all entries that have a particular slot, specify a path to that slot as the query spec's indexPath value. Note that in order to query on the presence of a particular slot, the soup must be indexed on that slot. For example, the following example of a query returns a cursor to all soup entries that have a name slot. The cursor sorts the entries according to the value of this slot. As first returned by the query, the cursor points to the first entry in index order.

```
// mySoup is a valid soup indexed on the 'name slot
nameCursor:= mySoup:Query({indexPath:'name});
```

You can also use the cursor method GoToKey to go directly to the first entry holding a specified name or value in an indexed slot. For examples of the use of this method, see "Moving the Cursor" beginning on page 11-55.

Using beginKey and endKey values to limit your search can improve query performance significantly. The following example is an index query that uses a beginKey value and an endKey value to return entries for which $(11 \geq \text{entry.number} \leq 27)$.

```
// mySoup is indexed on the 'number slot
local numCursor := mySoup:Query({indexPath: 'number,
                                    beginKey: 11,
                                    endKey: 27});
```

The index on the number slot potentially includes all entries that have a number slot. The index sorts entries on their index key values; unless otherwise specified, the default index order is ascending. Thus, the query can use a beginKey value of 11 to skip over entries holding a value less than 11 in the number slot. The test can be concluded quickly by specifying a maximum value beyond which the cursor generated by this query does not proceed. In this case, the endKey value specifies that the query result does not include entries having values greater than 27 in the number slot. When multiple entries hold a specified endrange value, all of them are included in the result of a query that specifies that endrange value; for example, if multiple entries in the mySoup soup hold the value 27 in their number slot, the previous example includes all of these entries in its result.

The beginKey specification evaluates to a value that occupies a unique position in the sorted index data for the soup. If no entry is associated with this value, the cursor is positioned at the next valid entry in index order. For example, if the mySoup soup in the previous code fragment does not contain an entry having a number slot that holds the value 11, the next valid entry in index order is the first entry in the range over which the cursor iterates.

Similarly, the endKey specification evaluates to a value that occupies a unique position in the sorted index data for the soup. If no entry is associated with this value, the cursor stops on the first valid entry in index order before the endKey value. For example, if the mySoup soup in the previous code fragment does not contain an entry having a number slot that holds the value 27, the last valid entry at or before the position that would be occupied by 27 in the index is the last entry in the range over which the cursor iterates.

To conduct the same query while excluding the endrange values, specify a beginExclKey value instead of a beginKey value, and specify an endExclKey value instead of an endKey value, as shown in the following code fragment:

```
// mySoup is indexed on the 'number slot
// return entries for which (11 > entry.number < 27 )
local numCursor := mySoup:Query({indexPath: 'number,
                                  beginExclKey: 11,
                                  endExclKey: 27});
```

Note that a query spec cannot include both the inclusive and exclusive forms of the same endrange selector; for example, you cannot specify beginKey and a beginExclKey values in the same query spec. However, you can specify, for example, a beginKey value and an endExclKey value in the same query spec.

Because the index sorts entries according to key values, a beginKey on a soup indexed in descending key order may appear to act like an endKey on a soup indexed in ascending order, and vice versa. For more information, see "Queries on Descending Indexes" beginning on page 11-46.

Another way to find all entries having a particular value in a specified slot is to use an indexValidTest method, which can test any index key value without reading its corresponding entry into the NewtonScript heap. The system passes index key values to this function as the cursor moves. Your indexValidTest must return a non-nil value if the entry associated with the key value should be included in the query result. For example, you could use an indexValidTest method to select entries that hold even-number values in a specified slot, as shown in the following code fragment:

```
// mySoup indexed on 'number slot
// select entries having a 'number slot that holds
// an even value between 19 and 58
local myCursor :=
        mySoup:Query({ beginKey: 19, endExclKey: 58,
                      indexValidTest: func (key)
                        (key MOD 2 = 0)});
```

A less-preferred way to test entries is to provide a validTest function to test entries individually. The use of a validTest increases the memory requirements of the search because the system must read soup entries into the NewtonScript heap in order to pass them to the validTest function. Whenever possible, you should avoid using validTest methods in favor of using indexValidTest methods. Generally, you need not use a validTest method unless you must read the entry's data to determine whether to include it in the query result.

The query passes the entire entry to the `validTest` method, rather than just the value of the indexed slot. The next code example reads the entry's `aSlot` and `otherSlot` slots in order to compare their values:

```
// select entries for which aSlot > otherSlot
local myCursor :=
        mySoup:Query({endKey: aKeyValue,
                      validTest: func (entry)
                      begin
                         entry.aSlot > entry.otherSlot
                      end});
```

Querying for Tags

In order to select soup entries according to their associated tag values, you need to include a tags query spec frame in the `tagSpec` slot of the query specification frame passed to the `Query` method. In addition to specifying one or more tags used to select entries, the tags query spec can specify set operators such as `not`, `any`, `equal`, and `all` to create complex filters based on tag values. For a complete description of the tags query spec frame, see "Tags Query Specification Frame" (page 9-13) in *Newton Programmer's Reference*.

You cannot query for tags on a soup that does not have a tags index. This index is usually specified by your soup definition and created along with the soup, but it can be added to an existing soup if necessary. Note that each soup or union soup has only one tags index; if you add a tags index to a soup that already has one, it replaces the original tags index. For more information, see "Tags Index Specification Frame" (page 9-8) in *Newton Programmer's Reference*.

The next several examples presume that the `mySoup` soup has a tags index on the `labels` slot. Note that queries need not specify the path to the slot from which tag values are extracted—in this case, the `labels` slot—because each soup has only one tags index and its index path is specified when the tags index is created. However, because a soup or union soup is allowed to have multiple soup indexes, queries must specify a path to the indexed slot; hence, these examples also presume that the `mySoup` soup has a soup index on the `name` slot.

The presence of any tag specified by the `any` set operator is sufficient to include its entry in the results of the query that uses this operator. For example, the following query selects entries having either the symbol `'flower` or `'tall` in the `labels` slot. Entries not marked with at least one of these symbols are not included in the query result.

```
local myCurs := mySoup:Query({indexPath:'name,
                     tagSpec: {any:['tall, 'flower]}});
```

The `equal` set operator specifies a set of tags an entry must match exactly to be included in the query result. The query in the following example uses the `equal` set operator to select entries marked with only the 'flower and 'tall tags; this query does not select entries missing either tag, nor does it select entries marked with additional tags:

```
local myCurs := mySoup:Query({indexPath:'name,
                        tagSpec: {equal: ['tall, 'flower]}});
```

Like the equal set operator, the all set operator specifies a set of tags that entries must have to be selected; however, the all set operator does not exclude entries marked with additional tags. For example, the query in the following example uses the all set operator to select entries marked with both the 'flower and 'tall tags. This query excludes entries missing either of these tags but includes entries marked with a superset of the 'flower and 'tall tags:

```
local myCurs := mySoup:Query({indexPath:'name,
                        tagSpec: {all: ['tall, 'flower]}});
```

The presence of any tag specified by the none set operator is sufficient to exclude that entry from the query result. For example, the following query matches entries having both of the tags 'flower and 'tall but excludes any entry marked with the 'thorns tag:

```
local myCurs := mySoup:Query({indexPath:'name,
                        tagSpec: {all:['flower, 'tall],
                            none:['thorns]}});
```

The following exceptions may be thrown when attempting to query using a tag spec. If the soup does not have a tags index, a "no tags" exception levt.ex.fr.store| -48027 is thrown. If the tag spec passed as an argument to the Query method has none of the slots equal, any, all, or none, an "invalid tag spec" exception levt.ex.fr.store| -48028 is thrown.

Querying for Text

This section describes how to select entries according to the presence of one or more strings in any slot. The current system allows you to search entries for string beginnings, entire strings, or substrings of larger strings.

To select entries according to the presence of one or more specified string beginnings, add to your query spec a words slot containing an array of string beginnings to be matched. For example, the following code fragment illustrates a query that returns entries having strings beginning with "bob":

```
// find words beginning with "bob"
local myCurs := mySoup:Query({words: ["bob"]});
```

Data Storage and Retrieval

This query finds entries containing the words `"Bob"`, `"Bobby"`, and so forth, but not words such as `"JoeBob"`. Text queries are not case sensitive—even though the original query spec is all lower case, this query finds entries such as `"Bob"` or `"BOB"`.

Because the `words` slot contains an array, it can be used to search for multiple string beginnings. For example, the following code fragment returns entries that contain both of the string beginnings `"Bob"` and `"Apple"`. Thus, an entry containing the strings `"Bobby"` and `"Applegate"` would be included in the results of the search, but an entry missing either of the word beginnings `"Bob"` or `"Apple"` is not included.

```
// find entries holding "bob" and "apple" word beginnings
// won't find entries having only one of these beginnings
local myCurs := mySoup:Query({words: ["bob", "apple"]});
```

Because each element in the array is a string, each "word" to be matched can actually contain multiple words and punctuation. For example, the following code fragment returns entries that contain both of the string beginnings `"Bob"` and `"Apple Computer, Inc."`:

```
// find word beginnings "bob" and "Apple Computer, Inc."
local myCursor := mySoup:Query({words: ["bob",
                                "Apple Computer, Inc."]});
```

Note

The more unique the search string is, the more quickly a `words` search proceeds. Thus, `words` queries are slow for search words that have only one or two characters in them. ◆

To search for entire strings, rather than string beginnings, the query spec must include an `entireWords` slot that holds the value `true`, as shown in the following code fragment:

```
// return entries holding entire words "bob" and "Apple Computer"
local myCursor := mySoup:Query({words: ["bob", "Apple Computer"],
                                entireWords: true });
```

This query returns entries that contain both of the strings `"Bob"` and `"Apple Computer"`. Because the `entireWords` slot holds the value `true`, this query does not match strings such as `"Apple Computer, Inc."` or `"Bobby"`. Entries containing only one of the specified words are not included in the results of the search.

To conduct a text search that is not constrained by word boundaries, add to your query spec a `text` slot containing a single string to be matched. For example, the following code fragment illustrates a query that returns entries having strings that contain the substring `"Bob"`:

```
// find strings containing the substring "Bob"
local myCursor := mySoup:Query({text: "bob"});
```

This query finds entries containing words such as `"JoeBob"`, as well as those containing words such as `"bob"` and `"Bobby"`.

Internationalized Sorting Order for Text Queries

Indexes are not normally sensitive to case, diacritical marks, or ligatures in string values; however, index and query specifications can request this behavior specifically. When internationalized index ordering is used, uppercase letters sort first, followed by lowercase letters, diacritical marks, and ligatures. Thus, the letter A sorts before the letter a, which sorts before the letter å, which sorts before the letter á, which sorts before the ligature æ.

To index string values in internationalized order, include an optional `sortID` slot holding the value 1 in the index specification frame used to build a soup's index. A cursor subsequently generated against that soup returns entries holding the following strings in the order listed here:

```
"AA", "aa", "åå", "EE", "ÉÉ", "ee"
```

This internationalized indexing order is available only for indexes on string values. When the `sortID` slot is missing from the index spec or this slot's value is `nil`, the index generated is not sensitive to case, diacritics, or ligatures; in other words, the index may not necessarily sort `"AA"` before `"aa"`, and so on.

If an index has internationalized ordering, find operations performed by cursors generated against that index can be made sensitive to case and diacritics. To request this behavior, include a non-nil `secOrder` slot in the query spec passed to the `Query` method of an internationally-indexed soup.

The value of the `secOrder` slot affects the use of the `beginKey`, `beginExclKey`, `endKey`, and `endExclKey` slots, as well as the `GoToKey` cursor method. For example, sending the `GoToKey("åå")` message to the cursor generated by this query returns the first entry found at or after the `"åå"` index value but does not return entries holding values that vary in case, diacritics, and so on.

When the `secOrder` slot is missing or holds the value `nil`, find operations carried out by cursor methods such as `GoToKey` ignore case and diacritics; that is, they may return entries holding case and diacritic variations on the requested value. For example, sending the `myCursor:GoToKey("åå")` message returns the first entry found that holds any of the `"AA"`, `"aa"`, or `"åå"` values. However, the cursor generated by this query still uses the sorting order provided by the internationalized index: cursor methods such as `Next` and `Prev` return entries in the internationally-indexed order.

Queries on Descending Indexes

Even though queries and cursors based on descending order indexes work just like normal queries and cursors, their behavior can seem confusing if you forget that it is a function of index order. It is always helpful to remember the following points when working with queries and cursors—especially when using descending indexes:

■ The "beginning" and "end" of a range of index values is a function of index key order.

■ The cursor navigates entries in index key order.

This section provides examples of the behavior of cursors that use descending indexes. These examples are based on a soup containing the entries shown in the following code fragment; although this example uses string values, any kind of index key value may be sorted in descending order.

```
{data: "able", …};
{data: "axe", …};
{data: "name", …};
{data: "noun", …};
```

Soup indexes normally sort string data in ascending alphabetical order; for example, `"able"`, `"axe"`, `"name"`, `"noun"`. A descending index sorts the same data in reverse alphabetical order; for example, `"noun"`, `"name"`, `"axe"`, `"able"`.

Figure 11-6 depicts the reversed ordering that a descending index provides, with examples of cursor behavior that is a function of index ordering.

Figure 11-6   Cursor operations on descending index

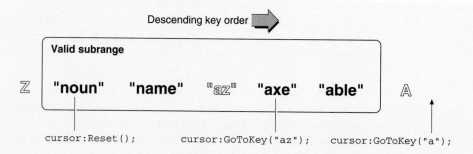

Data Storage and Retrieval

Sending the `Reset` message to the cursor positions it at the first valid entry in index order. In this case, the first entry is `"noun"` because the entries are sorted in descending alphabetical order.

The `GoToKey` cursor method steps through the set of valid entries in index order until it finds the first entry having a specified key value. If the specified key value is not found, this method returns the next valid entry found after the specified index position. Thus, sending the `GotoKey("az")` message to this cursor returns the value `"axe"` because it's the first valid entry that appears in the index after the unoccupied `"az"` position.

Sending the `GotoKey("a")` message to this cursor returns the value `nil` because this message positions the cursor beyond the end of the range of valid entries defined by the query that generated the cursor.

Figure 11-7 illustrates that specifying a `beginExclKey` value of `"b"` excludes from consideration every entry beginning with a letter that comes after `"b"` in the reverse alphabet; that is, this `beginExclKey` value causes the valid range of entries to include only entries beginning with `"a"`. As a result, sending the `GotoKey("n")` message causes this cursor to return the value `"axe"` because it is the first valid entry appearing in the index after the `"n"` position.

Note

The sort order for symbol-based indexes is the ASCII order of the symbol's lexical form. This sorting behavior is made available in NewtonScript by the `SymbolCompareLex` global function. ◆

Figure 11-7 Specifying ends of a descending index

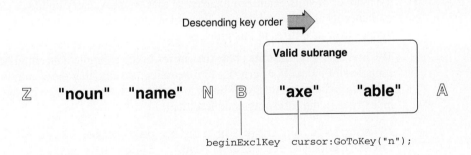

Querying on Multiple-Slot Indexes

Before reading this section, you should understand the contents of "Querying on Single-Slot Indexes" beginning on page 11-39.

Data Storage and Retrieval

A multiple-slot query can be performed only on a soup that has a multiple-slot index generated against the same set of keys in the same order as the query spec. For information on creating an index, see "Registering and Unregistering Soup Definitions" beginning on page 11-33 and "Adding an Index to an Existing Soup" beginning on page 11-36. For a description of the data structure that defines a multiple-slot index, see "Multiple-Slot Index Specification Frame" (page 9-6) in *Newton Programmer's Reference*.

In a general sense, queries on multiple-slot indexes are specified like queries on single-slot indexes and behave the same way. The "differences" you'll encounter are usually the result of misunderstanding how multiple index keys are used to sort and select indexed entries.

For purposes of discussion, assume that you have a soup containing the entries in the following code fragment, and that you want to sort these entries alphabetically by last name and then by first name:

```
// entries used for all examples in this section
{last: "Perry", first: "Bruce", num: 1}
{last: "Perry", first: "Ralph", num: 2}
{last: "Perry", first: "Barbara", num: 3}
{last: "Perry", first: "John", num: 4}
{last: "Bates", first: "Carol", num: 5}
{last: "Perry", first: "Daphne", num: 7}
```

A single-slot index sorts entries according to the value held in a single slot that you specify when the index is created. In contrast, a multiple-slot index may consider the values of multiple slots when sorting entries. It's important to understand that either kind of index imposes only one sort order on the indexed data, regardless of the number of slots examined to arrive at that order. A query on index values evaluates its associated entries in this order, and the cursor generated by this query iterates over its entries in this order, as well.

The first example illustrates how the entries in the example data could be sorted by a single-slot index. For purposes of discussion, assume that these entries are indexed on the value that each holds in its last slot, as specified by the single-slot index spec in the following code fragment:

```
// single-slot index on string data from 'last slot
{structure:'slot, path: 'last, type:'string}
```

Sorting the entries according to the value each holds in its last slot isn't very useful because all of the entries except one hold an identical value in this slot. Unfortunately, sorting the entries on the value of another slot does not produce a useful ordering, either: an index on any other single slot sorts the "Bates" entry in the midst of all the "Perry" entries.

A multiple-slot index solves this problem by sorting entries according to multiple key values. The key values are extracted from up to six index paths specified by the `path` array of the index specification frame. For example, the following code fragment specifies a multiple-slot index that sorts entries according to the values each holds in its `'last`, `'first`, and `'num` slots:

```
// multiple-slot index on data from three slots
myMultiSlotSpec :=
    {structure:'multiSlot,
    path: ['last,'first,'num],
    type: ['string, 'string, 'int }
```

The first key in the `path` array is called the primary key; subsequent lower-order keys, if they are present, are the secondary key, tertiary key, and so on, up to a total of six keys per array.

The primary key specifies a minimum criterion for inclusion in the index and provides a value used to sort the indexed entries initially. In the example, only entries having a `last` slot are indexed, and the value of the `last` slot is used to impose an initial ordering on the indexed entries. Thus, the multiple-slot index in the previous example sorts the `"Bates"` entry before all of the `"Perry"` entries.

The secondary key, if it is present, is used to sort entries having identical primary keys. In the previous example, the multiple-slot index imposes a secondary ordering on all `"Perry"` entries, according to the value each holds in its `first` slot. Similarly, the tertiary key, if present, is used to sort further any entries having identical secondary key values. Because none of the entries in the example have identical secondary key values (none of the `first` slots hold identical values), the value of each entry's `num` slot has no effect on how the index sorts the entries.

Thus, the multiple-slot index shown previously sorts the set of sample entries in the following order:

```
{last: "Bates", first: "Carol", num: 5}
{last: "Perry", first: "Barbara", num: 3}
{last: "Perry", first: "Bruce", num: 1}
{last: "Perry", first: "Daphne", num: 7}
{last: "Perry", first: "John", num: 4}
{last: "Perry", first: "Ralph", num: 2}
```

Now that you're familiar with the manner in which multiple-slot indexes sort entries, let's look at the way the `Query` method uses a multiple-slot index to select entries.

Missing slots in a multiple-slot query spec are treated as `nil` values, just as they are when querying on single-slot indexes. For example, if the query spec is missing an `endKey` slot, the upper end of the range of entries examined by the query is unbounded, just as it would be for a query on a single-slot index.

Instead of using single values for the indexPath, beginKey, beginExclKey, endKey, and endExclKey slots in the query spec, the Query method accepts arrays of keys or values as these arguments when it works with a soup having a multiple-slot index. The first key in the array is the primary key; subsequent lower-order keys, if they are present, are the secondary key, tertiary key, and so on, up to a total of six keys per array.

To get a better idea of how queries evaluate multiple-slot key selectors, consider how the beginKey value in the following code fragment would work with the example data:

```
myQSpec := {indexPath: ['last,'first,'num],
            beginKey:["Perry","Bruce",5]}
```

Querying the example data using this specification returns a cursor that initially references the following entry:

```
{last: "Perry", first: "Daphne", num: 7}
```

First, the query finds the primary key value of "Perry" in the index, skipping over the "Bates" entry in the process of doing so. Next, the query searches for an index value identical to the secondary key "Bruce", skipping over the "Barbara" entry in the process of doing so. Finally, the query searches for an index value identical to the tertiary key value 5. Because an entry having this value is not found, the cursor is positioned on the next valid entry in index order, which has the tertiary key value 7.

When specifying strings as bounding values for queries, don't forget that the beginKey, beginExclKey, endKey, and endExclKey slots in a query spec specify identical matches only. For example, the key value "P" is not identical to the key value "Perry".

When an identical index value cannot be found for a key specification, subordinate key values have no effect. For example, if the primary key value is not matched, the secondary and tertiary key values have no effect.

To demonstrate these points, imagine that you wrote the query spec in the previous example a bit differently. Instead of specifying a value of "Perry" for the primary element in the beginKey array, assume you specified a value of "P". This change would make the query spec look like the following code fragment:

```
myQSpec := {indexPath: ['last,'first,'num],
            beginKey:["P","Bruce",5]}
```

Querying our example data using this specification returns a cursor that initially references the following entry:

```
{last: "Perry", first: "Barbara", num: 3}
```

This time around, the query again skips over the `"Bates"` entry in the process of positioning the cursor at index value `"P"`. However, because no entry holds a primary index key value of `"P"`, the cursor stops at the next valid entry in index order. Further, because an identical index value was not found for the primary key specification, the secondary and tertiary key selectors have no effect at all. Thus the cursor stops on the first index value found after the position that `["P","Bruce",5]` would occupy if it were present in the index data.

When an element of an array in a query spec is missing or `nil`, the `Query` method does not test subordinate key values specified by the array. For example, the presence of the `nil` value in the `endKey` specification `{endKey : ["bob", nil, 55]}` makes it equivalent to the `{endKey : ["bob"]}` specification.

One result of this behavior is that it is impossible to make a query ignore higher-order sort keys while still testing on lower-order keys. For example, it is meaningless to specify a value such as `[nil,` *validKey, ...*`]` for the `beginKey, beginExclKey, endKey,` or `endExclKey` slot in a query spec—the `nil`-value primary element specifies that the query is to ignore subsequent elements of the array.

If you want to be able to ignore key specifiers in a query spec selectively, you need to define for your entries a default "`nil`-equivalent" value that does have a position in index order. For example, you could use the empty string (`""`) for string key values, either of the values `0` or `MININT` for integer key values, and the null symbol (`'||`) for symbolic key values.

Further, the presence of a `nil`-value index key in an entry suppresses the evaluation of lower-order keys in that entry for sorting in the multiple-slot index. For example, the entries in the following code fragment sort to the same position in the multiple-slot index because as soon as the system encounters the `nil` key value in each entry's `secondary` slot, it does not attempt to sort that entry any further:

```
{primary: "foo", secondary: nil, tertiary: "bar"}
{primary: "foo", secondary: nil, tertiary: "qux"}
```

Querying explicitly for `nil` key values (`nil`-value slots) is not supported. Your entries' indexed slots must hold non-`nil` values to participate in queries.

For cursors generated against multiple-slot indexes, the cursor method `GoToKey` accepts arrays of keys as its argument. You can use this method to experiment with multiple-slot key specifications.

Similarly, for queries on multiple-slot indexes, the input passed to the `indexValidTest` function is an array of key values, with the first key in the array being the primary key, followed by any subordinate key values held by the entry being tested.

▲ **WARNING**

Index keys are limited to a total of 39 unicode characters (80 bytes, 2 of which are used internally) per soup entry. Keys that exceed this limit may be truncated when passed to an `indexValidTest` function. This 80-byte limit applies to the entire key space allocated for an entry, not for individual keys. As a result, subordinate keys in multiple-slot indexes may be truncated or missing when the total key size for the entry is greater than 80 bytes. For more information, see the description of the `indexValidTest` function in "Query Specification Frame" (page 9-9) in *Newton Programmer's Reference*. See also the description of the `MakeKey` method (page 9-45) in *Newton Programmer's Reference*. ▲

Limitations of Index Keys

Under the following conditions, a string may not match its index key exactly:

- Keys of type `'string` are truncated after 39 unicode characters.

- Ink data is stripped from `'string` keys.

- Subkeys in multiple-slot indexes may be truncated or missing when the total key size is greater than 80 bytes.

You can use the `MakeKey` function to determine precisely the index key that the system generates for a particular string. The interface to this function looks like the following code fragment:

soup:MakeKey(*string*, *indexPath*)

The following examples presume that *mySoup* is a valid soup (not a union soup) having the multiple-slot index specified by the following code fragment:

```
myMultiSlotIndexSpec := {structure: ' multislot,
                    path: ['name.first,
                           'cardType,
                           'name.last],
                    type : ['string, 'int, 'string]};
```

Each of the soup's entries has a `name` slot and a `cardType` slot. The `name` slot holds a frame containing the slots `first` and `last`, which contain string data. The `cardType` slot holds integer data.

The first example illustrates the truncation of string keys longer than 39 characters. Evaluating the following code fragment in the Inspector

mySoup:MakeKey(["12345678901234567890", 3,
          "ABCDEFGHIJKLMNOPQRSTUVWXYZ"],
          ['name.first, 'cardType, 'name.last])

returns the key value

["12345678901234567890", 3, "ABCDEFGHIJKLMNO"]

The next example illustrates the truncation of subkeys when the total key size is greater than 80 bytes. In this example, the first string in the *string* array is so long that it uses up the entire 80 bytes allocated for the key, with the result that the first string is truncated and the remaining key values are `nil`. Evaluating the following code fragment in the Inspector

mySoup:MakeKey(["12345678901234567890abcdefghijjlmnopqrstuvwxyz",
    3, "ABCDEFGHIJKLMNOPQRSTUVWXYZ12345678901234567890"],
    ['name.first, 'cardType, 'name.last])

returns the key value

["12345678901234567890abcdefghijjlmnopqr", NIL, NIL]

Missing elements in the *string* array are treated as `nil` values. For example, the following code fragment is missing the second two elements of the *string* array:

mySoup:MakeKey(["12345678901234567890],
        ['name.first, 'cardType, 'name.last])

Evaluating this code fragment in the Inspector returns the key value

["12345678901234567890", NIL, NIL]

On the other hand, missing index paths cause this method to throw an exception. If one of the index paths in a multiple-slot index is missing from the array passed as the value of the *indexPath* parameter, the `MakeKey` method throws a "soup index does not exist" `evt.ex.fr.store -48013` exception.

Using Cursors

This section discusses the functions and methods used to work with cursor objects returned by the `Query` method of soups or union soups. Individual entries in soups and union soups are manipulated by the entry functions described in the section "Using Entries," later in this chapter. This section describes

- getting the cursor
- testing validity of the cursor
- getting the currently referenced soup entry from the cursor
- moving the cursor

- getting the number of entries in cursor data
- getting an index key from the cursor
- copying the cursor

Getting a Cursor

Cursor objects are returned by the `Query` method. For more information, see "Using Queries" beginning on page 11-38.

Testing Validity of the Cursor

When a storage card is inserted or a soup is created, union soups include new soups in the union automatically as is appropriate. A cursor on a union soup may not be able to include a new soup when the new soup's indexes do not match those present for the other soups in the union. In particular, this situation can occur when

- The new soup does not have the index specified in the `indexPath` of the query spec used to generate the cursor.
- The query spec used to generate the cursor included a `tagSpec` and the new soup does not have the correct tags index.

In such cases, the cursor becomes invalid. An invalid cursor returns `nil` when sent messages such as `Next`, `Prev`, `Entry`, and so on. Note that a valid cursor returns `nil` when it receives a message that positions it outside of the range of valid entries. (For an example, see the text accompanying Figure 11-6 on page 11-46.)

You can test the cursor's validity by invoking the `Status` cursor method. This method returns the `'valid` symbol for cursors that are valid and returns the `'missingIndex` symbol when a soup referenced by the cursor is missing an index. Your application needs to call this method when it receives either of the `'soupEnters` or `'soupCreated` soup change notification messages. If the `Status` method does not return the `'valid` symbol, the application must correct the situation and recreate the cursor.

For a detailed description of the `Status` cursor method, see the section "Query and Cursor Methods" (page 9-60) in *Newton Programmer's Reference*. For a discussion of soup change notification messages, see the section "Callback Functions for Soup Change Notification" (page 9-14) in *Newton Programmer's Reference*.

Getting the Entry Currently Referenced by the Cursor

To obtain the entry currently referenced by the cursor, send the `Entry` message to the cursor, as shown in the following code fragment:

```
// assume myCursor is valid cursor returned from a query
local theEntry := myCursor:Entry();
```

Moving the Cursor

This section describes various ways to position the cursor within the range of entries it references.

Sometimes the following discussion refers to the "first" entry in a cursor. As you know, the order imposed on cursor data is defined by the soup index used by the query that generated the cursor. When you see mentions of the "first" entry in a cursor, be aware that this phrasing really means "the first entry as defined by index order (ascending or descending order)."

When first returned by a query, the cursor points to the first entry in the data set that satisfies the query. Thus, to obtain the first entry in the data set referenced by a newly created cursor, just send the Entry message to the cursor.

You can also position the cursor on the first entry in its data set by sending the Reset message. The Reset method moves the cursor to the first valid entry in the query result and returns that entry. For example:

```
local cursor := mySoup:Query(nil);
// move the cursor ahead a bit
local anEntry := cursor:Move(3);
// go back to first entry
local firstEntry := cursor:Reset();
```

Note that if the query spec includes a beginKey value, the Reset method returns the first valid entry at or after the beginKey value in index order.

To obtain the last entry in the set of entries referenced by the cursor, send the ResetToEnd cursor message, as shown in the following example:

```
local cursor := mySoup: Query({indexPath: 'name,
                                endKey: "ZZ"});
local lastCursorEntry := cursor:ResetToEnd();
```

Note that if the query spec includes an endKey value, the ResetToEnd method positions the cursor on the last valid entry in index order at or before the specified endKey value. For example, if you specify an endKey value of "Z" but the last valid entry previous to that in index order has the key value "gardenia", the entry associated with the "gardenia" key value is returned.

The cursor can be advanced to the next entry in index order or moved back to the previous entry by the Next and Prev methods, respectively. After these methods move the cursor, they return the current entry. If sending either of these messages positions the cursor outside of the range of valid entries, it returns nil.

You can use the Move method to move the cursor multiple positions. For example, instead of coding incremental cursor movement as in the following example,

```
for i := 1 to 5 do myCursor:Next();
```

you can obtain faster results by using the Move method. The following code fragment depicts a typical call to this method. After positioning the cursor, the Move method returns the current entry.

```
// skip next four entries and return the fifth one or nil
local theEntry := myCursor:Move(5);
```

To move the cursor in large increments, it's faster to use the GoTo and GoToKey methods to position the cursor directly. You can use the GoToKey method to go directly to the first indexed slot that has a particular value and return the entry containing that slot, as shown in the following example:

```
// index spec for soup that generated myCursor
indxSpec: {structure: 'slot, path: 'name, type: 'string};

// go to the first entry that has
// the value "Nige" in the name slot
local theEntry := myCursor:GotoKey("Nige");
```

If the argument to the GoToKey method is not of the type specified by the soup's index spec, this method throws an exception. For example, the index spec in the previous example specifies that the name slot holds string data. If you pass a symbol to the GoToKey method, it signals an error because this soup's index holds string data:

```
// throws exception - arg doesn't match index data type
myCursor:GotoKey('name);
```

Counting the Number of Entries in Cursor Data

Because the user can add or delete entries at any time, it's difficult to determine with absolute certainty the number of entries referenced by a cursor. With that in mind, you can use the CountEntries cursor method to discover the number of entries present in the set referenced by the cursor at the time the CountEntries method executes.

To discover the number of entries in the entire soup, you can execute a very broad query that includes all soup entries in the set referenced by the cursor and then send a CountEntries message to that cursor. For example:

```
local allEntriesCursor := mySoup:Query(nil);
local numEntries := allEntriesCursor:CountEntries();
```

Note that if the query used to generate the cursor specifies a beginKey value, the CountEntries method starts counting at the first valid entry having an index key value equal to or greater than the beginKey value. Similarly, if the query that generated the cursor used an endKey value, the CountEntries method stops counting at the last valid entry having an index key value equal to or less than the endKey value.

Note that the use of the CountEntries method is somewhat time-consuming and may increase your application's heap space requirements; for performance reasons, use this method only when necessary.

Getting the Current Entry's Index Key

The EntryKey cursor method returns the index key data associated with the current cursor entry without reading the entry into the NewtonScript heap. Note, however, that under certain circumstances the value returned by this method does not match the entry's index key data exactly. For more information, see "Limitations of Index Keys" on page 11-52.

Copying Cursors

You can clone a cursor to use for browsing soup entries without disturbing the original cursor. Do not use the global functions Clone or DeepClone to clone cursors. Instead, use the Clone method of the cursor to be copied, as shown in the following code fragment:

```
local namesUSoup:= GetUnionSoupAlways(ROM_CardFileSoupName);
local namesCursor := namesUSoup:Query(nil);
local cursorCopy:= namesCursor:Clone();
```

Using Entries

This section discusses the functions and methods that work with soup entry objects returned by cursors. This section describes

- adding entries to soups
- removing entries from soups
- saving references to entries
- modifying entries
- replacing entries
- sharing entry data
- copying entry data
- using the entry cache effectively

Saving Frames as Soup Entries

To save a frame as a soup entry, pass the frame to either of the union soup methods `AddToDefaultStoreXmit` or `AddToStoreXmit`, or pass it to the `AddXmit` soup method. Each of these methods transforms the frame presented as its argument into a soup entry, returns the entry, and transmits a change notification message. The following code example illustrates the use of the `AddToDefaultStoreXmit` method:

```
local myFrame := {text: "Some info", color: 'blue};
// assume mySoupDef is a valid soup definition
local myUSoup := RegUnionSoup(mySoupDef)
myUSoup:AddToDefaultStoreXmit(myFrame,'|MyApp:MySig|);
```

The new soup entry that these methods create consists of the frame presented to the entry-creation method, along with copies of any data structures the frame references, as well as copies of any data structures those structures reference, and so on. Thus, you must be very cautious about making soup entries out of frames that include references to other data structures. In general, this practice is to be avoided—it can result in the creation of extremely large entries or entries missing slots that were present in the original frame.

For example, the presence of a `_parent` slot in the frame presented as an argument to these methods causes the whole `_parent` frame (and its parent, and so on) to be stored in the resulting entry, potentially making it extremely large. An alternative approach is to store a key symbol in the data and find the parent object in a frame of templates at run time.

Do not include `_proto` slots in frames presented to methods that create soup entries. These slots are not written to the soup entry and are missing when the entry is read from the soup.

Do not save magic pointers in soup entries. Because the objects they reference are always available in ROM, saving magic pointers is unnecessary and may cause the entries to exceed the maximum permissible size.

Circular pointers within an entry are supported, and an entry can refer to another by using an entry alias.

The size of an individual entry is not limited by the NewtonScript language; however, due to various practical limitations, entries larger than about 16 KB can impact application performance significantly. For best performance, it is recommended that you limit the size of individual entries to 8 KB or less. Note that this total does not include data held by virtual binary objects that the entry references; virtual binary objects save their data separately on a store specified when the virtual binary object is created. For more information, see "Virtual Binary Objects" on page 12-2 in Chapter 12, "Special-Purpose Objects for Data Storage and Retrieval."

No more than 32 KB of text (total of all strings, keeping in mind that one character is 2 bytes) can reside in any soup entry. Another practical limitation is that there must be space in the NewtonScript heap to hold the entire soup entry. You should also be aware that Newton Backup Utility and Newton Connection Kit do not support entries larger than 32K.

Keeping these limitations in mind, you can put any slots you need into your soup entries. Entries within the same soup need not have the same set of slots. The only slots to which you must pay special attention are those that are indexed. When you create a soup, you specify which of its entries' slots to index. Indexed slots must contain data of the type specified by the index. For example, if you specify that an index is to be built on slot `foo` and that `foo` contains a text string, it's important that every `foo` slot in every entry in the indexed soup contains a text string or `nil`. Entries that do not have a `foo` slot will not be found in queries on the `foo` index. Entries having a `foo` slot that contains data of some type other than `text` cause various exceptions. For example, if you should try to add this kind of frame to an indexed soup, the method that attempts to add the frame throws an exception; if you try to add a new index on a slot that varies in data type from entry to entry, the `AddIndex` method throws an exception, and so on. Soup entries can contain `nil`-value slots, but querying for such slots is not supported; that is, you can query only for slots that hold non-`nil` values.

Removing Entries From Soups

To remove an entry, pass it to the `EntryRemoveFromSoupXmit` function, as shown in the following code fragment. If you try to remove an invalid entry, this function throws an exception. An entry can become invalid when, for example, the user ejects the storage card on which it resides.

```
local myCursor := Query(nil);
local theEntry := myCursor:Entry();
if theEntry then
    EntryRemoveFromSoup(theEntry, '|MyApp:MySig|);
```

Modifying Entries

Only one instance of a particular entry exists at any time, regardless of how the entry was obtained. That is, if two cursors from two different queries on a particular soup happen to be pointing at identical entries, they are actually both pointing at the same entry.

When first retrieved from a soup, an entry is just an identifier. When the entry is accessed as a frame (by getting or setting one of its slots), the complete entry frame is constructed in the NewtonScript heap. The frame is marked to identify it as a member of the soup from which it came.

When the frame is constructed from the entry, it is cached in memory. At this point, you can add, modify, and delete slots just as you would in any other frame; however, the changes do not persist until the EntryChangeXmit function is called for that particular entry. The EntryChangeXmit function writes the cached entry frame back to the soup, replacing the original entry with the changed one.

If the EntryUndoChangesXmit function is called, the changes are thrown out and the entry is restored to its original state. This function disposes of the cached entry frame and restores the reference to the original uncached entry, just as if the original entry was never referenced. Note that you can use the FrameDirty function to determine whether a cached entry has been modified since it was read into the NewtonScript heap; however, this function does not detect changes to individual characters in a string (a common operation for clParagraphView views). For more information, see "FrameDirty" (page 9-69) in *Newton Programmer's Reference*.

The following code example gets an entry from the namesUSoup union soup, changes it, and writes the changed entry back to the soup:

```
local namesUSoup := GetUnionSoupAlways(ROM_CardFileSoupName);
local namesCursor := namesUSoup:Query(nil);
local theEntry := namesCursor:Entry();
if theEntry then
   begin
      theEntry.cardType := 4;
      EntryChangeXmit(theEntry, '|MyApp:MySig|);
   end;
```

It's not always easy to determine the best time to write a cached entry back to its soup. For example, it would be inappropriate to call a function like EntryChangeXmit from the ViewChangedScript method of a protoLabelInputLine view. When the user enters data on the input line with the keyboard, the ViewChangedScript is called after every key press. Calling the EntryChangeXmit function for every key press would be noticeably slow.

In some situations, the appropriate time to call EntryChangeXmit is more obvious. For example, a natural time to call EntryChangeXmit would be when the user dismisses an input slip.

Moving Entries

You can use the MoveTarget method of the root view to move (not copy) an entry into the same-named soup on another store. For example, you would use this method to move entries from one union soup member to another. For more information, see "System-Supplied Filing Methods" (page 12-11) in *Newton Programmer's Reference*.

Copying Entries

The `EntryCopyXmit` global function and the `CopyEntriesXmit` soup method enable you to copy entries from one soup to another and transmit appropriate change notifications.

The following code fragment uses the `CopyEntriesXmit` soup method to copy all the entries from a specified source soup into a specified destination soup. Note that this method is defined only for soups, not for union soups. The following code fragment uses the `GetMember` union soup method to retrieve the plain soup constituent of a union soup from a specified store. The `GetMember` method never returns `nil`; instead, it creates an empty member soup on the specified store if one does not already exist:

```
// myUsoup member on internal store is the source soup
local myUSoup := GetUnionSoupAlways("myUSoup:mySig");
local sourceSoup := myUSoup:GetMember(GetStores()[0])
// myUsoup member on another store is the destination soup
local destSoup :=  myUSoup:GetMember(GetStores()[1]);
// copy all entries from source soup to dest soup
local cursor := sourceSoup:Query(nil);
if (cursor:CountEntries() <> 0) then
    sourceSoup:CopyEntriesXmit(destSoup, '|MyApp:MySig|);
```

You can use the `EntryCopyXmit` function to copy an entry from a specified source soup to a specified destination soup and transmit a soup change notification message. Note that this function is defined only for soups, not for union soups. The following code fragment uses the `GetSoup` store method to retrieve a specified soup from its store. Because the `GetSoup` method returns `nil` when the soup to be retrieved is not available, you must at least ensure that this result is non-nil before using it. The following code fragment actually goes one step further and uses the `IsValid` soup method to test the validity of the `destSoup` soup in additional ways:

```
local myUSoup := GetUnionSoupAlways("myUSoup:mySig");
// get all entries having 'hot in 'temperature slot
local cursor := myUSoup:Query({indexPath: 'temperature,
                               beginKey: 'hot
                               endKey: 'hot});
local destSoup := GetStores()[0]:GetSoup("mySoup:mySig");
// make sure we actually got a valid soup
if destSoup:IsValid() then
    begin
        // xmit a single notification after all changes are made
        while e := cursor:Entry() do EntryCopyXmit(e,destSoup,nil);
        XmitSoupChange(destSoup, '|MyApp:MySig|, 'whatThe, nil);
    end;
```

Note

The `EntryCopyXmit` method copies the cached entry—not the original soup entry—into the destination soup. ◆

Sharing Entry Data

Shared soups and shared entries need to be in a well-documented format to allow other applications to use them. For an example of how to document the structure of your soup entries, refer to Chapter 19, "Built-in Applications and System Data." There you will see descriptions of the soups used by the built-in applications on Newton devices produced by Apple Computer, Inc.

Using the Entry Cache Efficiently

Whenever you access a slot in a soup entry, the system reads the entire entry into the NewtonScript heap if it is not already present. That is, simply testing or printing the value of a single slot causes the entire soup entry in which it resides to be read into the entry cache. For best performance, avoid creating cached entries when you don't need them, and flush the entry cache as soon as is appropriate. This section describes how you can avoid unnecessary caching and how you can reclaim cache memory explicitly. Table 11-1 on page 11-63 summarizes the use of the entry cache by the functions and methods described in this discussion.

Reading a soup entry into memory requires more heap space than testing tag or index values does. Whenever possible, work with index keys and tags rather than the contents of soup entries. Some suggested techniques for doing so include the following:

- Avoid using `validTest` functions in favor of using `indexValidTest` functions in your queries, as the latter can be performed without reading soup entries into memory.

- Query on index key values or tag values rather than on values that require reading soup entries into the NewtonScript heap.

- Use the cursor method `EntryKey` to retrieve an entry's key value without reading the entry into the NewtonScript heap.

Normally, adding or changing a soup entry creates a cached entry. If you do not plan on working further with an entry's data after you've added or modified it, you can reclaim heap space by releasing the memory used by the entry cache. You can use the `AddFlushedXmit` soup method to add a soup entry without creating a cached entry at all; in addition to saving heap space, this method saves you the time normally required to create the cached entry. When working with a cached entry, you can use the `EntryFlushXmit` function to write it back to its soup and clear the entry cache.

In contrast, the EntryUndoChanges function clears the entry cache without writing the cached entry to the soup. This function makes references to the entry point to the original, unmodified entry residing in the soup, instead of the cached entry.

Note that reading, printing, or modifying any slot in the entry after calling EntryFlushXmit, EntryUndoChanges, or AddFlushedXmit causes the entire entry to be read back into the NewtonScript heap; thus, use these functions only when you're sure you won't need to access the entry in the near future.

If you do need to work with the entry data after you've written it to the soup, you'll want to use functions and methods that don't clear the entry cache after writing the soup entry. The AddToDefaultStoreXmit and AddToStoreXmit union soup methods save frames as soup entries without clearing the entry cache afterward. When adding frames to single soups, you can use the AddXmit soup method for the same purpose. The EntryChangeXmit function also writes the cached entry back to its soup without flushing the cache afterward. Contrast this function with the EntryFlushXmit function, which clears the entry cache after writing the cached entry back to its soup. Table 11-1 summarizes the caching behavior of all methods that write entries to soups or union soups.

Table 11-1   Effect of functions and methods on entry cache

Function or method	Cached entry
uSoup:AddToDefaultStoreXmit (*frame*, *changeSym*)	Creates and returns
uSoup:AddToStoreXmit (*frame*, *changeSym*)	Creates and returns
soup:AddXmit (*frame*, *changeSym*)	Creates and returns
soup:AddFlushedXmit (*frame*, *changeSym*)	Does not create or return
EntryFlushXmit (*entry*)	Returns existing
EntryChangeXmit (*entry*)	Returns existing
EntryUndoChanges (*entry*)	Throws away existing

Using Soup Change Notification

When your application changes an entry in a shared soup, the system executes callback functions registered by applications using that soup, allowing them to take action in response to the change. The system-supplied soup change notification service allows applications to

■ notify each other when they make changes to soup entries

■ respond to notifications precisely

■ control how and when notifications are sent

The first part of this section describes how to register and unregister a callback function for execution in response to changes in a particular soup. The next part describes the various notifications that may be sent. The last part of this section describes how applications send soup change notifications.

Registering Your Application for Change Notification

The RegSoupChange global function registers a callback function for execution in response to changes in a particular soup. Note that this callback function must not call either of the RegSoupChange or UnRegSoupChange functions.

If your application needs to respond to changes in more than one soup, you'll need to call the RegSoupChange function once on each soup for which your application requires change notification. This approach is valid for any system-supplied soup except that used by the built-in Preferences application. For notification of changes to user preferences, you must call the RegUserConfigChange function.

You can call the RegSoupChange function at any time that makes sense for your application. For example, you might do so from within your base view's viewSetupDoneScript method; however, this is only a suggested guideline. In order to conserve available memory, your application should minimize the amount of time callback functions remain registered.

The following code example shows how to register your application for notification of changes to the soup used by the built-in Names application:

```
local myFn := func (soupName, appSym, changeType, changeData)
        begin
            if (changeType) then
                begin
                if (changeType <> 'whatThe) then
                    print (changeType && "in the" && soupName &&
                            "soup by the" && GetAppName(appSym) &&
                            "application.");
                else
                    print ("Unspecified changes occurred in the" &&
                            soupName && "soup.");
                end;
        end;
// register for changes to soup used by built-in "Names" app
RegSoupChange(ROM_CardFileSoupName, '|myFn1:MyApp:MySig|, myFn);
```

▲ **WARNING**

Any callback function registered by the `RegSoupChange`
function must not call either of the `RegSoupChange` or
`UnRegSoupChange` functions. ▲

The second argument to the `RegSoupChange` function can be any unique symbol
that identifies the callback to be registered. If your application registers only one
callback function, you can just use your application symbol as the callback
identifier (ID). A callback ID need only be unique within the registry that uses it.
For example, no two power registry callback functions can share the same callback
ID; on the other hand, your application's power registry callback can use the same
ID as your application's login screen callback. Thus, if your application only
registers one callback function with each of the various registries, all of your
callback functions can use your application symbol (with developer signature) as
their callback ID.

To generate unique identifiers for multiple callbacks within the same registry, you
can prefix an additional identifier to your application symbol. For example, the
symbol `'|myFn1:MyApp:MySig|` could be used to identify one of several
callback functions registered by the `MyApp:MySig` application.

Unregistering Your Application for Change Notification

When your application no longer needs to be notified of changes to a particular
soup, it needs to call the `UnRegSoupChange` function to unregister its callback
function for that soup.

```
// unregister my app's Names soup callback
UnRegSoupChange(ROM_CardFileSoupName, '|myFn1:MyApp:MySig|);
```

Normally, you can unregister your soup change callbacks in the `viewQuitScript`
method of your application's base view.

Responding to Notifications

When a soup changes in some way, the system executes the callback functions
registered for that soup. Note that the system does not consider the soup to have
changed until an entry is written to the soup. Thus, changing a cached entry is not
considered a change to the soup until the `EntryChangeXmit` function writes the
cached entry back to the soup.

Note
The system-supplied Preferences application sends
soup change notifications only if your application
uses the `RegUserConfigChange` function to register
for such notifications. ◆

Your callback function must take any action that is appropriate to respond to the change. Most applications have no need to respond to soup changes unless they are open, which is why it is recommended that you register your callbacks when your application opens and unregister them when it closes.

The arguments passed to your callback function include the name of the soup that changed, the symbol identifying the callback function to execute, the kind of change that occurred, and optional data such as changed soup entries. For a simple code example, see "Registering Your Application for Change Notification" beginning on page 11-64. For a complete description of the callback function and its parameters, see the section "Callback Functions for Soup Change Notification" (page 9-14) in *Newton Programmer's Reference*.

▲ **WARNING**

The `'soupEnters` and `'soupLeaves` messages are guaranteed to be sent only when a reference to the changed soup exists. These messages may not be sent for soups that are not in use. For example, if no cursor object references the soup, this message may not be sent. ▲

Sending Notifications

When your application alters a soup, it may need to notify other applications that the soup has changed. The best means of doing so depends on the exact nature of the change.

The system provides functions and methods that transmit change notification messages automatically after altering soups, union soups, or entries. The names of these auto-transmit routines end with the `-Xmit` suffix. They are described throughout this chapter in sections pertaining to the main behaviors they provide, such as adding frames to soups as entries, changing entries, and so on.

The auto-transmit (*fnOrMethodName*`Xmit`) routines provide the easiest and best way to send notifications when making a limited number of changes to a soup. For example, to save a frame in a union soup and transmit an appropriate notification message, use the `AddToDefaultStoreXmit` method as shown in the following code fragment:

```
// get soup in which to save the new entry
local myUSoup := GetUnionSoupAlways("myUSoup:mySig");
// frame to add as new entry
local myFrame := {name: Daphne, color: tabby};
// add the entry and transmit change notification
local ent := myUSoup:AddToDefaultStoreXmit(myFrame,'|MyApp:MySig|);
```

The auto-transmit methods and functions accept a *changeSym* parameter identifying the application that changed the soup. If you pass `nil` for the value of the *changeSym* parameter, the change notification is not sent, but the function or method does everything else its description specifies.

Sometimes it may not be not desirable to send notifications immediately after making each change to a soup; for example, when changing a large number of soup entries, you might want to wait until after you've finished making all the changes to transmit notification messages. You can use the `XmitSoupChange` global function to send soup change notifications explicitly, as shown in the following code example:

```
// assume cursor and destSoup are valid
// xmit a single notification after all changes are made
while e := cursor:Entry() do EntryCopyXmit(e,destSoup,nil);
XmitSoupChange("mySoup:mySig", '|MyApp:MySig|, 'whatThe, nil);
```

The first argument to the `XmitSoupChange` function specifies the name of the soup that has changed and the second argument specifies the application making the change. The third argument is a predefined symbol specifying the kind of change that was made, such as whether an entry was added, deleted, or changed. Where appropriate, the final argument is change data, such as the new version of the entry that was changed. Because this particular example makes multiple changes to the `destSoup` soup, it passes the `'whatThe` symbol to indicate unspecified changes, and passes `nil` as the change data. For a more detailed discussion of change type and change data, see the section "Callback Functions for Soup Change Notification" (page 9-14) in *Newton Programmer's Reference*.

Soup change notification messages are sent on a deferred basis. In most situations, this implementation detail has no practical impact; however, you should be aware that soup change messages are not sent until after the method that sends them returns. For example, if your `ButtonClickScript` method causes a soup change, the change notification message is not sent until after the `ButtonClickScript` method returns.

Summary of Data Storage

This section summarizes data structures, functions, objects and methods used for data storage on Newton devices.

Data Structures

Soup Definition Frame

```
mySoupDef :=
{   // string that identifies this soup to the system
    name: "appName:appSym",
    // string that is user visible name
    userName: "My Application soup",
    // application symbol
    ownerApp: '|myApp:mySig|,
    // user-visible name of app that owns this soup
    ownerAppName: "My Application",
    // user-visible string describing soup
    userDescr: "This soup is used by
                My Application.",
    // array of indexSpecs - default indexes
    indexes: [anIndexSpec, anotherIndexSpec]
    // optional function used to initialize the soup
    initHook: symbolOrCallBackFn
}
```

Single-Slot Index Specification Frame

```
{
    // must use this value - index keys are slot values
    structure:'slot,
    // entries indexed on this slot
    path: pathExpr,
    // data type found in the indexed slot
    type: symbol,
    // optional. 'ascending or 'descending
    order: symbol,
    // optional. pass 1 to use alternate sort table
    sortID: nil
}
```

Multiple-Slot Index Specification Frame

```
{
   // index keys may be multiple slot values
   structure: 'multiSlot, // must use this value
   // up to six path expressions specifying indexed slots
   path:[pathExpr1, pathExpr2, ... , pathExpr6],
   // data type found in each indexed slot
   type:[sym1, sym2, ... sym6]
   // optional. 'ascending or 'descending
   order: [sym1, sym2, ... sym6 ]
   // optional. pass 1 to use alternate sort table
   sortID: nil
}
```

Tags Index Specification Frame

```
{
   // must use this value - tags are slot values
   structure:'slot,
   // index values (tags) extracted from this slot
   path:'slotName,
   // must use this value
   type:'tags,
}
```

Query Specification Frame

```
// pass nil instead of a query spec frame
// to retrieve all entries in the soup

// this frame used for queries on single-slot indexes
// see next example for multiple-slot query spec frame
{
// use the specified single-slot index for this query
// required when querying for index values
indexPath : 'pathExpr,
// minimum index key value examined by this query
// for all entries, (beginKey ≤ entry.indexPath)
beginKey : keyValue, // optional
// excluded lower boundary of key range examined by query
// for all entries, (beginExclKey < entry.indexPath)
beginExclKey : keyValue, // optional
```

```
// maximum index key value examined by this query
// for all entries, (entry.indexPath ≤ endKey)
endKey: keyValue, // optional
// excluded upper boundary of key range examined by query
// for all entries, (beginExclKey < entry.indexPath)
endExclKey : keyValue, // optional
// returns non-nil to include entry in result
indexValidTest: func (keyValue) begin … end;, // optional
// returns non-nil to include entry in result
validTest: func (entry) begin … end; // optional
// optional tags query spec frame; see page 11-71
tagSpec: {equal:[t1, t2, …tN], all:[t1, t2, …tN],
         any:[t1, t2, …tN],none:[t1, t2, …tN]},
// when non-nil, match entire string in 'words slot
entireWords: Boolean, // optional
// string(s) to match w/ word beginnings in entries
words: string|[str1, str2, … , strN], // optional
// string to match w/ any substring in entries
text: string, // optional
}

// this frame used for queries on multiple-slot indexes
// see previous example for single-slot query spec frame
{
// use the specified multiple-slot index for this query
indexPath : ['pathExpr1, 'pathExpr2, …'pathExpr6], // required
// minimum index key value examined by this query
// for all entries, (beginKey ≤ entry.indexPath)
beginKey : [keyValue1,keyValue2 … keyValue6], // optional
// excluded lower boundary of key range examined by query
// for all entries, (beginExclKey < entry.indexPath)
beginExclKey : [keyValue1,keyValue2 … keyValue6], // optional
// maximum index key value examined by this query
// for all entries, (entry.indexPath ≤ endKey)
endKey: [keyValue1,keyValue2 … keyValue6], // optional
// excluded upper boundary of key range examined by query
// for all entries, (beginExclKey < entry.indexPath)
endExclKey : [keyValue1,keyValue2 … keyValue6], // optional
// optional; returns non-nil to include entry in result
indexValidTest: func ([keyValue1,keyValue2 … keyValue6])
                    begin … end;,
// optional; returns non-nil to include entry in result
validTest: func (entry) begin … end;
```

```
// optional tags query spec frame; see page 11-71
tagSpec: {equal: [t1, t2, ...tN], all: [t1, t2, ...tN],
        any: [t1, t2, ...tN], none: [t1, t2, ...tN]},
// when non-nil, match entire string in 'words slot
entireWords: Boolean, // optional
// string(s) to match w/ word beginnings in entries
words: string | [str1, str2, ... , strN], // optional
// string to match w/ any substring in entries
text: string, // optional
}
```

Tags Query Specification Frame

```
// this frame resides in tagSpec slot of query spec frame
// at least one of these slots must appear
// select only entries having identical set of tags
{equal: [t1, t2, ...tN],
// select only entries having identical tags or superset
all: [t1, t2, ...tN],
// select entries having any of these tags
any: [t1, t2, ...tN],
// select entries having none of these tags
none: [t1, t2, ...tN]}
```

Callback Functions for Soup Change Notification

```
func (soupNameString, appSymbol, changeTypeSymbol, changeData);
```

Data Storage Functions and Methods

Stores

```
store:AtomicAction (function)
store:BusyAction (appSymbol, appName, action)
store:CheckWriteProtect ()
GetDefaultStore ()
store:GetInfo (slotSymbol)
store:GetName ()
store:GetSoup (soupNameString)
store:GetSoupNames ()
GetStores ()
store:HasSoup (soupName)
store:IsReadOnly ()
```

store:IsValid()
SetDefaultStore(*newDefaultStore*)
store:SetInfo(*slotSymbol*, *value*)
store:TotalSize()
store:UsedSize()

Soups

These functions and methods allow you to work with soup-level data such as frames, soup indexes, soup information frames, and soup signatures.

Creating Soups
RegUnionSoup(*appSymbol*, *soupDef*);
UnRegUnionSoup(*name*, *appSymbol*);
store:CreateSoupXmit(*soupName*, *indexArray*, *changeSym*)
CreateSoupFromSoupDef(*soupDef*, *store*, *changeSym*)
uSoup:GetMember(*store*)

Adding and Copying Entries
uSoup:AddToDefaultStoreXmit(*frame*, *changeSym*)
uSoup:AddToStoreXmit(*frame*, *store*, *changeSym*)
soupOrUsoup:AddFlushedXmit(*frameOrEntry*, *changeSym*)
soup:AddXmit(*frame*, *changeSym*)
soup:CopyEntriesXmit(*destSoup*, *changeSym*)

Retrieving Entries
soupOrUSoup:Query(*querySpec*)

Change Notification
RegSoupChange(*soupName*, *callbackID*, *callBackFn*)
UnRegSoupChange(*soupName*, *callbackID*)
XmitSoupChange(*soupName*, *appSymbol*, *changeType*, *changeData*)

Manipulating Tags
soup:HasTags()
soup:GetTags()
soupOrUsoup:ModifyTagXmit(*oldTag*, *newTag*, *changeSym*)
soupOrUsoup:RemoveTagsXmit(*tags*, *changeSym*)
soupOrUsoup:AddTagsXmit(*tags*, *changeSym*)

Additional Functions and Methods
soupOrUsoup:AddIndexXmit(*indexSpec*, *changeSym*)
soup:GetIndexes()
soup:GetInfo(*slotSymbol*)
soupOrUsoup:GetName()
soup:GetSignature()

soupOrUsoup:GetSize()
uSoup:GetSoupList()
soup:GetStore()
GetUnionSoupAlways(*soupNameString*)
soup:MakeKey(*string*, *indexPath*)
IsSoupEntry(*object*)
soup:IsValid()
soup:RemoveAllEntriesXmit(*changeSym*)
soup:RemoveFromStoreXmit(*changeSym*)
soupOrUsoup:RemoveIndexXmit(*indexPath*, *changeSym*)
soup:SetInfoXmit(*slotSymbol*, *value*, *changeSym*)
soup:SetName(*soupNameString*)

Cursors

These functions and methods work with the cursor object returned by the
Query method.

Cursor Validity
cursor:Status()

Retrieving Entries and Manipulating the Cursor
cursor:Entry()
cursor:Next()
cursor:Prev()
cursor:Move(*n*)
cursor:EntryKey()
cursor:GoToKey(*key*)
cursor:GoTo(*entry*)
cursor:Reset()
cursor:ResetToEnd()
cursor:WhichEnd()

Additional Functions and Methods
MapCursor(*cursor*, *function*)
cursor:CountEntries()
cursor:Clone()

Entries

These functions allow you to work with individual soup entries returned by the
cursor object.

EntryChangeXmit(*entry*, *changeSym*)
EntryCopyXmit(*entry*, *newSoup*, *changeSym*)
EntryFlushXmit(*entry*, *changeSym*)

```
EntryIsResident(entry)
EntryModTime(entry)
EntryMoveXmit(entry, newSoup, changeSym)
EntryRemoveFromSoupXmit(entry, changeSym)
EntryReplaceXmit(original, replacement, changeSym)
EntrySize(entry)
EntrySoup(entry)
EntryStore(entry)
EntryTextSize(entry)
EntryUndoChangesXmit(entry, changeSym)
EntryUniqueId(entry)
FrameDirty(frame)
IsSameEntry(entryOralias1, entryOralias2)
```

Data Backup and Restore Functions

These functions are intended for use by special-purpose data backup and restoration programs only. Many of them intentionally defeat the error-checking features upon which the system relies to maintain values that identify entries to the system and specify when they were last modified.

```
store:Erase()
store:GetAllInfo()
store:GetSignature()
store:SetName(storeNameString)

soup:AddWithUniqueIdXmit(entry, changeSym)
soup:GetAllInfo()
soup:GetIndexesModTime()
soup:GetInfoModTime()
soup:GetNextUid()
soup:SetSignature(signature)
soup:SetAllInfoXmit (frame, changeSym)
EntryChangeWithModTimeXmit(entry, changeSym)
EntryReplaceWithModTimeXmit (original, replacement, changeSym)
```

Special-Purpose Objects for Data Storage and Retrieval

This chapter describes the use of special-purpose objects to augment or replace the behavior of the system-supplied store, soup, cursor, and entry objects. This chapter describes

- the use of entry alias objects to save references to soup entries

- the use of virtual binary objects to store large amounts of binary data

- the use of store parts to build read-only soup data into packages

- the use of mock entry objects to implement your own suite of objects that provide access to nonsoup data in the same manner as the system-provided store, soup, cursor, and entry objects.

Before reading this chapter, you should understand the contents of Chapter 11, "Data Storage and Retrieval," which provides an overview of the Newton data storage system and describes how to use stores, soups, queries, cursors, and entries to meet most applications' data storage needs.

About Special-Purpose Storage Objects

The special-purpose data storage objects described here can be used to augment or replace the behavior of stores, soups, cursors, and entries.

Entry Aliases

An entry alias is an object that provides a standard way to save a reference to a soup entry. Unless it uses an entry alias to do so, a soup entry cannot save a reference to an entry in another soup—the referenced entry is copied into the host entry when the host entry is written back to its soup. However, entry aliases may be saved in soup entries without causing this problem.

Entry aliases are also useful for providing convenient access to entries from multiple soups. For example, the built-in Find service uses entry aliases to present entries from multiple soups in a single overview view.

Virtual Binary Objects

The size of any NewtonScript object is limited by the amount of memory available in the NewtonScript heap. As a result, you cannot create binary objects larger than the amount of available NewtonScript heap space. For similar reasons, the amount of data that can be stored in a single soup entry is limited as well. (See "Saving Frames as Soup Entries" beginning on page 11-58 for details.) You can use virtual binary objects to work around these restrictions.

A **virtual binary object** or **VBO** is a special kind of object that is useful for holding binary data larger than the available space in the NewtonScript heap. VBOs can be used to store large amounts of raw binary data, such as large bitmaps, the samples of large digitized sounds, fax data, packages, or application-specific binary data. A package is actually a special kind of virtual binary object; however, a package is read-only and is created in a slightly different manner than a normal VBO.

In the following ways, VBOs are like normal NewtonScript binary objects:

- The VBO is not persistent until it is written to a soup. As with any soup entry data, if a VBO in a soup entry is modified, the changes are not persistent until the cached entry frame is written back to the soup. If a soup entry containing a VBO is moved to another store, the binary data associated with the VBO is moved to that store as well. For a discussion of the soup entry cache, see "Entries" on page 11-17.

- The space used by the VBO is made available for garbage collection when there are no more references to the VBO.

- Binary data—including VBO data—is not shared between soup entries, even when their respective soups reside on the same store. As a result, you may need to consider space issues when moving or duplicating entries that hold VBO data.

VBOs are different from normal NewtonScript binary objects in the following ways:

- VBO data does not reside in the NewtonScript heap—it resides in store memory.

- Store memory for VBO data is not allocated until it is needed to write data. "Using Virtual Binary Objects" on page 12-8 discusses this important point in detail.

- You cannot use a value stored in a virtual binary object as a soup index key.

- VBOs can be created in compressed or uncompressed form. If the VBO is compressed, the system compresses and decompresses its associated binary data on demand. The fact that a VBO is compressed is normally transparent to your code; however, the time required to compress and uncompress VBO data may affect performance.

- When passed a reference to a VBO residing on a store that is unavailable, methods that write VBO data throw exceptions rather than displaying the "Newton still needs the card" alert.

Normal binary objects encapsulate their data and reside entirely in the NewtonScript heap; thus, creating one of these objects or reading any of its data requires an amount of heap space sufficient to hold all its data. Therefore, the size of a normal binary object is limited by the amount of NewtonScript heap space available at the time it is created. For example, a binary object encapsulating 5 KB of data requires 5 KB of NewtonScript heap space. If sufficient heap space is not available, the binary object cannot be created.

In contrast, VBO data resides on a store specified when the VBO is created. The system manages VBO data automatically, providing NewtonScript objects with transparent access to it on demand. A VBO can hold more data than a normal binary object because it is not limited by the amount of free space available in the NewtonScript heap. Contrasting the previous example, a VBO holding 5 KB of data requires a negligible amount of heap space, because its data resides in store memory, rather than in the NewtonScript heap.

Note
The system does not allocate store memory for VBO data until it is needed to write data to the store. Testing the amount of store memory available when the VBO is created does not guarantee the future availability of this memory. Thus, it is possible to fail due to lack of store space when writing to a VBO, even though the VBO was created successfully. The only practical solution to this problem is to enclose in a `try` block any code that writes VBO data. ◆

Parts

Recall that a **package** is the basic unit of downloadable Newton software: it provides a means of loading code, resources, objects, and scripts into a Newton device. A package consists of one or more constituent units called **parts.**

The format of a part is identified by a four-character identifier called its **type** or its **part code.** Table 12-1 on page 12-4 lists the various kinds of parts and their associated
type identifiers.

Some of the parts described in Table 12-1 may already be familiar to you. `Form` parts are the Newton application packages you create with Newton Toolkit. `Book` parts are the interactive digital books described in the *Newton Book Maker User's Guide*. Store parts (parts of type `soup`) are useful for the storage of read-only data and are discussed later in this chapter. Dictionary parts (parts of type `dict`) supplement the built-in word lists used by the recognition subsystem. `Font` parts are used to add new typefaces to Newton devices; for more information about these parts, contact Newton Developer Technical Support. `Auto` parts are described in the *Newton Toolkit User's Guide*.

Table 12-1   Parts and type identifiers

Part	Type	Description
Application	`form`	Application.
Book	`book`	Book created by Newton Book Maker or Newton Press.
Auto part	`auto`	Background application/extension.
Store part	`soup`	Read-only soup.
Dictionary	`dict`	Custom dictionary for Newton recognition subsystem.
Font	`font`	Additional font.

Except for `soup` parts, all the parts listed in Table 12-1 are called **frame parts** because they include a part frame which holds the items comprising the frame part. Such items may include icons, scripts, other parts, binary data and so on. A `soup` part, on the other hand, does not have a part frame and is composed of soup data only.

When a frame part is loaded, the system disperses the contents of its part frame to the appropriate subsystems. For example, in addition to the application itself, which is a `form` part used by the Extras Drawer, the part frame in an application package might include a custom icon used by the Extras Drawer, a custom dictionary used by the recognition subsystem, a soup part that provides application data, and an `InstallScript` function that performs application-specific setup tasks.

Store Parts

A **store part** is a part that encapsulates a read-only store. Because you can build store parts into application packages, the store part is sometimes referred to as a **package store.**

Soups can reside on package stores, just as they do on normal stores; however, because package stores are read-only, soups residing on package stores must also be read-only. Store parts can be used to provide soup-like access to read-only data residing in an application package.

For more information about the characteristics of soups, see "Soups" on page 11-7 and "Using Soups" on page 11-32.

Mock Entries

A **mock entry** is a NewtonScript object that mimics the behavior of a soup entry. The mock entry is a foundation object you can use to build up a suite of objects that acts like the system-supplied store, soup, cursor, and entry objects. For example, you could create a mock entry object that uses a serial communications link to retrieve a record from a remote database; additional objects could implement methods to provide cursor-like access to these mock entries, just as if they resided in a local soup. Your mock entry could reside in a mock soup, which, in turn, could reside on a mock store.

The mock entry counterparts to the system-supplied Entry*Xxx* functions are implemented as the methods of a NewtonScript frame known as the mock entry's **handler.** You supply this frame, which implements these methods as well as any it requires for its own purposes. The handler may also hold information local to a specific mock entry or information required to retrieve the mock entry's data.

Like a normal soup entry, the mock entry caches its data in the NewtonScript heap when the entry is accessed; thus, the data associated with a mock entry is called its **cached frame.** As with normal soup entries, the cached frame appears to be the mock entry itself when accessed by other NewtonScript objects. Your handler provides an `EntryAccess` method that creates this frame in response to messages from the system.

The cached frame must be self-contained, just as a normal soup entry is. Therefore, the cached frame must not use `_proto` and `_parent` inheritance.

To create a mock entry, you call the `NewMockEntry` global function. Depending on your needs, you can create the mock entry with or without its associated cached frame. Either way, the mock entry object returned by this function manages other objects' access to its cached frame.

When the mock entry's cached frame is present, the system forwards entry accesses to it transparently. When the cached frame is not present, the system calls the handler's `EntryAccess` method to generate a cached frame before forwarding the access. You must supply this method, which creates and installs the cached frame in the mock entry.

The handler's `EntryAccess` method is called only when a slot in the mock entry is accessed. Simply referencing the mock entry does not cause the cached entry to be created. For example, in the following code fragment, assigning m to x does not create a cached entry—it just creates another reference to the mock entry. However, accessing the mock entry's `foo` slot from either of the variables m or x may cause the `EntryAccess` method of `myHandler` to be invoked.

```
local myHandler := {
      object: {foo: 'bar},
      EntryAccess: func (mockEntry)
        begin
            // install cached obj & notify system
            EntrySetCachedObject(mockEntry, object);
            // return cached obj
            object;
        end,
      // your additional slots and methods here
      …}
```

```
// create new mock entry w/ no cached frame
local m := NewMockEntry(myHandler, nil);
// referencing m doesn't create cached frame
local x := m;
// either statement could invoke myHandler:EntryAccess()
local a := x.foo;
local b := m.foo;
```

To almost all of the system, the mock entry appears to be a normal soup entry; for example:

- `m.foo` evaluates to `'bar`

- `ClassOf(m)` is `'frame`

- `m.baz := 42` adds a slot to the `handler.object` frame and this modified frame is returned the next time the mock entry is accessed.

Only the `IsMockEntry` global function can determine that `m` is a mock entry, rather than a soup entry. Note that the `IsSoupEntry` function returns `true` for both mock entries and normal soup entries.

Mock Stores, Mock Soups, and Mock Cursors

The current implementation of the Newton object system provides only mock entries; you must implement appropriate mock cursors, mock soups, and mock stores as required.

The **mock store** is a frame you supply which responds appropriately to all the messages that might normally be sent to a store object. For example, when the mock store's `GetSoup` method is invoked, it should return a mock soup.

The **mock soup** is a frame you supply which responds appropriately to all the messages that might normally be sent to a soup object. For example, when the mock soup's `Query` method is called, the mock soup should return a mock cursor. Mock soups cannot participate in union soups; however, you can implement your own mock union soup objects that manage the interaction of your mock soups with normal soups or union soups.

A **mock cursor** is a frame you supply that can respond appropriately to all the messages that might normally be sent to a cursor object. For example, when the mock cursor's `Entry` method is invoked, it should return a mock entry.

Using Special-Purpose Data Storage Objects

This section describes how to use entry aliases, virtual binary objects (VBOs), store parts, and mock entries. This section presumes understanding of the conceptual material presented in preceding sections.

Using Entry Aliases

This section describes how to create entry aliases, how to save them, and how to resolve them.

Aliases can be created for any entry that resides in a soup or union soup. Aliases cannot be created for mock entry objects.

You must not assume that an entry alias is valid. When the entry to which it refers is deleted or is moved to another store, an entry alias becomes invalid. Renaming a store renders invalid all aliases to entries residing on that store.

The `MakeEntryAlias` function returns an alias to a soup entry, as shown in the following code fragment:

```
// return entries that contain "bob" and "Apple"
local myCurs:= namesSoup:Query({ entireWords: true,
                              words:["Bob", "Apple"]});
// keep an alias to bob around
local bobAlias := MakeEntryAlias(myCurs:Entry());
// but get rid of the cursor
myCurs := nil;
```

To save an entry alias, simply save it in a soup entry.

You can use the `ResolveEntryAlias` function to obtain the entry to which the alias refers, as shown in the following code fragment:

```
// continued from previous example
local bobEntry := ResolveEntryAlias(bobAlias);
```

Note that the `ResolveEntryAlias` function returns `nil` if the original store, soup, or entry to which the alias refers is unavailable.

You can use the `IsSameEntry` function to compare entries and aliases to each other; this function returns `true` for any two aliases or references to the same entry. For example:

```
// return entries that contain "bob" and "Apple"
local myCurs:= namesSoup:Query({ entireWords: true,
                                 words:["Bob", "Apple"]});
local aBob:= myCurs:Entry();
// keep an alias to bob around
local bobAlias := MakeEntryAlias(aBob);
// the following comparison returns true
IsSameEntry(aBob, bobAlias)
```

The `IsEntryAlias` function returns `true` if its argument is an entry alias, as shown in the following example:

```
// return entries that contain "bob" and "Apple"
local myCurs:= namesSoup:Query({ entireWords: true,
                                 words:["Bob", "Apple"]});
// keep an alias to bob around
local bobAlias := MakeEntryAlias(myCurs:Entry());
// the following test returns true
IsEntryAlias(bobAlias);
```

Using Virtual Binary Objects

This section describes how to use a virtual binary object to store binary data that is too large to fit into the NewtonScript heap. Topics discussed include:

- creating compressed or uncompressed VBOs

- saving VBOs in soup entries

- adding data to VBOs

- undoing changes to VBO data

In addition to the subjects discussed here, see "VBO Functions and Methods" (page 9-74) in *Newton Programmer's Reference* for descriptions of VBO utility functions.

Creating Virtual Binary Objects

When you create a VBO, you specify whether its associated binary data is to be stored in compressed or uncompressed format. Whether you create compressed or uncompressed VBO objects is a question of space versus speed: uncompressed data provides faster access, but requires more store space than the equivalent compressed data.

The `NewVBO` and `NewCompressedVBO` store methods create virtual binary objects. Both methods require that you specify the class of the binary object to be created, as well as the store on which VBO data is to reside.

The following code fragment uses the store method `NewVBO` to create a new, uncompressed, "blank" virtual binary object on the default store:

```
// create new uncompressed VBO of size 5 KB and class 'samples
local binData := GetDefaultStore():NewVBO('samples,5000);
```

Another way to create an uncompressed VBO is to pass `nil` as the values of the *companderName* and *companderData* parameters to the `NewCompressedVBO` method, as the following code fragment shows:

```
// create new uncompressed VBO of size 5 KB and class 'samples
local binData := GetDefaultStore():NewCompressedVBO('samples, 5000,
                                                    nil, nil);
```

When you create a compressed VBO, you need to specify how the system is to expand and compress data moved to and from the store associated with the VBO. The system provides two compressor-expanders (also known as companders), which compress and expand raw binary data on demand. The *companderName* parameter to the `NewCompressedVBO` method indicates the compander to be used for that particular VBO's data.

The Lempel Ziv compander is a suitable for most data types; its use is specified by passing the string `"TLZStoreCompander"` as the value of the *companderName* parameter to the `NewCompressedVBO` method. The pixel map compander is specialized for use with pixel map data; its use is specified by passing the string `"TPixelMapCompander"` as the value of the *companderName* parameter to the `NewCompressedVBO` method.

▲ **WARNING**
The pixel map compander makes certain assumptions about the data passed to it; do not use it for any kind of data other than pixel maps. For more information, see the description of the `NewCompressedVBO` method (page 9-75) in *Newton Programmer's Reference*. ▲

Because both of the companders provided by the current implementation of the system initialize themselves automatically, you must always pass `nil` as the value of the *companderArgs* parameter to the `NewCompressedVBO` method.

To create a new compressed VBO, specify a compander and a store in the arguments to the `NewCompressedVBO` method, as shown in the following example:

```
// create new compressed VBO of size 5 KB and class 'pixMap
local binData := GetDefaultStore():NewCompressedVBO('pixMap,
                                 5000,"TPixelMapCompander", nil);
```

A VBO becomes permanent only when it is written to a soup entry, and its associated binary data always resides on the same store as the entry. Thus, when creating a VBO, it's usually best to specify that it use the same store as the soup entry into which you'll save the VBO. If you try to put the same VBO in two different soup entries, a duplicate VBO is created, even if both entries reside on the same store.

It is recommended that you enclose in a `try` block any code that writes VBO data. Store memory for VBO data is not allocated when the VBO is created; rather, it is allocated as needed to write VBO data. Thus, when writing an entry containing a VBO back to its soup, it is possible to fail due to lack of store space for new or changed VBO data, even though the VBO was created successfully.

Because the system manages store-backed VBO data transparently, calling a function such as `StuffByte` on a VBO does not necessarily cause the system to write new VBO data to the store. For similar reasons, VBOs may raise exceptions at seemingly unusual times, as the system moves VBO data to and from store memory as required to accommodate various objects' needs.

Finally, you may need to consider store space requirements when copying soup entries that hold VBOs. When moving or copying a soup entry containing a VBO, another copy of the VBO data is made by the destination soup's `Add` method because VBO data is not shared between entries.

For a short code example that creates a VBO, saves data in it, and writes the VBO to a soup, see the conclusion of the "Modifying VBO Data" section, immediately following.

Modifying VBO Data

Recall that examining or modifying any slot in a soup entry causes the entire entry to be read into the entry cache. When an entry containing a VBO is read into the entry cache, the VBO data is not read into the entry cache, but made available to the entry transparently.

Subsequently modifying the entry changes the cached data while leaving the original soup entry untouched. The changes to the entry (and any VBOs residing in it) are not saved until the entry is written back to the soup; for example, as the result of an `EntryChangedXmit` call.

Note
Because store space for VBO data is not allocated until the data is actually written, it's recommended that you enclose VBO write operations in exception handling code. ◆

To undo changes to binary data associated with a VBO that resides in a cached soup entry, call the `EntryUndoChanges` function. This function disposes of the cached soup entry and restores references to the original, untouched soup entry; it also undoes changes to VBO data referenced by the entry.

The following code fragment adds sound sample data to an empty VBO and demonstrates the use of the `EntryUndoChanges` function to undo those changes:

```
// create a temporary soup
mySoup := RegUnionSoup('|foo:myApp:mySig|,
        {name: "foo:myApp:mySig", indexes: '[]}) ;

// get a soup entry that is a sound
anEntry := mySoup:AddToDefaultStoreXmit('{sndFrameType: nil,
                                        samples:nil,
                                        samplingRate:nil,
                                        dataType:nil,
                                        compressionType: nil,
                                        userName: nil}, nil) ;

// make a VBO to use for the samples
myVBO := GetDefaultStore():NewCompressedVBO('samples,5000,nil, nil);

// grab some samples from ROM and fill in most of sound frame
romSound := Clone(ROM_FunBeep) ;
anEntry.sndFrameType := romSound.sndFrameType ;
anEntry.samplingRate := romSound.samplingRate ;
anEntry.dataType := romSound.dataType ;
anEntry.compressionType := romSound.compressionType ;
anEntry.samples := myVBO ;

// put the samples in the VBO
BinaryMunger(myVBO, 0, nil, romSound.samples, 0, nil) ;

// write the VBO to the soup
try
    EntryChangeXmit(anEntry, nil);
onException |evt.ex.fr.store| do
    :Notify(kNotifyAlert, "My App", "Sorry, can't save changes.");

// listen to the sound to verify change
PlaySound(anEntry);

// change the sound
BinaryMunger(anEntry.samples,0, nil, ROM_PlinkBeep.samples, 0, nil);

PlaySound(anEntry) ;
```

```
// decide to go back to the original
EntryUndoChanges(anEntry);

PlaySound(anEntry);

// clean up
foreach store in GetStores() do
begin
        mySoup := store:GetSoup("foo:myApp:mySig") ;
        if  mySoup then
                mySoup:RemoveFromStoreXmit(nil);
end ;
UnregUnionSoup("foo:myApp:mySig", '|foo:myApp:mySig|);
```

VBOs and String Data

In most cases, you should avoid using the & and && string-concatenation operators with VBO-based strings. These operators work by allocating a new string in the NewtonScript heap and copying data from its arguments into the new object. You can run out of heap space easily when attempting this operation with large strings.

Instead, use the StrMunger global function to concatenate two strings. The following code fragment appends the str2 string to the str1 string, increasing the size of str1 as necessary, regardless of whether str1 is VBO data or resident in the NewtonScript heap.

```
StrMunger(str1, MAXINT, nil, str2, 0, nil);
```

The value of MAXINT is $1<<29-1$ or 536870911; however, any number larger than StrLen(str1) works adequately.

Using Store Parts

This section describes how to create a store part and add soup data to it. This discussion is followed by a description of how to access the store part's soups from your application.

Note that other representations may provide better space efficiency or faster access to data. Store parts are useful when you wish to avoid recoding soup data in a more efficient representation, or when you need multiple indexes or some other convenience that soup-based queries provide.

Creating a Store Part

To create a store part, take the following steps using Newton Toolkit version 1.5 or greater:

- Create a new project.

- Select the Store Part radio button in the Output Settings dialog box. NTK disables all other settings in this dialog box when the Store Part option is selected.

- Configure the Package Settings dialog box as you normally would. The name specified in this dialog box identifies the store part to the system in much the same way that a package name identifies a package; thus, you need to ensure the uniqueness of this identifier by basing it on your developer signature in some way.

- Add a new text file to the project. You'll add to this document the NewtonScript code that creates one or more soups to reside on the store part.

At compile time, NTK provides a global variable named theStore, which represents the store part (package store) you are building. Any changes made to this variable are reflected in the store part that is produced as the output of the build cycle. Thus, to create your read-only soup, you can add to the text file some NewtonScript code similar to the following example:

```
// some useful consts; note use of developer signature
constant kStoreName := "MyStore:MYSIG" ;
constant kSoupName := "MySoup:MYSIG" ;
constant kSoupIndices := '[] ;

// theStore is a global var provided by NTK
theStore:SetName(kStoreName) ;

// create the soup but don't xmit at build time
local soup:=theStore:CreateSoupXmit(kSoupName,
                    kSoupIndices, nil);

// add a couple entries
soup:Add({anInteger: 1}) ;
soup:Add({anInteger: 2}) ;
```

When the package is built, NTK incorporates the store part in it.

Getting the Store Part

Store parts (also known as package stores) are made available by the GetPackageStore function. Package stores do not appear in the GetStores result array, which is reserved for normal store objects.

The GetPackageStore function retrieves the store by name, so each package store must be given a unique name when it is built. Generally, this is ensured by including the unique package symbol in the store name.

Accessing Data in Store Parts

Although store parts support most of the messages that normal soups do, remember that store parts are read-only. Sending to a store part those messages that would normally change a soup or its store (such as CreateSoupXmit, SetName and so on) throws an exception.

Another thing to keep in mind is that soups on store parts do not participate in union soups. You need to check explicitly for the presence of your store and soup.

The GetPackageStore and GetPackageStores functions provide two different ways to find a store part. Usually, you use the global function GetPackageStore and pass the name of the store part you created as its argument. Assuming the example code shown in "Creating a Store Part" on page 12-13 was used to create the store part, you could use code similar to the following example to check for the existence of the read-only soup residing on the store part:

```
local pStore := GetPackageStore(kStoreName) ;
if pStore then
    local pSoup := pStore:GetSoup(kSoupName) ;
```

Using Mock Entries

A mock entry has two parts: one is a cached frame, which the NewtonScript interpreter treats as the entry when doing assignment, slot lookup, and so on; the other is the handler frame that retrieves the actual entry data and implements a suite of methods that manipulate it.

Topics discussed in this section include

- implementing the EntryAccess method
- creating a mock entry
- testing the validity of a mock entry
- getting entry cache data
- getting and setting mock entry handlers
- implementing additional handler methods

Implementing the EntryAccess Method

Each of your mock entry handler frames must supply an `EntryAccess` method that creates a cached frame containing the mock entry's data, installs the cached frame in the mock entry, and returns the cached frame. This method is called when the system attempts to access a cached frame that is not present.

The system passes the mock entry to your `EntryAccess` method when it is invoked. This method calls the `EntrySetCachedObject` function to install the cached frame in the mock entry and then returns the cached frame.

The following code fragment provides a simple example of an `EntryAccess` method:

```
myHandler := {
   object: {foo: 'bar},
   EntryAccess: func (mockEntry)
      begin
         // install cached frame
         EntrySetCachedObject(mockEntry, object);
         // return cached frame
         object;
      end,
   // your additional slots and methods here
   ...}
```

Creating a New Mock Entry

The `NewMockEntry` global function creates a new mock entry object having a specified handler and cached frame. Your application can use this method to create a new mock entry; for example, in response to a *mockSoup*:Add() message.

The handler frame you pass to the `NewMockEntry` function must define an `EntryAccess` method, as described in "Implementing the EntryAccess Method" on page 12-15. The handler may also contain supporting methods or data used by the mock entry; for example, it might hold information local to a specific mock entry or information required to retrieve the mock entry's data.

Depending on your needs, you can create new mock entries with or without their corresponding cached frames. To create a mock entry with its cached frame already installed, pass both the handler and the cached frame to this function.

To create a mock entry without a cached frame, pass `nil` as the value of the *cachedObject* parameter to the `NewMockEntry` function. When a slot in the returned mock entry is accessed, the handler's `EntryAccess` method is invoked to create the cached entry if it is not present.

Testing the Validity of a Mock Entry

The `IsMockEntry` global function returns the value `true` for objects that are valid mock entries. You can use this function to distinguish between mock entry objects and other objects such as cache frames or soup entries. Note that the `IsSoupEntry` function returns `true` for both mock entries and normal soup entries.

Getting Mock Entry Data

The `EntryCachedObject` global function returns the cached frame associated with a specified mock entry. You can call this function to retrieve the cached frame associated with a specified mock entry. For example, your handler frame's `EntryChange` method must retrieve the cached frame in order to write it back to a mock soup.

Changing the Mock Entry's Handler

The `EntrySetHandler` function is a special-purpose function that you can use to replace a mock entry's handler. For example, you can use this function to install a handler that implements debug versions of methods present in the mock entry's original handler frame. Such methods might include breakpoints and print statements that would not be present in the commercial version of an application.

Getting the Mock Entry's Handler

The system supplies the `EntryHandler` function for debugging purposes. The `EntryHandler` function returns a reference to the handler frame associated with the mock entry specified by the value of the *mockEntry* parameter.

Implementing Additional Handler Methods

Your handler needs to provide additional methods that are the mock entry counterparts to system-supplied entry functions, such as `EntryUndoChangesXmit`, and others. For a list of suggested methods that your handler may implement, see "Application-Defined Mock Entry Handler Methods" on page 12-19.

Summary of Special-Purpose Data Storage Objects

This section summarizes data structures, objects, methods and global functions used by Newton devices for specialized data storage purposes.

Data Structures

Package Reference Information Frame

```
{
size: nBytes, // pkg's uncompressed size in bytes
store: aStore, // store on which pkg resides
title: string, // user-visible package name string
version: int, // version number
timeStamp: int, // date and time pkg was loaded
creationDate: int, // date pkg created
copyProtection: value, Non-nil means protected.
dispatchOnly: value, // Non-nil means dispatch-only pkg.
copyright: string, // copyright information string
compressed: value, // Non-nil value means pkg is compressed
cmprsdSz: int, // compressed size of pkg in bytes
numParts: int, // number of parts in pkg
parts: [p1, p2, … pN], // parts comprising this package.
partTypes: [sym1, sym2, … symN] // parallel to parts array.
```

Functions and Methods

Packages

```
GetPackageNames(store)
GetPackages()
GetPkgRef(name, store)
GetPkgRefInfo(pkgRef)
IsValid(obj)
IsPackage(obj)
IsPackageActive(pkgRef)
MarkPackageBusy(pkgRef, appName, reason)
MarkPackageNotBusy(pkgRef)
ObjectPkgRcf(obj)
```

Special-Purpose Objects for Data Storage and Retrieval

SafeFreezePackage(*pkgRef*)
SafeMovePackage(*pkgRef*, *destStore*)
SafeRemovePackage(*pkgRef*)
store:SuckPackageFromBinary(*binary*, *paramFrame*)
store:SuckPackageFromEndpoint(*endPoint*, *paramFrame*)
ThawPackage(*pkgRef*)

Store Parts (Package Stores)

GetPackageStore(*name*)
GetPackageStores()

Entry Aliases

IsEntryAlias(*object*)
MakeEntryAlias(*entry*)
ResolveEntryAlias(*alias*)
IsSameEntry(*entryOralias1*, *entryOralias2*)

Virtual Binary Objects (VBOs)

store:NewVBO(*class*, *size*)
store:NewCompressedVBO(*class*, *size*, *companderName*, *companderArgs*)
IsVBO(*vbo*)
GetVBOStore(*vbo*)
GetVBOStoredSize(*vbo*)
GetVBOCompander(*vbo*)

Mock Entries

EntryCachedObject(*mockEntry*)
EntryHandler(*mockEntry*)
EntrySetCachedObject(*mockEntry*, *newCachedObj*)
EntrySetHandler(*mockEntry*, *newHandler*)
IsMockEntry(*object*)
NewMockEntry(*handler*, *cachedObj*)
NewWeakArray(*length*)

Application-Defined Mock Entry Handler Methods

handler: EntryAccess (*mockEntry*)

handler: EntryChange (*mockEntry*)

handler: EntryChangeWithModTime (*mockEntry*)

handler: EntryCopy (*mockEntry*, *newSoup*)

handler: EntryModTime (*mockEntry*)

handler: EntryMove (*mockEntry*, *newSoup*)

handler: EntryRemoveFromSoup (*mockEntry*)

handler: EntryReplace (*original*, *replacement*)

handler: EntryReplaceWithModTime (*original*, *replacement*)

handler: EntrySize (*mockEntry*)

handler: EntrySoup (*mockEntry*)

handler: EntryStore (*mockEntry*)

handler: EntryTextSize (*mockEntry*)

handler: EntryUndoChanges (*mockEntry*)

handler: EntryUniqueID (*mockEntry*)

handler: EntryValid (*mockEntry*)

Drawing and Graphics

This chapter describes how to draw graphical objects such as lines and rectangles in Newton applications.

You should read this chapter if you are attempting to draw complex or primitive graphical objects in a view. Before reading this chapter, you should be familiar with the information in Chapter 3, "Views."

This chapter describes:

- the types of graphical objects supported and how to draw them
- drawing methods and functions used to perform specific tasks
- drawing classes and protos that operate on graphics and drawing methods and functions

About Drawing

The drawing interface provides a number of functions, methods, and protos that allow you to create graphic objects in Newton applications. Objects can be shapes, pictures, or rendered bitmaps. Additional functions and methods provide ways to scale, transform, or rotate the images. All objects are drawn into views. See "View Instantiation" (page 3-26) for complete details.

This section provides detailed conceptual information on drawing functions and methods. Specifically, it covers the following:

- supported shape objects
- the style frame
- new functions, methods, and messages added for Newton OS 2.0, as well as modifications to existing pieces of the drawing code

Note that for all of the functions described in this chapter:

- The coordinates you specify are interpreted as local to the view in which the object is drawn.

- The origin of the coordinate plane (0,0) is the upper-left corner of the view in which the object is drawn.

- Positive values are towards the right or the bottom of the screen from the origin. For additional information on the Newton coordinate system see "Coordinate System" (page 3-6).

Shape-Based Graphics

Newton system software provides functions for drawing primitive graphic objects in a view. These drawing functions return a data structure called a **shape** that is used by the drawing system to draw an image on the screen. The drawing system supports the following shape objects:

- lines

- rectangles

- rounded rectangles

- ovals (including circles)

- polygons

- wedges and arcs

- regions

- text

- pictures

- bitmaps

Complex graphics can be drawn by passing arrays of shapes to the various drawing functions. Primitive shapes can be combined procedurally by collecting them into a shape called a picture. The appearance will be the same except that, when drawn, the picture will not be affected by any style specifications. The styles are recorded into the picture when you make it with `MakePict`—with the exception of any transform or clipping slot. See "Controlling Clipping" (page 13-12) and "Transforming a Shape" (page 13-13) for more information.

Each type of shape is described in the following pages.

A **line** is defined by two points: the current *x* and *y* location of the graphics pen and the *x* and *y* location of its destination. The pen hangs below the right of the defining points, as shown in Figure 13-1, where two lines are drawn with two different pen sizes.

Figure 13-1   A line drawn with different bit patterns and pen sizes

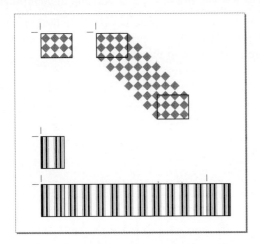

A **rectangle** can be defined by two points—its top-left and bottom-right corners, as shown in Figure 13-2, or by four boundaries—its upper, left, bottom, and right sides. Rectangles are used to define active areas on the screen, to assign coordinate systems to graphic entities, and to specify the locations and sizes for various graphics operations.

Figure 13-2   A rectangle

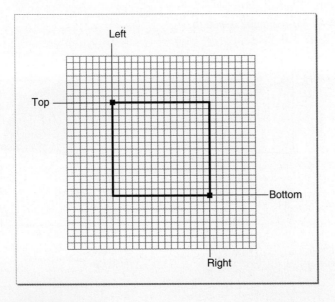

Drawing and Graphics

Drawing also provides functions that allow you to perform a variety of mathematical calculations on rectangles—changing their sizes, shifting them around, and so on.

An **oval** is a circular or elliptical shape defined by the bounding rectangle that encloses it. If the bounding rectangle is a square (that is, has equal width and height), the oval is a circle, as shown in Figure 13-3.

Figure 13-3   An oval

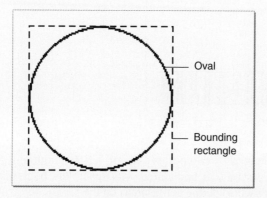

An **arc** is a portion of the circumference of an oval bounded by a pair of radii joining at the oval's center; a wedge includes part of the oval's interior. Arcs and wedges are defined by the bounding rectangle that encloses the oval, along with a pair of angles marking the positions of the bounding radii, as shown in Figure 13-4.

Figure 13-4   An arc and a wedge

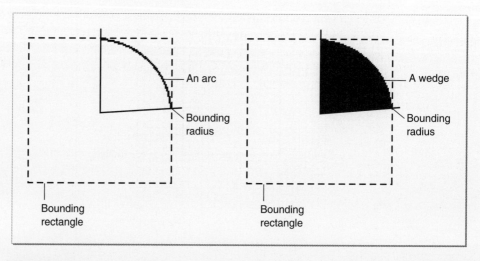

A **rounded rectangle** is a rectangle with rounded corners. The figure is defined by the rectangle itself, along with the width and height of the ovals forming the corners (called the diameters of curvature), as shown in Figure 13-5. The corner width and corner height are limited to the width and height of the rectangle itself; if they are larger, the rounded rectangle becomes an oval.

Figure 13-5   A rounded rectangle

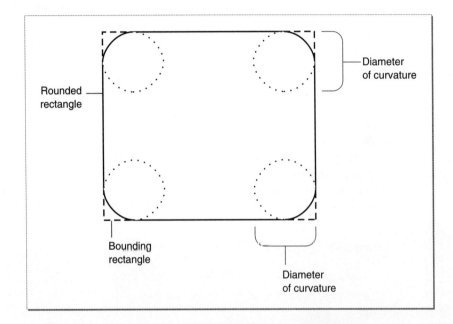

A **polygon** is defined by a sequence of points representing the polygon's vertices, connected by straight lines from one point to the next. You define a polygon by specifying an array of *x* and *y* locations in which to draw lines and passing it as a parameter to `MakePolygon`. Figure 13-6 shows an example of a polygon.

Drawing and Graphics

Figure 13-6   A polygon

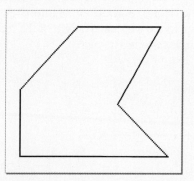

A **region** is an arbitrary area or set of areas, the outline of which is one or more closed loops. One of drawing's most powerful capabilities is the ability to work with regions of arbitrary size, shape, and complexity. You define a region by drawing its boundary with drawing functions. The boundary can be any set of lines and shapes (even including other regions) forming one or more closed loops. A region can be concave or convex, can consist of one connected area or many separate areas. In Figure 13-7, the region consists of two unconnected areas.

Figure 13-7   A region

Your application can record a sequence of drawing operations in a **picture** and play its image back later. Pictures provide a form of graphic data exchange: one program can draw something that was defined in another program, with great flexibility and without having to know any details about what's being drawn. Figure 13-8 shows an example of a picture containing a rectangle, an oval, and a triangle.

Figure 13-8   A simple picture

Manipulating Shapes

In addition to drawing shapes, you can perform operations on them. You can

- **offset** shapes; that is, change the location of the origin of the shape's coordinate plane, causing the shape to be drawn in a different location on the screen. Note that offsetting a shape modifies it; for example, the offset shape will have different viewBounds values than the original shape.

- **scale** shapes; that is, draw the shape to fill a destination rectangle of a specified size. The destination rectangle can be larger, smaller, or the same size as the original shape. Note that scaling a shape modifies it; for example, the scaled shape has different viewBounds values than the original shape.

- **hit-test** shapes to determine whether a pen event occurred within the boundaries of the shape. This operation is useful for implementing button-like behavior in any shape.

The Style Frame

Any shape can optionally specify characteristics that affect the way it is imaged, such as the size of the pen or the fill pattern to be used. These characteristics are specified by the values of slots in a style frame associated with the shape. If the value of the style frame is nil, the view system draws the shape using default values for these drawing characteristics. See "Style Frame" (page 10-1) in the *Newton Programmer's Reference* for complete details.

Drawing Compatibility

The following new functionality has been added for Newton OS 2.0. For complete details on the new drawing functions, see the "Drawing and Graphics Reference" in the *Newton Programmer's Reference*.

New Functions

The following functions have been added:

- GetShapeInfo—returns a frame containing slots of interest for the shape.

- DrawIntoBitmap—draws shapes into a bitmap in the same way that the DrawShape method draws shapes into a view.

- MakeBitmap—returns a blank (white) bitmap shape of the specified size.

- MungeBitmap—performs various destructive bitmap operations such as rotating or flipping the bitmap.

- ViewIntoBitmap—provides a screen-capture capability, writing a portion of the specified view into the specified bitmap.

New Style Attribute Slots

Version 2.0 of Newton system software supports two new slots in the style frame: clipping and the transform.

Changes to Bitmaps

Previous versions of Newton system software treated bitmaps statically. They were created only from compile-time data, and the operations one could perform on them were limited to drawing them.

Version 2.0 of Newton system software provides a more dynamic treatment of bitmaps. You can dynamically create and destroy them, draw into them, and perform such operations as rotating and flipping them. This more flexible treatment of bitmaps allows you to use them as offscreen buffers as well as for storage of documents such as fax pages.

Changes to the HitShape Method

Previous versions of HitShape returned a non-nil value if a specified point lies within the boundaries of one or more shapes passed to it. Version 2.0 of the HitShape function now returns additional information.

Changes to View Classes

The `icon` slot of a view of the `clPictureView` class can now contain a graphic shape, in addition to bitmap or picture objects.

Using the Drawing Interface

This section describes how to use the drawing interface to perform specific tasks. See "Drawing and Graphics Reference" (page 10-1) in the *Newton Programmer's Reference* for descriptions of the functions and methods discussed in this section.

How to Draw

Drawing on the Newton screen is a two-part process. You first create a shape object by calling one or more graphics functions, such as `MakeRect`, `MakeLine`, and so on. You then draw the shape object by passing any of the shapes returned by the shape-creation functions, or an array of such shapes optionally intermixed with style frames to the `DrawShape` method. If a style frame is included in the shape array, it applies to all subsequent shapes in the array, until overridden by another style frame.

In addition to the shape object, the `DrawShape` method accepts a **style frame** parameter. The style frame specifies certain characteristics to use when drawing the shape, such as pen size, pen pattern, fill pattern, transfer mode, and so on.

This system is versatile because it separates the shapes from the styles with which they are drawn. You can create a single shape and then easily draw it using different styles at different times.

`DrawShape` can also accept as its argument an array of shapes instead of just a single shape. Therefore, you can create a series of shapes and draw them all at once with a single call to the `DrawShape` method. Additional style frames can be included in the shape array to change the drawing style for the shapes that follow them. "Using Nested Arrays of Shapes" (page 13-10), discusses the use of arrays of shapes in more detail.

Responding to the ViewDrawScript Message

When the system draws a view, it sends a `ViewDrawScript` message to the view. To perform your own drawing operations at this time, you must provide a `ViewDrawScript` method that calls the appropriate drawing functions.

The system also sends the `ViewDrawScript` message to the view whenever it is redrawn. Views may be redrawn as the result of a system notification or a user action.

If you want to redraw a view explicitly at any particular time, you need to send it the `Dirty` message. This message causes the system to add that view to the area of the screen that it updates in the next event loop cycle. To make the update area redraw before the next event loop cycle, you must call the `RefreshViews` function after sending the `Dirty` message.

Drawing Immediately

If you want to draw in a view at times other than when the view is being opened or redrawn automatically, you can execute drawing code outside of the `ViewDrawScript` method by using `DoDrawing`. For example, you might need to perform your own drawing operations immediately when the user taps in the view.

You can use the `DoDrawing` method for this purpose. The `DoDrawing` method calls another drawing method that you supply as one of its arguments.

▲ **WARNING**
Do not directly use `DrawShape` to draw shapes outside of your `ViewDrawScript`. Standard drawing in `ViewDrawScript` and `DoDrawing` automatically set up the drawing environment. If you use `DrawShape` without setting up the drawing environment, your application could accidentally draw on top of other applications, keyboards, or floaters. ▲

Using Nested Arrays of Shapes

The `DrawShape` method can draw multiple shapes when passed an array of shapes as its argument. Style frames may be included in the shape array to change the drawing style used to image subsequent elements of the array. Each element of the array can itself be an array as well; this section refers to such an array as a **nested array.**

Styles are maintained on a per-array basis in nested arrays, and the *startStyle* parameter of `DrawShape` is always treated as though it were the first array element of the topmost array. Therefore, compound shapes and multiple styles remain intact when nested arrays are combined into larger groupings.

When the `DrawShape` method processes a nested array, the shapes are drawn in ascending element order and drawing begins with the style of the parent array. Although the drawing style may change while processing the elements of an individual array, that style applies only to the elements of that particular array. Therefore, if an array happens to be an element of another array—that is, a nested array—style changes in the nested array affect the processing of its subsequent elements but the drawing style of the parent array is restored after the last element of the nested array is processed.

For example, you might nest arrays to create the hierarchy of shapes and styles depicted in Figure 13-9.

Figure 13-9   Example of nested shape arrays

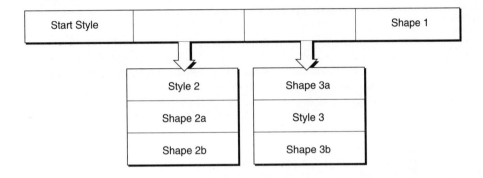

If the nested shape array depicted in Figure 13-9 were passed to the DrawShape function, the results summarized in Table 13-1 would occur.

Table 13-1   Summary of drawing results

Shape	Style
2a	2
2b	2
3a	*startStyle*
3b	3
1	*startStyle*

The Transform Slot in Nested Shape Arrays

Within a single shape array, the transform slot is treated like a style frame: only one transform is active per array; if another transform is specified within the array, the previous transform is overridden. Within nested arrays, however, the transform slot is treated a little differently than most style slots. As the DrawShape method descends into nested arrays of shapes, changes to the transform slot are cumulative; the resulting transform is the net sum of all the transforms in the hierarchy. For example, if in Figure 13-9 *startStyle* has a transform of 10,10 and Style 3 has a transform 50,0 then shapes 2a, 2b, 1, 3a would be drawn offset by 10,10 but Shape 3b would be drawn offset by 60,10.

Default Transfer Mode

The default transfer mode is actually a split state: bitmaps and text are drawn with a `modeOR` transfer mode, but other items (geometric shapes, pens, and fill patterns) are drawn with a `modeCOPY` transfer mode. However, when you actually specify a transfer mode (with a non-`nil` value in the `transferMode` slot of the style frame), all drawing uses the specified mode.

Transfer Modes at Print Time

Only a few transfer modes are supported for printing. Only `modeCOPY`, `modeOR`, and `modeBIC` may be used; other modes may produce unexpected results.

Note
Most problems occur when using PostScript printers, so you should test your code on LaserWriters as well as StyleWriters. ◆

Controlling Clipping

When the system draws a shape in a view for which the `vClipping` flag is set, it draws only the part that fits inside the view in which drawing takes place. Any parts of the shape that fall outside the boundaries of that view are not drawn, as if they have been cut off or clipped. The term **clipping** refers to this view system behavior; in common usage, the shape is said to have been "clipped to the destination view."

Note
Although the view system allows drawing outside the boundaries of a view for which the `vClipping` flag is not set, it does not guarantee that drawing outside the boundaries of the view will occur reliably. You need to make your destination view large enough to completely enclose the shapes you want to draw. You could also set the destination view's `vClipping` flag to clip drawing to the bounds of the destination view. Note also that an application base view that is a child of the root view always clips drawing to its boundaries. ◆

When no other clipping region is specified and `vClipping` is set, the boundaries of the destination view define the region outside of which drawing does not occur. This area is known as the **clipping region.** If you want to specify different clipping regions, you can use the style frame's `clipping` slot to do so. Because drawing is always clipped to the boundaries of the destination view, regardless of any other clipping region you specify, you cannot use the `clipping` slot to force drawing outside the boundaries of a view.

If the style frame includes a `clipping` slot, the drawing of all shapes affected by this style frame is clipped according to the value of the `clipping` slot. If the value of the `clipping` slot is `nil` or if the `clipping` slot is not supplied, the clipping behavior of the destination view is used.

If the `clipping` slot contains a region shape, that region is used as the clipping boundary for drawing operations affected by this style frame. If the `clipping` slot contains an array of shapes or regions, the system passes the contents of the `clipping` slot to the `MakeRegion` function to automatically create a new clipping region from the contents of this slot.

Note
Although putting an array of shapes in the `clipping` slot may seem convenient, it significantly increases the time required to process the style frame. For best performance from the view system, do not use this shortcut in style frames that are used repeatedly. ◆

Transforming a Shape

The `transform` slot changes the size or location of a shape without altering the shape itself. It accepts an array specifying an *x*, *y* coordinate pair or a pair of rectangles. The *x*, *y* coordinate arguments relocate a shape by specifying an offset from the origin of the destination view's coordinate plane. The rectangle arguments specify a mapping of the source and destination views that alters both the size and location (offset) of the source view when it is drawn in the destination view.

The rectangle arguments work the same way as the parameters to the `ScaleShape` function (although transforms won't accept `nil` for the boundaries of the source rectangle): the size of the shape is changed proportionately according to the dimensions of the destination rectangle, and the coordinates of the destination rectangle can also be used to draw the shape in a new location.

The following code fragments demonstrate the use of offset coordinates and mapping rectangles as the value of the `transform` slot:

```
    transform: [30,50],// offset shapes by 30 h and 50 v
```

or

```
    transform:
[SetBounds(0,0,100,100),SetBounds(25,25,75,75)],
// half width and height, centered in relation to
// the original object(not the view) assuming that
// the first rect actually specified correct bounds
```

Using Drawing View Classes and Protos

Four view classes and three protos, which you can use to create your own templates, are built into the system. The view classes include:

- `clPolygonView` —displays polygons or ink, or accepts graphic or ink input.

- `clPictureView`—displays a bitmap or picture object shape.

- `clEditView`—edits views that can accept both text and graphic user input.

- `clRemoteView`—displays a scaled image of another view.

The protos include:

- `protoImageView`—provides a view in which you can display, magnify, scroll, and annotate images.

- `protoThumbnail`—is used in conjunction with a `protoImageView`. It displays a small copy of the image with a rectangle representing the location and panel in the image.

- `protoThumbnailFloater`—provides a way to use a thumbnail, but also adjusts the thumbnail's size to reflect the aspect ratio of the image that it contains.

Displaying Graphics Shapes and Ink

Use the `clPolygonView` class to display polygons and ink, or to accept graphic or ink input. The `clPolygonView` class includes these features:

- Shape recognition and editing, such as stretching of shapes from their vertices, view resizing, scrubbing, selection, copying to clipboard, duplicating, and other gestures, as controlled by the setting of the `viewFlags` slot.

- Snapping of new line endpoints to nearby vertices and midpoints of existing shapes.

- Automatic resizing to accommodate enlarged shapes (when the view is enclosed in a `clEditView`). This feature is controlled by the `vCalculateBounds` flag in the `viewFlags` slot.

Views of the `clPolygonView` class are supported only as children of views of the `clEditView` class. In other words, you can put a `clPolygonView` only inside a `clEditView`.

You don't need to create polygon views yourself if you are accepting user input inside a `clEditView`. You simply provide a `clEditView` and when the user draws in it, the view automatically creates polygon views to hold shapes.

Displaying Bitmaps, Pictures, and Graphics Shapes

You can use a view of the `clPictureView` class to display a bitmap, picture, or graphic shape (polygon). The icon slot in this view can contain a bitmap, a picture object, or a graphic shape.

Displaying Pictures in a clEditView

Use the `clEditView` view class to display and accept text and graphic data in a view. Views of the `clEditView` class contain no data directly; instead, they have child views that contain the individual data items. Pictures are contained in child views of the class `clPictureView`. For details on displaying text, see "Using Views and Protos for Text Input and Display" (page 8-6).

To add a picture to a `clEditView`, you need to create an appropriate template of the `clPictureView` class, add the template to the `viewChildren` array, and then open the view or call `RedoChildren`. You can also use the `AddView` method to add the picture to an existing view, and then mark the view as dirty so that it will be redrawn.

The template holding the PICT items must contain the following slots:

- `viewStationery`—which must have the symbol `'pict`

- `viewBounds`—which is a bounds frame; for example,

  `RelBounds(0,0,40,40)`

- `icon`—which is a bitmap frame, a picture object, or a graphic shape

Displaying Scaled Images of Other Views

Use the `clRemoteView` view class to display a scaled image of another view. This class can be used to show a page preview of a full-page view in a smaller window, for example.

The view that you want to display inside the remote view should be specified as the single child of the remote view. This child is always hidden, and is used internally by the remote view to construct the scaled image.

A `clRemoteView` should never have more than one view, the scaled view, otherwise the results are undefined and subject to change.

Here is an example of a view definition of the `clRemoteView` class:

```
myRemoteView := {...
   viewclass: clRemoteView,
   viewBounds: {left: 75, top: 203, right: 178,
               bottom: 322},
   viewFlags: vVisible+vReadOnly,
```

```
viewFormat: nil,
ViewSetupFormScript: func()
    begin
    // aView is the view to be scaled
    self.stepchildren := [aView];
    end,
...};
```

Translating Data Shapes

You can use the global functions PointsToArray and ArrayToPoints to translate points data between a polygon shape ('polygonShape) and a NewtonScript array.

Finding Points Within a Shape

Use the HitShape function to determine whether a pen event occurred within the boundaries of the shape. This operation is useful for implementing button-like behavior in any shape. Possible results returned by the HitShape function include:

```
nil    // nothing hit
true   // the primitive shape passed was hit
[2,5]  // X marks the shape hit in the following array
       // shape := [s,s,[s,s,s,s,s,X,s],s,s]
```

You can retrieve the shape by using the value returned by the HitShape method as a path expression, as in the following code fragment:

```
result := HitShape(shape,x,y);
if result then // make sure non-nil
    begin
    if IsArray(result) then // its an array path
        thingHit := shape.(result);
    else
        thingHit := shape;// its a simple shape
    end
```

Although the expression shape.(result) may look unusual, it is perfectly legitimate NewtonScript. For further explanation of this syntax, see the "Array Accessor" discussion in *The NewtonScript Programming Language*.

Using Bitmaps

You can dynamically create and destroy bitmaps, draw into them, and perform operations on them such as rotating, flipping, and sizing. This flexible treatment of bitmaps allows you to use them as offscreen buffers and for storage of documents such as fax pages.

You can create and use bitmap images with the drawing bitmap functions. To create a bitmap you first allocate a bitmap that will contain the drawing with the MakeBitmap function. Then create a shape with the MakeShape function. DrawIntoBitmap takes the drawing and draws it into the bitmap. The final step is to draw the bitmap on the Newton screen with the DrawShape function.

The following example shows how to draw a bitmap. It creates a bitmap by drawing a shape and draws it onto the screen. This example then rotates the shape, scales it, and redraws it on the Newton:

```
bitmapWidth := 90;
bitmapHeight := 120;
vfBlack := 5;

// allocate a new bitmap
bitmap := MakeBitmap(bitmapWidth, bitmapHeight, nil);

// make a shape and draw it into the bitmap
shapes := MakeOval(0, 0, 50, 75);
DrawIntoBitmap(shapes, {fillPattern: vfBlack}, bitmap);

// draw the bitmap
GetRoot():DrawShape(bitmap, {transform: [100, 100]});

// Rotation is a destructive operation:  it replaces the
// old bitmap with the new rotated bitmap.
MungeBitmap(bitmap, 'rotateRight, nil);

// translate and scale the bitmap
fromRect := SetBounds(0, 0, bitmapWidth, bitmapHeight);
toRight := 100 + floor(bitmapWidth * 1.25);
toBottom := 200 + floor(bitmapHeight * 1.25);

toRight := 100 + bitmapWidth * 5 div 4;
toBottom := 200 + bitmapHeight * 5 div 4;

toRect := SetBounds(100, 200, toRight, toBottom);

// draw the bitmap again
GetRoot():DrawShape(bitmap, {transform: [fromRect,
toRect]});
```

Making CopyBits Scale Its Output Bitmap

CopyBits uses the bounds of the bitmap passed to it to scale the bitmap that it draws; so, by changing the bounds of the bitmap passed to CopyBits, you can make this method scale the bitmap it draws. If you want to scale the output bitmap without changing the bounds of the original, call ScaleShape on a clone of the original bitmap and pass the modified clone bitmap to the CopyBits method.

Storing Compressed Pictures and Bitmaps

NTK supports limited compression of pictures and bitmaps. If you store your package compressed (using the "optimize for space" setting), all items in your package are compressed in small (approximately 1 KB) pages, rather than object by object.

You can use the NTK compile-time function GetNamedResource to get a Macintosh PICT resource that can be drawn on the Newton in a view of the clPictureView class. PICT resources are generally smaller than bitmap frames because each bitmap within the PICT resource contains compressed bitmap data.

Note
This information applies to the Mac OS version of NTK; the Windows version differs. See the *Newton Toolkit User's Guide* for details. ◆

Capturing a Portion of a View Into a Bitmap

Use the ViewIntoBitmap method to capture a portion of a specified view into a specified bitmap. This function does not provide scaling capability, although scaling can be accomplished by passing the *destBitmap* bitmap returned by this method to the DrawIntoBitmap function as the value of its *shape* parameter. Figure 13-10 shows the relationships between the view to be captured, the source rectangle, the destination bitmap, and the destination rectangle.

Figure 13-10 Example of `ViewIntoBitmap` method

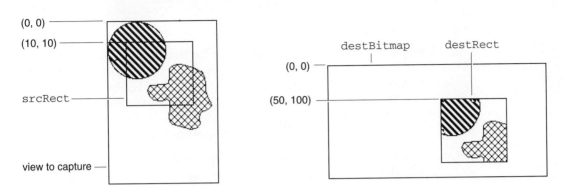

Rotating or Flipping a Bitmap

Use the `MungeBitmap` function (page 10-22) to perform various bitmap operations such as rotating or flipping the bitmap. These operations are destructive to the bitmap passed as an argument to this function; the bitmap is modified in place and the modified bitmap shape is returned. Figure 13-11 illustrates how the `MungeBitmap` function works. See "Using Bitmaps" (page 13-17) for a code example.

Figure 13-11 Example of `MungeBitmap` method

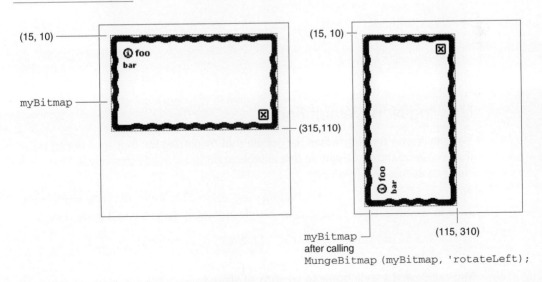

Importing Macintosh PICT Resources

The following information applies to the Mac OS version of NTK; the Windows version differs. See the *Newton Toolkit User's Guide* for details.

A Macintosh PICT resource can be imported into the Newton in two ways: as a bitmap or as a picture object. A Macintosh PICT resource is stored much more compactly on the Newton as a picture object; however, it may be slower to draw than a bitmap. The same Macintosh PICT resource may occupy much more space when imported as a bitmap, but may draw significantly faster. The method you should use depends on whether you want to optimize for space or speed.

A Macintosh PICT resource is imported as a bitmap by using the slot editor for the `icon` slot (an editor of the picture type). Alternatively, the resource can be imported as a picture object by using the `GetResource` or `GetNamedResource` compile-time functions available in NTK. In this case, you must use an `AfterScript` slot to set the value of the `icon` slot to the picture object obtained by one of these resource functions.

Note

The constant `clIconView` can also be used to indicate a view of the `clPictureView` class. These two constants have identical values. ◆

Here is an example of a template defining a view of the `clPictureView` class:

```
aPicture := {...
   viewClass: clPictureView,
   viewBounds: {left:0, top:75, right:150, bottom:175},
   viewFlags: vVisible+vClickable,
   icon: myPicture,
...}
```

Drawing Non-Default Fonts

You can draw a font other than the default font by putting the font specifier style frame close to the text shape so that another style frame won't override it. Use either `DrawShape` or `MakePict`.

There are several places where it might seem reasonable to put the style frame with the font specifier. `DrawShape` takes a style argument, so you could place it there:

```
:DrawShape(myText, {font: '{family: someFont,
   face: 0, size: 9 }});
```

You can embed a style frame in an array of shapes:

```
:DrawShape ([{font:        ...}, myText, shape ], nil);
```

You can also use `MakePict`:

```
myText := MakePict([{penpattern: 0, font: ...}, rect,
    {font: ...}, txtshape], {font: ...});
```

You can set the font in locations with `MakePict`. In this case the font gets "encapsulated" into the PICT.

If the `{penpattern}` frame was not present in the picture shape, any of the above places should suffice to set the font.

PICT Swapping During Run-Time Operations

To set a default picture for a `clPictureView`, use NTK's picture slot editor to set the `icon` slot of the `clPictureView`. You may select a PICT resource from any resource file that has been added to your project. The picture will be converted on the Macintosh from a type 1 or 2 PICT into a bitmap, and stored in your package at compile time. To change this picture at run time, you need to keep a reference to each alternate picture or bitmap. This is done using `DefConst` at compile time in a text file as follows:

```
OpenResFile(HOME & "Photos Of Ralph.rsrc");
// Here we convert a PICT 1 or PICT 2 into a BitMap.
// This is what NTK's picture slot editor does.
DefConst('kPictureAsBitMap,
        GetPictAsBits("Ralph", nil));

// Here the picture is assumed to be in PICT 1 format.
// If it is not, the picture will not draw and you may
// throw exceptions when attempting to draw the object.
DefConst('kPictureAsPict,
        GetNamedResource("PICT", "Ralph", 'picture));

// Verify this is a Format 1 PICT object!
if ExtractWord('kPictureAsPict, 10) <> 0x1101 then
    print("WARNING: Ralph is not a Format 1 PICT
resource!");

// This is one way to get the picture's bounds
// information. You can also extract it from the
// picture's own bounds rectangle at either compile time
// or run time, by using ExtractWord to construct each
// slot of a bounds frame.
DefConst('kPictureAsPictBounds,
        PictBounds("Ralph", 0, 0));


CloseResFile();
```

Notice that there are two types of pictures: bitmaps (a frame with `bits`, a `bounds`, and `mask` slots) and Format 1 PICTs (binary objects of class picture). `clPictureView` can draw both of these types of objects, so you just need to choose a format and use `SetValue` on the `icon` slot, as follows:

```
SetValue(myView, 'icon, kPictureAsBitMap);
```
or
```
SetValue(myView, 'icon, kPictureAsPict);
```

Optimizing Drawing Performance

You can use several methods to make drawing functions execute faster.

If you have a fairly static background picture, you can use a predefined PICT resource. Create the PICT in your favorite drawing program, and use the PICT as the background (`clIconView`). The graphics system also has a picture-making function that enables you to create pictures that you can draw over and over again.

If you want to improve hit-testing of objects, use a larger view in combination with a `ViewDrawScript` or a `ViewClickScript` rather than using smaller views with an individual `ViewClickScript`. This is especially true of a view that consists of regular smaller views.

Summary of Drawing

Data Structure

Style Frame

```
aStyle := {
transferMode : constant, // transfer mode for the pen
penSize : integer, // size of the pen in pixels
penPattern : constant, // the pen pattern
fillPattern : constant, // the fill pattern
font : string, // font to use for drawing text
justification : symbol, // alignment of text
clipping : shape, region, or array of shapes, // specifies clipping
transform : array, // offsets or scales the shape
```

View Classes

clPolygonView

```
clPolygonView := {
viewbounds : int, // size of view and location
points : struct, // binary data structure containing
                      polygon data
ink : struct, // binary data structure containing ink data
viewFlags : const, // controls the recognition behavior of
                  the view
viewFormat : const, // controls appearance of the view
```

clPictureView

```
clPictureView := {
icon : bitmap, graphic shape, picture, // icon to display
viewBounds: int, // size and location of the view
viewFlags : const, // controls the recognition behavior of
                  the view
viewFormat : const, // controls appearance of the view
```

Drawing and Graphics

clRemoteView

```
clRemoteView := {
stepChildren : int, // specifies a single view
viewBounds: int, // size and location of the view
viewFlags : const, // controls the recognition behavior of
                    the view
viewFormat : const, // controls appearance of the view
```

Protos

protoImageView

```
aProtoImageView := {
_proto: ProtoImageView,
Image : shape,
Annotations : array,
scalingInfo : frame,
viewBounds : boundsFrame,
viewJustify: justificationFlags,
viewFormat : formatFlags,
zoomStops : array,
dragCorridor : integer,
grabbyHand : shape,
myImageView:penDown : function, // drags image
myImageView:ScalingInfoChanged : function, // called when
                                    scaling changes
myImageView:Setup : function, // initializes the image
myImageView:OpenImage : function, // opens image
myImageView:ToggleImage : function, // closes image
myImageView:GetScalingInfo : function, // returns scaling
                                  information
myImageView:HasAnnotations : function, // returns annotation
                                  information
myImageView:GetAnnotations : function, // returns an array of
                                  views
myImageView:SetAnnotationMode : function, // sets display
                                  behavior
myImageView:GetAnnotationMode : function, // returns a symbol
myImageView:TargetChanged : function, // called when
                                annotation is changed
myImageView:CanScroll : function, // returns scrolling
                                information
myImageView:ScrollTo : function, // scrolls an image
```

Drawing and Graphics

```
myImageView:ScrollBy : function, // scrolls an image
myImageView:ZoomBy : function, // makes an image larger
                                    or smaller
myImageView:ZoomTo : function, // changes the size of
                                    the image
myImageView:CanZoomBy : function, // changes the size of
                                    the image
myImageView:ZoomToBox : function, // resizes the image
...
}
```

protoThumbnail

```
protoThumbnail : = {
_proto: protoThumbnail,
ImageTarget : view,
Image : shape or bitmap,
viewBounds : boundsFrame,
viewJustify : justificationFlags,
trackWhileScrolling : integer, // tracks the grey box
myThumbnail:Setup : function, // prepares thumbnail
myThumbnail:OpenThumbnail : function, // opens thumbnail
myThumbnail:ToggleThumbnail : function, // opens or closes
                                    thumbnail
myThumbnail:Update : function, // renders thumbnail view
myThumbnail:GetScalingInfo : function, // returns scaling
                                    information
myThumbnail:PrepareToScroll : function, // prepares for
                                    scrolling
myThumbnail:ScrollTo : function, // scrolls a view
myThumbnail:DoneScrolling : function, // cleans up a scroll
operation
...
}
```

protoThumbnailPointer

```
protoThumbnailPointer : = {
_proto: protoThumbnailPointer,
ImageTarget : view,
Image : shape,
viewBounds : boundsFrame,
viewJustify : justificationFlags,
```

```
trackWhileScrolling : integer, // tracks the grey box
...
}
```

Functions and Methods

Bitmap Functions

MakeBitmap (*widthInPixels, heightInPixels, optionsFrame*)
DrawIntoBitmap (*shape, styleFrame, destBitmap*)
MungeBitmap (*bitmap, operator, options*)
view:ViewIntoBitmap (*view, srcRect, destRect, destBitmap*)

Hit-Testing Functions

HitShape (*shape, x, y*)
PtInPicture (*x, y, bitmap*)

Shape-Creation Functions

MakeLine (*x1, y1, x2, y2*)
MakeRect (*left, top, right, bottom*)
MakeRoundRect (*left, top, right, bottom, diameter*)
MakeOval (*left, top, right, bottom*)
MakeWedge (*left, top, right, bottom, startAngle, arcAngle*)
MakePolygon (*pointArray*)
MakeShape (*object*)
MakeRegion (*shapeArray*)
MakePict (*shapeArray, styleFrame*)
MakeText (*string, left, top, right, bottom*)
MakeTextLines (*string, bounds, lineheight, font*)
TextBox (*text, fontFrame, bounds*)

Shape Operation Functions and Methods

GetShapeInfo (*shape*)
*view:*DrawShape (*shape, styleFrame*)
OffsetShape (*shape, deltaH, deltaV*)
ScaleShape (*shape, srcRect, dstRect*)
ShapeBounds (*shape*)
InvertRect (*left, top, right, bottom*)
InsetRect (*rect, deltax, deltay*)

IsPtInRect(*x*, *y*, *bounds*)
FitToBox(*sourceBox*, *boundingBox*, *justify*)
OffsetRect(*rect*, *deltaX*, *deltaY*)
SectRect(*rect1*, *rect2*)
UnionRect(*rect1*, *rect2*)
RectsOverlap(*rect1*, *rect2*)

Utility Functions

*view:*DoDrawing(*drawMethodSym*, *parameters*)
*view:*CopyBits(*picture*, *x*, *y*, *mode*)
DrawXBitmap(*bounds*, *picture*, *index*, *mode*)
*view:*LockScreen(*lock*)
IsPrimShape(*shape*)
PointsToArray(*polygonShape*)
ArrayToPoints(*pointsArray*)

Sound

This chapter describes how to use sound in your application and how to manipulate Newton sound frames to produce pitch shifting and other effects.

You should read this chapter if you are attempting to use sound in an application.

This chapter provides an introduction to sound, describing:

- sounds, sound channels, and sound frames
- specific tasks such as creating a sound frame, playing a sound, and manipulating sound frames
- methods, functions, and protos that operate on sound

About Newton Sound

This section provides detailed conceptual information on sound functions and methods. Specifically, it covers the following:

- overview of sound and the sound channel
- sounds related to user events
- a brief description of the sound frame
- new functions, methods, and messages added for NPG System Software 2.0, as well as extensions to sound code

Newton devices play only sampled sounds; sound synthesis is not supported. However, a number of built-in sounds are supplied in the Newton ROM that you can use in your application. See "Sound Resources" (page 11-10) in the *Newton Programmer's Reference* for complete details. You can also use the Newton Toolkit (NTK) to create custom sounds on desktop computers.

A Newton sound is represented as a sound frame. You can easily associate any sound with a certain events or play sound frames programmatically. The system allows you to play sound frames synchronously or asynchronously.

All operations on sound frames are created by sending messages to a sound channel that encapsulates the sound frame and the methods that operate on it. Sound channels can play sampled sounds starting from any point within the data. For more advanced uses of sound you can open a sound channel which allows multiple channels to play simultaneously, or multiple sounds to be queued in a single channel. You use a sound channel by sending messages to a sound channel frame. Additionally, playback can be paused at any point in the sample data and later resumed from that point.

Sound channels have the following characteristics:

- There is no visual representation of a sound to the user.

- Sound channels must explicitly be created and destroyed.

The creation and disposal of sound channels follow this model:

- To create a sound channel, you send the Open message to a sound channel frame.

- To dispose of the sound channel, you send the Close message to it.

Event-related Sounds

Views can play sounds to accompany various events. For example, the system plays certain sounds to accompany user actions such as opening the Extras Drawer, scrolling the Notepad, and so forth.

Sounds in ROM

The system provides a number of sounds in ROM that are played to accompany various events. See "Sound Resources" (page 11-10) in the *Newton Programmer's Reference* for complete details.

Sounds for Predefined Events

All views recognize a set of predefined slot names that specify sounds to accompany certain system events. To add a ROM-based sound to one of these events, store the name of the ROM-based sound in the appropriate view slot.

The following predefined slots can be included in views to play event-related sounds:

showSound	The sound is played when the view is shown.
hideSound	The sound is played when the view is hidden.
scrollUpSound	The sound is played when the view receives a ViewScrollUpScript message.
scrollDownSound	
	The sound is played when the view receives a ViewScrollDownScript message.

For example, to play a sound in ROM when the view opens, place its name in the view's showSound slot.

In fact, all ROM_*soundName* constants are pointers to Newton sound frames stored in ROM. Instead of using one of these constants; however, you can store a Newton sound frame in a slot, causing the sound stored in that frame to play in accompaniment to the event associated with that slot. The next section describes the format of a Newton sound frame.

Sound Data Structures

Three data structures are related to sounds: a sound frame, a sound result frame, and a protoSoundChannel.

A sound frame stores sound sample data and additional information used internally by the system. A sound result frame returns information to the sound frame when the sound channel stops or pauses. Like any other frame, a sound frame and sound result frame cannot be greater than 32 KB in size. See "Sound Data Structures" (page 11-1) in the *Newton Programmer's Reference*, for a complete list of slots required by for both types of frames.

The protoSoundChannel provides methods that implement pause and playback of sounds and completion callbacks. It also provides query methods that return whether the sound is running or paused.

If you are providing custom sounds, you can store them as virtual binary objects. An example of storing a sound as a VBO is given in Chapter 11, "Data Storage and Retrieval."

Compatibility

Sound frames have been extended so that those in version 1.*x* can be played without modification by devices based on version 2.0 of the Newton ROM. Not all Newton 2.0 sound frames can be played by older Newton devices.

Two new functions have been added: PlaySoundAtVolume and PlaySoundIrregardless. PlaySoundAtVolume plays a sound specified by the sound frame at a specific volume level. PlaySoundIrregardless plays a sound no matter what the user's settings are.

Using Sound

This section describes how to use sound to perform specific tasks. See *Newton Toolkit User's Guide* for descriptions of the functions and methods discussed in this section.

Creating and Using Custom Sound Frames

The following information applies to the Mac OS version of NTK. The Windows version differs; see the *Newton Toolkit User's Guide* for details.

The compile-time functions `GetSound` and `GetSound11` allow you to use the Newton Toolkit to create Newton sound frames from Mac OS `'snd '` resource data. This section summarizes the main steps required to create custom sound frames from Mac OS `'snd '` resources in NTK; for a complete discussion of this material, see the *Newton Toolkit User's Guide*.

Follow these steps to add a custom sound to your application:

1. Include the sound resource file in your application's NTK project.

2. In your application, create an evaluate slot to reference the sound frame through a compile-time variable.

3. In your Project Data file

   ☐ Open the sound resource file with `OpenResFile` or `OpenResFileX`.

   ☐ If using `OpenResFileX`, store the file reference it returns.

   ☐ Use the functions `GetSound11` or `GetSound` to obtain the sound frame.

   ☐ Use a compile-time variable to store the sound frame returned by `GetSound` or `GetSound11`.

   ☐ Use the function `CloseResFile` or `CloseResFileX`, as appropriate, to close the sound resource file. If you use the `CloseResFileX` function, you need to pass as its argument the saved file reference originally returned by `OpenResFileX`.

4. In your application

   ☐ Set the value of the evaluate slot to the name of the compile-time variable that stores the sound frame.

   ☐ Pass the name of the evaluate slot as the argument to the `PlaySoundSync` function. These run-time functions play sound from anywhere in your code.

Creating Sound Frames Procedurally

To create a sound frame, you usually need to create a copy of the sound frame you wish to modify. Because you cannot modify sound frames in ROM, you must copy the sound frame in order to modify the binary sample data.

Cloning the original version of a sound frame you want to modify also allows you to reset values to their original state and provides a means of recovering the original sound frame easily if an operation fails.

Cloning Sound Frames

You can use the `Clone` function to make a modifiable copy of the sound frame by passing the frame or its reference to `Clone` and saving the result in a variable, as in the following example:

```
clonedSound := clone(ROM_simpleBeep);
```

This technique is an extremely efficient means of creating a modifiable sound frame, because the copy created is a shallow clone; that is, the cloned frame `clonedSound` does not actually store a copy of the `ROM_simpleBeep` binary data. Instead, the `clonedSound` frame stores a pointer to the ROM data in its `samples` slot. Thus, the `clonedSound` frame is fairly lightweight in terms of overhead in the NewtonScript heap.

Playing Sound

Newton system software plays sound in two ways. The first is to use the global sound functions `PlaySoundAtVolume` or `PlaySoundIrregardless`. The other way is to instantiate a sound playback channel and send messages to it. Each approach has benefits and drawbacks. Using the global functions is the simplest and most efficient approach, but it offers less control than sending messages to a sound channel.

Sound channels are appropriate for applications that require greater control over playback, such as one that allows pausing playback and sound completion. Sound channels are also useful for games, which might require having many sounds available on short notice or playing multiple sounds at the same time.

Using a Sound Channel to Play Sound

Using a sound channel to play a sound is accomplished by creating a sound channel and sending the `Start` message to it.

Creating a Sound Channel for Playback

You create a sound channel by sending it the `Open` function.

The code that creates a sound channel for playback might look like the following example:

```
mySndChn := {_proto:protoSoundChannel};
mySndChn:Open();
```

Playing Sounds

Once you create the sound channel, you can use any of the following methods to control the sound.

`Schedule`—queues the sound for play.

`Start`—starts playing the sounds in the order that they were scheduled.

`Stop`—stops all scheduled sounds including currently playing sounds, if any.

`Pause`—temporarily stops the current playback process in the specified sound channel.

`IsPaused`—checks to see if the sound channel is paused.

`IsActive`—checks to see if the sound channel is playing.

Deleting the Sound Channel

When finished with the sound channel, you need to dispose of it by sending the `Close` message to it. Most applications can dispose of the sound channel as soon as playback is completed; the callback function associated with a sound frame is an appropriate way to send the `Close` message to the channel.

Note

The system sound channel is never automatically disposed of even if the sound channel frame is garbage collected. You must send the `Close` message to the channel to dispose of the system sound channel. ◆

Playing Sound Programmatically

You can use any of the global functions to play sound programmatically. For example, you might want to play a sound when the user taps a button, or when a lengthy operation is complete. Sounds can be played synchronously or asynchronously, as described in the following section.

Synchronous and Asynchronous Sound

When a sound is played asynchronously, the playback can be intermixed with other tasks because the system does not wait for the sound to finish before beginning another task (such as updating the user interface, allowing user feedback; for example with buttons, or playing a subsequent sound).

When playback must be allowed to complete, use the `PlaySoundSync`, `PlaySoundAtVolume`, or `PlaySoundIrregardless` to guarantee uninterrupted playback. Synchronous playback is generally preferred unless the sound is so long as to be tedious or the application requires a high degree of responsiveness to the user. The NewtonScript interpreter can do nothing else until it completes synchronous playback.

Both approaches have benefits and drawbacks: synchronous playback can block other NewtonScript code from running when it's inconvenient to do so; on the other hand, asynchronous playback is never guaranteed to complete. Your use of synchronous or asynchronous sound playback depends on your application's needs.

Differences Between Synchronous Asynchronous Playback

The following code example demonstrates the difference between asynchronous playback and synchronous playback. To hear the demonstration of the two types of sound playback, type following code example into the Inspector as it is shown here, select all of these lines, and press Enter:

```
print ("Synchronous sound demo");
call func()
    begin
        for i := 0 to 20 do
        PlaySoundSync(ROM_simplebeep);
    end with();

print ("Async sound demo");
call func()
    begin
        for i := 0 to 20 do
        PlaySoundSync(ROM_simplebeep);
    end with();
```

The synchronous sound playback example plays the ROM_simplebeep sound twenty times; the sound plays its entire length each time. Twenty repetitions may seem a bit laborious until you hear how quickly the same calls are made in asynchronous mode.

Note that the asynchronous version can call the sound chip so fast that the sound does not have enough time to finish playing; as a result, part of the playback is clipped off with each new call to the `PlaySoundSync` function. In fact, it's likely that you won't hear twenty sounds in the asynchronous playback demo; the calls occur faster than the Newton sound chip can respond.

About the Sound Chip

The Newton sound chip requires about 50 milliseconds to load a sound and begin playing it. It also requires about 50 milliseconds to clear its registers and ready itself for the next call after playback completes. Although most applications are not affected by this timing information, it is included for interested developers, along with the caveat not to rely on the ramp-up and ramp-down times specified here because they may change in future Newton devices.

Generating Telephone Dialing Tones

Applications can use the `Dial` view method and the `RawDial` global function to generate telephone dialing tones from NewtonScript. It is strongly recommended that you use these functions rather than attempt to generate dialing tones yourself. These functions produce dialing tones that meet the standards for all countries in which Newton devices are available, sparing the application developer the effort of dealing with widely varying telephone standards.

If you need to perform other actions while generating dialing tones, such as posting status messages as various parts of the phone number are dialed, you can use the global function `RawDial` to dial asynchronously. The `RawDial` function accepts the same arguments as the `Dial` method; however, it dials asynchronously.

Note that both dialing functions map alphanumeric characters to the dialing tones that a standard telephone keypad produces for these characters. Standard telephone keypads do not implement the letters Q and Z; the `Dial` method and `RawDial` function map these letters to the tone for the digit 1. Pound (#) and asterisk (*) characters are mapped to the same tones that a standard telephone keypad provides for these characters.

Certain phone systems, such as those used for PBX and military applications, also generate special tones (DTMF dialing tones) for the letters A–D. Because the Newton ROM does not generate these special tones, its dialing functions map the characters A, B, C, and D to the tones they generate on a standard telephone keypad.

Advanced Sound Techniques

This section describes advanced techniques for manipulating the sound frame or its playback. The topics discussed include pitch shifting and manipulating sample data to produce altered sounds.

Pitch Shifting

In general, you can set the value of a sound frame's `samplingRate` slot to any float value less than that specified by the `kFloat22kRate` constant. However, this usually results in poor sound quality. What generally works best is to take an 11 kHz sound and play it at some higher rate. Of course, 22 kHz sound resources cannot be played at any higher sampling rate.

You can experiment with pitch shifting by playing sounds in the Inspector using the `PlaySoundSync` function. You can use any of the ROM sounds or your own custom sounds. The following example shows how to shift a sound's pitch by altering the value of the sound frame's `samplingRate` slot. Remember when setting this slot that `samplingRate` must be a value of type `float`.

```
// keep a copy of original for future use
origSound := clone(ROM_simpleBeep);

// make a copy to modify
mySound := Clone(origSound);

// play the original sound
PlaySoundSync(mySound);

// play at half original pitch
mySound.samplingRate := origSound.samplingRate/2;
PlaySoundSync(mySound);

// note how easily we can return to normal pitch
mySound.samplingRate := origSound.samplingRate;

// play at twice speed
mySound.samplingRate := origSound.samplingRate*2;
PlaySoundSync(mySound);
```

By using the output from a control view to alter the value of the sound frame's `samplingRate` slot, you can allow the user to interactively modify the pitch of playback. The following example code changes the value of the `samplingRate` slot according to the setting of a `protoSlider` view:

```
theSlider.changedSlider := func()begin
if viewValue = maxValue then
   mySound.samplingRate := originalRate
   else mySound.samplingRate := (viewValue*1.01);
PlaySoundSync(mySound);
end
```

For an example that uses output from a view based on the `protoKeypad`
prototype, see the Newton DTS sample code on this topic.

Manipulating Sample Data

This section describes how to use the utility functions `ExtractByte` and
`StuffByte` to manipulate individual bytes in sound sample data. Because of
performance considerations, you'll want to manipulate sample data on the Newton
only when it's absolutely necessary. Even simple operations, like the example here,
can take a long time to perform on a relatively small sound sample.

The following example, extracts bytes from the end of the sample data and adds
them to its beginning, thus reassembling the samples in reverse order to create a
"backwards" sound.

```
// backwardSound is a slot in the app's base view
// if it's nil then create the backward sound
if (not backwardSound) then
begin
// get a frame to work with
   backwardSound := deepclone(ROM_funbeep);
// a var to store the modified sample data
   local sampleHolder := Clone(backwardSound.samples);
   local theSize := Length(sampleHolder) -1 ;
// Copy bytes from one end of the binary object
// to the other.
   for i := 0 to theSize do
      StuffByte(backwardSound.samples,i,
               ExtractByte(sampleHolder,theSize-i));
end;
```

A better solution is to provide the backwards sound as a resource that can be
played just like any other sound; a number of sound editors are available to create
such a resource on a desktop computer.

Summary of Sound

Data Structures

SndFrame Structure

```
mySndFrame := {
_proto: mySndFrame,
sndFrameType : symbol, // specifies format
samples : frame, // contains sampled binary data
samplingRate : integer /floating point, // specifies playback rate
compressionType : integer, // indicates no compression
dataType : integer, // indicates size of sample in bits
start : integer, // index of first sample to play
count : integer, // number of samples to play
loops : integer, // time to repeat sound
Callback : function, // indicates the state of the sound
```

SndResult Structure

```
mySndResult := {
_proto: mySndResult,
sound : integer, // reference to soundFrame that was paused
index : function, // index of sample that was paused/stopped
```

Protos

protoSoundChannel

```
aProtoSoundChannel := {
_proto: protoSoundChannel,
Open : function, // opens sound channel
Close : function, // closes sound channel
Schedule : function, // queues sound for play
Start : function, // starts sound channel
Stop : function, // stops sound channel
Pause : function, // pauses playback
IsPaused : function, // checks if sound channel is paused
IsActive : function, // checks if  sound channel is active
...
}
```

Functions and Methods

view:Dial(*numberString*,*where*)
GetVolume()
PlaySoundSync(*soundFrameRef*)
RawDial(*number*, *where*)
SetVolume(*volume*)
PlaySoundAtVolume(*soundFrameRef*, *volume*)
PlaySoundIrregardless(*soundFrameRef*)
PlaySoundIrregardlessAtVolume(*soundFrameRef*, *volume*)
PlaySoundEffect(*soundFrameRef*, *volume*, *type*)
Clicker()

Sound Resources

ROM_alarmWakeup // alarm sound
ROM_click // click sound
ROM_crumple // paper crumpling sound
ROM_drawerClose // drawer closing sound
ROM_drawerOpen // drawer opening sound
ROM_flip // page flipping sound
ROM_funBeep // trill sound
ROM_hiliteSound // squeek sound
ROM_plinkBeep // xylo sound
ROM_simpleBeep // bell sound
ROM_wakeupBeep // power on sound
ROM_plunk // paper hitting trash sound
ROM_poof // puff of air sound

CHAPTER 15

Filing

This chapter describes how your application can support the Filing service. This service allows the user to

- associate data items with folders displayed by the user interface
- create, edit, or delete folders at will
- specify the store on which a soup entry is to reside when it is filed

Before reading this chapter, you should understand the use of views to image data, as explained in Chapter 3, "Views." You should also understand the contents of Chapter 11, "Data Storage and Retrieval," which describes the soup-based storage model on which the Filing service is based. If your application does not save data as soup entries, you need to implement mock entries and related objects to provide soup-like access to your data, as described in Chapter 12, "Special-Purpose Objects for Data Storage and Retrieval."

A related service called the Soupervisor allows the user to file or move all entries in a specified soup at once. For more information, see the description of this service in Chapter 19, "Built-in Applications and System Data."

About Filing

The Filing service enables the user to associate data items with tags that represent folders in the user interface. In most cases, the filed items are soup entries that reside in their respective soups, rather than in any sort of directory structure. Filing an item displayed on the screen simply associates its corresponding soup entry with the tag that represents a particular folder. Soup entries hold this tag in their labels slot. The Filing service also allows the user to move entries to a specified store when they are filed.

The currently displayed application data to be filed is referred to as the **target** of the filing action. The target may consist of multiple data items; for example, most applications provide an overview view from which the user can file and move multiple items simultaneously.

Your application must provide a **target view** that can manipulate the target. The target view is usually the same view that images the target data. Although the application base view is often an appropriate target view, it may not be under all circumstances. For example, each of these common situations has specialized targeting needs:

- Most applications allow the user to file and move multiple data items from within an overview view. In this situation, the target may consist of multiple items, and the overview view is usually the appropriate target view.

- Applications that display more than one data item at a time, such as the built-in Notes application, may need to specify which of several equal child views is actually the target.

- You might want the target view to be a floating window when one is present, and the application's base view at all other times.

You can override the system-supplied GetTargetInfo method to vary the target and target view according to circumstances.

Applications with less-elaborate targeting needs can use the default GetTargetInfo method supplied by the system. To use the default GetTargetInfo method, your application base view must supply target and targetView slots. You are responsible for updating the values of these slots whenever the target changes; that is, whenever the data item on display changes.

To file the target, the user taps a file folder button you provide. This view, which is based on the protoFilingButton system prototype, looks like a button with a picture of a paper file folder on it. Figure 15-1 provides two examples of views based on the protoFilingButton system prototype.

Figure 15-1   Two examples of filing button views

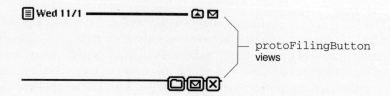

Filing

When the user taps the `protoFilingButton` view, it displays the Filing slip shown in Figure 15-2.

Figure 15-2   Filing slip

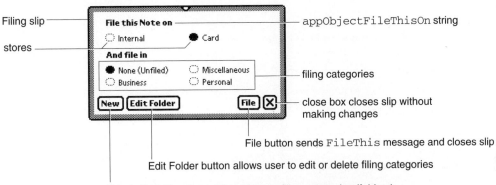

The Filing slip displays a set of categories in which the target can be filed. These filing categories include all folders available to the application that displayed the Filing slip, as well as the Unfiled category. This slip also provides a close box that dismisses it without making any changes.

The user can create new folders and edit the names of existing ones by means of buttons the Filing slip provides for this purpose. When a new folder is created, it may be designated as visible only from within a specified application; such a folder is said to be a **local folder** belonging to the application that created it. Any folder not created as a local folder is visible from all applications, and is called a **global folder.** The system permits the creation of a maximum of twelve local folders per application and twelve global folders system-wide. The system does not permit the creation of local and global folders having the same name.

Most applications allow the user to create and view any combination of local and global folders; however, you can suppress the display of either kind of folder if necessary. For example, the Extras Drawer displays only its own filing categories because those created by other applications are not likely to be useful for organizing the display of application packages, soups, and so on.

When the user adds, removes, or edits filing categories, the folder change notification service executes your previously registered callback function to respond appropriately to these changes. You use the `RegFolderChanged` global function to register a callback function with this service. The companion function `UnRegFolderChanged` unregisters a specified callback function.

Filing and other system services display user messages containing a string that is the user-visible name of your application. For example, this string is used to complete the text displayed when the user creates a local folder. You need to create in your application's base view an appName slot that holds this string. Figure 15-3 depicts the text displayed when the user creates a folder that is local to the Notepad application.

Figure 15-3   Creating a local folder

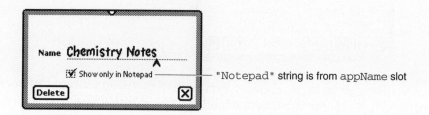

The system determines whether to display global or local folders by testing the values of optional slots you can supply in the application's base view. You can set the value of the localFoldersOnly slot to true to cause the Filing slip and folder tab views to display only the current application's local folders. You can set the value of the globalFoldersOnly slot to true to cause the Filing slip and folder tab views to display only global folders. When these slots are both nil or missing, the Filing slip and folder tab display global folders and the current application's local folders.

▲ **WARNING**
The localFoldersOnly and globalFoldersOnly must not both hold non-nil values at the same time. ▲

Your target view can provide an optional doCardRouting slot to control the display of the buttons that specify the store on which to file the target. When an external store is available and the value of the doCardRouting slot is true, the Filing slip includes buttons that represent available stores.

You must supply the full text of the string that labels this group of store buttons. This string is held in an appObjectFileThisOn slot that you provide. Similarly, you must supply the full text of the string labelling the group of buttons that represent filing categories. This string is held in an appObjectFileThisIn slot that you provide. Figure 15-2 shows where the Filing slip displays these strings.

When no external store is available or the value of the doCardRouting slot
is nil, the system displays the simplified version of the Filing slip shown in
Figure 15-4.

Figure 15-4   Filing slip without external store

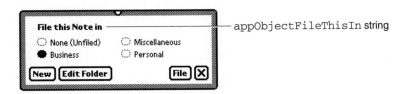

— appObjectFileThisIn string

This simplified version of the Filing slip does not include the buttons that allow
the user to choose a store. Note that the string labelling the group of buttons
representing filing categories differs slightly in this version of the Filing slip. This
string is provided by an appObjectFileThisIn slot that your application's base
view supplies.

Regardless of other options you may have implemented, the Filing slip always
opens with the current filing category selected; for example, the 'business
folder is selected in Figure 15-4. If you include a non-nil
dontStartWithFolder slot in your target view, the Filing slip opens with no
default folder selected. This feature is intended for use when you cannot
necessarily determine a useful default filing category, such as when the target view
is an overview that displays the contents of multiple folders.

When the value of the doCardRouting slot is the 'onlyCardRouting symbol,
the Filing slip does not include the filing category buttons but allows the user to
move the target between available stores without changing its filing category.
Figure 15-5 shows the Filing slip when an external store is available and the value
of the target view's doCardRouting slot is the 'onlyCardRouting symbol.

Figure 15-5   Filing slip for 'onlyCardRouting

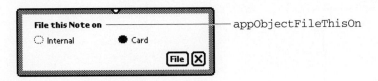

— appObjectFileThisOn

Filing

When the user taps the File button, the system

- invokes the `GetTargetInfo` method to discover the target and the target view
- sends the `FileThis` message to the target view

Your target view must supply a `FileThis` method that performs any tasks necessary to file the target, such as the following:

- moving its soup entry to a different store
- redrawing the current view
- setting the target's `labels` slot to its new value
- performing any additional tasks that are appropriate

Your application must provide a folder tab view that

- indicates the filing category of currently displayed data.
- allows the user to choose a new filing category to display

The system provides `protoNewFolderTab` and `protoClockFolderTab` system prototypes you can use to create your folder tab view. Views based on either proto can display a title text string in the area to the left of the folder tab. The `protoNewFolderTab` view displays a text string that you may supply optionally, as shown in Figure 15-6.

Figure 15-6   A `protoNewFolderTab` view

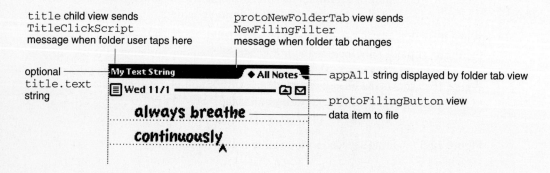

title child view sends
TitleClickScript
message when folder user taps here

protoNewFolderTab view sends
NewFilingFilter
message when folder tab changes

optional — title.text string

My Text String   ◆ All Notes

📄 Wed 11/1

always breathe

continuously

appAll string displayed by folder tab view

protoFilingButton view

data item to file

The `protoClockFolderTab` is a variation on `protoNewFolderTab`
that displays the current time as its title text. Do not attempt to replace this
text; if you want to display your own title text in a folder tab view, use a
`protoNewFolderTab` view rather than a `protoClockFolderTab` view.
Figure 15-7 depicts a typical `protoClockFolderTab` view.

Figure 15-7   A `protoClockFolderTab` view

Either kind of folder tab view sends a `TitleClickScript` message to your
application when the user taps its title text. The `protoClockFolderTab` view's
default `TitleClickScript` method opens the built-in Clock application. The
`protoNewFolderTab` view provides no default `TitleClickScript` method.
Your folder tab view can provide its own `TitleClickScript` method to
customize the action it takes in response to a tap on its title text. Your
`titleClickScript` method accepts no arguments.

Both kinds of folder tab views rely on an `appObjectUnfiled` slot that you
provide in your application's base view. This slot contains the full text of the string
"Unfiled *items*", in which *items* is the plural form of the target your application
manipulates; for example, "Unfiled Notes." This string appears in the folder tab
view when the application displays data items not associated with any filing
category. This string is also displayed in the picker that opens when the user taps
the filing tab.

Both kinds of folder tab views also rely on the use of an `appAll` slot that you
provide in your application's base view. This slot contains the full text of the string
"All *items*" in which *items* is the plural form of the target your application manipulates; for example, "All Notes." This string appears in the folder tab view when
the application displays all its data items (including those that are not filed). This
string is also displayed in the picker that opens when the user taps the folder tab.

Tapping the folder tab displays a picker from which the user can choose a filing
category. Your application must filter the display of filed items according to the
category selected in this list; hence, the value retrieved from this list is referred to
as the filing filter. A check mark appears next to the currently selected filing filter;
the user can tap an item in the list to select a new filing filter. In addition to
selecting a filing filter in this picker, the user can specify whether to display items

on the internal store, the external store or both; that is, the user can specify a stores filter in addition to a labels filter. Figure 15-8 shows the folder tab picker in a view based on the `protoClockFolderTab` proto.

Figure 15-8   Choosing a filing filter

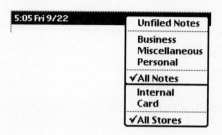

To display items according to the user's choice of store, your target view must supply a `storesFilter` slot. When the target view has a `storesFilter` slot and more than one store is available, the folder tab views allow the user to specify a store in addition to a folder from which data items are retrieved for display. For example, the user might choose to display only entries in the `'business` folder on the internal store.

When the user chooses any filter from this picker, the system updates the `storesFilter` or `labelsFilter` slot and sends the target view a `NewFilingFilter` message. The argument passed to this method by the system tells you what changed—the stores filter or the labels filter—but not its new value.

You must supply a `NewFilingFilter` method that examines the `storesFilter` or `labelsFilter` slot and queries your application's soups appropriately. If the value of the `labelsFilter` slot is `nil`, your `NewFilingFilter` method must display all target items. Similarly, if the value of the target view's `storesFilter` slot is `nil`, your `NewFilingFilter` method must display items on all available stores.

Your `NewFilingFilter` method must also perform any other actions necessary to display the appropriate data, such as redrawing views affected by the new filter value.

You can use the `RegFolderChanged` function to register your own callback function to be executed when the user adds, deletes, or edits folder names. You cannot respond adequately to these kinds of changes from within your `NewFilingFilter` or `FileThis` methods alone.

Filing Compatibility Information

Version 2.0 of the Newton operating system supports earlier versions of the Filing interface completely—no code modifications are required for older filing code to continue working under the version 2.0 operating system. However, it is strongly suggested that you update your application to the version 2.0 Filing interface to take advantage of new features and to remain compatible with future versions of the Newton operating system. This section provides version 2.0 compatibility information for applications that use earlier versions of the Filing interface.

Users can now create folders visible only to a specified application; the folders are said to be local to that application. Folders created using previous versions of the Filing interface are visible to all applications when first read on a 2.0-based system. Applications can now filter the display of items according to the store on which they reside and according to whether they are filed in local or global folders.

The symbols that represent folders are no longer tied to the strings that represent them to the user, as they were in previous versions of the Newton operating system. This new scheme allows you to use the same folder symbol everywhere for a particular concept, such as a business, while varying the user-visible string representing that folder; for example the user-visible string could be localized for various languages.

Applications can now route items directly to a specified store from the Filing slip. In addition, registration for notification of changes to folder names has been simplified.

The `protoFolderTab` proto is replaced by the `protoNewFolderTab` and `protoClockFolderTab` protos.

The `protoFilingButton` proto now supplies its own borders. You do not need to enclose the filing button in another view to produce a border around the button.

The `FolderChanged` and `FilingChanged` methods are obsolete. They are replaced by the `FileThis` method and the folder change notification mechanism. If your application supplies a `FileThis` method, the system does not send `FolderChanged` and `FilingChanged` messages to your application. Instead of supplying a `FolderChanged` method, your application should register a callback function with the folder change notification mechanism to perform tasks when the user adds, deletes, or edits folders.

The `FilterChanged` method is obsolete; your application should supply a `NewFilingFilter` method instead. Your `NewFilingFilter` method must update the query that retrieves items matching the current filing category and perform any other actions that are appropriate, such as redrawing views affected by the change of filing filter. If your application supplies a `NewFilingFilter` method, the system does not send `FilterChanged` messages to your application.

The new slots `appObjectFileThisIn` and `appObjectFileThisOn` support localization of your application's Filing messages into languages having masculine and feminine nouns.

The `DefaultFolderChanged` function is obsolete. Do not use this function.

The `target` and `targetView` slots are superseded by your override of the `GetTargetInfo` method. However, if you do not override the system-supplied `GetTargetInfo` method, you must include these slots in your application's base view.

Registration for notification of changes to folder names has been simplified. Use the new functions `RegFolderChanged` and `UnRegFolderChanged` to register for folder change notification.

Using the Filing Service

To support the Filing service, your application must

- provide three views (a folder tab view, a filing button view, and a view that images the filing target)
- respond to two messages (`FileThis` and `NewFilingFilter`)
- register a callback function with the folder change notification service

Additionally, you can

- support the use of multiple target items
- customize the Filing slip and folder set that your application uses

The remainder of this section describes these tasks in detail.

Overview of Filing Support

You need to take the following steps to support the Filing service:

- Add a `labels` slot to your application's soup entries.
- Create in your application's base view the slots `appName`, `appAll`, `appObjectFileThisIn`, `appObjectFileThisOn`, and `appObjectUnfiled`.
- Supply a filing target. It is recommended that you override the `GetTargetInfo` method; if you do not, your application base view must supply `target` and `targetView` slots for use by the default method. You are responsible for keeping the values of these slots current.
- Create a `labelsFilter` slot in your application's target view.

- Create a `storesFilter` slot in your application's target view
- Implement the `FileThis` and `NewFilingFilter` methods.
- Add a filing button view and a folder tab view to your application.
- Register a callback function with the folder change notification mechanism.

Optionally, you can

- create a `doCardRouting` slot in your application's base view
- create a `dontStartWithFolder` slot in your target view
- implement support for local or global folders only
- customize the title text in your `protoNewFolderTab` view
- provide a `TitleClickScript` method to customize the action your folder tab view takes when the user taps its title text

The sections immediately following describe these tasks in detail.

Creating the Labels Slot

Each of your application's soup entries must contain a `labels` slot. It is recommended that you make this slot part of a default soup entry created by a frame-constructor function you supply. (For information on the use of frame-constructor functions, see "Programmer's Overview" on page 11-25 in Chapter 11, "Data Storage and Retrieval.")

When the user files a soup entry, the system stores a value in its `labels` slot. Setting the value of the `labels` slot is really the only "filing" that is done—the entry still resides in the soup, but your `FileThis` and `NewFilingFilter` methods provide the user-interface illusion that the data has been put in a folder.

The `labels` slot can store either a symbol or the value `nil`. If the value stored in this slot is `nil`, your `FileThis` method must treat the item as unfiled. If a symbol is stored in this slot, your `FileThis` method must test the value of this slot to determine whether the entry should be displayed and then redraw the display appropriately. Similarly, your `NewFilingFilter` method tests the value of this slot to determine whether to display the item when the filing filter changes.

Creating the appName Slot

You must create in your application's base view an `appName` slot containing a string that is the user-visible name of your application.

Creating the appAll Slot

You must create in your application's base view an `appAll` slot containing a string of the form

`"All `*`Items`*`"`

where *Items* is the plural for the items to be filed, such as cards, notes, and so on. For example, when the user taps the folder tab view in the built-in Notes application, the last item in the picker is "All Notes."

The following code fragment defines a typical `appAll` slot:

```
myAppBase := {… appAll: "All Notes", …}
```

Creating the appObjectFileThisIn Slot

You must define the `appObjectFileThisIn` slot in your application's base view. This slot holds the full text of the message to be displayed to the user when filing a single item; for example,

`"File this widget in"`

This string is shown at the top of the Filing slip pictured in Figure 15-2 (page 15-3).

Creating the appObjectFileThisOn Slot

You must define the `appObjectFileThisOn` slot in your application's base view. This slot holds the full text of the string labelling the group of buttons that represent stores in the Filing slip; for example,

`"File this `*`item`*` on"`

where *item* is the singular case of the target your application files, such as a card, a note, and so on.

For an example of this string, see Figure 15-5 (page 15-5).

Creating the appObjectUnfiled Slot

You must define an `appObjectUnfiled` slot in your application's base view. This slot holds a string of the form

`"Unfiled `*`Items`*`"`

where *Items* is the plural case of the items to be filed, such as cards, notes, and so on. For example, if the user taps the folder tab view in the built-in Notes application, the first item in the picker is "Unfiled Notes."

The following code fragment defines a typical `appObjectUnfiled` slot:

```
myAppBase := {… appObjectUnfiled: "Unfiled Notes", …}
```

Specifying the Target

The `GetTargetInfo` method identifies the current target and target view to the system. Depending on your needs, you can use the default version of this method or override it.

If you use the default version, your application's base view must supply `target` and `targetView` slots that you update whenever the target or target view changes. If you override this method, you provide these slots in the result frame that it returns, rather than in your application's base view. These slots provide the same information regardless of whether they reside in the `GetTargetInfo` method's result frame or in the application's base view.

Creating the Target Slot

The `target` slot contains the data item with which the user is working, such as the soup entry that represents the currently displayed note to file. If there is no active item, this slot must have the value `nil`.

Your application must update the value of the `target` slot every time the user views a new item. Because the selection of a new item is an application-specific detail, it is difficult to recommend a means of updating this slot that is appropriate for every application; however, it is common to update the value of this slot from the `ViewClickScript` method of the active view.

Creating the TargetView Slot

The `targetView` slot contains the view that receives messages from the Filing service and can manipulate the target. The application's base view is usually an appropriate value for this slot.

Overriding the GetTargetInfo Method

You can implement your own `GetTargetInfo` method if the default version supplied by the system is not suitable for your application's needs. For example, if your application images data items in floating windows or displays more than one data item at a time, you probably need to supply a `GetTargetInfo` method that can return an appropriate target and target view in those situations.

You must override the `GetTargetInfo` method in order to move an item to another store when it is filed. The result frame returned by your `GetTargetInfo` override can include an optional `targetStore` slot that specifies the store on which an item is to reside when it is filed.

To override this method, create in your application base view a slot named `GetTargetInfo` and implement this method as specified in the description of the `GetTargetInfo` method (page 12-11) in *Newton Programmer's Reference*.

Creating the labelsFilter slot

Your application's target view must supply a `labelsFilter` slot. This slot holds a value indicating the current filing filter selected by the user in the picker displayed by the folder tab view. This slot can store either a symbol indicating the currently displayed filing category or the value `nil` (which specifies that the Unfiled category is currently displayed).

The system sets the value of the `labelsFilter` slot for you. Your `NewFilingFilter` method must update the display of your application's data according to the value of this slot.

To display a predetermined filing category when your application opens, you can set an initial value for the `labelsFilter` slot from within the application base view's `ViewSetupFormScript` method.

Creating the storesFilter slot

Your application's target view must supply a `storesFilter` slot. This slot stores a value indicating the current store filter selected by the user from the picker displayed by the folder tab view. This slot can store either a symbol or the value `nil`.

The system sets the value of the `storesFilter` slot for you. Your `NewFilingFilter` method must update the display of your application's data according to the value of this slot.

To display items on a particular store when your application opens, you can set an initial value for the `storesFilter` slot from within the application base view's `ViewSetupFormScript` method.

Adding the Filing Button

You need to take the following steps to add the `protoFilingButton` view to your application:

- In NTK, sketch the filing button using the `protoFilingButton` proto and declare it to the application's base view.

- Set appropriate values for the button's `viewBounds` slot.

Adding the Folder Tab View

Your application's base view must provide a view that displays the currently selected filing category and allows the user to select a new filing category. This view is based on either the `protoNewFolderTab` or `protoClockFolderTab` system proto.

Adding the folder tab view to your application is easy. In NTK, sketch the folder tab in your application's base view using the `protoNewFolderTab` proto and declare your folder tab view to the application's base view. The system sets the folder tab view's bounds for you at run time, positioning the folder tab relative to its parent, near the top of the screen.

Customizing Folder Tab Views

The `protoNewFolderTab` proto supplies a child view named `title` that images a string that you may supply optionally. To display your own string as the title text in a `protoNewFolderTab` view, use the global function `SetValue` to set the value of the `text` slot in the `title` view child of your folder tab view.

For example,

```
SetValue(myNewFolderTab.title, 'text, "My text");
```

▲ **WARNING**
Do not create a `title` slot in any folder tab view. Do not replace the title text in a `protoClockFolderTab` view. ▲

Defining a TitleClickScript Method

The folder tab view's `TitleClickScript` method is invoked when the user taps the title text in a `protoNewFolderTab` view or the time displayed as title text in a `protoClockFolderTab` view. The default `TitleClickScript` method provided for `protoNewFolderTab` views does nothing. The default `TitleClickScript` method provided by the `protoClockFolderTab` view displays the built-in Clock application.

You can provide your own `TitleClickScript` method to customize the action your folder tab views take when the user taps them.

Implementing the FileThis Method

When the user taps the File button in the Filing slip, the system sends the `FileThis` message to the target view. Your `FileThis` method must perform any actions necessary to file the target and redraw the current display appropriately.

For example, if your application is displaying an overview list of unfiled items when it receives this message, your `FileThis` method needs to redraw the list without the newly filed item in it, providing the user-interface illusion that the item has been moved.

Your `FileThis` method must also handle the case in which the user re-files an item in the category under which it already resides. In this case, the appropriate response is to do nothing; unnecessarily redrawing views that have not changed makes the screen appear to flicker or flash. Because the value of the target's `labels` slot does not change unless you change it, you can test this slot's current value to determine whether the new value is different.

Filing

The arguments to the FileThis method supply all the information necessary to file a soup entry, including the item to file (the target), the category under which to file it (the value to which you set the target's labels slot), and the store on which to file it.

If the value of the labelsChanged parameter to the FileThis method is true, your FileThis method must use the value of the newLabels parameter to update the value of the target's labels slot. However, if the value of the labelsChanged parameter is nil, the value of the newLabels parameter is undefined—don't use it!

Similarly, if the value of the storesChanged parameter is true, your FileThis method must move the target to the new store. However, if the value of the storesChanged parameter is nil, the value of the destStore parameter is undefined.

The following code example shows the implementation of a typical FileThis method. Remember to call EntryChangeXmit from this method so your changes to filed entries are saved!

```
FileThis: // example code - your mileage may vary
func(target, labelsChanged, newLabels, storesChanged, destStore)
   begin
      if labelsChanged AND target.labels <> newLabels then
      begin
         target.labels := newLabels;
         EntryChangeXmit(target, kAppSymbol);
      end // labelsChanged
      if storesChanged and (EntryStore(target) <> destStore) and
         not destStore:IsReadOnly() then
         begin
            // move the entry to the new store & xmit change
            // make sure you handle locked stores too
            if EntryStore(target):IsReadOnly() then
               EntryCopyXmit(target, destStore, kAppSymbol);
            else
               EntryMoveXmit(target, destStore, kAppSymbol);
         end; //storesChanged
   end; // FileThis
```

Implementing the NewFilingFilter Method

When the user changes the current filing filter in the folder tab view, the system calls your application's NewFilingFilter method. You need to define this method in your application's base view. Your NewFilingFilter method must update the query that retrieves items matching the current filing category and perform any other actions that are appropriate, such as redrawing views affected by the change in filing filter.

The symbol passed as the sole argument to your NewFilingFilter method specifies which of the storesFilter or labelsFilter slots changed in value. This argument does not specify the slot's new value, however. Your NewFilingFilter method must use the current value of the specified slot to retrieve those soup entries that fall into the new filing category.

The following code example shows the implementation of a typical NewFilingFilter method, which queries the application soup for the entries that match the current filing category and then redraws views affected by the change in filing category.

```
NewFilingFilter: func(newFilterPath)
begin
    // first figure out if query should be done on
    // a union soup or on a specific store soup
    // this is to make filter by store more efficient

    local querySoup := GetUnionSoupAlways(kSoupName) ;

    if storesFilter and storesFilter:IsValid() then
        querySoup := querySoup:GetMember(storesFilter) ;

    // now construct the query based on the labelsFilter
    // and set my application cursor (called myCursor)
    // to the new query

    // the default is to show all items, i.e.,
    // labelsFilter is '_all
    local theQuery := nil ;

    if NOT labelsFilter then
        // labelsFilter is NIL, so show only those entries
        // that do not have a valid tag in the labels
        // slot
        theQuery := {none: GetFolderList(appSymbol, nil)};
    else if labelsFilter <> '_all then
        // labelsFilter is some specific folder
        theQuery := {all: labelsFilter} ;

    myCursor := querySoup:Query(theQuery) ;
```

```
    // now redraw views affected by the change
    // NOTE: You could keep track of the original
    //         labelsFilter and storesFilter to see
    //         whether you need to actually do work.
end
```

Using the Folder Change Notification Service

You can use the RegFolderChanged global function to register callback functions that are executed when the user adds, removes, or edits folders. Most applications register these functions only while the application is actually open, so the application base view's ViewSetupFormScript is an ideal place from which to call the RegFolderChanged function. For example,

```
myCallback1 := func (oldFolder, newFolder);
begin
    // retag entries
end;
myAppBase.viewSetupFormScript := func ()begin
RegFolderChanged('|myFnId1:myApp:mySig|, myCallback1);
end;
```

The UnRegFolderChanged function removes a specified callback from use by the folder change mechanism. Most applications unregister their folder change callback functions when they close, making the application base view's ViewQuitScript method an appropriate place to unregister folder change callback functions. For example,

```
myAppBase.viewQuitScript := func ()begin
UnRegFolderChanged('|myFnId1:myApp:mySig|);
end;
```

Creating the doCardRouting slot

If you want to move items between stores from within the Filing slip, you need to create a doCardRouting slot in your application's base view. When an external store is available and the value of this slot is non-nil, the Filing slip displays buttons allowing the user to route the target to a specified destination store. If this slot has a non-nil value but no external store is available, these "card-routing" buttons are not displayed.

Using Local or Global Folders Only

To suppress the display of either local or global folders in the Filing slip and the folder tab views, you can set the values of optional localFoldersOnly and globalFoldersOnly slots that you supply in your application's base view. Note that the use of local or global folders only is intended to be an application design decision that is made once, rather than a user preference that can change.

When the localFoldersOnly slot holds the value true, the Filing slip and folder tab views do not display the names of global folders. When the globalFoldersOnly slot holds the value true, the Filing slip and folder tab views do not display the names of local folders.

▲ **WARNING**
The localFoldersOnly and globalFoldersOnly must not both hold non-nil values at the same time. ▲

Adding and Removing Filing Categories Programmatically

You can use the AddFolder and RemoveFolder global functions to modify the set of folders (filing categories) available to your application. Note that the RemoveFolder function does not remove any folder that is also used by other applications. For more information, see the descriptions of these methods in the *Newton Programmer's Reference*.

Interface to User-Visible Folder Names

Symbols that represent folders are not tied to the strings that represent those folders to the user. As a result, you can use the same folder symbol everywhere for a particular concept, such as a business, while varying the user-visible string representing that folder; for example the user-visible string could be localized for various languages.

You can use the GetFolderStr function to retrieve the user-visible string associated with a folder symbol.

Summary

This section summarizes the data structures, protos, functions, and methods used by the Filing service.

Data Structures for Filing

Application Base View Slots

```
myAppBaseView :=
        {_parent: {…},// root view
        _proto:  {// myAppBaseViewTemplate
                _proto: {…}, // protoApp,
                // slots you supply in myAppBaseViewTemplate
                appObjectUnfiled: "Unfiled Items",
                appAll: "All Items",
                appObjectFileThisOn: "File this item on",
                storesFilter: NIL,
                doCardRouting: 1,
                GetTargetInfo: <function, 1 arg(s) #6000F951>,
                labelsFilter: NIL,
                appObjectFileThisIn: "File this item in",
                appSymbol: |myApp:mySig|,
                …},
        // my filing button template, defined in app base view
        myfilingButton: {_parent: <2> // myAppBaseView,
                        _proto: protoFilingButton, …},
        // my new folder tab template, defined in app base view
        myNewFolderTab: {…}, // see summary on page 15-21
        …}
```

Target Information Frame

```
// returned by the GetTargetInfo method
{target: item,// the item to file or route
targetView: view, // filing messages are sent to this view
targetStore: store, // store on which target resides
// this frame may also include your own slots
…}
```

Filing Protos

protoFilingButton

```
myFilingButtonView :=
// do not override ViewClickScript; use ButtonClickScript instead
   { _parent:{ // MyAppBaseView
              _parent: {…}, // root view
              _proto: {…}, // myAppBaseViewTemplate
            …},
     _proto:  {// myFilingButtonTemplate
              // set your own viewBounds in NTK view editor
              viewBounds: {left: 10, top: 250,
                        right: 27, bottom: 263},
              _proto: {// protoFilingButton
                      _proto: {…}, // protoPictureButton
                      // your ButtonClickScript must call inherited
                      ButtonClickScript:<function, 0 arg(s) …>,
                      // your Update must call inherited
                       Update: <function, 0 arg(s) …>,
                      // your viewSetupFormScript must call inherited
                       viewSetupFormScript:<function, 0 arg(s)…>
                      …},
              …},
   …}
```

protoNewFolderTab

```
myNewFolderTabView := {
   {_parent: myAppBaseView, // see summary on page 15-20
    _proto: { protoNewFolderTab,
             // your folder tab's viewSetupFormScript must
             // call this inherited method using conditional send
             viewSetupFormScript: <function, 0 arg(s) …>,
             …},
   // do not alter this slot; set only the text slot
   title: {_parent: <2> // myNewFolderTabView,
             _proto: {viewClass: clTextView, …},
             // string displayed at left of newFolderTab view
             text: "My Text",
             …},
   }
```

protoClockFolderTab

```
myClockFolderTabView := {
   {_parent: myAppBaseView, // see page 15-20
   _proto: { protoClockFolderTab,
            // your folder tab's viewSetupFormScript must
            // call inherited:?viewSetupFormScript()
            viewSetupFormScript: <function, 0 arg(s) …>, …},
   // do not attempt to alter the time display text
   …}
```

Filing Functions and Methods

view:GetTargetInfo(*reason*) // override for multiple targets
view:MoveTarget (*target*, *destStore*) // move target between stores
RegFolderChanged(*callbackID*, *callBackFn*)// register folder change callback
UnRegFolderChanged(*callbackID*) // unregister folder change callback
AddFolder(*newFolderStr*, *appSymbol*) // add local folder
RemoveFolder(*folderSym*, *appSymbol*) // remove local folder
GetFolderStr(*folderSym*) // get user-visible folder name from app sym
RemoveAppFolders(*appSym*) // remove specified app's local folders
GetFolderList(*appSymbol*, *localOnly*) // list the app's local folders

Application-Defined Filing Functions and Methods

// Optional. Specify filing target, target view, target store
GetTargetInfo(*reason*)
// Required. Respond to changes in filing filter or store filter
targetView:NewFilingFilter(*newFilter*)
// Required. File the item as specified
targetView:FileThis (*target*, *labelsChanged*, *newLabels*, *storesChanged*, *newStore*)

Find

This chapter describes how your application can support finding text, dates, or your own data types in its data. If you want users to be able to use the system's Find service to locate data in your application, you should be familiar with the material discussed in this chapter.

Before reading this chapter, you should understand the concept of the target of an action, explained in Chapter 15, "Filing." Familiarity with using views to image data, covered in Chapter 3, "Views," is also helpful. If your application stores data as soup entries, you should understand the contents of Chapter 11, "Data Storage and Retrieval."

This chapter is divided into two main parts:

- "About the Find Service" describes the core user interface to the Find service, along with variations and optional features. A compatibility section covers differences between the current version of the Find service and previous ones.

- "Using the Find Service" provides a technical overview of Find operations, with code examples to show how to implement support for this service in your application.

In addition, the "Find Reference" (page 13-1) in *Newton Programmer's Reference* provides complete descriptions of all Find service data structures, functions, and methods.

About the Find Service

The Find service searches for occurrences of data items the user specifies on a Find slip. The Find slip may be supplied by the system or by the developer. Figure 16-1 illustrates the system-supplied Find slip.

Figure 16-1   The system-supplied Find slip

The system-supplied Find slip contains an input line that specifies a search string, several buttons indicate the scope of the search, and a Look For picker (pop-up menu) that specifies the kind of search to perform. By choosing from the Look For picker (pop-up menu) you may specify whether the search string is a text item or a date, as shown in Figure 16-2.

Figure 16-2   Specifying text or date searches in the Find slip

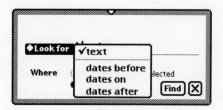

Text searches are case insensitive and find only string beginnings. That is, a search for the string "smith" may return the items "Smith" and "smithers," but not "blacksmith." Date searches find items dated before, after, or on the date specified by the search string.

From the application developer's perspective, text finds and date finds are nearly identical. The only significant difference between them is the test an item must pass to be included in the result of the search.

The system-supplied Find slip always contains an Everywhere button and Selected button. If the current application supports the Find service, a button with the application's name appears in this slip as well.

Find

Searching for data in the current application only is called a **Local find** operation.
Figure 16-3 depicts a Local find in the Notepad application.

Figure 16-3   A local Find operation

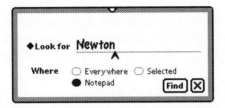

The Everywhere and Selected buttons specify that the system perform searches in
applications other than the currently active one. Applications must register with the
Find service to participate in such searches.

Tapping the Everywhere button tells the system to conduct searches in all currently
available applications registered with the Find service. This kind of search is called
a **Global find.** Applications need not be open to participate in a Global find.

A Global find is similar to a series of Local find operations initiated by the system.
When the user requests a Global find, the system executes a Local find in each
application registered with the Find service.

Tapping the Selected button causes a checklist to appear at the top of the Find slip.
The list includes all currently available applications registered with the Find
service. Tapping items in the list places a check mark next to applications in which
the system should conduct a Local find. This kind of search is called a **Selected
find.** The slip in Figure 16-4 depicts a search for the string "Daphne" in the Notes
and Dates applications.

Figure 16-4   Searching selected applications

About the Find Service

In addition, an application can support searches of multiple data sets. For example, a personal finance program might allow you to search the check ledger, the account list, and the credit charges list as separate searches, even though all the data resides in a single application. For more information on how to implement this in your application see "Adding Application Data Sets to Selected Finds" beginning on page 16-19.

In addition, you can replace the Find slip in the currently active application. Typically, you would do this to provide a customized user interface for specialized searches. For more information, see "Replacing the Built-in Find Slip" beginning on page 16-24.

After setting the parameters of the search with the Find slip, the user initiates the search by tapping the Find button. Alternatively, the user can cancel the search by tapping the close box to dismiss the Find slip.

While the search executes, the system provides user feedback through a Progress slip. This slip provides a Stop button that allows the user to cancel a search in progress. Figure 16-5 shows a typical Progress slip.

Figure 16-5   Progress slip

When the search is completed, the Find service displays an overview list of items that match the search criteria. Figure 16-6 shows the Find overview as it might appear after searching all applications for the string "Daphne".

Figure 16-6   The Find overview

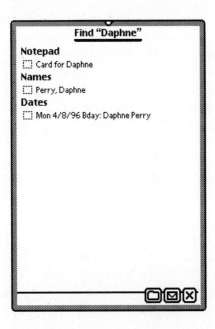

The user can tap items in the Find overview to display them. As items are displayed, a status message at the top of the Find slip indicates which item is displayed and whether there are more results to display. Figure 16-7 depicts this status message.

Figure 16-7   Find status message

When more than one item is found, the status message indicates that there are more items to display.

Between uses, the Find service stores the setting of the Look For picker. The next time this service is used, it reopens in the most recently set find mode. Note that in order to conserve memory, the list of found items is not saved between finds.

Compatibility Information

The current version of the Find service opens in the text or date find mode last used. The Find slip in versions of Newton System Software prior to 2.0 always opened in text find mode, regardless of the mode last used.

Find now performs "date equal" finds, and returns control to the user more quickly than previous versions did. The Find slip no longer displays the total number of items in the search result; that is, instead of displaying user feedback such as "This is item 24. There are 36 items" the Find slip displays "This is item 24. There are (no) more items."

The Find service now offers routines that allow you to include multiple data sets from a single application in Selected find operations. Three new methods support this functionality: AppFindTargets, FindTargeted, and DateFindTargeted. You use the AppFindTargets method to add identifying strings for the data sets to the Selected picker. The two new Find methods with which you implement targeted finds are FindTargeted and DateFindTargeted. They are identical to their nontargeted counterparts, except the last parameter, *indexPath*, is a path to a data set within an application.

Do not modify any system data structures directly to register or unregister an application with the Find service. Instead, use the RegFindApps and UnRegFindApps functions provided for this purpose. Applications running on older Newton devices can use the kRegFindAppsFunc and kUnregFindAppsFunc functions provided by NTK for this purpose.

The ShowFoundItem method now has two parameters, a data item and a finder frame. However, the old ShowFoundItem method, with one parameter (*item*) is still supported.

The SetStatus method is obsolete; use the SetMessage method instead. In addition, the FileAs and MoveTo methods are also obsolete; you should use FileAndMove instead.

Using the Find Service

This section includes a technical overview of Find operations and describes how to implement Find support in your application.

Technical Overview

When the user taps the Find button, the system invokes your application's search method. This can be a date find method (DateFind) or a text find method (Find).

The only significant difference between a date find and a text find is that a different search method locates the items that are returned. To support text searches, you must supply a `Find` method. To support searching by date, you must supply a `DateFind` method.

You can support any of these search methods independently of one another; for example, you can implement the `Find` method without implementing the `DateFind` method.

You may also customize searches by adding a subset of data items from one application to the Selected picker menu in the Find slip. Items added here may be, for instance, a checkbook and ledger from a personal finance program.

A **finder** is a frame that enumerates items resulting from a Find operation. The general characteristics of your finder are defined by the proto it's based on. The system supplies two protos on which to base your finder: the `ROM_SoupFinder` or the `ROM_CompatibleFinder`.

The `ROM_SoupFinder` proto supports searching soup data. The `ROM_CompatibleFinder` proto provides a framework, which you should override, that supports searching data that is not soup based. When a finder based on the `ROM_SoupFinder` proto completes a search, it returns with a cursor which is used to retrieve the found items from the application soup. When a finder based on the `ROM_CompatibleFinder` proto completes a search, it returns with the actual found items in an array (the `items` array).

If you store data in soups, there are standard find methods defined for the `ROM_SoupFinder` proto that you can use. When you devise a different scheme, you must use the `ROM_CompatibleFinder` proto and define versions of the finder methods that are tailored to your type of data storage.

After a search method scans your application's data and returns a finder frame, you must append it to the system-supplied `results` array. Global and Selected finds usually append more than one frame to this array, as multiple applications complete their searches.

While a search continues, the system automatically provides user feedback on its progress. When the search method completes, the system displays an overview list of the items that were found.

For Global or Selected finds, each application (or data set, for a targeted data set find) in which items were found is identified by a heading, with the found items listed under it. The application name that appears in this heading is supplied by the `title` slot each application provides in its base view.

The system sends a `FindSoupExcerpt` message to your application, which must have a `FindSoupExcerpt` method to respond to it. This method must extract and return a string for the Find overview to display. If no items are found, the `FindSoupExcerpt` message is not sent. If you are using the

ROM_CompatibleFinder proto, the string to display for each found item is contained in the title slot of each of the items in the items array in your finder.

When the user taps scroll buttons to scroll through this list of found items, the system keeps track of the user's place in the array of found items. Figure 16-8 depicts the strings from both the title slot and the FindSoupExcerpt method as they are used in a typical Find overview.

Figure 16-8   Strings used in a Find overview

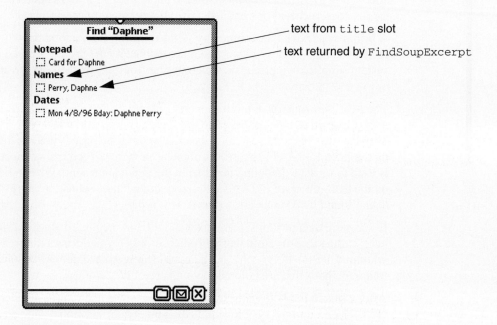

When the user taps an item in the overview, the system sends a ShowFoundItem message to the view specified by the owner slot in your finder frame (which you appended to the system's results array). In the template of the specified owner view, you define a ShowFoundItem method that must locate the found item in your application's data and perform any actions necessary to display it, including scrolling or highlighting the item as appropriate. Although the interface to the ShowFoundItem method varies according to the finder proto your finder is based on, you can often use the same method to display the results of both text and date searches. If you are using a finder based on ROM_CompatibleFinder, you must override its ShowFakeEntry method to call your ShowFoundItem method.

Figure 16-9   The `ShowFoundItem` method displays the view of an overview item

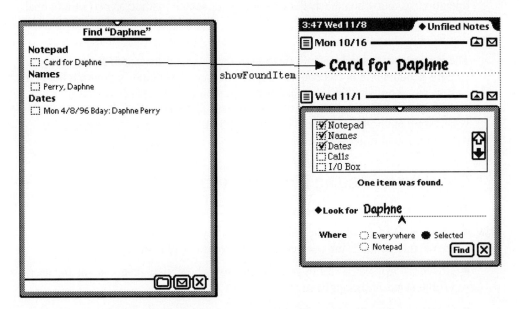

The Find overview provides Routing and Filing buttons. If you are using the `ROM_SoupFinder` the system will file, move, and delete your entries in the overview of found items. In such an occurrence, the soup-change notification mechanism notifies your application. (The soup-change notification mechanism is described in Chapter 11, "Data Storage and Retrieval.")

If you are using the `ROM_CompatibleFinder` you may either not allow your found item to be routed or override the relevant methods.

Note that if the system routes your soup-based data, your application is notified via the soup-change notification mechanism. For a complete description of this mechanism, see Chapter 11, "Data Storage and Retrieval."

Global and Selected Finds

When the user taps the Find button, the system invokes find methods in the appropriate applications. For a Local find, only the currently active application is sent a message. For a Global find, all applications registered with the Find service are sent messages. Selected finds send messages to a user-specified subset of all applications registered for Global finds. In terms of the messages sent, Global finds and Selected finds are similar to Local finds; however, there are some differences in these operations that your application needs to address.

The most important difference between Local finds and other kinds of find operations is that when the system invokes your search method as part of a Global or Selected find, your application may not be open. Therefore, you must test to see that the application soup is available before searching it.

The system informs your search method of the scope of the search through the *scope* parameter. You can choose to ignore it or you can modify your application's actions based on whether the value of this parameter is `'localFind` or `'globalFind`. The system passes the `'globalFind` symbol when it invokes your search method for a Global or Selected find. The `'localFind` symbol is passed for Local find operations.

Checklist for Adding Find Support

To add application support for the Find service, you need to do the following:

- Create a `title` slot, in the view referenced by the `owner` slot of your finder frame, that contains the user-visible name of the application.

- Create the `appName` slot in your application's base view that contains the user-visible name of the application.

- Choose a finder proto on which to base your application's frame. You should use `ROM_SoupFinder` if your data is stored in a single soup, and `ROM_CompatibleFinder` otherwise.

- Supply at least one search method (`Find`, `DateFind`).

- Append the resultant finder frame to the system-supplied `results` array at the end of your search method(s).

- Supply a `FindSoupExcerpt` method that extracts strings from soup entries for display in the Find overview. This method is required only if you use the `ROM_SoupFinder` proto. If you use the `ROM_CompatibleFinder` proto you must add a `title` slot with a string defining each found item to the frame representing the item.

- Supply a `ShowFoundItem` method that displays an individual entry from the found items.

- When using a `ROM_CompatibleFinder` proto, write a `ShowFakeEntry` method to call your `ShowFoundItem` method.

- When using the `ROM_CompatibleFinder`, you should either not allow your found items to be selected (and thus not routed), or override the relevant routing methods.

Optionally, you may also do the following:

- Register and unregister for participation in Global and Selected finds.

■ Employ multiple data sets from one application in a Selected find by adding the method `AppFindTargets`, and one or both of the search methods `FindTargeted` and `DateFindTargeted`.

■ Replace the system-supplied Find slip with one of your own by supplying a `CustomFind` method in your application's base view. This method will be called when the user taps Find and your application is frontmost.

The sections immediately following describe these tasks in detail.

Creating the title Slot

A string that is your application's user-visible name must be available in a text slot called `title`. You need to create this slot in the view referenced by the `owner` slot of the finder frame returned by your search method. Commonly, the `owner` slot references the application's base view and the `title` slot resides in this view.

The Find service uses this string in the list of application names displayed for Selected finds as well as in the overview of found items.

Creating the appName Slot

Your application's base view must contain an `appName` text slot. This slot holds a string that is your application's user-visible name. The value of this slot is used to name the Find slip button that represents your application when it is the current application. It is also employed by other system services to obtain a user-visible name for your application.

Using the Finder Protos

You use a finder proto as the basis from which to construct the finder frame returned by your search method. The two system-supplied finder protos are employed according to the data type you use for your application's data storage. You can create your own customizations at compile time by creating an item like the following example:

```
kMySoupFinder:= {
            _proto: ROM_SoupFinder,

            Delete: func()
            begin
               print("About to delete " &
                       Length(selected) && "items");
               inherited:Delete();
            end
            }
```

Find

The full complement of slots in the finder frame resulting from your searches varies according to the finder proto it's based on. A finder frame based on the ROM_SoupFinder proto returns a finder containing a cursor with which to retrieve found items from the application soup. A finder frame based on the ROM_CompatibleFinder proto results in a frame containing an array of the actual found items.

The ROM_CompatibleFinder proto is meant to serve as a guideline for creating a finder that works on a data storage set that does not use soups. The methods included must be overridden to fit the data type in which your application data is stored.

Several methods and slots are included by both system protos; they include:

- The selected array stores selected items from the Find overview in an internal format. All you can do is pass the array to the Length function to determine the number of selected items.

- The Count method returns an integer with the total number of found items.

- The Resync method resets the finder to the first found item.

- The ShowFoundItem method displays the overview data item that resides in the overview's items array.

- The ShowOrdinalItem method displays an item based on the ordinal number or symbol ('first, 'prev, or 'next) passed to it.

Whenever possible, you should store your application's data in soups and use the ROM_SoupFinder proto to support the Find service, as shown in the following code fragment:

```
if cursor:Entry() then begin
   myFinder := {
      _proto: ROM_SoupFinder,
      owner: self,
      title:"My Application",
      findType:'text, //other possible values are
                      //'dateBefore,'dateOn, and 'dateAfter
      findWords: [searchedForTheseStrings],
      cursor: myCursor,};
```

Table 16-1 provides quick reference descriptions of the ROM_SoupFinder methods. Most should not be overridden, but those that may be are indicated.

Table 16-1   Overview of `ROM_SoupFinder` methods

Method	Description	Override?
Reset	Resets cursor to first found entry. In general you should use ReSync to reset a finder.	No
ZeroOneOrMore	Returns 0 if no found entries, 1 for one found entry, or other number for more.	No
ShowEntry	Causes the finding application to display entry, which is passed to it as an argument. Does not close the Find overview.	No
SelectItem	Marks the item, passed in as an argument, as selected. If this method is set to nil a checkbox does not appear in front of the item.	No
IsSelected	Returns true if the item, passed in as an argument, is selected.	No
ForEachSelected	Calls the callback function, passed in as an argument, with each selected item. The function has one argument: the entry from the cursor.	No
FileAndMove	File and/or move the selected items. Has four arguments: *labelsChanged, newLabel, storeChanged, newStore*. If *labelsChanged* or *storeChanged,* is true *newLabel* and *newStore* indicate the new label and store. If overridden you must check for selected items as in `if selected then // do work;`	Yes, but should call inherited method to do work.
Delete	Deletes all selected items from writeable stores.	Yes, but crumple effect still occurs.
GetTarget	Returns cursor for routing.	Yes

Note

The `ROM_SoupFinder` and `ROM_CompatibleFinder` methods `MakeFoundItem` and `AddFoundItem` are internal methods, which should not be called or overridden under any circumstances. ◆

If your application does not store data as soup entries, you can use the ROM_CompatibleFinder proto as the framework from which to create your finder frame. Although ROM_CompatibleFinder provides most of the services that ROM_SoupFinder does, it does not respond to messages sent by the system when the user files, deletes, or moves items in the Find overview. The following methods have the same definitions in the ROM_CompatibleFinder as they have in the ROM_SoupFinder. If you use ROM_CompatibleFinder proto, in most cases, you must define the following methods to work on your data structures:

- FileAndMove
- Delete
- IsSelected
- SelectItem
- ForEachSelected
- GetTarget

The commonality of definition between these methods causes problems in some cases. For instance, when used with the ROM_CompatibleFinder proto, the ForEachSelected method must be overridden because it is expected to return an array of soup entries.

The ROM_CompatibleFinder proto has the two following methods which are not found in the ROM_SoupFinder proto:

- ShowFakeEntry
- ConvertToSoupEntry

When you use the ROM_CompatibleFinder proto, you should define a ShowFakeEntry method that makes sure your application is open, and calls your ShowFoundItem method.

The convenience method, ConvertToSoupEntry, returns a soup entry when given a data item as a parameter.

Implementing Search Methods

Your application conducts searches in response to messages that it receives from the system. You must supply a search method for each message that your application supports. These methods are usually defined in your application's base view; they include:

- Find
- DateFind
- FindTargeted
- DateFindTargeted

Although the implementation of a search method is for the most part application specific, some general requirements apply to all search methods. This section describes these requirements and advises you of potential problems your search methods may need to handle.

Your search method must be able to search for data in internal RAM as well as in RAM or ROM on a PCMCIA card. Using union soups, which allow you to treat multiple soups as a single soup regardless of physical location, to store your data makes it easier to solve this problem.

As a search method proceeds through the application data, it must test items against criteria specified in the Find slip and collect the ones meeting the test criteria. It also needs to call the SetMessage method to provide a status string that the system displays to the user while the search is in progress. Each of the code examples included later in this section shows how to do this.

When the search is completed, it must append its finder frame to the system-supplied results array. This task is described in detail in "Returning Search Results" (page 16-21).

If your application registers for participation in Global finds, your search methods may be invoked when your application is not open. Thus, your search methods must not rely on your application being open when they are invoked.

Using the StandardFind Method

You can use the system-supplied StandardFind method to search for text in soup-based application data. This method makes the necessary calls to display the status message, gather matching data items, and to append the finder frame that contains the cursor with which to fetch found items to the system's results array. The parameters are described in detail in "StandardFind" (page 13-13) in *Newton Programmer's Reference*.

You must call the GetUnionSoupAlways function, saving the result, before calling StandardFind. Note that your Find method must be defined in your application's base view. Its use is illustrated in the following code example:

```
MyApplicationBase.Find :=
func(what, results, scope, statusView)
begin
   // The following assignment forces the existence of
   // a union soup. Always all GetUnionSoupAlways
   //(saving the result in a local variable) before
   // calling StandardFind.

   local temp := GetUnionSoupAlways (kMySoupName);
   :StandardFind(what, kMySoupName, results,
                 statusView, nil);
end;
```

Using Your Own Text-Searching Method

The following code example illustrates the kinds of tasks you must perform when the StandardFind method is not used. (However, it is strongly suggested that you use the StandardFind method to implement your Find routine, if possible.) This example searches for text in soup-based application data using the ROM_SoupFinder proto:

```
// This routine MUST be named Find; it is called by
// the system when the user chooses Find.
MyApplicationBase.Find :=
func(what, results, scope, statusView)
begin
    local myFinder;

    // Report status to the user;
    // note use of GetAppName and Unicode ellipsis.
    if statusView then
        statusView:SetMessage("Searching in " &
                GetAppName(kAppSymbol)& $\u2026);

    // Presume our soup def is registered,
    // however, app may be closed so get our own soup.
    local mySoup:= GetUnionSoupAlways("My Soup");

    // Make sure a member soup exists so query won't
    // fail (GetMember creates the soup if necessary).
    mySoup:GetMember(GetDefaultStore());

    //Retrieve entries with strings beginning with "what".
    local myCursor := mySoup: Query({text: what});

    // Append finder to system-supplied results array
    if cursor:Entry() then
    begin
        myFinder :=
        {
            _proto: ROM_SoupFinder,
            owner: self,
            title:"My Application",
            findType: 'text,
            findWords: :MyStringSplittingFn(what),
            cursor: myCursor,
        };
        AddArraySlot(results, myFinder);
    end;
end;
```

Finding Text With a ROM_CompatibleFinder

The following example shows how to use the ROM_CompatibleFinder proto to search for text in application data that is not soup based. The sample code immediately following doesn't contain code that actually searches application data, because the implementation of such a search would be specific to the data type used to store the application data.

```
MyAppplicationBase.Find:=
func(what, results, scope, statusView)
begin
    local item, foundItems, massagedFoundItems, myFinder;

    // Set the message in the Find slip.
    if statusView then
        statusView:SetMessage("Searching in " &
            GetAppName(kAppSymbol) & $\u2026);

    // MyFindMethod does the actual searching, since
    // this is too app-specific to do here. It returns
    // an array of all the data items that match 'what.
    foundItems := MyFindMethod(what);

    // Now we create an array with frames of the form
    // mandated for ROM_CompatibleFinder.
    massagedFoundItems :=
        foreach item in foundItems collect
            {
                // Use proto inheritance to protect data
                _proto    : item,
                // This is seen by the user in the Overview
                // (pretend our data is frames w/'name slots)
                title     : item.name,
                // We may add any other slots here our
                // methods may want later
            };

    // Construct the finder frame.
    myFinder :=
        {_proto: ROM_CompatibleFinder, // For non-soup data
        owner: self,// View receiving ShowFoundItem message
        title: "My App",
        items: massagedFoundItems,
        findType : 'text,
        findWords: :MyStringSplittingFn(what),
```

```
    // We may also add slots here...
    };

  // Append myFinder frame to system's results array
  AddArraySlot(results, myFinder);
end;
```

Implementing the DateFind Method

Date-based searches have a lot in common with their text-based counterparts; in fact the only significant difference between these two operations is the search criteria. Rather than matching a text string, the DateFind method tests items against a time value according to the value of the findType parameter. This parameter indicates whether the search should include results for items dated on, after, or before a specified date.

You can simplify the implementation of date-based searches by time-stamping your application's data when it is stored. If you store application data as frames that hold the time they were created or modified in a particular slot, the DateFind method simply tests the value of this slot to accept or reject the entry.

The sample code immediately following shows the implementation of a typical DateFind method using the ROM_SoupFinder proto. This code assumes that soup entries have a timeStamp slot:

```
MyApplicationBase.DateFind :=
func(findTime, findType, results, scope, statusView)
begin
  local myCursor ;
  local querySpecFrame;
  local querySpec;
  local ourFinder;
  local mySoup;
  constant kOneDay := 60*24;

  // report status to the user
  if statusView then
    statusView:SetMessage("Searching in " &
              GetAppName(kAppSymbol) & $\u2026);

  // Get the soup
  mySoup:= RegUnionSoup(kAppSymbol, kSoupDef);
```

Find

```
querySpecFrame :=
{
    dateBefore   :   {
                indexPath : 'timeStamp,
                endKey: findTime,
                },
    dateAfter    :   {
                indexPath : 'timeStamp,
                beginKey: findTime,
                },
    dateOn       :   {
                indexPath : 'timeStamp,
                beginKey: kOneDay *
                        (findTime div kOneDay) ,
                endKey: kOneDay + kOneDay *
                        (findTime div kOneDay) ,
                }
};
local querySpec := querySpecFrame.(findType);

// Get the cursor.
myCursor := mySoup:Query(querySpec);

// Set up finder frame and add it to the results
// array.
if myCursor:Entry() then
begin
    ourFinder := {
                _proto: ROM_SoupFinder,
                owner: self,
                title: "My Application",
                findType: findType,
                findWords: [DateNTime(findTime)],
                cursor: myCursor
            };
    AddArraySlot(results, ourFinder);
    end;
end;
```

Adding Application Data Sets to Selected Finds

You can allow users to choose data sets in an application to search by adding the
AppFindTargets method and either or both of the FindTargeted or
DateFindTargeted methods. This functionality is useful when you want to

limit a Find operation to certain data sets of an application. For example, a personal finance program may have a check ledger, an account list, and a credit card charges list. Another example is an online sales catalog program that could allow users to separately search different catalogs. Even though a single application is receiving the Find message, a Selected find operation from the Find slip allows the user to designate any or all of the associated data sets for the Find operation.

To enable multiple data sets in a find operation, first add the method AppFindTargets to your application's base view. This method must return an array of frames that specify the data sets for the application. These data set frames consist of a name and target pair of slots for each data set, in the following form:

[{name: "*userVisibleText*", target: *thisDataForYourUse*}, {...}]

The name slot of the data set frame holds the string to be displayed in the picker which displays when the Find slip's Selected button is tapped. The target slot, of the data set frame, can be set to anything; it is passed to your FindTargeted (or DateFindTargeted) method. There may be any number of these data set frames included.

An example AppFindTargets method may be defined as follows:

```
MyApplicationBase.AppFindTargets: func()
begin
        [{name:"Check Book", target:'check},
        {name:"Accounts", target: 'accounts},
        {name "Credit Cards", target:'credit}];
end;
```

You must then add the search methods to your finder frame. These methods leverage from the built-in Find and DateFind methods, adding the data set you refer to in the target slot as an additional parameter. You define a FindTargeted method as shown in the following example:

```
MyApplicationBase.FindTargeted:
func (what,sysResultArray,scope, statusView,target)
   // N.B. Scope for Selected find is always 'globalFind
begin
   local mySoup;
   // Assume the target parameter is the name of the
   // soup to search... (We provided this value in
   // base.AppFindTargets.)

   // Must include the following line... See "Using the
   // StandardFind Method."
   local temp := GetUnionSoupAlways(target)
   :StandardFind( what, target, sysResultArray,
                  statusView, 'text);
end;
```

Note

Applications implementing these methods must also implement the usual `Find` and `DateFind` methods since a find operation may be dispatched as other than a Selected find. ◆

Returning Search Results

After constructing the finder frame, your search method needs to append it to the system-supplied `results` array. Each element in this array is a finder frame. In the case of a finder based on the `ROM_SoupFinder`, the array the frame has a cursor for obtaining the items found in the search. In the case of a finder based on the `ROM_CompatibleFinder` proto, your finder frame contains an array of the found items themselves. You need to use the global function `AddArraySlot` to append your finder frame to the `results` array.

The following example shows a line of code that would be placed at the end of your application's search method to store the results of the search. In this code fragment, the `results` parameter is the system-supplied array passed to the `Find` method, and the `myFinder` parameter is the finder frame resulting from the search. The following call to `AddArraySlot` places the finder frame, `myFinder`, at the end of the `results` array:

```
AddArraySlot(results, myFinder);
```

Note that the system's `results` array is cleared when the Find slip closes.

Implementing Find Overview Support

The messages described in this section are sent to your application when the user taps buttons in the Find overview. These include:

- the `FindSoupExcerpt` message
- the `ShowFoundItem` message

If your finder frame is based on `ROM_CompatibleFinder`, you do not need to write a `FindSoupExcerpt` method, but you must also write a `ShowFakeEntry` method to call your `ShowFoundItem` method.

The FindSoupExcerpt Method

If you use the `ROM_SoupFinder` proto to construct a finder frame, your application must supply a `FindSoupExcerpt` method. This methods must extract the name of a found item when it is given the soup entry and the finder frame, and return it to the system as a string to display in the Find overview.

Your `FindSoupExcerpt` method may also extract extra information if the finder frame has been set up to hold additional data. For example, if the date associated with each found item was saved, you could use this information to build more descriptive titles for overview items.

The following example shows the implementation of a simple `FindSoupExcerpt` method:

```
myApplication.FindSoupExcerpt:=
func(entry, myFinder)
begin
   //We simply return the string in our entry's name slot
   entry.name;
end
```

For a complete description of the `FindSoupExcerpt` method, see "FindSoupExcerpt" (page 13-19) in *Newton Programmer's Reference*.

If you are using the `ROM_CompatibleFinder` proto, this finder must contain the strings that a `ROM_SoupFinder`'s `FindSoupExcerpt` method would return. For more information see the description of the `items` array in "ROM_CompatibleFinder" (page 13-7) in *Newton Programmer's Reference*.

The ShowFoundItem Method

This method locates the specified item in your application's data and displays it, performing any scrolling or highlighting that is appropriate. A typical `ShowFoundItem` method may need to

- open a view appropriate for displaying the target
- set the cursor or the `target` slot to reference the target
- scroll the contents of the display view to make the target visible
- highlight the target in the display view

The implementation of a `ShowFoundItem` method depends on which finder proto you use. This section describes an example `ShowFoundItem` method suitable for use with the `ROM_SoupFinder` proto.

If you've based your finder frame on the `ROM_SoupFinder` proto, the `ShowFoundItem` method is passed two arguments: the soup entry that the user tapped in the Find overview, and the finder frame your application added to the `results` array of finder frames.

The system expects your application's `ShowFoundItem` method to look like the following example:

```
ShowFoundItem: func(myEntry, myFinder) begin . . . end
```

In the body of this method, you need to do whatever is necessary to display the soup entry myEntry. Typically, you first send a Close message to the Overview and then open the view that displays the entry. The following code fragment shows the implementation of a typical ShowFoundItem method.

```
// For use with ROM_SoupFinder proto
myApplication.ShowFoundItem:=
func(entry, myFinder)
begin // close my overview if it's open
    if currentView = myOverview then begin
        myOverView:Close();
        myDisplayView:Open();
        // open view that displays the entry
    end;
    // scroll, highlight, etc. as necessary
    // to display the entry
    myDisplayView:DisplayEntry(entry, cursor);
end
```

Your application is always open when the ShowFoundItem message is sent to it. For example, this message is sent when the user scrolls between found items from within the Find slip. The system also invokes this method when the user taps an item in the Find overview. In this case, the system opens your application, if necessary, before sending the ShowFoundItem message to it.

Note that if no items are found this message is never sent.

Using ShowFoundItem with ROM_CompatibleFinder

If you are using a finder based on ROM_CompatibleFinder, you still need to implement a ShowFoundItem in your application's base view. Your finder also needs to override the ShowFakeEntry method. Your ShowFakeEntry method needs to call your ShowFoundItem method, making sure that your application is open first. Your ShowFoundItem method should accept an element of the finder's items array as its first parameter, instead of a soup entry. It should perform the same actions as a ShowFoundItem method that expects a soup entry, as described in "The ShowFoundItem Method" (page 16-22).

The following example demonstrates a typical ShowFakeEntry method:

```
myFinder :=
{
    _proto : ROM_CompatibleFinder,
    ShowFakeEntry : func (index)
    begin
        local myApp;
        if myApp := GetRoot.(kAppSymbol) then
```

```
    begin
       myApp:Open();
       myApp:ShowFoundItem (items[index], self);
    end;
 end,
 ....
}
```

Replacing the Built-in Find Slip

Applications can replace the system-supplied Find slip with a customized version, which is called when the application is frontmost. To implement a custom Find slip that displays in your application, include a method named `CustomFind` in the application's base view. This `CustomFind` method must open the Find slip you constructed and do anything else that's appropriate, including displaying found items.

Reporting Progress to the User

It is strongly recommended that your status messages be consistent with those that the built-in Newton applications display while a Find operation is in progress; for example, you can use a message such as "Searching in *appName*."

Your search method is passed a *statusView* parameter which is the view the system is using to report progress. You can display a string in this view, by calling its `SetMessage` method. Figure 16-10 depicts a typical status message from the Find service.

Figure 16-10   Typical status message

The following code fragment shows how to use the `statusView` parameter to display a progress message to the user:

```
MyAppplicationBase.Find:=
func(what, results, scope, statusView)
begin
    if statusView then
        statusView:SetMessage("Searching in" &
                              GetAppName(kAppSymbol)&
                              $/u2026);

    ...
end;
```

There are several ways to obtain the application name string that replaces the *appName* variable; they are listed here in order of recommended use:

- You can retrieve this string from the `appName` slot in your application's base view.

- You can retrieve this string from the `title` slot in your finder frame.

- You can retrieve this string by calling `GetAppName(kAppSymbol);`

Registering for Finds

Applications registered with the Find service participate in Global finds; they also participate in selective finds when specified by the user.

You do not need to register with the Find service to support Local finds. Global and Local find support use the same mechanism, which relies on the `Find` and `ShowFoundItem` methods that your application supplies. A Global find is simply a series of Local finds initiated by the system in applications that have registered for participation in Global finds.

Use the `RegFindApps` function to register your application with the Find service and its counterpart, the `UnRegFindApps` function, to reverse the effect. You should call these functions from your application part's `InstallScript` and `RemoveScript` functions.

Summary

Finder Protos

```
mySoupFinder:= {        // Use to find soup entries.
   _proto: ROM_SoupFinder,
   owner:self, // View that gets ShowFoundItem message
                 // usually your app's base view
   title: "My Application",// Displayed in Find overview
                      // usually inherited from owner
   cursor:myCursor,// Returned by search method's query
   findType:'text// Must use this value for text search
   findWords:[search strings] // Array of words to match
   selected: [], // Internal array of selected items
   Count: func(),//Returns # found items; don't override
   Delete: func(), // Deletes all selected items
   FileAndMove: func
                   (labelsChanged, newLabel, storeChanged, newStore),
                 // Files and/or moves selected items
   ForEachSelected: func(callbackFunction), // Calls callback
      // func for each selected found item; dont override
   GetTarget: func(), //Returns target frame; for routing
   IsSelected: func(item), // Returns true if item
                      // selected; don't override.
   Reset: func(), // Resets cursor; don't override.
   ReSync: func(), // Resets soupFinder; do not override.
   SelectItem: func(item), // Marks item as selected
   ShowFoundItem:func(item, finder),
   ShowEntry: func(entry), // Displays entry;
                      // don't override
   ShowOrdinalItem: func(ordinal), //Shows found item
                         // specified by integer
   ZeroOneOrMore: func(), // Returns number of items;
                      // don't override
}
```

Find

```
myCompatibleFinder:= {// Use to find data stored in
                      // non-soup data structures.
                      //Override most to fit your data.
   _proto: ROM_CompatibleFinder,
   owner:self, // Required. View that gets ShowFoundItem
             // message;usually your app's base view.
   title: "My Application",// Displayed in Find overview;
                         // usually inherited from owner.
   findType:'text// Can also be 'dateBefore,
                        //'dateOn, or 'dateAfter.
   findWords:[textOrDate]// Text or date to find.
   items:[// Array of the items found by your search.
         {_proto: myFoundItem, //Optional; but better
                        //to reference data as it
                      //gets altered destructively.
         title: "My Application",//String displayed in
                              //Find overview.
         },
         { /* and other such frames... */ },
         ]
   selected: [], // Internal array of selected items.
   ConvertToSoupEntry: func(item),//Return a soup entry
                        //corresponding to data item.
   Count: func(),//Returns number of found items;
             // don't override.
   Delete: func(), // Deletes all selected items.
   FileAndMove: func(labelsChanged,newLabel,
                              storeChanged,newStore),
               // Files and/or moves selected items
   ForEachSelected: (callbackFunction), // Calls callback
             // function for each selected
             // found item; don't override.
   GetTarget: func(), //Returns target frame; for routing
   IsSelected: func(item), // Returns true if item is
                        // selected; don't override.
   ReSync: func(), // Resets finder to its initial
             // state; do not override.
   SelectItem: func(item), // Marks item as selected
   ShowFakeEntry: func(index), // Displays the index(th)
             // number found item. Replaces
             // ShowFoundItem in compatabile finder.

}
```

Functions and Methods

```
RegFindApps(appSymbol)      //registers app. for global &
                            //selected finds
UnRegFindApps(appSymbol)  //unregs. app for non-local finds
statusView:SetMessage(msg)//sets string in progress view
view:StandardFind (what,soupName,results,statusView,indexPath)
                            //searches soups
```

Application-Defined Methods

```
appBase:Find (what,results,scope,statusView) //text find
appBase:FindTargeted (what,results,scope,statusView, target)
                        // targeted text find
appBase:DateFind (findTime,compareHow,results,scope,statusView)
                        // date find
appBase:DateFindTargeted (what,results,scope,statusView, target)
                        // targeted date find
appBase:AppFindTargets ()//sets targets for targeted finds
targetView:FindSoupExcerpt(entry,resultFrame)// returns string
                        // to display in find overview
targetView:ShowFoundItem (foundItem, myFinder) //show found
                                               //item
appBase:CustomFind() //Does all find work
```

CHAPTER 17

Additional System Services

This chapter discusses system services not covered elsewhere in this book. The topics covered in this chapter are

- Providing the capability to undo and redo user actions.
- Using idler objects to perform periodic operations.
- Using the notification service to respond to soup, folder, or user configuration change messages.
- Using the alerts and alarms service to display user messages and execute callback functions at specified times.
- Using progress indicators to provide user feedback.
- Using the power registry to execute callback functions when the Newton is powered on or off.
- Using a custom help book to provide online help to the user.

If you are developing an application that utilizes any of these objects or services, you should familiarize yourself with the material discussed in this chapter.

About Additional System Services

This section briefly describes the undo, idler objects, alerts and alarms, change notification, progress reporting, and power registry services. These are discussed in greater detail later in this chapter.

Undo

The Undo service is the mechanism the system provides for undoing and redoing the user's most recent action. From within each function or method that must support Undo, your application registers a function object that can reverse the actions of that function or method. This function object is called an **undo action,** and is called when the user taps the Undo button. The undo action can then register a function object to redo the original function or method. Thus tapping the Undo button twice completes an undo/redo cycle.

Undo Compatibility

The user interface standards for version 2.0 of the Newton operating system call for the user's second tap on the Undo button to provide a Redo rather than a second level of Undo. Your undo action must create an undo action for itself to implement this interface. For more information, see the section "Using Undo Actions" beginning on page 17-8.

The global function `AddUndoAction` is obsolete, replaced by the view method of the same name that provides similar functionality. Existing code that uses the global function can be converted by prefixing a colon to the message selector. For example:

```
AddUndoAction(....)
```

becomes

```
:AddUndoAction(...)
```

Idler Objects

An idler object sends a message to your view periodically to execute the `ViewIdleScript` method you provide for that view. This allows you to perform periodic tasks from any view for which you have installed an idler object.

Note, however, that the time the `ViewIdleScript` message is sent is not guaranteed to be the exact interval you specify. This is because the idler may be delayed if a method is executing when the interval expires. The `ViewIdleScript` message cannot be sent until an executing method returns.

Change Notifications

The system provides notification services send your application a message when a soup, folder, or user configuration variable has been changed. These are described in the following chapters:

■ The soup change notification service is discussed in Chapter 11, "Data Storage and Retrieval."

■ The folder change notification service is discussed in Chapter 15, "Filing."

■ The user configuration change notification service is discussed in Chapter 19, "Built-in Applications and System Data."

Online Help

Your application can provide a `protoInfoButton` view that displays customized online help to the user (or a `newtInfoButton` if working in the NewtApp framework). Help can also be displayed from the Intelligent Assistant. For a complete description of how to create a help book and integrate it with your application, see version 2.0 of the *Book Maker User's Guide*. For a description of the `protoInfoButton`, see Chapter 7, "Controls and Other Protos." For a description of the `newtInfoButton` proto, see Chapter 4, "NewtApp Applications." For information about displaying online help from the Assistant, see Chapter 18, "Intelligent Assistant."

Alerts and Alarms

The Alert service enables you to display messages to the user. The Alarms service in addition to displaying a user alert, provides applications with a way to perform actions at specified times.

User Alerts

The view method `Notify` displays a user alert slip similar to the one shown in Figure 17-1. The system saves the last four alert messages. The user can scroll through them by tapping the universal scroll arrows while the alert view is open. Also, the user can tap the circled "i" to display the date and time of the message.

Figure 17-1   User alert

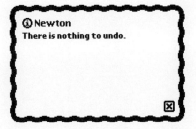

User Alarms

The Alarms service can be used to display an alert slip and execute a callback function at a specified time. If the Newton is asleep at the time the alarm is to execute, the alarm powers up the Newton and executes the callback function. The user can temporarily dismiss the alert for a specified time period by tapping the Snooze button included in the alarm slip, as shown in Figure 17-2.

Figure 17-2   Alarm slip with Snooze button

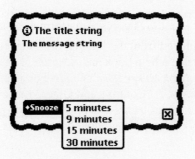

Periodic Alarms

The periodic alarm service sends messages to your application at a specified time. This can be used, for example, by an email client application to periodically log on to a server to check for incoming messages.

The interface to the periodic alarm service is the system-supplied `protoPeriodicAlarmEditor`, shown in Figure 17-3. You can create views from this proto to allow the user of your application to schedule periodic alarms. When the alarm times scheduled in this view come up, a message is sent to your application.

Figure 17-3   A view based on `protoPeriodicAlarmEditor`

Alarms Compatibility

All alarm information described here is new to the Newton 2.0 system. Alarm functionality for 1.x devices is provided by the NTK platform file. See the platform file release notes for the 1.x platform for important compatibility information.

Progress Indicators

This section describes the automatic busy cursor, the notification icon, and the status slip, which you can use to provide feedback to the user during lengthy operations.

Automatic Busy Cursor

When the system is temporarily unavailable for user input, it displays the busy cursor shown in Figure 17-4. Your application need not do anything extra to support the busy cursor; the system displays it automatically. There is a function, ShowBusyBox, however, which shows or hides the busy cursor.

Figure 17-4   Busy cursor

Notify Icon

The notify icon is a small blinking star you can display at the top of the screen to remind the user that an operation is in progress without using the amount of screen space a progress slip requires. The notify icon allows you to register callback functions that are accessible to the user from a pop-up menu that the notify icon displays. For example, you would normally register a function that allows the user to cancel the operation in progress. Figure 17-5 illustrates the notify icon and a menu typical of those it can display.

Figure 17-5   Notify icon

Notify icon's
popup menu

Notify icon

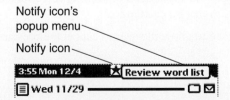

Status Slips With Progress Indicators

For complex operations requiring more user feedback than the automatic busy cursor offers, you can provide a status slip. You can use the `DoProgress` function to call the function that implements that operation. The `DoProgress` function displays a status slip with graphical progress indicators and informative messages. Figure 17-6 depicts a typical progress slip displayed by the `DoProgress` global function.

Figure 17-6   Progress slip with barber pole gauge

The status slip that this function displays is based on the `protoStatusTemplate` system prototype. You can also use this system prototype to provide your own status slips.

Status slips based on the `protoStatusTemplate` may contain any of the following optional items:

- Title text; for example, the name of the application or the operation in progress.

- Message text; for example, "Searching in *ApplicationName*...", "Connecting to modem…" and so on.

- Either a bar gauge, barber pole, or progress indicator that displays relative completeness of the current operation as a shaded portion of the entire gauge. A bar gauge is a horizontal rectangle which is filled from left to right. A barber pole gauge animates a set of diagonal stripes while the operation progresses but does not indicate how much of the operation has been completed. A progress indicator looks like a piece of paper which is progressively filled in.

- An icon; visually identifying the application or present operation. The Find slip in Figure 17-6 on (page 17-6) uses a custom icon.

- A button; this is usually used to allow the user to cancel the present operation.

Power Registry

The Power Registry implements a cooperative model for powering the Newton on and off. When power is turned on or off, this service

- notifies registered applications of the impending change in power status
- allows applications to temporarily halt the shutdown process
- executes registered callback functions

The Power Registry model is based on the registration of callback functions to execute when the Newton is powered on or off. You can use the `RegPowerOn` function to register a callback function for execution when the Newton is powered on. The `UnRegPowerOn` function reverses the action of the `RegPowerOn` function; that is, it removes the specified function from the registry of functions called when the Newton is powered on.

Power-on functions can also be tied to the login screen. The login screen appears when the user powers on a Newton device. Password-protected Newton devices display the login screen until the password is correctly entered. If your power-on function has a visible component, you should tie this function into the login screen, instead of as a regular power-on function. The `RegLogin` and `UnRegLogin` methods are used to register and unregister login functions respectively.

You can use the `RegPowerOff` function to register a callback function for execution when the Newton is powered off. The `UnRegPowerOff` function removes the specified function from the registry of functions called when the Newton is powered off.

Note that "power-off" callback functions can delay an impending shutdown when necessary. For example, your callback function might delay an impending power-off operation until it can successfully tear down a communications endpoint.

Power Compatibility Information

Applications can now register callback functions to execute when the Newton powers on or off. All of the functions that provide this service are new.

The `BatteryLevel` function is obsolete. It has been replaced by the `BatteryStatus` function.

Using Additional System Services

This section discusses how to use the undo, idler objects, alerts and alarms, change notification, progress reporting, and power registry services.

Using Undo Actions

The following code example shows how to provide undo capability in a view. Imagine you have a view that uses cards. The view has a particular method, `DeleteCard`, that it uses to delete a card. Within the `DeleteCard` method, you call the `AddUndoAction` method, passing as its arguments the name of the card deleted and a different method that will add the card (thereby undoing the delete operation). Your call to *view*:`AddUndoAction` would look like the one in the following code fragment:

```
DeleteCard: func(theCard)
        begin
            // statements that delete a card
            . . .

            // call AddCard as an undo action
            :AddUndoAction ('AddCard, [theCard])
        end,
```

You also need to supply the `AddCard` method, which would look similar to the following example. It too provides an undo action—one that calls the original action, thereby completing the Undo/Redo cycle.

```
AddCard: func(theCard)
        begin
            // statements that add a card
             . . .

            // call DeleteCard as an undo action
            :AddUndoAction ('DeleteCard, [theCard])
        end,
```

The Various Undo Methods

The `AddUndoAction` method ties an undo action to a specific view. If that view is no longer open when the user taps Undo, the action does not take place. Because an undo action should generally cause a visible change, it is often desirable to tie the undo actions to views.

When it is not desirable or feasible to tie an undo action to an open view, you can use the `AddUndoCall` or `AddUndoSend` functions to execute the undo action unconditionally. For example, view methods usually use the `AddUndoAction` view method to post their undo action; however, if the view will not be open when the user taps Undo, you may need to use the `AddUndoCall` or `AddUndoSend` functions to post the undo action. If your action relies on the view being open or some other condition, it must test that condition explicitly.

Avoiding Undo-Related "Bad Package" Errors

The `AddUndoAction` method saves the current context (`self`) so that later it can send the "redo" message (the argument to the *methodName* parameter of the `AddUndoAction` method) to the appropriate object. As a result, it is possible that references to your application can stay in the system inside the Undo mechanism's data structures after the application has been removed. These references can cause -10401 (bad package) errors when the user taps Undo after ejecting the card on which the application resides. Using the `EnsureInternal` function on all parameters passed to the `AddUndoAction` function does not remedy this problem.

You can use the `ClearUndoStacks` function to clean up dangling references to `self` that are left behind by the `AddUndoAction` method. The `ClearUndoStacks` function is generally called from the `ViewQuitScript` method of the application base view. You can call this function elsewhere as necessary but you must do so very cautiously to avoid damaging other applications' undo actions.

Note

The `ClearUndoStacks` function deletes all pending undo actions—including those posted by other applications. Use this function cautiously. ◆

Using Idler Objects

This section describes how to install an idler object for a specified view. An idler object sends `ViewIdleScript` messages to the view periodically.

Note that an idler object cannot guarantee its `ViewIdleScript` message to be sent at precisely the time you specify. The `ViewIdleScript` message cannot be sent until an executing method returns; thus the idler's message may be delayed if a method is executing when the interval expires.

Using an idler object is straightforward; you need to

- Send the `SetUpIdle` message to the view that is to receive the `ViewIdleScript` message. This message takes a single parameter: the number of milliseconds to wait before sending the first `ViewIdleScript` message.

- Implement the `ViewIdleScript` method that is to be executed. This method should return the number of milliseconds before the next `ViewIdleScript` message is sent.

- Call `SetUpIdle` again, this time passing in the value 0, or return `nil` from your `ViewIdleScript`. This removes the idler object.

The idler object is removed in any case when the view is closed.

Note
Do not install idler objects having idle time intervals of
less than 100 milliseconds. ◆

The following example prints a random five-letter word in the Inspector until the
view is closed:

```
myButton := {
    _proto : protoTextButton,
    ButtonClickScript : func() :SetUpIdle(100);//start the
                                            //cycle
    text : "Print silly words",
    ViewIdleScript: func()
            begin
                print( GetRandomWord (5,5) );
                //this function's return value
                //determines when it is called next
                2 * 1000; //come back in 2 secs.
            end;
    ...
}
```

Using Change Notification

For a complete description of these services, see the appropriate chapter:

- For information on soup change notification, see Chapter 11, "Data Storage
  and Retrieval."

- For information on folder change notification, see Chapter 15, "Filing."

- For information on user configuration change notification, see Chapter 19,
  "Built-in Applications and System Data."

Using Online Help

You create online help by creating a help book using Newton Book Maker. For
information on how to do this see version 2.0 of the *Book Maker User's Guide*. The
help book can then be displayed from the information ("i") button. This button is
based on protoInfoButton, or newtInfoButton if you are working within
the NewtApp framework. For a description of the protoInfoButton proto, see
Chapter 7, "Controls and Other Protos." For a description of the newtInfoButton
proto, see Chapter 4, "NewtApp Applications."

Help can also be displayed from the Intelligent Assistant. For information about
this, see Chapter 18, "Intelligent Assistant."

Using Alerts and Alarms

This section describes the use of functions and methods that provide alerts and alarms, and the `protoPeriodicAlarmEditor`.

Using the Notify Method to Display User Alerts

The `Notify` method offers a simple way to display a message to the user. This method takes three arguments. The first specifies which type of alert is displayed; some alerts beep, some only log their notice instead of displaying it, and so on. The other two arguments are strings shown to the user in the alert.

The following code fragment creates the slip shown in Figure 17-7:

```
:Notify(kNotifyAlert,"LlamaCalc",
    "You've run out of Llamas!");
```

Figure 17-7   A user alert

Creating Alarms

The `AddAlarm` and `AddAlarmInSeconds` functions are used to schedule a new alarm. You can also use these functions to substitute a new alarm for one that is currently scheduled but has not yet executed.

The `AddAlarm` function creates each new alarm as a soup entry (thus, alarms persist across restarts) and returns an **alarm key** that uniquely identifies the new alarm. This alarm key is a string you provide as one of the arguments to the function that creates the alarm; it includes your developer signature as a suffix. For example, a typical alarm key might be the string `"lunch:myApp:mySig"` or something similar. Note that only the first 24 characters of an alarm key are significant.

IMPORTANT

Do not manipulate the alarm soup or its entries directly. Use only the interface described in this chapter to manipulate alarms. ▲

The following code example adds an alarm set to execute in five minutes:

```
AddAlarm("Alarm1:MyApp:MySig", Time()+5,
   ["Title String","Message String"], nil, nil);
```

The first argument is the alarm key (which this function call returns). The second is when the alarm is to execute. The third is an array of strings to use as arguments to the `AlarmUser` function that displays the alarm slip. If a three-element array is passed in as `AddAlarm`'s third argument, these array elements are used as arguments to the `Notify` function that is used to display the slip. The fourth and fifth arguments are a callback function, and its arguments, which is executed when the alarm executes.

If an installed alarm has the key specified in the call to `AddAlarm`, the installed alarm is removed, and the new alarm is installed.

After an alarm executes, it is made available for garbage collection; thus, alarms that have already executed may no longer exist. For this reason, it is unwise to store references to alarms or try to manipulate them by any means other than the interface the system provides.

Obtaining Information about Alarms

The `GetAlarm` function returns a frame with information about an alarm. The alarm is identified by its key. The frame returned has the following slots:

key	The alarm key.
time	The time at which the alarm is to execute.
notifyArgs	The array of arguments to pass to `Notify` or `AlarmUser`.
callBackFunc	The function object to execute, or `nil`.
callBackParams	Array of arguments to `callBackFunc`, or `nil`.

This frame may contain other slots; do not rely on the values (or future existence) of these slots. You must also not modify this frame in any way.

Retrieving Alarm Keys

The `GetAppAlarmKeys` function returns an array containing the alarm keys of all alarms installed by an application. These keys can be used to pass to the `AddAlarm`, `GetAlarm`, and `RemoveAlarm` functions.

This function relies on all of your application's alarms ending with the same suffix. For this reason it is important for all alarms created by a particular application to use alarm keys ending with the same suffix.

The following code example removes all alarms an application has scheduled for the next five minutes:

```
foreach alarmKey in GetAppAlarmKeys(":MyApp:MySig") do
    if not (GetAlarm(alarmKey).time > Time() + 5) then
        RemoveAlarm (alarmKey);
```

Removing Installed Alarms

The functions `RemoveAlarm` and `RemoveAppAlarms` remove a particular alarm and all of an application's alarms, respectively. The `RemoveAlarm` function takes the alarm key of the alarm to remove as its single argument. Use of this function is demonstrated in the code example in "Retrieving Alarm Keys" beginning on page 17-12.

The `RemoveAppAlarms` function takes an alarm key suffix as an argument and removes all alarms whose key ends with this suffix. For this reason it is important for all alarms created by a particular application to use alarm keys ending with the same suffix. If your application's alarm are not meaningful if your application is not installed, you should call this function in your application's `RemoveScript` function.

Common Problems With Alarms

This section describes common problems encountered with use of the alarm service.

Problems With Alarm Callback Functions

Alarms are kept in a soup; thus, they persist across restarts and installation or removal of packages. This means that the arguments you pass to your callback function are also stored in a soup; hence, these arguments are also copied deeply. (See the description of the `DeepClone` function in *Newton Programmer's Reference*.) Therefore, you must avoid indirectly referencing large objects lest they unnecessarily inflate the size of your entries in the alarm soup.

A classic example of accidentally referencing a large object is in dynamically creating the function object executed with the alarm. Function objects may contain references to the lexical environment and the current receiver (`self`) at the time they are created. For example, function objects created from a view method reference the root view through their parent chain. If you pass such a function object to the `AddAlarm` function, the system attempts to copy the entire root view into the alarm soup. One way to minimize the size of your callback function object is to pass as your callback a one-line function that invokes a method in your application package to actually do the work.

In any case, debugging your callback function is difficult because any exceptions it raises are caught and ignored by the alarm mechanism. Thus, you need to debug your callback functions thoroughly before passing them to the `AddAlarm` function.

Since your application may not be open, or even installed when its alarm executes, your code needs to handle these eventualities appropriately. The following code fragment shows how to test for the presence of an application before sending a message to it:

```
if GetRoot().(kAppSymbol) then
    GetRoot().(kAppSymbol):DoSomething()
else
    GetRoot():Notify(...)
```

Alarms and Sound

The Alarm panel in user preferences controls the volume of alarm sounds. Do not change preferences without the user's knowledge.

Courteous Use of Alarms

Each alarm you schedule uses space in the internal store. You need to exercise reasonable judgment when creating multiple alarms. Your application needs to schedule and use alarms in a way that does not hamper the activities of other applications residing on the user's Newton. While limiting your application to a single alarm might be too restrictive, scheduling a daily wake-up alarm for the next year by creating 365 different alarms would use up a lot of the internal store.

Similarly, your alarm actions should be brief, so they don't interfere with other alarms. If you need to do something time consuming or repetitive, use a deferred action or set up a `ViewIdleScript`.

Using the Periodic Alarm Editor

There is no way to set a periodic alarm programmatically. You can, however, create a view from `protoPeriodicAlarmEditor`, and allow your application's users to set periodic alarms. To attain the functionality of periodic alarms without using the `protoPeriodicAlarmEditor`, you would need to programmatically add new alarms from the callback functions executed when your alarms go off.

There are three steps required to support the alarm editor:

1. Add a method in your application's base view called `AlarmsEnabled`. This method takes no arguments, and should return a Boolean indicating whether your application should be sent the `PeriodicAlarm` message (see next item). If the alarms are not a feature that can be disabled, you can simply define your `AlarmsEnabled` method as:

```
func() true;
```

2. Define another method in your application's base view named `PeriodicAlarm`. This method is called whenever the alarm "goes off." This method is passed a single parameter, *alarm*, that contains information about the present alarm. For information on the *alarm* parameter, see `PeriodicAlarm` in *Newton Programmer's Reference*.

3. Create a view that is based on `protoPeriodicAlarmEditor`. You need to set three slots in this view:

   □ A `title` slot set to a string that is displayed at the top of the view.

   □ An `ownerSymbol` slot set to your application symbol. The system sends `PeriodicAlarm` messages are sent to `GetRoot().(ownerSymbol)`.

   □ An `ownerApp` slot set to a string that names of your application.

IMPORTANT

Do not add child views to a view that is based on `protoPeriodicAlarmEditor`. ▲

Using Progress Indicators

This section describes how to use the automatic busy cursor, the notify icon, the `DoProgress` function, and `protoStatusTemplate` views.

Using the Automatic Busy Cursor

Your application need not do anything extra to support the busy cursor; it is displayed automatically when the system is temporarily unavailable for user input. If you want the busy cursor to appear, or to suppress it's appearance, you may call the `ShowBusyBox` function. This global function takes one parameter, *showIt*, which is a Boolean that determines whether the busy cursor is shown.

Using the Notify Icon

To report progress to the user, most applications display a status slip based on `protoStatusTemplate`. Normally, this slip includes a close box you can use to hide the status slip and add an action to the notify icon. The action shows the status slip again.

Note

Status views that use the `DoProgress` function are an exception to this rule. Do not include a close box in these views. ◆

The notify icon maintains a list of these actions. When the user taps the notify icon, a pop-up menu of actions appears. Choosing an item from the menu invokes that action and removes it.

To add an action to the notify icon and display it, call the `AddAction` method as in the following example:

```
myFunc := func() GetRoot():SysBeep();
theAct := GetRoot().notifyIcon:AddAction("Beep", myFunc,
    nil);
```

You can remove an action by calling the `KillAction` method—for example, if your task in progress completes while the `protoStatusTemplate` view is hidden, you should close the status view and remove the action from the notify icon's menu. You need to save the result the `AddAction` method returns. Pass this object to the `KillAction` method to remove the action from the notify icon's list of actions, as in the following example:

```
GetRoot().notifyIcon:KillAction(theAct);
```

Using the DoProgress Function

To provide user feedback during a lengthy operation, you can use the `DoProgress` function to display a status view and call the function that implements that operation. The `DoProgress` function is suitable only for tasks that complete synchronously. To report the progress of asynchronous work, you must display your own `protoStatusTemplate` view and update it yourself, as described in "Using protoStatusTemplate Views" beginning on page 17-18.

The `DoProgress` function accepts as its arguments a symbol specifying the kind of progress indicator to display (a thermometer gauge or a barber pole), an options frame that allows you to customize the progress-reporting view further, and a function that actually performs the operation on which you are reporting progress.

You must not allow the user to close the progress slip without cancelling the progress-reporting operation—if the `DoProgress` method sends status messages to a nonexistent view, the Newton hangs. You must hide the Close button normally provided by the `DoProgress` method. You can do this by including a `closebox` slot having the value `nil`, in the options frame that you pass to `DoProgress` as shown in the following code fragment:

```
local myOpts := { closebox:nil,
                  icon: kMyIcon,
                  statusText: kAppName,
                  gauge: 10,
                  titleText:"One moment, please..."}
```

The function you pass to `DoProgress` must accept as its sole argument the view that displays `SetStatus` strings to the user. For example, to report status while performing the myFunc function, pass it as the value of the *workFunc* parameter to the DoProgress function, as illustrated in the following code fragment:

```
// options and data are accessible from workFunc because
// the workFunc "closes over" this context
myOpts := { wFnData:"Confabulating",
            closebox:nil,
            icon: kMyIcon,
            statusText: kAppName,
            gauge: 10,
            titleText:"One moment, please."};

workFunc := func (theContextView)
    begin
        for x := 1 to 10 do
            begin
                myOpts.titleText:= :SomeWork(myOpts.wFnData);
                myOpts.gauge := x * 10;
                try
                    theContextView:SetStatus('vGauge,myOpts);
                // handle any exceptions you anticipate
                onexception |evt.ex.foo| do
                    // handle & possibly rethrow if it's fatal
                onexception |evt.ex.bar| do
                    // handle & possibly rethrow if it's fatal
                onexception |evt.ex| do
                    // either an unexpected exception has been
                    // thrown or the user has canceled our
                    // operation. Perform any cleanup
                    // necessary, and be sure to rethrow..
                    ReThrow();
            end; // for loop
    end; // workFunc

progress := DoProgress('vGauge, myOpts, workFunc);
if progress = 'cancelled then
    // this is another place to clean up after being
    // cancelled
```

The workFunc function's argument, theContextView, is the status slip that contains the gauge. A reference to this view is passed to your work function so that you can send it SetStatus messages. Note that workFunc is structured in a way that permits it to call the progress slip's SetStatus method at regular intervals, passing values used to update the progress slip's gauge and message string.

The code above shows the two ways in which your code can respond when the user cancels the operation. If the user taps the Stop button an exception is thrown by SetStatus. You may catch this exception and perform any clean-up necessary. (In the code above the all-inclusive |evt.ex| onexception clause catches this exception.) You must, however, rethrow this exception so the system can perform its own cleanup, otherwise the Newton device appears to hang. You must ensure that any exceptions you do not specifically anticipate are rethrown by your exception-handling code.

You may also perform any necessary housecleaning after an uncompleted operation by comparing the result of the DoProgress function. If the user tapped the Stop button, DoProgress returns the symbol 'cancelled.

Using DoProgress or Creating Your Own protoStatusTemplate

The DoProgress function creates a view based on the protoStatusTemplate to report progress to the user. Using this function is the simplest way to create a protoStatusTemplate view. However, it is not suitable for all applications.

You should use DoProgress if

- Your code is structured synchronously; that is, DoProgress does not return until the *workFunc* function has completed or the user cancels the operation.

- The built-in bar gauge or barber pole status slips which DoProgress uses are suitable for your needs.

- The action is modal; that is, the user cannot do anything until the action finishes or is canceled.

If any of these is not true, use protoStatusTemplate; that is you should create your own protoStatusTemplate if

- Your code is structured asynchronously; that is, it allows user events to be processed normally.

- Your code uses communications; these usually have asynchronous components.

- Your code requires a custom status template type; possibly for a transport.

- Your actions are not modal; that is, the user could proceed in your application or other applications while the action is in progress.

Using protoStatusTemplate Views

You need to take the following steps to use a protoStatusTemplate view to report progress to the user:

1. Specify the components of the status slip and their initial values. You can use one of the system-supplied templates or create your own template.

2. Open the status slip. There are three parts to this process:

☐ Instantiate your status view by passing its template to the `BuildContext` function.

☐ Initialize the status slip by passing the template's setup frame to the status slip's `ViewSet` method.

☐ Invoke the status slip's `Open` method to display the slip.

3. Perform the operation on which you are reporting progress, updating the status slip periodically by invoking the status view's `UpdateIndicator` or `ViewSet` method.

4. Write a `CancelRequest` method which is executed when the user cancels your operation with a "Cancel" or "Stop" button. If your action cannot be cancelled, do not provide such a button.

Each of these steps is described in detail in the following sections.

Defining Status View and Component View Templates

You can create a status slip view from the system-supplied templates `vStatus`, `vGauge`, `vBarber`, `vConfirm`, `vProgress`, or `vStatusTitle` (shown in Figure 17-8), or you can create your own template for this view.

Your status view template must have a `_proto` slot that holds the value `protoStatusTemplate`. It may also include

■ Methods and data that must be available to the status view or its child views.

■ An optional `initialSetup` slot. If this slot is present, the view system uses its contents to initialize the status slip automatically when the slip is opened.

■ A frame describing a custom component template. This is needed only if you do not wish to use one of the built-in templates. This frame must contain the following slots:

height   Height of the status slip, (not the component view) expressed in pixels. Making this value part of the component view template allows status slips to resize themselves based on the height specified by their component views.

name   A symbol representing this template to the `ViewSet` method. For example, if the name of your component template is `'vMyBarber`, this slot should hold the `'vMyBarber` symbol.

kids   Array of frames specifying the view templates used to instantiate the components of this view. These templates should be based on one of the protos described in "Status View Components" (page 14-14) in *Newton Programmer's Reference*.

Figure 17-8 Built-in status view configurations

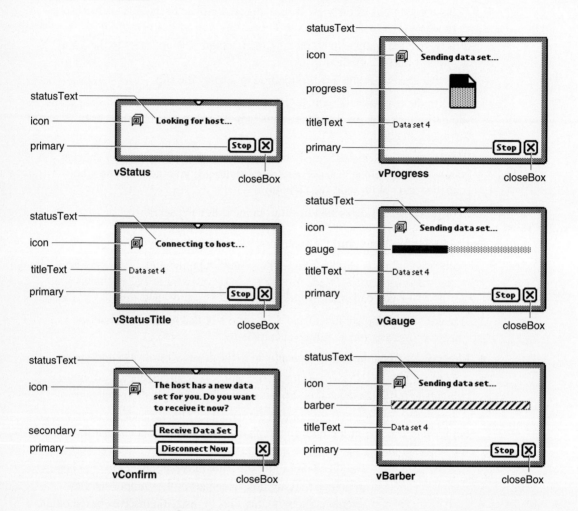

If you want to use a system-supplied template, you can simply define your status template as

```
myStatusTemplate := {_proto : protoStatusTemplate};
```

The definition of myStatusTemplate above does not include an initialSetup slot, so it is necessary to call the ViewSet method to initialize the view when it is instantiated. (This is discussed in "Opening the Status Slip" beginning on page 17-23.)

The following status template defines a more complicated, self-animating, custom barber pole gauge. The myStatusTemplate template defined in this example includes an InitialSetup frame initializes this view automatically before it opens.

```
myStatusTemplate := {
    _proto: protoStatusTemplate,
    // custom self-animating barber pole
    vMyBarber:
        {
        height:105,
        name:'vMyBarber,
        kids:
            [
                protoStatusText,
                { _proto: protoStatusBarber,
                    //we animate ourself in this script
                    ViewIdleScript: func()
                        begin
                            // if hidden, don't bother with updating barber
                            if Visible(self) then
                                // animate barber pole
                                base:UpdateIndicator({name: 'vMyBarber,
                                                values: {barber: true}});
                            // return number of ticks to wait
                            // before returning to ViewIdleScript
                            300;
                        end,
                    ViewSetupDoneScript: func()
                        begin
                            inherited:?ViewSetupDoneScript();
                            :SetupIdle(100);// kick off idle script
                        end,
                },
                { _proto: protoStatusButton,
                    text: "Stop",
                    // ButtonClickScript: func() ...
                    // default is statusView:CancelRequest()...
                },
            //Note that we do not need to include a closebox or an
            //icon these are provided by the protoStatusTemplate,
            //All views created from protoStatusTemplate have
            //these two children.
            ],
```

```
initialSetup: // used to initialize view automatically
    {
    name: 'vMyBarber,
    appSymbol: kAppSymbol,
    values:
        {
        icon: kDummyActionIcon,
        statusText: "Computing IsHalting…",
        closeBox: func()
            begin
                base:Hide(); //close the status view
                //add an action to the Notify Icon, this allows
                //the user to reopen the status view, which is
                //necessary to allow the user to cancel the
                //operation... (we save a reference to the
                //action in the app base view to kill later)
                GetRoot().(kAppSymbol).theNotifyIconAction :=
                        GetRoot().notifyIcon:AddAction(
                            "IsHalting",kNotifyCallbackFunc,nil)
                //the notify icon will need this reference to
                //the status slip
                GetRoot().(kAppSymbol).theStatusSlip := base;
            end;
        }, //values
    }, //initialSetup
} //myStatusTemplate
```

We defined kNotifyCallbackFunc at compile time, so as to avoid creating run-time functions (closures) as:

```
DefConst ('kNotifyCallbackFunc,
    func()
        begin
            if not Visible ( GetRoot().(kAppSymbol) ) then
                GetRoot().(kAppSymbol):Open();
            GetRoot().(kAppSymbol).theStatusView:Show();

            //won't need any more
            GetRoot().(kAppSymbol).theStatusView := nil;
        end);
```

And be sure to include this in your application's `ViewQuitScript` to get rid of the notify icon's action:

```
if theNotifyIconAction then
begin
   GetRoot().notifyIcon:KillAction(theNotifyIconAction);
   theNotifyIconAction := nil;
end;
```

Opening the Status Slip

To instantiate a status slip view from its template, pass the template to the `BuildContext` function, as shown in the following code fragment:

```
statusView := BuildContext(myStatusTemplate);
```

You should use only the `BuildContext` function to instantiate this template.

Next, you need to initialize the view. If your status view template provided an `initialSetup` slot containing a setup frame, the system uses the frame in this slot to perform this initialization automatically. Otherwise, you need to set some initial values for the status view from within its `ViewSetupDoneScript` method. Pass the `ViewSet` method a setup frame, as described in `ViewSet` in *Newton Programmer's Reference.*

Once the view has been initialized, send it the `Open` message to display it, as in the following code fragment:

```
statusView:Open();
```

Reporting Progress

Once your status slip is open you can perform the task on which you report progress. You should structure the task to alternate between performing some work and updating the status slip.

You can use the status slip's `UpdateIndicator` method to update the gauge view only, as in the following example:

```
statusView:UpdateIndicator({values:{gauge: 50}});
```

To update other items in the status slip, you need to use the `ViewSet` method. Although you can use the `ViewSet` method to initialize all the status slip's components, you need not always pass all of these values. Once the status slip is open you need only pass to this method the values to be changed.

```
statusView:ViewSet({
             name: 'vGauge,
             values: {statusText: "Waiting for host...",
                 gauge: 30} // 30% filled
               });
```

Because the ViewSet method rebuilds and updates all the status slip's child views, you'll obtain better performance by calling UpdateIndicator rather than ViewSet when you just need to update the gauge view. The UpdateIndicator method rebuilds and updates only the gauge, barber pole, and progress sheet views.

Implementing a CancelRequest Method

If your status slip provides a "Stop" or "Cancel" button, you may include a ButtonClickScript with the button or write a CancelRequest method to handle the necessary housekeeping. The CancelRequest method can be implemented either in the status slip or in the application (or transport) base view. The system checks if the status slip has a CancelRequest method, and if not sends this message to the application (or transport) base view.

Using the Power Registry

This section describes the cooperative model that Newton devices use to turn power on and off, and the battery information functions.

Registering Power-On Functions

You may register functions to be called when a Newton device is powered on with the RegPowerOn function. When the Newton device is powered on, the system calls your "power-on" callback function passing it a symbol indicating the reason it was called. This allows your code to condition its actions accordingly. For example, you might perform one set of actions when the user presses the power switch and another set of actions when the device is powered on by the execution of an alarm.

The 'user symbol indicates that the user pressed the power switch. The 'emergencyPowerOn symbol is passed any time the Newton device is powered up after an emergency power-off. An emergency power-off is any shutdown in which one or more power-off scripts did not execute. The 'serialgpi symbol indicates the presence of +5 volts on the serial port general-purpose input pin (pin 7). The 'alarm symbol indicates that the power-on was caused by the execution of an alarm. The 'cardlock symbol indicates that a PCMCIA card was inserted or removed.

The UnRegPowerOn function unregisters functions added with RegPowerOn.

IMPORTANT

The callback function registered with RegPowerOn must not itself call RegPowerOn nor UnRegPowerOn. ▲

Registering Login Screen Functions

If you want a power-on function that brings up some sort of visible component, you should register that function as login function. These functions are only called after the login screen has been displayed and the password entered (if the user has installed a password). Note that future Newton devices may not support the login screen. In this case the login functions will still be executed.

The methods that register login functions are defined in the sleepScreen view, to get a reference to the sleepScreen view to send it RegLogin and UnRegLogin messages, use code such as:

```
GetRoot().sleepScreen:RegLogin(callBackFn,callBackFnArgs);
```

IMPORTANT

The callback function registered with RegLogin must not itself call RegLogin nor UnRegLogin. ▲

Registering Power-Off Functions

You may register callback functions to be called when a Newton device is powered off with the RegPowerOff function. As with power-on functions, when the Newton is powered off, the system passes a symbol to your "shutdown" callback function indicating the reason it was called. This symbol, passed as the value of your callback's *why* parameter, allows it to condition its actions according to the way the system was powered off. The 'user symbol indicates that the user initiated the shutdown. The 'idle symbol indicates the system initiated shutdown after the Newton was left idle for the period of time specified by the user's Sleep preferences. The 'because symbol indicates that the Newton powered off for some other unspecified reason.

The system also passes a symbol to your callback function indicating the current status of the shutdown operation. This symbol is passed as the value of your callback's *what* parameter. The value of this parameter is used as the basis for the cooperative shutdown process. Your callback function must return a value indicating whether to continue the power-off sequence or delay it. This value is passed to all registered shutdown functions, allowing each to indicate whether it is ready to shut down or needs time to complete a task.

The 'okToPowerOff symbol indicates that the system has received a request to shut down. In response to the 'okToPowerOff symbol, your callback can return true to specify that shutdown may continue, or it can return nil to cancel the shutdown process. Note that an 'okToPowerOff symbol does not guarantee that shutdown will occur—another callback function may cancel the power-off sequence.

The 'powerOff symbol indicates that shutdown is imminent. If the callback function must first perform an operation asynchronously, such as the disposal of a communications endpoint, it can return the 'holdYourHorses symbol to delay shutdown. After completing the task for which you delayed shutdown, you must call the PowerOffResume function as soon as possible to resume the power-off sequence.

Returning nil in response to the 'powerOff symbol allows the power-off sequence to continue. Your callback function must return the value nil in response to any symbols other than those described here.

The UnRegPowerOff function unregisters functions added with RegPowerOff.

IMPORTANT

The callback function registered with RegPowerOff must not itself call RegPowerOff nor UnRegPowerOff. ▲

Using the Battery Information Functions

Two functions return battery-related information. The BatteryCount function returns the count of installed battery packs. The BatteryStatus function returns a frame with information about the status of a battery pack. This frame contains information about the battery type and charge status, whether the Newton device is plugged in, and other power-related data. Note that the contents of this frame differ depending on the hardware responsible for the battery's operation.

Summary of Additional System Services

This section summarizes the services documented in this chapter.

Undo

Functions and Methods

```
AddUndoCall(callBackFn, argArray) //registers a function to
                                  //call for Undo
AddUndoSend(receiver, message, argArray) //registers a message
                                         //to be sent for Undo
view:AddUndoAction(methodName, argArray) //registers an Undo
                                 //action for a specific view
ClearUndoStacks() // clears Undo stack
```

Idlers

Method

```
view:SetupIdle(milliseconds) //sets up an idler object
```

Notification and Alarms

Proto

```
aProtoPeriodicAlarmEditor := { //creates periodic alarms
   _proto: protoPeriodicAlarmEditor,
   title : string,                 //text at top of view
   ownerSymbol : symbol,           //your appSymbol
   ownerApp : string,              //your app's name
   viewBounds : frame,             //bounds frame

   //don't add child views
...
}
```

Functions and Methods

myApp:AlarmsEnabled() //call PeriodicAlarms?

myApp:PeriodicAlarms(*alarm*) //called when periodic alarm
                              //triggers
AddAlarm(*alarmKey*, *time*, *argsArray*, *callBackFn*, *callBackParams*) //adds
                                              //an alarm
AlarmUser(*title*, *message*) //brings up slip
RemoveAlarm(*alarmKey*) //removes alarms
GetAlarm(*alarmKey*) //gets an alarm
GetAppAlarmKeys(*alarmKeySuffix*) //gets an app's alarm keys
RemoveAppAlarms(*alarmKeySuffix*) //removes an app's alarms
view:Notify(*level*, *headerStr*, *messageStr*) //brings up slip

Reporting Progress

Proto

```
aProtoStatusTemplate := { // report asynch task progress
_proto: protoStatusTemplate,
viewBounds : boundsFrame,       //bounds of slip
initialSetup: frame,            // initial setup values frame
ViewSet: func(setup),           // update the view
UpdateIndicator: func(setup),   // change progress indicator
CancelRequest: func(why),       // called on cancel
...
}
```

Functions and Methods

contextView:SetMessage(*msgText*)// for user msgs in find slip
DoProgress(*kind*, *options*, *workFunc*) // for synchronous tasks
notifyIcon:AddAction(*title*, *cbFn*, *args*) //adds action to notify
                                          //icon
notifyIcon:KillAction(*obj*) //removes action from notify icon
ShowBusyBox(*showIt*) //shows/hides busy box - Platform file
                //function

Power Registry

Functions and Methods

```
BatteryCount() //returns battery count
BatteryStatus(which) //returns info about battery
RegPowerOff(callbackID,callBackFn) //registers a power-off
                                    //callback fn.
UnRegPowerOff(callBackID) //unregisters a power-off
                           //callback fn.
PowerOffResume(appSymbol) //resumes power-off sequence
RegPowerOn(callbackID,callBackFn) //registers a power-on
                                   //callback fn.
UnRegPowerOn(callbackID) //unregisters a power-on handler
loginScreen:RegLogin(appSymbol,callBackFn) //registers a login
                                    //screen callback fn.
loginScreen:UnRegLogin(callbackID) //unregisters a login
                                    //screen callback fn.
```

Intelligent Assistant

The Intelligent Assistant is a system service that attempts to complete actions specified by the user's written input. You can think of the Assistant as an alternate interface to Newton applications and services.

The Assistant can use the built-in applications to complete predefined tasks such as calling, faxing, printing, scheduling, and so on. You can also program the Assistant to execute any task that your application performs. In addition, you can display your application's online help from the Assistant.

This chapter describes how to make application behaviors and online help available from the Assistant. If you want to provide a textual interface to your application or its online help, you should become familiar with the Assistant and the concepts discussed in this chapter.

Before reading this chapter, you should be familiar with the concept of the target of an action, as explained in Chapter 15, "Filing," and you should understand the behavior or service that your application provides through the Assistant. Although it is not essential, it is helpful if you are familiar with lexical dictionaries. Lexical dictionaries are described in Chapter 9, "Recognition."

About the Assistant

This section describes the Assistant's behavior in a variety of user scenarios, and then provides an overview of the templates, frames, and methods that provide this behavior.

Introduction

When the user invokes the Assistant, the system passes the current text selection to it. If no text is selected, the system passes to the Assistant the contents of a buffer that holds the most recent text input.

The Assistant then attempts to match words in the input string with templates and dictionaries that classify the words as actions, targets, or unknown entities. The templates may be supplied by the system or by your application. Some system-supplied templates make use of lexical dictionaries, which are also supplied by the system. For more information about lexical dictionaries, see Chapter 9, "Recognition."

Depending on the amount of information that parsing the input string provides, the Assistant either attempts to complete a task or prompts the user to supply additional information.

Input Strings

The Assistant is preprogrammed with a list of words representing tasks that the built-in applications can perform. In addition to using these words, you can program the Assistant to associate your own words with tasks your application performs. The user cannot add words to the Assistant's vocabulary.

You can associate multiple verbs with a single action; for example, the system supplies a template that maps the words `"call"`, `"dial"`, `"phone"`, and `"ring"` to the same task.

The Assistant uses some of the same dictionaries as the recognition system when attempting to classify items in the input string. For example, it uses the system's built-in lexical dictionaries to classify strings as phone numbers.

The word order in the input phrase is not significant— for example, the input phrase `"Bob fax"` produces the same result as the phrase `"Fax Bob"`. This syntax-independent architecture allows easier localization of applications for international audiences.

Note

The input string passed to the Assistant must not contain more than 15 words. The Assistant does not attempt to interpret strings containing more than 15 words. ◆

No Verb in Input String

If the Assistant cannot determine the user's intended action, it displays an Assist slip that prompts the user to tap the Please picker for more options. The Please picker allows the user to specify an action when the Assistant cannot determine one by parsing the input string.

For example, using the string `"Bob"` as partial input, the Assistant can perform a number of actions: it can find Bob, fax Bob, call Bob, schedule a meeting with Bob, and so on. However, this input string does not indicate which of these actions is the user's actual intent. Figure 18-1 shows the Assist slip as it would appear if the string `"Bob"` were the only input provided to the Assistant.

Figure 18-1   Assist slip

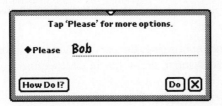

When prompted by the Assist slip, the user must provide additional information on its input line or choose an action from the Please picker. The top portion of the Please picker displays all of the actions currently registered with the Assistant. The Please picker is shown in Figure 18-2.

Figure 18-2   The Please picker

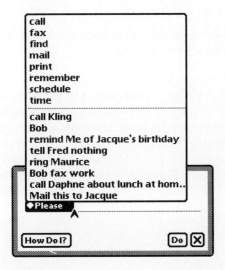

The built-in tasks that the Assistant can complete include calling, faxing, finding, mailing, printing, remembering (adding To Do items), scheduling (adding meetings), getting time information from the built-in Time Zones application and displaying online help. Note that the top portion of this menu displays only one word for each action the Assistant can perform. For example, the word `"call"` appears here but the synonyms `"ring"` and `"phone"` do not. Recently used synonyms may appear in the bottom half of the slip, however.

To allow the user to repeat recent actions easily, the bottom portion of the Please picker displays the eight strings most recently passed to the Assistant. Thus, the string "ring Maurice" appears here, even though the action of placing a phone call is represented only by the verb "call" in the top portion of the picker.

After making corrections to the input string, the user can tap the Do button in the Assist slip to pass the corrected string to the Assistant once again.

Ambiguous or Missing Information

If the input string specifies an action, the Assistant does not display the Assist slip containing the Please picker, but may still need to obtain additional information in order to complete the task.

When an action is specified but required information is still missing, the Assistant tries to supply as much of the required information as possible. For example, if the input string is "fax bob", the Assistant can query the Names soup for information such as Bob's name and fax number. However, the user may still need to correct the input if the Assistant chooses the wrong Bob from the Names soup, cannot find Bob in the Names soup, or cannot find Bob's fax number in this soup.

The user can resolve ambiguities or provide additional information from within a task slip that the Assistant displays for this purpose.

The Task Slip

The task slip provides the user with a final opportunity to correct input to the Assistant and confirm or dismiss execution of the task before the Assistant actually takes action. Although it's recommended that you always provide this opportunity to confirm, modify, or cancel the task before taking action, it's especially important to do so when execution of the task will open other applications or otherwise inconvenience the user.

Figure 18-3   Calling task slip

Programmer's Overview

This section describes how the templates, frames and methods used by the Assistant interact to provide services to the user.

You can think of any user operation as a set of one or more actions to complete. A single action is represented to the Assistant by an **action template.** You can use action templates supplied by the system and you can also define your own action templates.

Some actions require data or objects on which to operate. For example, a phone-dialing action requires a phone number to dial. The data or object on which an action operates is represented to the Assistant by a **target template.** The system provides a variety of target templates, and you can define your own as well.

Each action template or target template defines a set of one or more strings known as its **lexicon.** In general, an action template's `lexicon` slot holds one or more verbs, while the `lexicon` slot of a target template holds one or more nouns.

When any of the words in a template's lexicon appear in the input string passed to the Assistant, the Assistant builds a frame based on that template. For example, the lexicon for the built-in `call_act` template includes the strings `"call"`, `"ring"`, and `"dial"`. When any of these strings appear in the Assistant's input string, the Assistant builds a frame based on the `call_act` template. Frames created from action templates are called **action frames;** frames created from target templates are called **target frames.**

A **task** is a behavior (such as calling, printing, faxing, and so on) that is made available to the user by the Assistant. Usually a task consists of multiple actions and targets, although a task can be as simple as a single action having no target.

You define a task to the Assistant by using the `RegTaskTemplate` function to register a **task template** with the system. A task template is like a recipe: it specifies everything required to perform a particular task, including

- the actions and targets required to provide a specified behavior

- the behavior to provide

- supporting methods and data structures

The task template must specify all of the actions and targets required to perform the task it defines. You provide this information as an array of action templates and target templates residing in your task template's `signature` slot. When the task template is registered with the Assistant, all of the templates in the `signature` slot are registered as well. Once your task template is registered, the Assistant can match user input with words in any of the lexicons of templates specified in the task template's `signature` slot.

Your task template designates one action template as its **primary action.** The primary action is the one that the Assistant associates with a specified verb in its input string. The primary action is represented by an action template that resides in the task template's primary_act slot. Because task templates do not provide lexicons, the designation of a primary action provides the Assistant with a way to associate a verb in the input string with a task template.

In addition to items required by the Assistant, your task template can hold any additional methods or data structures you require to perform the task.

Recall that the Assistant creates an action frame or target frame for each word in the input string that matches a lexicon item in a registered template. If the Assistant can match an action frame with the primary_act slot in a task template, it uses that template to create a **task frame.** The task frame holds all the information defined in the task template, as well as some additional slots that the Assistant provides.

The Assistant creates slots in the task frame to hold action frames and task frames that are created as templates in the signature slot are matched. These slots are named using symbols that reside in a preConditions slot that your task template provides.

Each element of the preConditions array specifies the name of the slot that is to hold the frame created from the template in the corresponding element of the signature array. For example, presume that the fourth element of the signature array holds the call_act template and the fourth element of the preConditions array holds the 'myCallAction symbol. When the call_act template is matched, the Assistant creates in a slot named 'myCallAction in the task frame and places in that slot the action frame created from the call_act template. Later in this chapter, the section "The Signature and PreConditions Slots" (page 18-10) discusses this process in more detail.

If the Assistant cannot match an action frame with any of the task templates currently registered, it displays the Assist slip, which prompts the user to specify an action.

If the Assistant matches more than one action frame with a currently registered task template's primary_act slot, it attempts to resolve the conflict by determining whether additional frames required by the task template are present. The conflict resolution process is described in "Resolving Template-Matching Conflicts" (page 18-13).

Once the Assistant has matched as many templates as possible and stored the resulting frames in the task frame, it sends the PostParse message to the task frame.

Figure 18-4 illustrates a simple example of how the Assistant builds a task frame by matching user input strings with registered templates.

Figure 18-4   Simplified overview of the Assistant's matching process

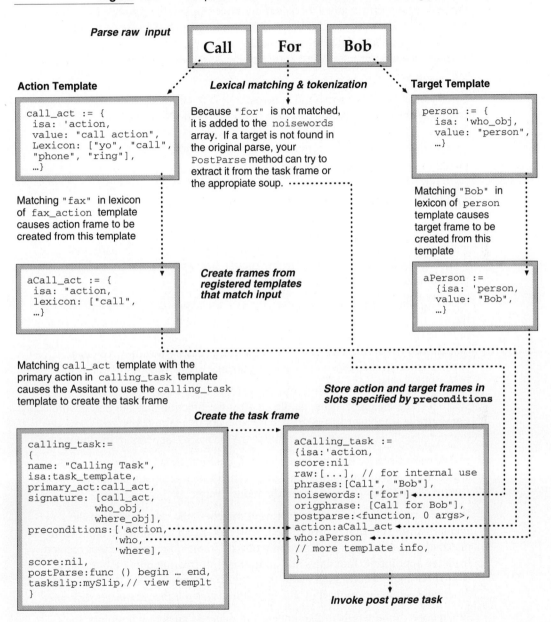

Parse raw input

| Call | For | Bob |

Action Template

Lexical matching & tokenization   **Target Template**

```
call_act := {
  isa: 'action,
  value: "call action",
  Lexicon: ["yo", "call",
  "phone", "ring"],
  …}
```

Because `"for"` is not matched, it is added to the `noisewords` array. If a target is not found in the original parse, your `PostParse` method can try to extract it from the task frame or the appropiate soup.

```
person := {
  isa: 'who_obj,
  value: "person",
  …}
```

Matching `"fax"` in lexicon of `fax_action` template causes action frame to be created from this template

Matching `"Bob"` in lexicon of `person` template causes target frame to be created from this template

```
aCall_act := {
  isa: "action,
  lexicon: ["call",
  …}
```

Create frames from registered templates that match input

```
aPerson :=
  {isa: 'person,
  value: "Bob",
  …}
```

Matching `call_act` template with the primary action in `calling_task` template causes the Assitant to use the `calling_task` template to create the task frame

Store action and target frames in slots specified by `preconditions`

Create the task frame

```
calling_task:=
{
name: "Calling Task",
isa:task_template,
primary_act:call_act,
signature: [call_act,
          who_obj,
          where_obj],
preconditions:['action,
              'who,
              'where],
score:nil,
postParse:func () begin … end,
taskslip:mySlip,// view templt
}
```

```
aCalling_task :=
{isa:'action,
score:nil
raw:[...], // for internal use
phrases:[Call", "Bob"],
noisewords: ["for"]
origphrase: [Call for Bob"],
postparse:<function, 0 args>,
action:aCall_act
who:aPerson
// more template info,
}
```

Invoke post parse task

You define the `PostParse` method in your task template. Your `PostParse` method must perform any actions required to complete the primary task. The `PostParse` method usually acts as a dispatching method that executes the subtasks comprising the primary action. In doing so, the `PostParse` method may validate data and retrieve information that the Assistant was unable to find on its own.

IMPORTANT

Once your `PostParse` method is invoked, it is in complete control of the error-handling and user interface on the Newton. Your `PostParse` method must include any code necessary to complete the primary action, such as code required to display a task slip, validate input, and handle errors. ▲

Matching Words With Templates

This section discusses the process of extracting words or phrases from user input and matching them to templates registered with the Assistant. In particular, this section provides more detail regarding unmatched words, partially matched phrases, and words that match multiple templates.

When the user taps the Assist button, the system passes the current input string to the `ParseUtter` function, which matches words in the input string with elements in the lexicons of templates currently registered with the Assistant. Normally, you do not need to call the `ParseUtter` function yourself; however, you can experiment with the Assistant by passing strings to this function in the NTK Inspector window.

When parsing the input string, the `ParseUtter` function matches entire words only. For example if the word `"telephone"` appears in a template's `lexicon` slot, that template is not matched when the word `"phone"` appears in the input string.

The Assistant's matching process is case insensitive; thus, if the word `"phone"` appears in a registered template's `lexicon` slot, that template is matched when `"Phone"` or `"phone"` appears in the input string.

If absolutely nothing in the input string is matched, the return result of the `ParseUtter` function is unspecified. However, if any word in the input string is matched, the `ParseUtter` function returns a frame containing frames created from the appropriate templates and additional information about the matched words. For more information about the result frame returned by the `ParseUtter` function, see the description of this function in *Newton Programmer's Reference*.

When none of the words in the input string matches an action template, the Assistant may use the information it did match to try to determine a likely action. For example, when the user enters the phrase `"buzz 555-1234"`, the Assistant does not match the word `"buzz"` to an action template but it can identify

"555-1234" as having the format of a telephone number. Based on that information, the Assistant creates a task frame from the built-in call_act template and displays a call slip to prompt the user for additional information.

When no action template is matched, or more than one is matched, the Assistant compares the number of matched target templates for each task with the total number of targets for that task. The Assistant creates the task frame from the task template having the highest percentage of targets matched and then invokes that task frame's PostParse method.

If two or more tasks have the same percentage of matched target templates, then the Assistant displays the slip containing the Please picker and prompts the user to choose an action. Under these circumstances, the Please picker contains only words representing the candidate templates.

To permit more natural interaction, the Assistant ignores words that do not appear in any registered template's lexicon. Rather than limiting the user to terse commands, the Assistant extracts meaningful words from phrases such as "Make a call to Bob at work" and ignores the others. For example, the words "call", "Bob" and "work" are meaningful to the Assistant because they appear in the lexicons of registered templates. (In this case, the templates are supplied and registered by the system.) On the other hand, because the words "a", "to", and "at" do not appear in the lexicons of any registered templates, they are not matched and are therefore ignored.

Unmatched words appear in the noiseWords slot of the frame that the ParseUtter function returns. Your PostParse method may be able to use the contents of this array to determine further information about the user's intended action. For example, if there are no entries for Bob in the Names soup, the word "bob" is not matched and is returned as an element of the noiseWords array. The word "to" is also likely to show up in this array. Because words are added to this array in the order they were parsed, your PostParse method can extract the word following "to" from the noiseWords array and attempt to use it as a target. The recommended action in this situation is to use this information to fill out a task slip that is displayed to the user for confirmation.

When a word appears in the lexicon of more than one template, it can cause the Assistant to match the wrong template. For example, two games might both register action templates having the word "play" in their lexicon, or you might attempt to register a template that duplicates a word in the lexicon of one of the system-supplied templates. A strategy for resolving these kinds of conflicts is described in "Resolving Template-Matching Conflicts" (page 18-13).

The Signature and PreConditions Slots

Your task template must define two slots, called `signature` and `preConditions`, which store arrays of templates and symbols, respectively.

The `signature` slot holds action templates and target templates that must be matched to complete the primary action. The `preConditions` slot specifies the names of slots that the Assistant creates in the task frame as templates in the `signature` slot are matched.

Each element of the `preConditions` array is related to the corresponding element of the `signature` array. Specifically, an element of the `preConditions` array specifies the name of the slot that the Assistant creates in the task frame when the template in the corresponding element of the `signature` array is matched.

For example, to send a fax the Assistant needs frames representing the action of faxing, a fax number, the name of the person to whom the fax is sent, and the time at which the fax is to be sent. The `signature` slot in the following code fragment specifies by name the templates required to create these frames.

```
{...
// example: when fax_number is matched, Assistant creates
// a 'number slot in task frame & puts target frame in it
signature: [fax_action, fax_number, who_obj, when_obj],
preConditions: ['action, 'number, 'recipient, 'when],
...}
```

The corresponding elements of the `preConditions` slot specify the names of slots that the Assistant creates in the task frame to hold the frames created as the templates in the `signature` slot are matched. For example, the `preConditions` array in the previous code fragment specifies that the Assistant creates slots named `action`, `number`, `recipient` and `when` in the task frame as necessary.

Continuing with the example based on the previous code fragment, when the Assistant parses the input phrase `"fax Bob"`, it matches the word `"fax"` to the `fax_action` template in the first element of the `signature` array and creates an action frame from this template. The Assistant places this action frame in an `action` slot (named for the symbol in the first element of the `preConditions` array) that it creates in the task frame. Similarly, the Assistant creates a target frame when the word `"Bob"` is matched to the `who_obj` template in the third element of the `signature` array. The Assistant places this target frame in a `recipient` slot (named for the symbol in the third element of the `preConditions` array) that it creates in the task frame.

Words representing elements of the `signature` array do not necessarily need to appear in the input string in order to be matched to a template; for example, your `PostParse` method might supply Bob's fax number by finding it in the Names soup.

The Assistant creates a slot in the task frame only when a template is matched. For example, if the `when_obj` template is not matched, the `when` slot is not created.

If any frame represented in the `signature` array is not present (that is, if its lexicon was not matched) the Assistant may still call your `PostParse` method if it can match an action frame with your task template's primary action. Your `PostParse` method must validate all input and deal with missing objects appropriately. For example, if your `PostParse` method cannot obtain the missing information by parsing the task frame or looking elsewhere for it (such as in the appropriate soup), it can display a task slip to solicit further input from the user.

The Task Frame

When your `PostParse` method is called, the `ParseUtter` function will have added slots to the task frame. You can use the information in these slots for your own purposes. For example, your `PostParse` method can extract additional information for use in displaying a task slip.

This section describes the `entries`, `phrases`, `noiseWords`, `value` and `origPhrase` slots that the `ParseUtter` function adds to the task frame. These slots are added only when they are needed to hold information. For example, if no soup entries are matched in the parsing process, the `entries` slot is not added to the task frame.

The Entries Slot

If a template matches a soup entry, an alias to that entry is returned as an element of the array residing in the `entries` slot of the task frame. To retrieve an entry from this array, use the `GetMatchedEntries` global function.

The Phrases Slot

The result frame returned by the `ParseUtter` function contains a `phrases` slot that holds an array of strings. Each word in the input phrase that matches a template is returned as an element of the `phrases` array.

For example the following code fragment depicts the `phrases` array that might be returned after parsing the input string `"call Bob"`.

```
// input string is "call Bob"
{...
phrases: ["call", "Bob"],
...}
```

Elements of the `phrases` array can store more than a single word. For example, if the parser searches the Names soup for an object of the type `who_obj` having the value "Bob Anderson", that element of the phrases array stores the entire string "Bob Anderson", as the following code fragment shows:

```
// input string is "call bob anderson"
{...
phrases: ["bob anderson", "call"],
...}
```

Note that strings may appear in the phrases array in a different order than they did in the original input to the Assistant.

The OrigPhrase Slot

The original input phrase is returned as a single string that resides in the task frame's origPhrase slot. You can examine this slot to determine the number and ordering of words in the original input string.

The Value Slot

Some values can be parsed correctly only by using a lexical dictionary that describes their format. These values include formatted numbers such as phone numbers, currency values, dates, and times.

When the Assistant uses a lexical dictionary to parse an object, it returns the parsed phrase as a single string in the value slot. For example, if the user had entered the phrase "Call 555-1212" the Assistant would store the phone number in the value slot, as shown in the following example:

```
{...
input: [{isa: {value: "action"},
        Lexicon: [["call", "phone", "ring", "dial"]],
        value: "call"},
        {isa: {isa: {isa: {#4B9F1D},
                     value: NIL,
                     Lexicon: [#4B9FA1]}},
        value: "555-1212"}],
...}
```

Note that the value slot is created only when the Assistant uses a lexical dictionary to parse a formatted string such as a time, date, phone number, or monetary value.

Resolving Template-Matching Conflicts

Template matching conflicts may arise when a template's lexicon includes a word that appears in the lexicon of another registered template. This section describes the means by which the Assistant attempts to resolve such conflicts.

When a verb matches more than one action template, the Assistant must choose the appropriate action template. For example, imagine that two games, Chess and Checkers, are currently loaded in the Extras Drawer. If both games specify the word "play" in their action template's lexicon, the Assistant cannot open the correct application by simply matching this verb; the correct game to open must be determined by some other means. For example, the code fragment below shows the template for an action, play_act, that might conceivably be defined by both games:

```
play_act := { value: "play action",
              isa: 'dyna_user_action,
          lexicon: [ "play"  ]
              }
```

The task templates for each of these games might look like the following example. Note that both templates define play_act as the primary action:

```
chessTemplate := {
            value:  "Chess Template",
            isa:  'task_template,
            primary_act:  play_act,
            preConditions:  ['generic_action,'action, 'game],
            signature:  ['dyna_user_action, play_act,
                         chess_obj],
            PostParse: func()
                     begin
                         print("we made it, chess!");
                     end,
            score:  nil},

checkersTemplate := { value:  "Checkers Template",
              isa: 'task_template,
              primary_act: play_act,
              preConditions: ['generic_action, 'action,
                                'game],
              signature: ['dyna_user_action, play_act,
                           chkrs_obj],
              PostParse: func()
                       begin
                           print("we made it, checkers!");
                       end,
              score:  nil},
```

If you specify the `'dyna_user_action` symbol as the first element of your task template's `signature` slot, any target that distinguishes one template from another enables the Assistant to select the correct template. For example, the two target templates in the following code fragment represent the games Chess and Checkers, respectively:

```
chess_obj := {value: "chess obj",
              isa: 'dyna_user_obj,
              lexicon: [ "chess" ]
              }

chkrs_obj := {value: "checkers obj",
              isa: 'dyna_user_obj,
              lexicon: [ "checkers" ]
              }
```

The fact that the lexicons in these templates do not match allows the Assistant to resolve the ambiguity. When the string `"play chess"` is passed to the Assistant, the word `"play"` is matched to the `play_act` template and the Assistant creates an action frame from that template. Similarly, the Assistant matches the word `"chess"` with the `chess_obj` template's lexicon and creates a target frame from that template.

Note that the `play_act` action frame can be matched to the `primary_act` of either the `chess_Template` or the `checkers_Template`. Because the signatures of both of these templates specify the `dyna_user_action` and `play_act` frame types as their first two elements, the conflict is not resolved until the third element of one of these `signature` arrays is matched.

The `chess_obj` target frame matches the third element of the signature for the `chess_template`. It does not match any elements of the signature in the `checkers_Template`. Thus, matching the word `"chess"` resolves the conflict because the only `signature` array that has been matched completely is that of the `chess_Template`.

Compatibility Information

The Assistant now matches entire words only, instead of allowing partial matches.

The Assistant no longer uppercases the words that it returns.

The Assistant now adds the eight most recently parsed phrases to the bottom of the Please pop-up menu. Phrases do not need to be interpreted successfully by the Assistant to be included in this list.

The result frame returned by the `ParseUtter` function contains a new slot named `entries`, which holds an array of aliases to soup entries that were matched when parsing the input string. To retrieve these entries, you must use the new `GetMatchedEntries` global function.

Using the Assistant

This section describes how to make an application behavior available through the Assistant, as well as how to display online help from the Assistant. This material presumes understanding of the conceptual material provided in previous section.

Making Behavior Available From the Assistant

You need to take the following steps to make an application behavior available through the Assistant:

1. Create an action template for your primary action. If necessary, create additional action templates that define subtasks of the primary action.

2. Create zero or more target templates. (Some actions require no target; others may use system-supplied target templates.)

3. Implement your `PostParse` method.

4. Create a task template.

5. Register and unregister your task template with the Assistant at the appropriate times.

The sections immediately following describe these tasks in detail.

It is recommended that you begin by defining the action and target templates required to complete the primary action. After doing so, you will have a better idea of the tasks your `PostParse` method needs to handle. After creating all the necessary templates and writing a suitable `PostParse` method, defining the task template itself is likely to be a trivial chore.

Defining Action and Target Templates

Action templates and target templates are simply frames that contain a specified set of slots and values. You need to define templates for all the actions and targets required to complete a task. One of the action templates must define the primary action.

Take the following steps to define an action template or a target template:

1. Define a frame containing the `value`, `isa` and `lexicon` slots.

2. Assign the frame to a slot or variable that is the name of the template.

3. Place in the `value` slot a string that identifies the action or target that this template defines.

4. If the template defines an action, place the symbol `'dyna_user_action` in its `isa` slot. If the template defines a target, place the symbol `'dyna_user_obj` in its `isa` slot.

5. Define the words or phrases this template is to match as an array of strings in its lexicon slot. If you place the name of a system-supplied template in your template's isa slot, your template inherits its lexicon from the system-supplied template. You should be aware, however that isa slot values other than the symbols 'dyna_user_action and 'dyna_user_obj may interfere with the system's ability to match your template successfully. For more information, see the section "Defining Your Own Frame Types to the Assistant," immediately following.

Sample Action Template

The following code fragment defines an action template called myPayAction that might be used by a home banking application:

```
myPayAction := {
    value:   "Pay Action",      // name of action
    isa:     'dyna_user_action  // must use this value
    lexicon: ["pay", "paid"]    // words to match
}
```

Sample Target Template

The following code fragment defines a target template called cbPayee that a home banking application might use:

```
myPayee := {
    value:   "Who Object",      // name of target
    isa:     'dyna_user_obj     // must use this value
    lexicon: ["to", "Bob"]      // words to match
    }
```

Defining Your Own Frame Types to the Assistant

The conflict resolution mechanism relies on the use of system-supplied dynamic user object templates. You can define your own symbol for your template's isa slot as long as it ultimately refers to a template with the symbol 'dyna_user_action or 'dyna_user_obj as the value of its isa slot. For example, you can define a my_action template that is a 'dyna_user_action, as shown in the following code fragment:

```
my_action := {
    value:   "my action"        // name of this action
    isa:     'dyna_user_action,  // must use this value
    lexicon: ["jump", "hop"]     // words to match action
}
```

Based on the definition above, you can derive a `my_other_action` template that holds the value `'my_action` in its `isa` slot, as in the following example:

```
my_other_action := {
    // name of this action
    value:    "my other action",
    // subclass of 'dyna_user_action
    isa:      'my_action,
    // words matching this action
    lexicon: ["leap", "lunge"]
}
```

You can take a similar approach to define your own target object types by placing the `'dyna_user_obj` symbol in your target template's `isa` slot. For example, you can define a template `my_target` that is a `dyna_user_obj` and use its symbol in this slot also, as in the following code fragment:

```
my_target := {
    value:    "my target"     // name of this target
    isa:      'dyna_user_obj // must use this value
}
```

Based on the definition above, you can derive another target template from `my_target`, and store the value `'my_target` in its `isa` slot, as in the following example:

```
my_other_target := {
    value:"my other target",// name of this targe
    isa:  'my_target,        // subclass of 'dyna_user_obj
}
```

Implementing the PostParse Method

Your `PostParse` method implements the behavior your application provides through the Assistant. This method resides in the `PostParse` slot of your task template. It is called after all the templates in the `signature` slot have been matched.

Your `PostParse` method must provide any behavior required to complete the specified task, such as obtaining additional information from the `ParseUtter` result frame as necessary, and handling error conditions.

Sample PostParse Method

The following code fragment is an example of a `PostParse` method that tests for the existence of the `value` slot and accesses its content:

```
PostParse: func()
begin
  local thePhraseText;
      // self is the task frame
    if hasSlot(self, 'value) then
    thePhraseText := self.value;
    else
    // handle missing input
  end;
  // display phrase text in task slip
  end;
end;
```

Defining the Task Template

Your task template defines a primary action and its supporting data structures.

Take the following steps to define a task template:

1. Define a frame containing the `value`, `isa`, `primary_act`, `PostParse`, `signature`, `preConditions`, and `score` slots. Subsequent bullet items in this section describe the contents of these slots.

2. Assign the frame to a slot, variable, or constant that is the name of the task template.

3. Place a string in the `value` slot that identifies the task that this template defines.

4. Place the `'task_template` symbol in the `isa` slot.

5. Place the name of the slot or variable defining your primary action in the `primary_act` slot.

6. Place the name of the slot, variable or constant defining your `PostParse` method in the `PostParse` slot.

7. Place in the `signature` slot an array of the names of all action and target templates required to complete this task.

8. Place an array of symbols in the `preConditions` slot that specifies the names of slots the Assistant must create to hold frames built from the templates specified in the `signature` array. The `preConditions` and `signature` arrays must have the same number of elements. Furthermore, the symbols in the `preConditions` array must appear in the same ordinal position as their counterparts in the `signature` array; that is, the first element of the

preConditions array is related to the first element of the signature array, the second element of the preConditions array is related to the second element of the signature array, and so on. For more information, see the section "The Signature and PreConditions Slots" (page 18-10).

9. Place the value nil in the score slot. This slot is used internally by the Assistant.

Sample Task Template

The following code fragment is an example of a task template. This template might be used to implement an action in a home banking application:

```
payTemplate := {
    value:        "Pay Template",   // name of this template
    isa:          'task_template,   // must use this value
    primary_act: myPayAction,       // primary action
    PostParse:    func () begin … end, // PostParse method
    // required templates
    signature:    [myPayAction, myWho, myAmount, myWhen],
    // slots to create as required templates are matched
    preConditions: ['action, 'name, 'amount, 'when],
    score:        nil               // for internal use
}
```

Registering and Unregistering the Task Template

To register your task template, call the RegTaskTemplate function from your application part's InstallScript function. When the task template is registered successfully, the value returned by RegTaskTemplate is a reference to the task frame. You need to save a reference to the value returned by this function, because you'll need that value later to unregister the task template. If RegTaskTemplate returns nil, the template was not registered successfully.

To unregister your task template, call the UnRegTaskTemplate function, passing as its argument the result that was returned by RegTaskTemplate when you first registered the task template. It is recommended that you call the UnRegTaskTemplate function from your application part's RemoveScript method.

Displaying Online Help From the Assistant

Application help takes the form of a help book created with Newton Book Maker. You need to take the following steps to open a help book from the Assistant:

1. In your application's base view, define a viewHelpTopic slot. The value of this slot is a string that is the name of a topic in the help book to be opened.

2. Define an action template for opening the appropriate help book. The global functions ShowManual and OpenHelpTo open the system-supplied help book. The OpenHelpBook and OpenHelpBookTo functions open a help book that you supply. The ShowManual function is described in "Utility Functions" (page 26-1). All of these functions are described in version 1.1 of the *Newton Book Maker User's Guide* .

3. Define a task template that holds the name of your action template as the value of its primary_act slot.

4. Register and unregister the task template at the appropriate times.

For information on defining, registering, and unregistering templates, see the preceding section, "Making Behavior Available From the Assistant" (page 18-15).

For information on displaying online help from an information button that your application provides, see "protoInfoButton" (page 6-10) in *Newton Programmer's Reference*.

Routing Items From the Assistant

When routing an item from the Assistant—for example, when filing, faxing, printing, or mailing the item—the Assistant sends a GetTargetInfo message to your application. The root view supplies a default GetTargetInfo method that returns information such as the item to be routed and the view that is able to manipulate it. This method relies on target and targetView slots supplied by your application's base view. You can define your own GetTargetInfo method if you need to supply different target information. For more information, see "Specifying the Target" (page 15-13). For detailed information on supporting routing in your application, see "Routing Interface" (page 21-1).

Normally the GetTargetInfo message is sent to the application's base view; however, such behavior may not be appropriate for applications having more than one view with user data. For example, the built-in Notepad application can display multiple active Notes.

To specify that the GetTargetInfo message be sent to a view other than your application base view, your application's base view must provide a GetActiveView method that returns the view to which the GetTargetInfo message is sent. The GetTargetInfo message is sent to the view specified by the return result of the GetActiveView method.

Summary

Data Structures

Task Frame

```
// Returned by ParseUtter function
{
    // original user input phrase
    origphrase: ["str1", "str2", … "strN"],
    // strings that matched registered templates
    phrases: ["aStr1", "aStr2", … "aStrN"],
    // strings that did not match registered templates
    noisewords: ["noiseStr1", "noiseStr2", … "noiseStrN"],
    // Aliases to soup entries that were matched
    // You must use GetMatchedEntries fn to retrieve
    entries: [alias1, alias2, … aliasN],
    // formatted strings returned by lexical parse, if any
    value : ["lexStr1", "lexStr2", … "lexStrN"],
    // method that performs primary act
    PostParse : func() begin … end,
    // additional slots & methods defined in task template
    …}
```

Templates

Task Template

```
// defines task and provides supporting objects & methods
myTask := {
    isa: 'task_template, // Required. Must use this value
    // Action template that defines lexicon for this task
    primary_act: myAct, // Required.
    // Required. Templates used by this task
    signature: [myTarget1, myAct1, … , myTargetN, myActN],
    // Required. Names of slots created in the task frame
    // as templates are matched
    preconditions : ['mySlot1, 'mySlot2, … 'mySlotN],
    // Required. Method that performs the task
    PostParse: func() begin … end,
```

```
// Optional. View template that defines task slip
taskslip : myTaskSlipView,
// internal use only - always put nil in this slot
score: nil,
// your additional slots and methods
...}
```

Action Template

```
// defines action words to Assistant
my_act := {
   // string may be replaced in lexical parse
   value: string , //Required.
   // object type that this template creates
   // must use this value or one descended from it
   isa: 'dyna_user_action, // Required.
// Words or phrases to match with this template
lexicon: [string1, string2,...stringN],// Required.
}
```

Target Template

```
// defines object of an action to Assistant
my_Target := {
   // string may be replaced in lexical parse
   value: string , //Required.
   // object type that this template creates
   // must use this value or one descended from it
   isa: 'dyna_user_obj, // Required.
   // Words or phrases to match with this template
   lexicon: [string1, string2,...stringN],// Required.
   // your template can include your own slots as well
   ...}
```

Developer-Supplied Task Template

You must always supply a task template, which defines the application behavior
made available through the Assistant.

System-Supplied Action Templates

```
// base your action templates on this generic action
dyna_user_action:= {
   // this template has no lexicon
   ...}

// Action template for dialing the telephone
call_act:= {
   // Words or phrases to match with this template
   // lexicon: ["call", "phone", "ring","dial"],
   ...}

// Action template for using the Find service.
find_act := {
   lexicon :["find", "locate", "search for", "look for"],
   ...}

//Action template for faxing the target data item
fax_act:= {
   lexicon: ["fax"],
   ...}

//Action template for printing the target data item
print_act:= {
   lexicon: ["print"],
   ...}

// Action template for displaying the About box
about_act := {
   lexicon: ["about newton"],
   ...}

// Action template for retrieving time values
// from the Time Zones application
time_act := {
   lexicon: ["time", "time in","the time in",
             "what time is it", "what time is it in",
             "the time in", "what time",
             "what is the time", "what is the time in"],
   ...}
```

Intelligent Assistant

```
// Action template for creating To Do items
remind_act := {
    lexicon: ["remember", "remind", "remind me",
              "to do", "todo", "don't forget to",
              "don't let me forget to"],
    …}

// Action template for sending electronic mail
mail_act := {
    lexicon: ["mail", "send", "email"],
    …}

// Action template for scheduling meetings
// and events in the Dates application
schedule_act := {
    lexicon: ["schedule"],
    …}

// Action template for scheduling meetings
// and events in the Dates application
meet_act := {
    lexicon: ["meet", "meet me", "see", "talk to"],
    …}

// Action template for scheduling meals in Dates app
meal_act := {…}
```

Meals

```
// Action template for scheduling breakfast in Dates app
breakfast_act := {
    isa: 'meal_act,
    usualTime:"7:00 am",
    lexicon: ["breakfast"],
    …}

// Action template for scheduling brunch in Dates app
brunch_act := {
    isa: 'meal_act,
    usualTime:"10:00 am",
    lexicon: ["brunch"],
    …}
```

```
// Action template for scheduling lunch in Dates app
lunch_act := {
    isa: 'meal_act,
    usualTime:"12:00 pm",
    lexicon: ["lunch"],
    ...}
```

```
// Action template for scheduling dinner in Dates app
dinner_act := {
    isa: 'meal_act,
    usualTime:"7:00 pm",
    lexicon: ["dinner"],
    ...}
```

Special Events

```
birthday := {
    isa: 'special_event_act,
    Lexicon: ["birthday","bday","b-day"],
    ...}
```

```
anniversary := {
    isa: 'special_event_act,
    Lexicon: ["anniversary"],
    ...}
```

```
holiday := {
    isa: 'special_event_act,
    Lexicon: ["holiday"],
    ...}
```

Developer-Supplied Action Templates

You must supply the action template specified by the value of your task template's `primary_act` slot.

You must supply any additional templates specified by the `signature` slot of the task template.

Intelligent Assistant

System-Supplied Target Templates

Places

```
// list of system-supplied where_obj target templates
// system uses lexical dictionaries to match these
// templates so they do not provide lexicons
address, city, region, country, postal_code,
phone,parsed_phone, phone_tag, faxPhone, homePhone,
workPhone, carPhone, mobilePhone, beeper, places, company,
city, county, state, country, town, province
```

Times

```
// list of system supplied when_obj frames
// system uses lexical dictionaries to match these
// templates so they do not provide lexicons

time, date
```

User Objects

```
// System supplied generic target template has no lexicon
// your target templates must be based on this template
dyna_user_obj:= {
   isa: 'user_obj
   ...}

// System supplied generic person template has no lexicon
// do not base your target templates on this template
who_obj:= {
   isa: 'user_obj
   ...}

// System supplied generic object template has no lexicon
// do not base your target templates on this template
what_obj:= {
   isa: 'user_obj
   ...}

// System supplied generic place template has no lexicon
// do not base your target templates on this template
where_obj:= {
   isa: 'user_obj
   ...}
```

Intelligent Assistant

People

```
person := { // generic person template
   isa: 'who_obj,
   value: nil // system use only
   ...}

title := { // "owner", "manager", and so on
   isa: 'who_obj,
   ...}

affiliate:= { // "friend", "brother", "sister", and so on
   isa: 'person,
   ...}

group := { // "Engineering", "Marketing", and so on
   isa: 'person,
   ...}

custom := { // customized 'person template
   isa: 'person,
   ...}
```

Miscellaneous

```
salutationPrefix := {
   ISA: 'parser_obj,
   Lexicon: ["dear", "to", "attention", "attn",
            "attn." , "hey"],
...}
```

Developer-Supplied Target Templates

You must supply any target template your task template requires that is not supplied by the system. Required target templates are specified by the task template's signature slot.

Assistant Functions and Methods

```
ParseUtter(inputString)          // matches input to templates
tmpltRef := RegTaskTemplate(myTemplt)//register w/ Assistant
UnRegTaskTemplate(tmpltRef)      // unregister task template
GetMatchedEntries(which, entries) // returns array of aliases
```

Developer-Supplied Functions and Methods

taskFrame:`PostParse()`   `// called after input is parsed`

Application Base View Slots

`viewHelpTopic`   `// topic in help book`

Built-in Applications and System Data

This chapter describes the interfaces to the built-in applications. It also describes the soup formats used by the built-in applications and the soup format of the System soup.

You should read the appropriate section of this chapter if your application needs to interact with any of the built-in applications, receive faxes, use auxiliary buttons, or access system data. Specifically, the following areas are covered in this chapter:

- interacting with the Names application and its soup

- interacting with the Dates application and its soups

- interacting with the To Do List application and its soup

- interacting with the Time Zones application

- interacting with the Notes application and its soup

- retrieving entries from the Fax soup

- adding panels to the Prefs and Formula rolls

- adding auxiliary buttons to other applications

- creating and managing icons in the Extras Drawer

- accessing user configuration data and storing application preferences in the System soup

At the end of this chapter is a summary of all the functions, methods, data structures, protos, and soup formats that are associated with the material discussed in this chapter. Everything listed in this summary section is described in more detail in *Newton Programmer's Reference*.

IMPORTANT

Soup formats are subject to change. Applications that rely on soup
formats risk incompatibility with future versions of Newton
software. To avoid future compatibility problems with soup
format changes, you should use the methods provided by the
built-in applications (if any exist) or the global functions
`GetSysEntryData` and `SetSysEntryData` to get or change
entries in any of the built-in soups. They allow you to get and set
the values of slots in a soup entry. ▲

Familiarity with Chapter 1, "Overview," Chapter 5, "Stationery," and Chapter 11,
"Data Storage and Retrieval," of this manual is particularly valuable in reading
this chapter.

Note

Future Newton devices may not include all the built-in
applications described in this chapter. ◆

Names

This section describes the application program interface (API) to the Names
application. The Names application manages a database of people and places. It
presents information either as a business card, or as a list of all the available
information. These two views are shown in Figure 19-1.

About the Names Application

The Names application is built with the NewtApp framework using data definitions
(commonly called "dataDefs") and view definitions (commonly called "viewDefs").
This architecture allows extensibility—the addition of new data views, card types,
and card layout styles—without altering the Names application itself. For more
information on dataDefs and viewDefs, see Chapter 4, "NewtApp Applications,"
and Chapter 5, "Stationery."

The Names application interface allows you to programmatically add complete cards
and add information to an existing card. In addition, several Names methods let
you access information in a Names soup entry.

The Names application can be extended by adding auxiliary buttons, as described
in "Auxiliary Buttons" beginning on page 19-36.

The application is called Names, because that is what the user sees, but in programming the term "cardfile" is used interchangeably and appears in the code.

Figure 19-1 Names application Card and All Info views

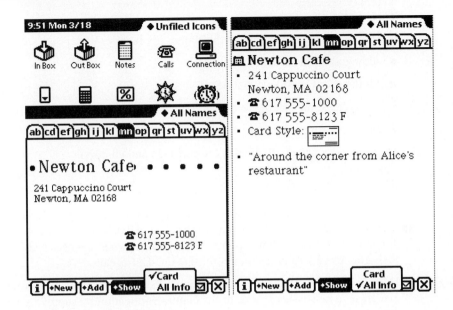

Names Compatibility

All the Names methods, variables, and constants are new in this version. The `'group`, `'owner`, and `'worksite` types are new. The `'person` and `'company` types include many new slots.

The Names application converts incoming soup entries that contain 1.x data into soup entries that conform to the 2.0 data format. Conversion includes adding particular slots to soup entries and, in some cases, removing slots. The data conversion occurs when the Newton receives 1.x entries by beaming, synchronizing using Newton Connection, restoring from a backup, or updating a 1.x card to 2.0.

A user can beam a card created in version 2.0 to a Newton running an earlier version of the system and it will read and edit the card, and *vice versa*.

In addition to changes in the programmatic interface, the 2.0 version has extensive changes in the user interface to accommodate the increased number of card types, layout styles, and data.

Using the Names Application

This section describes

- adding a new type of card to the Names application
- adding a new data item to a card
- adding a new card layout style
- using the Names methods
- using the Names soup
- using two protos with pickers for personae and emporia

Adding a New Type of Card

The New button on the Names status bar creates its picker by looking at the registered dataDefs for the Names application. All dataDefs whose superSymbol slot is set to 'Names show up in the New picker. When the user picks a choice, the MakeNewEntry routine defined for that dataDef is called.

Built-in choices on the New picker include Person, Company, and Group. You can create a new type of card for the Names application by supplying a new data definition.

In addition to the usual slots found in a dataDef frame, Names dataDefs contain two special slots, overviewIcon and viewsToDisplay.

These slots are described in "Names Data Definition Frame" (page 16-2) in *Newton Programmer's Reference*. For information on dataDefs in particular, and stationery in general, see Chapter 5, "Stationery."

Adding a New Data Item

The Add button on the Names status bar allows the user to add new items of information to a card, such as a phone number or an address for a person. There is a Custom choice on the Add picker (pop-up menu), through which the user can create special data items that contain a simple text field. However, you can programmatically add new choices to the picker by creating and registering new view definitions with the Names application.

The Add button creates its picker from the viewDefs registered for the card type of the current card. Of these, only viewDefs whose type slot is set to 'editor show up in the Add picker.

Names viewDefs must contain a special slot called infoFrame, in addition to those slots required of all viewDefs. The infoFrame slot is described in "Names View Definition Frame" (page 16-3), and the slots common to all viewDefs are described in "viewDef Frame" (page 4-1) in *Newton Programmer's Reference*.

Here is an example of an `infoFrame` for a Names viewDef defining a view that
has two fields, `Make` and `Model`:

```
infoFrame:{checkPaths: '[carMake, carModel],
        checkPrefix: '[true, [pathExpr: carInfo]],
        stringData: nil,
        format: "^?0Make: ^0\n||^?1Model: ^1||" }
```

When chosen from the Add picker the first time, this view initially fills in the
`carMake` and `carModel` slots in the soup entry with the user's entries. If chosen
again, this view creates an array called `carInfo` containing one frame for each
additional data set. These frames would look like this:

```
{carMake: make, carModel: model}
```

The reason this is necessary is that after information for the first car is entered, the
soup entry will contain the slots `carMake` and `carModel`. The information for the
second car could not also be stored in the `carMake` and `carModel` slots of the
soup entry. Instead a `carInfo` slot is added to the soup entry, this slot holds a
frame containing `carMake` and `carModel` slots.

When a view from the Add picker is instantiated, the system creates a slot called
`selectedPath` in the view that was instantiated. This slot is set to the path
expression where data should be entered (or to `nil` if the data should be entered
directly into the soup entry). For example, when chosen from the Add picker the
first time, the view in this example would have its `selectedPath` slot set to `nil`,
meaning that the information should be put directly into the soup entry. When
chosen from the picker the second time, the `selectedPath` slot is set to
`[pathExpr: carInfo, 0]`, to indicate that the new car information should go
into the first frame in the `carInfo` array. The third time, `selectedPath` is set to
`[pathExpr: carInfo, 1]`, and so on.

Adding a New Card Layout Style

When the "Card" layout is selected in the Show picker, the Names application
looks at the `cardType` slot of the current card to determine which kind of business
card layout to use for that card. You can create new viewDefs and register them
with the Names application to use a custom card layouts. Card viewDefs must have
the `type` slot set to `'bizcard`, and must contain a `bizCardNum` slot and a
`bizCardIcon` slot.

The `bizCardNum` slot contains an integer that corresponds to the value stored in
the `cardType` slot of the card entries. The values 0-6 correspond to the business
card layouts that are built into the system. You should pick integers over 1,000 to
use as a `bizCardNum`, and register your number with Newton DTS.

The bizCardIcon slot contains an icon representing the new layout, to be shown in the Card Style view, where the user can change the type of card layout to use for a particular card. This icon should be 38x23 since this is the size of the built-in icons.

Adding New Layouts to the Names Application

The Show picker allows the user to chose from the two built-in layouts: Card and All Info. You can programmatically add a new layout by calling the Names method AddLayout. It takes a single parameter, which is the layout to add. This layout should be based on the newtLayout proto, and must include the following slots:

name	A string shown in the Show picker.
symbol	A symbol, which includes your developer signature, uniquely identifying this layout. This symbol must be passed to the EnsureInternal function.
type	Set this slot to the symbol 'viewer.
protection	Set this slot to the symbol 'private.

For more details see AddLayout (page 16-8), and its counterpart function SafeRemoveLayout (page 16-13) in *Newton Programmer's Reference*.

Using the Names Methods and Functions

There are a number of methods provided by the Names application. To obtain a reference to the Names application in order to send these methods, use the following code:

```
GetRoot().cardfile
```

Note that future Newton devices may not include the Names application. You should therefore check for the existence of the Names application before trying to access it. Use the following code to test for this:

```
if GetRoot().cardfile then ...
```

The methods provided allow you to

- add a new card (AddCard)
- add data to an existing card (AddCardData)
- turn to a particular card if Names is open (ShowFoundItem)
- open the Names application to a particular card (OpenTo)
- replace ink data in a card with a string (ReplaceInkData)
- add an action to the Action picker (RegNamesRouteScript)

- get information from Names soup entries
  - □ for credit/phone card information (BcCreditCards)
  - □ for custom fields information (BcCustomFields)
  - □ for e-mail address information (BcEmailAddress)
  - □ for e-mail network information (BcEmailNetwork)
  - □ for phone number information (BcPhoneNumber)

These functions and methods are all described in *Newton Programmer's Reference*.

Using the Names Soup

The Names application stores its data in the ROM_CardFileSoupName ("Names") soup. Entries in this soup are frames for either a person, an owner, a group, a company, or a worksite card.

The soup formats for each of these types of entries are described in "Names Soup Format" (page 16-15) in *Newton Programmer's Reference*. A list of these frames is available in the Summary; see "Names Soup" (page 19-49).

To avoid future compatibility problems with soup format changes, you should use the Names methods provided for getting or setting information in the Names soup. If none is available for getting the information you want, use the global functions GetSysEntryData and SetSysEntryData to get or change entries in any of the built-in soups. They allow you to get and set the values of slots in a soup entry. If you don't use these functions to get and set entry slots in the built-in soups, your application may break under future versions of system software.

Using the Names Protos

The Names application uses two protos which are available to you: protoPersonaPopup and protoEmporiumPopup. These protos provide pickers that maintain lists of **personae** and **emporia.** Personae are people who use the Newton device, and emporia are places where the Newton device is used.

Note that you can get the information on the current owner and worksite from the user configuration data stored by the system. This data is described in "System Data" beginning on page 19-44.

protoPersonaPopup

This proto is used for a picker that lets the user maintain and switch between different owner cards, or "**personae.**" Here's an example:

◆ Christopher Bent

✓Christopher Bent
Chris Bent-Smith

The diamond appears only if there is more than one owner card; otherwise you see just a name without a diamond. Tapping the name produces a picker showing the names of all owner cards stored by the Names application in this Newton device.

protoEmporiumPopup

This proto is used for a picker that lets the user maintain and switch between different information relevant to various locations where she may be. Here's an example:

◆ San Francisco

```
√San Francisco
Mountain View
··········
Other City
```

When the user chooses a different city, information like time zone, area code, and so on is changed to reflect the different location. Choosing "Other City" allows the user to pick a different city anywhere in the world.

Dates

This section describes the Dates API. The Dates application manages meetings and events, and is closely integrated with the To Do List application. Dates can display the user's schedule by day, week, month, and year. It also integrates its information with the To Do List in the Day's Agenda view. Figure 19-2 shows the Day and the Day's Agenda views.

About the Dates Application

The Dates application interface consists of many methods of the calendar object (for a list, see "Summary" beginning on page 19-46). Always use these methods to access or modify Dates application data. Even though the soup format is documented for your information, do not directly modify Dates soup entries, except for any special slots that you might want to add and maintain yourself.

The Dates application can schedule **meetings** and **events.**

- A **meeting** is an entry for a specific time during the day. People can be invited and the meeting can be scheduled for a particular location. Note that meetings use two kinds of icons, one for regular meetings and a special icon for weekly meetings (meetings that repeat at the same time each week).

- An **event** is an entry for a day but not for a particular time during that day. Examples include a birthday, an anniversary, or a vacation. Events are entered into the blank space at the top of the Dates application while in the Day view. Events use three kinds of icons: one for single-day events, one for multiday events, and one for annual events (such as birthdays).

Figure 19-2 Dates application Day and Day's Agenda views

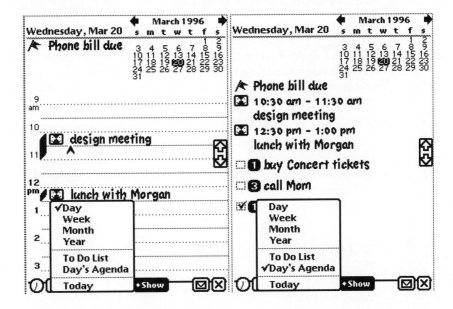

Meetings and events can repeat. That is, they can recur on one or more days in addition to the original meeting or event date.

The application is called Dates, because that is what the user sees, but in programming the term "calendar" is used interchangeably and appears in the code.

Dates Compatibility

This section describes Dates features that are new, changed, or obsolete in system software version 2.0, compared to 1.x versions.

■ All the Dates methods, variables, and constants described in this chapter are new.

■ The following slots are new in Dates soup meeting frames: `class`, `instanceNotesData`, `mtgIconType`, `mtgInvitees`, `mtgLocation`, and `version`. In addition, the `mtgText` slot may contain a rich string instead of a plain string.

■ Dates soup notes frames are new; see "Notes Frames" (page 16-62) in *Newton Programmer's Reference*.

■ The Dates application converts incoming soup entries that contain 1.x data into soup entries that conform to the 2.0 data format. Conversion includes adding particular slots to soup entries and, in some cases, removing slots. The data conversion occurs when the Newton receives 1.x entries by beaming, synchronizing using the Newton Connection Kit, or restoring from a backup.

■ In addition to changes in the programmatic interface, the 2.0 version has extensive changes in the user interface.

■ In system software version 1.x, the Dates application allowed notes (text and graphics) to be written without an associated meeting marker. In system software 2.0, such notes, previously called annotations, cannot be written. Annotations imported via Newton Connection Kit from a 1.x system are still visible and editable, however. As in version 1.x, these objects are stored in the `ROM_CalendarSoupName` soup.

■ In 1.x versions, all instances of a repeating meeting or repeating events share the same set of notes. A repeating meeting is one that recurs at a periodic time interval. In 2.0, notes of a repeating meeting and repeating events are local to each occurrence of the meeting. When a 1.x repeating meeting is converted to 2.0 format, all the notes are typically added to the meeting instance whose meeting slip the user opens first.

Using the Dates Application

This section describes

■ adding meetings or events

■ deleting meeting or events

■ finding meetings or events

■ moving meetings or events

■ getting and setting information for meetings or events

■ creating and using a new meeting type

■ performing miscellaneous operations

■ controlling the Dates display

■ using the Dates soups

To get a reference to the Dates application, in order to send it the messages described in this section, use this code:

```
GetRoot().calendar;
```

Note that future Newton devices may not include the Dates application. You should therefore check for the existence of the Dates application before trying to access it. Use the following code to test for this:

```
if GetRoot().calendar then ...
```

Adding Meetings or Events

You can programmatically add meetings and events by using the
`AddAppointment` and `AddEvent` methods. You should use these methods rather
than adding entries in the Dates soups directly.

Here are some examples of adding meetings. Note that the parameters to
`AddAppointment` are (*mtgText, mtgStartDate, mtgDuration, repeatPeriod,
repeatInfo*).

■ To schedule a one-hour lunch appointment:

```
GetRoot().calendar:AddAppointment("lunch with Ellen",
    StringToDate("6/30/95 11:30am"), 60, nil, nil);
```

■ To schedule a twice weekly meeting on Mondays and Wednesdays:

```
GetRoot().calendar:AddAppointment("design meeting",
    StringToDate("11/6/95 10:30am"), 60, 'weekly, [1, 3]);
```

■ To schedule a yearly party engagement at New Year's Eve:

```
GetRoot().calendar:AddAppointment("New Year's Eve Party",
    StringToDate("12/31/96 9:00pm"), 120, 'yearly, nil);
```

Here are some examples of adding events; note that the parameters to `AddEvent`
are: (*mtgText, mtgStartDate, repeatPeriod, repeatInfo*).

■ To schedule an event:

```
GetRoot().calendar:AddEvent("buy flowers",
    StringToDate("6/30/95"), nil, nil);
```

■ To schedule a birthday that repeats yearly:

```
GetRoot().calendar:AddEvent("George's birthday",
    StringToDate("2/22/95"), 'yearly, nil);
```

■ To schedule Mother's Day:

```
GetRoot().calendar:AddEvent("Mother's Day",
    StringToDate("5/14/95"), 'yearlyByWeek, nil);
```

Deleting Meetings and Events

The Dates application provides three methods for deleting meetings or events: DeleteAppointment, DeleteRepeatingEntry, and DeleteEvent.

These three methods all take the same parameters, as in DeleteAppointment (*mtgTextOrFrame*, *mtgStartDate*, *deleteOneOnly*). The meeting or event to be deleted can be identified in one of two ways:

- By matching the title (in the *mtgTextOrFrame* parameter) and the start date (in the *mtgStartDate* parameter) of the meeting or event.

- By passing in a meeting frame for the *mtgTextOrFrame* parameter. A meeting frame can be obtained either by calling one of two searching methods (FindAppointment or FindExactlyOneAppointment) described in "Finding Meetings or Events" (page 19-13), or by querying one of the Dates soups, described in "Dates Soup Formats" (page 16-56) in *Newton Programmer's Reference*.

As is explained in "Using the Dates Soups" (page 19-22), repeating meetings and events are stored as a single soup entry (meeting frame) in either the "Repeat Meetings" or "Repeat Notes" soups. Calling DeleteAppointment or DeleteEvent with a meeting title and start date (as in the first bullet above) deletes only that instance of a repeating meeting or event. However, calling one of these methods with a meeting frame (as in the second bullet above) stored in one of these two soups deletes the entire series. DeleteRepeatingEntry deletes the entire series of repeating events or meetings, regardless of whether a meeting frame or the title and start date of an event or meeting is used.

Here are some examples of deleting meetings or events of different types:

- To delete a meeting by title/start time:

```
GetRoot().calendar:DeleteAppointment ("lunch with Ellen",
    StringToDate("6/30/95 11:30am"), true);
```

- To delete the same meeting passing in a meeting frame returned by FindExactlyOneAppointment:

```
GetRoot().calendar:DeleteAppointment
        (GetRoot().calendar:FindExactlyOneAppointment
                    ("lunch with Ellen",
                    nil,
                    StringToDate("6/30/95 11:30am"),
                    'Meeting),
        nil,  // these last two params. are ignored when
        nil); // supplying a meeting frame.
```

- To delete a single instance of the repeating event created in "Adding Meetings or Events":

```
GetRoot().calendar:DeleteEvent ("George's birthday",
   StringToDate("2/22/95"), true);
```

- To delete the whole series of George's birthdays by passing in a meeting frame for a repeating meeting:

```
GetRoot().calendar:DeleteEvent
        ( GetRoot().calendar:FindAppointment
                  ("George's birthday",
                  nil,
                  StringToDate("2/22/95"),
                  'RepeatingEvent,
                  nil)
            [0], //FindAppointment returns an array
      nil,   // again, these two params. are ignored
      nil);
```

- The preferred way to delete the repeating event series is by calling DeleteRepeatingEntry:

```
GetRoot().calendar:DeleteRepeatingEntry
   ("George's birthday", StringToDate("2/22/95"), true);
```

Finding Meetings or Events

The Dates application provides two methods to find meetings or events in one of the Dates soups: FindAppointment and FindExactlyOneAppointment.

The FindAppointment method takes the following parameters: FindAppointment(*mtgText*, *findWords*, *dateRange*, *type*, *maxNumberToFind*). The FindExactlyOneAppointment method shares the same first four parameters, but (not surprisingly) does not use a *maxNumberToFind* parameter. The FindExactlyOneAppointment method functions exactly like FindAppointment, except that if more than one meeting or event fits the search criteria, an exception (error –48418) is thrown.

The following examples show how to find meetings with these two methods:

- To find all meetings in the month of June 1995 with the word "lunch" in the title or the notes:

```
GetRoot().calendar:FindAppointment
        (nil,
        '["lunch"],
```

```
        [StringToDate("6/1/95 12:00am"),
            StringToDate ("6/30/95 11:59pm")],
    nil,
    nil);
```

■ To find the unique meeting in the month of June with the word "lunch" in the title or the notes, and handle the possibility of an exception being thrown if this criterion is not unique:

```
try
    GetRoot().calendar:FindExactlyOneAppointment
            (nil,
            '["lunch"],
            [StringToDate("6/1/95 12:00am"),
            StringToDate("6/30/95 11:59pm")],
            nil);
onexception |evt.ex| do
    if CurrentException().data.errorCode = -48418
        then //handle this case
        else Rethrow()
```

The Dates application also provides a method, FindNextMeeting, which returns an array with the meeting start date and duration, for the first meeting after a specified time. The FindNextMeeting method is thus particularly useful for finding an open time slot in the user's schedule.

■ Here is an example, which finds the next meeting after 2 P.M. on November 1, 1996:

```
GetRoot().calendar:FindNextMeeting
        (StringToDate("11/1/96 2pm"));
```

Moving Meetings and Events

To move an appointment programmatically you employ the MoveAppointment method.

■ Here is an example; note that the parameters to MoveAppointment are: (*mtgText,mtgStartDate,newStartDate,newDuration*).

```
GetRoot().calendar:MoveAppointment(
                "Job Review",
                StringToDate("9/1/96 9:30am"),
                StringToDate("9/8/96 4:00pm"),
                nil //do not change duration
            );
```

■ To move a meeting half an hour earlier and give it a different (90 minute) duration:

```
GetRoot().calendar:MoveAppointment(
          "lunch with Ellen",
          StringToDate("6/30/95 12:00pm"),
          StringToDate("6/30/95 11:30am"),
          90);
```

`MoveOnlyOneAppointment` works just like `MoveAppointment` except that if it finds a nonexception instance of a repeating meeting or event that fits the criteria, it moves only that instance. `MoveAppointment` would move all the nonexceptions in that case.

■ To move a single occurrence of a repeating meeting:

```
GetRoot().calendar:MoveOnlyOneAppointment(
          "design meeting",
          StringToDate("11/13/95 10:30am"),
          StringToDate("11/14/95 2:00pm"),
          nil);
```

The `IncrementMonth` function can be especially useful when moving appointments.

■ This example moves an appointment two months ahead.

```
GetRoot().calendar:MoveAppointment(
      "lunch with Ellen",
      StringToDate("6/30/95 12:00pm"),
      IncrementMonth(StringToDate("6/30/95 11:30am"),2),
      nil);
```

Getting and Setting Information for Meetings or Events

There are a number of Dates methods that get/set information stored in the Dates soups:

■ Set a stop date for a repeating meeting with `SetRepeatingEntryStopDate`.

■ Set an alarm for a meeting with `SetEntryAlarm`.

■ Get or set the meeting invitees with `GetMeetingInvitees` and `SetMeetingInvitees`.

■ Get or set a meeting location with `GetMeetingLocation` and `SetMeetingLocation`.

■ Get or set the meeting notes with `GetMeetingNotes` and `SetMeetingNotes`.

Built-in Applications and System Data

■ Get or set the meeting icon type with `GetMeetingIconType` and `SetMeetingIconType`.

The remainder of this section presents sample code that uses these methods. You may wish to look at the summary section at the end of this chapter to see what the parameters to these methods are.

```
// useful abbreviations
cal         := GetRoot().calendar;
mtgName     := "App Design Mtg";
mtgDur      := 60;
startDate   := StringToDate("2/20/96 12:00pm");
appDueDate  := StringToDate("7/23/96 12:00pm");

// schedule a weekly meeting at noon Tuesdays (2/20/96
// falls on a Tuesday)
cal:AddAppointment(mtgName,startDate,mtgDur,'weekly,nil);

// we stop having these meetings when app is due
cal:SetRepeatingEntryStopDate(mtgName,startDate,
    appDueDate);

// set a 15-minute advance notice alarm for the meeting
cal:SetEntryAlarm (mtgName, startDate, 15);

// Add an invitee to the meeting. We know that there are
// presently no invitees, since we have just created this
// meeting. But in general, you would add to the present
// list of invitees. Here we add to the (empty) array.

invitees := cal:GetMeetingInvitees(mtgName,startDate);

AddArraySlot(invitees,{name:{first:"Jan",last:"Smith"}});

cal:SetMeetingInvitees(mtgName, startDate, invitees);

// set the location of a meeting to a place not in the
// Names soup
cal:SetMeetingLocation(mtgName, startDate, "Blue Room");

// if the meeting is not in the Blue Room beep
theRoom = cal:GetMeetingLocation(mtgName, startDate)

if not strEqual ("Blue Room", theRoom.company)
    then GetRoot():SysBeep();
```

```
// get the notes of the last meeting. If there are no
// meeting notes, GetMeetingNotes returns nil
meetingNotes := cal:GetMeetingNotes(mtgName, appDueDate);

// add a paragraph to these notes, then set the meeting
// notes to this new array. Note, how care is taken
// not to overwrite any existing notes.

newNote    := {viewStationery :    'para,
                text           :    "Last Design Meeting",
                viewBounds     :    SetBounds(5, 5, 10, 10)
                };                  //Bounds will be expanded
                                    //by system
if meetingNotes then
   begin
      lowestBottom := 0;
      foreach elem in meetingNotes do
         if elem.viewBounds.bottom > lowestBottom then
            lowestBottom := elem.viewBounds.bottom;

      newNote.viewBounds.top := lowestBottom + 5;
      newNote.viewBounds.bottom := lowestBottom + 50;
      AddArraySlot(meetingNotes, newNote);
   end;

   else
      meetingNotes := [newNote];

// Now add the new note array to the meeting
cal:SetMeetingNotes (mtgName,AppDueDate,meetingNotes);

// check if the icon is of type 'WeeklyMeeting
// if it isn't make it so
if NOT (cal:GetMeetingIconType( mtgName, startDate)
        = 'WeeklyMeeting)
   then cal:SetMeetingIconType(mtgName, startDate,
                                'WeeklyMeeting);
```

Creating a New Meeting Type

You can programmatically add new meeting types by calling the Dates method RegMeetingType. The meeting type will appear in the New picker in the Dates status bar. The RegMeetingType method takes two parameters, a symbol identifying the meeting type—which should include your developer signature—

and a frame containing the definition of the new meeting type. This frame has the following slots; see "RegMeetingType" (page 16-48) in *Newton Programmer's Reference* for full details:

Slot description

item	Required. A string that is the meeting type name to appear in the New picker.
icon	Required. The icon shown in the New picker. It should be no larger than 24x15 pixels.
NewMeeting	Required. Method called if the user chooses this meeting type in the New picker.
smallIcon	Optional. The icon displayed in the meeting slip. It should be no more than 12 pixels high. If this icon is not provided, icon is used, which may look ugly.
OpenMeeting	Optional. Method called when user taps an icon for a meeting or event of this type. If this method is not provided, Dates opens the default meeting slip.
memory	Optional. Where to store meeting titles of this type.

The NewMeeting method is passed in the date and time the note was created and the viewBounds of the Dates application. It must create a meeting (or event) using either AddAppointment (or AddEvent), and must add a slot to the appointment created called meetingType. This slot must be set to the symbol that identified the meeting type in the call to RegMeetingType. Remember to call EntryChange to save this new slot.

If NewMeeting returns the meeting (or event) created, Dates then opens the default meeting slip. You may also return nil from NewMeeting, in which case you must have already opened the meeting slip from within NewMeeting. The meeting slip should be opened by using the Dates method RememberedOpen, which records this so that Dates can close the view, if Dates is closed. Use RememberedClose to close this view.

If you do define a custom meeting slip, you should also define an OpenMeeting method. This method is called when the user taps an icon of the type you have created. For more information see OpenMeeting (page 16-50) in *Newton Programmer's Reference*.

Examples of Creating New Meeting Types

The following example code registers a new meeting type for a monthly meeting:

```
GetRoot().calendar:RegMeetingType (
   '|MonthlyMeeting:MySig|,
   {  item: "Monthly Meeting",
      icon: myIcon,
      smallicon: mySmallIcon,
      NewMeeting: func(date, parentBox)
         begin
            local appt:= GetRoot().calendar
                        :AddAppointment ("",date, 60,
                                         'monthly, nil);
            appt.meetingType:=
                        '|MonthlyMeeting:MySig|;
            EntryChange(appt);
            appt; // the calendar will open the
                  // default meeting slip if we
                  // return the new appointment
         end,
   });
```

To register a new meeting type for a monthly event with a custom meeting slip:

```
GetRoot().calendar:RegMeetingType (
   '|Monthly Event:MySig|,
   {  item: "Monthly Event",
      icon: myIcon,
      smallicon: mySmallIcon,
      NewMeeting: func(date, parentBox)
      begin
         local appt := GetRoot().calendar
                     :AddEvent("", date, 'monthly, nil);
         appt.meetingType := '|MonthlyEvent:MySig|;
         EntryChange(appt);
         :OpenMeeting(appt,date,cal:GlobalBox());
         nil;  // tells calendar not to open
               // default meeting slip
      end,
      OpenMeeting: func(meeting, date, parentBox)
      begin
         local cal := GetRoot().calendar;
```

```
        local slip :=
            BuildContext(
                {_proto: protoFloater
                viewFlags:vClickable + vFloating +
                        vApplication + vClipping,
                viewJustify:0,
                viewBounds:SetBounds (
                            parentBox.left+40,
                            parentBox.top+40,
                            parentBox.right-40,
                            parentBox.bottom-100),
                declareSelf:'base,
                stepChildren:
                [
                    {viewStationery: 'para,
                    text:     "test slip",
                    viewBounds:RelBounds(10, 10,50, 20)
                    },
                    {_proto: protoCancelButton,
                    buttonClickScript: func()
                    //closes the view and tells
                    //calendar the view was closed
                        AddDeferredSend(
                            cal,
                            'RememberedClose,
                            [base]),
                    }
                ],
            });
        // open the view and tell Dates it was opened
        GetRoot().calendar:RememberedOpen(slip);

        nil;              // tells Dates not to open
                          // default meeting slip
    end,
});
```

Miscellaneous Operations

Dates provides a number of methods that have not been mentioned elsewhere:

- `DisplayDate` displays meetings in the Dates application, To Do items, or the agenda for a specified date.

- `GetSelectedDates` returns an array of the currently selected and displayed dates.

- `OpenMeetingSlip` opens the meeting slip for a specific meeting or event.

- `RegInfoItem` adds and `UnRegInfoItem` or deletes an item in the Info picker in the base view of the Dates application. This example shows how to add a command that displays the next day's To Do List to the Info button:

```
GetRoot().calendar:RegInfoItem('|NextDayToDo:MyApp|,
        {  item: "Next Day's To Do",
            doAction: func()
                begin
                    local cal := GetRoot().calendar;
                    cal:DisplayDate
                        (cal:GetSelectedDates() [0]
                                  +(24*60),'ToDoList);
                end;
        });
```

Controlling the Dates Display

There are two system variables you can set to control specific features of the Dates display: `firstDayOfWeek` and `useWeekNumber`.

The Dates variable `firstDayOfWeek` specifies what the first day of the week should be, for display purposes. It holds an integer value from 0 to 6, where 0 means Sunday, 1 means Monday, and so on. The default value is 0, which means that by default all months show Sunday as the first day of the week.

Once this value has been set, all new views of the class `clMonthView` and views that display meeting frequency reflect the new value, but existing views must be closed and reopened to reflect the new value. This variable is part of the system-stored user configuration data (the Dates application checks there first), or in the locale bundle frame (Dates checks there next).

The Dates variable `useWeekNumber` controls display of a week number in the upper-left corner of the Dates view. If this slot is non-`nil`, the Dates application displays the week number there. The first week of the year is number 1 and the last week is number 52. This variable is a slot in the locale bundle frame.

To get and set the value of user configuration variables, use the functions `GetUserConfig` and `SetUserConfig`; this frame and the two functions are described in "System Data" (page 19-44). To return the current locale bundle frame, use the global function `GetLocale`.

Using the Dates Soups

The Dates application stores meeting and event information and notes in the following soups:

Soup (name string)	Description
ROM_CalendarSoupName ("Calendar")	Entries are meeting frames for nonrepeating meetings.
ROM_RepeatMeetingName ("Repeat Meetings")	Entries are meeting frames for repeating meetings and notes frames for notes associated with specific instances of a repeating meeting. A single meeting frame entry describes all the instances of a repeating meeting.
ROM_CalendarNotesName ("Calendar Notes")	Entries are meeting frames for nonrepeating events.
ROM_RepeatNotesName ("Repeat Notes")	Entries are meeting frames for repeating events and notes frames for notes associated with specific instances of a repeating event.

The slot structures of meeting frames and note frames are described in "Meeting Frames" (page 16-57) and "Notes Frames" (page 16-62) in *Newton Programmer's Reference*. A list of these frames is available in the Summary; see "Dates Soups" (page 19-52).

Although the format of the various Dates soups is documented in this section, you should not directly change entries. It is best to use the methods supplied by the Dates application to get and set entries.

To Do List

This section describes the To Do List API. The To Do List application is integrated into the Dates application; it is accessed through the Dates Show button. The To Do List is shown in Figure 19-3.

About the To Do List Application

The To Do List API allows you to create To Do List items programmatically, check them off, obtain them according to date and other criteria, and remove them by date and other criteria.

Figure 19-3   The To Do List application

To Do List Compatibility

Version 2.0 reads and converts all 1.x To Do List soups. It does not reproduce styling of text, because 2.0 doesn't support styling. It does not allow shapes and sketches in a task, so shapes and sketches are thrown away.

Because the internal structure of the 2.0 To Do List soup is completely different from that of the 1.x version, when you transmit a 2.0 soup to a 1.x system it creates a 1.x entry.

Using the To Do List Application

This section provides information about the use of the To Do List soup and methods. To obtain a reference to the To Do List in order to send it messages, use the following code:

```
GetRoot().calendar:GetToDo();
```

Note that future Newton devices may not include the To Do List application. You should therefore check for the existence of the To Do List application before trying to access it. Use the following code for this test:

```
if GetRoot().calendar then
    if GetRoot().calendar:?GetToDo() then ...
```

Also, note that some of these methods only work when the To Do List is open. You can ensure the To Do List is open by calling the Dates method `DisplayDate` passing in `'toDoList` for the *format* parameter as in the following code:

```
//open Dates and make it show today's To Do List
GetRoot().calendar:Open();
GetRoot().calendar:DisplayDate(time(),'toDoList);
```

This section describes

- creating and removing To Do tasks
- accessing tasks
- checking-off tasks
- using miscellaneous To Do List methods
- using the To Do List soup

Creating and Removing Tasks

There are two To Do List methods that add a task: `CreateToDoItem` and `CreateToDoItemAll`. The `CreateToDoItem` method takes four parameters, as in `CreateToDoItem`(*date*, *richString*, *reminder*, *frequency*). The `CreateToDoItemAll` method takes two additional parameters, *priority* and *completed*, which set the priority and completion status of the new task.

The following code example adds a task to today's To Do List:

```
GetRoot().calendar:GetToDo():CreateToDoItem (time(),
        "test", nil, nil);
```

The To Do List `GetToDoEntry` method (discussed in "Accessing Tasks" beginning on page 19-24) will also create a soup entry if one does not exist for that date.

To remove tasks, use the To Do List method `RemoveOldToDoItems`, which removes either all or those tasks that have been marked-off before a specific date. The following code sample removes all the nonrepeating To Do List tasks in the twentieth century:

```
GetRoot().calendar:GetToDo():
   RemoveOldToDoItems(StringToDate("1/1/2000"),'all,nil);
```

Accessing Tasks

The To Do List provides three methods for accessing tasks:

- `GetToDoItemsForThisDate`
- `GetToDoEntry`
- `GetToDoItemsForRange`.

`GetToDoItemsForThisDate` returns an array of tasks. Tasks are elements of the array stored in the `topics` slot of a day's soup entry. For the structure of these frames, see "To Do List Soup Format" (page 16-77) in *Newton Programmer's Reference*. The following code example obtains today's tasks:

```
todaysTasksArray := GetRoot().calendar:GetToDo():
    GetToDoItemsForThisDate(time());
```

`GetToDoEntry` returns an array of soup entries for a specific day. Since the To Do List stores tasks in a soup entry for each day, this array will contain an element for each store that has a task stored under that day. The following code example obtains today's soup entries:

```
todaysEntries := GetRoot().calendar:GetToDo():
    GetToDoEntry(time(),nil);
```

Note

The `GetToDoEntry` method requires that the To Do List be open. ◆

`GetToDoItemsForRange` returns an array of frames for each day in the range passed in. The following code example retrieves the tasks for the next seven days:

```
nextWeeksTasks := GetRoot().calendar:GetToDo():
    GetToDoItemsForRange(time(), time() + 7*24*60);
```

There is also a To Do List method, `NextToDoDate(`*date*`)`, which returns the date of the next task on or after *date*. This method can be useful in this context.

Checking-Off a Task

A tasks is marked as completed with the To Do List method `SetDone`. This method requires the To Do List to be open; you can make sure the To Do List is open by calling the Dates method `DisplayDate`. The following code sample marks off a task:

```
//open Dates and make it show today's To Do List
GetRoot().calendar:Open();
GetRoot().calendar:DisplayDate(time(),'toDoList);

//get a reference to today's tasks
todaysTasksArray := GetRoot().calendar:GetToDo():
    GetToDoItemsForThisDate(time());

//find a task that says "test"
for i := 0 to length(todaysTasksArray) - 1 do
    if StrEqual (todaysTasksArray[i].text, "test") then
```

```
begin
    theTask  := todaysTasksArray[i];
    theIndex := i;
end;

//and mark it as done
GetRoot().calendar:GetToDo():
    SetDone(theIndex,theTask,true,nil,nil);
```

The third parameter to SetDone determines whether a task is checked off; passing nil unchecks it.

Miscellaneous To Do List Methods

The To Do List also provides the following methods:

- GetTaskShapes and GetToDoShapes return the shapes necessary to draw tasks, which are used for printing.

- LastVisibleTopic returns the index in the topics array of the last task drawn.

- SetPriority sets the priority of a task. (This method requires the To Do List to be open.)

- EnsureVisibleTopic scrolls the To Do List as necessary to ensure that a task is visible. (This method requires the To Do List to be open.)

Using the To Do List Soup

The To Do List stores its data in the "To Do List" soup. Entries in this soup are frames for either a particular day, or for all repeating to do items.

In this soup, each day has a single entry that includes a topics slot, which is an array of tasks for that day. All repeating tasks are saved in a single entry, with a date slot of 0.

If one day is represented by an entry on each of several stores of the soup—for example, if there was one entry in internal store and one on a storage card—the To Do List merges the entries for display purposes. The entries are not actually moved from one store to another in this process.

For information about the structure of entries in this soup, see "To Do List Soup Format" (page 16-77) in *Newton Programmer's Reference*. A list of these frames is available in the Summary; see "To Do List Soup" (page 19-53).

To avoid future compatibility problems with soup format changes, you should use the global functions GetSysEntryData and SetSysEntryData to get or change entries in any of the built-in soups. They allow you to get and set the values of slots in a soup entry. If you don't use these functions to get and set entry slots in the built-in soups, your application may break under future versions of system software.

Time Zones

This section describes the Time Zones API. The Time Zones application is shown in Figure 19-4.

Figure 19-4   The Time Zones application

About the Time Zones Application

The Time Zone application lets the user access information about locations, which may come from the system, the user, or from another application. The user can browse the cities of the world for the time and other travel information, such as network access phone numbers. The user can define a **Home City,** an **Away City,** and other locations of interest (**emporia**). Information the user specifies is available to your application. When the user specifies that the Newton device is in a new location, local information, such as network phone numbers, is available to your application. For more information on localization, see Chapter 20, "Localizing Newton Applications."

Time Zone Compatibility

The Time Zone application runs only on version 2.0, and is fully compatible with older versions back to 1.3.

Using the Time Zone Application

The application program interface provides functions for retrieving information about cities and countries, a method to add a city to a Newton device's list of cities, and a method to set the home city. To call a Time Zones method, you need a reference to the application. To obtain this reference, use the following code:

```
GetRoot().worldClock
```

Note that future Newton devices may not include the Time Zones application. You should therefore check for the existence of the Time Zones application before trying to access it. Use the following code to test for this:

```
if GetRoot().worldClock then ...
```

Obtaining Information About a City or Country

The `GetCityEntry` and `GetCountryEntry` global functions return information about a number of cities and countries around the world. This information is available to the user by picking All Info from the Show picker, shown in Figure 19-5.

Figure 19-5 Time Zones application's All Info view

Both these functions take a string as an argument for the city or country to return information about. The search is conducted by string comparison with this argument. You should be aware that although there may be variations of the name of a city or country, only one name is stored on the Newton device. For example, `GetCityEntry("Los Angeles")` returns a frame with information about Los Angeles, but `GetCityEntry("LA")` does not. You should check the spelling in the Time Zones application of city or country names you wish to use. Keep in mind though that the list of cities and countries is not necessarily the same on your Newton device and the user of your application. Your application should also check string names for cities and countries entered by the user.

The GetCountryEntry function performs an additional search based on the class of the string passed in. This is done in order to take into account the language of the ROM used; the symbols are all in English. To set the class of a string, use the SetCountryClass function, described in Chapter 20, "Localizing Newton Applications."

The frame returned by the GetCityEntry function is the same as the *newCityFrame* parameter to the NewCity function described in "Adding a City to a Newton Device" beginning on page 19-29. For information on the frame returned by the GetCountryEntry function see the description of this function in *Newton Programmer's Reference*.

Adding a City to a Newton Device

The Time Zones NewCity method adds a city to a Newton device. It takes a *newCityFrame* parameter which is a frame with the following slots:

Slot descriptions

name	Required. A string containing the name of the location.
longitude	Required. The longitude of the location. The formula for generating this value appears in "Using Longitude and Latitude Values" beginning on page 19-30.
latitude	Required. The latitude of the location.
gmt	Required. The offset in minutes from Greenwich Mean Time.
country	Required. A symbol representing the country in which the city is located.
areaCode	Optional. A string for the area code of the location.
region	Optional. A string for the region of the location. For cities in the U.S. this should be the state; for cities in Canada the province.
airport	Optional. A string for the airport designation for the city, or an array of strings if the city is served by multiple airports.

Here is an example of such a frame:

```
{name:"Portland",
longitude:354036540,
latitude:67929083,
gmt:  -28800,
country:'USA,
```

```
areaCode: "503",
region:"OR",
airport:"PDX"}
```

Using Longitude and Latitude Values

To calculate the latitude or longitude of a location, create and use the
following function:

```
CalcLngLat := func(dgrs, min, secs, westOrSouth) begin
    local loc;
    loc := dgrs / 180 + min / (180 * 60) + secs
        / (180 * 60 * 60);
    loc := rinttol(loc * 0x10000000);
    if westOrSouth then
        loc := 0x20000000 - loc;
    loc;
end;
```

The built-in utility functions LatitudeToString and LongitudeToString
return a string representation of an encoded integer latitude or longitude value. For
information on these functions see *Newton Programmer's Reference*.

Setting the Home City

The SetLocation method sets the home city. It takes a single parameter
whichCity which is the same as the *newCityFrame* parameter of the NewCity
method; see "Adding a City to a Newton Device" beginning on page 19-29. The
following code makes Los Angeles the home city:

```
GetRoot().worldClock:SetLocation( GetCityEntry
    ("Los Angeles") [0] );
```

Notes

This section describes the Notes API. The Notes application uses three types of
stationery: regular notes, checklists, and outlines. Figure 19-6 shows a note and a
checklist; an outline (not shown) is like the checklist without the checkboxes.

Figure 19-6   Notes note and Checklist views

About the Notes Application

Notes is a simple application based on NewtApp that allows the user to create new stationery, scroll up and down, route and file notes, and scan an overview.

The Notes API is limited to a few methods which allow you to create new notes.

The Notes application can be extended by adding auxiliary buttons, as described in "Auxiliary Buttons" beginning on page 19-36.

The name of the application is Notes, which is what the user sees, but in programming the term `paperroll` is also used and appears in the code.

Notes Compatibility

There are some anomalies in converting ink from system software 2.0 to earlier versions of the system. Version 2.0 ink text is converted to straight ink when viewed in 1.x versions. Paragraphs with mixed regular and ink text are converted so that the regular text loses any styles; for example in 1.x versions, it becomes 18-point user font. Any paragraph that contains ink text is reflowed in 1.x versions so that line layouts (breaks) are different from the original. This means that the paragraph may grow taller. Ink works converted from 2.0 to 1.x straight ink appear in the size originally drawn, not in the 2.0 scaled size.

Using the Notes Application

This section describes the methods that add new notes, and the Notes soup format.

To obtain a reference to the Notes application in order to send it messages, use the following code:

```
GetRoot().paperroll
```

Note that future Newton devices may not include the Notes application. You should therefore check for the existence of the Notes application before trying to access it. Use the following code to test for this:

```
if GetRoot().paperroll then ...
```

Creating New Notes

The Notes method MakeTextNote(*string*, *addIt*) creates a note that consists of a single string. The *addIt* parameter is a Boolean; pass true for *addIt* to add the note to the Notes soup. The following code adds a note programmatically:

```
GetRoot().paperroll:MakeTextNote
     ("Isn't this easy?",true);
```

If you want to add a more sophisticated note, follow these steps:

1. Create a note with MakeTextNote, but pass nil for the *addIt* parameter. MakeTextNote returns a note frame.

2. Modify the data slot of the frame returned by MakeTextNote. The data slot must be an array of frames that have the format described in "Notes Soup Format" (page 16-82) in *Newton Programmer's Reference*.

3. Call the Notes method NewNote with the modified note frame.

Below is an example of this procedure:

```
// create a note frame
notes    := GetRoot().paperroll;
theNote  := notes:MakeTextNote ( "", nil);

// modify the data slot. Note that the data array now
// contains a frame for the empty string.
theNote.data :=
   [{viewStationery :'para, // a text object
    viewBounds : {top:3, left:3, right:97, bottom:97},
    text : "I'm just a string."},
   {viewStationery :'poly, //a polygon object
```

```
points :ArrayToPoints ([11, // a rectangle
                        5,     //how many points
                        0,0,   //first point
                        0,25, //second
                        150,25,//third
                        150,0,//fourth
                        0,0]),//back home
   viewBounds : {top:0, left:0, right:100, bottom:100}}
];
```

```
//Add the note to the Notes application
notes:NewNote ( theNote, true, nil);
```

This creates the note shown in Figure 19-7.

Figure 19-7   Note added using `NewNote` method

Adding Stationery to the Notes Application

The Notes application includes three types of built-in stationery: notes, outlines, and checklists. In addition, you can create your own stationery. For information on how to do this see Chapter 5, "Stationery," which includes an extended example of adding stationery to the Notes application.

Using the Notes Soup

The Notes soup holds individual entries for the different kinds of built-in stationery as follows:

- note—the lined paper used for the Notes
- outline—paper with automated outlining
- checklist—outline paper with a box to check off completed items

Detailed information on the data structures that support these stationeries is provided in "Notes Soup Format" (page 16-82) in *Newton Programmer's Reference*. A list of these frames is available in the Summary; see "Notes Soup" (page 19-53).

To avoid future compatibility problems with soup format changes, you should use the global functions GetSysEntryData and SetSysEntryData to make change entries in any of the built-in soups. These allow you to get and set the values of slots in a soup entry. If you don't use these functions to get and set entry slots in the built-in soups, your application may break under future versions of system software.

Fax Soup Entries

This section describes Fax soup entries.

About Fax Soup Entries

If you want to use a received fax in your application, you can find it in the In/Out Box soup or set up a process to route it to your application by means of the PutAwayScript or the AutoPutAway messages, both described in *Newton Programmer's Reference*.

The PutAwayScript message results from a user action. An application can register to handle putting away fax data by using the RegAppClasses function, see RegAppClasses in *Newton Programmer's Reference*.

The AutoPutAway message requires no user action. The In Box checks for an AutoPutAway method in the base view of the application whose appSymbol slot matches that in the item. If the AutoPutAway method exists, the In Box sends the AutoPutAway message to the application, passing the incoming item as a parameter.

In either case, the body slot from the In/Out Box entry is passed to the application. All the fax data that an application needs is embedded within the body slot; see "Using Fax Soup Entries" (page 19-34).

You may also want to use the system prototypes that relate to viewing and manipulating images with your fax data. They are protoImageView, protoThumbnail, and protoThumbnailFloater.

Using Fax Soup Entries

When an entry is submitted to the In/Out Box from a transport such as fax receive, or from an application, the fax is stored in the body slot of the In/Out Box soup entry. The In/Out Box stores the original application soup entry in a frame called `body` within the In/Out Box soup entry, where a user can view it. Applications may be passed an In/Out Box soup entry as part of the putting away process. For more information on handling items coming from the In/Out Box, see "Receiving Data" beginning on page 21-31 in *Newton Programmer's Guide.*

The structure of the `body` frame is described in "Fax Soup Entries Reference" (page 16-94) in *Newton Programmer's Reference.*

Prefs and Formulas Rolls

This section describes the Prefs and Formulas API's. Figure 19-8 shows custom panels added to these two applications by DTS sample code.

Figure 19-8   Custom Prefs and Formulas Panels

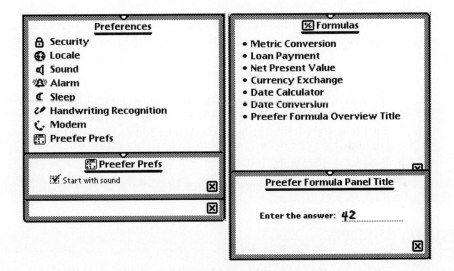

About the Prefs and Formulas Rolls

The Prefs application presents the user with a list of items for which such preferences as handwriting recognition and sound levels can be set. These are system-wide or system-level preferences, do not add application-specific preferences to the Prefs roll. The Formulas application contains a list of items that perform some sort of calculation for the user.

You can extend the Prefs and Formulas rolls through the registry functions: `RegPrefs` and `RegFormulas`.

Prefs and Formulas Compatibility

The functions RegPrefs, UnRegPrefs, RegFormulas, and UnRegFormulas are new to the 2.0 system.

Using the Prefs and Formulas Interfaces

This section describes how to add panels to the Prefs and Formulas rolls.

Adding a Prefs Roll Item

The RegPrefs function adds a panel to the Prefs rolls. This roll is not intended for application-specific preferences, but rather for system-wide preferences. Application-specific preferences should be set through an information button (an "i" button) in the application base view's status bar. For more on the information button, see newtInfoButton or protoInfoButton, depending on whether you are working in the NewtApp framework or not.

The item added to the Prefs roll should be based on protoPrefsRollItem. The UnRegPrefs function reverses the effects of the RegPrefs function.

Adding a Formulas Roll Item

The RegFormulas function adds a panel to the Formulas roll. There is no proto tailored for use as a Formulas panel. Instead, you should attempt to make your panel look and act like the system-supplied panels. For an example of a template with the look of the built-in Formulas panels, see the DTS sample code related to the Prefs and Formulas rolls.

The UnRegFormulas function reverses the effects of the RegFormulas function.

Auxiliary Buttons

This section describes the use of auxiliary buttons. Figure 19-9 shows the effect of adding an auxiliary button to the Notes application.

About Auxiliary Buttons

A set of functions allow you to add buttons to the status bars of the Notes and Names applications. Third-party applications can use this mechanism to allow themselves to be extended.

Auxiliary Buttons Compatibility

The auxiliary buttons mechanism is new to the Newton 2.0 system.

Figure 19-9 The Notes application with and without an auxiliary button

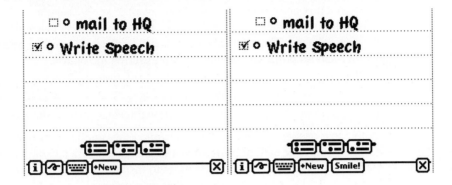

Using Auxiliary Buttons

You can add buttons to the status bars or other locations in the Notes and Names applications. Your application may also use this mechanism to allow itself to be extended.

RegAuxButton and UnRegAuxButton are the functions that add and remove a button from the auxiliary button registry; they are called by **button providers.** Button providers can ignore the descriptions of the other functions, which are called by **button hosts.**

Here is an example of registering a button with the Notes application:

```
RegAuxButton('|smileButton:PIEDTS|,
    {destApp: 'paperroll,// Add buttons to Notes
    _proto: protoTextButton,
    text: "Smile!",
    viewBounds: RelBounds(0,0,40,10),
    buttonClickScript: func() print("Cheese!")
    });
```

This code added the auxiliary button shown in Figure 19-9.

The following code shows how this button should be removed:

```
UnRegAuxButton('|smileButton:PIEDTS|);
```

You should be careful what assumptions you make about the environment where the button will appear. The buttons may not be on a protoStatusBar or have a base slot available by inheritance, and the implementation details of the built-in applications may well change in the future. Remember to check your assumptions and catch exceptions.

Any application that adds buttons to another application should provide a preference that allows the user to enable or disable the display of the source application buttons in the destination application. The user may want to suppress buttons because the buttons from several source applications may be too many to fit in a single destination application. The user should be able to choose which should appear, and the preference should normally default to *not* registering the button.

Note that a button you register might not appear at all if too many buttons are already registered in the destination application, so you must ensure alternative access to your application through conventional means, such as the Extras Drawer.

Also note that packages that install buttons into other applications may cause the system to display the card reinsertion warning if they are on a card that has been ejected. It is wise to advise or require users to install packages on the internal store if they are going to register buttons in other applications.

The functions `GetAuxButtons`, `AddAuxButton`, and `RemoveAuxButton` are for use by button hosts that are adding the buttons to their own status bars (or wherever is appropriate). You should call `GetAuxButtons` in your base view's `ViewSetupChildrenScript` and merge the resulting array with the buttons that always appear on your status bar. You should probably also override the `viewBounds` or `viewJustify` slots of the buttons, to place them correctly.

If your application is the backdrop application, this array contains both the buttons specific to your application and any designated for the backdrop application. You do not need to write any special code to detect whether your application is the backdrop application.

Icons and the Extras Drawer

This section describes the Extras Drawer's API for icon management.

About Icons and the Extras Drawer

As you may know, you can design custom icons for your application in NTK. Information on how to do this is provided in the *Newton Toolkit User's Guide*. You can also programmatically change the picture of the icon and the text displayed under it.

There are two special purpose icons you can add to the Extras Drawer—**script icons** and **soup icons.** A script icon is an icon that executes a function object when tapped. A soup icon acts as a container, under which the icons of various soups are combined. You should create a soup icon if your application creates more than one soup, since this will unclutter the Extras Drawer. You also need to create soup icons to support the soupervisor mechanism (described later in this section).

This section also covers creating a cursor that iterates over icons in the Extras Drawer, and a number of functions that manipulate the entries these cursors iterate over. With these functions you can programmatically open an icon (which has the same effect as a user tapping the icon), and get information about the package the icon represents.

In addition, the Newton 2.0 system creates an icon for any soup on a mounted store in the Storage folder of the Extras Drawer. Tapping this icon brings up a slip that displays information about the memory consumption of the soup (see Figure 19-10). It also provides a delete button, which can delete the soup. And, without too much work, you can provide a filing button that allows the user to move the soup to a different store or folder. This is accomplished through what is called the **soupervisor mechanism.**

Figure 19-10 The information slips for an application's soup that do and do not support the soupervisor mechanism (note extra filing button)

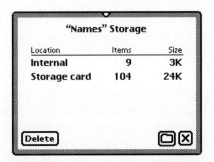
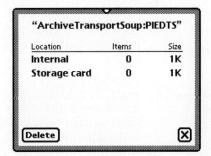

Extras Drawer Compatibility

Everything described in this section is new to the Newton 2.0 system.

Using the Extras Drawer's Interface for Icon Management

This section covers the following topics:

- creating cursors that iterate over the icons in the Extras Drawer

- changing an icon's information

- creating script and soup icons

- supporting the soupervisor mechanism

To accomplish some of these tasks, you need to send messages to the Extras Drawer. Use this code to get a reference to the Extras Drawer:

```
GetRoot().extrasDrawer
```

Using Extras Drawer Cursors

The Extras Drawer method `GetPartCursor` creates a cursor that can iterate over parts (icons) in the Extras Drawer. You can create a cursor that iterates over parts in a specific store, a particular folder of the Extras Drawer, a particular package, or a combination of these criteria. This cursor is a normal soup cursor, as described in Chapter 11, "Data Storage and Retrieval."

Entries returned by part cursors are subject to change. These entries should be manipulated only with one of the following three Extras Drawer methods:

- `GetPartEntryData` returns information about a part.

- `LaunchPartEntry` has the same effect as the user tapping the icon.

- `SetExtrasInfo` sets data in a part entry; see "Changing Icon Information."

Changing Icon Information

The Extras Drawer method `SetExtrasInfo` can be used to change the icon or text under an icon. It can also change the `labels` slot of an icon, which has the effect of filing the icon. If the icon is a soup icon, you may also change the array of soups that this icon represents and the application that owns these soups.

Adding a Soup Icon

If your application uses more than one soup or you want to file or move entire soups through the soupervisor mechanism, you should consider using a soup icon, so that only one icon appears in the Extras Drawer. You should store this icon in the internal store, otherwise all the component soups will reappear when the external store is removed. Also, you should give the icon a different package name from your application in your call to `AddExtraIcon`, both as the *pkgName* parameter and in the `app` slot of the *paramFrame* parameter. Again, this is so that it is not removed when your application is.

You add a soup icon to the Extras Drawer by calling its `AddExtraIcon` method. Passing the symbol `'soupEntry` for the first parameter specifies that the icon to add is a soup icon.

The rest of this section provides sample code for installing a soup icon. Before trying to understand this code, you should read the description of `AddExtraIcon` (page 16-88) in *Newton Programmer's Reference*.

```
//Useful constants
constant kMySoupNamesArray := '["soup1:NDTS",
    "soup2:NDTS", "soup3:NDTS" ];
constant kMySoupUserName := "Souper Thing";
DefConst('kSoupPackageName, "Soups:" & kPackageName);
```

```
InstallScript := func (partFrame)
begin
   local ed        := GetRoot().extrasDrawer;
   local iStore    := GetStores()[0];

   //check if our icon is already installed
   if Length (ed:GetExtraIcons ('soupEntry,
         kSoupPackageName, iStore)) = 0 then
      call kAddExtraIconFunc with
         ('soupEntry,
         {  //soups we are combining
            soupNames: kMySoupNamesArray,
            //title shown under the icon
            text : kMySoupUserName,
            //for the soupervisor mechanism
            ownerApp : kAppSymbol,
            //for access via SetExtrasInfo
            app : kSoupPackageName,
         }
         //Note, we do not use kPackageName since
         //we don't want the icon moved when the
         //package is moved.
         kSoupPackageName,
         iStore);
end;
```

The Extras Drawer method GetExtraIcons used in the above code to obtain an array of soup icons that match the package name is described in GetExtraIcons (page 16-90) in *Newton Programmer's Reference*.

Removing a Soup Icon

Use the Extras Drawer method RemoveExtraIcon to remove your soup icon, as in the following code:

```
//A good place for this would be in a DeletionScript
local ed := GetRoot().extrasDrawer;
foreach icon in ed:GetExtraIcons ('soupEntry,
      kSoupPackageName, GetStores()[0]) do
   ed:RemoveExtraIcon (icon);
```

Creating a Script Icon

Installation of a script icon is basically the same as that for a soup icon. The two main differences are that the symbol 'scriptEntry is passed in for the *iconType* parameter of AddExtraIcon, and the *paramFrame* argument contains different slots. However, with a script icon it is not important to keep this icon in the internal store. Instead, you should ensure that the icon is installed on the same store as the package with which it is associated.

The most likely use for a script icon is for a transport to bring up an interface for user preferences. The code sample shown below brings up a such a slip:

```
//Useful constants.
DefConst('kMyConfigSlipSym,
        Intern("configSlip:" & kAppSymbol));
constant kScriptIconName    := "ScriptIcon Slip";
constant kScriptIconPkgName:= Intern ("Script:" &
   kAppSymbol);

// get the icon picture
r := OpenResFileX(HOME & "pictures");
DefConst('kMyScriptIcon, GetPictAsBits("TARDIS", nil));
CloseResFileX(r);

// the tap action, small and simple
DefConst('kTapScript, func()
        GetGlobalVar(kMyConfigSlipSym):Open() );

DefConst('kScriptIconParamFrame,
        {
        // name in the Extras Drawer
        text: kScriptIconName,
         // icon in the Extras Drawer
        icon: kMyScriptIcon,
        // to allow access via SetExtrasInfo
        app:kScriptIconPkgName,
        // function to call when icon is tapped
        tapAction: kTapScript
        }
);
```

```
InstallScript := func(partFrame, removeFrame)
begin
   local mySlip := GetLayout("MySlip.t") ;

   // install the slip
   DefGlobalVar (kMyConfigSlipSym, BuildContext(mySlip));

   local ed := GetRoot().extrasDrawer;

   //Figure out which store our package is in. This code
   //will work for a form part, as long as the argument
   //to ObjectPkgRef is a reference type (i.e., a
   // pointer).
   local myStore := GetVBOStore(ObjectPkgRef(mySlip));

   //check if our icon is already installed
   if Length(ed:GetExtraIcons('ScriptEntry, kPackageName,
             myStore)) = 0 then
        call kAddExtraIconFunc with
             ('ScriptEntry,
              kScriptIconParamFrame,
              kPackageName,
              myStore);
end;

RemoveScript := func(removeFrame)
   // remove the slip
   UnDefGlobalVar(kMyConfigSlipSym);
```

Note that you do not have to remove the script icon, since it is associated with your package. When the package is removed, the icon is removed as well. But if you wish to remove it at some other time, you can do so with a call to the Extras Drawer method `RemoveExtraIcon`.

Using the Soupervisor Mechanism

In order to take advantage of the soupervisor mechanism, you need to do the following:

1. At build time, add an `ownerApp` slot to your part frame. This slot should be set to your application symbol. You can do this with a call to `SetPartFrameSlot`, as in the following code:

```
call SetPartFrameSlot with ('ownerApp, kAppSymbol);
```

2. Add a frame called `soupervisor` to your application's base view. Note that this means you cannot add a `soupervisor` frame to an autopart unless `GetRoot.(kAppSymbol)` exists. This frame must have a slot called `type`. The possible values for the `type` slot are

`'moveOnly`	Allows a user to move all soup entries to a different store.
`'fileOnly`	Allows a user to file all soup entries to a different folder.
`'all`	Allows a user to move and file all soup entries.

3. Create a soup icon whose `ownerApp` slot is your application's application symbol; see "Adding a Soup Icon" beginning on page 19-40.

If you wish to gain control over this process (or some part of it), you may define one or more of the following optional methods in your soupervisor frame: `FileSoup`, `FileEntry`, and `MoveEntry`. These three methods are described in "The Soupervisor Frame" (page 16-86) in *Newton Programmer's Reference*.

System Data

This section describes the API to system stored data and how to store application preferences in the system soup.

About System Data

The system stores user preferences and other system information in a soup called "System," which you should reference with the constant `ROM_SystemSoupName`. This soup holds information such as the user's address and phone number, the currently selected printer, and handwriting recognition settings.

Your application can use this data to customize itself to the user's current situation, and save the user some writing or tapping. Your application can be registered to be notified when changes are made to this data.

You may also store a single entry in this soup with application-specific preferences.

Using System Data

This section describes

■ The functions used to access user configuration data, and to register an application to be notified of changes to this data.

■ How to create an entry in the system soup for your application's preferences.

Functions for Accessing User Configuration Data

The global functions `GetUserConfig` and `SetUserConfig` get and set the values of user configuration variables in the system soup. These variables, see "User Configuration Variables" (page 16-101) in *Newton Programmer's Reference*. A list of these variables is available in the Summary; see 19 "User Configuration Variables."

Your application can also register with the system to receive notification of changes to these variables. To do this, use the functions `RegUserConfigChange` and `UnRegUserConfigChange` described in *Newton Programmer's Reference*.

IMPORTANT

The `RegUserConfigChange` global function registers a callback function for execution in response to changes the user configuration variables. This callback function must not call `RegUserConfigChange` or `UnRegUserConfigChange`. ▲

Storing Application Preferences in the System Soup

Each application that needs to save user preference or state information should create a single entry in the system soup to store its data. Each entry in the system soup must contain a slot named `tag` whose value is a string uniquely identifying the application to which the entry belongs. The system soup is indexed on the `tag` slot, allowing quick access to your application's entry.

Use the utility function `GetAppPrefs` to add your application's preferences entry to the system soup. `GetAppPrefs` takes a default frame as a parameter, so you do not need to create an entry in the system soup. The default is used if one doesn't already exist. The following sample code illustrates how this is done:

```
//define a default frame
constant kDefaultPrefs :=
          '{curCity : "Cupertino",
          //... and other application specific slots.
          // Note: we do not include a 'tag slot,
          // this will be added by GetAppPrefs.
          }


// then when we have information to store...
ourPrefsEntry := GetAppPrefs(kAppSymbol, kDefaultPrefs);
ourPrefsEntry.curCity := newCity;
EntryChange(ourPrefsEntry);
```

The `GetAppPrefs` function is described in *Newton Programmer's Reference*.

Summary

Constants and Variables

Names Card Layouts

Constant	Value
kSquiggle	0
kPlain	1
kSeparate	2
kCross	3

Dates Variables

firstDayOfWeek
useWeekNumber

Dates Constants for the Day of the Week

Constant	Value
kSunday	0x00000800
kMonday	0x00000400
kTuesday	0x00000200
kWednesday	0x00000100
kThursday	0x00000080
kFriday	0x00000040
kSaturday	0x00000020
kEveryday	0x00000FE0

Built-in Applications and System Data

Dates Constants for repeatType

Constant	Value
kDayOfWeek	0
kWeekInMonth	1
kDateInMonth	2
kDateInYear	3
kPeriod	4
kNever	5
kWeekInYear	7

Other Date Constants

Constant	Value
kForever	0x1FFFFFFF
kMaxyear	2919
kYearMissing	2920

Dates Constants for the Weeks in a Month

Constant	Value
kFirstWeek	0x00000010
kSecondWeek	0x00000008
kThirdWeek	0x00000004
kFourthWeek	0x00000002
kLastWeek	0x00000001
kEveryWeek	0x0000001F

User Configuration Variables

```
address
cityZip
company
country
countrySlot
currentAreaCode
```

```
currentCountry
currentEmporium
currentPersona
currentPrinter
dialingPrefix
doAutoAdd
doInkWordRecognition
doTextRecognition
doShapeRecognition
emailPassword
faxPhone
homePhone
leftHanded
learningEnabledOption
lettersCursiveOption
letterInFieldsOption
letterSetSelection
letterSpaceCursiveOption
location
mailAccount
mailNetwork
mailPhone
name
paperSize
paperSizes
phone
signature
speedCursiveOption
timeoutCursiveOption
userFont
```

Protos

protoPersonaPopup

```
myPersonaPopup := {
_proto: protoPersonaPopup,
SetUpText: function,// returns string to display as current
                    // persona
JamIt: function, // calls SetUpText and updates screen
...}
```

protoEmporiumPopup

```
myEmporiumPopup := {
_proto: protoEmporiumPopup,
SetUpText: function, // returns string to display as current
                  // emporium
JamIt: function, // calls SetUpText and updates screen
...}
```

protoRepeatPicker

```
myRepeatPicker := {
_proto: protoRepeatPicker,
selectedMeeting: meetingFrame, // the selected meeting
originalMtgDate: date, // if a repeating meeting, date of
                    // instance, else ignored
newMtgDate: date, // the mtgStartDate of the selected
                  // meeting
viewBounds: boundsFrame, // the bounds frame
...}
```

protoRepeatView

```
myRepeatView := {
_proto: protoRepeatView,
viewFlags: integer, // defaults to vClickable+vFloating
viewFormat: integer, // defaults to vfFillWhite +
                   // vfFrameDragger + vfPen(7) +
                   // vfInset(1) + vfRound(5)
viewJustify: integer, // defaults to vjParentCenterH
viewBounds: boundsFrame , // defaults to RelBounds
                       // (0, 0, 204, 190)
GetRepeatSpec: function, // returns a frame with repeating
                       // info
...}
```

Soup Formats

Names Soup

Person Entries

```
aPersonEntry := {
version: integer,
class: symbol,
```

```
cardType: integer,
name: frame,
names: array,
company: stringOrRichString,
title: stringOrRichString,
companies: array,
address: stringOrRichString,
address2: stringOrRichString,
addresses: array,
city: stringOrRichString,
region: stringOrRichString,
postal_code: stringOrRichString,
country: stringOrRichString,
phones: array,
email: stringOrRichString,
emailAddrs: array,
emailPassword: nil,
pagers: array,
bday: integerOrStringOrRichString,
bdayEvent: entryAlias,
anniversary: integerOrStringOrRichString,
anniversaryEvent: entryAlias,
notes: array,
sorton: string,
...}
```

Owner Entries

```
anOwnerEntry := {
version: integer,
class: symbol,
cardType: integer,
name: frame,
names: array,
company: stringOrRichString,
title: stringOrRichString,
companies: array,
address: stringOrRichString,
address2: stringOrRichString,
addresses: array,
city: stringOrRichString,
region: stringOrRichString,
postal_code: stringOrRichString,
country: stringOrRichString,
```

```
phones: array,
email: stringOrRichString,
emailAddrs: array,
emailPassword: string,
pagers: array,
bday: integerOrStringOrRichString,
bdayEvent: entryAlias,
anniversary: integerOrStringOrRichString,
anniversaryEvent: entryAlias,
notes: array,
sorton: string,
owner: frame,
...}
```

Group Entries

```
aGroupEntry := {
version: integer,
class: symbol,
cardType: integer,
group: stringOrRichString,
goupInfo: frame,
members: array,
notes: array,
sorton: string,
...}
```

Company Entries

```
aCompanyEntry := {
version: integer,
class: symbol,
cardType: integer,
name: frame,
names: array,
company: stringOrRichString,
address: stringOrRichString,
address2: stringOrRichString,
addresses: array,
city: stringOrRichString,
region: stringOrRichString,
postal_code: stringOrRichString,
country: stringOrRichString,
phones: array,
```

```
email: stringOrRichString,
emailAddrs: array,
notes: array,
sorton: string,
...}
```

Worksite Entries

```
aWorksiteEntry := {
version: integer,
class: symbol,
cardType: integer,
place: stringOrRichString,
dialingPrefix: stringOrRichString,
areaCode: stringOrRichString,
printer: string,
mailAccess: array,
connectionPhone: string,
connectionNetwork: string,
cityAlias: entryAlias,
countrySymbol: symbol,
country: stringOrRichString,
notes: array,
sorton: string,
...}
```

Dates Soups

Meeting Frames

```
aMeetingFrame := {
viewStationery: symbol,
mtgStartDate: integer,
mtgDuration: integer,
mtgText: stringOrRichString,
mtgStopDate: integer,
repeatType: integer,
mtgInfo: frame,
mtgAlarm: integer,
mtgIconType: symbol,
mtgInvitees: array,
mtgLocation: nameReference,
notesData: array,
instanceNotesData: array,
```

```
version: integer,
viewBounds: frame,
exceptions: array,
...}
```

Notes Frames

```
aNotesFrame := {
notes: array,
repeatingMeetingAlias: entryAlias,
...}
```

To Do List Soup

```
aToDoListEntry := {
class: symbol,
needsSort: Boolean,
date: integer,
topics: array,
...}
```

Notes Soup

```
aNotesEntry := {
viewStationery: symbol,
class: symbol,
height: integer,
timeStamp: integer,
labels: symbol,
data: array,
topics: array,
...}
```

Functions and Methods

Names Application Methods

cardfile:AddCard(*dataDefType*, *entryFrame*) // creates a new
    // card in the Names application
cardfile:AddCardData(*entry*, *layoutSym*, *newData*) // adds data
    // to an existing card
cardfile:AddLayout(*layout*) // adds a view definition to
    // the Show picker

Built-in Applications and System Data

cardfile:BcCreditCards(*inEntry*, *inWhich*) // returns the
    // credit card information
cardfile:BcCustomFields(*inEntry*, *inWhich*) // returns custom
    // field information
cardfile:BcEmailAddress(*entry*, *which*) // returns e-mail
    // information
cardfile:BcEmailNetwork(*entry*, *type*)// returns e-mail
    // network information
cardfile:BcPhoneNumbers(*inEntry*, *inWhich*) // returns an
    // array of phone numbers
cardfile:OpenTo(*entry*, nil) // opens Names to a card
cardfile:ReplaceInkData(*entry*, *layoutSym*, *oldString*, *checkPath*,
newString) // replaces a specified ink string with a
    // recognized string
RegNamesRouteScript(*symbol*, *routeScriptFrame*) // adds an
    // action to the Action picker (platform file func)
cardfile:SafeRemoveLayout(*layout*) // removes a layout added
    // with AddLayout (platform file function)
cardfile:ShowFoundItem(*entry*, nil) // opens a card if Names
    // is open
UnRegNamesRouteScript(*symbol*) // removes an action added
    // with RegNamesRouteScript (platform file function)

Dates Application Methods

calendar:AddAppointment(*mtgText*, *mtgStartDate*, *mtgDuration*,
    repeatPeriod, *repeatInfo*) // adds a meeting to a Dates soup
calendar:AddEvent(*mtgText*, *mtgStartDate*, *repeatPeriod*, *repeatInfo*)
    // adds an event to a Dates soup
calendar:DeleteAppointment(*mtgTextOrFrame*, *mtgStartDate*,
    deleteOneOnly) // deletes specified meeting(s)
calendar:DeleteEvent(*mtgTextOrFrame*, *mtgStartDate*,
    deleteOneOnly) // deletes specifed event
calendar:DeleteRepeatingEntry(*mtgTextOrFrame*, *mtgStartDate*,
    deleteOneOnly) // deletes specified repeating meeting or
    // event series
calendar:DisplayDate(*date*, *format*)// displays meetings,
    // events, or To Do tasks for a date
calendar:FindAppointment(*mtgText*, *findWords*, *dateRange*, *type*,
    maxNumberToFind) // returns specified mtgs or events
calendar:FindExactlyOneAppointment(*mtgText*, *findWords*,
    dateRange, *type*) // returns a specified mtg or event
calendar:FindNextMeeting(*date*) // returns startDate and
    // duration of next meeting after a date

calendar:GetMeetingIconType(*mtgTextOFrame*, *mtgStartDate*)
    // returns the type of icon of a meeting or event
GetCalendarMeetingType() // returns an array of meeting
    // types registered with Dates (platform file func)
GetCalendarMeetingTypeInfo(*typeSymbol*) // returns
    // information about a meeting type registered with
    // Dates (platform file function)
calendar:GetMeetingInvitees(*mtgText*, *mtgStartDate*) // returns
    // list of invitees
calendar:GetMeetingLocation(*mtgText*, *mtgStartDate*) // returns
    // meeting location
calendar:GetMeetingNotes(*mtgText*, *mtgStartDate*) // returns
    // notes for a meeting
calendar:GetSelectedDates() // returns currently selected
    // date(s)
calendar:MoveAppointment(*mtgText*, *mtgStartDate*, *newStartDate*,
    newDuration) // changes date or duration of specified
    // meetings or events or repeating series
calendar:MoveOnlyOneAppointment(*mtgText*, *mtgStartDate*,
    newStartDate, *newDuration*) // changes date or duration of
    // a specified meeting or event or repeating meeting
    // or event instance
calendar:OpenMeetingSlip(*meetingFrame*, *date*, *openDefaultSlip*)
    // opens slip for specified meeting
calendar:RegInfoItem(*symbol*, *frame*) // adds item to info
    // picker
calendar:RegMeetingType(*symbol*, *frame*) // adds meeting type
    // to New picker
myMeetingType:NewMeeting (*date*, *parentBox*) // creates a new
    // meeting for custom meeting type
myMeetingType:OpenMeeting(*meeting*, *date*, *parentBox*) // opens
    // meeting slip for custom meeting type
calendar:RememberedClose(*view*)// closes view opened with
    // RememberedOpen
calendar:RememberedOpen(*view*) // opens view and sets up
    // closing of view with calendar
calendar:SetEntryAlarm(*mtgText*, *mtgStartDate*, *minutesBefore*)
    // sets alarm for specified meeting
calendar:SetMeetingIconType(*mtgText*, *mtgStartDate*, *newIconType*)
    // sets icon type for specified meeting or event
calendar:SetMeetingInvitees(*mtgText*, *mtgStartDate*, *invitees*)
    // sets list of invitees for specified meeting
calendar:SetMeetingLocation(*mtgText*, *mtgStartDate*, *location*)
    // sets location for specified meeting

calendar : SetMeetingNotes (*mtgText, mtgStartDate, notes*)
    // sets notes for specified meeting or event
calendar : SetRepeatingEntryStopDate (*mtgText, mtgStartDate, mtgStopDate*)
    // sets last date for specified repeating
    // meeting or event
calendar : UnRegInfoItem (*symbol*) // removes item from info
    // picker
calendar : UnRegMeetingType (*symbol*) // removes meeting type
    // from New picker

To Do List Methods

toDoFrame : CreateToDoItem (*date, richString, reminder, frequency*)
    // adds a task on specified date
toDoFrame : CreateToDoItemAll (*date, richString, reminder, frequency,*
    priority, completed) // Adds a task with
    // priority and completion information
toDoFrame : EnsureVisibleTopic (*index*) // Scrolls the To Do
    // List as necessary to display a task
toDoFrame : GetToDoItemsForRange (*beginDate, endDate*) //Returns
    // topics for a range of dates
toDoFrame : GetToDoItemsForThisDate (*date*) // Returns
    // topics for date
toDoFrame : GetTaskShapes (*originalShapes, task, yOffset, width, font*)
    // Returns an array of shapes for the task
toDoFrame : GetToDoShapes (*date, yOffset, width, font*) // Returns
    // an array of shapes for the task
toDoFrame : LastVisibleTopic () // Returns the index of the
    // last topic drawn in the view
toDoFrame : NextToDoDate (*date*) // Returns the date of the
    // next task
toDoFrame : RemoveOldTodoItems (*beforeDate, removeWhich, nil*)
    // Removes tasks from before a sppecified date
toDoFrame : SetDone (*index, topic, done, nil, nil*) // Marks a task
    // completed
SetPriority (*index, priority, undo*) //Sets the priority of a task

Time Zone Functions

```
GetCityEntry(name) // returns information about the
   // specified city
GetCountryEntry(name) // returns information about the
   // specified country
worldClock:SetLocation(whichCity) // sets the current city
worldClock:NewCity(newCity, nil, makeHome) // adds a city
```

Notes Methods

```
paperroll:MakeTextNote(string, addIt) // adds a text note to
    // Notes soup
paperroll:NewNote(note, goto, store) // adds a note to
    // Notes soup
```

Prefs and Formulas Functions

```
RegFormulas(appSymbol, formulasTemplate) //registers a template
   // to be added to the Formulas roll
UnRegFormulas(appSymbol) //unregisters a template added
   // with RegFormulas
RegPrefs(appSymbol, prefsTemplate) //registers a template
   // to be added to the Prefs roll
UnRegPrefs(appSymbol) //unregisters a template added
   // with RegPrefs
```

Auxiliary Button Functions

```
app:AddAuxButton(buttonFrame) // message sent when
   // RegAuxButton is called with your app as destApp
GetAuxButtons(appSymbol) // returns array of your app's
   // buttons
RegAuxButton(buttonSymbol, template) // registers a button to
   // be added to another application
app:RemoveAuxButton(buttonSymbol) // message sent when
   // UnRegAuxButton is called for one of your app's
   // buttons
UnRegAuxButton(buttonSymbol) // removes an auxilary button
   // added with RegAuxButton
```

Extras Drawer Functions and Methods

extrasDrawer:AddExtraIcon(*iconType*, *paramFrame*, *pkgName*, *store*)
    // adds an icon (platform file function)
extrasDrawer:GetExtraIcons(*iconType*, *pkgName*, *store*)
    // returns array of icons added with AddExtraIcon
extrasDrawer:GetPartCursor(*packageName*, *store*, *folderSym*)
    // returns cursor that iterates over parts (icons)
    // (platform file function)
extrasDrawer:GetPartEntryData(*entry*) // returns information
    // about a part (platform file function)
extrasDrawer:LaunchPartEntry(*entry*) // launches a part entry
    // (platform file function)
extrasDrawer:RemoveExtraIcon(*extraIcon*) // removes an icon
    // added with AddExtraIcon
extrasDrawer:SetExtrasInfo(*paramFrame*, *newInfo*) //changes
    // information about an icon (platform file function)

System Data and Utility Functions

GetSysEntryData(*entry*, *path*) // returns the value of a
    // specified slot in a built-in soup entry
GetUserConfig(*configSym*) // returns the value of a user
    // configuration variable
RegUserConfigChange(*callbackID*,*callBackFn*) // registers
    // a function called when a user configuration
    // variable changes
SetSysEntryData(*entry*, *path*, *value*) // sets the value of a
    // specified slot in a built-in soup entry
SetUserConfig(*configSym*, *theValue*) // sets the value of a
    // user configuration variable
UnRegUserConfigChange(*appSymbol*) // unregisters a
    // function registered by RegUserConfigChange
UseCurrentEmporium() //makes system update user
    // configuration variables based on the value of the
    // currentEmporium variable
UseCurrentPersona() //makes system update user
    // configuration variables based on the value of the
    // currentPersona variable

CHAPTER 20

Localizing Newton Applications

This chapter discusses how to support multiple languages and use locale-specific user preferences to customize the way an application handles numbers, dates, and times.

This chapter also discusses how locale settings affect the set of dictionaries the system uses for handwriting recognition. The recognition information in this chapter assumes a basic understanding of handwriting recognition issues. If you need more information on this subject, you should read Chapter 9, "Recognition."

About Localization

The goal of localization functions is to let you set up applications so you can build versions in different languages without changing the source files.

There are two basic approaches to localization:

- You can fully localize your application at compile time, replacing objects in English with objects in other languages. This is discussed in "Defining Language at Compile Time" (page 20-3).

- You can check preferences that the user sets to indicate preferred formats for output of dates and currency amounts. The next section discusses these user settings. "Determining Language at Run Time" (page 20-6) discusses this and related issues.

The Locale Panel and the International Frame

The Locale panel lets a user tell the Newton device the conventions that should be used to interpret input and display information. The user can specify values for the country, keyboard type, and paper size in this panel, which is shown in Figure 20-1. The system stores the Locale panel settings in the International Frame.

Figure 20-1   The Locale settings in Preferences

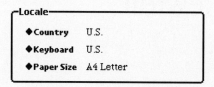

The most important of these settings is the Country pop-up menu. Every Newton device contains a number of frames for tailoring the system's responses to match the conventions of a specified location. These frames are called **locale bundles.** At any time, one and only one of these locale bundles is active; that is called the **active locale bundle.** The user can change the active locale bundle by using the Country pop-up menu from the Locale panel.

The values in a locale bundle specify a variety of items, such as locally popular formats for displaying currency values and other numbers.

Each Newton device may contain different locale bundles:

- Every Newton device contains locale bundles in its ROM, which vary depending on what ROM the device has. For example, the German version of the Newton MessagePad does not have the same built-in locale bundles as the English version.

- Applications can add locale bundles to provide locale settings for additional countries, or to override built-in locale bundles. For information on how to do this, see "Adding a New Bundle to the System" (page 20-8).

Locale and ROM Version

Newton devices are sold with ROMs in different versions, such as an English ROM and a German ROM. However, it is the active locale, rather than the ROM version, that controls localized information.

How Locale Affects Recognition

As you change settings in the Locale panel, the set of dictionaries used for word recognition does not change. However, altering the locale changes the set of system lexical dictionaries and change the recognizable formats for dates, times, and numbers.

For entering dates, times, and numbers, you can think of the entry process as consisting of three stages:

- Recognizing the handwriting. This uses the recognition lexical dictionaries.

- Understanding what the recognized text means. This uses the system lexical dictionaries.

■ Displaying the text. This uses the date, time, and number formatting attributes of the active locale bundle.

The recognition lexical dictionaries need to be, and are, most tolerant. Because the formats specified in these dictionaries are more loosely defined, you can actually combine the different formats being used in different countries. These dictionaries accept constructs such as "77/34/56", a string that doesn't make much sense.

The system lexical dictionaries are used to interpret (that is, parse) recognized text, so they need to be more strict about accepted formats. For example, if given the string "12/10/96", the parser needs to know whether the user means that to represent December 10 or October 12. The system lexical dictionaries impose these restrictions, and are local-specific.

For more information about dictionary-based recognition, see Chapter 9, "Recognition."

Using the Localization Features of the Newton

This section describes how to localize your applications using the built-in features of the Newton.

Defining Language at Compile Time

You can write an application so that the language used in strings and other objects is determined at compile time. There are essentially three parts to doing this:

■ You define objects called **localization frames** that define the objects for different languages. "Defining a Localization Frame" (page 20-4) discusses how to do this.

■ You use the LocObj function in place of using the language-dependent object directly. "Using LocObj to Reference Localized Objects" (page 20-4) discusses how to do this.

■ You define the language for a build by using the Project Settings item in the Project menu. See the *Newton Toolkit User's Guide* for information on project settings.

When you do this, you may also want to build strings from components and measuring the lengths of strings at compile time so that you can arrange your displays. "Use ParamStr Rather Than "&" and "&&" Concatenation" (page 20-5) and "Measuring String Widths at Compile Time" (page 20-6) discuss how to do those tasks.

Defining a Localization Frame

You define the alternative language frames with the `SetLocalizationFrame` function in a text file included in the project. Here is an example:

```
SetLocalizationFrame({
    Swedish: {
        find: {
            searchFor:
                "Söker efter ^0…",    // "Searching for ^0…"
        . . .}},
    French: {
        find: {
            searchFor:
                "Recherche dans ^0…",// "Searching for ^0…"
        . . .}}
});
```

When the Language setting in the Project Settings dialog box is English, NTK uses the string included in the code itself ("Searching for *name*"). When the Language setting is Swedish, NTK looks for the string contained in the slot `Swedish.find.searchFor` in the language frame.

You can place other kinds of objects in localization frames. For example, suppose that you have an integer value that varies by language:

```
SetLocalizationFrame({
    French: {
        languageInt: 1,
    },
    Swedish: {
        languageInt: 2,
    },
    German: {
        languageInt: 3.
    }
});
```

To avoid name collisions, it's a good idea to use at least one extra naming level, such as in the first example, which uses `find`. You can set up data objects in as complex a hierarchy as you need within the language frame.

Using LocObj to Reference Localized Objects

The `LocObj` function takes two parameters:

- A string or other object; this is used in the English-language version of the application.

■ A frames path the compiler uses to find the alternative object when the Language setting in the Project Settings dialog box is for anything other than English. You should avoid having reserved words in the path—refer to Appendix A of *The NewtonScript Programming Language* for a complete list of reserved words in NewtonScript.

If you display a message while searching for an object, for example, you can set up the message for any language by wrapping the string in the LocObj function:

```
msg := LocObj("Searching for ^0…", 'find.searchfor)
```

When an English-language version of the application is compiled, the LocObj function simply returns its first argument; this implementation helps keep code readable by allowing you to use English strings in your code. For non-English versions of the application, the LocObj function uses the value of the language slot in NTK Package Settings and the path expression passed as its second argument to return the appropriate object from the localization frame.

As another example, an application that is not localized might provide user feedback by passing the string "Not found." to the SetStatus function, as in the following code fragment:

```
:SetStatus("Not found.");
```

The localized version of the same code uses the LocObj function to return a path expression based on the 'find.nope argument and the language for which the application is compiled. The SetStatus function then uses this path expression to reference the localized string. Because the LocObj function returns this path expression as its result, the argument to SetStatus can be "wrapped" in a call to the LocObj function, as in the following line of code:

```
:SetStatus( LocObj("Not found", 'find.nope) );
```

The object passed to the LocObj method doesn't have to be a string; it can be an array or an immediate value.

The path expression that references the object must be unique across the entire system. Thus, to avoid name collisions, it's recommended that you use additional naming levels based on your application symbol; for example, 'myApp.find.nope introduces a third naming level to the path expression.

Use ParamStr Rather Than "&" and "&&" Concatenation

While it is often convenient to use the ampersand string concatenators & and &&, the ParamStr function provides a much more flexible and powerful way to parameterize the construction of strings, which helps you customize your strings for different languages by, for example, varying word order.

Measuring String Widths at Compile Time

When the size of a screen element depends on the size of associated text, you can use the MeasureString function to determine, at compile time, how big to make the screen element. If you want to determine the size at runtime, use StrFontWidth.

You could establish the width of the search message, for example, by using MeasureString and LocObj together.

```
MeasureString(LocObj("What is your name?",
                     'find.nameQ), simpleFont12);
```

At compile time, the MeasureString call is replaced with a constant as long as the arguments to MeasureString are also constant. (LocObj produces a constant result at compile time.) You could access the width at run time from the view's ViewDrawScript method with this function:

```
func()
   begin
   local newBounds := deepClone(viewBounds);
   newBounds.right := newBounds.left +
        MeasureString("This is a string", simpleFont12);
   SetValue(self, 'viewBounds, newBounds);
end
```

Determining Language at Run Time

You can determine the language at run time, and your program can use that information to modify its behavior.

There are two ways to determine the current language:

- Examine the active locale bundle. You can also add new locale bundles to give the user new locale options and can set the locale from within your program. The sections that follow discuss how to examine the active locale bundle.

- Use the GetLanguageEnvironment function to find out the native language for which the ROMs on the Newton device are implemented.

Note that you need to decide which of these methods your application should use in order to determine its behavior.

Examining the Active Locale Bundle

The global function GetLocale returns the active locale bundle, which is the locale bundle that the Country pop-up is currently set to. Use this function rather than accessing the frame directly.

For example:

```
activeLocale:=GetLocale();
```

Once you've obtained a bundle, you can examine it to see how your application should interpret user input or display output.

See "Contents of a Locale Bundle" (page 17-1) in *Newton Programmer's Reference* for information on the slots of a locale bundle.

Changing Locale Settings

You cannot change settings in the active locale bundle. To change locale settings, you need to create a new locale bundle that has the values you want and make it the active locale. This is called a **custom locale bundle.** See the next section for information on how to create on of those.

Creating a Custom Locale Bundle

Every custom locale bundle has a _proto slot that references another locale bundle. To create your application's custom locale bundle, use the FindLocale function to get the frame to be referenced by your custom locale bundle's _proto slot.

IMPORTANT

Your custom bundle's _proto slot must ultimately reference a system-supplied locale bundle. That does not have to be direct— you can reference a custom bundle that you know references a system-supplied bundle, for example. ▲

Your custom locale bundle is simply a frame that includes this _proto reference and any additional slots you wish to define to override the values of those inherited from the prototype. Your custom locale bundle should look like the code in the following example:

```
usLocaleBundle := FindLocale('usa);
myLocaleBundle :=
        {
        _proto: usLocaleBundle,
        // add slots to be modified
        title: "myLocaleBundle:PIEDTS",
        localeSym: '|myLocaleBundle:PIEDTS|,
        };
```

The FindLocale function accepts as its argument a symbol specifying the locale bundle it is to return. This function returns the locale bundle that has this value in its localeSym slot.

In the preceding code example the `myLocaleBundle` frame is based on the U.S. locale bundle. It gives a new `title` and `localeSym` value, as it must, but implements no functional changes to the locale. To make changes to the locale bundle, you can add your own slots in place of the comment that says

```
// add slots to be modified
```

Your custom locale bundle must have a `localeSym` slot of its own, as well as a `title` slot that gives the string that you want to appear in the Country pop-up menu. Since there can't be another locale bundle in the system with the same symbol as your new bundle, and shouldn't be one with the same title, be careful to avoid name clashes when creating your bundle's `title` and `localeSym` values. The problems associated with creating a unique name string for a locale bundle are similar to those you might encounter when creating a name for a soup; for suggestions regarding the creation of unique name strings, see "Naming Soups" (page 11-32). Basically, you should incorporate your developer or application symbol in the bundle's title and symbol slots.

Adding a New Bundle to the System

Once you have created a locale bundle, you need to make it available to the system by using the `AddLocale` function. The following code sample shows how to pass the previously created locale bundle `myLocaleBundle` to this function:

```
Call kAddLocaleFunc with (myLocaleBundle);
```

(You call this function in this way because it is a platform file function.)

If the `localeSym` slot in `myLocaleBundle` is not unique, the new locale overrides the existing locale with the same symbol. You can override a built-in locale bundle.

Removing a Locale Bundle

To remove the custom locale bundle you have installed use the system-supplied `RemoveLocale` function.

As with any shared data, the appropriate time to remove your locale bundle is left up to you because it can be difficult to determine whether other applications are using a bundle. Even if your own application is the only one using the custom locale bundle, it can be difficult to decide whether to remove it. You wouldn't necessarily want to install it every time the application opened and remove it every time the application closed.

If you remove the active locale bundle, `RemoveLocale` makes one of the built-in locales the active locale; the locale it chooses depends on the ROM version. If your application makes a new bundle active, you may want to save the symbol of the previously active bundle, so that you can reset the value before you remove your locale bundle.

The `RemoveLocale` function accepts as its argument a symbol specifying the locale bundle it is to remove. The following code shows how to pass the locale bundle's symbol to this function:

```
RemoveLocale('|myLocaleBundle:PIEDTS|);
```

Changing the Active Locale

The `SetLocale` function searches for a specified locale bundle and makes that bundle the active locale bundle. This is equivalent to the user setting the Country value from the Country pop-up menu, and overrides the user's action. You should, therefore, save the previous setting and reset it when you finish using your locale.

This function accepts as its argument a symbol identifying the bundle to install. The following code example shows how to use the `SetLocale` function to install the custom locale frame created in "Defining a Localization Frame" (page 20-4):

```
SetLocale('|myLocaleBundle:PIEDTS|);
```

Using a Localized Country Name

When the name of a country is stored in a soup, the program that stores it should call `SetCountryClass` on the name string. That function sets the string to a class that represents the country so that if the soup entry is read on a Newton with a different ROM, a program can use `GetCountryEntry` to get the name of the country in that ROM's language. See "Obtaining Information About a City or Country" (page 19-28) for information on using `GetCountryEntry`.

Summary: Customizing Locale

The following code sample summarizes the information discussed in the preceding sections:

```
// get a bundle to use as a proto
usLocaleBundle := FindLocale('usa);

// define your custom locale bundle
myLocaleBundle :=
        {
        _proto: usLocaleBundle,
        // add slots to be modified here
        title: "myLocaleBundle:PIEDTS",
        localeSym: '|myLocaleBundle:PIEDTS|,
        }

// add myLocaleBundle to the system
AddLocale(myLocaleBundle);
```

```
//save the current locale setting
previousLocale:=GetLocale().localeSym;

//install myLocaleBundle as the active locale bundle
SetLocale('|myLocaleBundle:PIEDTS|);

//reset the previous locale setting
SetLocale(previousLocale);

//remove your locale
RemoveLocale('|myLocaleBundle:PIEDTS|);
```

Localized Output

Your application should employ locale-specific user preferences to customize its handling of numbers, dates, and times. In addition to information available from the active locale bundle, your application should use the utility functions described here to display localized strings representing dates, times, and monetary values.

Date and Time Values

The Newton system deals with dates and times as either the number of minutes since midnight, January 1, 1904 or the number of seconds since midnight, January 1, 1993. Those functions are listed in "System Clock Functions" (page 20-15) in this manual and detailed in "System Clock Functions" (page 17-20) in *Newton Programmer's Reference*.

Obviously, you generally need date and time values in formatted strings that the user can enter or read. The system has several ways of helping you get these strings:

- Some functions use the current locale setting to determine the proper format

- Some functions take a format specification as a parameter; in this case, some of the output (such as the words used for days of the week) are still determined by the locale setting)

- Some functions convert system clock values to and from date frames that have the pieces of date and time information broken into individual slots

Some parts of the strings returned are always determined by the locale bundle. In particular, the active locale bundle determines:

- The order in which date elements appear

- The delimiters that separate the various elements of the date or time string

- Words used for months and days of the week

Times always appear in hour/minute/seconds order, although you can use format specifications to vary the display of individual elements and delimiters in the time string.

Functions that Use the Locale Setting To Determine Format

These functions are quite simple. You pass in a system clock value or a string, and the function uses the date and time format information in the current locale bundle to produce a string or a system clock value. Here are the functions of this type:

```
DateNTime(time)
HourMinute(time)
ShortDate(time)
StringToDate(dateString)
StringToTime(timeString)
```

For example:

```
DateNTime(Time());
```

Depending on the locale, this might return the string:

```
"04/17/1996 10:53am"
```

See the *Newton Programmer's Reference* for more information on these functions.

Functions that Take Format Specifications

These functions take a time value and a string format specification and return a string formatted accordingly:

```
LongDateStr(time, dateStrSpec)
ShortDateStr(time, dateStrSpec)
TimeStr(time, timeStrSpec)
```

You can pass three kinds of format specifications:

- You can use one of the pre-defined format specifications in ROM_dateTimeStrSpecs

- You can use the GetDateStringSpec function to create a new format specification

- You can use the kIncludeAllElements constant, which tells the functions to use the format in the active locale

In all cases, the active locale bundle determines certain features of date and time strings, specifically the order of elements and the separators used.

Using Formats from ROM_dateTimeStrSpecs

For commonly used format specifications, the system defines formats that can be passed directly to the functions that accept format specifications. These formats are stored in ROM_dateTimeStrSpecs. See Table 17-5 (page 17-12) in *Newton Programmer's Reference* for the list of available formats.

To use one of these values, access the appropriate slot by dereferencing
ROM_dateTimeStrSpecs with a dot operator, as in the following example:

```
LongDateStr(Time(),ROM_datetimestrspecs.longDateStrSpec);
```

Using these predefined format specifications also saves the trouble of defining them
at compile time and initializing slots with the compile-time variables at run time.

Format specifications available from the ROM_dateTimeStrSpecs object are
listed in "System-Defined Format Specifications" (page 17-11) in *Newton
Programmer's Reference*

Using GetDateStringSpec

A date or time format specification is an array, the elements of which are
themselves two-element arrays. The first element in each two-element array is a
constant specifying the item to display. The second element is a constant specifying
the format in which to display that item.

The complete set of constants is listed in "Constants to Create Your Own
Specification" (page 17-13) in *Newton Programmer's Reference*.

For example, the two-element array [kElementDayOfWeek, kFormatAbbr]
specifies that the day in a date string is to be displayed in abbreviated format, such
as "Wed". On the other hand, the two-element array [kElementDayOfWeek,
kFormatLong] specifies that the day of the week is to be displayed in long
format, such as "Wednesday".

The following code example uses system-supplied constants to build an array of
[*element*, *format*] pairs specifying the output of a date string. This array is
supplied as the argument to the GetDateStringSpec function, which returns the
format specification passed to the LongDateStr function. The LongDateStr
function returns a string with the current time (returned by the Time function)
formatted as specified by the format specification:

```
// at compile time, define my array of
// element and format pairs
DefConst('myArray,
    [
        [kElementYear, kFormatNumeric],// year
        [kElementDay, kFormatNumeric],// day of month
        [kElementMonth, kFormatLong],// name of month
        [kElementDayOfWeek, kFormatLong]// day of week
    ]);
// create the formatSpec
// this spec returns a string such as "February 1, 1994"
DefConst('kmyDateSpec, GetDateStringSpec(myArray));
```

```
// get the current time
theTime:= Time();
// pass the time and the format to LongDateStr
LongDateStr(theTime,kmyDateSpec);
```

This example is deliberately verbose for purposes of illustrating how to build a format specification array.

The kIncludeAllElements Constant

If you want to use the default format for time or date strings as specified by the active locale bundle, you can pass the kIncludeAllElements constant to the functions LongDateStr, ShortDateStr, and TimeStr. You'll get the results summarized in Table 20-1.

Table 20-1   Using the kIncludeAllElements constant

Function	Format of output
LongDateStr	day of week, month, day, year in locale's default format
ShortDateStr	year, month, day in locale's default short date format
TimeStr	hour, minute, second, AM/PM, and suffix

Currency Values

Currency strings reflect localized formatting characteristics that distinguish them from other number strings. They

■ typically display a prefix or suffix indicating their denomination

■ may require an additional prefix and/or suffix that indicates whether the amount is negative.

Currency strings must also adhere to regional conventions for

■ grouping numbers

■ the delimiter that indicates these groupings

■ the character that represents the decimal point

These values are stored in a frame in the active locale bundle's numberFormat slot.

For example, the currencyPrefix slot stores the value "$" for the U.S. locale and "£" for the United Kingdom locale, while in the French Canadian locale, the currencyPrefix slot has no value and the currencySuffix slot stores the value "$".

Summary of Localization Functions

This section categorizes the date, time, locale, and utility functions in this chapter according to task.

Compile-Time Functions

These functions allow you to build an application for various language environments.

```
LocObj(obj, pathexpr)
MeasureString(str, fontSpec)
```

Locale Functions

These functions manipulate locale bundles:

```
AddLocale(theLocaleBundle) // platform file function
FindLocale(locSymbol) // platform file function
GetLocale()
RemoveLocale(locSymbol) // platform file function
SetLocale(locSymbol)
SetLocalizationFrame(frame)
```

Date and Time Functions

These functions return date or time information from the system clock. They are grouped into two categories: those that return formatted strings and those that do not.

Formatted Date/Time Functions

These functions return formatted date or time strings. Some of the functions in this list format the string according to a format specification supplied as one of their arguments; others format the string according to values stored in the active locale bundle. See the descriptions of individual functions for more information.

```
DateNTime(time)
HourMinute(time)
LongDateStr(time, dateStrSpec)
ShortDate(time)
ShortDateStr(time, dateStrSpec)
StringToDate(dateString)
StringToDateFrame(str)
```

```
StringToTime(timeString)
TimeStr(time, timeStrSpec)
```

Date Frame Functions

These functions convert system clock values to or from date frames. A system clock value is an integer giving the number of minutes since midnight, January 1, 1904 or the number of seconds since midnight, January 1, 1993; a date frame has slots with day, date, year, and so on. See Table 17-8 (page 17-27) in *Newton Programmer's Reference* for details of a date frame.

```
Date(time)
DateFromSeconds(timeInSeconds)
TotalMinutes(dateFrame)
TotalSeconds(dateFrame)
```

System Clock Functions

These functions get and set system clock values, and convert those values between seconds and minutes.

```
IncrementMonth(time, numMonths)
SetTime(time)
SetTimeInSeconds(time)
Ticks()
Time()
TimeInSeconds()
TimeInSecondsToTime(seconds)
TimeToTimeInSeconds(minutes, extraSeconds)
```

Utility Functions

These functions perform tasks related to the presentation of data in regionalized formats.

```
GetDateStringSpec(formatArray)
GetLanguageEnvironment() // platform file function
IsValidDate(date)
SetCountryClass(countryName)
```

Routing Interface

This chapter describes the Routing interface in Newton system software. The Routing interface allows applications to send, receive, and perform other operations on data, such as deleting or duplicating. The Routing interface provides a common user interface mechanism that all applications should use to provide routing services.

You should read this chapter if your application needs to provide routing services to the user. This chapter describes how to

- route items through the Out Box using transport-supplied actions
- route items using application-supplied actions
- receive incoming items through the In Box
- support viewing items in the In/Out Box

About Routing

Routing is a term that describes nearly any action taken on a piece of data. Some typical routing actions include printing, faxing, mailing, beaming (infrared communication), deleting, and duplicating. In addition to system-supplied routing services, applications can implement their own routing actions that operate on data.

Routing also describes the process of receiving data through the In Box.

The Routing interface provides the link between an application and the In/Out Box for sending and receiving data using transports. The Routing interface also provides a standard mechanism for an application to make available its own routing actions that do not use transports, such as deleting and duplicating.

The In/Out Box

The In/Out Box is a central repository for incoming and outgoing data handled by the Routing and Transport interfaces. The In/Out Box application is accessed through the In Box or Out Box icons in the Extras Drawer. The user can tap either icon to open the In/Out Box to view and operate on its contents. Once it's open, the user can switch between the In Box and the Out Box by tapping radio buttons in the application.

When open, the In/Out Box displays either the In Box, containing incoming items, or the Out Box, containing outgoing items. The user can choose to sort items in both the boxes in various ways, such as by date, transport type, or status. A transport is a type of communication service such as fax, e-mail, or beam. Figure 21-1 shows the In Box and Out Box overviews where the items are sorted by transport type.

Figure 21-1   In Box and Out Box overviews

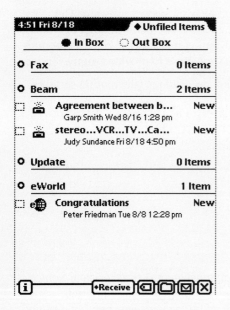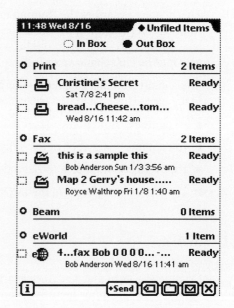

The In/Out Box uses the Transport interface internally to perform its operations.

The In Box

Incoming data items are received into the In Box and stored there. For example, the user may receive beamed items, e-mail, or fax messages. Many kinds of In Box items can be viewed in the In Box and then put away into another application residing on the Newton device. For example, the user may receive an e-mail message, read it in the In Box, and then put it away into the Notes application. The act of putting away an item transfers it to the selected application. The user can optionally delete the item from the In Box at the same time.

The In Box also supports an automatic "put away" feature. An application can register to automatically receive items designated for it. In this case, as soon as the

In Box receives such an item, it is automatically transferred from the In Box to the application, without user intervention. For example, incoming stock quotes from a wireless modem could be automatically transferred to a stock tracking application.

The In Box itself also supports routing certain items. For example, you can read incoming e-mail, reply to it, print it, or fax it directly from within the In Box.

The Out Box

Outgoing data items are stored in the Out Box until a physical connection is available or until the user chooses to transmit the items. For example, the user may fax and e-mail several items while aboard an airplane. These items are stored in the Out Box until the user reaches a destination, connects the Newton to a phone line, and sends the items.

While items are stored in the Out Box, most can be viewed, some can be edited, and routing or addressing information can be changed. For example, you can add more recipients to an e-mail message or change a fax number.

Individual transports can support automatic connection features. For example, the transport could be configured to automatically connect and send items at a certain time each day.

The Out Box itself also supports routing actions. Items in the Out Box can be sent through other transports directly from there. For example, if a fax is queued to send, the user can also print it from the Out Box.

Action Picker

Routing actions are accessed in an application from the Action button—the small envelope icon. When the user taps this button, a picker (pop-up menu) listing routing actions appears, as shown in Figure 21-2. These routing actions apply to the current target object. The **target** object typically consists of one or more selected items or the data in a view, such as the current note in the Notes application. Usually this corresponds to a soup entry or to multiple soup entries.

Figure 21-2   Action picker

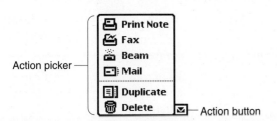

About Routing

In the user interface of your application, the Action button should be positioned differently, depending on how your application displays individual items. If your application can have more than one selectable item on the screen at a time (like Notes), the Action button should be attached to the top of the view it will act on. For example, each note in the Notes application has its own Action button, which applies just to that note. If your application displays only one data item at a time, the Action button must be on the status bar at the bottom of the screen.

You can add an Action button to the user interface of your application by adding a view based on the `protoActionButton` proto. This proto contains the functionality to create and pop up the picker.

The picker displayed when a user taps the Action button lists the routing actions available for the particular type of data selected. There are two kinds of routing actions that can appear on the Action picker:

■ routing actions that correspond to transports installed in the Newton device

■ application-defined actions that do not use the Out Box and a transport to perform the routing operation, such as Delete and Duplicate

Transport-based actions that support the type of data being routed are shown at the top of the Action picker. Application-defined routing actions appear at the bottom of the picker, below a separator line.

Note that the first action listed in the Action picker has the name of the target item appended to it (for example, "Print Note"). The Action picker obtains the name of the item from the `appObject` slot. Most applications define this slot in their base view. It holds an array of two strings, the singular and plural forms of the name of the item (for example, `["Entry", "Entries"]`).

The system builds the list of routing actions dynamically, at the time the Action button is tapped. This allows all applications to take advantage of new transports that are added to the system at any time. Applications and transports need know nothing about each other; the Routing interface acts as the bridge, creating the picker at run time.

Applications don't specify that particular transports be included on the picker. Instead, applications enable transports based on the class of data to route and the types of formats available for that data class: for example, view formats (for printing and faxing), frame formats (for beaming), text formats (for e-mail), and so on.

Here's a summary of the main steps that occur when the user taps the Action button:

1. The system obtains the target by sending the `GetTargetInfo` message to the Action button view, and then determines the class of the target.

2. Using the class of the target, the system builds a list of routing formats that can handle that class of data by looking them up in the view definition registry using the `GetRouteFormats` function. Note that only routing formats are included in the list; other view definitions are ignored.

3. Using the list of formats, the system builds a list of transports that can handle at least one of the data types supported by any of the formats. The matching transports are shown on the Action picker. Application-defined actions such as delete or duplicate are also added to the picker.

4. If the user chooses a transport-based action from the picker, the system sends the SetupItem message to the current (last-used) format for that transport and the data type being routed. Then the routing slip is opened, where the user can supply addressing information and confirm the routing action. If the user switches formats from among those available, the SetupItem message is sent to the new format.

5. If the user chooses an application-defined action from the picker, the system sends the Action button view the message defined by the application for that action (in the RouteScript slot of the routeScripts frame).

The following section describes routing formats in more detail and explains how they're used to determine what transport-based routing actions appear on the Action picker. The steps in this summary are explained in greater detail in the section "Providing Transport-Based Routing Actions" beginning on page 21-9.

Routing Formats

To implement the sending of data using the Routing interface and a transport, an application uses one or more routing formats that specify how data is to be formatted when it is routed. A routing format is a frame specifying items such as the title of the format, a unique identifying symbol, the type of data the format handles, and other information controlling how the data is handled. Some types of routing formats, such as print formats, are view templates that contain child views that lay out the data being printed. Other types of routing formats, such as frame formats, simply control how a frame of data is sent; these have no visual representation.

Here is an example of a routing format frame:

```
{_proto: protoPrintFormat,// based on this proto
title: "Two-column", // name of format
symbol: '|twoColumnFormat:SIG|, // format id

// construct child views that do the actual layout
ViewSetupChildrenScript: func() begin ... end,

// handle multiple pages
PrintNextPageScript: func() begin ... end,
...}
```

The dataTypes slot in the format indicates the types of data handled by the format. This slot and the class of the data object being routed are used to determine which transports show up in the Action picker. The system builds a list of all routing formats registered under the symbol matching the class of the object being routed. This list contains all the formats that can be used with that class of object. Remember that the class of a frame object is simply the value of the `class` slot in the frame. So, to route a frame, it must have a `class` slot that contains a value corresponding to one of the classes under which routing formats are registered. For more details about registering routing formats, see the section "Registering Routing Formats" beginning on page 21-16.

Each transport installed in the system contains a `dataTypes` array that indicates the data types it can handle, for example, `['text, 'frame]`. For the item being routed, the Action picker lists every transport whose `dataTypes` slot includes one of the types specified by the `dataTypes` slots of the routing formats associated with that item. This selection mechanism is illustrated in Figure 21-3.

For more information about transports, see Chapter 22, "Transport Interface."

Figure 21-3   Transport selection mechanism for action picker

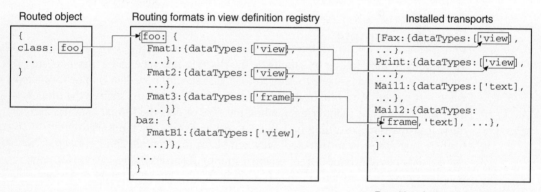

Resulting Action picker lists the transports Fax, Print, and Mail2

Once the user chooses a transport from the Action picker, the routing slip for that transport is displayed. All the routing formats that support the class of data being routed and are handled by that transport are listed in the format picker in the routing slip, as shown in Figure 21-4. The last used format for that transport in that application is set as the current format; if no last format is found, the first format found is used.

If there is an auxiliary view associated with a format, it is opened automatically when that format is selected. For more details on auxiliary views, see "Displaying an Auxiliary View" (page 21-15).

Figure 21-4   Format picker in routing slip

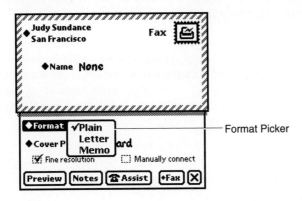

The built-in applications and transports support routing of the basic data types listed in Table 21-1. Other data types may be defined by applications, but only those transports aware of them can use them. If you do create a custom data type, you must append your developer signature to make it unique.

Table 21-1   Routing data types

Data type	Description	Built-in transport support[1]
`'view`	Data is exported in page-by-page views for operations such as printing and faxing.	print, fax
`'frame`	Data is exported as a NewtonScript frame.	beam
`'text`	Data is exported as a string.	mail
`'binary`	Data is exported as a binary object.	not applicable

[1] This column lists the built-in transports that support each of the routing data types. Note that this information is firmware-dependent. All Newton devices may not have all these transports built in, and some devices may have additional transports not listed here.

Typically, an application defines multiple routing formats to allow routing that uses different types of transports. For example, an application might define one `'frame` format, one `'text` format, and two `'view` formats.

An application may make use of built-in routing formats and other routing formats that have been registered in the system, if the application sends data of the class handled by those formats. But typically an application registers unique formats of its own that are custom designed for its own data.

You must register all routing formats that you define with the system, usually in your application part InstallScript function. Registration is discussed in the section "Registering Routing Formats" beginning on page 21-16.

Current Format

The routing system maintains a "current format," which is the last routing format used by your application for a specific transport, or the first routing format available otherwise. The current format sets the format picker in the routing slip the next time the user chooses to route an item using the same transport.

The current format is saved in a slot in the application base view. It is your responsibility to save this information to a soup if you want to preserve it. For more information, see the section "Getting and Setting the Current Format" (page 21-11).

Routing Compatibility

The Routing interface described in this chapter is entirely new in system software 2.0. The previous Routing interface, documented in the original edition of *Newton Programmer's Guide*, is obsolete, but still supported for compatibility with older applications. Do not use the old Routing interface, as it will not be supported in future system software versions.

Note that if a Newton 1.x application that includes the routing capability is run under system software version 2.0, the names of routing actions in the Action pickers may appear slightly differently than they do under Newton 1.x because of the way the picker is constructed in Newton 2.0.

Also, note that custom transports designed using the Transport interface will not be available to Newton 1.x applications.

Print Formats

In the Newton 1.x system, print formats have left and right default margins of 60 pixels. In Newton 2.0, the default margins are 0. In Newton 2.0, you must let the print format set up its own view bounds and design its child views to be positioned relative to their parent's bounds. In other words, do not modify the viewBounds and viewJustify slots of the print format.

Using Routing

This section describes how to use the Routing interface to perform these specific tasks:

- provide transport-based routing actions
- provide application-specific routing actions

- send items programmatically
- receive items
- allow items to be viewed in the In/Out Box

Providing Transport-Based Routing Actions

Here's a summary of the minimum things you need to do to support routing by the Action button in an application:

- Include the Action button in your application (or in individual views) by adding a view based on the `protoActionButton` proto.

- Supply a `GetTargetInfo` method in your application (or in individual views) or ensure that the `target` and `targetView` slots are set up correctly with the target object and target view, so the system can determine what is being routed.

- Ensure that the target data object has a meaningful class (for frame objects, this is the `class` slot). The data class is used to determine the appropriate formats, and thus transports, available to an item.

- Create one or more routing formats, using one of the routing format protos. Give your formats unique `symbol` and `title` slots, and supply the `SetupItem` method, if necessary. View formats may need a `PrintNextPageScript` method for multiple pages, and may need a `FormatInitScript` method if much preparation must be done before printing or faxing. Text formats may need a `TextScript` method.

- Register your routing formats in the application part `InstallScript` function and unregister them in the `RemoveScript` function.

To support routing through transports, your application uses one or more routing formats. These may be custom formats registered by your application or other formats built into the system or installed separately. For more information about routing formats, see the section "Routing Formats" beginning on page 21-5. There are some prototype formats built into the system that you must use to create your own formats:

- To create a format for routing a `'view` data type, use the `protoPrintFormat`; see "Creating a Print Format" (page 21-18).

- To create a format for routing `'frame` and `'text` data types, use the `protoFrameFormat`; see "Creating a Frame Format" (page 21-21).

- To create a new kind of format for data types other than `'view` or `'frame`, you can use the `protoRoutingFormat`; see "Creating a New Type of Format" (page 21-22).

The following sections describe the more detailed aspects of supporting transport-based routing.

Getting and Verifying the Target Object

When the user first taps the Action button, but before a choice is made from the picker, the Routing interface sends the Action button view the GetTargetInfo message, passing the symbol 'routing as a parameter. The purpose of this message is to get the target object to be routed and the target view in which it resides. Usually, these items are stored in slots named target and targetView in your application. If you set up and use such slots in your views, you don't need to implement the GetTargetInfo method because this is a root view method that is found by inheritance. The root view method simply looks for the slots target and targetView, starting from the receiver of the message, which is the Action button view. It returns these slots in a frame called the target information frame. If you don't use these slots in your views, you'll need to implement the GetTargetInfo method to return them.

You'll need to implement the GetTargetInfo method if the user has selected multiple items to route. In this case, you'll need to construct a single object that encapsulates the multiple items selected for routing, because the target must be a single object and it can't be a standard cursor. In your GetTargetInfo method you can use the function CreateTargetCursor to create a multiple-item target object from the selected items.

Note

In most cases the target object is a frame. In some cases you might want to route a nonframe object such as a string or binary. The Routing interface supports nonframe target objects; however, other system services such as Filing may require target objects that are frames, so you may not be able to use the same target with them. Note also that nonframe target objects must have a meaningful class for use with the Routing interface. ◆

Once the user chooses a transport-based routing action from the Action picker, the system creates a new item frame containing some default slots and values for the target item. This is done by means of the transport method NewItem. One slot that is initialized by NewItem is the appSymbol slot of the item frame. The value for this slot is obtained from the appSymbol slot of the application doing the routing (through inheritance from the Action button view).

Then, just before the routing slip is opened, the Routing interface sends the message VerifyRoutingInfo to the view identified by the appSymbol slot in the item frame. This is normally your application base view. However, if you are doing routing from a view created by BuildContext, for example, the appSymbol slot might be missing because such views don't automatically include this slot. You must include an appSymbol slot in such a view, if you need to use the VerifyRoutingInfo message, since the appSymbol slot determines where this message is sent.

The VerifyRoutingInfo method is passed two parameters, the target information frame obtained by GetTargetInfo, and the partially initialized item frame obtained from NewItem. The VerifyRoutingInfo method allows you a chance to verify or change the target item before the routing slip is opened. Normally you would return the same target frame that was passed in, possibly modified. To cancel the routing operation, you can return nil from this method.

Note that the system sends the VerifyRoutingInfo message only if it is implemented by your application; otherwise, the routing operation continues without it.

If multiple items are being routed, the target object (constructed by CreateTargeCursor) encapsulates them all. In your VerifyRoutingInfo method, you can use the function GetTargetCursor to return a cursor to navigate the items. Then you can iterate through the cursor using the cursor methods Entry, Next, and Prev, as described in Chapter 11, "Data Storage and Retrieval." Note that only these three cursor methods are supported for use with cursors returned by GetTargetCursor.

Getting and Setting the Current Format

Next, the Routing interface sends your application base view the GetDefaultFormat message. The purpose of this message is to get the default format so that when the routing slip is opened, the format can be initially set to the default. Normally, the default format for a particular transport is simply the last format used with that transport from that application. This information is stored in the lastFormats slot of your application base view. Unless you want to do something special, you don't need to implement the GetDefaultFormat method because this is a root view method that is found by inheritance. The root view method simply gets the default format symbol from the lastFormats slot.

The format can be changed by the user, or by the system (if no last format is found, the default is set to the first one that is found). When the format is changed, the Routing interface sends your application base view the SetDefaultFormat message. The purpose of this message is to store the default format symbol for later use. Normally, this is stored in the lastFormats slot in the application base view. Unless you want to do something special, you don't need to implement the SetDefaultFormat method because this is a root view method that is found by inheritance. The root view method simply sets the new format symbol in the lastFormats slot of your application base view.

The lastFormats frame contains a slot for each transport that has been used from your application. Whenever a transport is selected, the system first checks your application for the lastFormats frame and for a slot within that frame named with the symbol of the transport being used. If the slot is found, it contains the symbol of the last format used by that transport. Then the system searches for a format whose symbol slot matches it.

If your application does not have a `lastFormats` slot, or if a matching format is not found (the format was unregistered), the first format found becomes the current format.

It is your responsibility to save the `lastFormats` frame to a soup if you want to maintain it, since this information is cleared on a system reset or if your application is uninstalled.

Supplying the Target Object

Next, the Routing interface sends the `SetupItem` message to the current format. This message informs the format that it is selected and an item is being routed. The `SetupItem` method is passed two parameters: a partially initialized item frame, and a target information frame, as returned by `GetTargetInfo`. The item frame is obtained from the transport method `NewItem`, which creates a new Out Box item frame containing some default slots and values. This is the frame that is to be stored in the Out Box. It must be filled in with the data object being sent.

The target information frame contains two important slots, `target` and `targetView`, which define the data object to be routed and the view that contains it, respectively. The `SetupItem` method must set the `body` slot of the item frame to the value contained in the `target` slot of the target information frame. This fills in the item frame with the actual data to be sent.

You are not required to provide a `SetupItem` method in routing formats since this method is defined in the routing format protos. The `SetupItem` method defined in the protos simply assigns the `target` slot in the target information frame to the `body` slot of the item frame. You can override this method if you want to perform additional operations and still call the inherited `SetupItem` method. Note that there's a potential problem with not copying the target object. If the object is viewable and editable and the user edits the object in the Out Box, that potentially changes the original object stored by the application, since there are potentially not two separate objects, but two pointers to the same object.

If you want to modify the `body` slot of the item in some way, you should supply your own `SetupItem` method instead of calling the inherited version. Then in your own `SetupItem` method, clone the `target` slot of the target information frame into the `body` slot of the item frame.

When sending data to another Newton device (for example, by beaming) it's a good idea to ensure that the sent object contains a `version` slot (inside the `item.body` frame) that holds the current version of your application. This will help to reduce compatibility problems in future versions of your application. If the data format changes, your application can easily identify older and newer data formats.

Storing an Alias to the Target Object

When there is a single target object, if there is not enough storage space, or the target object is larger than a specified size, you can specify that an alias to the target object, rather than the target object itself, be stored in the `item.body` slot. This can be a soup entry alias or you can implement your own alias handling. You enable the storing of an alias by setting the `storeAlias` slot in the routing format frame to `true`. Additionally, you can specify a maximum size limit for target objects by setting the `sizeLimit` slot in the routing format frame. If any target object is larger than the size specified in this slot, and `storeAlias` is also `true`, an alias to the target object is stored in the `item.body` slot. To store every target as an alias, set `sizeLimit` to 0.

The default `SetupItem` method provided in the routing format protos reads the `storeAlias` slot and performs the appropriate operations if this slot is `true`; otherwise, it assigns the actual target object to the `item.body` slot, as usual. If an alias to the target object is stored in the `item.body` slot, the routing interface also sets the `item.needsResolve` slot to `true`, to signal that the `body` slot contains an alias that needs to be resolved.

When it's time to send an item, the format `ResolveBody` method is used to resolve an alias before the item is sent. The item won't be sent until the alias is resolved (`ResolveBody` returns a non-`nil` value), since there's no point in sending an alias.

If an alias to an item is stored, the item can still be viewed and operated upon in the In/Out Box, just like any other item.

Note that there are some potential problems if an alias to the target object is stored. If the target entry resides on a card store, and the card is removed before the item is actually sent from the Out Box, the alias cannot be resolved and the send operation on that item will fail. No matter where the original object resides, even if it is simply deleted, the send operation on that item will fail. Therefore, whenever an alias is stored, the user is warned by an alert slip explaining that the original item must be available when the routed item is actually sent. You can set the routing format slot `showMessage` to `nil` to prevent the warning message from being displayed.

Another problem with storing an alias is that the alias is just a pointer to the original data. For example, say the user faxes a note and chooses to send it later, and you store an alias to the note in the Out Box. Then the user opens the fax item in the Out Box and changes the note. This actually changes the original note in the Notes application, since the alias is a pointer to the original soup entry. Similarly, if the user changed the original note before the fax was sent, then the fax text would be changed without the user being aware of it.

Most target objects are soup entries, for which the routing format protos can handle the operations of determining the object size, making an alias, and resolving the alias when needed. However, in some cases, you may want to route objects that are not soup entries. If you want to create custom aliases to such objects, you must override the routing format methods that handle the alias operations: `TargetSize`, `MakeBodyAlias`, and `ResolveBody`.

The `TargetSize` method must determine the size of the target object passed to it. The default method does this for soup entries, but you must override it and do it yourself for other kinds of objects. The size of the object is used to determine if the object is greater than the size specified by the `sizeLimit` slot in the routing format, or greater than the available space on the store. If either of these conditions is true, an alias is created for the object.

Storing Multiple Items

You may want to send multiple items in one routing operation. This allows you to use a single routing slip to address several items at once, for example, if the user selects multiple items from an overview. If you've constructed a multiple-item target object for a group of items, you can specify that these items be stored as individual items in the Out Box or that the single multiple-item target object be stored in the Out Box. The `storeCursors` slot in the routing format controls this feature, along with the transport. This feature works only if the transport also supports it and is able to handle a multiple-item target (the transport `allowBodyCursors` slot is also `true`). For example, the built-in beam transport does not support the storing of a multiple-item target for multiple items, so the `storeCursors` slot in the routing format is ignored for that transport.

The default value of the `storeCursors` slot is `true`.

Set the `storeCursors` slot to `true` to store a single multiple-item target object for the items in the Out Box. When the items are sent, the cursor is resolved into its component entries.

Set the `storeCursors` slot to `nil` to store each of the selected items as a separate item in the Out Box. Each item can later be sent or operated on individually from the Out Box.

Using the Built-in Overview Data Class

The system includes a built-in overview data class, `'newtOverview`, that you can use to simplify routing from overviews. Special formats that handle the data types `'view`, `'frame`, and `'text` are registered under this data class. (You should not register any other formats under the `'newtOverview` class.)

At the time data is actually sent from the Out Box, these special formats handle each item from the overview separately, looking for the first nonoverview format registered in the system that can handle the data class of that item. At this time, formats you have registered would be invoked separately for the individual items in the overview selection. For example, for printing, each item would be printed on a new page.

If your `GetTargetInfo` method returns a multiple-item target object by using the function `CreateTargetCursor`, you can set the class of that target object to `'newtOverview` to enable this special behavior. You'd do this using code like this:

```
CreateTargetCursor('newtOverview, myItemArray);
```

There is a limitation to using the `'newtOverview` data class, which is that this data class handles data types of `'view`, `'frame`, and `'text` only. If you want to enable other data types, or restrict the data types to just a subset of these, you'll need to create your own overview data class and register formats under that class.

Note that the overview-handling code discussed here is contained in `protoRoutingFormat`, so any format that you create can support this same functionality. To use it, you must define a multiple-item data class and then register formats under that data class.

Displaying an Auxiliary View

When the user chooses a format in the format picker, you may need to get additional information from the user in the routing slip view. You can do this by means of an auxiliary view template that you specify in the `auxForm` slot of the routing format. If you specify a view template in this slot, when the format is selected, this auxiliary view template is instantiated with the function `BuildContext` and is sent an `Open` message.

Figure 21-5 shows an example of the auxiliary view used with the built-in Memo format for Note stationery in the Notes application. This view gets information to be used for the Name and Subject fields of the memo header.

Figure 21-5   Auxiliary view example

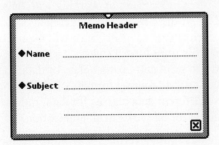

If you need access to information about the item being routed, you can access the `fields` slot in the auxiliary view. The system sets the `fields` slot to the frame that becomes the In/Out Box entry for the item being routed. For details on this frame, see "Item Frame" (page 18-1) in *Newton Programmer's Reference*.

If you need to read the `body` slot within the `fields` frame, note that it might contain an alias. In order to access it you must get the format and send it the `ResolveBody` message, like this:

```
theFormat := GetCurrentFormat(fields);
resolvedBodySlot := theFormat:ResolveBody(fields);
```

The `ResolveBody` method returns the data in the `body` slot whether or not it is referenced by an alias, so you can always use it.

You can store information you obtain from an auxiliary view in the `fields` frame, preferably in the `body` slot (or if `body` contains an alias, in the entry the alias points to). If you store data from the auxiliary view in a different slot, be sure the slot name has your developer signature appended to avoid future slot name conflicts.

Registering Routing Formats

All routing formats are specified as view definitions and are registered with the system by means of the global function `RegisterViewDef`. The formats that handle data types other than `'view` are not actually views, but they are registered as view definitions to take advantage of the central registration mechanism. Registering formats in this way makes them available to all applications in the system. Routing formats are specially identified in the view definition registry because the `type` slot of all routing formats is set to the symbol `'routeFormat` (or `'printFormat` in some ROM versions).

Register formats with the class of the object you want them to act on. Here is an example of registering a format:

```
RegisterViewDef(myPrintFormat, '|myDataClass:SIG|);
```

This call registers the format `myPrintFormat` as working with data whose class is `'|myDataClass:SIG|`. If the class of any target data object is `'|myDataClass:SIG|`, the format `myPrintFormat` will be available when that item is routed. The fact that this print format (with a `'view` data type) has been registered means that you can print and fax that class of data items. This mechanism enables you to have separate routing formats (and thus routing actions) for individual views, if they use different data classes for data, rather than using the same formats (and routing actions) for all views in an application.

Typically, your application registers routing formats when it is installed, in its part `InstallScript` function, and unregisters formats in its `RemoveScript` function. You use the function `UnRegisterViewDef` to unregister routing formats.

In an application part `InstallScript` function, when registering your routing formats, you must not use the Newton Toolkit function `GetLayout` to obtain a reference to the routing format layout, so that you can pass it to

RegisterViewDef. Nor should you use DefConst, or any other method that directly references the routing format. This is because the entire InstallScript function is passed to EnsureInternal (for application parts). Your routing format layouts would be copied into the NewtonScript heap, wasting precious memory.

Instead, you should use an indirect method to reference your routing format layouts. One way is to store a reference to your routing format layouts (by using GetLayout) in a slot in your application base view (for example, myRoutingFormat). Then in the InstallScript function, you can reference that slot through the expression partFrame.theForm.myRoutingFormat. Because the reference to the layout is found at run time through an argument to InstallScript, it is not copied into NewtonScript memory by EnsureInternal when your application is installed.

For example, first you could store the routing format layout in an application base view slot:

```
myRoutingFormat: GetLayout("MyNiceLayout");
```

Then in the InstallScript function, you could use code like this to register the format:

```
InstallScript(partFrame)
begin
    local myApp := partFrame.theForm;
    . . .
    RegisterViewDef(myApp.myRoutingFormat,
                    kMyMainDataClassSym);
end;
```

For more information about view definitions and the functions that act on them, refer to Chapter 5, "Stationery."

Note
If your application uses the NewtApp framework, registering routing formats is much easier. The NewtApp framework does it for you. All you have to do is add your formats to the allViewDefs frame in the application base view (that is based on the newtApplication proto). For more information, see "Using the Required NewtApp Install and Remove Scripts" beginning on page 4-21. ◆

Creating a Print Format

You create a print format by using `protoPrintFormat`. This proto is required for routing formats with a `'view` data type, such as views that you would print or fax. This proto format is actually a view template, which displays the target object visually. The data to be displayed is laid out as child views of the `protoPrintFormat` view.

Here is an example of a format based on this proto:

```
// in NTK you create a new layout for view formats
MyPrintFormat := {
    _proto: protoPrintFormat,
    symbol: '|myPrintFormat:SIG|,
    title: "PrintIt",
    ViewSetupChildrenScript: func() begin
        // construct child views for first page here
        end,
    PrintNextPageScript: func() begin
        nil;
        // construct child views for next page here
        end,
};
```

For more information about the slots and methods provided by this proto, see "Routing Format Protos" (page 18-9) in *Newton Programmer's Reference*.

Topics unique to `protoPrintFormat` are discussed in the following subsections.

Page Layout

The view based on the `protoPrintFormat` proto is automatically sized (in the `ViewSetupFormScript` method) to fit the dimensions of a page on the output device to which it is being routed. Do not change the values of the `viewBounds` or `viewJustify` slots in the print format view.

You can increase the margins used on the page by setting the `margins` slot. Set this slot to a bounds rectangle frame, like this:

```
{left: 25, top: 20, right: 25, bottom: 30}
```

Each slot in this frame is interpreted as an inset from each edge of the printable area of the paper in pixels. You must specify only non-negative values, to make sure that you don't print off the page. The default value of the `margins` slot is `{left:0, top:0, right:0, bottom:0}`.

Also, you can control the orientation of the data on the paper by setting the `orientation` slot. Specify a symbol indicating whether to use the paper vertically in portrait mode ('portrait) or horizontally in landscape mode ('landscape). The default value of the orientation slot is 'portrait. Your format should always use relative view justification and/or check the actual bounds of the print format by using the LocalBox view method. Note that you cannot change the orientation between a series of pages being printed by a single print format.

If multiple items are being routed (as from a multiple selection in an overview), you may want to print each item on a separate page or print the items one after another, placing multiple items on the same page before starting a new page. You can control this feature by setting the usesCursors slot. The default setting of this slot is nil.

If you want to lay out multiple items on a page, set the usesCursors slot of the format to true. In this case, the target object encapsulates all the items being routed in a single multiple-item object created by CreateTargetCursor. Your format should call the GetTargetCursor method to return a cursor for this object, on which you can iterate over the individual items to be routed using the cursor methods Entry, Next, and Prev. If your format can use other print formats, you can use the GetCursorFormat method of the protoPrintFormat to find formats for the individual items.

If you want to lay out each item on a separate page, or if this format cannot handle a multiple-item target object, set the usesCursors slot to nil. In this case, this format is invoked multiple times, once for each item being routed, and each item begins on a separate page.

Printing and Faxing

When an item in the Out Box is actually printed or faxed using your print format, the view represented by the print format is instantiated and drawn to the output device. As when any view is instantiated, the system sends the print format view standard messages and also routing-specific messages. For optimal printing performance, and to avoid timing out a fax connection, you need to be aware of the sequence of events and know which operations are time-critical.

Here is the sequence of events during a printing or faxing operation:

1. The transport sends the print format the FormatInitScript message, to give you an opportunity to perform initialization operations. You must perform any lengthy initialization operations in this method, before the transport connection is made. You can store initialized data in self. For more information about using FormatInitScript, see *Newton Programmer's Reference.*

2. For sending a fax only, the transport sends the print format the CountPages message. If you can determine the number of pages in the fax ahead of time, you should override this method in your print format and have it return the number of pages (not including the cover page). If you don't override this message, the transport opens the print format view in an offscreen window and performs steps 3, 4, and 6, below, to go through each page so it can count the number of pages.

Then the print format view is closed. Note that the `ViewShowScript` and `ViewDrawScript` messages are not sent to the view. This takes a lot of time for the transport to determine the number of pages, so if you can, override the `CountPages` method with one of your own.

3. The transport instantiates the print format view and sends it the `ViewSetupFormScript` message. Depending on certain factors, the transport connection might be made at the beginning of this step or in step 4. You can rely only on the connection being made sometime after step 2.

4. The transport sends the `ViewSetupChildrenScript` message to the print format view, then the child views are instantiated (and sent the standard view messages), and finally the transport sends the `ViewSetupDoneScript` and `ViewShowScript` messages to the view.

5. The transport draws the print format view and sends the `ViewDrawScript` message to the view. Note that each child view on the page is also drawn and sent the `ViewDrawScript` message, in hierarchical order. The page might be printed or faxed in "bands" (sections), so this step may repeat several times for the page.

   If you need to draw something in your `ViewDrawScript` method, you can call the view method `GetDrawBox` to determine the band that is currently being drawn. Then you can draw just those shapes that are necessary for the current band. The transport does not draw any views or shapes outside the current band. Any shapes extending outside the current band are automatically clipped.

IMPORTANT

The `ViewDrawScript` message is sent at a time-critical point in a fax operation. It is imperative that you do as little work as possible in the `ViewDrawScript` method. ▲

6. The transport sends the `PrintNextPageScript` message to the print format view. If your print format handles more than a single page of data, you must define the `PrintNextPageScript` method in your print format. The transport sends this message each time it reaches the end of a page, to allow you to construct the next page of data. While there is more data to route, this method should return a non-`nil` value; in that case, the printing process continues with the next page at step 4. When there is no more data to route, the `PrintNextPageScript` method should return `nil`; in that case the printing process ends and the connection is closed.

You set up the child views containing the data for the first page in the `ViewSetupChildrenScript` method of your print format. Typically, you do this by setting the value of the `stepChildren` array. Don't forget to call the inherited method (`inherited:?ViewSetupChildrenScript`) so that the proto behavior is preserved.

The `PrintNextPageScript` method should construct the view for the next page of data so that the message `self:Dirty()` shows the view. Typically, you do this by keeping track of what data has been routed so far. When the format receives this message, you select a new set of child views representing the next page of data to send. Then you call the view method `RedoChildren`, which closes and then reopens the child views. This method also causes the transport to send your print format view the `ViewSetupChildrenScript` message again.

Note that in the `PrintNextPageScript` method, you can also change the content of child views on the current page. For example, you might want to change the content of a text field. To do this, use the `SetValue` function to pass in a new value for the view content, like this:

```
SetValue(myParagraphView, 'text, newRichString);
```

When faxing, it's best not to perform lengthy operations in the `PrintNextPageScript` method, since the connection stays open between pages. However, this is less time critical than the `ViewDrawScript` method. If possible, execute lengthy operations in the `FormatInitScript` method, which is called just once before the connection is opened.

If you need to create any custom shapes to be drawn on the page by the `ViewDrawScript` method, create the shapes in the `FormatInitScript` method. Alternatively, you can create shapes at compile time, if they are static. Because of fax connection time-out issues, minimize shape creation in the `ViewDrawScript` method, as shape creation takes too much time and the connection might time out as a result.

Creating a Frame Format

You create a frame format by using `protoFrameFormat`. This is the standard format for routing objects with `'frame` or `'text` data types, such as for beaming and e-mail. To enable these types of transports for your data, you must register at least one format based on this proto. Here is an example of a format based on this proto:

```
MyFrameFormat := {
    _proto: protoFrameFormat,
    symbol: '|myFrameFormat:SIG|,
    title: "No comments",
    SetupItem: func(item, targetInfoFrame) begin
        local myData := clone(myTargetInfo.target);
        RemoveSlot(myData, 'comments); // remove some stuff
        item.body := myData;
        // this item.body is not a soup entry.
        // if it MIGHT be a soup entry, call
        // inherited:SetupItem(item, targetInfoFrame)
```

```
      // which takes targetInfoFrame.target and makes an
      // alias, if appropriate
      end,
    TextScript: func(item,target) begin . . . end,
    ...
};
```

Note that one application can have multiple frame formats. You would simply supply a different SetupItem method for the different formats (as well as unique symbol and title slots), to construct the item frame differently.

If your frame format doesn't support the 'text data type, you should override the dataTypes slot and set it to ['frame].

For routing formats that support the 'text data type, you must override the default TextScript method that obtains the string data, if there are no data definitions for the data that contain their own TextScript method.

For more information about the slots and methods provided by this proto, see "Routing Format Protos" (page 18-9) in *Newton Programmer's Reference*.

Creating a New Type of Format

You create a new type of routing format by using protoRoutingFormat. This is the base routing format, which serves as a proto for the other routing format protos.

Here is an example of a format based on this proto:

```
MyNewFormat := {
   _proto: protoRoutingformat,
   dataTypes: ['binary],
   symbol: '|myFormat:SIG|,
   title: "Custom",
   SetupItem: func(item, targetInfoFrame) begin
      call kMyFunkySetup with (item, targetInfoFrame);
      end,
   ...
};
```

For more information about the slots and methods provided by this proto, see "Routing Format Protos" (page 18-9) in *Newton Programmer's Reference*.

Providing Application-Specific Routing Actions

First, to provide the Action button in the user interface of your application, you must include a view based on the protoActionButton proto. For details, see protoActionButton (page 18-7) in *Newton Programmer's Reference*.

Your application can provide internal application-defined actions, such as deleting and duplicating, that do not use the Out Box and a transport to perform the routing operation. These routing actions appear at the bottom of the Action picker.

You define these routing actions by providing a slot named routeScripts in your application. The Action button searches its own context for the first routeScripts slot that it finds. Usually you define routeScripts in the base view of your application. That way, all child views can find it by inheritance. But if you want to have different routing actions active for different views, you can define a routeScripts slot in each child view definition, where it will override the one in the base view.

Alternatively, instead of defining an array of application-specific routing actions in the routeScripts slot, you may want to build the array dynamically. To do this, you can override the root view method GetRouteScripts, which is used by the Routing interface to obtain the routeScripts array from your application. The default version of this method simply returns the contents of the routeScripts slot to the Routing interface. In the GetRouteScripts method, build and return an array like one you would define in the routeScripts slot.

If you provide a routeScripts slot, it must contain an array of frames, one for each routing action item, that look like this:

```
{title: "MyAction", // name of action
icon: GetPictAsBits("MyActionIcon",nil), // picker icon
RouteScript: 'MyActionFunc, // called if action selected
// other slots and methods you need
...}
```

To include a separator line in the Action picker's list of application-specific routing actions, include the symbol 'pickSeparator in the routeScripts array between the two items you want to separate. Alternatively, you can include a nil value to include a separator line.

For delete and duplicate actions, there are bitmaps available in ROM that you can use as icons. For the icon slot of a delete action, you can specify the magic pointer constant ROM_RouteDeleteIcon. For the icon slot of a duplicate action, you can specify the magic pointer constant ROM_RouteDuplicateIcon.

If your application registers view definitions with the system, note that each view definition can define its own routeScripts array. The routing action items that apply to the individual view definition are added below those that apply to the whole application in the Action picker. See the following section for more information about specifying routeScripts in stationery.

Performing the Routing Action

The important slot in each frame in the `routeScripts` array is the `RouteScript` slot. This slot contains either a symbol identifying a method, or a function directly, that is called if the user chooses this action from the Action picker. This function is where you perform the routing action. The function you define is passed two parameters, *target* and *targetView*, which define the data object to be routed and the view that contains it, respectively.

The two values, *target* and *targetView*, are obtained from your application by the Routing interface. As soon as the Action button is first tapped, the Routing interface sends the Action button view the `GetTargetInfo` message to obtain these two values. The `GetTargetInfo` method returns a frame containing these and other slots.

If you set up and use `target` and `targetView` slots in your views, you don't need to implement the `GetTargetInfo` method because this is a root view method that is found by inheritance. The root view method looks for the slots `target` and `targetView`, starting from the receiver of the message, which is the Action button view. It returns these slots in a frame called the target information frame. If you don't use these slots in your views, you'll need to implement the `GetTargetInfo` method to return them.

The `RouteScript` slot can contain either a symbol identifying a function or it can contain a function directly. If you are defining the `routeScripts` array in a registered view definition, the `RouteScript` slot must contain a function directly. Alternatively, if your view definition is used only within your application, you can specify an `appSymbol` slot in the `routeScripts` frame and specify a symbol for the `RouteScript` slot. The `appSymbol` slot tells the system in what application to find the method identified by the `RouteScript` slot. Using the latter alternative ties the view definition to a single application.

Here is an example of how you might define the function identified by the `RouteScript` slot shown in the example frame above:

```
MyActionFunc: func(target,targetView) begin
    targetView:DeleteStuffFunc(target);
    end,
```

Handling Multiple Items

The target item, as returned by `GetTargetInfo`, may actually be a multiple-item target object that encapsulates several individual items to be routed. You can check if this is the case by using the function `TargetIsCursor`. If the target item is a multiple-item target object, and you need to act separately on the individual items, you can obtain a cursor for the items by using the function `GetTargetCursor`. Then you can use the standard cursor methods `Entry`, `Next`, and `Prev` to iterate over the cursor and return individual items. For more information about using cursors, refer to Chapter 11, "Data Storage and Retrieval." Note that only these three cursor methods are supported for use with cursors returned by `GetTargetCursor`.

Note that `GetTargetCursor` works with any kind of target data, whether or not it's a cursor. So you don't need to call `TargetIsCursor` to check before calling `GetTargetCursor`.

Here's an example of a `RouteScript` method that uses `GetTargetCursor` to operate on multiple items:

```
MyActionFunc := func(target,targetView)
   begin
      local curs := GetTargetCursor(target,nil);
      local e := curs:Entry();
      while e do begin
         :DoMyAction(e); // do the operation
         e := curs:Next();
      end;
      // update display here
   end;
```

Handling No Target Item

If the target item returned by `GetTargetInfo` is `nil`, this indicates that no target item is selected or there is nothing to do when the Action button is pressed. In this case, the system displays a warning message to inform the user of that fact. To take advantage of this warning message feature, all application-specific routing actions must be disabled when there is no target. (You may want to include some actions even when there is no target; in this case, you can ignore this section.)

To disable application-specific routing actions when there is no target, you can do one of two things:

- Define a `GetTitle` method in the `routeScripts` frame for each action, instead of a `title` slot. Then return `nil` from the `GetTitle` method to prevent that action from showing up on the picker.

- Define a `GetRouteScripts` method in your application, instead of a `routeScripts` slot. Then return `nil` or an empty array from the `GetRouteScripts` method to prevent any actions from showing up on the picker.

Note that there are different messages displayed when there is no target item (the target is `nil`) and when there are no actions available for the target item.

Sending Items Programmatically

Your application can send an item programmatically, using a specific transport or transport group, without any user intervention. The Action button is not used in this case. This is done using the global function Send.

Here is an example of how to use the Send function:

```
myItem := {
   toRef: [nameRefObject, ...], // array of fax name refs
   title: "The Subject", // title of item
   body: {class: kMyDataSym, // fax data frame
         myData: ...},
   appSymbol: kAppSymbol,
   currentFormat: kOtherPrintFormatSym
   };
Send('fax, myItem);
```

You must construct an item frame containing the data and other slots that you want to set in the item. You then pass this item frame as an argument to the Send function.

Before calling the Send function, you may want to allow the user to choose a format for the item being sent. To do this, you'll need a list of formats that can handle the item. To get a list of appropriate formats, you can use the GetRouteFormats function. Using this list, you could display a picker from which the user can choose a format.

You may also want to allow the user to choose a transport for the item being sent. To do this, you'll need a list of transports that can handle specific formats. To get a list of appropriate transports, you can use the GetFormatTransports function.

In the Send function, it's best to specify a transport group or let the user choose the transport. If you specify a specific transport, it may not be installed and the operation will fail.

In the Send function, the Routing interface obtains a default item frame from the selected transport by sending the NewItem message to the transport. The slots you specify in your item frame are copied into the default item frame obtained from the transport. Note that the default frame supplied by the transport may contain other slots used by the transport.

The slots you include in the item frame vary, depending on the transport. The In/Out Box and transports ignore slots they don't care about. Applications can use this feature to communicate information to multiple transports with the same item frame. For a comprehensive list of slots and detailed descriptions, see "Item Frame" (page 18-1) in *Newton Programmer's Reference*.

The following frame shows a summary of the slots you can include in the item frame. Note that some of the slots shown are specific to a particular transport, and you should include them only if you are sending to that transport. Also, don't include any additional slots in the item frame unless they are specific to a particular transport.

```
itemFrame := {
appSymbol: symbol, // appSymbol of sender
destAppSymbol: symbol, // receiving app, if different
body: frame, // the data to send
title: string, // item title, e-mail subject
toRef: array, // array of name refs for recipients
cc: array, // array of name refs for copied recipients
bcc: array, // array of name refs for blind copies
currentFormat: symbol, // routing format to use
connect: Boolean, // try to connect immediately?
hidden: Boolean, // hide in Out Box?
covert: Boolean, // not logged or saved in Out Box?
completionScript: Boolean, // notify app of state change?
needsResolve: Boolean, // body slot contains an alias?
// transport-specific slots
printer: frame, // the printer to use for printing
coverPage: Boolean, // use a cover page for fax?
faxResolution: symbol, // 'fine or 'normal fax resolution
phoneNumber: string, // phone number, for call transport
name: string, // name, for call transport
serviceProvider: symbol, // call; 'modem, 'speaker, or nil
saveAsLog: Boolean, // log call in Calls app?
}
```

Note that you can set any of the Boolean slots in the SetupItem method of the routing format.

Applications implementing their own custom sending functionality apart from the Action button may need to open the transport routing slip view for the user. If you need to do this, you can use the global function OpenRoutingSlip, as described in the section "Opening a Routing Slip Programmatically" beginning on page 21-29.

Creating a Name Reference

For the built-in fax and call transports, and for e-mail and other transports that use addresses, addressing information for an item to send is stored in the toRef slot of the item frame, and certain other slots such as cc, bcc, and so on. These slots contain arrays of one or more name reference objects. A name reference is simply a frame that serves as a wrapper for a soup entry (often from the Names soup, thus the term "name reference"). The name reference may contain an alias to a soup entry and even some of the slots from the soup entry. Note that you must use name references; you cannot specify soup entries directly.

To create a name reference object, use name reference data definitions registered with the system in the data definition registry. There are built-in name reference data definitions for e-mail (' |nameRef.email|), fax (' |nameRef.fax|), and call (' |nameRef.phone|) information associated with names from the Names file. These data definitions contain a method, MakeNameRef, that creates and returns a name reference.

You can pass a Names soup entry directly to MakeNameRef, or you can construct your own simple frame of information that contains the appropriate slots. Fax and call name references should include the slots name, phone, and country. E-mail name references should include the slots name, email, and country. For more information about these slots, see "Names Soup Format" (page 16-15) in *Newton Programmer's Reference*.

Here's an example of how to create a name reference for a fax phone number or an e-mail address:

```
// use a Names file entry directly
local myData := aNamesFileEntry; // entry from Names soup

// or create your own fake entry frame based on other info
local myData := {
    name:{first:"Juneau", last:"Macbeth"},
    phone: "408-555-1234", // fax phone string
    email: "jmacbeth@acompany.com", // e-mail address string
    country: "USA",
}


// then create the fax name reference
aToRef := GetDataDefs(' |nameRef.fax|):MakeNameRef(myData,
                                                ' |nameRef.fax|);
// or create the e-mail name reference
aToRef := GetDataDefs(' |nameRef.email|):MakeNameRef(myData,
                                                ' |nameRef.email|);
```

For more information about name references and the MakeNameRef method, see the documentation of protoListPicker in Chapter 6, "Pickers, Pop-up Views, and Overviews."

Specifying a Printer

For print operations, the printer slot of the item frame specifies which printer to use. This slot must contain a printer frame. The only valid way of obtaining a printer frame is from the currentPrinter variable of the user configuration data. That variable holds the printer selected by the user as the current printer. You can use this function to obtain the current printer for the item:

```
item.printer := GetUserConfig('currentPrinter);
```

If you want to provide a way for the user to select a different printer, you can use the printer chooser proto, protoPrinterChooserButton. This proto changes the setting of the current printer in the system; it actually changes the currentPrinter variable.

If you don't want to change the current printer in the user's system, but just want to let them select a printer for this one print job, then you'll need to do the following things:

1. Get and temporarily save the current value of the currentPrinter variable in the user configuration data, using GetUserConfig.

2. Display the printer chooser button, allowing the user to select a printer for this print job. When they select one, the printer chooser proto automatically changes the currentPrinter variable to the chosen one.

3. Retrieve the new value of the currentPrinter variable, using GetUserConfig, and use that for the printer slot in the item frame.

4. Reset the user's original printer choice by resetting the currentPrinter variable in the user configuration data to the value you saved in step 1. To do this you must use the function SetUserConfig.

Opening a Routing Slip Programmatically

To open a routing slip programmatically for a transport, use the OpenRoutingSlip function. First, create a new item by using the transport's NewItem method; then add routing information such as the recipient or other information to the new item frame; and finally, use OpenRoutingSlip to open the routing slip for the transport.

Here's an example of how to do these steps to open a routing slip for the built-in Call transport:

```
// opening the Call Transport routing slip
local curs, item, anEntry, class, nameRef;

// get a new item frame from the transport
// '|phoneHome:Newton| identifies the Call transport
item := TransportNotify('|phoneHome:Newton|, 'NewItem, [nil]);
if item = 'noTransport or not item then
    return 'noTransport;
```

```
// get an entry from the Names soup to use for the recipient
curs:=GetUnionSoupAlways(ROM_CardfileSoupName):Query(nil);
if curs:Entry() then
    begin
    // set the toRef slot in the item frame
    class := '|nameRef.phone|; // transport addressing class
    nameRef := GetDataDefs(class):MakeNameRef(anEntry, class);
    item.toRef :=  [nameRef];
    targetInfo := {
        targetView: getroot(),
        target: {}, // for non-Call transports, add your data here
        appsymbol: '|my:SIG|
        };
    // open the routing slip
    OpenRoutingSlip(item, targetInfo);
    // returns view (succeeded), or fails with
    // nil or 'skipErrorMessage
    end;
```

For the built-in fax and call transports, and for e-mail transports, addressing information for an item is stored in the toRef slot of the item frame. E-mail transports may also store addresses in additional slots such as cc and bcc. These slots contain arrays of one or more name reference objects. The example code above illustrates a name reference created from the data definition registered for the addressing class of the transport (in this case the Call transport). For more information about creating name references, see "Creating a Name Reference" beginning on page 21-27.

For transports that handle data (unlike the Call transport example here), you must also pass a target information frame to the OpenRoutingSlip function. The target slot in this frame contains the data to send. Note that the target slot can contain a multiple-item target object, which you can create using the function CreateTargetCursor.

Supporting the Intelligent Assistant

Besides using the standard interface for routing (the Action button), the user can also invoke routing actions by using the Intelligent Assistant and writing the name of the action. In order to determine what item to route, the Intelligent Assistant sends the GetActiveView message to your application. This method returns the view to which the GetTargetInfo message should be sent.

The GetActiveView method is implemented by default in the root view and simply returns self, the current receiver. If this return value is not appropriate for your application, you must override this method in your application base view.

Receiving Data

Incoming data arrives first as an entry in the In Box. If there is a public view definition registered for the class of the entry, the item may then be viewed directly in the In Box.

IMPORTANT

Generally, the `body` slot of every received item must have a meaningful class. (This is not strictly required if the item has an `appSymbol` slot.) If `body` contains a frame, its `class` slot identifies its data class. Items received from other Newton devices generally have a `body.class` slot. For items received from other systems, the transport must assign a meaningful class (use `SetClass`). ▲

An incoming item may be stored in the In Box until the user chooses to manually put away the item into an application, or an incoming item may be transferred automatically to an application as soon as the item arrives in the In Box. This is controlled by the applications present on the Newton and described in detail in the following sections.

If an In Box item contains an `appSymbol` slot, that slot identifies the receiving application for the item. The system uses this slot to identify the default application to which the item should be put away (if any). If the original item contained a `destAppSymbol` slot when submitted to the In Box, that slot is copied into the `appSymbol` slot to identify the application that should receive it. The receiving transport does this before the item is passed to the In Box by using the transport method `NewFromItem`.

These are the minimum steps you need to take to support receiving items through the In/Out Box in your application:

- Supply a `PutAwayScript` method in your application base view. When a user chooses to put away an item to your application from the In/Out Box, the item is passed to this method.

- Register the data classes that your application can accept by using the `RegAppClasses` function in the application part `InstallScript` function. Unregister using `UnRegTheseAppClasses` or `UnRegAppClasses` in the application part `RemoveScript` function.

Automatically Putting Away Items

The first thing the In Box does with an incoming item is to determine which applications might want to accept the item immediately. The In Box does this by checking the In Box application registry to find out if any applications have registered to accept such items; see the section "Registering to Receive Foreign

Data" (page 21-34). If a matching application is found in the registry, the appSymbol slot of the item is set to the value of the appSymbol slot in the matching application. If no matching applications are found in the registry, the item may have a pre-existing appSymbol slot, which determines the application to which it belongs. If no matching application is located in the registry and the item has no existing appSymbol slot, it cannot be put away automatically.

Next, the In Box checks for an AutoPutAway method in the base view of the application whose appSymbol slot matches that in the item. If the AutoPutAway method exists, the In Box sends the AutoPutAway message to the application, passing the incoming item as a parameter. In this way, items can be automatically transferred to an application, with no user intervention.

If the AutoPutAway method returns nil, this signals that the item could not be put away and the item is left in the In Box.

If the AutoPutAway method returns a non-nil value, it is assumed that the application handled the item. The item is either saved in the In Box or deleted from the In Box, depending on the user's preference.

If your application implements the AutoPutAway method, it can inform the system of this fact when it is installed, to receive any items that may have arrived for it while it was uninstalled. In the application part InstallScript function, call the global function AppInstalled to let the system know that the application is present. The AppInstalled function prompts the In Box to send an AutoPutAway message to the application for each In Box item that may have arrived for the application before the application was installed. Note that you must call the AppInstalled function using a deferred action, like this:

```
AddDeferredCall(GetGlobalFn('AppInstalled),[kAppSymbol]);
```

This feature is useful in cases where the application resides on a card that is not always installed in the system. Messages are held in the In Box while the application is not installed, and then when it is installed, those received messages are sent to the application with the AutoPutAway message.

The item passed to your application's AutoPutAway method is the entry from the In Box. It has several slots that are used by the In Box or the transport. The data your application uses is contained in the body slot.

If the item was sent by a custom transport that sends multiple-item target objects (such as those created by CreateTargetCursor), you might need to check if the body slot contains such an object by using TargetIsCursor. If so, you can get a cursor for the object by using GetTargetCursor, and then iterate over the cursor to handle individual items.

Manually Putting Away Items

If an item is not put away automatically, it resides in the In Box until the user chooses to put it away manually by tapping the Put Away button. When the user taps the Put Away button, the In Box displays a slip showing to which application the item will be put away. This application is the one that matches the appSymbol slot in the item. The In Box sends the PutAwayScript message to the base view of that application. The item is passed as a parameter.

The item passed to your application's PutAwayScript method is the entry from the In Box. It has several slots in it that are used by the In Box or the transport. The data your application uses is contained in the body slot.

Because the item could have been sent by a custom transport that sends multiple-item target objects (such as those created by CreateTargetCursor), you might need to check if the body slot contains such an object by using TargetIsCursor. If so, you can get a cursor for the object by using GetTargetCursor, and then iterate over the cursor to handle individual items.

If the PutAwayScript method returns nil, this signals that the item could not be put away and the In Box leaves the item in the In Box and an alert is displayed telling the user that the item could not be put away.

If the PutAwayScript method returns a non-nil value, it is assumed that the application handled the item. The item is either saved in the In Box or deleted from the In Box, depending on the user's preference as set in the Put Away slip.

If multiple applications have registered to accept data of the item's class, the system displays a picker listing those applications in the Put Away slip. The application that matches the appSymbol slot of the item is listed as the default choice. If there is no appSymbol slot, or the application is missing, then a different application is the default choice. The user can choose the application to which the data is to be sent, and the PutAwayScript message is sent to that application.

The registry used for this operation is called the application data class registry; note that it is different from the In Box application registry mentioned above. Applications can register to accept data of one or more classes by using the RegAppClasses function.

It is recommended that all applications wanting to receive items through the In Box register their capability to receive data of particular classes by calling the RegAppClasses function. If your application is no longer interested in data of these classes, or your application is being uninstalled, you can unregister to receive these data classes by using the UnRegTheseAppClasses function.

You can check which applications can accept data of a particular class by using the ClassAppByClass function.

Registering to Receive Foreign Data

To receive data from a different application or from a non-Newton source, your application must register its interest in such data with the In Box application registry. To do this, use the RegInboxApp function.

If your application is no longer interested in foreign data, or is being uninstalled, you can unregister to receive foreign data by using the UnRegInboxApp function.

Note that your application can register to receive data from a different application. If you register a test function with RegInBoxApp, and that test function returns true for a particular item, the Routing interface changes the value of the appSymbol slot in the item to be the value of the appSymbol slot in your application.

Be careful not to intercept incoming items that should be destined for other applications when using this feature. The In Box application registry overrides the appSymbol slot of the item. The system uses the appSymbol slot as well as the application data class registry (RegAppClasses) to find applications to which an incoming item can be put away. The application identified by the appSymbol slot is used as the default for the automatic put away feature (AutoPutAway) and for the Put Away picker.

Filing Items That Are Put Away

When an item is put away by an application, by default it is filed in the same folder on the receiving Newton as it was in on the sending Newton. This often makes it difficult for users to find new items, since they may be put away in folders that are undefined. To alleviate this problem, it is recommended that all incoming items be put away unfiled, so that users can more easily find items and file them where they want to. Incoming items should be put away unfiled even if the recipient has a folder of the same name as the sender.

For most applications, you put away an item unfiled by setting the item.body.labels slot to nil. However, filing techniques vary, so this may not work for all applications.

Viewing Items in the In/Out Box

When data is queued in the Out Box, or has been received in the In Box and not automatically put away, the user can view the data directly in the In/Out Box. When the user chooses to view an item in the In/Out Box by tapping the item, the system looks for a view definition of the type 'editor or 'viewer that is registered for the class of that item.

Your application should register such view definitions with the system if you want users to be able to view items from your application in the In/Out Box. If you do not provide a view definition, and there are no other view definitions available for that data class, the In/Out Box displays a generic blank view for the item. Items formatted with the 'view data type do not need a separate view definition because the In/Out Box itself provides a page preview view for these items.

Of the view definitions registered by your application, you can identify which should be made available to the In/Out Box and which should be hidden from the In/Out Box, by setting the protection slot in the view definition. Set the protection slot to 'public to make the view definition available to the In/Out Box. Set the protection slot to 'private to hide the view definition from the In/Out Box.

If more than one view definition is available to the In/Out Box for viewing an item, the In/Out Box lets the user choose which view they want to see.

Note that view definitions for In Box items are opened by the In Box in a read-only state. That is, if the view definition is of the type 'editor, the user won't be able to edit existing fields or write in new information. In other words, all child views based on the clParagraphView class are read-only. However, views can receive and respond to taps; that is, ViewClickScript messages are sent. If you want to prevent your view definition from receiving all pen input, you can place a transparent view of the clView class over the top of it to catch any taps.

Out Box items are opened in a writable state, if they are normally writable; that is, the Out Box does nothing special to prevent editing if the view is editable. You may want to make your out box items writable or not, depending on whether or not you want the user to be able to change them in the out box.

You can use the newtEntryView method EntryCool to test if an item in the In/Out Box is writable or not. This method returns nil for all In Box items, since they are read-only.

Note also that application view definitions used in the In/Out Box must not expect data defined within the context of the application.

For more information about writing and registering view definitions, refer to Chapter 5, "Stationery." Note that the In/Out Box does not need data definitions, only view definitions.

View Definition Slots

View definitions to be used by the In/Out Box have other slots of interest besides the target slot.

One other slot of interest is named fields. When the view is open, the fields slot contains a reference to the In/Out Box entry. If the entry has a body slot and the body slot contains a frame with a class slot, then the In/Out Box sets target to the body slot of the entry. This allows view definitions written for your application to be used by the In/Out Box without modification. If you need to access addressing or other information in the entry besides the actual data being routed, look at the frame in the `fields` slot. However, use of the `fields` slot is for special cases only and is generally discouraged. This is because it works only in the In/Out Box, and so ties your stationery to it. If you need to use the `fields` slot in your stationery, you should always check for the existence of this slot before using it, and you must be able to handle the case where it is missing.

Also, view definitions to be used by the In/Out Box can have a `rollScrolling` slot. This slot contains a Boolean value. If you set this slot to `true`, the view is treated as a paper roll-based view that specifies its height. In this case, the In/Out Box handles scrolling within the view for you, when the user taps the built-in scroll arrows. If the `rollScrolling` slot is set to `nil`, scrolling functionality must be provided by the view definition itself, typically with scroll arrows inside the view.

If the `rollScrolling` slot is set to `true`, the target item must have a `height` slot that specifies the height of the item in pixels.

Note that the `newtEditView` proto sets the `rollScrolling` slot to `true`, and is useful for creating a paper roll-based view definition.

Advanced Alias Handling

For sending data, an application may register a routing format that stores a sent object as an alias in the In Box. In fact, you can set a slot, `storeAlias`, in the routing format that allows this to happen. When such an object is to be sent by the transport, the Routing interface automatically resolves the alias into the actual object that is sent.

However, in some circumstances, you might want to provide your own custom alias handling. For example, you might want to store an object in the In Box as a complex frame consisting of some directly stored data and some slots that contain aliases. In this case, you would override the routing format method `MakeBodyAlias` to construct your own object.

When the system needs to access the item, such as when it is viewed in the In/Out Box, it sends the message `ResolveBody` to the format. You must override this method and use it to resolve the alias you constructed in the `MakeBodyAlias` method.

Note that if the send operation fails, the Out Box continues to store the original unresolved entry.

Summary of the Routing Interface

Constants

```
ROM_RouteDeleteIcon      // bitmap for delete icon
ROM_RouteDuplicateIcon   // bitmap for duplicate icon
```

Data Structures

Item Frame

```
itemFrame := {
appSymbol: symbol,        // appSymbol of sender
destAppSymbol: symbol,    // receiving app, if different
body: frame,              // the data to send
title: string,            // item title, e-mail subject
toRef: array,             // array of name refs for recipients
cc: array,      // array of name refs for copied recipients
bcc: array,     // array of name refs for blind copies
fromRef: frame,           // name ref for sender
currentFormat: symbol,    // routing format to use
connect: Boolean,         // try to connect immediately?
hidden: Boolean,          // hide in Out Box?
covert: Boolean,          // not logged or saved in Out Box?
completionScript: Boolean,    // notify app of state change?
needsResolve: Boolean,    // body slot contains an alias?
// transport-specific slots
printer: frame,           // printer frame; the printer to use
coverPage: Boolean,       // use a cover page for fax?
faxResolution: symbol,    // 'fine or 'normal fax resolution
phoneNumber: string,      // phone number, for call transport
name: string,             // name, for call transport
serviceProvider: symbol,  // 'modem, 'speaker, or nil
saveAsLog: Boolean,       // log call in Calls app?
}
```

RouteScripts Array Element

```
RouteScriptsArrayElement := {
title: string,          // string name of picker item
icon: bitmap object,    // icon for picker item
appSymbol: symbol,      // used if defined in a view def
RouteScript: symbol or function,// function called if this
                                // action is chosen
GetTitle: function,     // supplied instead of title slot
...
}
```

Protos

protoActionButton

```
aProtoActionButton := {
_proto: protoActionButton,
viewBounds : boundsFrame,
...
}
```

protoPrinterChooserButton

```
aPrinterChooserButton := {
_proto: protoPrinterChooserButton,
viewBounds : boundsFrame,
}
```

protoRoutingFormat, protoPrintFormat, and protoFrameFormat

```
aFormat := {
_proto: protoRoutingFormat, // or one of the other protos
type: 'routeFormat,   // some ROMs also use 'printFormat
title: string,            // name of format
symbol: symbol,           // unique id - include signature
dataTypes: ['frame, 'text],// supports frame & text data
version: integer,         // version number
auxForm: viewTemplate,    // for auxiliary view
storeAlias: Boolean,      // store alias?
showMessage: Boolean,     // warn user when aliasing?
sizeLimit: integer,       // maximum size without aliasing
storeCursors: Boolean,    // store cursor to multiple items?
SetupItem: function,      // puts target into item frame
```

```
TextScript: function,        // gets text data
TargetSize: function,        // determines target size
MakeBodyAlias: function,     // makes an alias
ResolveBody: function,       // resolves alias body slot

// for protoPrintFormat variant only
dataTypes: ['view],   // print formats support view data
usesCursors: Boolean,   // handles multiple items on a page?
orientation: symbol,      // 'portrait or 'orientation
margins: boundsFrame,     // inset from edges
pageWidth: integer,       // width of view
pageHeight: integer,      // height of view
ViewSetupChildrenScript: function,   // set up the children
PrintNextPageScript: function,       // for multiple pages
GetCursorFormat: function, //returns format for next item
FormatInitScript: function,          // initialization
CountPages: function,      // counts pages for a fax
...
}
```

Functions and Methods

Send-Related Functions and Methods

```
Send(transportSym, item)
GetRouteFormats(item)
GetFormatTransports(formatArray, target)
app:GetDefaultFormat(transportSym, target)
app:SetDefaultFormat(transportSym, target, formatSym)
OpenRoutingSlip(item, targetInfo)
```

Cursor-Related Functions

```
CreateTargetCursor(class, dataArray)
GetTargetCursor(target, param2)
TargetIsCursor(target)
```

Utility Functions and Methods

```
AppInstalled(appSymbol)
ClassAppByClass(dataClass)
app:GetActiveView()
```

GetItemTransport(*item*)
view:GetRouteScripts(*targetInfoFrame*)
RegAppClasses(*appSymbol*, *dataClasses*)
RegInboxApp(*appSymbol*, *test*)
TransportNotify(*transportSym*, *message*, *paramArray*)
UnRegAppClasses(*appSymbol*)
UnRegInboxApp(*appSymbol*)
UnRegTheseAppClasses(*appSymbol*, *dataClasses*)

Application-Defined Methods

app:AutoPutAway(*item*)
app:PutAwayScript(*item*)
app:ItemCompletionScript(*item*)
app:VerifyRoutingInfo(*targetInfo*, *item*)

Transport Interface

This chapter describes the Transport interface in Newton system software. The Transport interface lets you provide additional communication services to the system.

You should read this chapter if you are writing a low-level communication tool or special endpoint that you want to make available as a transport for applications to use. If you are writing only an application, you need only use the Routing interface described in Chapter 21, "Routing Interface."

This chapter describes how to

- create a transport and make it available to the system

- create a routing information template, for use by the In/Out Box

- control the built-in status templates, if you need to provide status information to the user

- create a routing slip template, if your transport sends data

- create a transport preferences template, if your transport has user-configurable options

About Transports

A **transport** is a NewtonScript object that provides a communication service to the Newton In/Out Box. It usually interfaces between the In/Out Box and an endpoint (see Figure 1-2 on page 1-12), moving data between the two. This chapter describes the transport object and its interface to the In/Out Box.

Applications interact with transports through the Routing interface and the In/Out Box. The In/Out Box serves as the bridge between applications and transports, neither of which knows about the other.

Most transports are visible as items in the Action picker menu. The transports available in the picker are not specified directly by an application, but consist of all the transports found that can handle the kind of data the application routes. Because this menu is constructed dynamically, applications can take advantage of additional transports that might be installed in the system at any time. An application need not know anything about the transports available. Likewise, transports can be removed from the system without any effect on applications.

Transport Parts

In writing a transport, you need to supply the following parts:

- the transport object itself, created from `protoTransport`
- an optional routing information template for the In/Out Box, created from `protoTransportHeader`
- an optional status template for displaying status information to the user, created from `protoStatusTemplate` (if you don't provide one, a default status view is used)
- a routing slip template for obtaining routing information from the user, created from `protoFullRouteSlip` (used only for transports that send data)
- a preferences template for user-configuration settings, created from `protoTransportPrefs` (needed only for transports that have user-configurable options that you want to store as preferences)

Item Frame

Anything sent or received through the In/Out Box by a transport is passed as a single frame, called the item frame, though it may contain references to multiple objects to send or receive. The frame can contain any number of slots. Some slots are required, and others are optional. Some slots (`body`) have meaning only to the application that created the item, others have meaning only to the In/Out Box itself, and still others are reserved for the transport. You should ignore any slot not documented, since it may be used internally.

The following are slots in the item frame that you should know about:

`timestamp`	The time this item was submitted to the In/Out Box. For e-mail transports and other kinds of transports where the sent and received times are typically different, the transport should set this slot to the time the item was originally sent, for incoming items. For more information, see the section "Setting the timeStamp Slot of an Item" (page 22-11). Other transports or applications shouldn't change this value.
`appSymbol`	A symbol identifying the owner application. For an incoming item, if this symbol is missing, or the application cannot be located, the `class` slot inside the `body` frame is used to find an application that can put away the item.

destAppSymbol	Optional. A symbol identifying the application to receive the item, if it is different from the sending application. Applications that send data should set this slot to identify the receiving application, if it is different from the sending one. On the receiving side, the transport method NewFromItem copies this value into the appSymbol slot of the received item frame.
body	The frame being sent (or references to the data). This is supplied by the application. This can be a multiple-item target object that references more than one data object to send. All application-specific data should be stored within the body slot.
title	Optional. This string is used in the In/Out Box as the item's title. The transport may provide this for received items that do not contain a data definition. If this slot is not provided, the transport obtains a title from the item's data definition.
remote	A value interpreted as a Boolean. Any non-nil value indicates an item whose body is stored remotely. The transport must set this slot if it downloads just the title of an item but leaves the body stored remotely. When the user tries to view the item, the In Box alerts the transport to download the body of the item from the remote host by sending it the ReceiveRequest message.
connect	A Boolean used for items to be sent. This slot is set to true if the user chooses to send the item immediately with the Send button in the routing slip. If the user chooses to send the item later, this slot is set to nil. Note that this slot can also be set by the format method SetupItem or the Send function.
error	An integer error code; non-nil indicates an error. This is usually set by ItemCompleted.
currentFormat	A symbol identifying the selected format for this item.
hidden	A Boolean; if true, the item is not displayed in the In/Out Box. If set to true, the completionScript slot must also be set to true and the application must have an ItemCompletionScript method.
covert	A Boolean; if true, the item is not logged or saved.
state	A symbol indicating status: 'ready, 'sent, 'received, 'read, 'inLog, 'outLog, or 'pending. This is usually set by ItemCompleted. Do not set this slot directly.

completionScript

A Boolean; if `true`, the transport sends the `ItemCompletionScript` message to the application when the item's state changes or when errors occur. For more details on this mechanism, see the section "Completion and Logging" beginning on page 22-16.

needsResolve

A Boolean that is set to `true` if the `body` slot contains an alias, rather than the actual data. This means that the format method `ResolveBody` must be called before the item is sent.

For transports that need addressing information, this is usually encapsulated in name references. A **name reference** is a frame that contains a soup entry or an alias to one, usually from the Names soup, hence the term name reference. The system includes built-in data definitions that can access name references, along with associated view definitions to display the information stored in or referenced by a name reference. For more information about using name references for addressing information, see the section "Creating a Name Reference" beginning on page 21-27. For more on name references in general, see "Name References" (page 5-1) in *Newton Programmer's Reference*.

The following slots in the item frame define the recipient and sender addresses:

toRef

An array containing one or more name references used to identify the recipient(s) of the item.

fromRef

A frame containing a name reference that identifies the sender. This information is usually extracted from the sender's current owner card, or current persona. The transport normally sets this slot in its `NewItem` method. For more information, see the section "Obtaining an Item Frame" beginning on page 22-13.

cc

An array containing one or more name references used to identify recipients of copies of the item. Typically, this slot is used by e-mail transports.

bcc

An array containing one or more name references used to identify recipients of blind copies of the item. Typically, this slot is used by e-mail transports.

In addition, there may be other address slots used by some transports.

For a detailed description of all the item frame slots that are important to the Routing interface, see "Item Frame" (page 18-1) in *Newton Programmer's Reference*.

Using the Transport Interface

This section describes how to use the Transport interface to perform these specific tasks:

■ create a new transport object

■ create a routing information template, for use by the In/Out Box

■ control the built-in status template, if you need to provide status information to the user

■ create a routing slip template, if your transport sends data

■ create a transport preferences template, if your transport has user-configurable options

Providing a Transport Object

To make a new transport object, create a frame with a prototype of protoTransport.

Transports are not built as applications, but are built as auto parts. This means that when installed, they add their services to the system but do not add an application to the Extras Drawer. (They are represented by an icon in the Extras Drawer, but you can't tap it to open it like you can an application icon.)

For a complete description of the protoTransport object, see "protoTransport" (page 19-2) in *Newton Programmer's Reference*.

The following subsections describe operations that a transport can perform, and the methods that you must supply or call in your transport object to support these operations.

Installing the Transport

To install a new transport in the system, call the RegTransport function from the InstallScript function of your transport part and pass it the transport appSymbol and transport template. The RegTransport function additionally sends your transport object the InstallScript message; this message is unrelated to the InstallScript function used by package parts. The InstallScript message sent to your transport object lets the transport perform initialization operations when it is installed.

Here is an example of installing a transport in the part `InstallScript` function:

```
InstallScript := func(partFrame,removeFrame)
   begin
   RegTransport(kAppSym, partFrame.partData.(kAppSym));
   // assumes that partData.(kAppSym) holds the transport
   end;
```

When your transport is removed, use the `UnRegTransport` function to unregister the transport from the system. You pass the `UnRegTransport` function the transport `appSymbol` like this:

```
RemoveScript := func(removeFrame)
   begin
   UnRegTransport(kAppSym);
   end;
```

If your transport is scrubbed by the user from the Extras Drawer, the system also calls the `DeletionScript` function in its package part. In the `DeletionScript` function, you should call the `DeleteTransport` function, which removes user configuration information related to the transport. Here's an example of a `DeletionScript` function:

```
SetPartFrameSlot('DeletionScript,func(removeFrame)
   begin
   // delete prefs and other temporary data
   DeleteTransport(kAppSym);
   end)
```

Setting the Address Class

The transport object contains a slot, `addressingClass`, that holds a symbol. This symbol identifies the class of the address information used by the transport, such as that stored in the `toRef` and `fromRef` slots of an item. (See the section "Item Frame" beginning on page 22-2.) The In/Out Box uses this symbol to look up and display the to and from address information based on soup entries (usually from the Names soup).

The class of address information is defined by name reference data definitions registered in the system. You can specify one of the following built-in name reference data definitions in the `addressingClass` slot:

- `'|nameRef.email|`, for use with a transport that handles e-mail
- `'|nameRef.fax|`, for use with a transport that handles fax phone calls
- `'|nameRef.phone|`, for use with a transport that handles other phone calls

Or you can specify a custom name reference data definition that you have created and registered with the system. Note that all name reference data definitions must be registered under a symbol that is a subclass of `'nameref`.

The default setting of the addressingClass slot is the symbol
'|nameRef.email|

For more information about how to use name references for addressing information, see the section "Creating a Name Reference" beginning on page 21-27. For more on name references in general, see "Name References" (page 5-1) in *Newton Programmer's Reference*.

Grouping Transports

Two or more transports can be grouped together in the Action picker under a single action. For example, there might be several different e-mail transports grouped together under the single action "Mail." The user selects a particular e-mail transport from a picker supplied by the system in the routing slip, if there are multiple transports registered for that group. (The picker doesn't appear if there is only one installed transport in the group.)

Each group of transports is identified by a common symbol, called the group symbol. You indicate that your transport should be a member of a group by specifying its group symbol in the group slot, its title in the groupTitle slot, and its icon in the groupIcon slot. All transports in the same group should specify the same group icon. This icon is shown in the Action picker for that transport group. The individual transport icon (specified in the icon slot) is shown in the routing slip when the transport is selected from the transport group picker.

You can use the following built-in bitmaps in the groupIcon slot of your transport, if it belongs to one of the predefined groups. Here are the magic pointer constants:

Group	Icon bitmap constant
'mail	ROM_RouteMailIcon
'print	ROM_RoutePrintIcon
'fax	ROM_RouteFaxIcon
'beam	ROM_RouteBeamIcon

After the user chooses a particular transport in a group from the picker in the routing slip, the system remembers the last choice and sets the routing slip to that choice when the user later chooses the same routing action from the Action picker. If the user changes the transport in the routing slip group picker, the system closes and reopens the routing slip for the current target item, since the routing slip may be different for a different transport.

Before the routing slip is closed, it is sent the TransportChanged message. This allows the routing slip to take any necessary action such as alerting the user that addressing information might be lost as a result of changing transports. If TransportChanged returns a non-nil value, the transport is not changed and the routing slip is not closed. If `TransportChanged` returns `nil`, then the transport is changed and operations continue normally.

You can use the function `GetGroupTransport` to determine the name of the current (last-used for sending by the user) transport in a group. Note that when you install a grouped transport, it becomes the current transport for that group.

Transports that are part of a group are individually selectable on the Send, Receive, and Preferences pickers in the In/Out Box.

Sending Data

The Out Box sends the `SendRequest` message to your transport when data needs to be sent. If your transport supports sending data, you must define this method to actually send the data. For a complete description of the `SendRequest` method, see "SendRequest" (page 19-33) in *Newton Programmer's Reference*.

The Out Box puts its own query information in the *request* frame argument to `SendRequest`. Your `SendRequest` method must pass this frame to the `ItemRequest` message to get the item (or next item) to send. In your `SendRequest` method, keep calling `ItemRequest` until it returns `nil`, signalling no more items to send. For a complete description of the `ItemRequest` method, see "ItemRequest" (page 19-26) in *Newton Programmer's Reference*.

If the `body` slot of an item originally contained an alias, the alias is automatically resolved by `ItemRequest`. That is, items returned by `ItemRequest` always contain a `body` slot that is not an alias.

Note that you can save entry aliases to items returned by `ItemRequest`, if you want. Later, when using them, make sure that `ResolveEntryAlias` returns a non-`nil` value, and that the item `state` slot is set as expected.

You can choose to comply with or ignore any request to send, depending on the communication resources available and their status. If you choose to comply, your `SendRequest` method must obtain one or more items from the Out Box by using the `ItemRequest` method, and send them by whatever means the transport uses to communicate. For example, most transports use the Endpoint interface to establish and operate a connection.

If *request*.cause is `'submit`, the item is queued in the Out Box for later sending, but the Out Box still notifies the transport by sending it this `SendRequest` message so that the transport knows there are items waiting to be sent. Typically, a transport doesn't need to take any immediate action on items where *request*.cause is `'submit`, so you can use code like this to simply return:

```
If request.cause = 'submit then return nil;
```

The `item.connect` slot contains a Boolean value indicating if the user chose to send the item now (`true`) or later (`nil`).

After sending an item (successfully or unsuccessfully), you must call
`ItemCompleted` to inform the In/Out Box. If there was an error,
the `ItemCompleted` method informs the In/Out Box that an item was not sent.
`ItemCompleted` uses `HandleError` to inform the user of an error. If you want
to perform your own error notification, you can override the `HandleError` method.

Sending All Items

If your transport establishes a connection, and you want to take advantage of it to
send all queued items from the Out Box, you can send your transport the message
`CheckOutbox`. This method is defined in `protoTransport` and it causes the
In/Out Box to send your transport a `SendRequest` for all queued items waiting to
be sent. The `SendRequest` message sent back to your transport includes a *request*
argument in which the `cause` slot is set to `'user`.

Applications can also send the `CheckOutbox` message directly to transports by
using the `TransportNotify` global function.

Note that a side effect of the `CheckOutbox` message is that if there is nothing to
send, an alert explaining that is displayed to the user. If you want to perform this
operation but avoid the alert in that case, you can use the function `QuietSendAll`.
This function causes the In/Out Box to send your transport a `SendRequest` for all
queued items waiting to be sent, however the `cause` slot of the `SendRequest`
request argument is set to `'periodic`.

Converting an E-Mail Address to an Internet Address

If you are implementing a new e-mail transport that communicates with another
e-mail system, you may need to convert e-mail addresses from that system to
Internet-compatible addresses. The transport method `NormalizeAddress` allows
you to do this. You pass it a name reference containing an e-mail address, and it
returns a string containing an Internet-compatible e-mail address.

To register a new e-mail system so that it shows up on e-mail pickers throughout
the system and to register a conversion for Internet addresses, use the function
`RegEmailSystem`.

Receiving Data

The Out Box sends the `ReceiveRequest` message to your transport to request
the transport to receive items. If your transport supports receiving data, you must
define this method to receive it. For a complete description of the
`ReceiveRequest` method, see "ReceiveRequest" (page 19-32) in *Newton
Programmer's Reference*.

The `ReceiveRequest` method takes one parameter, a frame containing a `cause`
slot whose value is a symbol.

Some transports may ignore the `ReceiveRequest` message, since they receive data continuously. Others may use this message as a trigger to initiate a connection.

You can choose to comply with or ignore any request to receive, depending on the communication resources available and their status. If you choose to comply, the `ReceiveRequest` method should establish a connection and begin receiving by whatever means the transport uses to communicate. For example, many transports use the Endpoint interface to establish and operate a connection. After receiving the item, you should call the transport method `NewFromItem` to copy it into a standard item frame used by the In/Out Box. Finally, you must call `ItemCompleted` to write the item to the In Box.

If your transport creates virtual binary objects, you must use the method `GetDefaultOwnerStore` to determine on which store to create them.

Note

The `body` slot within every received item must have a `class` slot to identify its data class. Data objects received from other Newton devices always have a `class` slot. For data received from other systems, your transport must assign a meaningful class to the `item.body` object. ◆

Deferring Reception of the Item Data

Some transports might want to download just part of an item initially, such as its title, then download the actual item data when a user requests it. For example, upon connection an e-mail transport might download just the titles of messages or other data objects. When the user attempts to view one of these items in the In Box, the transport then downloads the body of the item from the remote host.

This feature is accomplished by the use of the `cause` slot in the parameter passed to the `ReceiveRequest` method, and by the use of a `remote` slot in the item frame.

If a transport initially downloads just a part of each item, such as its title, it must insert a slot called `remote`, whose value is `true` in the item frame of those items. This slot serves as a flag to tell the In/Out Box that the body of the item is stored remotely and has not yet been downloaded.

When the user attempts to view one of these items in the In Box, the In Box sees the `remote` slot, and sends the transport the `ReceiveRequest` message with the `'remote` cause. This alerts the transport to download the body of the item from the remote host. If the user selected multiple remote items for downloading, you must use the `ItemRequest` method to retrieve subsequent requested items and download them. Keep calling `ItemRequest` until it returns `nil`, which signals that there are no more items to retrieve.

After downloading all the remote data, you must refresh the In Box view, so the items are updated. To do so, send the `Refresh` message to the application identified by the `ownerApp` slot in the transport, like this:

```
ownerApp:Refresh();
```

Note
In Newton OS version 2.0, the `ownerApp` slot in the transport must first be set up by using the NTK platform file function `kSetupOwnerAppFunc` in the transport `InstallScript` method. ◆

To delete partially downloaded (remote) items from the In Box, send the `RemoveTempItems` message to the application identified by the `ownerApp` slot in the transport, like this:

```
ownerApp:RemoveTempItems(transportSym);
// then refresh the in box view
ownerApp:Refresh();
```

Typically, after disconnecting, transports that handle remote items delete those items from the In Box that the user has not chosen to fully download. Also, you must send the `Refresh` message following `RemoveTempItems`.

Setting the timeStamp Slot of an Item

The `timeStamp` slot of the item frame holds the time that an item was submitted to the In/Out Box. This slot is ordinarily set by the In/Out Box when an item is received or submitted for sending. Many transports won't need to do anything special, but some transports must set this slot themselves. Such transports include those that receive data that contains internal information about when an item was sent, and where the time the item was sent typically differs from the time it was received by the transport.

For example, this applies to most e-mail transports. Typically an e-mail message is sent by a user to a mail system where it waits to be downloaded by a client transport running on a Newton device. The time the item was originally sent always differs from the time the item is eventually received by the Newton transport.

In this case, your transport will need to set the `item.timeStamp` slot to the time the original mail was sent. You must decode this information however it is stored in the mail message and set it in the `item.timeStamp` slot before you call the `ItemCompleted` method. The `timeStamp` slot must contain the time in the same format as returned by the `Time` function; that is, the number of minutes since midnight, January 1, 1904.

If your transport sets the `timeStamp` slot, the In/Out Box does not override it.

Handling Requests When the Transport Is Active

While the transport is actively sending or receiving data in the background, the user might request another send or receive operation from the In/Out Box. One way to handle such requests is to queue them up and append them to the current communication transaction or to start another connection when the transport is finished.

You can use the transport method QueueRequest to queue up requests for sending or receiving, if the transport already has an active communication session in progress. Call QueueRequest from the SendRequest or ReceiveRequest method, whichever one you receive as a result of a user request.

Depending on how you call it, you can make QueueRequest append the new request to a request in progress or start another connection when the current request is finished. To append the new request to one in progress, for the first parameter, specify the request frame of a request already in progress. A request frame is the frame passed to SendRequest or ReceiveRequest to begin the request in progress. The second parameter is the new request frame.

The following is an example of a SendRequest method in which QueueRequest is called to append the new request to the one in progress.

```
// SendRequest method
func (newRequest)
begin
if status <> 'idle then // check if I'm active
    // append to current request
    :QueueRequest(currentRequest, newRequest);
else
    // do a normal send here
end,
```

When a new request is appended to an in-progress request, items from the new request are returned from the ItemRequest method after all items from the in-progress request are exhausted. In this way, new items are sent as part of the current communication session.

To queue a new request so that the transport finishes its current transaction before beginning a new one, specify a symbol for the first parameter of QueueRequest. The symbol should be the name of a method that you want the system to call when the transport state returns to idle. Usually this is another SendRequest or ReceiveRequest method. The following is an example of a SendRequest method in which QueueRequest is called to defer a new request until the transport returns to the idle state.

```
// SendRequest method
func (newRequest)
begin
if status <> 'idle then // check if I'm active
    // wait for idle and then call SendRequest again
    :QueueRequest('SendRequest, newRequest);
else
    // do a normal send here
end,
```

Canceling an Operation

The system sends the `CancelRequest` message to the transport when the user cancels the current transaction or for other reasons, such as when the system wants to turn off. This method must be defined by all transports.

When a transport receives this message, it must terminate the communication operation as soon as possible.

The `CancelRequest` method should return non-`nil` if it is OK to turn off power immediately after this method returns, or `nil` if it is not OK to turn off power immediately. In the latter case, the system waits until your transport returns to the idle state before turning off. This allows you to send an asynchronous cancel request to your communication endpoint, for example, and still return immediately from the `CancelRequest` method. When you receive the callback message from your endpoint cancel request confirming cancellation, use the `SetStatusDialog` method to set the transport status to idle to alert the system that it is OK to turn off.

Obtaining an Item Frame

The system sends the `NewItem` message to the transport to obtain a new item frame to make a new In/Out Box entry.

This method is supplied by the `protoTransport`, but should be overridden by your transport to fill in extra values your transport uses. If you override this method, you must first call the inherited `NewItem` method, as shown in the example below. The item frame returned by the `NewItem` method should contain default values for your transport.

The item frame returned by the default method supplied in `protoTransport` is not yet a soup entry. The `item.category` slot is initialized to the `appSymbol` slot in your transport. For more information on the `item` frame, see the section "Item Frame" beginning on page 22-2.

The `NewItem` message is sent to your transport during both send and receive operations. When the user sends an item, the system sends the `NewItem` message to the transport to create a new In/Out Box entry before opening a routing slip for the item. This allows the transport an opportunity to add its own slots to the item frame.

Most transports will want to add a `fromRef` slot to the item frame. This slot must contain a name reference that identifies the sender. This information is usually extracted from the sender's current owner card, or persona. You shouldn't just use the value of `GetUserConfig('currentPersona)` because it is simply an alias to a names file entry. Instead, construct a name reference from this value. For example:

```
persona := GetUserConfig('currentPersona);
dataDef := GetDataDefs(addressingClass);
fromRef := dataDef:MakeNameRef(persona,addressingClass);
```

Most transports will want to extract and send only the needed information from the `fromRef` name reference. For example, an e-mail transport would typically just extract the sender name and e-mail address from the name reference and send them as strings. One method of name reference data definitions that you can use to extract useful information from a name card includes `GetRoutingInfo`. Here is an example of using this method:

```
// extract just routing info using GetRoutingInfo
routeInfo:= datadef:GetRoutingInfo(fromRef);
// returns an array like this:
[{name: "Chris Smith", email: "cbsmith@apple.test.com"}]
```

The `GetRoutingInfo` method returns an array of at least one frame that has at least a `name` slot containing a string. Depending on the `addressingClass` slot passed to the `GetDataDefs` function, the returned frame also contains other information particular to the type of address used for the transport. In the example above, the frame also contains an `email` slot with an e-mail address.

If you want to add other slots to the `fromRef` frame, you can either define your own name reference data definition and override the method `GetItemRoutingFrame` (called by `GetRoutingInfo`), or add the slots you want to the `fromRef` frame by extracting them from the original name reference with the `Get` method. For example:

```
// use Get to extract info from certain slots
fromRef.myInfo := dataDef:Get(fromRef,'myInfo,nil);
```

Note that a sender may have multiple e-mail addresses and the transport should set the e-mail address in the `fromRef` frame to the one that is appropriate to itself. For example, for an internet e-mail transport, you would typically set the `fromRef` e-mail address to the sender's internet address. Here's an example of code that sets the appropriate e-mail address in the `fromRef` object:

```
owner:=ResolveEntryAlias(GetUserConfig('currentPersona));
    if owner and GetRoot().cardfile then begin
        addrs := GetRoot().cardfile:BcEmailAddress(owner,
                            ['|string.email.internet|]);
        if addrs then
            fromRef := clone(addrs[0]);
    end
```

You can find a description of `BcEmailAddress` and other similar functions that extract information from Names soup entries in "Names Functions and Methods" (page 16-5) in *Newton Programmer's Reference*.

If, instead of extracting the address and sending it as a string, your transport sends addressing information as a frame, like the beam transport, you must remove any soup entry aliases from the name reference before it is transmitted. You can do this by using the name reference data definition method `PrepareForRouting`, as follows:

```
// strip the aliases from a name ref
fromRef := datadef:PrepareForRouting(fromRef);
```

In general, however, you should not send all the information in a user's persona with a message, since it can include personal or confidential information such as credit card numbers.

For more information about name references and the methods of name reference data definitions, see the section "Creating a Name Reference" beginning on page 21-27, and "Name References" (page 5-1) in *Newton Programmer's Reference*.

The following is an example of how to override the `NewItem` method during a send operation to add a `fromRef` slot:

```
// a sample overridden NewItem method
mytransport.NewItem := func(context) begin
    // first call inherited method to get default frame
    local item := inherited:NewItem(context);

    // get sender info and insert fromRef slot
    local persona:= GetUserConfig('currentPersona);
    local dataDef := GetDataDefs(addressingClass);
```

```
if dataDef then
   begin
   item.fromRef := dataDef:MakeNameRef(persona,
                                  addressingClass);
   // add other slots or extract routing info here
   end;
   item;
end;
```

During a receive operation, the transport itself must invoke the NewFromItem method to get a new In/Out Box item frame. This method copies most slots from the received item to the new In/Out Box item frame. Additionally, it inserts the destAppSymbol slot value (if included) in the received frame into the appSymbol slot in the new frame.

Finally, the transport should call ItemCompleted to register the item in the In Box (see the following section).

Completion and Logging

After your transport finishes processing an item (either sending or receiving, with or without errors), you must send the transport the message ItemCompleted. This method must be used when an item is altered in any way. It performs several operations, including setting the state and error status of the item; sending the ItemCompletionScript callback message to the application; handling error conditions; and saving, logging, or deleting the item, depending on the logging preferences.

Send the ItemCompleted message only after your transport has completely processed an item. If you send this message before you know that the item was delivered successfully, for example, there's a possibility that the item will be lost.

If ItemCompleted was called as the result of an error, it calls HandleError to translate the error code and notify the user. If you want to perform your own error notification, you can override the HandleError method.

Note that the ItemCompleted method in protoTransport sends the ItemCompletionScript callback message to the application only if the item contains a completionScript slot that is set to true. You must set this slot if you want the callback message to be sent. For more information on ItemCompletionScript see *Newton Programmer's Reference* (page 18-33).

To perform logging, ItemCompleted sends your transport the message MakeLogEntry, passing a log entry to which you can add slots. The protoTransport object includes a default MakeLogEntry method, but you should override this method to add transport-specific slots to the log entry.

The default method simply adds a title slot to the log entry. The GetItemTitle transport method is called to get the title.

Storing Transport Preferences and Configuration Information

Transports can store user-configurable preferences and other configuration information. Typically, you store several chunks of data that correspond to individual preferences or other kinds of configuration information that you want to save for your transport. You must use the transport methods `GetConfig` and `SetConfig` to retrieve and set configuration information for your transport.

Default preferences for a transport are set by the `defaultConfiguration` slot in the transport object. This slot holds a frame containing values that correspond to items in a preferences slip that lets the user set preferences for your transport. For more information about displaying a preferences slip to the user, see the section "Providing a Preferences Template" beginning on page 22-33.

If you don't want to use this preferences dialog or the setting of the `defaultConfiguration` slot in `protoTransport`, override the initial setting by creating your own default preferences frame and including it in the `defaultConfiguration` slot of your transport object. Note that you can't use a `_proto` slot in the default frame since the contents of the `defaultConfiguration` slot are stored in a soup and `_proto` slots can't be stored in soup entries.

Extending the In/Out Box Interface

Your transport can extend the In/Out Box interface if items the transport handles can be viewed in the In/Out Box. You can add additional actions to the In/Out Box Tag picker in the In/Out Box. The In/Out Box Tag picker is displayed when the user taps the Tag button in the In/Out Box, as shown here:

In/Out Box
Tag picker
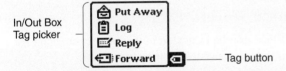
Tag button

The In/Out Box Tag picker includes only the Put Away and Log items by default. You can add other transport-dependent items by implementing the `GetTransportScripts` method. For example, the picker shown above includes Reply and Forward items added by an e-mail transport to let the user perform those operations on e-mail directly in the In/Out Box.

When the user taps the Tag button, the system sends your transport the `GetTransportScripts` message, if you've implemented it. This method must return an array of frames that describe new items to be added to the In/Out Box Tag picker. The array is exactly the same as the `routeScripts` array that adds items to the Action picker in an application. Here is an example of a return value that adds two items to the picker:

```
[ {title: "Reply", // name of action
icon: ROM_RouteReply, // picker icon
// called if action selected
RouteScript: func(target, targetView) begin ... end,
},
{title: "Forward", // name of action
icon: ROM_RouteForward, // picker icon
// called if action selected
RouteScript: func(target, targetView) begin ... end,
} ]
```

The `RouteScript` slot contains a method that is called if the user selects that item from the picker. Alternatively, in the `RouteScript` slot you can specify a symbol identifying a transport method, and then supply your transport symbol in another slot named `appSymbol`.

For more detailed information about the items in the array, see the section "Providing Application-Specific Routing Actions" beginning on page 21-22.

For the `icon` slot of each frame in the array, you can specify an icon that appears next to the name of the action in the picker. There are standard bitmaps available in the ROM for the following actions:

- reply, ROM_RouteReply
- forward, ROM_RouteForward
- add sender to the Names application, ROM_RouteAddSender
- copy text to Notes application, ROM_RoutePasteText

If you are adding one of these actions, use the indicated magic pointer constant for the standard bitmap, to keep the interface consistent among transports.

Also, when the user taps the Tag button, the system sends your transport the `CanPutAway` message, if you've implemented it. This method allows your transport to add a put away option for the item to the Put Away picker. This hook allows a transport to put away items that could not otherwise be put away. Remember that applications (or transports) that need to put away items must implement the `PutAwayScript` method.

Whenever an item belonging to your transport is displayed in the In/Out Box, the In/Out Box also sends your transport the `IOBoxExtensions` message. This hook lets your transport add functionality to items in the In/Out Box by adding to the list of view definitions available for an item.

Application Messages

Applications can send messages directly to a single transport or to all transports by using the `TransportNotify` global function. This mechanism serves as a general way for applications to communicate with transports. Here is an example of using this function:

```
TransportNotify('_all,'AppOpened,[appSymbol])
```

The In/Out Box uses this mechanism to send three different messages to transports: `AppOpened`, `AppClosed`, and `AppInFront`. The `AppOpened` message notifies the transport that an application has opened and is interested in data from the transport. The In/Out Box sends this message to all transports when it opens. This method is not defined by default in `protoTransport` since it's transport-specific. If you want to respond to the `AppOpened` message, you must define this method in your transport.

This message is designed to support applications that might poll for data, such as a pager. For example, when the application is open, it can notify the transport with this message so that the transport can poll more frequently (and use more power) than when the application is closed. Another use might be for an application to notify a transport that automatically makes a connection whenever the application is open.

The `AppClosed` message notifies the transport that an application has closed. The In/Out Box sends this message to all transports when it closes. Again, this method is not defined by default in `protoTransport` since there is no default action—it's transport-specific. If you want to respond to the `AppClosed` message, you must define this method in your transport.

Note that more than one application can be open at a time in the system. If you want your transport to do something like disconnect when it receives this message, keep track of how many times it's received the `AppOpened` message and don't actually disconnect until it receives the same number of `AppClosed` messages.

The `AppInFront` message notifies the transport of a change in the frontmost status of an application—either the application is no longer frontmost, or it now is. The In/Out Box sends this message to all transports when another application is opened in front of the In/Out Box view, or when the In/Out Box view is brought to the front. Note that the `AppInFront` message is not sent when an application is opened or closed, so you need to check for the `AppOpened` and `AppClosed` messages to catch those occurrences.

Again, this method is not defined by default in `protoTransport` since there is no default action—it's transport-specific. If you want to respond to the `AppInFront` message, you must define this method in your transport. Not that this method is used only in special circumstances and is not needed by most transports.

Error Handling

The default exception handling method implemented by protoTransport is
HandleThrow, which catches and handles exceptions resulting from any supplied
transport methods such as SendRequest and ReceiveRequest. You must
provide your own exception handler for any methods that you define, or you can
pass them to HandleThrow, as follows:

```
try begin
   ... // do something
   Throw();
onException |evt.ex| do
   :HandleThrow();
end
```

When handling an exception, HandleThrow first calls IgnoreError to give
your transport a chance to screen out benign errors. If IgnoreError returns
true, HandleThrow returns nil and stops.

Assuming the error is not rejected by IgnoreError, HandleThrow next checks
to see if an item is currently being processed. If so, it sends your transport the
ItemCompleted message and returns true. Note that ItemCompleted calls
HandleError to display an error alert to the user. If no item is currently being
processed, HandleThrow sends the HandleError message itself to display an
error alert.

The HandleError method calls TranslateError to give your transport a
chance to translate an error code into an error message that can be displayed to the
user. If your transport can't translate the error (for example, because it's a
system-defined error) you should simply call the inherited TranslateError
method, which handles system-defined errors.

Power-Off Handling

The protoTransport object registers a power-off handler with the system
whenever the transport is not in the idle state. If the system is about to power off,
this power-off handler sends the transport the PowerOffCheck message.

The default PowerOffCheck method in protoTransport displays a slip
asking the user to confirm that it is OK to break the connection. Then, when the
power is about to be turned off, the system sends the transport the
CancelRequest message and waits until the transport is idle before turning the
power off.

You can override the default PowerOffCheck method if you wish.

There is also a power-on handler that sends a CancelRequest message to the
transport when the system turns on after shutting down unexpectedly while
the transport is active.

Providing a Status Template

A status template for a transport is based on the proto `protoStatusTemplate`.
The status template displays status information to the user. A transport should
generally display a status view whenever it is sent the `ReceiveRequest` or
`SendRequest` messages.

You probably won't need to create your own status template. The `protoTransport`
is defined with a default status template named `statusTemplate` (based on
`protoStatusTemplate`), which includes six predefined subtypes, described in
Table 22-1 and shown in Figure 22-1. Each subtype consists of a set of child views
that are added to the base status view. The base status view includes a transport
icon and a close box, to which different child views are added, depending on the
specified subtype name.

Table 22-1   Status view subtypes

Subtype name	Important values	Description
vStatus	statusText (top string)	A view that incorporates a status line. This is the default subview created by `SetStatusDialog`.
vStatusTitle	statusText (top string), titleText (lower string)	A view that incorporates a status line and a line for the item's title.
vConfirm	statusText (top string), primary (lower-button text and method: {text: *string*, script: *function*}), secondary (upper-button text and method: {text: *string*, script: *function*})	A view that has space for three lines of text, and two buttons. This view is suitable for situations where the user must choose between two options.
vProgress	statusText (top string), titleText (lower string), progress (integer, percentage completed)	A view that incorporates status and title lines, as well as a dog-eared page image that fills from top to bottom, based on the progress of the transfer.
vGauge	statusText (top string), titleText (lower string), gauge (integer, percentage completed)	A view that incorporates status and title lines, as well as a horizontal gauge that fills from left to right, based on the progress of the transfer.
vBarber	statusText (top string), titleText (lower string), barber (set to true)	A view that incorporates status and title lines, as well as a horizontal barber pole-like image that can be made to appear to move from left to right.

Figure 22-1   Status view subtypes

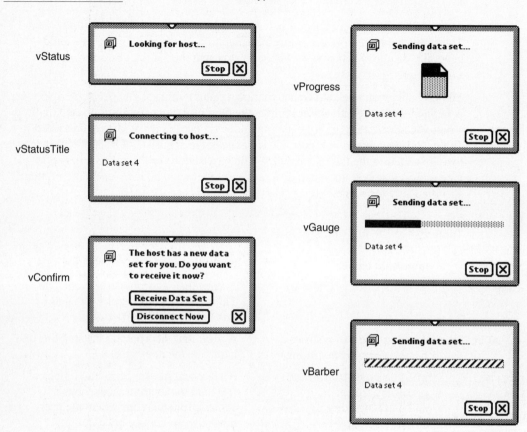

Each child view included in a subtype has one important value that controls the appearance of that child element. For example, the vProgress subtype consists of three child views that have these important values: statusText (the string displayed at the top of the view), titleText (the string displayed at the bottom of the view), and progress (an integer indicating the percentage of the page that should be shown filled with black). The important values for each subtype appear in Table 22-1. This information is necessary for use in the SetStatusDialog method.

A transport specifies the use of a subtype in the status view by passing the subtype name in the *name* parameter to the SetStatusDialog transport method. Transports can dynamically switch from one status subtype to another without closing the status view, and can easily update the contents of the status view as well (for example, updating the progress indicator).

Using this set of predefined status templates gives all transports a similar user interface and matches the use of other status views throughout the system.

For more detailed information on `protoStatusTemplate` and the predefined subtypes, refer to Chapter 17, "Additional System Services."

Controlling the Status View

Your transport should display a status view to the user whenever it is engaged in a lengthy activity such as sending or receiving data. In general, this means you must display a status view as part of the processing you do whenever you receive a `SendRequest` or `ReceiveRequest` message that results in the transmission of data.

To display a status view, use the transport method `SetStatusDialog`. If the `autoStatus` slot of the transport preferences frame is `true`, the status view opens automatically when you send the `SetStatusDialog` message with a status other than `'idle` as the first parameter. If the status view is already open, `SetStatusDialog` updates the status view with the new status information you pass to it. If `autoStatus` is `nil`, the status view does not open because the user has set a preference that it not be shown.

Here is an example of how to use the `SetStatusDialog` method:

```
:SetStatusDialog('Connecting, 'vStatus, "Looking for host...");
```

The `SetStatusDialog` method takes three parameters. The first is a symbol indicating what the new transport status is. This is typically one of the slots in the `dialogStatusMsgs` frame, such as `'Connecting`, or `'Idle`. The second parameter is the name of the status subtype you want to use. You can specify one of the built-in subtypes described in the previous section, or the name of a custom subtype that you have constructed. (You specify the value of the `name` slot in the subtype template.) For information on constructing custom `protoStatusTemplate` view subtypes, see Chapter 17, "Additional System Services."

The third parameter is typically a frame that contains one or more slots of values. Each slot corresponds to a single child view within the subtype you are using, and it sets the value of that child view. A slot name is the value of the `name` slot in the child view you are setting, and the value is whatever important value that type of view uses. The slot names and the expected values for the predefined status subtypes are listed in the "Important values" column in Table 22-1.

The following examples show how you'd use the `SetStatusDialog` method to set the different status subtypes to create the status views shown in Figure 22-1.

```
// vStatus subtype
:SetStatusDialog('Connecting, 'vStatus, "Looking for host...");

// vStatusTitle subtype
:SetStatusDialog('Connecting, 'vStatusTitle, {statusText: "Connecting
to host...", titleText: "Data set 4"});

// vConfirm subtype
:SetStatusDialog('Confirming, 'vConfirm, {statusText: "The host has a
new data set for you. Do you want to receive it now?",
secondary:{text:"Receive Data Set", script: func() ... },
primary:{text:"Disconnect Now", script: func() ... }});

// vProgress subtype
:SetStatusDialog('Sending, 'vProgress, {statusText: "Sending data
set...", titleText: "Data set 4", progress:40});

// vGauge subtype
:SetStatusDialog('Sending, 'vGauge, {statusText: "Sending data
set...", titleText: "Data set 4", gauge:40});

// vBarber subtype
:SetStatusDialog('Sending, 'vBarber, {statusText: "Sending data
set...", titleText:"Data set 4", barber:true});
```

Once the status view is open, each time you call SetStatusDialog, the system closes and reopens all its child views. This is fairly fast, but if you just want to update a progress indicator that is already visible in the subtypes vProgress, vGauge, or vBarber, you can use the alternate method UpdateIndicator. This protoStatusTemplate method updates the progress indicator child of the status view: the page image for the vProgress subtype, the horizontal bar for the vGauge subtype, and animation of the barber pole for the vBarber subtype.

For example, you'd use UpdateIndicator to update the vGauge subtype as follows:

```
statusDialog:UpdateIndicator({name:'vGauge, values:{gauge: 50,}});
```

Note that the frame of data you pass to UpdateIndicator consists of two slots, name and values, that hold the name of the subtype and the value(s) you want to set, respectively. The values slot is specified just like the *values* parameter to SetStatusDialog.

Also, note that UpdateIndicator is a method of protoStatusTemplate, and you need to send this message to the open status view. A reference to the open status view is stored in the statusDialog slot of the transport frame, so you can send the message to the value of that slot, as shown above.

The vBarber subtype shows a barber pole-like image, but it doesn't animate automatically. To make it appear to move, use the UpdateIndicator method in a ViewIdleScript method, as shown here:

```
// create the initial vBarber status view
:SetStatusDialog('Sending, 'vBarber, {statusText: "Sending data
set...", titleText:"Data set 1", barber:true});

...
// set up the status view data frame
statusDialog.barberValueFrame:={name:'vBarber,values:{barber:true}};
...
// set up the idle script
statusDialog.ViewIdleScript:= func()
   begin
   :UpdateIndicator(barberValueFrame); // spin the barber
   return 500; // idle for 0.5 seconds
   end;
...
// start the idler
statusDialog:Setupidle(500);
```

If the autoStatus slot of the transport preferences frame is true, the status view closes automatically when you send the SetStatusDialog message with 'idle as the first parameter.

You can force the status view to close manually by sending the transport the message CloseStatusDialog. However, the next time you send the message SetStatusDialog with a state other than 'idle as the first parameter, the dialog reopens.

Providing a Routing Information Template

When viewing an item in the In/Out Box, the user can tap the transport icon to the left of the item title to display a view that gives routing information about the item. For example, for a fax item, the fax phone number is displayed; for a mail item, the e-mail header is shown. Figure 22-2 (page 22-26) shows an example of a routing information view.

You should create a template for a routing information view for your transport, using protoTransportHeader. If you don't specify a header view, your transport uses the default view, which displays the item title, the transport icon and name, and the item's size in the In/Out Box soup (the first three elements in the picture above).

Figure 22-2   Routing information view

Tap
transport
icon next to

Routing
information
view is

In your transport object, store a reference to your routing information template in the `transportInfoForm` slot.

To add your own information to the routing information view, you can supply a `BuildText` method. From `BuildText`, call the `AddText` method for each additional line of text you want to add below the existing elements. Alternatively, you can add child views to the routing information view.

If you do add additional lines or views to the routing information view that cause it to increase in height, you must also set the `addedHeight` slot in the routing information view or in your `BuildText` method (or anywhere before the inherited `ViewSetupFormScript` method is called). In this slot, specify the number of pixels by which you are increasing the height of the view.

The header view may include editable fields. If the user changes something in an editable field, you probably want to know about it so that you can save the new information or perform other operations. The `InfoChanged` message is provided for this purpose. This message is sent to whatever object you designate when the header view is closed.

Providing a Routing Slip Template

A transport uses a routing slip when sending an item in order to get all the information necessary to transmit the item. Since the user interface for the routing slip is provided by the transport, the application does not need to know anything about what is required to send the item.

Store a reference to your routing slip template in the `routingSlip` slot in your transport object.

Use the `protoFullRouteSlip` template, described in the following section, to create a routing slip.

One additional proto for use in routing slips is described in the section "Using protoAddressPicker" (page 22-31).

Using protoFullRouteSlip

This routing slip proto already includes most of the elements required in a routing slip. Figure 22-3 shows an example of this proto. For a complete description of the slots and methods in this proto, see "protoFullRouteSlip" (page 19-38) in *Newton Programmer's Reference*.

Figure 22-3   `protoFullRouteSlip` view

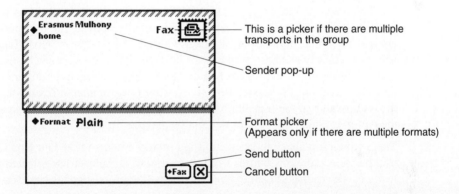

The transport name and stamp icon in the upper-right corner of the routing slip are automatically supplied. They are based on the *transport*.`actionTitle` and *transport*.`icon` slots.

The format picker child in `protoFullRouteSlip` provides the picker list for choosing among multiple formats. The current format is initially displayed. The picker provides for opening an auxiliary view if one is associated with the current format. This child view uses the `currentFormat` slot in the item (the `fields.currentFormat` slot in the routing slip), a list of routing formats compatible with the item, and the `activeFormat` slot in the routing slip to set up the picker with the correct choices. These slots are set up by the system.

When the user picks another format, the `activeFormat` slot is updated, which changes the format choice shown next to the label. Additionally, the `SetDefaultFormat` message is sent to the application, and `currentFormat` in the item is updated. The format picker also sends the `SetupItem` message to the format itself. If the format contains an `auxForm` slot, the view specified in the `auxForm` slot opens when the format is selected.

The sender pop-up child view allows the sender of the item to select a different owner persona or worksite from a picker, which might affect how the owner's name and address appear and how the item is sent. For example, if you choose a worksite location with a different area code from your company worksite, and send a fax to your company, the system automatically inserts a "1" and the company area code before the phone number, which it wouldn't do if you told the system you were at a location in that area code.

The default owner name (or persona as it is sometimes called) shown by this picker is the one corresponding to the last-used owner name for a routing operation. The default worksite for the owner is the one corresponding to the last worksite used for a routing operation, or the setting of the home location in the Time Zones application (whichever was done last). Note that additional owner names and worksites can be created by users in the Owner Info application.

The Send button child in `protoFullRouteSlip` provides the button that actually sends the item to the Out Box, and can also activate the transport. When tapped, the button may display a picker with the choices "Now" and "Later," or it may immediately send the item now or later. Its operation depends on the user preference setting of the `nowOrLater` slot in the preferences configuration frame described in Table 19-1 (page 19-7) in *Newton Programmer's Reference*, and on the return value of the transport `ConnectionDetect` method, which can force the button to send now or later without displaying a picker.

The Send button also handles submitting multiple items to the Out Box when the user has selected many entries from an overview. If the user has selected multiple items but the transport cannot handle cursors (the `allowBodyCursors` transport slot is `nil`), the system sends the transport the `VerifyRoutingInfo` method. This method allows the transport to modify the individual items, if necessary. When only a single item (not a multiple-item target object) is submitted to the Out Box, `VerifyRoutingInfo` is not called. In this case, if you need to modify the item before it is sent, you can do this in the routing slip method `PrepareToSend`.

The function of the Send button is to submit the contents of the `fields` slot in the routing slip to the Out Box. (The `fields` slot holds the item being routed and other information about it.) After the item is submitted, the Out Box sends the transport the `SendRequest` message to alert it that an item is waiting to be sent. If the `cause` slot in the *request* argument to `SendRequest` is set to `'submit`, this indicates the user chose to send the item later from the Send button. If the `cause` slot is `'item`, this indicates the user chose to send the item immediately. Additionally, the `connect` slot in the item contains a Boolean value indicating if the user chose to send the item now (`true`) or later (`nil`).

The name of the current transport appears in the upper-right corner of the `protoFullRouteSlip` view. If that transport belongs to a group, the transport name is actually a picker, from which the user can choose any of the other transports in the group. The picker is displayed only if there is more than one transport that belongs to the group. If the user changes the transport, the system closes and reopens the routing slip for the current target item, since the routing slip may be different for a different transport. Before the routing slip is closed, it is sent the `TransportChanged` message. This allows the routing slip to take such necessary action as alerting the user that addressing information might be lost as a result of changing transports. For more information on grouped transports, see the section "Grouping Transports" beginning on page 22-7.

Besides the supplied elements, your transport needs to add additional transport-specific elements to the routing slip view. For example, transports are responsible for adding the views that occupy the middle of the envelope area, to obtain routing or addressing information for the item. And transports typically add other elements to the area below the envelope. Figure 22-4 shows what a complete routing slip might look like, after you add transport-specific items.

Figure 22-4   Complete routing slip

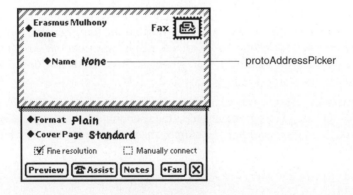

The middle of the envelope portion of a routing slip template typically includes a view that gathers and displays recipient information for the item being sent. You'll probably want to use the `protoAddressPicker` to allow the user to choose recipients for the item. For details on how to use this proto, see the section "Using protoAddressPicker" beginning on page 22-31.

Positioning Elements in the Lower Portion of the Routing Slip

The height of the lower portion of the routing slip is controlled by the `bottomIndent` slot. Placing your own user interface elements in this portion of the routing slip is complicated by the fact that the format picker may or may not be inserted by the system. It is included only if there is more than one format for the item. Also, the system performs animation on the routing slip, changing the location of the bottom bounds.

Any user interface elements you add to this portion of the routing slip must be positioned relative to the bottom of the slip dynamically, at run time. You can determine the position of the bottom of the slip by calling the routing slip method `BottomOfSlip`. An alternative method of positioning elements dynamically is to make them sibling bottom-relative to the last child of the routing slip proto, which is the Send button.

Note that only the first child element you add needs to follow these rules. Additional elements can be positioned sibling-relative to it.

Using Owner Information

The `protoFullRouteSlip` view sends the `OwnerInfoChanged` callback method to itself if the user changes the selection of owner name or worksite location in the sender pop-up view. The `OwnerInfoChanged` method provides the chance to update any information in the routing slip that depends on data in the sender's current owner card or worksite. In addition, the `fromRef` slot in the item will probably need to be updated with new sender information. For more information about setting the `fromRef` slot, see the section "Obtaining an Item Frame" beginning on page 22-13.

In your `OwnerInfoChanged` method, you can obtain any changes by checking variables in which you are interested in the user configuration data, using the `GetUserConfig` function. For example, the area code at the user's location can be found by using this code:

```
GetUserConfig('currentAreaCode);
```

For a list of variables in the user configuration data, see "User Configuration Variables" (page 16-101) in *Newton Programmer's Reference*.

One issue to consider when saving items in the Out Box for later transmission is when to read the sender's owner card and worksite information. In general, data from the owner card should be obtained from the current persona at the time the item is queued by the user. Such information might include the sender's name, return address, credit card information, and so on.

However, if you use worksite information (for example, for addressing), you may want to wait until the item is actually transmitted to obtain the most current information based on the user's current worksite setting, and modify addressing information at that time. For example, if a user queued several fax items from home but didn't send them until she got to work, the area code information for telephone numbers might need to be changed.

Using protoAddressPicker

This proto consists of a labeled field that you can use in the routing slip to allow the user to choose the recipient(s) of the item being sent. The first time the user taps on the address picker, it opens a view that displays a list of names from the Names file, from which the user can choose one or more recipients (Figure 22-5).

Figure 22-5   protoPeoplePicker view

This view uses the protoPeoplePicker to provide the name picking facility. The address picker is customizable so that you can substitute a name picking service other than protoPeoplePicker by setting the _picker slot. For example, an e-mail transport might use this facility to provide an alternate directory service.

When the user picks a name, the information is saved, and the next time the address picker opens, it displays a small picker with the saved name and the choice "Other Names." The user can choose "Other Names" to reopen the protoPeoplePicker view and select from the comprehensive list of names. Each time a new name is selected, it is saved and added to the initial address picker list, giving the user a convenient way to select from recently used addresses, as shown in Figure 22-6. The address picker remembers the last eight names selected.

Figure 22-6 Address picker with remembered names

The Intelligent Assistant also interacts with the address picker. If the user invokes a routing action such as "fax Bob" with the Intelligent Assistant, the Intelligent Assistant sets up the address picker with a list of alternatives from the Names file, as shown in Figure 22-7.

Figure 22-7 Address picker set up by Intelligent Assistant

The `protoAddressPicker` uses name references to refer to individual names. A name reference is a frame that contains a soup entry or an alias to a soup entry, usually from the Names soup, hence the term name reference. The system includes built-in data definitions that can access name references and has associated view definitions that can display the information stored in or referenced by a name reference. The built-in data definitions and view definitions are registered under subclasses of the symbol `'nameRef`. For more information about name references, see "Name References" (page 5-1) in *Newton Programmer's Reference*.

Most transports can use the built-in name reference data and view definitions to handle and display name references. For example, one place you might need to use these is if you need to build a string representing the address or addresses chosen in the `protoAddressPicker`. The `selected` slot of the `protoAddressPicker` contains an array of name references for the names selected by the user in the picker. You can use the name reference data definition method `GetRoutingTitle` to return a string representing all the selected addresses, truncated to the length you specify. Alternately, you can use the transport method `GetNameText` to do the same thing.

Providing a Preferences Template

Transport preferences are accessed and changed from the information button in the In/Out Box. (The information button is the small button with an "i" in it.) Each transport with a preferences view is listed in the information picker, as shown in Figure 22-8.

Figure 22-8   Information picker and preferences view

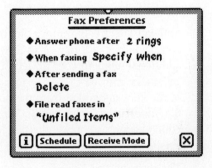

Information picker   Preferences view

To make a preferences view for a transport, create a template with a prototype of `protoTransportPrefs`. In your transport object, store a reference to your preferences view template in the `preferencesForm` slot. When the information picker is displayed, it automatically includes an item for each transport that has a preferences template registered in the transport's `preferencesForm` slot.

Each transport may add its own preferences view for configuring any options that apply to that transport. Some common options include

- enable/disable logging
- deferred/immediate send
- enable/disable listening

- default folders for new and read or sent items
- show/hide status and progress dialogs

The `protoTransportPrefs` proto provides a dialog containing the preferences items shown in Figure 22-9.

Figure 22-9   `protoTransportPrefs` view

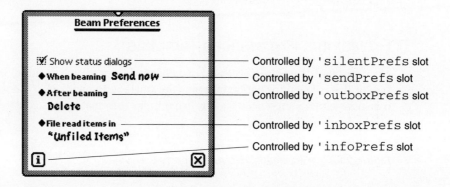

You can selectively remove any of the elements shown above by setting the corresponding slot to `nil` in the `protoTransportPrefs` view. To include additional items in your preferences view, add child views to the `protoTransportPrefs` view. The default child elements positioned in the center of the view are added from the bottom up and are justified relative to the bottom of the preferences view or to the top of their preceding sibling view. To add other child elements, increase the height of the view and add your elements above the existing ones, except for the title.

The `protoTransportPrefs` template also automatically checks your transport and displays or hides the In/Out Box preference elements. If your transport does not contain a `SendRequest` method, the Out Box preference element is not displayed; if your transport does not contain a `ReceiveRequest` method, the In Box preference element is not displayed. If the latter element is missing, the Out Box element is automatically drawn at the bottom of the preferences view.

For example, the built-in Print transport uses the `protoTransportPrefs` proto for its preferences view. Since the `ReceiveRequest` method does not exist in the Print transport, the In Box preference element is not displayed, as shown in Figure 22-10.

Figure 22-10   Print preferences

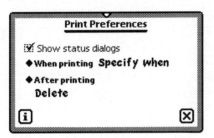

The Info button is included in the `protoTransportPrefs` template so you can give the user access to About and Help views for the transport. The button is built from the standard `protoInfoButton` proto. To include items on the Info picker, you must provide handler methods in the `infoPrefs` slot of your transport preferences view. The `protoTransportPrefs` template includes a handler for the "Help" item that displays the system help book, open to the routing section. You'll need to override this method if you want to provide your own help information.

You can add custom items to the Info picker by supplying `GenInfoAuxItems` and `DoInfoAux` methods in the `infoPrefs` frame. For more information about these methods and how the Info button works, see "protoInfoButton" (page 6-10) in *Newton Programmer's Reference*.

The `defaultConfiguration` slot in the `protoTransport` holds the initial preferences associated with the transport. This slot is set up by default with a frame holding an initial selection of preferences items. The child views of the `protoTransportPrefs` proto are designed to manipulate the slots in this frame.

If you want to override the default preferences frame, you need to construct an identical one with different values. You can't use a _proto slot in your default frame since the contents of the `defaultConfiguration` slot are stored in a soup and _proto slots can't be stored in soup entries.

Summary of the Transport Interface

Constants

```
ROM_RouteMailIcon // bitmap for mail group icon
ROM_RoutePrintIcon // bitmap for print group icon
ROM_RouteFaxIcon // bitmap for fax group icon
ROM_RouteBeamIcon // bitmap for beam group icon
ROM_RouteReply // bitmap for reply action icon
ROM_RouteForward // bitmap for forward action icon
ROM_RouteAddSender // bitmap for add sender to Names icon
ROM_RoutePasteText // bitmap for copy text to Notes icon
```

Protos

protoTransport

```
myTransport := {
_proto: protoTransport, // proto transport object
appSymbol: symbol, // transport symbol
title: string, // transport name
dataTypes: array, // symbols for routing types supported
actionTitle: string, // name of transport action
icon: bitmapFrame, // transport icon
group: symbol, // transport group symbol
groupTitle: string, // group name
groupIcon: bitmapFrame, // group icon
routingSlip: viewTemplate, // routing slip template
transportInfoForm: viewTemplate, // routing info template
preferencesForm: viewTemplate, // preferences template
statusTemplate: viewTemplate, // status template
statusDialog: view, // status view
modalStatus: Boolean, // modal status dialogs?
dialogStatusMsgs: frame, // status strings
status: symbol, // current status
addressingClass: symbol, // name reference symbol
addressSymbols: array, // don't translate e-mail classes
allowBodyCursors: Boolean, // allow cursors in body slot?
defaultConfiguration: frame, // user preferences defaults
AppClosed: function, // notifies transport of app closing
```

Transport Interface

```
AppInFront: function, // notifies transport of change in
                         app frontmost status
AppOpened: function, // notifies transport of app opening
CancelRequest: function, // cancels in-progress operation
CanPutAway: function, // put away hook for transport
CheckOutbox: function, // invokes SendRequest operation
CloseStatusDialog: function, // closes status dialog
ConnectionDetect: function, // force send now or later
GetConfig: function, // returns a prefs value
GetDefaultOwnerStore: function, // returns default store
GetFolderName: function, // gets folder name for item
GetFromText: function, // hook to supply item sender
GetItemInfo: function, // returns item to or from info
GetItemStateString: function, // returns item status string
GetItemTime: function, // returns item time stamp info
GetItemTitle: function, // returns item title
GetNameText: function, // returns name string from namerefs
GetStatusString: function, // returns transport status
GetTitleInfoShape: function, // returns info shape
GetToText: function, // hook to supply item recipient(s)
GetTransportScripts: function,// extends In/Out Box actions
HandleError: function, // displays error alert
HandleThrow: function, // handles exceptions
IgnoreError: function, // screens errors
InstallScript: function, // notification of installation
IOBoxExtensions: function, // extends In/Out Box view defs
IsInItem: function, // is item in the In or Out Box?
IsLogItem: function, // has item been logged?
ItemCompleted: function, // processes an item
ItemDeleted: function, // called when item is deleted
ItemDuplicated: function, // called when item is duplicated
ItemPutAway: function, // called after item is put away
ItemRequest: function, // gets next queued item
MakeLogEntry: function, // makes log entry
MissingTarget: function, // notification of missing target
NewFromItem: function, // gets item frame for received data
NewItem: function, // gets new item frame
NormalizeAddress: function, // translates e-mail address
PowerOffCheck: function, // notification of power-off
QueueRequest: function, // queues item for later handling
ReceiveRequest: function, // receives data
SendRequest: function, // sends data
SetConfig: function, // sets a prefs value
SetStatusDialog: function, // opens/updates status dialog
```

```
TranslateError: function, // returns a string translation
VerifyRoutingInfo: function, // called on send of multiple
                    // item target that is being split
...
}
```

protoTransportHeader

```
aHeader := {
_proto: protoTransportHeader, // proto header object
transport: frame, // transport object
target: frame, // target object
addedHeight: integer, // height you're adding to header
context: view, // view to notify with InfoChanged msg
changed: Boolean, // user changed a field?
BuildText: function, // builds additional header lines
AddText: function, // adds lines to header
InfoChanged: function, // notifies view of changed field
...
}
```

protoFullRouteSlip

```
aFullRoutingSlip := {
_proto: protoFullRouteSlip, // proto full routing slip
viewJustify: integer, // viewJustify flags
envelopeHeight: integer, // height of envelope portion
envelopeWidth: integer, // width of envelope portion
bottomIndent: integer, // height of lower portion
fields: frame, // item frame
target: frame, // target object
activeFormat: frame, // currently selected format
transport: frame, // transport object
formatPicker: frame, // the format picker child view
sendButton: frame, // the send button child view
BottomOfSlip: function, // returns bottom of slip
FormatChanged: function, // notifies slip of new format
OwnerInfoChanged: function, // notifies slip of new sender
PrepareToSend: function, // notifies slip when item is sent
ContinueSend: function, // continues send process
TransportChanged: function, // notifies of transport change
...
}
```

protoAddressPicker

```
anAddressPicker := {
_proto: protoAddressPicker, // address picker
viewBounds: boundsFrame, // location and size
text: string, // picker label
otherText: string, // last item (pops up people picker)
selected: array, // name refs to be initially selected
alternatives: array, // name refs to be shown in picker
class: symbol, // name ref data def class
_picker: viewTemplate, // picker for other addresses
...
}
```

protoTransportPrefs

```
myTransportPrefs := {
_proto: protoTransportPrefs, // transport prefs proto
viewBounds: boundsFrame, // location and size
title: string, // transport name
appSymbol: symbol, // transport appSymbol
silentPrefs: frame, // controls checkbox element in prefs
sendPrefs: frame, // controls send element in prefs
outboxPrefs: frame, // controls out box prefs element
inboxPrefs: frame, // controls in box prefs element
infoPrefs: frame, // defines more info button choices
...
}
```

Functions and Methods

Utility Functions

```
RegTransport(symbol, transport)
UnRegTransport(symbol)
DeleteTransport(symbol)
GetCurrentFormat(item)
GetGroupTransport(groupSymbol)
QuietSendAll(transportSym) // platform file function
ownerApp:Refresh()
ownerApp:RemoveTempItems(transportSym)
```

Endpoint Interface

This chapter describes the basic Endpoint interface in Newton system software. The Endpoint interface allows you to perform real-time communication using any of the communication tools available in the system. The Endpoint interface is well suited for communication needs such as database access and terminal emulation.

You should read this chapter if your application needs to perform real-time communications—that is, communication operations that do not use the Routing and Transport interfaces described in the previous chapters. This chapter describes how to

- set options to configure the underlying communication tool

- establish a connection

- send and receive data

- set up an input specification frame to control how data is received

- cancel communication operations

This chapter describes the general approach to using the Endpoint interface, but does not discuss details specific to using individual communication tools. For specific details on using particular built-in communication tools, see Chapter 24, "Built-in Communications Tools."

About the Endpoint Interface

The Endpoint interface is based on a single proto—`protoBasicEndpoint`—which provides a standard interface to all communication tools (serial, modem, infrared, AppleTalk, and so on). This proto provides methods for

- interacting with the underlying communication tool

- setting and getting endpoint options

- opening and closing connections

- sending and receiving data

The **endpoint** object created from this proto encapsulates and maintains the details of the specific connection. It allows you to control the underlying communication tool to perform your communication tasks.

The Endpoint interface uses an asynchronous, state-driven communications model. In asynchronous operation, communication requests are queued, and control is returned to your application after each request is made but before it is completed. Many endpoint methods can also be called synchronously. In synchronous operation, execution of your application is blocked until the request completes; that is, the endpoint method does not return until the communication operation is finished.

The Endpoint interface supports multiple simultaneous connections. That is, you can have more than one active endpoint at a time. Each endpoint object controls an underlying communication tool, and these tools run as separate operating system tasks. However, remember that the endpoint objects you create and control all execute within the single Application task.

The number of simultaneously active endpoints you can use is limited in practice by available system memory and processor speed. Each communication tool task requires significant memory and processor resources. Note that memory for the communication tools that underlie endpoints is allocated from the operating system domain, whereas memory for the endpoint objects is allocated from the NewtonScript heap.

Asynchronous Operation

Almost all endpoint methods can be called asynchronously. This means that calling the method queues a request for a particular operation with the underlying communication tool task, and then the method returns. When the operation completes, the communication tool sends a callback message to notify the endpoint that the request has been completed. The callback message is the CompletionScript message, and it is defined by your application in a frame called the callback specification, or **callback spec**. (For more details, see "Callback Spec Frame" (page 20-9) in *Newton Programmer's Reference*.)

You define the callback spec frame in your application and pass it as an argument to each endpoint method you call asynchronously. The callback spec frame contains slots that control how the endpoint method executes, and it contains a CompletionScript method that is called when the endpoint operation completes. The CompletionScript method is passed a result code parameter that indicates if the operation completed successfully or with an error.

A special type of callback spec, called an **output spec**, is used with the Output method. An output spec contains a few additional slots that allow you to pass special protocol flags and to define how the data being sent is translated. Output specs are described in "Output Spec Frame" (page 20-10) in *Newton Programmer's Reference*.

This kind of asynchronous operation lends itself nicely to creating state-machine based code, where each part of the communication process is a state that is invoked by calling an endpoint method. The CompletionScript method of each state invokes the next state, and the state machine automatically progresses from one state to the next in a predefined fashion.

Synchronous Operation

Many endpoint methods can be called synchronously as well as asynchronously. Synchronous operation means that invoking a method queues a request for a particular operation with the underlying communication tool task, and the method does not return until the operation is completed. This means that your application is blocked from execution until the synchronous method returns.

Only a few endpoint methods must be called synchronously. Most can be called either asynchronously or synchronously. For methods that can be called in either mode, it is recommended that you use the asynchronous mode whenever possible. If you call such a method synchronously, the communication system spawns a separate task associated with the method call, while putting your application task on hold. This results in higher system overhead and can reduce overall system performance if you use many synchronous method calls.

Input

In the Endpoint interface, you receive data by defining a frame called an input specification, or **input spec,** and then waiting for input. The input spec defines how incoming data should be formatted, termination conditions that control when the input should be stopped, data filtering options, and callback methods. The main callback method is the InputScript method, which is passed the received data when the input operation terminates normally. Receiving data with the Endpoint interface is *always asynchronous*.

Here is an overview of the way you can use input spec methods to obtain the received data:

- Let the termination conditions specified in the input spec be triggered by the received data, thus calling your InputScript method. For example, when a particular string is received, the InputScript method is called.

- Periodically sample incoming data by using the input spec PartialScript method, which is called periodically at intervals you specify in the input spec.

- Cause the system to send the InputScript callback method by using the Input method. This immediately returns the contents of the input buffer and clears it.

- Immediately return the input buffer contents without terminating the active input spec and without clearing the buffer by using the Partial method.

If the input operation terminates normally—that is, the InputScript method is called—the system automatically reposts the input spec for you to receive additional input. Of course, you can alter this process if you want to.

Data Forms

All NewtonScript data needs to be transformed whenever it is sent to or received from a foreign environment. That foreign environment may be a server or host computer at the other end of the connection, or it may even be the communication tool that's processing the configuration options you've passed to it. Typically, communication tools expect C-type option data.

Whether you're sending, receiving, or using data to set endpoint options, you can tag the data with a **data form.** A data form is a symbol that describes the transformations that need to take place when data is exchanged with other environments. When you send data or set endpoint options, the data form defines how to convert the data from its NewtonScript format. When you receive data or get endpoint options, the data form defines the type of data expected.

Data forms are used in output specs, input specs, and endpoint option frames. The data form is defined by a slot named form in these frames. If you don't define the data form in a particular case, a default data form is used, depending on the type of operation and the type of data being handled.

Note that when sending data, you can take advantage of the default data forms by not explicitly specifying a data form. Because NewtonScript objects have type information embedded in their values, the system can select appropriate default data forms for different kinds of data being sent. For example, if you send string data and don't specify the data form, the 'string data form is used by default.

The symbols you use to indicate data forms are 'char, 'number, 'string, 'bytes, 'binary, 'template, and 'frame. Each is best suited to certain data and operations.:

- For simple scalar values, use 'char for characters and 'number for integers.

- For semi-aggregate forms of these kinds of data, use 'string for a concatenation of characters plus a terminating byte, and use 'bytes for an array of bytes.

- For binary data, use 'binary. This is the fastest option for sending and receiving, since the data processing is minimal.

- For more complex data, there are two aggregate data forms. You may want to use the 'template form if you're communicating with a remote procedure call service that expects C-type data and that follows the exact same marshalling restrictions the Newton does. The 'frame form is convenient if you're exchanging frames with another Newton.

The different types of data forms and the defaults are described in more detail in "Data Form Symbols" (Table 20-1 on page 20-2) in *Newton Programmer's Reference*.

Only a subset of data form values is applicable for any particular operation. Table 23-1 enumerates the data forms and their applicability to output specs, input specs, and endpoint option frames.

Table 23-1 Data form applicability

Data form	Output spec	Input spec	Option frame
`'char`	default for characters	OK	OK
`'number`	default for numbers	OK	OK
`'string`	default for strings	default	OK
`'bytes`	OK	OK	OK
`'binary`	default for binary objects; output spec can include optional `target` slot	OK; input spec must include `target` slot	OK
`'template`	OK	OK; input spec must include `target` slot	default
`'frame`	OK	OK	not applicable

Template Data Form

The `'template` data form enables you to pass data as if you were passing C structures, and is thus extremely useful in communicating with the lower level communication tools in getting and setting endpoint options.

When you set options or send data using the `'template` data form, the data is expected to be a frame containing two slots, `arglist` and `typelist`. The `arglist` slot is an array containing the data, the list of arguments. The `typelist` slot is a corresponding array containing the types that describe the data.

To get endpoint options, the data in the `data` slot must be a frame containing the `arglist` and `typelist` arrays. The `arglist` array should contain placeholder or default values. The system supplies the actual `arglist` values when the option list is returned.

In the same manner, to receive data, you must add a `target` slot to your input spec containing the `arglist` and `typelist` arrays. The `arglist` array contains placeholder or default values, which the system fills in when the data is received. For more information, see the section "Specifying the Data Form and Target" beginning on page 23-13.

The data types that can be used in the `typelist` array are identified by these symbols: `'long`, `'ulong`, `'short`, `'byte`, `'char`, `'unicodechar`, `'boolean`, `'struct`, and `'array`. They are described in detail in "Data Type Symbols" (Table 20-2 on page 20-3) in *Newton Programmer's Reference*.

Note that the `'struct` and `'array` data types are not used alone, but in conjunction with other elements in a `typelist` array. They modify how the other elements are treated. The `'struct` data type defines the array as an aggregate structure of various data types that is padded to a long-word boundary (4 bytes in the Newton system). Note that the whole structure is padded, not each array element. You must specify the `'struct` data type in order to include more than one type of data in the array.

The `'array` data type defines the array as an aggregate array of one or more elements of a single data type. The `'array` data type is specified as a NewtonScript array of three items, like this:

```
['array, dataTypeSymbol, integer]
```

Replace the *dataTypeSymbol* with one of the other simple data types. And *integer* is an integer specifying the number of units of that data type to convert. To convert an entire string, including the terminator, specify zero for *integer*. A nonzero value specifies the exact number of units to be converted, independent of a termination character in the source string.

Here are some examples of how to use the `'array` data type to represent C strings and Unicode strings in NewtonScript. The first example shows how to convert between a NewtonScript string of undefined length and a C string (translated to/from Unicode):

```
['array, 'char, 0]
```

This example shows how to convert a four-character NewtonScript string to a C string:

```
['array, 'char, 4]
```

This example shows how to convert between a NewtonScript string and a Unicode string:

```
['array, 'unicodechar, 0]
```

The `'template` data form is intended primarily as a means of communicating with the lower level communication tools in the Newton system. You can use this data form to communicate with a remote system, however, you must be careful and know exactly what you are doing to use it for this purpose. Remember that the lengths of various data types and the byte order may be different in other systems and may change in future releases of the Newton operating system.

Endpoint Options

You configure the communication tool underlying an endpoint object by setting endpoint options. An endpoint option is specified in an **endpoint option frame** that is passed in an array as an argument to one of the endpoint methods. Options select the communication tool to use, control its configuration and operation, and return result code information from each endpoint method call. An alternative way to set options is to directly call the endpoint Option method.

There are three kinds of options you can set, each identified by a unique symbol:

■ 'service options, which specify the kind of communication service, or tool, to be controlled by the endpoint

■ 'option options, which control characteristics of the communication tool

■ 'address options, which specify address information used by the communication tool

For details on the particular options you can use with the built-in communication tools, see Chapter 24, "Built-in Communications Tools."

Compatibility

The protoBasicEndpoint and protoStreamingEndpoint objects and all the utility functions described in this chapter are new in Newton system software version 2.0. The protoEndpoint interface used in system software version 1.x is obsolete, but still supported for compatibility with older applications. Do not use the protoEndpoint interface, as it will not be supported in future system software versions.

Specific enhancements introduced by the new endpoint protos in system software 2.0 include the following:

■ **Data forms.** You can handle and identify many more types of data by tagging it using data forms specified in the form slot of an option frame.

■ **Asynchronous behavior and callback specs.** Most endpoint methods can now be called asynchronously.

■ **Flexible input specs.** Enhancements include support for time-outs and the ability to specify multiple termination sequences.

■ **Better error handling.** Consistent with other system services, errors resulting from synchronous methods are signaled by throwing an exception.

■ **Binary data handling.** The way binary (raw) data is handled has changed significantly. For input, you can now target a direct data input object, which results in significantly faster performance. For output, you can specify offsets and lengths, which allows you to send the data in chunks.

■ **Multiple communication sessions.** The system now supports multiple simultaneous communication sessions. In other words, you can have more than one active endpoint at a time.

Using the Endpoint Interface

This section describes

- setting endpoint options
- initializing and terminating an endpoint
- establishing a connection
- sending data
- receiving data
- sending and receiving streamed data
- working with binary data
- canceling operations
- handling errors
- linking the endpoint with an application

Setting Endpoint Options

Endpoint options are specified in an endpoint option frame that is passed as an argument to an endpoint method. Typically you specify an array of option frames, setting several options at once. Note that you cannot nest an option array inside another one.

You must specify a single `'service` option, to select a communication tool. Then you usually specify one or more `'option` options to configure the communication tool—for example, to set the baud rate, flow control, and parity of the serial tool. Note that if you are using the modem communication tool, you can use the utility function `MakeModemOption` to return a modem dialing option for use with the built-in modem tool.

You may also need to specify an `'address` option, depending on the communication tool you are using. The only built-in tools that use an `'address` option are the modem and AppleTalk tools. Note that you should use the global functions `MakePhoneOption` and `MakeAppleTalkOption` to construct `'address` options for the modem and AppleTalk tools.

The slots in an endpoint option frame are described in detail in "Endpoint Option Frame" (page 20-7) in *Newton Programmer's Reference*.

All option data you set gets packed together into one block of data. Each option within this block must be long-word aligned for the communication tools. So, when using the `'template` data form, you need to use the `'struct` type (at the beginning of the `typelist` array) to guarantee that the option is long-word aligned and padded. To set the serial input/output parameters, for instance, the option frame might look like this:

```
serialIOParms := {
    type: 'option,
    label: kCMOSerialIOParms,
    opCode: opSetNegotiate,
    data: {
        arglist: [
            kNoParity,   // parity
            k1StopBits, // stopBits
            k8DataBits, // dataBits
            k9600bps,   // bps
        ],
        typelist: [
            'struct,
            'uLong,
            'long,
            'long,
            'long
        ]
    }
};
```

To get the connection information, the option frame you construct might look like this:

```
connectInfoParms := {
    type: 'option,
    label: kCMOSerialIOParms,
    opCode: opGetCurrent,
    data: {
        arglist: [
            0, // parity placeholder
            0, // stopBits placeholder
            0, // dataBits placeholder
            0, // bps placeholder
        ],
        typelist: [
            'struct,
            'ulong,
            'long,
```

```
        'long,
        'long
    ]
  }
};
```

When you set endpoint options, the cloned option frame is returned to you so that you can check the result codes for individual options. If you set options with an asynchronous method call, the cloned option frame is returned as a parameter to the CompletionScript callback method. If you set options with a synchronous method call, the cloned option frame is returned as the value of the synchronous method itself.

The result slot in each option frame is always set for returned options. It can be set to any of the error codes listed in "Option Error Code Constants" (Table 20-5 on page 20-5) in *Newton Programmer's Reference*. If an option succeeds without errors, the result slot is set to nil.

Exceptions are not thrown when individual options fail. This allows a request to succeed if, for example, every specified option except one succeeds. If you need to determine whether a particular option succeeds or fails, you must check the result slot of the option in question.

Note that in one array of option frames, you can specify options that are of the same type, and that seem to conflict. Since options are processed one at a time, in order, the last option of a particular type is the one that is actually implemented by the communication tool.

Note
When instantiating an endpoint for use with the modem tool, you can have options specified by the *options* parameter to the Instantiate method, as well as options specified by a modem setup package (see Chapter 25, "Modem Setup Service."). Any options from a modem setup package are appended to those set by the Instantiate method. ◆

For details on the specific options you can set for the built-in communication tools, see Chapter 24, "Built-in Communications Tools."

Initialization and Termination

Before using an endpoint, you must instantiate it using the Instantiate method. This method allocates memory in the system and creates the endpoint object. Then, you must bind the endpoint object to the communication hardware by calling the Bind method. This allocates the communication tool resources for use by the endpoint.

When you are finished with an endpoint, you must unbind it using the UnBind method, then dispose of it using the Dispose method.

Establishing a Connection

After instantiating and binding an endpoint, you establish a connection.

There are two ways you can create a connection. One way is to call the Connect method. If the physical connection is serial, for instance, you don't even need to specify an address as an option. The Connect method immediately establishes communication with whatever is at the other end of the line.

Certain communication tools—for example, the modem and AppleTalk tools—require you to specify an option of type 'address in order to make a connection. The modem tool requires a phone number as an 'address option. You should use the global function MakePhoneOption to return a proper phone number 'address option. The AppleTalk tool requires an AppleTalk Name Binding Protocol (NBP) 'address option. You should use the global function MakeAppleTalkOption to return a proper NBP 'address option.

To establish a connection where you expect someone else to initiate the connection, you need to call the Listen method. Once the connection is made by using Listen, you need to call the Accept method to accept the connection, or the Disconnect method to reject the connection and disconnect.

Sending Data

To send data, use the Output method. This method is intelligent enough to figure out the type of data you're sending and to convert it appropriately for transmission. This is because NewtonScript objects have type information embedded in their values, allowing the system to select appropriate default data forms for different kinds of data being sent.

You can specify output options and a callback method by defining an output spec, which you pass as a parameter to the Output method.

Certain communication tools may require or support the use of special flags indicating that particular protocols are in use. For example, the built-in infrared and AppleTalk tools expect framed (or packetized) data, and there are special flags to indicate that this kind of protocol is in use. If you are using such a communication tool to send data, you need to specify the sendFlags slot in the output spec frame. In this slot, you specify one or more flag constants added together.

To send packetized data, you set sendFlags to kPacket+kMore for each packet of data that is not the last packet. For the last packet, set sendFlags to kPacket+kEOP.

Receiving Data Using Input Specs

The most common way to receive data is to use input specs. An input spec is a frame that defines what kind of data you are looking for, termination conditions that control when the input should be stopped, and callback methods to notify you when input is stopped or other conditions occur.

An input spec consists of many pieces. It contains slots that define

- the type of data expected (form slot)

- the input target for template and binary data (target slot)

- the data termination conditions (termination slot)

- protocol flags for receiving data (rcvFlags slot)

- an inactivity time-out (reqTimeout slot)

- the data filter options (filter slot)

- the options associated with the receive request (rcvOptions slot)

- a method to be called when the termination conditions are met (InputScript method)

- a method to be called periodically to check input as it accumulates (PartialScript method, partialFrequency slot)

- a method to be called if the input spec terminates unexpectedly (CompletionScript method)

Table 23-2 summarizes the various input data forms and the input spec slots that are applicable to them. Input spec slots not included in the table apply to all data forms. For more details on the input spec frame, see "Input Spec Frame" (page 20-11) in *Newton Programmer's Reference*.

After you've connected or accepted a connection, you set up your first input spec by calling SetInputSpec. When one input spec terminates, the system automatically posts another input spec for you when the InputScript method defined in the previous input spec returns. This new input spec duplicates the one that just terminated. If you don't want this to happen, you can call the SetInputSpec method from within the InputScript method of your input spec to change the input spec or terminate the input. Pass nil to SetInputSpec to terminate the input.

You also use the SetInputSpec method if you need to set up an input spec at some other point. Note that if you want to terminate a current input spec to set up a new one, you must call the Cancel method before calling SetInputSpec with your new spec. (This applies inside an InputScript that is called as a result of calling the Input method.)

Table 23-2   Input spec slot applicability

Data form	target slot	termination slot	discard After slot*	filter slot	partial Frequency and partial Script slots†
`'char`	na (not applicable)	determined automatically	na	OK	na
`'number`	na	determined automatically	na	OK	na
`'string`	na	OK	OK	OK	OK
`'bytes`	na	OK	OK	OK	OK
`'binary`	`data` and `offset` slots only	all slots except `endSequence`	na	na	na
`'template`	`typelist` and `arglist` slots only	determined automatically	na	na	na
`'frame`	na	determined automatically	na	na	na

  * `discardAfter` is written as one word, broken here because of space limitations.
  † `partialFrequency` and `partialScript` are written as one word, broken here because of space limitations.

The following sections describe how to set the various slots in the input spec to accomplish specific tasks.

Specifying the Data Form and Target

You can choose how you want the received data formatted by setting the `form` slot in the input spec. In this slot, you specify one of the standard data forms described in "Data Form Symbols" (Table 20-1 on page 20-2) in *Newton Programmer's Reference*.

In preparation for receiving data, the system creates an input buffer. The buffer's size is based on the input spec slot `termination.byteCount`, on the slot `discardAfter`, or on the intrinsic size of the data. The system receives all the data in to this buffer, then translates the data into a newly created object whose type is specified by the input spec's `form` slot. It is this object that is passed back to the `InputScript` method.

If you specify the form 'template or 'binary, you also must specify a target slot in the input spec. The target slot is a frame used to define additional information pertaining to the data form.

If your input form is 'template, then you must set the arglist and typelist slots in the target frame. The arglist array contains placeholder data, which is filled in with actual data when it is received, and the typelist array contains the template's array of types.

If your input form is 'binary, data is written directly into the binary object that you specify in the data slot of the target frame. You can specify a binary object, virtual binary object, or string. Note that the binary object must be the same size as the received data; the system will not expand or shrink the object. For information on virtual binary objects, see Chapter 11, "Data Storage and Retrieval."

The offset slot in the target frame allows you to specify an offset in the binary object at which to write incoming data. For instance, if you want to write the received data in consecutive blocks in a binary object that already exists, you must set the data slot to the binary object, and set the offset slot to the byte offset at which you want the new data to be written for each block.

Specifying Data Termination Conditions

For 'string and 'bytes data forms, you must indicate when the input terminates by specifying a termination slot. You can terminate the input on these conditions:

- when a certain number of bytes has been received (set the byteCount slot)

- when a specific set of characters in the input stream has been found (set the endSequence slot)

- when the communication tool returns an end-of-packet indicator (set the useEOP slot)

Normally with the 'binary data form, the input is terminated when the target object fills up. However, you can also use the termination slot with binary data to specify a byte count that causes the input to terminate after a certain number of bytes has been received. This feature is useful when you want to provide user feedback as a large binary object is being received. Set the byteCount slot in the termination frame, and, when the input terminates, repost the input spec with the target.offset slot offset by the value of the termination.byteCount slot.

If you want to receive data that ends with a particular sequence of data, define that sequence in the endSequence slot in the termination frame. The endSequence slot allows you to terminate input based on a particular sequence of incoming data called the termination sequence. You can specify a single termination sequence, or an array of items, any one of which will cause the input to terminate. A termination sequence can be a single character, a string, a number, or an array of bytes. If you don't want to look for a termination sequence, don't define this slot.

For the `binary` data form, you cannot use the endSequence slot to specify a termination condition.

Note
Note that the system executes byte-by-byte comparisons between the termination sequence and the input stream. To facilitate this process, the termination sequence (or elements within the endSequence array) is converted to a byte or binary format to speed the comparison. Internally, single characters are converted to single bytes using the translation table specified by the endpoint encoding slot. Numbers are converted to single bytes; strings are converted to binary objects. An array of bytes is also treated as a binary object. For large numbers, you must encode your number as an array of bytes if there are significant digits beyond the high order byte of the number. ◆

If you want to terminate input based on a transport-level end-of-packet (EOP) indicator, then you can set the useEOP slot in the termination frame. This slot holds a Boolean value specifying whether or not to look for EOP indicators. Specify this slot only if the input spec rcvFlags slot includes the kPacket flag. Moreover, if the rcvFlags slot includes the kPacket flag and you do not specify the termination.useEOP slot, the system effectively sets useEOP to the default value true. For more information, see the following section, "Specifying Flags for Receiving."

It is not appropriate to specify the termination slot for data forms other than `string`, `bytes`, and `binary`. The `char` and `number` data forms automatically terminate after 1 and 4 bytes, respectively. The `frame` data form is terminated automatically when a complete frame has been received, and the `template` data form terminates when the number of bytes received matches the typelist specification in the target frame.

To limit the amount of accumulated data in the input buffer, you can define a discardAfter slot in the input spec. You can do this only when you have not specified a termination.byteCount slot for `string` and `bytes` data forms. The discardAfter slot sets the input buffer size. If the buffer overflows, older bytes are discarded in favor of more recently received bytes.

Specifying Flags for Receiving

For certain communication tools, it may be necessary to use special protocol flags when receiving data. You do this by specifying one or more flag constants in the rcvFlags slot in the input spec. You can use such flags only if the communication tool supports them.

For example, some of the built-in communication tools, such as the infrared and AppleTalk tools, support only framed receiving (packetized data). In order to use framed receiving, you must set the rcvFlags slot to the constant kPacket. With the infrared tool, if you do not specify a rcvFlags value of kPacket, the tool will behave unexpectedly.

Do not define the rcvFlags slot if the underlying communication tool does not support EOP indicators. If you do so, your input will terminate after each physical buffer of data is received. If you wish to terminate an input spec based on an EOP indicator, set the useEOP slot in the termination frame to true.

Of the built-in communication tools, only the infrared, AppleTalk, and framed asynchronous serial tools support framed packets and the kPacket flag.

If you set the kPacket flag and set the useEOP slot to true, you cannot also use the byteCount slot in the termination frame—if you do, byteCount will be ignored. In this case, only an EOP indicator will terminate input. If you do want to use the byteCount slot with the kPacket flag, set the useEOP slot to nil. In the latter case, the remote system should send an EOP indicator with every packet, though input won't terminate until the byteCount condition is met.

Specifying an Input Time-Out

You can specify a time-out for input in the reqTimeout slot of the input spec. In this slot, you specify the time, in milliseconds, of inactivity to allow during input. If there is no input for the specified interval, the time-out expires, the input is terminated, and the CompletionScript message is sent to the input spec frame. In this case, the result code passed with the CompletionScript message is –16005.

Don't specify a reqTimeout value less than 30 milliseconds.

Note that if a time-out expires for an asynchronous request such as receiving, that request and *all* outstanding requests are canceled.

Specifying Data Filter Options

As incoming data is received in the input buffer, the data can be processed, or filtered. This filtering can occur on all types of received data, except binary data (defined by the 'binary data form). This filtering of data is defined by the filter slot in the input spec. The `filter` slot is a frame containing two slots, `byteProxy` and `sevenBit`, which allow you to perform two different kinds of processing.

The `byteProxy` slot allows you to identify one or more characters or bytes in the input stream to be replaced by zero or one characters. You may, for instance, replace null characters (`0x00`) with spaces (`0x20`). Note that if your input data form is set to `'string`, you are encouraged to use this slot. Otherwise, null characters embedded in your string may prematurely terminate that string. (Remember, NewtonScript strings are null-terminated.)

The `byteProxy` slot contains an array of one or more frames. Each frame must have a `byte` slot, identifying the single-byte character or byte to be replaced, and a `proxy` slot, identifying the single-byte character or byte to be used instead. The `proxy` slot can also be `nil`, meaning that the original byte is to be removed completely from the input stream.

Note

Note that the system executes byte-by-byte comparisons and swaps between the bytes in the input stream and the replacements in the `proxy` slot. To facilitate this process, the values in the `byte` and `proxy` slots are converted to a byte format to speed the comparison and swap. Internally, single characters are converted to single bytes using the translation table specified in the endpoint `encoding` slot. Numbers are converted to single bytes. If a number has significant digits beyond the high-order byte, they will be dropped during the comparison and swap. ◆

You can also specify the `sevenBit` slot in the `filter` frame. Set this slot to `true` to specify that the high-order bit of every incoming byte be stripped ("zeroed out"). This is a convenient feature if you plan to communicate over links (particularly private European carriers) that spuriously set the high-order bit.

Specifying Receive Options

You can also set communication tool options associated with the receive request. To do this, specify an option frame or an array of option frames in the `rcvOptions` slot in the input spec. The options are set when the input spec is posted by the `SetInputSpec` method. The processed options are returned in the *options* parameter passed to the `InputScript` method.

Note that the options are used only once. If your `InputScript` method is called, for example, and it returns expecting the input spec to remain active, the options are not reposted. To explicitly reset the options in this example, you must call `SetInputSpec` within your `InputScript` method.

Handling Normal Termination of Input

The `InputScript` message is sent to the input spec frame when one of the termination conditions is met. You define the `InputScript` method in the input spec frame.

The received data is passed as a parameter to the `InputScript` method. Another parameter describes the specific condition that caused the input to terminate, in case you had specified more than one in the input spec.

When the `InputScript` method returns, the system automatically posts another receive request for you using the same input spec as the last one. You can prevent this by calling `SetInputSpec` within the `InputScript` method. In the `SetInputSpec` method, you can set a different input spec, or you can prevent a new input spec from being posted by setting the *inputSpec* parameter to `nil`. Note that while the input spec is `nil`, incoming data may be lost.

Periodically Sampling Incoming Data

You can sample the incoming data without meeting any of the termination conditions by specifying a `PartialScript` method in the input spec. The system sends the `PartialScript` message to the input spec frame periodically, at the frequency you define in the `partialFrequency` slot in the input spec, as long as there are one or more bytes of data in the input buffer. The system passes to the `PartialScript` method all of the data currently in the input buffer, but the data is not removed from the input buffer. If you want to remove this data from the input buffer, you can call the `FlushPartial` method.

Note that the sending of `PartialScript` messages is controlled by system idle events and is in no way triggered by receive request completions. The current input spec remains in effect after the `PartialScript` method returns.

You typically would use a `PartialScript` method to detect abnormal or out-of-band data not found by any of the usual input termination conditions.

You can specify `PartialScript` methods only for those input data forms that allow termination conditions —specifically, the `'string` and `'bytes` data forms.

To use the `PartialScript` method, you must also include the `partialFrequency` slot in the input spec. The `partialFrequency` slot specifies the frequency, in milliseconds, at which the input data buffer should be checked. If new data exists in the buffer, the `PartialScript` message is sent to the input spec frame.

Handling Unexpected Completion

The `CompletionScript` message is sent to the input spec frame when the input spec completes unexpectedly—for example, because of a time-out expiring or a `Cancel` message.

If you do not specify a `CompletionScript` method in your input spec frame, an exception is forwarded to the endpoint `ExceptionHandler` method.

Special Considerations

If you want to set up an input spec, but you never want to terminate the input, you can set up the input form to be either `'string` or `'bytes` data, and not define any of the data termination conditions. In this case, it is up to you to read and flush the input. You can do this by using a `PartialScript` method that calls the `FlushPartial` method at the appropriate times. Note that if the input exceeds the `discardAfter` size, the oldest data in the buffer is deleted to reduce the size of the input.

Alternatively, if you omit the `InputScript` method, yet define the input data form and termination conditions, the input continues to be terminated and flushed at the appropriate times. The only difference is that without an `InputScript` method, you'll never see the complete input.

Receiving Data Using Alternative Methods

The methods described in this section allow you to receive data in ways other than letting an input spec terminate normally. You may not need to use these methods; they're provided for flexibility in handling special situations.

You can force the system to send a pending input spec the `InputScript` message by calling the `Input` method. Note that this method is appropriate to use only when receiving data of the forms `'string` and `'bytes`. Also, in an `InputScript` method that is called as a result of calling `Input`, you cannot use `SetInputSpec` to change or terminate the input spec. Instead, you must first send the `Cancel` message to cancel the current input spec.

You can look at incoming data outside the scope of your `InputScript` or `PartialScript` method by calling the method `Partial`. This method returns data from the input buffer but doesn't remove it from the buffer. You can use this method to sample incoming data without affecting the normal operation of your input spec and its callback methods. Note that this method is appropriate to use only when receiving data of the forms `'string` and `'bytes`.

IMPORTANT

Do not call the `Input` or `Partial` methods in a polling loop to look for incoming data. The Newton communications architecture requires a return to the main event loop in order to process incoming data from the endpoint's underlying communication tool. These methods are included as an alternate way of retrieving data from the incoming data buffer, not as a way to implement synchronous data receives. ▲

To flush data from the input buffer, you can use the methods `FlushInput` and `FlushPartial`. The `FlushInput` method discards all data in the input buffer, and `FlushPartial` discards all data read by the last call to the `Partial` method.

Streaming Data In and Out

Besides `protoBasicEndpoint`, there is another type of endpoint proto called `protoStreamingEndpoint`. The purpose of this streaming endpoint is to provide a way to send and receive large frames without having first to flatten or unflatten them.

Flattening refers to the process of converting a frame object into a stream of bytes. Unflattening refers to the process of converting those bytes back into a frame object.

With the streaming endpoint, frame data is flattened or unflattened in chunks as it is sent or received. This allows large objects to be sent and received without causing the NewtonScript heap to overflow as a result of having to convert an entire object at once.

The `protoStreamingEndpoint` proto is based on `protoBasicEndpoint` and includes a method, `StreamIn`, that allows you to receive streamed data. This method automatically unflattens received data into a frame object in memory, and can place embedded virtual binary objects directly on a store. Another method, `StreamOut`, allows you to send frame data as a byte stream. Note that these two methods are synchronous; that is, they don't return until the operation is complete. However, they do provide progress information during the operation by means of a periodic callback.

Working With Binary Data

For receiving binary data, the data is returned as a raw byte stream. The data is not converted and is block-moved directly into a binary object that you have preallocated and specified as the target for the input.

To create this target object, specify a `target` frame in your input spec. This frame contains a `data` slot and optionally an `offset` slot. The `data` slot contains the preallocated binary (or virtual binary) object, while the `offset` slot is the offset within the binary object at which to stream data. For more information on receiving binary data and using the `target` frame, see the section "Specifying the Data Form and Target" beginning on page 23-13.

For sending data, the data is expected to be a binary object and is interpreted as a raw byte stream. That is, the data is not converted and is passed directly to the communication tool. This is the default data form for sending binary objects.

If you wish to send only a portion of your binary data at once, you can specify a `target` frame in the output spec. Within the `target` frame, the `offset` slot defines the offset from the beginning of the binary object at which to begin sending data, and the `length` slot defines the length of the data to send.

These binary capabilities are very useful if you wish to send and receive flattened frames "packetized" for a communication protocol. By using the global function `Translate`, you can flatten a frame. Then you can packetize the transmission by using the `target` frame in the output spec.

On the receiving end, you can preallocate a virtual binary object, and then assemble the packets using the `target` frame in the input spec. Once all binary data has been received, you can unflatten the frame using the `Translate` function again.

Canceling Operations

To stop endpoint operations, you can use the endpoint method `Cancel` or `Disconnect`. Endpoint operations can also be canceled indirectly as a result of a time-out expiring. Remember that you can set a time-out for a request in the callback spec that you pass to most endpoint methods, and you can set a time-out in an input spec.

Note that you cannot specify what is canceled. When you or the system cancel operations, all outstanding synchronous and asynchronous requests are canceled.

The cancellation process proceeds differently depending on whether you are canceling asynchronous or synchronous requests that you have previously queued. Following a cancellation, it is safe to proceed with other endpoint operations at different times, according to the following rules:

- If you use only asynchronous calls in your application, you can safely proceed after you receive the `CompletionScript` message resulting from the `Cancel` call (or from the method whose time-out expired).

- If you use only synchronous calls in your application, you can safely proceed after the cancelled synchronous call throws an exception as a result of the cancellation.

Mixing asynchronous and synchronous methods in your application is not recommended. However, if you do so, you should treat the cancellation process as if you had used all synchronous calls, and proceed only after an exception is thrown.

The cancellation itself can be invoked asynchronously or synchronously, and is handled differently in the system depending on how it's done. The details are explained in the following subsections.

Asynchronous Cancellation

Cancellation can be invoked asynchronously in the following ways:

- calling the `Cancel` method asynchronously, or calling the `Disconnect` method asynchronously with the *cancelPending* parameter set to `true`

- having a time-out expire for an asynchronous request

When cancellation is invoked asynchronously, the system first cancels all pending asynchronous requests. This means that the `CompletionScript` message is sent to the callback spec for each of these requests, and the `CompletionScript` *result* parameter is set to –16005.

Note
When calling `Cancel` asynchronously, it is possible that additional asynchronous requests might be queued (by a `CompletionScript` method) after the `Cancel` request is queued but before it is executed. These additional requests will fail with error –36003 since they will be processed after the cancel process begins. In fact, any endpoint request that is made while a cancel is in progress will fail with error –36003. ◆

Next, the cancel request itself completes by sending the `CompletionScript` message. This message is sent to the callback spec passed to the `Cancel` (or `Disconnect`) method. Or, if the cancellation was invoked as the result of a time-out expiration, the `CompletionScript` message is sent to the callback spec of whatever method timed out (or to the input spec, if input was in progress).

Finally, any pending synchronous request is canceled by throwing an exception that contains error code –16005.

Synchronous Cancellation

Cancellation can be invoked synchronously in the following ways:

- calling the `Cancel` method synchronously, or calling the `Disconnect` method synchronously with the *cancelPending* parameter set to `true`

- having a time-out expire for a synchronous request

When cancellation is invoked synchronously, the system first cancels any pending asynchronous requests. This means that the `CompletionScript` message is sent to the callback spec for each of these requests, and the `CompletionScript` *result* parameter is set to –16005.

Next, the `Cancel` (or `Disconnect`) method returns, and any pending synchronous request is canceled by throwing an exception that contains error code –16005. Or, if the cancellation was invoked as the result of a time-out expiration, then whatever method timed out throws an exception containing error code –16005.

Other Operations

The `Option` method allows you to get and set options apart from the *options* parameter to the `Bind`, `Connect`, `Listen`, `Accept`, and `Output` methods.

You can check the state of a connection by calling the `State` method.

Custom communication tools can return special events to the endpoint object through the `EventHandler` message. This message is sent to the endpoint whenever an event occurs that is not handled by one of the usual endpoint event handlers. A custom communication tool and an endpoint can use this mechanism to pass events from the communication tool up to the endpoint layer.

Error Handling

By specifying an `ExceptionHandler` method in your endpoint, you can handle exception conditions not caught by local `try...onexception` clauses, as well as exceptions not caught by `CompletionScript` methods.

When you call an endpoint method synchronously, and an error occurs in that method, the system throws an exception (usually of type `|evt.ex.comm|`). You can catch these exceptions in your application by using the `try...onexception` construct. It's a good idea to bracket every endpoint method call with this exception catching construct.

If an error occurs as a result of an asynchronous request, no exception is thrown, but the error is returned in the *result* parameter to the `CompletionScript` method associated with that request. If you did not define a `CompletionScript` method, or if the error is unsolicited, the error is forwarded to your `ExceptionHandler` method. If you did not define an `ExceptionHandler` method, then the communication system throws an exception. This exception is caught by the operating system, which displays a warning message to the user.

Constants for error codes generated by the Endpoint interface are defined in "Endpoint Error Code Constants" (Table 20-4 on page 20-4) in *Newton Programmer's Reference*.

When you use the `Option` method (or any method that takes options as a parameter), not only can the method itself fail, but a failure can occur in processing each of the individual option requests. If the latter happens, the `result` slot in the returned option frame is set to one of the option error codes listed in "Option Error Code Constants" (Table 20-5 on page 20-5) in *Newton Programmer's Reference*. If an option succeeds without errors, the `result` slot is set to `nil`. For more general information on setting options, see the section "Endpoint Options" beginning on page 23-7.

Power-Off Handling

During send and receive operations, you may want to protect against the system powering off so that the connection is not broken. The system can power-off unexpectedly as a result of the user inadvertently turning off the power or as a result of a low battery. If you want to be notified before the system powers off, you can register a callback function that the system will call before the power is turned off. Depending on the value you return from your callback function, you can prevent, delay, or allow the power-off sequence to continue.

For details on registering power handling functions, see Chapter 17, "Additional System Services."

Linking the Endpoint With an Application

If your endpoint is going to be driven by an application, you'll have a reference to the endpoint frame in your application. Also, you'll probably want to have a reference to your application base view in the endpoint frame, so you can handle endpoint messages in your application through inheritance.

The easiest way to link the endpoint and application together is to create a slot in your application base view like this:

```
ViewSetupFormScript: func ()
   begin
   self.fEndPoint: {_proto: protoBasicEndpoint,
                    _parent: self};
   end
```

This creates an endpoint frame as a slot in the application base view at run time, and makes the application base view (`self` here) the parent of the endpoint frame, so it can receive endpoint messages through inheritance.

Summary of the Endpoint Interface

Constants and Symbols

Data Form Symbols

```
'char
'number
'string
'bytes
'binary
'template
'frame
```

Data Type Symbols

```
'long
'ulong
'short
'byte
'char
'unicodechar
'boolean
'struct
'array
```

Option Opcode Constants

opSetNegotiate	256
opSetRequired	512
opGetDefault	768
opGetCurrent	1024

Endpoint State Constants

`kUninit`	0
`kUnbnd`	1
`kIdle`	2
`kOutCon`	3
`kInCon`	4
`kDataXfer`	5
`kOutRel`	6
`kInRel`	7
`kInFlux`	8
`kOutLstn`	9

Other Endpoint Constants

`kNoTimeout`	0
`kEOP`	0
`kMore`	1
`kPacket`	2

Data Structures

Option Frame

```
myOption := {
type: symbol, // option type
label: string, // 4-char option identifier
opCode: integer, // an opCode constant
form: 'template, // default form for options
result: nil, // set by the system on return
data: {
   arglist: [], // array of data items
   typelist:[], // array of data types
   }
}
```

Callback Spec Frame

```
myCallbackSpec := {
async: Boolean, // asynch request?
reqTimeout: integer, // time-out period, or 0
CompletionScript: // called when request is done
    func(endpoint, options, result)...,
}
```

Output Spec Frame

```
myOutputSpec := {
async: Boolean, // asynch request?
reqTimeout: integer, // time-out period, in milliseconds
sendFlags: integer, // flag constant(s)
form: symbol, // data form identifier
target: { // used for 'binary data forms
    offset: integer, // offset to begin sending from
    length: integer // number of bytes to send
    },
CompletionScript: // called when request is done
    func(endpoint, options, result)...,
}
```

Input Spec Frame

```
myInputSpec := {
form: symbol, // data form identifier
target: { // used with 'template and 'binary data forms
    typelist: [], // array of data types
    arglist: [], // array of data items
    data: object, // binary object to receive data
    offset: integer // offset at which to write data
    },
termination: { // defines termination conditions
    byteCount: integer, // number of bytes to receive
    endSequence: object, // char,string,number,or byte array
    useEOP: Boolean // terminate on EOP indicator?
    },
discardAfter: integer, // buffer size
rcvFlags: integer, // receive flag constant(s)
reqTimeout: integer, // time-out period, in milliseconds
```

```
filter: { // used to filter incoming data
    byteProxy: [{ // an array of frames
        byte: char, // char or byte to replace
        proxy: char // replacement char or byte, or nil
        }, ...],
    sevenBit: Boolean // strip high-order bit
    },
rcvOptions: [], // array of options, or a single frame
partialFrequency: integer, // freq, in milliseconds, to call
                           // PartialScript
InputScript: // called when input is terminated
    func(endpoint, data, terminator, options)...,
PartialScript: // called at partialFrequency interval
    func(endpoint, data)...,
CompletionScript: // called on unexpected completion
    func(endpoint, options, result)...,
}
```

Protos

protoBasicEndpoint

```
myEndpoint := {
_proto: protoBasicEndpoint, // proto endpoint
encoding:integer,//encoding table,default=kMacRomanEncoding
Instantiate: // instantiates endpoint object
    func(endpoint, options) ...,
Bind: // binds endpoint to comm tool
    func(options, callbackSpec) ...,
UnBind: // unbinds endpoint from comm tool
    func(options, callbackSpec) ...,
Dispose: // disposes endpoint object
    func(options, callbackSpec) ...,
Connect: // establishes connection
    func(options, callbackSpec) ...,
Listen: // passively listens for connection
    func(options, callbackSpec) ...,
Accept: // accepts connection
    func(options, callbackSpec) ...,
Disconnect: // disconnects
    func(cancelPending, callbackSpec) ...,
Output: // sends data
    func(data, options, outputSpec) ...,
SetInputSpec: // sets input spec
    func(inputSpec)...,
```

Endpoint Interface

```
Input: // returns data from input buffer and clears it
    func() ...,
Partial: // returns data from input buffer
    func() ...,
FlushInput: // flushes whole input buffer
    func() ...,
FlushPartial: // flushes input buffer previously read
    func() ...,
Cancel: // cancels operations
    func(callbackSpec) ...,
Option: // sets & gets options
    func(options, callbackSpec) ...,
ExceptionHandler: // called on exceptions
    func(error) ...,
EventHandler: // called on unhandled events
    func(event) ...,
State: // returns endpoint state
    func() ...,
...
}
```

protoStreamingEndpoint

```
myStreamEndpoint := {
_proto: protoStreamingEndpoint, // proto endpoint
StreamIn: // receives stream data
    func({   form: 'frame, // required
             reqTimeout: integer, // time-out in ms.
             rcvFlags: integer, // receive flag constant(s)
             target: {
                 store: store}, // store for VBOs
             ProgressScript: // progress callback
                 func(bytes, totalBytes)...
    }) ...,
StreamOut: // sends stream data
    func(data,
             {form: 'frame, // required
             reqTimeout: integer, // time-out in ms.
             sendFlags: integer, // send flag constant(s)
             ProgressScript: // progress callback
                 func(bytes, totalBytes)...
    }) ...,
...
}
```

Functions and Methods

Utility Functions

```
MakeAppleTalkOption(NBPaddressString)
MakeModemOption()
MakePhoneOption(phoneString)
Translate(data, translator, store, progressScript)
```

Built-in Communications Tools

This chapter describes the built-in communications tools provided in Newton system software 2.0. The following tools are built into the system:

- Serial
- Modem
- Infrared
- AppleTalk

These communications tools are accessed and used through the Endpoint interface. This chapter provides an introduction to each tool and the options that you use with each. For detailed descriptions of the options, see "Built-in Communications Tools Reference" (page 21-1) in *Newton Programmer's Reference.*

For basic information on using communications endpoints, see "Endpoint Interface" (page 23-1).

Serial Tool

Three varieties of the serial tool are built into Newton system software:

- a standard asynchronous serial tool
- a standard asynchronous serial tool with Microcom Networking Protocol (MNP) compression
- a framed asynchronous serial tool

These serial tool varieties are described in the following three subsections.

Standard Asynchronous Serial Tool

You use the standard asynchronous serial communications tool to perform standard, asynchronous communications, including sending and receiving data.

The following is an example of how to create an endpoint that uses the standard asynchronous serial tool:

```
myAsyncEP := {_proto:protoBasicEndpoint};
myOptions := [
    { label:   kCMSAsyncSerial,
      type:    'service,
      opCode:  opSetRequired } ];
returnedOptions:= myAsyncEP:Instantiate(myAsyncEP,
    myOptions);
```

Table 24-1 summarizes the standard serial options. Each of these options is described in detail in "Options for the Standard Asynchronous Serial Tool" (page 21-2) in *Newton Programmer's Referencee*.

Table 24-1   Summary of serial options

Label	Value	Use when	Description
kCMOSerialHWChipLoc	"schp"	Before or at binding	Sets which serial hardware to use.
kCMOSerialChipSpec	"sers"	Before or at binding	Sets which serial hardware to use and returns information about the serial hardware.
kCMOSerialCircuitControl	"sctl"	After connecting	Controls usage of the serial interface lines.
kCMOSerialBuffers	"sbuf"	Before or at binding	Sets the size of the input and output buffers.
kCMOSerialIOParms	"siop"	Any time	Sets the bps rate, stop bits, data bits, and parity options.
kCMOSerialBitRate	"sbps "	Any time	Changes the bps rate.
kCMOOutputFlowControlParms	"oflc"	Any time	Sets output flow control parameters.
kCMOInputFlowControlParms	"iflc"	Any time	Sets input flow control parameters.

continued

Table 24-1   Summary of serial options (continued)

Label	Value	Use when	Description
kCMOSerialBreak	"sbrk"	After connecting	Sends a break.
kCMOSerialDiscard	"sdsc"	After connecting	Discards data in input and/or output buffer.
kCMOSerialEventEnables	"sevt"	Any time	Configures the serial tool to complete an endpoint event on particular state changes.
kCMOSerialBytesAvailable	"sbav"	After connecting	Read-only option returns the number of bytes available in the input buffer.
kCMOSerialIOStats	"sios"	After connecting	Read-only option reports statistics from the current serial connection.
kHMOSerExtClockDivide	"cdiv"	After binding	Used only with an external clock to set the clock divide factor.

You can get or set most of the standard serial options in the endpoint method that established the state, as shown in Table 24-1. You set the endpoint options by passing an argument to the communications tool when calling one of the endpoint methods such as Instantiate, Bind, and Connect. For example, when you pass an option to the Bind method, the system sets the option and then does the binding.

Many of the communications options can only be used when the communications tool is in a certain state. For example, the first option in Table 24-1, kCMOSerialHWChipLoc, can only be used after the endpoint has been instantiated and before the binding is made. That means you could use it in the Instantiate and Bind methods, but not in the Connect method.

All of these options have default values, so you may not need to use an option if the default values provide the behavior you want. However, the default values do not apply partially. This means that if you do use an option, you must specify a value for each field within it.

Serial Tool with MNP Compression

The asynchronous serial communications tool with MNP compression works just like a standard asynchronous serial endpoint, except that it uses MNP data compression.

The following is an example that shows how to create an endpoint that uses the serial tool with MNP compression:

```
myMnpEP := {_proto:protoBasicEndpoint};
myOptions := [
    { label:    kCMSMNPID,
      type:     'service,
      opCode:   opSetRequired } ];
returnedOptions:= myMnpEP:Instantiate(myMnpEP,
      myOptions);
```

The serial tool with MNP endpoint uses all of the standard serial options, as well as two MNP options, which are summarized in Table 24-2. These options are described in detail in "Options for the Serial Tool with MNP Compression" (page 21-27) in *Newton Programmer's Reference*.

Table 24-2   Summary of serial tool with MNP options

Label	Value	Use when	Description
kCMOMNPCompression	"mnpc"	Before connecting	Sets the data compression type.
kCMOMNPDataRate	"eter"	Any time	Configures internal MNP timers.

Framed Asynchronous Serial Tool

The framed asynchronous serial communications tool is a superset of the standard asynchronous serial communications tool. This tool supports the sending and receiving of framed data. If you use this tool and do not specify framing for a send or receive operation, the framed asynchronous serial tool works exactly like the standard asynchronous serial tool.

When you use framing for input, the framed asynchronous serial tool discards characters until a start of frame sequence is detected and terminates input with an end-of-file (EOF) indication when the end-of-frame sequence is detected. The tool reports an error is if a CRC error is detected.

When you use framing for output, the data is prefixed with the start-of-frame sequence. The end-of frame-sequence and the calculated CRC are sent at the end of the data. The escape character is used for data transparency during framed operations.

An endpoint can include kPacket, kEOP, and kMore flags to control the sending and receiving of framed (packetized) data with the framed asynchronous serial tool. For more information on these flags, see "Sending Data" (page 23-11).

The following is an example that shows how to create an endpoint that uses the framed asynchronous serial tool:

```
myFramedEP := {_proto:protoBasicEndpoint};
myOptions := [
    { label:    kCMSFramedAsyncSerial,
      type:     'service,
      opCode:   opSetRequired } ];
returnedOptions:= myFramedEP:Instantiate(myFramedEP,
myOptions);
```

The framed asynchronous serial tool uses the standard asynchronous serial tool options, as well as two framing options, which are summarized in Table 24-3. These options are described in detail in "Options for the Framed Asynchronous Serial Tool" (page 21-29) in *Newton Programmer's Reference*.

Table 24-3   Summary of framed serial options

Label	Value	Use when	Description
kCMOFramingParms	"fram"	Any time	Configures data framing parameters.
kCMOFramedAsyncStats	"frst"	Any time	Read-only option returns the number of bytes discarded while looking for a valid header.

The default settings for the kCMOFramingParms option implement BSC framing, as shown in Figure 24-1.

Figure 24-1   Default serial framing

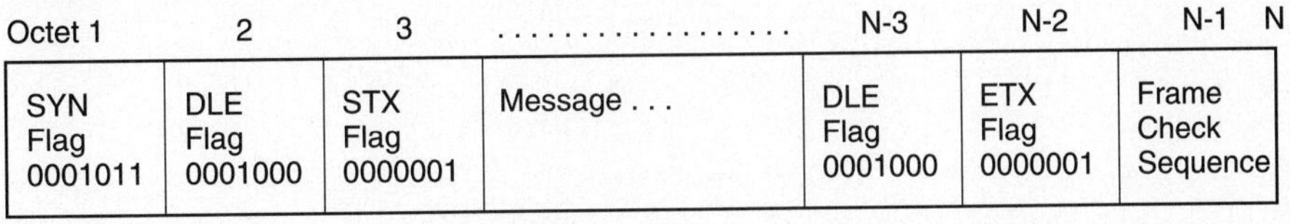

Octet 1	2	3	. . . .	N-3	N-2	N-1 N
SYN Flag 0001011	DLE Flag 0001000	STX Flag 0000001	Message . . .	DLE Flag 0001000	ETX Flag 0000001	Frame Check Sequence

Each packet is framed at the beginning by the 3-character SYN-DLE-STX header. The packet data follows; if a DLE (escape character) occurs in the data stream, both that character and an additional DLE character are sent; conversely, two consecutive DLE characters on input are turned into a single DLE data byte. The packet is framed at the end by the 2-character DLE-ETX trailer. Finally, a 2-character frame check sequence is appended. This frame check is initialized to zero at the beginning, and calculated on just the data bytes and the final ETX character, ignoring the header bytes, any inserted DLE characters, and the DLE character in the trailer.

The frame trailer is sent when an output is done that specifies end of frame. Conversely, on input, when a trailer is detected, the input is terminated with an end of frame indication; if a CRC error is detected, kSerErr_CRCError is returned instead.

Modem Tool

The modem communications tool includes built in support of V.42 and V.42bis. The alternate error-correcting protocol in V.42, also known as MNP, is supported (LAPM is not implemented). V.42bis data compression and MNP Class 5 data compression are supported.

The following is an example of how to create an endpoint that uses the built-in modem communications tool:

```
myModemEP := {_proto:protoBasicEndpoint};
myOptions := [
    { label:   kCMSModemID,
      type:    'service,
      opCode:  opSetRequired } ];
results := myModemEP:Instantiate(myModemEP, myOptions);
```

Table 24-4 summarizes the modem options you can use to configure the modem communications tool. These options are described in detail in "Options for the Modem Tool" (page 21-31) in *Newton Programmer's Reference*.

Table 24-4   Summary of modem options

Label	Value	Use When	Description
kCMOModemPrefs	"mpre"	Any time	Configures the modem controller.
kCMOModemProfile	"mpro"	Any time	Override modem setup selected in preferences. Use when instatiating.
kCMOModemECType	"mecp"	Any time	Specifies the type of error control protocol to be used in the modem connection.
kCMOModemDialing	"mdo"	Any time	Controls the parameters associated with dialing.
kCMOModemConnectType	"mcto"	Any time	Configures the modem endpoint for the type of connection desired (voice, fax, data, or cellular data).
kCMOModemConnectSpeed	"mspd"	After connecting	Read-only option indicating modem-to-modem raw connection speed.
kCMOModemFaxCapabilities	"mfax"	After bind, before connecting	Read-only option indicating the fax service class capabilities and modem modulation capabilities.
kCMOModemFaxEnabledCaps	"mfec"	Any time	Determines or sets which fax and modem capabilities are enabled. This option is available only for System Software version 2.1 or later.
kCMOModemVoiceSupport	"mvso"	After bind, before connecting	Read-only option indicating if the modem supports line current sense (LCS).
kCMOMNPSpeedNegotiation	"mnpn"	Any time	Sets MNP data rate speed.
kCMOMNPCompression	"mnpc"	Before connecting	Sets the data compression type.
kCMOMNPStatistics	"mnps"	After connecting	Read-only option reporting performance statistics from the current MNP connection.

Infrared Tool

You use the infrared (IR) communications tool to perform half-duplex infrared communications. Since the infrared tool does not support full-duplex communications, you cannot activate an input specification and expect to output data.

The infrared tool supports packetized data, which means that an endpoint can include kPacket, kEOP, and kMore flags to control sending and receiving framed (packetized) data. For more information on these flags, see "Sending Data" (page 23-11).

The following is an example of how to create an endpoint that uses the infrared communications tool:

```
myIrEP := {_proto:protoBasicEndpoint};
myOptions := [
    { label:    kCMSSlowIR,
      type:     'service,
      opCode:   opSetRequired }
];


returnedoptions:= myIrEP:Instantiate(myIrEP, myOptions);
```

The infrared tool supports three options, which are summarized in Table 24-5. These options are described in detail in "Options for the Infrared Tool" (page 21-65) in *Newton Programmer's Reference*.

Table 24-5   Summary of Infrared Options

Label	Value	Use when	Description
kCMOSlowIRConnect	"irco"	When initiating, connecting, or listening	Controls how the connection is made
kCMOSlowIRProtocolType	"irpt"	After connecting or accepting	Read-only option returns the protocol and speed of the connection
kCMOSlowIRStats	"irst"	After connecting or accepting	Read-only option returns statistics about the data received and sent

The infrared tool uses the Sharp Infrared protocol. Because of the characteristics of this protocol, Apple recommends setting sendFlags to kPacket and to kEOP every time you send data. For more information on sendFlags see, "Sending Data" (page 23-11).

If you don't set sendFlags as recommended above, the tool only sends data after it queues 512 bytes of data, which means that input scripts do not terminate as you might expect. On the receiving side, the queuing means you terminate after every output if you set useEOP to true. If you are using byteCount, you should set useEOP to nil to trigger on byteCount instead of EOP. For more information on useEOP and byteCount, see "Specifying Data Termination Conditions" (page 23-14).

AppleTalk Tool

The AppleTalk tool enables access to the ADSP (Apple Data Stream Protocol component of the AppleTalk protocol stack.

The following is an example of how to create an AppleTalk endpoint:

```
myATalkEP := {_proto:protoBasicEndpoint};
myOptions := [
   { label:    kCMSAppleTalkID,
     type:     'service,
     opCode:   opSetRequired
   },
   { label:    kCMSAppleTalkID,
     type:     'option,
     opCode:   opSetRequired,
     data:     { arglist: ["adsp"],// or KCMOAppleTalkADSP
                 typelist:[
                    'struct
                    ['array, 'char, 4]
                    ]
                }
   },
   { label:    kCMOEndpointName,
     type:     'option,
     opCode:   opSetRequired,
     data:     { arglist: [kADSPEndpoint],
                 typelist:[
                    'struct
                    ['array, 'char, 0]
                    ]
```

```
        }
    } ];
results := myATalkEP:Instantiate(myATalkEP, myOptions);
```

The AppleTalk tool options are summarized in Table 24-6. These options are described in detail in "Options for the AppleTalk Tool" (page 21-71) in *Newton Programmer's Reference*.

Table 24-6   Summary of AppleTalk options

Label	Value	Use When	Description
kCMARouteLabel	"rout"	When connecting or listening	Sets an AppleTalk NBP address.
kCMOAppleTalkBuffer	"bsiz"	When connecting, listening, or accepting	Sets the size of the send, receive, and attention buffers.
kCMOSerialBytesAvailable	"sbav"	After connecting	Read-only option returns the number of bytes available in the receive buffer.
kCMSAppleTalkID	"atlk"	For instantiation	Specifies AppleTalk tool type.
kCMOEndpointName	"endp"	For instantiation	Specifies AppleTalk endpoint. Must be used as above.

Resource Arbitration Options

You can construct a communications tool to share its resources with other communications tools. For example, you might need to use a hardware port that other tools want to use. This section describes how you can implement resource sharing in your communications tool.

The communications tool base provides a default implementation of resource arbitration that uses two options to control the release of a tool's resources:

■ The resource-passive claim option (kCMOPassiveClaim) has a Boolean value that specifies whether or not a communications tool is claiming its resources passively or actively. If this value is true, the communications tool is claiming its resources passively and will allow another tool to claim it. If this value is nil, the communications tool is claiming its resources actively and will not allow another tool to claim it.

■ The resource-passive state option (kCMOPassiveState) has a Boolean value that specifies whether or not the current state of the communications tool supports releasing resources. If this value is set, and kCMOPassiveClaim is true, your communications tool is willing to relinquish use of its passively claimed resources. If this value is nil, the communications tool is not willing to relinquish use of its passively claimed resources.

Table 24-7 shows the resource arbitration options. These options are described in detail in "Options for Resource Arbitration" (page 21-82) in *Newton Programmer's Reference*.

Table 24-7   Resource arbitration options

Label	Value	Use when	Description
kCMOPassiveClaim	"cpcm"	Before bind	Specifies whether your tool claims resources actively or passively
kCMOPassiveState	"cpst"	Typically on listen	Specifies whether your tool releases resources

The following example demonstrates how to instruct a communications tool to claim its resources passively. You must do this before binding the tool. By default all tools are claimed actively.

```
{
    label:  kCMOPassiveClaim,
      type:   'option,
    opCode: opSetRequired,
    data: {
       arglist: [
          true,   // passively claim modem
       ],
       typelist: [
          kStruct,
          kBoolean,
       ]
    }
}
```

The following example shows how to instruct a communications tool to allow its resources to be claimed by another tool. For instance, you might send this option with an `arglist` value of `true` if you are listening for an incoming connection. The default for all tools is to be in an active state.

```
{
    label:  kCMOPassiveState,
    type:   'option,
    opCode: opSetRequired,
    data: {
        arglist: [
            true,    // passively claim modem
        },
        typelist: [
            kStruct,
            kBoolean,
        ]

    }
}
```

AppleTalk Functions

The Newton system software provides a number of global functions for obtaining the addresses of other devices on the network.

If you are using an endpoint with the AppleTalk tool, the AppleTalk drivers are opened automatically when you call the endpoint `Bind` method. The drivers are closed when you call the endpoint `UnBind` method.

To manually open the AppleTalk drivers, you need to call the `OpenAppleTalk` function. When you are done with AppleTalk, call the `CloseAppleTalk` function to close the drivers.

Note that you call the AppleTalk zone access functions without first calling `OpenAppleTalk`. Each of the AppleTalk zone access functions opens the drivers (if necessary), performs its operations, and closes the drivers (if necessary). If you are making multiple AppleTalk calls, it is more efficient for you to manually open the drivers, make your calls, and then close the drivers.

Table 24-8 summarizes the AppleTalk functions. These functions are described in detail in "AppleTalk Functions" (page 21-76) in *Newton Programmer's Reference*.

Table 24-8   AppleTalk functions

Function	Description
OpenAppleTalk	Opens the AppleTalk drivers.
CloseAppleTalk	Closes the AppleTalk drivers.
AppleTalkOpenCount	Returns the open count for the AppleTalk drivers.
HaveZones	Returns true if a connection exists and zones are available. Returns nil if there are no zones.
GetMyZone	Returns a string naming the current AppleTalk zone.
GetZoneList	Returns an array containing strings of all the existing zone names
GetNames	Returns the name for a network address or an array of names for an array of network addresses.
GetZoneFromName	Returns the zone name for a network address.
NBPStart	Begins a lookup of network entities.
NBPGetCount	Returns the number of entities the currently running NBP lookup has found.
NBPGetNames	Returns an array of names found by NBPStart.
NBPStop	Terminates a lookup started by NBPStart.

The Net Chooser

The Newton system provides a NetChooser as part of the root view. The Net Chooser is similar in operation to the Mac OS Chooser. You can use the function GetRoot().NetChooser:OpenNetChooser to display a list of network entities from which the user can make a selection. This function is declared as follows:

```
NetChooser:OpenNetChooser(zone,  lookupName,  startSelection,
                          who,  connText,  headerText,  lookforText)
```

The OpenNetChooser method displays the NetChooser view on the user's screen. The following is an example that shows the use of this function:

```
GetRoot().NetChooser:openNetChooser(nil,"=:LaserWriter@",
nil, self, "Use printer, sir", "Printer", "printers");
```

This example opens the NetChooser view and displays the *lookforText* string while the search is in progress, as shown in Figure 24-2 (page 24-14).

Figure 24-2   NetChooser view while searching

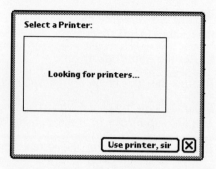

When the search has been completed, the NetChooser fills in the available choices and allows the user to make a selection, as shown in Figure 24-3.

Figure 24-3   NetChooser view displaying printers

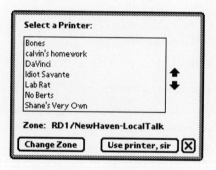

After the user has made a selection, the system calls a method that you provide named `NetworkChooserDone`. The system fills in the parameters to this method with the name of the selection and zone chosen by the user. The `NetworkChooserDone` method must have the following format:

myChooser:`NetworkChooserDone`(*currentSelection*, *currentZone*)

The two parameters, *currentSelection* and *currentZone,* are filled in by the system after the user makes a choice.

The following is an example that shows the use of this function:

```
ChooserSample := {
        // open network connection
openNetworkScript: func()
begin
GetRoot().NetChooser:openNetChooser(nil,"=:LaserWriter@",ni
l, self, "Use printer, sir", "Printer", "printers");
end,

        // called when the user selects an item
networkChooserDone: func(currentSelection, currentZone)
begin
Print("Current Selection =" && currentSelection);
Print("Current Zone =" && currentZone);
end
};
```

The following is an example of running this code in the inspector:

```
ChooserSample:OpenNetworkScript()
#1A        TRUE

        // select the network entity, close the Chooser
"Current Selection = Idiot Savante"
"Current Zone = RD1/NewHaven-LocalTalk"
```

The NetChooser methods are described in detail in "NetChooser Methods" (page 21-81) in *Newton Programmer's Reference*.

Summary

Built-in Communications Tool Service Option Labels

kCMSAsyncSerial	"aser"
kCMSMNPID	"mnps"
kCMSModemID	"mods"
kCMSSlowIR	"slir"
kCMSFramedAsyncSerial	"fser"
kCMSAppleTalkID	"atlk"

Options

Asynchronous Serial Tool Options

kCMOSerialHWChipLoc	"schp"
kCMOSerialChipSpec	"sers"
kCMOSerialCircuitControl	"sctl"
kCMOSerialBuffers	"sbuf"
kCMOSerialIOParms	"siop"
kCMOSerialBitRate	"sbps "
kCMOOutputFlowControlParms	"oflc"
kCMOInputFlowControlParms	"iflc"
kCMOSerialBreak	"sbrk"
kCMOSerialDiscard	"sdsc"
kCMOSerialEventEnables	"sevt"
kCMOSerialBytesAvailable	"sbav"
kCMOSerialIOStats	"sios"
kHMOSerExtClockDivide	"cdiv"

Serial with MNP Tool Options

kCMOMNPCompression	"mnpc"
kCMOMNPDataRate	"eter"

Framed Serial Tool Options

kCMOFramingParms	"fram"
kCMOFramedAsyncStats	"frst"

Modem Options

kCMOModemPrefs	"mpre"
kCMOModemProfile	"mpro"
kCMOModemECType	"mecp"
kCMOModemDialing	"mdo"
kCMOModemConnectType	"mcto"
kCMOModemConnectSpeed	"mspd"
kCMOModemFaxCapabilities	"mfax"
kCMOModemFaxEnabledCaps	"mfec"
kCMOModemVoiceSupport	"mvso"
kCMOMNPSpeedNegotiation	"mnpn"
kCMOMNPCompression	"mnpc"
kCMOMNPStatistics	"mnps"

Infrared Tool Options

kCMOSlowIRConnect	"irco"
kCMOSlowIRProtocolType	"irpt"
kCMOSlowIRStats	"irst"

AppleTalk Tool Options

kCMARouteLabel	"rout"
kCMOAppleTalkBuffer	"bsiz"
kCMOSerialBytesAvailable	"sbav"
kCMSAppleTalkID	"atlk"
kCMOEndpointName	"endp"

Resource Arbitration Options

kCMOPassiveClaim	"cpcm"
kCMOPassiveState	"cpst"

Constants

Serial Chip Location Option Constants

kHWLocExternalSerial	"extr"
kHWLocBuiltInIR	"infr"
kHWLocBuiltInModem	"mdem"
kHWLocPCMCIASlot1	"slt1"
kHWLocPCMCIASlot2	"slt2"

Serial Chip Specification Option Constants

kSerCap_Parity_Space	0x00000001
kSerCap_Parity_Mark	0x00000002
kSerCap_Parity_Odd	0x00000004
kSerCap_Parity_Even	0x00000008
kSerCap_DataBits_5	0x00000001
kSerCap_DataBits_6	0x00000002
kSerCap_DataBits_7	0x00000004
kSerCap_DataBits_8	0x00000008
kSerCap_DataBits_All	0x0000000F
kSerCap_StopBits_1	0x00000010
kSerCap_StopBits_1_5	0x00000020
kSerCap_StopBits_2	0x00000040
kSerCap_DataBits_All	0x00000070
kSerialChip8250	0x00
kSerialChip16450	0x01
kSerialChip16550	0x02
kSerialChip8530	0x20
kSerialChip6850	0x21
kSerialChip6402	0x22
kSerialChipUnknown	0x00

Serial Circuit Control Option Constants

kSerOutDTR	0x01
kSerOutRTS	0x02
kSerInDSR	0x02
kSerInDCD	0x08
kSerInRI	0x10
kSerInCTS	0x20
kSerInBreak	0x80

Serial Configuration Option Constants

k1StopBits	0
k1pt5StopBits	1
k2StopBits	2
kNoParity	0
kOddParity	1
kEvenParity	2
k5DataBits	5
k6DataBits	6
k7DataBits	7
k8DataBits	8
kExternalClock	1
k300bps	300
k600bps	600
k1200bps	1200
k2400bps	2400
k4800bps	4800
k7200bps	7200
k9600bps	9600
k12000bps	12000
k14400bps	14400
k19200bps	19200
k38400bps	38400
k57600bps	57600
k115200bps	115200
k230400bps	230400

Serial Event Configuration Option Constants

kSerialEventBreakStartedMask	0x00000001
kSerialEventBreakEndedMask	0x00000002
kSerialEventDCDNegatedMask	0x00000004
kSerialEventDCDAssertedMask	0x00000008
kSerialEventHSKiNegatedMask	0x00000010
kSerialEventHSKiAssertedMask	0x00000020
kSerialEventExtClkDetectEnableMask	0x00000040

Serial External Clock Divide Option Constants

kSerClk_Default	0x00
kSerClk_DivideBy_1	0x80
kSerClk_DivideBy_16	0x81
kSerClk_DivideBy_32	0x82
kSerClk_DivideBy_64	0x83

Modem Error Control Type Option Constants

kModemECProtocolNone	0x00000001
kModemECProtocolMNP	0x00000002
kModemECProtocolExternal	0x00000008

Modem Fax Capabilities Option Constants

kModemFaxClass0	0x00000001
kModemFaxClass1	0x00000002
kModemFaxClass2	0x00000004
kModemFaxClass2_0	0x00000008
kV21Ch2Mod	0x00000001
kV27Ter24Mod	0x00000002
kV27Ter48Mod	0x00000004
kV29_72Mod	0x00000008
kV17_72Mod	0x00000010
kV17st_72Mod	0x00000020
kV29_96Mod	0x00000040
kV17_96Mod	0x00000080
kV17st_96Mod	0x00000100

kV17_12Mod	0x00000200
kV17st_12Mod	0x00000400
kV17_14Mod	0x00000800
kV17st_14Mod	0x00001000

MNP Compression Option Constants

kMNPCompressionNone	0x00000001
kMNPCompressionMNP5	0x00000002
kMNPCompressionV42bis	0x00000008

Infrared Protocol Type Option Constants

kUsingNegotiateIR	0
kUsingSharpIR	1
kUsingNewton1	2
kUsingNewton2	4
kUsing9600	1
kUsing19200	2
kUsing38400	4

Functions and Methods

AppleTalk Driver Functions

```
OpenAppleTalk()
CloseAppleTalk()
AppleTalkOpenCount()
```

AppleTalk Zone Information Methods

```
HaveZones()
GetMyZone()
GetZoneList()
GetNames(fromWhat)
GetZoneFromName(fromWhat)
NBPStart(entity)
NBPGetCount(lookupID)
NBPGetNames(lookupID)
NBPStop(lookupID)
```

NetChooser Function

`NetChooser:OpenNetChooser(`*zone*`,` *lookupName*`,` *startSelection*`,`
who`,` *connText*`,` *headerText*`,` *lookforText*`)`

CHAPTER 25

Modem Setup Service

This chapter contains information about the modem setup capability in Newton system software. You need to read this chapter if you want to define a modem setup package for your application. The built-in modem communications tool uses these packages for communicating with modems. For more information about the built-in modem communications tool, see "Built-in Communications Tools" (page 24-1).

This chapter describes:

■ The modem setup service and how it works with modem setup packages.

■ The user interface for modem setup.

■ The modem characteristics required by the Newton modem tool.

■ The constants you use in defining a modem setup. These constants are described in detail in "Modem Setup Service Reference" (page 22-1) in *Newton Programmer's Reference*.

About the Modem Setup Service

This section provides detailed conceptual information on the modem setup service. Specifically, it covers the following:

■ a description of the modem setup user interface

■ the programmatic process by which a modem is setup

■ modem requirements

The modem setup service allows many different kinds of modems to be used with Newton devices. Each kind of modem can have an associated modem setup package, which can configure a modem endpoint to match the particular modem.

A modem setup package is installed on the Newton as an automatically loaded package. This means that when the package is loaded, the modem setup information is automatically stored in the system soup and then the package is removed. No icon appears for the modem setup in the Extras Drawer. Instead, modem setups are accessed through a picker in the Modem preferences view.

Modem setup packages can be supplied by modem manufacturers, or can be created by other developers.

A modem setup package can contain four parts:

- **General information.** The beginning of a modem setup package specifies general information about the modem corresponding to the package—for example, the modem's name and version number.

- **A modem tool preferences option.** The part of the package that contains specifications that configure the modem controller. For a description of this option, see "Modem Preferences Option" (page 21-34) in *Newton Programmer's Reference*.

- **A modem tool profile option.** This part of the package describes the characteristics of the modem—for example, whether the modem supports error correction protocols. For more information on this option, see the section "Modem Profile Option" (page 21-38) in *Newton Programmer's Reference*.

- **A fax profile option.** This part of the package describes the characteristics of the fax—for example, the speed at which faxes can be sent and received. This option is particularly useful to limit fax speeds over cellular connections.

If a modem supports both cellular and landline operations and does not automatically configure itself, you need to create a separate modem profile or setup for each operation. If you want to give the user the option to limit fax speeds, which is a common practice with cellular connections, you may want a third profile that specifies the fax profile option.

Note
The constants and code shown in this chapter apply to the NTK project that is provided by Newton Technical Support. This project provides an easy way to create modem setups. ◆

The Modem Setup User Interface

The user chooses the current modem setup in the Modem preferences, as shown in Figure 25-1 (page 25-3). The Modem Setup item is a picker, which when tapped displays all of the modem setups installed in the system. The chosen modem setup is the default used by all applications.

Figure 25-1   Modem preferences view

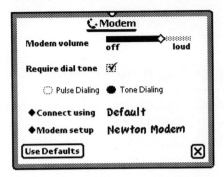

The Modem Setup Process

All communication applications that use a modem endpoint make use of the modem setup service. The current modem setup is automatically invoked when an application calls the modem endpoint's `Instantiate` method.

Note
If the modem endpoint option list includes the modem profile option (`kCMOModemProfile`), the modem setup is not invoked. This allows modem applications to override the modem setup when configuring the modem for special purposes. ◆

Here is what happens in the `Instantiate` method when the modem setup is invoked:

1. The `kCMOModemPrefs` option is added to the endpoint configuration options, and the `fEnablePassThru` field is set to `true`. This enables the endpoint to operate in pass-through mode. In this mode, the modem endpoint is functionally equivalent to a serial endpoint for input and output.

2. The modem endpoint is instantiated and connected in pass-through mode.

3. The Newton system software sets the modem preferences (`kCMOModemPrefs`), modem profile (`kCMOModemProfile`), and fax profile (`kCMOModemFaxCapabilities`) options as defined in the modem setup.

Note
A modem setup method is executed only once—when the endpoint is instantiated—even if the endpoint is subsequently used for multiple connections. ◆

4. The modem endpoint is reconfigured with pass-through mode disabled, and control is returned to the client application, which can proceed with its `Bind` and `Connect` calls.

"Defining a Modem Setup" (page 25-5) describes how to define a modem setup.

Modem Communication Tool Requirements

The Newton modem communication tool expects certain characteristics from a modem. These characteristics are described here.

- The modem tool expects a PCMCIA modem to use a 16450 or 16550 UART chip.

- The modem tool expects hardware flow control in both serial and PCMCIA modems. In modems not supporting hardware flow control, direct connect support is required, and the modem profile constant `kDirectConnectOnly` must be set to `true`. This means that the modem tool and the modem must be running at the same bit rate, allowing for no compression or error correction protocols to be used by the modem. (When operating in direct connect mode, the data rate of the modem tool is automatically adjusted to the data rate stated in the "CONNECT SEXTETS" message.)

- The modem tool expects control signals to be used as follows:
  - □ The modem tool uses RTS to control data flow from the modem.
  - □ The modem uses CTS to control data flow from the modem tool.
  - □ Support of the DCD signal is optional. In general, the modem tool expects DCD to reflect the actual carrier state. The usage of this signal by the modem tool is governed by the `kUseHardwareCD` constant.

- The modem tool expects non-verbose textual responses from the modem.

- The modem tool expects no echo.

- The modem tool currently supports the Class 1 protocol for FAX connections; under some circumstance (see the note below), the modem tool supports the Class 2 protocol. The configuration string defined by the constant `kConfigStrNoEC` is used for sending and receiving FAX documents. Additionally, these other requirements apply to the FAX service:
  - □ Flow control is required. In modems not supporting hardware flow control (where `kDirectConnectOnly` = `true`), XON/XOFF software flow control must be enabled.
  - □ Buffering must be enabled.
  - □ The `kConfigSpeed` constant must be set to higher than the highest connect rate of which the modem is capable. For example, if the modem supports 14400, set `kConfigSpeed` to 19200; if the modem supports 28800, set `kConfigSpeed` to 54600.

Note

The modem tool has been upgraded to support the Class 2 and Class 2.0 FAX protocols in release 2.1 of the Newton System Software. This upgrade is also available in the German version of release 2.0 of the Newton System Software. To enable the use of these protocols, you must define the fax profile in your modem setup. ◆

Defining a Modem Setup

The parts of a modem setup are specified in a Newton Toolkit (NTK) text file, which is provided by Newton Technical Support. The modem preferences and profile options are specified by setting constants. The following sections describe each part of the modem setup.

Setting Up General Information

The beginning of a modem setup contains general information about the setup and the modem to which it corresponds. Here is an example:

```
constant kModemName       := "Speedy Fast XL";
constant kVersion         := 1;
constant kOrganization    := "Speedy Computer, Inc.";
```

The value of kModemName appears in the Modem preferences. It is usually the name of the modem. The constant kVersion identifies the (integer-only) version of the modem setup package. The constant kOrganization indicates the source of the modem setup package. For detailed descriptions of these constants, see "Modem Setup General Information Constants" (page 22-2) in *Newton Programmer's Reference*.

Setting the Modem Preferences Option

This modem option configures the modem controller. Here is an example:

```
constant kIdModem            := nil;
constant kUseHardwareCD      := true;
constant kUseConfigString    := true;
constant kUseDialOptions     := true;
constant kHangUpAtDisconnect := true;
```

For detailed descriptions of these constants, see "Modem Setup Preference Constants" (page 22-3) in *Newton Programmer's Reference*. For more information about the modem preferences option, see "Modem Preferences Option" (page 21-34) in *Newton Programmer's Reference*.

Setting the Modem Profile Option

This modem profile option describes the modem characteristics, to be used by the modem controller. Here is an example:

```
constant kSupportsEC        := true;
constant kSupportsLCS       := nil;
constant kDirectConnectOnly:= nil;
constant kConnectSpeeds     := '[300, 1200, 2400, 4800,
                               7200, 9600, 12000, 14400];
constant kConfigSpeed       := 38400;
constant kCommandTimeout    := 2000;
constant kMaxCharsPerLine   := 40;
constant kInterCmdDelay     := 25;
constant kModemIDString     := "unknown";
constant kConfigStrNoEC        :=
                "ATE0&A0&B1&C1&H1&M0S12=12\n";
constant kConfigStrECOnly      :=
                "ATE0&A0&B1&C1&H1&M5S12=12\n";
constant kConfigStrECAndFallbac  :=
                "ATE0&A0&B1&C1&H1&M4S12=12\n";
constant kConfigStrDirectConnec  :=
                "ATE0&A0&B0&C1&H0&M0S12=12\n";
```

For detailed descriptions of these constants, see "Modem Setup Profile Constants" (page 22-4) in *Newton Programmer's Reference*. For more information about the modem preferences option, see "Modem Profile Option" (page 21-38) in *Newton Programmer's Reference*.

When the modem tool establishes communication with a modem through an endpoint, the tool normally sends a configuration string to the modem (as long as kUseConfigString is true). Several configuration strings are defined in a typical modem profile; the one that is sent depends on the type of connection requested and other parameters set in the modem profile. Table 25-1 summarizes when each kind of configuration string is used:

Table 25-1   Summary of configuration string usage

Configuration string	When used
kConfigStrNoEC	The default configuration used for data connections when kDirectConnectOnly is nil. Also used for FAX connections. See "The No Error Control Configuration String" (page 22-7) in *Newton Programmer's Reference* for an example.
kConfigStrECOnly	Used for data connections that require error correction. This configuration string is used only if requested by an application. The constant kSupportsEC must be true for this configuration string to be used. See "The Error Control Configuration String" (page 22-8) in *Newton Programmer's Reference* for an example.
kConfigStrECAndFallback	Used for data connections that allow error correction, but that can fall back to non-error-corrected mode. This configuration string is used only if requested by an application. See "The Error Control with Fallback Configuration String" (page 22-9) in *Newton Programmer's Reference* for an example.
kConfigStrDirectConnect	The default configuration used for data connections when kDirectConnectOnly is true. See "The Direct Connect Configuration String" (page 22-9) in *Newton Programmer's Reference* for an example.

Setting the Fax Profile Option

The fax profile option describes the fax characteristics to be used by the fax tool. Here is an example:

```
constant kTransmitDataMod   :=
            kV21Ch2Mod + KV27Ter24Mod+ kV27Ter48Mod;
constant kReceiveDataMod:=
            kV21Ch2Mod + KV27Ter24Mod + kV27Ter48Mod;
constant kServiceClass   :=
            kModemFaxClass1 + kModemFaxClass2;
```

This example limits the faxing to 4800 bps for both send and receive messages. If neither of these constants is defined, then the fax send and receive speeds are not restricted.

Note

You can only set the service class (use the `kServiceClass`
constant) for versions of the software that support the Class 2 fax
protocol. Newton System Software version 2.1 and the German
version of Newton System Software version 2.0 support the Class
2 fax protocol. ◆

For detailed descriptions of these constants, see "Fax Profile Constants"
(page 22-10) in *Newton Programmer's Reference*.

The constants that you can use to specify speeds in defining your fax profile values
are shown in Table 22-5 (page 22-11) in *Newton Programmer's Reference*.

Summary of the Modem Setup Service

Constants

Constants for Modem Setup General Information

```
kModemName
kVersion
kOrganization
```

Constants for Modem Setup Preferences

```
kIdModem
kUseHardwareCD
kUseConfigString
kUseDialOptions
kHangUpAtDisconnect
```

Constants for the Modem Setup Profile

```
kSupportsEC
kSupportsLCS
kDirectConnectOnly
kXonnectSpeeds
kXommandTimeout
kMaxCharsPerLine
kInterCmdDelay
kModemIDString
kConfigStrNoEC
kConfigStrECOnly
kConfigStrECAndFallback
kConfigStrDirectConnect
```

Constants for the fax profile

```
kTransmitDataMod
kReceiveDataMod
kServiceClass
```

Fax Speed Constants

```
kV21Ch2Mod
kv27Ter24Mod
kV27Ter48Mod
kV29_72Mod
kV17_72Mod
kV17st_72Mod
kV29_96Mod
kV17_96Mod
kV17st_96Mod
kV17_12Mod
kV17st_12Mod
kV17st_14Mod
```

Fax Class Constants

```
kModemFaxClass0
kModemFaxClass1
kModemFaxClass2
kModemFaxClass2_0
```

Utility Functions

This chapter provides a listing of a number of utility functions documented in the "Utility Functions Reference" in the *Newton Programmer's Reference*. The following groups of functions are included:

- Object system

- String

- Bitwise

- Array and sorted array

- Integer Math

- Floating point math

- Control of floating point math

- Financial

- Exception handling

- Message sending and deferred message sending

- Data extraction

- Data stuffing

- Getting and Setting Global Variables

- Miscellaneous

Four of the functions described in the Object system section are designed to clone, or copy, objects. These functions each behave slightly differently. Table 26-1 summarizes their actions. The "Recurs" column indicates if references within the object are copied. The "Follows magic pointers" column indicates if objects referenced through magic pointers are copied. The "Ensures object is internal" column indicates if the function ensures that all parts of the object exist in internal RAM or ROM. The "Copies object" column indicates if the object is copied.

Table 26-1   Summary of copying functions

Function name	Recurs	Follows magic pointers	Ensures object is internal	Copies object
Clone	—	—	—	yes
DeepClone	yes	yes	—	yes
EnsureInternal	yes	—	yes	as needed
TotalClone	yes	—	yes	yes

Compatibility

This section describes the changes to the utility functions for Newton System Software 2.0.

New Functions

The following new functions have been added for this release.

New Object System Functions

The following new object system functions have been added.

```
GetFunctionArgCount
IsCharacter
IsFunction
IsInteger
IsNumber
IsReadOnly (existed in 1.0 but now documented)
IsReal
IsString
IsSubclass (existed in 1.0 but now documented)
IsSymbol
MakeBinary
SetVariable
SymbolCompareLex
```

New String Functions

The following new string functions have been added.

```
CharPos
LatitudeToString
LongitudeToString
StrExactCompare
StrFilled (existed in 1.0 but now documented)
StrTokenize
StyledStrTruncate
SubstituteChars
```

New Array Functions

The following new array functions have been added.

```
ArrayInsert
InsertionSort
LFetch
LSearch
NewWeakArray
StableSort
```

New Sorted Array Functions

The following new functions have been added that operate on sorted arrays. These functions are based on binary search algorithms, hence the "B" prefix to the function names.

```
BDelete
BDifference
BFetch
BFetchRight
BFind
BFindRight
BInsert
BInsertRight
BIntersect
BMerge
BSearchLeft
BSearchRight
```

New Integer Math Functions

The following new functions related to integer math have been added.

```
GetRandomState
SetRandomState
```

New Financial Functions

The following new functions that perform operations related to the currency exchange rate have been added.

```
GetExchangeRate
SetExchangeRate
GetUpdatedExchangeRates
```

New Exception Handling Functions

The following new exception handling function has been added.

```
RethrowWithUserMessage
```

New Message Sending Functions

The following new utility functions for sending immediate messages have been added.

```
IsHalting
PerformIfDefined
ProtoPerform
ProtoPerformIfDefined
```

New Deferred Message Sending Functions

The following new utility functions for delayed and deferred actions have been added.

```
AddDeferredCall
AddDelayedCall
AddProcrastinatedCall
AddDeferredSend
AddDelayedSend
AddProcrastinatedSend
```

These new functions replace `AddDelayedAction` and `AddDeferredAction` (although both remain in the ROM for compatibility with existing applications). These two older functions have several problems, and you should not use them— they will likely be removed in future versions of system software.

New Data Stuffing Functions

The following new data stuffing functions have been added.

```
StuffCString
StuffPString
```

New Functions to Get and Set Globals

The following new functions that get, set, and check for the existence of global variables and functions have been added.

```
GetGlobalFn
GetGlobalVar
GlobalFnExists
GlobalVarExists
DefGlobalFn
DefGlobalVar
UnDefGlobalFn
UnDefGlobalVar
```

New Debugging Functions

The following debugging functions have been added.

```
StrHexDump
TrueSize
ViewAutopsy
```

The following debugging functions have been changed.

```
StackTrace
BreakLoop
```

New Miscellaneous Functions

The following miscellaneous functions have been added.

```
AddMemoryItem
AddMemoryItemUnique
Backlight
BacklightStatus
BinEqual
Gestalt
GetAppName
GetAppPrefs
GetMemoryItems
```

```
GetMemorySlot
MakePhone
MakeDisplayPhone
ParsePhone
PowerOff
Translate
```

Enhanced Functions

The following string function has been enhanced in Newton 2.0.

ParamStr has been enhanced to support conditional substitution.

Obsolete Functions

Some utility functions previously documented in the *Newton Programmer's Guide* are obsolete, but are still supported for compatibility with older applications. Do not use the following utility functions, as they may not be supported in future system software versions:

AddDeferredAction (use AddDeferredCall instead)
AddDelayedAction (use AddDelayedCall instead)
AddPowerOffHandler (use RegPowerOff instead)
ArrayPos (use LSearch instead)
GetGlobals (use GetGlobalVar or GetGlobalFn instead)
RemovePowerOffHandler (use UnRegPowerOff instead)
SmartStart (use other string manipulation functions)
SmartConcat (use other string manipulation functions)
SmartStop (use other string manipulation functions)
StrTruncate (use StyledStrTruncate instead)
StrWidth (use StrFontWidth instead)

Summary of Functions and Methods

Object System Functions

ClassOf (*object*)
Clone (*object*)
DeepClone (*object*)
EnsureInternal (*obj*)
GetFunctionArgCount (*function*)
GetSlot (*frame*, *slotSymbol*)
GetVariable (*frame*, *slotSymbol*)
HasSlot (*frame*, *slotSymbol*)
HasVariable (*frame*, *slotSymbol*)
Intern (*string*)
IsArray (*obj*)
IsBinary (*obj*)
IsCharacter (*obj*)
IsFrame (*obj*)
IsFunction (*obj*)
IsImmediate (*obj*)
IsInstance (*obj*, *class*)
IsInteger (*obj*)
IsNumber (*obj*)
IsReadOnly (*obj*)
IsReal (*obj*)
IsString (*obj*)
IsSubclass (*sub*, *super*)
IsSymbol (*obj*)
MakeBinary (*length*, *class*)
Map (*obj*, *function*)
PrimClassOf (*obj*)
RemoveSlot (*obj*, *slot*)
ReplaceObject (*originalObject*, *targetObject*)
SetClass (*obj*, *classSymbol*)
SetVariable (*frame*, *slotSymbol*, *value*)
SymbolCompareLex (*symbol1*, *symbol2*)
TotalClone (*obj*)

String Functions

BeginsWith(*string*, *substr*)

Capitalize(*string*)

CapitalizeWords(*string*)

CharPos(*str*, *char*, *startpos*)

Downcase(*string*)

EndsWith(*string*, *substr*)

EvalStringer(*frame*, *array*)

FindStringInArray(*array*, *string*)

FindStringInFrame(*frame*, *stringArray*, *path*)

FormattedNumberStr(*number*, *formatString*)

IsAlphaNumeric(*char*)

IsWhiteSpace(*char*)

LatitudeToString(*latitude*)

LongitudeToString(*longitude*)

NumberStr(*number*)

ParamStr(*baseString*, *paramStrArray*)

SPrintObject(*obj*)

StrCompare(*a*, *b*)

StrConcat(*a*, *b*)

StrEqual(*a*, *b*)

StrExactCompare(*a*, *b*)

StrFilled(*string*)

StrFontWidth(*string*, *fontSpec*)

Stringer(*array*)

StringFilter(*str*, *filter*, *instruction*)

StringToNumber(*string*)

StrLen(*string*)

StrMunger(*dstString, dstStart, dstCount, srcString, srcStart, srcCount*)

StrPos(*string*, *substr*, *start*)

StrReplace(*string*, *substr*, *replacement*, *count*)

StrTokenize(*str*, *delimiters*)

StyledStrTruncate(*string*, *length*, *font*)

SubstituteChars(*targetStr*, *searchStr*, *replaceStr*)

SubStr(*string*, *start*, *count*)

TrimString(*string*)

Upcase(*string*)

Bitwise Functions

Band(*a*, *b*)
Bor(*a*, *b*)
Bxor(*a*, *b*)
Bnot(*a*)

Array Functions

AddArraySlot (*array*, *value*)
Array(*size*, *initialValue*)
ArrayInsert(*array*, *element*, *position*)
ArrayMunger(*dstArray*, *dstStart*, *dstCount*, *srcArray*, *srcStart*, *srcCount*)
ArrayRemoveCount(*array*, *startIndex*, *count*)
InsertionSort(*array*, *test*, *key*)
Length (*array*)
LFetch(*array*, *item*, *start*, *test*, *key*)
LSearch(*array*, *item*, *start*, *test*, *key*)
NewWeakArray(*length*)
SetAdd (*array*, *value*, *uniqueOnly*)
SetContains(*array*, *item*)
SetDifference(*array1*, *array2*)
SetLength (*array*, *length*)
SetOverlaps(*array1*, *array2*)
SetRemove (*array*, *value*)
SetUnion(*array1*, *array2*, *uniqueFlag*)
Sort(*array*, *test*, *key*)
StableSort(*array*, *test*, *key*)

Sorted Array Functions

BDelete(*array*, *item*, *test*, *key*, *count*)
BDifference(*array1*, *array2*, *test*, *key*)
BFetch(*array*, *item*, *test*, *key*)
BFetchRight(*array*, *item*, *test*, *key*)
BFind(*array*, *item*, *test*, *key*)
BFindRight(*array*, *item*, *test*, *key*)
BInsert(*array*, *element*, *test*, *key*, *uniqueOnly*)
BInsertRight(*array*, *element*, *test*, *key*, *uniqueOnly*)
BIntersect(*array1*, *array2*, *test*, *key*, *uniqueOnly*)

Utility Functions

```
BMerge(array1, array2, test, key, uniqueOnly)
BSearchLeft(array, item, test, key)
BSearchRight(array, item, test, key)
```

Integer Math Functions

```
Abs(x)
Ceiling(x)
Floor(x)
GetRandomState()
Max( a, b )
Min( a, b )
Real(x)
Random (low, high)
SetRandomSeed (seedNumber)
SetRandomState(randomState)
```

Floating Point Math Functions

```
Acos(x)
Acosh(x)
Asin(x)
Asinh(x)
Atan(x)
Atan2(x,y)
Atanh(x)
CopySign(x,y)
Cos(x)
Cosh(x)
Erf(x)
Erfc(x)
Exp(x)
Expm1(x)
Fabs(x)
FDim(x,y)
FMax(x,y)
FMin(x,y)
Fmod(x,y)
Gamma(x)
Hypot(x,y)
```

Utility Functions

```
IsFinite (x)
IsNaN (x)
IsNormal (x)
LessEqualOrGreater (x, y)
LessOrGreater (x, y)
LGamma (x)
Log (x)
Logb (x)
Log1p (x)
Log10 (x)
NearbyInt (x)
NextAfterD (x, y)
Pow (x, y)
RandomX (x)
Remainder (x, y)
RemQuo (x, y)
Rint (x)
RintToL (x)
Round (x)
Scalb (x, k)
SignBit (x)
Signum (x)
Sin (x)
Sinh (x)
Sqrt (x)
Tan (x)
Tanh (x)
Trunc (x)
Unordered (x, y)
UnorderedGreaterOrEqual (x, y)
UnorderedLessOrEqual (x, y)
UnorderedOrEqual (x, y)
UnorderedOrGreater (x, y)
UnorderedOrLess (x, y)
FeClearExcept (excepts)
FeGetEnv ()
FeGetExcept (excepts)
FeHoldExcept ()
FeRaiseExcept (excepts)
FeSetEnv (envObj)
FeSetExcept (flagObj, excepts)
```

Summary of Functions and Methods

```
FeTestExcept (excepts)
FeUpdateEnv (envObj)
```

Financial Functions

```
Annuity (r, n)
Compound (r, n)
GetExchangeRate (country1, country2)
SetExchangeRate (country1, country2, rate)
GetUpdatedExchangeRates ()
```

Exception Functions

```
Throw (name, data)
Rethrow ()
CurrentException ()
RethrowWithUserMessage (userTitle, userMessage, override)
```

Message Sending Functions

```
Apply (function, parameterArray)
IsHalting (functionObject, args)
Perform (frame, message, parameterArray)
PerformIfDefined (receiver, message, paramArray)
ProtoPerform (receiver, message, paramArray)
ProtoPerformIfDefined (receiver, message, paramArray)
```

Deferred Message Sending Functions

```
AddDeferredCall (functionObject, paramArray)
AddDelayedCall (functionObject, paramArray, delay)
AddDeferredSend (receiver, message, paramArray)
AddDelayedSend (receiver, message, paramArray, delay)
AddProcrastinatedCall (funcSymbol, functionObject, paramArray, delay)
AddProcrastinatedSend (msgSymbol, receiver, message, paramArray, delay)
```

Data Extraction Functions

ExtractByte(*data*, *offset*)
ExtractBytes(*data*, *offset*, *length*, *class*)
ExtractChar(*data*, *offset*)
ExtractLong(*data*, *offset*)
ExtractXLong(*data*, *offset*)
ExtractWord(*data*, *offset*)
ExtractCString(*data*, *offset*)
ExtractPString(*data*, *offset*)
ExtractUniChar(*data*, *offset*)

Data Stuffing Functions

StuffByte(*obj*, *offset*, *toInsert*)
StuffChar(*obj*, *offset*, *toInsert*)
StuffCString(*obj*, *offset*, *aString*)
StuffLong(*obj*, *offset*, *toInsert*)
StuffPString(*obj*, *offset*, *aString*)
StuffUniChar(*obj*, *offset*, *toInsert*)
StuffWord(*obj*, *offset*, *toInsert*)

Getting and Setting Global Variables and Functions

GetGlobalFn(*symbol*)
GetGlobalVar(*symbol*)
GlobalFnExists(*symbol*)
GlobalVarExists(*symbol*)
DefGlobalFn(*symbol*, *function*)
DefGlobalVar(*symbol*, *value*)
UnDefGlobalFn(*symbol*)
UnDefGlobalVar(*symbol*)

Debugging Functions

BreakLoop()
DV(*view*)
GC()
ExitBreakLoop()
StackTrace()

Stats()
StrHexDump(*object*, *spaceInterval*)
TrueSize(*object*, *filter*)
ViewAutopsy(*functionSpec*)

Miscellaneous Functions

AddMemoryItem(*memSymbol*, *value*)
AddMemoryItemUnique(*memorySlot*, *value*, *testFunc*)
Backlight()
BacklightStatus(*state*)
BinEqual(*a*, *b*)
BinaryMunger(*dst*, *dstStart*, *dstCount*, *src*, *srcStart*, *srcCount*)
Chr(*integer*)
Compile(*string*)
Gestalt(*selector*)
GetAppName(*appSymbol*)
GetAppParams( )
GetAppPrefs(*appSymbol*, *defaultFrame*)
GetMemoryItems(*memSymbol*)
GetMemorySlot(*memorySlot*, *op*)
GetPrinterName(*printerFrame*) //platform file function
MakePhone (*phoneFrame*)
MakeDisplayPhone(*phoneStr*)
rootView:MungePhone(*inNum*, *country*)
ParsePhone(*phoneStr*)
PowerOff(*reason*)
Ord (*char*)
RegEmailSystem(*classSymbol*, *name*, *internet*)
RegPagerType(*classSymbol*, *name*)
RegPhoneType with (*classSymbol*, *name*, *number*)
ShowManual()
Sleep(*ticks*)
rootView:SysBeep()
Translate(*data*, *translator*, *store*, *callback*)
UnRegEmailSystem(*classSymbol*)
UnregPagerType(*classSymbol*)
UnregPhoneTypeFunc(*classSymbol*)

The Inside Story on Declare

This appendix describes the technical details of the declare mechanism. Knowing these technical details is not necessary to understanding what declaring a view means; they are provided primarily for completeness and to help you when you are debugging. You shouldn't write code that depends on these details.

For a basic discussion of the declare mechanism, see the section "View Instantiation" beginning on page 3-26. You should be familiar with that material before reading this appendix.

To serve as an example here, imagine a calculator application whose base view is named "Calculator." It has (among others) a child view named "Display." The Display view is declared in the Calculator view. See Figure A-1 for an illustration of this example.

In the following sections, we'll explain what happens at compile time and at run time as a result of the declare operation. A number of slots are created, which you may see in the Newton Toolkit (NTK) Inspector if you are examining the view templates.

Compile-Time Results

As a result of the declare operation, at compile time, NTK creates a slot in the place where the view is declared—that is, in the Calculator template. The name of the slot is the name of the declared view, `Display`. This slot's value is initially set to `nil`.

Another slot, called `stepAllocateContext`, is also created in the Calculator template. This slot holds an array of values (two for each view declared there). The first value in each pair is a symbol used by the system at run time to identify the name of the slot in the Calculator view that holds a reference to the declared view. This symbol is simply the name of the declared view, `Display`.

The second value in each pair is a reference to the template for the declared view. At run time, the system will preallocate a view memory object for the declared view from this template.

Note

Protos built into the system use an analogous slot called
`allocateContext`, that holds the same thing as
`stepAllocateContext`. The `allocateContext` slot is for
declared children from the `viewChildren` array and the
`stepAllocateContext` slot is for declared children from the
`stepChildren` array. ◆

Also, as a result of the declare operation, NTK creates a slot in the Display template
called `preallocatedContext`. This slot holds a symbol that is the name of the
template, in this case `'Display`. This symbol will be used by the system when the
view is instantiated to find the preallocated view memory object for the Display view.

Run-Time Results

When the Calculator view is opened (even before its `ViewSetupFormScript`
method is executed), a view memory object is preallocated for each view declared
in Calculator. (The information required to do this is obtained from the
`allocateContext` and `stepAllocateContext` slots.) In our example, a view
memory object is created for the Display view.

The `Display` slot in the Calculator view is updated so that it points to the newly
allocated Display view object.

Later in the instantiation process for the Calculator view, its child views are created
and shown, including the Display view. At this time, the view system looks at the
template for the Display view, sees the `preallocatedContext` slot, and knows
that a view memory object has been preallocated for this view. Using this slot, the
system can find the preallocated view.

The value of the `preallocatedContext` slot is the name of another slot in the
Calculator view. The system locates this slot in the Calculator view, and finds there
a reference to the preallocated view object. Instead of creating a new view object
for the Display view, the system uses the preallocated view.

Figure A-1   Declare example

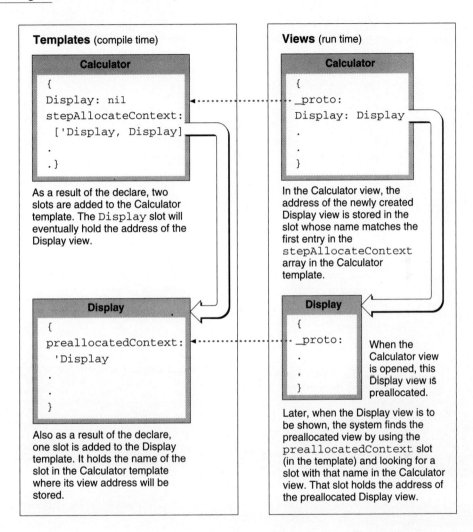

Templates (compile time)

Calculator

```
{
Display: nil
stepAllocateContext:
 ['Display, Display]
.

.}
```

As a result of the declare, two slots are added to the Calculator template. The Display slot will eventually hold the address of the Display view.

Display

```
{
preallocatedContext:
 'Display
.
.
}
```

Also as a result of the declare, one slot is added to the Display template. It holds the name of the slot in the Calculator template where its view address will be stored.

Views (run time)

Calculator

```
{
_proto:
Display: Display
.

.
}
```

In the Calculator view, the address of the newly created Display view is stored in the slot whose name matches the first entry in the stepAllocateContext array in the Calculator template.

Display

```
{
_proto:
.

.
}
```

When the Calculator view is opened, this Display view is preallocated.

Later, when the Display view is to be shown, the system finds the preallocated view by using the preallocatedContext slot (in the template) and looking for a slot with that name in the Calculator view. That slot holds the address of the preallocated Display view.

Glossary

Action button   The small envelope button used in applications to invoke routing functions. When tapped, it displays a picker listing routing actions available for the current item.

alias   An object that consists of a reference to another object. An alias saves space, since the alias object is small, and can be used to reference very large objects. Resolving an alias refers to retrieving the object that the alias references. See also **entry alias.**

application base view   The topmost parent view in an application. The application base view typically encloses all other views that make up the application.

arc   A portion of the circumference of an oval bounded by a pair of radii joining at the oval's center. Contrast a **wedge,** which includes part of the oval's interior. Arcs and wedges are defined by the bounding rectangle that encloses the oval, along with a pair of angles marking the positions of the bounding radii.

array   A sequence of numerically indexed slots (also known as the array elements) that contain objects. The first element is indexed by zero. Like other nonimmediate objects, an array can have a user-specified class, and can have its length changed dynamically.

away city   The **emporium** that's displayed as a counterpoint to your **home city.** It defines such information as dialing area, time zone, and so on. Sometimes it is called the "I'm here" city.

binary object   A sequence of bytes that can represent any kind of data, can be adjusted dynamically in size, and can have a user-specified class. Examples of binary objects include strings, real numbers, sounds, and bitmaps.

Boolean   A special kind of immediate value. In NewtonScript, there is only one Boolean, called `true`. Functions and control structures use `nil` to represent false. When testing for a true/false value, `nil` represents false, and any other value is equivalent to `true`.

button host   An application that receives buttons from other applications (**button providers**).

button provider   An application that adds a button to another application (the **button host**).

callback spec   A frame passed as an argument to an endpoint method. The callback spec frame contains slots that control how the endpoint method executes, along with a completion method that is called when the endpoint operation completes. See also **output spec**.

card   Short for a **PCMCIA** card. Also, a view of information about an entry in the Names soup, formatted as a business card.

child   A frame that references another frame (its parent) from a `_parent` slot. With regard to views, a child view is enclosed by its parent view.

class   A symbol that describes the data referenced by an object. Arrays, frames, and binary objects can have user-defined classes.

constant   A value that does not change. In NewtonScript the value of the constant is substituted wherever the constant is used in code.

cursor An object returned by the Query method. The cursor contains methods that iterate over a set of soup entries meeting the criteria specified in the query. The addition or deletion of entries matching the query specification is automatically reflected in the set of entries referenced by the cursor, even if the changes occur after the original query was made.

data definition A frame containing slots that define a particular type of data and the methods that operate on it. The entries defined are used by an application and stored in its soup. A data definition is registered with the system. The shortened term dataDef is sometimes used. See also **view definition**.

data form A symbol that describes the transformations that must occur when data is exchanged with other environments. When you send data or set endpoint options, the data form defines how to convert the data from its NewtonScript format. When you receive data or get endpoint options, the data form defines the type of data expected.

declaring a template Registering a template in another view (usually its parent) so that the template's view is preallocated when the other view is opened. This allows access to methods and slots in the declared view.

deferred recognition The process of recognizing an ink word that was drawn by the user at an earlier time. Deferred recognition is usually initiated when the user double-taps on an ink word. See also **ink** and **ink word.**

desktop computer Either a Mac OS or Windows-based computer. Sometimes called simply "desktop."

emporium The permanent internal descriptions of places the user works with the Newton PDA. (Home and Office are obvious examples, but so might be "Tokyo Office" if the user travels a lot.) Choosing an emporium sets up information such as local area code, dialing prefixes, time zone, and so on. This term is sometimes called "locale." The plural is "emporia."

endpoint An object created from protoBasicEndpoint, or one of its derivative protos, that controls a real-time communication session. This object encapsulates and maintains the details of the specific connection, and allows you to control the underlying communication tool.

endpoint option An endpoint option is specified in a frame passed in an array as an argument to one of the endpoint methods. Endpoint options select the communication tool to use, control its configuration and operation, and return result code information from each endpoint method call.

entry A frame stored in a soup and accessed through a cursor. An entry frame contains special slots that identify it as belonging to a soup.

entry alias An object that provides a standard way to save a reference to a soup entry. Entry aliases themselves may be stored in soups.

enumerated dictionary A list of words that can be recognized when this dictionary is enabled. See also **lexical dictionary.**

EOP End of packet indicator.

evaluate slot A slot that's evaluated when NTK (Newton Toolkit) compiles the application.

event An entry in the Dates application for a day, but not a particular time during that day.

field An area in a view where a user can write information.

finder A frame containing methods and/or objects that enumerate data items found to match criteria specified via the Find slip.

flag   A value that is set either on or off to enable a feature. Typically, flag values are single bits, though they can be groups of bits or a whole byte.

font spec   A structure used to store information about a font, including the font family, style, and point size.

frame   An unordered collection of slots, each of which consists of a name and value pair. The value of a slot can be any type of object, and slots can be added or removed from frames dynamically. A frame can have a user-specified class. Frames can be used like records in Pascal and structs in C, and also as objects that respond to messages.

free-form entry field   A field of a `protoCharEdit` view that accepts any characters as user input.

function object   A frame containing executable code. Function objects are created by the function constructor:

func (*args*) *funcBody*

An executable function object includes values for its lexical and message environment, as well as code. This information is captured when the function constructor is evaluated at run time.

gesture   A handwritten mark that is recognized as having a special meaning in the Newton system, such as tap, scrub, caret, and so on.

global   A variable or function that is accessible from any NewtonScript code.

grammar   A set of rules defining the format of an entity to be recognized, such as a date, time, phone number, or currency value. Lexical dictionaries are composed of sets of grammars. See also **lexical dictionary.**

home city   The **emporium** the system uses to modify dialing information, time zone, and so on. It is usually the user's home, but the user may set it to another city when traveling.

immediate   A value that is stored directly rather than through an indirect reference to a heap object. Immediates are characters, integers, or Booleans. See also **reference.**

implementor   The frame in which a method is defined. See also **receiver.**

In/Out Box   The application that serves as a central repository for all incoming and outgoing data handled by the Routing and Transport interfaces.

inheritance   The mechanism by which attributes (slots or data) and behaviors (methods) are made available to objects. Parent inheritance allows views of dissimilar types to share slots containing data or methods. Prototype inheritance allows a template to base its definition on that of another template or prototype.

ink   The raw data for input drawn by the user with the stylus. Also known as raw ink or sketch ink.

ink word   The grouping of ink data created by the recognition system, based on the timing and spacing of the user's handwriting. Ink words are created when the user has selected "Ink Text" in the Recognition Preferences slip. Ink words can subsequently be recognized with **deferred recognition.**

input spec   A frame used in receiving endpoint data that defines how incoming data should be formatted; termination conditions that control when the input should be stopped; data filtering options; and callback methods.

instantiate   To make a run-time object in the NewtonScript heap from a template. Usually this term refers to the process of creating a view from a template.

item frame   The frame that encapsulates a routed (sent or received) object and that is stored in the In/Out Box soup.

lexical dictionary   A list of valid grammars, each specifying the format of an entity to be recognized, such as a date, time, phone number or currency value. See also **enumerated dictionary** and **grammar.**

line   A shape defined by two points: the current x and y location of the graphics pen and the x and y location of its destination.

local   A variable whose scope is the function within which it is defined. You use the `local` keyword to explicitly create a local variable within a function.

magic pointer   A constant that represents a special kind of reference to an object in the Newton ROM. Magic pointer references are resolved at run time by the operating system, which substitutes the actual address of the ROM object for the magic pointer reference.

meeting   An entry in the Dates application for a specific time during the day. People can be invited and the meeting can be scheduled for a particular location.

message   A symbol with a set of arguments. A message is sent using the message send syntax *frame*:*messageName*(), where the message *messageName* is sent to the receiver *frame*.

method   A function object in a frame slot that is invoked in response to a message.

name reference   A frame that contains a soup entry or an alias to a soup entry, often, though not necessarily, from the Names soup. The frame may also contain some of the individual slots from the soup entry.

NewtonScript heap   An area of RAM used by the system for dynamically allocated objects, including NewtonScript objects.

`nil`   A value that indicates nothing, none, no, or anything negative or empty. It is similar to `(void*)0` in C. The value `nil` represents "false" in Boolean expressions; any other value represents "true."

object   A typed piece of data that can be an immediate, array, frame, or binary object. In NewtonScript, only frame objects can hold methods and receive messages.

option frame   A frame passed as a parameter to an endpoint method that selects the communication tool to use; controls its configuration and operation; and returns result code information from the endpoint method.

origin   The coordinates of the top-left corner of a view, usually (0, 0). The origin can be shifted, for example, to scroll the contents of a view.

output spec   A special type of **callback spec** used with an endpoint method. An output spec contains a few additional slots that allow you to pass special protocol flags and to define how the data being sent is translated.

oval   A circular or elliptical shape defined by the bounding rectangle that encloses it.

package   The unit in which software can be installed on and removed from the Newton. A package consists of a header containing the package name and other information, and one or more **parts** containing the software.

package file   A file that contains downloadable Newton software.

package store   See **store part.**

parent   A frame referenced through the `_parent` slot of another frame. With regard to views, a parent view encloses its child views.

part   A unit of software—either code or data—held in a part frame. The format of the part is identified by a four-character identifier called its type or its part code.

part frame   The top-level frame that holds an application, book, or auto part.

PCMCIA   Personal Computer Memory Card International Association. This acronym is used to describe the memory cards used by the Newton PDA. Newton memory cards follow the PCMCIA standards.

persona   The permanent internal description of an individual person that uses a particular Newton PDA, or a particular public image of the Newton owner. The owner is the obvious example, but there can be many others. Choosing a persona sets up information such as name, title, birthday, phone numbers, e-mail addresses, and so on. The plural is "personae."

picker   A type of Newton view that pops up and contains a list of items. The user can select an item by tapping it. This type of view closes when the user taps an item or taps outside the list without making a selection.

picture   A saved sequence of drawing operations that can be played back later.

polygon   A shape defined by a sequence of points representing the polygon's vertices, connected by straight lines from one point to the next.

pop-up   See **picker.**

project   The collected files and specifications that NTK uses to build a package that can be downloaded and executed on the Newton.

proto   A frame referenced through another frame's _proto slot. With regard to views, a proto is not intended to be directly instantiated—you reference the proto from a template. The

system supplies several view protos, which an application can use to implement user interface elements such as buttons, input fields, and so on.

protocol   An agreed-upon set of conventions for communications between two computers, such as the protocol used to communicate between a desktop computer and a Newton device.

raw ink   See **ink.**

receiver   The frame that was sent a message. The receiver for the invocation of a function object is accessible through the pseudo-variable self. See also **implementor.**

recognized text   Ink words processed by the recognition system. Ink drawn by the user is converted into recognized text when the user has selected "Text" in the Recognition Preferences slip or after deferred recognition takes place. See also **ink word**.

rectangle   A shape defined by two points—its top-left and its bottom-right corners—or by four boundaries—its upper, left, bottom, and right sides.

reference   A value that indirectly refers to an array, frame, or binary object. See also **immediate.**

region   An arbitrary area or set of areas on the coordinate plane. The outline of a region should be one or more closed loops.

resource   Raw data—usually bitmaps or sounds—stored on the development system and incorporated into a Newton application during the project build.

restore   To replace all the information in a Newton with information from a file on the desktop.

restricted entry field   A field of a protoCharEdit view that accepts as user input only the values specified in the view's template slot. For example, a field for entering phone numbers might restrict acceptable user input to numerals.

rich string   A string object that contains imbedded ink words. Rich strings create a compact representation for strings that contain ink words and can be used with most of the string-processing functions provided in the system software. See also **rich string format.**

rich string format   The internal representation used for rich strings. Each ink word is represented by a special placeholder character (kInkChar) in the string. The data for each ink word is stored after the string terminator character. The final 32 bits in a rich string encode information about the rich string.

root view   The topmost parent view in the view hierarchy. All other views descend from the root view.

rounded rectangle   A rectangle with rounded corners. The shape is defined by the rectangle itself, along with the diameter of the circles forming the corners (called the diameter of curvature).

routing format   A frame that describes how to format an object that is to be sent (routed). Examples include print routing formats, which describe how to visually format data, and frame routing formats, which describe the internal structure of a frame.

routing slip   A view that looks like an envelope. The transport displays this view after the user selects a transport-based action from the Action picker. This view is used by a transport to collect information needed to send the item.

script icon   An icon that executes a function object when tapped.

self   A pseudo-variable that is set to the current receiver.

shape   A data structure used by the drawing system to draw an image on the screen.

siblings   Child frames that have the same parent frame.

sketch ink   See **ink.**

slot   An element of a frame or array that can hold an immediate or reference.

soup   A persistently stored object that contains a series of frames called entries. Like a database, a soup has indexes you can use to access entries in a sorted order.

soupervisor mechanism   The system service that presents the user with information about a soup when the user taps its icon in the Extras Drawer. It allows for filing or moving all soup entries.

soup icon   An icon that represents one or more soups, usually in the Storage folder of the Extras Drawer.

stationery   Refers to the capability of having different kinds of data within a single application (such as plain notes and outlines in the Notepad) and/or to the capability of having different ways of viewing the same data (such as the Card and All Info views in the Names file). Implementing stationery involves writing data definitions and view definitions. See also **data definition** and **view definition.**

store   A physical repository that can contain soups and packages. A store is like a volume on a disk on a personal computer.

store part   A part that encapsulates a read-only store. This store may contain one or more soup objects. Store parts permit soup-like access to read-only data residing in a package. Store parts are sometimes referred to as package stores.

target   The object being acted upon. Sometimes the target consists of multiple items, for example, when multiple items are selected from an overview for sending.

template   A frame that contains the data description of an object (usually a view). A template is intended to be instantiated at run time. See also **proto.**

text run   A sequence of characters that are all displayed with the same font specification. Text is represented in paragraph views as a series of text runs with corresponding style (font spec) information. See also **font spec.**

tick   A sixtieth of a second.

transport   A NewtonScript object that provides a communication service to the Newton In/Out Box. It interfaces between the In/Out Box and an endpoint. Examples include the print, fax, beam, and mail transports. See also **endpoint.**

transport   A special type of Newton application used to send and/or receive data. Transports communicate with the In/Out Box on one end and typically to an endpoint object on the other end. Examples include the built-in transports such as print, fax, and beam. See also **endpoint.**

user proto   A proto defined by an application developer, not supplied by the system.

view   The object instantiated at run time from a template. A view is a frame that represents a visual object on the screen. The _proto slot of a view references its template, which defines its characteristics.

view class   A primitive building block on which a view is based. All view protos are based directly or indirectly (through another proto) on a view class. The view class of a view is specified in the viewClass slot of its template or proto.

view definition   A view template that defines how to display data from a particular data definition. A view definition is registered with the system under the name of the data definition to which it applies. The shortened term viewDef is sometimes used. See also **data definition**.

wedge   A pie-shaped segment of an oval, bounded by a pair of radii joining at the oval's center. Contrast with **arc**.

Index

B

C

D

G

H

I, J

Q

R

S

U

W, X, Y, Z

This Apple manual was written, edited, and composed on a desktop publishing system using Apple Macintosh computers and FrameMaker software. Proof pages were created on an Apple LaserWriter Pro 630 printer. Final page negatives were output directly from the text and graphics files. Line art was created using Adobe™ Illustrator. PostScript™, the page-description language for the LaserWriter, was developed by Adobe Systems Incorporated.

Text type is Palatino® and display type is Helvetica®. Bullets are ITC Zapf Dingbats®.

Special thanks to J. Christopher Bell, Gregory Christie, Bob Ebert, Mike Engber, Dan Peterson, Maurice Sharp, and Fred Tou.

NEWTON PROGRAMMER'S REFERENCE
CD TEAM
Gary Hillerson, Gerry Kane, Christopher Bey

LEAD WRITER
Christopher Bey

WRITERS
Bob Anders, Christopher Bey,
Cheryl Chambers, Gary Hillerson,
John Perry, Jonathan Simonoff,
Yvonne Tornatta, Dirk van Nouhuys,
Adrian Yacub

PROJECT LEADER
Christopher Bey

ILLUSTRATOR
Peggy Kunz

EDITORS
Linda Ackerman, David Schneider,
Anne Szabla

PRODUCTION EDITOR
Rex Wolf

PROJECT MANAGER
Gerry Kane